CONTEMPORARY MANAGEMENT SCIENCE

WITH SPREADSHEETS

David R. Anderson
University of Cincinnati

Dennis J. Sweeney
University of Cincinnati

Thomas A. Williams
Rochester Institute of Technology

SOUTH-WESTERN College Publishing

An International Thomson Publishing Company

Publishing Team Director: John Szilagy
Acquisitions Editor: Charles E. McCormick, Jr.
Developmental Editor: Alice C. Denny
Production Editor: Amy C. Hanson
Media Production Editor: Robin Browning
Production House: BookMasters, Inc.
Marketing Manager: Joseph A. Sabatino
Technology Coordinator: Kevin von Gillern
Manufacturing Coordinator: Sue Kirven
Internal and Cover Design: Michael H. Stratton
Cover Photo: FPG International

Component ISBN: 0-538-87609-3
Text ISBN: 0-324-00054-5

        2   3   4   5   7   8   9   C1   6   5   4   3   2   1   0   9
Printed in the United States of America

Library of Congress Cataloging-in-Publications Data:

Anderson, David Ray, 1941-
      Contemporary management science : with spreadsheets / David R.
   Anderson, Dennis J. Sweeney, Thomas A. Williams.
         p.   cm.
      Includes bibliographical references and index.
      ISBN 0-538-87609-3
      1. Management science.   I. Sweeney, Dennis J. II. Williams,
   Thomas Arthur, 1944–   . III. Title.
   HD30.25.A527   1998
   658—dc21   98-13629
                                                         CIP

I(T)P®

International Thomson Publishing
South-Western College Publishing is an ITP Company.
The trademark ITP is used under license.

To Our Students

CONTENTS IN BRIEF

CONTENTS

CONTEMPORARY MANAGEMENT SCIENCE WITH SPREADSHEETS will provide both undergraduate and graduate students with a conceptual understanding of the role of management science in the decision-making process. We have written a text that covers what we believe to be the core topics in management science. The contemporary, or new, aspect of this text is an emphasis on how spreadsheet packages (we use Microsoft's Excel) can be used to implement the techniques of management science and bring timely decision-making information to the screen of a personal computer.

We have written the book with the non-mathematician in mind; it is applications oriented. A problem scenario approach is used to teach modeling and the proper managerial interpretation of the solution to a model. Our experience has shown that if we start with a challenging managerial problem, students are much more interested in learning how a particular management science technique can be used to provide useful decision-making information. Once a problem is introduced, we first formulate a mathematical model, and then develop a spreadsheet model of the problem. Solving the spreadsheet model transforms the data and mathematical description of the problem into easily interpreted decision-making information.

A big advantage of spreadsheets is that they offer a convenient means for dealing with both the data associated with a problem, and a model of the problem. Many students entering management science courses are already familiar with spreadsheets, and their use to organize data and solve problems is appreciated and well accepted. However, this text is written for the course in management science, not a course in spreadsheets. We do not feel that the use of spreadsheets has eliminated the need to understand the mathematical models that underlie management science. Researchers have made tremendous strides in the past 50 years developing mathematical models of practical problems. We seek to build on that work. Our focus is on developing a smooth interface between mathematical modeling and the use of spreadsheets in management science.

The mathematical prerequisite for this text is a course in algebra. In addition, it is assumed that the student has at least a beginning understanding of and the ability to use a spreadsheet package such as Microsoft® Excel. Although the text is ideally suited to a one-term introductory course, instructors will find that the wide variety of application exercises and case problems provide the flexibility for longer and more in-depth courses.

Throughout the text we utilize generally accepted notation for the topics being covered. Students who pursue study beyond the level of this text should have little difficulty reading more advanced material.

Excel Spreadsheet Files

The disks at the back of this text contain 100 spreadsheets in both Excel 97 and Excel 5.0 formats. These disks include every example spreadsheet presented in the text as well as all spreadsheets used to solve the self-test problems. Students may use these disks to review the cell formulas and details of the spreadsheet models.

Some instructors may choose to use the example spreadsheets to demonstrate the flexibility of spreadsheets in analyzing a problem. Student assignments might involve using these existing spreadsheets as templates. Input data and other parameters can be varied to show how changes impact the solution and decision recommendations. For more emphasis on the development of spreadsheet models for new problems, the instructor may use the spreadsheets in the text for illustration purposes and then make class assignments which ask students to develop their own spreadsheet models for the problems and/or cases at the end of the chapters.

Ancillary Teaching Materials

The following support materials are available from the ITP Academic Resource Center at 800-423-0563 or through *www.swcollege.com*:

● **Solutions Manual with Solutions Disks**   The *Solutions Manual* (ISBN: 0-538-87610-7), prepared by the authors, includes solutions for all problems in the text. In addition, the *Solutions Manual* includes disks containing 125 spreadsheets which were developed to solve the text problems.

● **Instructor's Manual with Case Solutions Disk**   The *Instructor's Manual* (ISBN: 0-538-87613-1), also prepared by the authors, contains solutions to all case problems presented in this text. A disk containing the spreadsheets used to solve the case problems is included with the *Instructor's Manual*. The manual also provides brief annotations for each problem in the text. These annotations will help instructors select homework problems designed to meet their course objectives.

● **PowerPoint Presentation Slides**   Prepared by John Loucks, the presentation slides (ISBN: 0-538-87614-X) contain a teaching outline that incorporates graphics to help instructors create even more stimulating lectures. The PowerPoint 7.0 slides may be adapted using PowerPoint software to facilitate classroom use.

● **Test Bank** and **World Class Test**   Prepared by Jack B. Jensen and Sener Erdem of the University of South Maine, the *Test Bank* (ISBN: 0-538-87611-5) includes true/false, multiple choice, short answers, and problems for each chapter. *World Class Test* (ISBN: 0-324-00048-0) computerized testing software allows instructors to create, edit, store and print exams.

Acknowledgments

We would like to say thanks to the colleagues who provided helpful comments and suggestions during the development of this manuscript. These reviewers include Phillip C. Fry, Boise State University; Robert E. Johnson, Greenville College; Sameer Kumar, University of St. Thomas; Ruth A. Maurer, Walden University; Charlene Robert, Louisiana State University; Marie Yetimyan, San Jose State University; Mustafa R. Yilmaz, Northeastern University; and Zhiwei Zhu, University of Southwestern Louisiana.

Our associates from organizations who supplied the Management Science in Practice applications also made a significant contribution to this text. These individuals are cited in a credit line of the first page of each application.

We are also indebted to our acquisitions editor, Charles McCormick, Jr., our developmental editor, Alice Denny, our production editor, Amy Hanson, and others at South-Western College Publishing for their counsel and support during the preparation of this product.

David R. Anderson
Dennis J. Sweeney
Thomas A. Williams

David R. Anderson. David R. Anderson is Professor of Quantitative Analysis in the College of Business Administration at the University of Cincinnati. Born in Grand Forks, North Dakota, he earned his B.S., M.S., and Ph.D. degrees from Purdue University. Professor Anderson has served as Associate Dean of the College of Business Administration. In addition, he was the coordinator of the College's first Executive Program.

At the University of Cincinnati, Professor Anderson has taught introductory statistics for business students as well as graduate level courses in regression analysis, multivariate analysis, and management science. He has also taught statistical courses at the Department of Labor in Washington, D.C. He has been honored with nominations and awards for excellence in teaching and excellence in service to student organizations.

Professor Anderson has coauthored six textbooks in the areas of statistics, management science, linear programming, and production and operations management. He is an active consultant in the field of sampling and statistical methods.

Dennis J. Sweeney. Dennis J. Sweeney is Professor of Quantitative Analysis at the University of Cincinnati. Born in Des Moines, Iowa, he earned a B.S.B.A. degree from Drake University, graduating summa cum laude. He received his M.B.A. and D.B.A. degrees from Indiana University where he was an NDEA Fellow. Since receiving his doctorate in 1971, Professor Sweeney has spent all but 2 years at the University of Cincinnati. During 1978–79, he spent a year working in the management science group at Procter & Gamble; during 1981–82, he was a visiting professor at Duke University. Professor Sweeney served 5 years as Head of the Department of Quantitative Analysis and 4 years as Associate Dean at the University of Cincinnati.

Professor Sweeney has published over 30 articles in the general area of management science. The National Science Foundation, IBM, Procter & Gamble, Federated Department Stores, and Cincinnati Gas & Electric have funded his research, which has been published in *Management Science, Operations Research, Mathematical Programming, Decision Sciences,* and other journals.

Professor Sweeney has coauthored six textbooks in the areas of statistics, management science, linear programming, and production and operations management.

Thomas A. Williams. Thomas A. Williams is Professor of Management Science in the College of Business at Rochester Institute of Technology. Born in Elmira, New York, he earned his B.S. degree at Clarkson University. He did his graduate work at Rensselaer Polytechnic Institute, where he received his M.S. and Ph.D. degrees.

Before joining the College of Business at RIT, Professor Williams served for 7 years as a faculty member in the College of Business Administration at the University of Cincinnati, where he developed the undergraduate program in Information Systems and then served as its coordinator. At RIT he was the first chairman of the Decision Sciences Department. He teaches courses in management science and statistics, as well as more advanced courses in regression and decision analysis.

Professor Williams is the coauthor of seven textbooks in the areas of management science, statistics, production and operations management, and mathematics. He has been a consultant for numerous Fortune 500 companies and has worked on projects ranging from the use of elementary data analysis to the development of large-scale regression models.

I

INTRODUCTION

This book is concerned with the use of quantitative methods in the decision-making process. The emphasis is not on the methods themselves, but rather on how they can contribute to better decision making. A variety of names exists for this body of knowledge, including Management Science (MS), Operations Research (OR), and Decision Science. All are concerned with rational approaches to decision making based on the scientific method.

The scientific management revolution of the early 1900s, initiated by Frederic W. Taylor, provided the foundation for the use of quantitative methods in management. But modern usage of quantitative methods is generally considered to have originated during the World War II period, when teams were formed to deal with strategic and tactical problems faced by the military. These teams, which often consisted of people with diverse specialties (e.g., mathematicians, engineers, and behavioral scientists), joined together to solve a common problem through the use of the scientific method. After the war, many of these team members continued their research in the field of management science.

Two developments that occurred during the post–World War II period led to the growth and use of management science in nonmilitary applications. First, continued research resulted in numerous methodological developments. Probably the most significant development was the discovery by George Dantzig, in 1947, of the simplex method for solving linear programming problems. Many more methodological developments followed, and in 1957 the first book on operations research was published by Churchman, Ackoff, and Arnoff.[1]

Concurrently with these methodological developments, a virtual explosion in computing power was made available through digital computers. Computers enabled practitioners to use methodological advances to solve successfully a large variety of problems. The computer technology explosion continues; personal computers are now more powerful than earlier mainframe computers. Today, variants of the post–World War II methodological developments are being used on personal computers to solve problems larger than those solved on mainframe computers in the early 1990s.

N O T E S
and Comments

1. Operations research analyst is listed by the Bureau of Labor Statistics as one of the fastest growing occupations for careers requiring a bachelor's degree; they predict a growth from 57,000 jobs in 1990 to 100,000 jobs in 2005, an increase of 73%.

2. The Institute for Operations Research and the Management Sciences (INFORMS) and the Decision Sciences Institute (DSI) are two professional societies that publish journals and newsletters dealing with current research and applications of quantitative methods.

I.I   PROBLEM SOLVING AND DECISION MAKING

Problem solving can be defined as the process of identifying a difference between the actual and the desired state of affairs and then taking action to resolve the difference. For problems important enough to justify the time and effort of careful analysis, the problem-solving process involves the following seven steps:

1. Identify and define the problem.
2. Determine the set of alternative solutions.
3. Determine the criterion or criteria that will be used to evaluate the alternatives.
4. Evaluate the alternatives.
5. Choose an alternative.
6. Implement the selected alternative (the decision).
7. Evaluate the results and determine if a satisfactory solution has been obtained.

Decision making is the term generally associated with the first five steps of the problem-solving process. Thus, the first step of decision making is to identify and define the problem. Decision making ends with the choosing of an alternative, which is the act of making the decision.

Let us consider the following example of a decision-making process. For the moment, assume that you are currently unemployed and would like a position that will lead to a satisfying career. Suppose that your job search has resulted in offers from companies located in Rochester, New York; Dallas, Texas; Greensboro, North Carolina; and Pittsburgh, Pennsylvania. Thus, the alternatives for your decision problem can be stated as follows:

1. C. W. Churchman, R. L. Ackoff, and E. L. Arnoff, *Introduction to Operations Research* (New York: Wiley, 1957).

1. Accept the position in Rochester.
2. Accept the position in Dallas.
3. Accept the position in Greensboro.
4. Accept the position in Pittsburgh.

The next step of the decision-making process involves determining the criteria that will be used to evaluate the four alternatives. Obviously, the starting salary is going to be a factor of some importance. If salary were the only criterion of importance to you, the alternative selected as "best" would be the one with the highest starting salary. Problems in which the objective is to find the best solution with respect to one criterion are referred to as **single-criterion decision problems.**

Suppose that you have also concluded that the potential for advancement and the location of the job are two other criteria of major importance. Thus, the three criteria in your decision problem are starting salary, potential for advancement, and location. Problems that involve more than one criterion are referred to as **multicriteria decision problems.**

The next step of the decision-making process is to evaluate each alternative with respect to each criterion. For example, evaluating each alternative relative to the starting salary criterion is done simply by recording the starting salary for each job alternative. Evaluating each alternative with respect to the potential for advancement and the location of the job is more difficult to do, however, since these evaluations are based primarily on subjective factors that are often difficult to quantify. Suppose that for now you have decided to measure potential for advancement and job location by rating each of these criteria as poor, fair, average, good, or excellent and that the data you have compiled are shown in Table 1.1.

You are now ready to make a choice from the available alternatives. What makes this choice so difficult is that the criteria are probably not all equally important, and no one alternative is "best" with regard to all criteria. Although a method for dealing with situations like this is presented later in the text, for now let us suppose that after a careful evaluation of the data in Table 1.1, you have decided to select alternative 3 (Greensboro); alternative 3 is thus referred to as the **decision.**

At this point in time, the decision-making process is complete. In summary, we see that this process involved five steps:

1. Define the problem.
2. Identify the alternatives.
3. Determine the criteria.
4. Evaluate the alternatives.
5. Choose an alternative.

Note that missing from this list are the last two steps in the problem-solving process: implementing the selected alternative and evaluating the results to determine whether a

Table 1.1   DATA FOR THE JOB EVALUATION DECISION-MAKING PROBLEM

Alternative	Starting Salary	Potential Advancement	Job Location
Rochester	$38,500	Average	Average
Dallas	$36,000	Excellent	Good
Greensboro	$36,000	Good	Excellent
Pittsburgh	$37,000	Average	Good

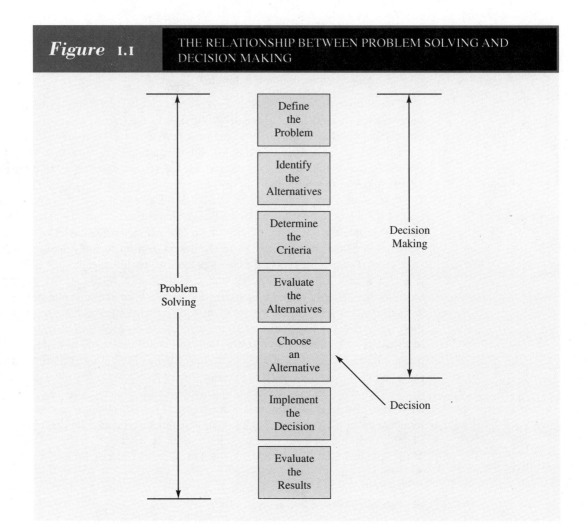

Figure 1.1 THE RELATIONSHIP BETWEEN PROBLEM SOLVING AND DECISION MAKING

satisfactory solution has been obtained. This omission is not meant to diminish the importance of each of these activities but to emphasize the more limited scope of the term *decision making* as compared to the term *problem solving*. Figure 1.1 summarizes the relationship between these two concepts.

1.2 QUANTITATIVE ANALYSIS AND DECISION MAKING

Consider the flowchart presented in Figure 1.2. Note that the first three steps of the decision-making process are combined under the heading "Structuring the Problem" and the latter two steps under the heading "Analyzing the Problem." Let us now consider in more detail how to carry out the set of activities that make up the decision-making process.

Figure 1.3 shows that the analysis phase of the decision-making process may take on two basic forms: qualitative and quantitative. Qualitative analysis is based primarily on a manager's judgment and experience; it includes a manager's intuitive "feel" for the problem and is more an art than a science. If a manager has had experience with similar problems, or if the problem is relatively simple, heavy emphasis may be placed upon a

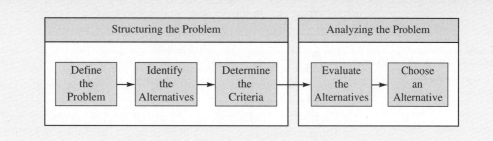

Figure 1.2 — AN ALTERNATE CLASSIFICATION OF THE DECISION-MAKING PROCESS

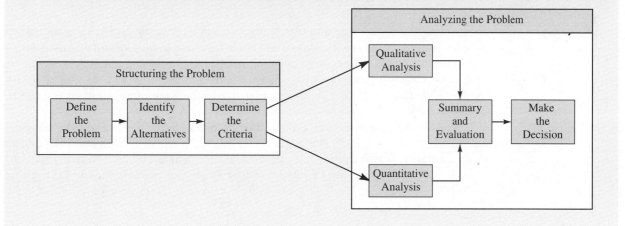

Figure 1.3 — THE ROLE OF QUALITATIVE AND QUANTITATIVE ANALYSIS

qualitative analysis. However, if a manager has had little experience with similar problems, or if the problem is sufficiently complex, then a quantitative analysis of the problem can be an especially important consideration in the manager's final decision.

When using the quantitative approach, an analyst will concentrate on the quantitative facts or data associated with the problem and develop mathematical expressions that describe the objectives, constraints, and other relationships that exist in the problem. Then, by using one or more quantitative methods, the analyst will make a recommendation based on the quantitative aspects of the problem.

Although skills in the qualitative approach are inherent in the manager and usually increase with experience, the skills of the quantitative approach can be learned only by studying and using quantitative methods. A manager can increase decision-making effectiveness by learning more about quantitative methodology and by better understanding its contribution to the decision-making process. A manager who is knowledgeable in quantitative decision-making procedures is in a much better position to compare and evaluate qualitative and quantitative sources of recommendations and ultimately to combine the two sources in order to make the best possible decision.

Quantitative methods are especially helpful with large, complex problems. For example, in the coordination of the thousands of tasks associated with landing the Apollo eleven safely on the moon, quantitative techniques helped to ensure that over 300,000 pieces of work performed by over 400,000 people were integrated smoothly.

The box in Figure 1.3 entitled "Quantitative Analysis" encompasses most of the subject matter of this text. We will consider a managerial problem, introduce the appropriate quantitative methodology, and then develop the recommended decision.

In closing this section, let us briefly state some of the reasons that a quantitative approach might be used in the decision-making process:

You should understand why quantitative approaches might be needed in a particular problem. Try Problem 4.

1. The problem is complex, and the manager cannot develop a good solution without the aid of quantitative analysis.
2. The problem is very important (e.g., a great deal of money is involved), and the manager desires a thorough qualitative and quantitative analysis before attempting to make a decision.
3. The problem is new, and the manager has no previous experience from which to draw.
4. The problem is repetitive, and the manager saves time and effort by relying on computerized quantitative procedures to make routine decision recommendations.

1.3   QUANTITATIVE ANALYSIS

From Figure 1.3 we see that quantitative analysis begins once the problem has been structured. Imagination, teamwork, and considerable effort are usually required to transform a rather general problem description into a well-defined problem that can be approached via quantitative analysis. The more the analyst is involved in the process of structuring the problem, the more likely the ensuing quantitative analysis will make an important contribution to the decision process.

When both the manager and the quantitative analyst agree that the problem has been adequately structured, work can begin on developing a model to represent the problem mathematically. Solution procedures can then be employed to find the best solution for the model. This best solution for the model then becomes a recommendation to the decision maker. The process of developing and solving models is the essence of the quantitative analysis process. Let's see how it works.

Model Development

Models are representations of real objects or situations. They can be presented in various forms. For example, a scale model of an airplane is a representation of a real airplane. Similarly, a child's toy truck is a model of a real truck. The model airplane and toy truck are examples of models that are physical replicas of real objects. In modeling terminology, physical replicas are referred to as **iconic models.**

A second classification of models includes those that are in physical form but do not have the same physical appearance as the object being modeled. Such models are referred to as **analog models.** The speedometer of an automobile is an analog model; the position of the needle on the dial represents the speed of the automobile. A thermometer is another analog model representing temperature.

A third classification of models—the type we will primarily be studying—includes those that represent a problem by a system of symbols and mathematical relationships or expressions. Such models are referred to as **mathematical models** and are a critical part of any quantitative approach to decision making. For example, the total profit from the sale of a product can be determined by multiplying the profit per unit by the quantity sold. If we let x represent the number of units sold and P the total profit, then, with a profit of \$10 per unit, the following mathematical model defines the total profit earned by selling x units:

$$P = 10x \qquad (1.1)$$

The purpose, or value, of any model is that it enables us to make inferences about the real situation by studying and analyzing the model. For example, an airplane designer might test an iconic model of a new airplane in a wind tunnel to learn about the potential flying characteristics of the full-size airplane. Similarly, a mathematical model may be used to make inferences about how much profit will be earned if a specified quantity of a particular product is sold. According to the mathematical model of equation (1.1), we would expect that selling three units of the product ($x = 3$) would provide a profit of $P = 10(3) = \$30$.

In general, experimenting with models requires less time and is less expensive than experimenting with a real object or situation. A model airplane is certainly quicker and less expensive to build and study than a full-size airplane. Similarly, the mathematical model in equation (1.1) allows a quick identification of profit expectations without actually requiring the manager to produce and sell x units. Models also have the advantage of reducing the risk associated with experimenting with a real situation. In particular, bad designs or bad decisions that cause a model airplane to crash or a mathematical model to project a \$10,000 loss can be avoided in a real situation.

Herbert A. Simon, a Nobel prize winner in economics and an expert in decision making, said that a mathematical model does not have to be exact; it just has to be close enough to provide better results than can be obtained by common sense.

The value of model-based conclusions and decisions is dependent on how well a model represents a real situation. The more closely a scale model represents a real airplane, the more accurate the conclusions and predictions will be. Similarly, the more closely a mathematical model represents a company's true profit-volume relationship, the more accurate the profit projections will be.

Because this text deals with quantitative analysis based on mathematical models, let us look more closely at the mathematical modeling process. When initially considering a managerial problem, we usually find that the problem-structuring phase leads to a specific objective, such as maximization of profit or minimization of cost, and possibly a set of restrictions or **constraints,** such as production capacities. The success of the mathematical model and quantitative approach will depend heavily on how accurately the objective and constraints can be expressed in terms of mathematical equations or relationships.

A mathematical expression that describes the problem's objective is referred to as the **objective function.** For example, the profit equation $P = 10x$ would be an objective function for a firm attempting to maximize profit. A production capacity constraint would be necessary if, for instance, 5 hours are required to produce each unit and only 40 hours are available per week. Let x indicate the number of units produced each week. The production time constraint is given by

$$5x \leq 40 \qquad (1.2)$$

The value of $5x$ is the total time required to produce x units; the $\leq$ symbol indicates that the production time required must be less than or equal to the 40 hours available.

The decision problem or question is the following: How many units of the product should be scheduled each week to maximize profit? A complete mathematical model for this simple production problem is

$$\text{Maximize} \qquad P = 10x \qquad \text{objective function}$$
$$\text{subject to (s.t.)}$$
$$\left. \begin{array}{l} 5x \leq 40 \\ x \geq 0 \end{array} \right\} \text{constraints}$$

The $x \geq 0$ constraint requires the production quantity x to be greater than or equal to zero, which simply recognizes the fact that manufacturing a negative number of units is not possible. The optimal solution to this model can be easily calculated and is given by $x = 8$, with an associated profit of $80. This model is an example of a linear programming model. In subsequent chapters we discuss more complicated mathematical models and learn how to solve them in situations where the answers are not nearly so obvious.

In the preceding mathematical model, the profit per unit ($10), the production time per unit (5 hours), and the production capacity (40 hours) are environmental factors that are not under the control of the manager or decision maker. Such environmental factors, which can affect both the objective function and the constraints, are referred to as **uncontrollable inputs** to the model. Inputs that are controlled or determined by the decision maker are referred to as **controllable inputs** to the model. In the example given, the production quantity x is the controllable input to the model. Controllable inputs are the decision alternatives specified by the manager and thus are also referred to as the **decision variables** of the model.

Once all controllable and uncontrollable inputs are specified, the objective function and constraints can be evaluated, and the output of the model determined. In this sense, the output of the model is simply the projection of what would happen if those particular environmental factors and decisions occurred in the real situation. A flowchart of how controllable and uncontrollable inputs are transformed by the mathematical model into output is shown in Figure 1.4. A similar flowchart showing the specific details of the production model is shown in Figure 1.5.

As stated earlier, the uncontrollable inputs are those the decision maker cannot influence. The specific controllable and uncontrollable inputs of a model depend on the particular problem or decision-making situation. In the production problem, the production time available (40), is an uncontrollable input. However, if hiring more employees or using overtime were possible, the number of hours of production time would become a controllable input and therefore a decision variable in the model.

Uncontrollable inputs can either be known exactly or be uncertain and subject to variation. If all uncontrollable inputs to a model are known and cannot vary, the model is referred to as a **deterministic model.** Corporate income tax rates are not under the influence of the manager and thus constitute an uncontrollable input in many decision models. Since these rates are known and fixed (at least in the short run), a mathematical model with corporate income tax rates as the only uncontrollable input would be a deterministic model. The distinguishing feature of a deterministic model is that the uncontrollable input values are known in advance.

Figure 1.4   FLOWCHART OF THE PROCESS OF TRANSFORMING MODEL INPUTS INTO OUTPUT

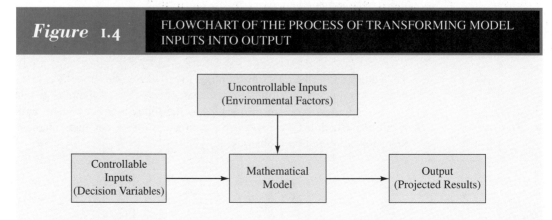

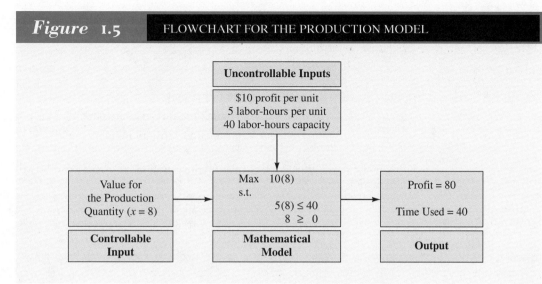

Figure 1.5   FLOWCHART FOR THE PRODUCTION MODEL

If any of the uncontrollable inputs are uncertain and subject to variation, the model is referred to as a **stochastic** or **probabilistic model.** An uncontrollable input to many production planning models is demand for the product. Because future demand may be any of a range of values, a mathematical model that treats demand with uncertainty would be called a *stochastic model.* In the production model, the number of hours of production time required per unit, the total hours available, and the unit profit were all uncontrollable inputs. Because the uncontrollable inputs were all known to take on fixed values, the model is deterministic. If, however, the number of hours of production time per unit could vary from 3 to 6 hours depending on the quality of the raw material, the model would be stochastic. The distinguishing feature of a stochastic model is that the value of the output cannot be determined even if the value of the controllable input is known because the specific values of the uncontrollable inputs are unknown. In this respect, stochastic models are often more difficult to analyze.

Data Preparation

Another step in the quantitative analysis of a problem is the preparation of the data required by the model. Data in this sense refer to the values of the uncontrollable inputs to the model. All uncontrollable inputs or data must be specified before we can analyze the model and recommend a decision.

In the production model, the values of the uncontrollable inputs or data were $10 per unit for profit, 5 hours per unit for production time, and 40 hours for production capacity. In the development of the model, these data values were known and incorporated into the model as it was being developed. If the model is relatively small and the uncontrollable input values or data required are few, the quantitative analyst will probably combine model development and data preparation into one step. That is, in these situations the data values are inserted as the equations of the mathematical model are developed.

However, in many mathematical modeling situations, the data or uncontrollable input values are not readily available. In these situations the quantitative analyst may know that the model will need profit per unit, production time, and production capacity data, but the values will not be known until the accounting, production, and engineering departments can be consulted. Rather than attempting to collect the required data as the model is being developed, the analyst will usually adopt a general notation for the model development step and then perform a separate data preparation step to obtain the uncontrollable input values required by the model.

Using the general notation

$$c = \text{profit per unit}$$
$$a = \text{production time in hours per unit}$$
$$b = \text{production capacity in hours}$$

the model development step of the production problem would result in the following general model:

$$\text{Max} \quad cx$$
$$\text{s.t.}$$
$$ax \leq b$$
$$x \geq 0$$

A separate data preparation step to identify the values for c, a, and b would then be necessary to complete the model.

Many inexperienced quantitative analysts assume that once the problem has been defined and a general model developed, the problem is essentially solved. These individuals tend to believe that data preparation is a trivial step in the process and can be easily handled by administrative assistants. Actually, this assumption could not be farther from the truth, especially with large-scale models that have numerous data input values. For example, a moderate-size linear programming model with 50 decision variables and 25 constraints could have over 1300 data elements that must be identified in the data preparation step. The time required to prepare these data and the possibility of data collection errors will make the data preparation step a critical part of the quantitative analysis process. Because a fairly large database is needed to support a mathematical model, often information systems specialists also become involved in the data preparation step.

Model Solution

Once the model development and data preparation steps have been completed, we can proceed to the model solution step. In this step, the analyst will attempt to identify the values of the decision variables that provide the "best" output for the model. The specific decision-variable value or values providing the "best" output will be referred to as the **optimal solution** for the model. For the production problem, the model solution step involves finding the value of the production quantity decision variable x that maximizes profit while not causing a violation of the production capacity constraint.

One procedure that might be used in the model solution step involves a trial-and-error approach in which the model is used to test and evaluate various decision alternatives. In the production model, this would mean testing and evaluating the model under various production quantities or values of x. Referring to Figure 1.5, note that we could input trial values for x and check the corresponding output for projected profit and satisfaction of the production capacity constraint. If a particular decision alternative does not satisfy one or more of the model constraints, the decision alternative is rejected as being an **infeasible solution** regardless of the objective function value. If all constraints are satisfied, the decision alternative is a **feasible solution** and a candidate for the "best" solution or recommended decision. Through this trial-and-error process of evaluating selected decision alternatives, a decision maker can identify a good—and possibly the best—feasible solution to the problem. This solution would then be the recommended decision for the problem.

Table 1.2 shows the results of a trial-and-error approach to solving the production model of Figure 1.5. The recommended decision is a production quantity of 8 since the feasible solution with the highest projected profit occurs at $x = 8$.

Although the trial-and-error solution process is often acceptable and can provide valuable information for a manager, it has the drawbacks of not necessarily providing the best solution and of being inefficient in terms of requiring numerous calculations if many decision alternatives are tried. Thus, quantitative analysts have developed special solution procedures for many models that are much more efficient than the trial-and-error approach. Throughout this text, you will be introduced to solution procedures that are applicable to the specific mathematical models that will be formulated. Although some relatively small models or problems can be solved by hand computations, most practical applications require the use of a computer.

Model development and model solution steps are not completely separable. An analyst will want to develop an accurate model or representation of the actual problem situation, and the analyst will also want to be able to find a solution to the model. If we approach the model development step by attempting to find the most accurate and realistic mathematical model, we may find the model so large and complex that obtaining a solution is impossible. In this case, a simpler and perhaps more easily understood model with a readily available solution procedure is preferred even if the recommended solution is only a rough approximation of the best decision. As you learn more about quantitative solution procedures, you will have a better idea of the types of mathematical models that can be developed and solved.

After a model solution has been obtained, both the quantitative analyst and the manager will be interested in determining how good the solution really is. Although the analyst has undoubtedly taken many precautions to develop a realistic model, often the goodness or accuracy of the model cannot be assessed until model solutions are generated. Model testing and validation are frequently conducted with relatively small "test" problems that have known or at least expected solutions. If the model generates the expected solutions and if other output information appears correct, the go-ahead may be given to use the model on the full-scale problem. However, if the model test and validation identify potential problems or inaccuracies inherent in the model, corrective action, such as model modification

> You should now understand the concept of a mathematical model and what is referred to as the optimal solution to the model. Try Problem 8.

Table 1.2	TRIAL-AND-ERROR SOLUTION FOR THE PRODUCTION MODEL OF FIGURE 1.5		
Decision Alternative (Production Quantity) x	Projected Profit	Total Hours of Production	Feasible Solution? (Time Used ≤ 40)
0	0	0	Yes
2	20	10	Yes
4	40	20	Yes
6	60	30	Yes
8	80	40	Yes
10	100	50	No
12	120	60	No

and/or collection of more accurate input data, may be taken. Whatever the corrective action, the model solution will not be used in practice until the model has satisfactorily passed testing and validation.

Report Generation

An important part of the quantitative analysis process is the preparation of managerial reports based on the model's solution. Referring to Figure 1.3, we see that the solution based on the quantitative analysis of a problem is one of the inputs the manager considers before making a final decision. Thus, the results of the model must appear in a managerial report that can be easily understood by the decision maker. The report should include the recommended decision and other pertinent information about the results that may be helpful to the decision maker.

A Note Regarding Implementation

As discussed in Section 1.2, the manager is responsible for integrating the quantitative solution with qualitative considerations in order to make the best possible decision. After doing this, the manager must oversee the implementation and follow-up evaluation of the decision. During the implementation and follow-up, the manager should continue to monitor the contribution of the model. At times, this process may lead to requests for model expansion or refinement that will cause the quantitative analyst to return to one of the earlier steps of the quantitative analysis process.

Successful implementation of results is critical to the quantitative analyst as well as to the manager. If the results of the quantitative analysis process are not correctly implemented, the entire effort may be of no value. It doesn't take too many unsuccessful implementations before the quantitative analyst is out of work. Because implementation often requires people to do things differently, it often meets with resistance. People want to know, "What's wrong with the way we've been doing it?" One of the most effective ways to ensure a successful implementation is to secure as much user involvement as possible throughout the modeling process. A user who feels involved in identifying the problem and developing the solution will more enthusiastically implement the results. The success rate for implementing the results of a quantitative analysis project is much greater for those projects that include extensive user involvement.

1.4   MODELS OF COST, REVENUE, AND PROFIT

Some of the most basic quantitative models arising in business and economic applications are those involving the relationship between a volume variable—such as production volume or sales volume—and cost, revenue, and profit. Through the use of these models, a manager can determine the projected cost, revenue, and/or profit associated with an established production quantity or a forecasted sales volume. Financial planning, production planning, sales quotas, and other areas of decision making can benefit from such cost, revenue, and profit models.

Cost and Volume Models

The cost of manufacturing or producing a product is a function of the volume produced. This cost can usually be defined as a sum of two costs: fixed cost and variable cost. **Fixed cost** is the portion of the total cost that does not depend on the production volume; this cost remains the same no matter how much is produced. **Variable cost,** on the other hand, is the portion of the total cost that is dependent on and varies with the production volume. To illustrate how cost and volume models can be developed, we will consider a simple manufacturing problem faced by Nowlin Plastics.

Nowlin Plastics produces a variety of compact disc (CD) storage cases. Nowlin's best selling product is the CD-50, a slim, plastic CD holder with a specially designed lining that protects the optical surface of the disk. Several products are produced on the same manufacturing line and a setup cost is incurred each time a changeover is made for a new product. Suppose that the setup cost for the CD-50 is $3,000. This setup cost is a fixed cost that is incurred regardless of the number of units eventually produced. In addition, suppose that variable labor and material costs are $2 for each unit produced. The cost-volume model for producing x units of the CD-50 can be written as

$$C(x) = 3000 + 2x \tag{1.3}$$

where

$$x = \text{production volume in units}$$
$$C(x) = \text{total cost of producing } x \text{ units}$$

Once a production volume is established, the model in equation (1.3) can be used to compute the total production cost. For example, the decision to produce $x = 1200$ units would result in a total cost of $C(1200) = 3000 + 2(1200) = \$5400$.

Marginal cost is defined as the rate of change of the total cost with respect to production volume. That is, it is the cost increase associated with a one-unit increase in the production volume. In the cost model of equation (1.3), we see that the total cost $C(x)$ will increase by $2 for each unit increase in the production volume. Thus, the marginal cost is $2. With more complex total cost models, marginal cost may depend on the production volume. In such cases, we could have marginal cost increasing or decreasing with the production volume x.

Revenue and Volume Models

Management of Nowlin Plastics will also want information on the projected revenue associated with selling a specified number of units. Thus, a model of the relationship between revenue and volume is also needed. Suppose that each CD-50 storage unit sells for $5. The model for total revenue can be written as

$$R(x) = 5x \tag{1.4}$$

where

$$x = \text{sales volume in units}$$
$$R(x) = \text{total revenue associated with selling } x \text{ units}$$

Marginal revenue is defined as the rate of change of total revenue with respect to sales volume. That is, it is the increase in total revenue resulting from a one-unit increase in sales volume. In the model of equation (1.4), we see that the marginal revenue is $5. In this case, marginal revenue is constant and does not vary with the sales volume. With more complex models, we may find that marginal revenue increases or decreases as the sales volume x increases.

Profit and Volume Models

One of the most important criteria for managerial decision making is profit. Managers need to be able to know the profit implications of their decisions. If we assume that we will only produce what can be sold, the production volume and sales volume will be equal. We can combine equations (1.3) and (1.4) to develop a profit-volume model that will determine profit associated with a specified production-sales volume. Since total profit is total revenue minus total cost, the following model provides the profit associated with producing and selling x units:

$$P(x) = R(x) - C(x) \qquad\qquad (1.5)$$
$$= 5x - (3000 + 2x) = -3000 + 3x$$

Thus, the model for profit $P(x)$ can be derived from the models of the revenue-volume and cost-volume relationships.

Break-Even Analysis

Using equation (1.5), we can now determine the profit associated with any production volume x. For example, suppose that a demand forecast indicates that 500 units of the product can be sold. The decision to produce and sell the 500 units results in a projected profit of

$$P(500) = -3000 + 3(500) = -1500$$

In other words, a loss of $1500 is predicted. If sales are expected to be 500 units, the manager may decide against producing the product. However, a demand forecast of 1800 units would show a projected profit of

$$P(1800) = -3000 + 3(1800) = 2400$$

This profit may be enough to justify proceeding with the production and sale of the product.

We see that a volume of 500 units will yield a loss, whereas a volume of 1800 provides a profit. The volume that results in total revenue equaling total cost (providing $0 profit) is called the **break-even point.** If the break-even point is known, a manager can quickly infer that a volume above the break-even point will result in a profit, while a volume below the break-even point will result in a loss. Thus, the break-even point for a product provides valuable information for a manager who must make a yes/no decision concerning production of the product.

Let us now return to the Nowlin Plastics example and show how the profit model in equation (1.5) can be used to compute the break-even point. The break-even point can be found by setting the profit expression equal to zero and solving for the production volume. Using equation (1.5), we have

$$P(x) = -3000 + 3x = 0$$
$$3x = 3000$$
$$x = 1000$$

You should now be able to determine the break-even point for a quantitative model. Try Problem 15.

With this information, we know that production and sales of the product must be at least 1000 units before a profit can be expected. The graphs of the total cost model, the total revenue model, and the location of the break-even point are shown in Figure 1.6.

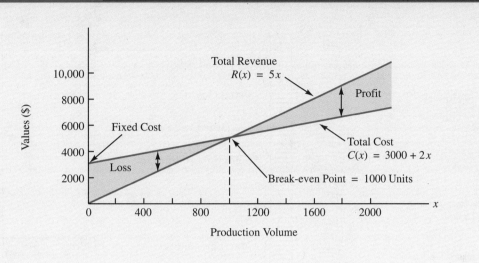

Figure 1.6 GRAPH OF THE BREAK-EVEN ANALYSIS FOR THE NOWLIN PLASTICS PRODUCTION EXAMPLE

1.5 SPREADSHEETS FOR MANAGEMENT SCIENCE

In Section 1.3 we stated that the process of developing and solving models is the essence of the quantitative analysis process. In this section we illustrate how spreadsheet software packages, such as Microsoft Excel®, can be used to perform a quantitative analysis of the Nowlin Plastics production example presented in Section 1.4.

Refer to the spreadsheet shown in Figure 1.7. We begin by entering the problem data into the top portion of the spreadsheet. The value of 3000 in cell B3 is the setup cost, the value of 2 in cell B5 is the variable labor and material costs per unit, and the value of $5 in cell B7 is the selling price per unit. In general, whenever we perform a quantitative analysis using a spreadsheet, we will enter the problem data in the top portion of the spreadsheet and reserve the bottom portion for model development. The label "Models" in cell B10 helps to provide a visual reminder of this convention.

Cell B12 in the models portion of the spreadsheet contains the proposed production volume in units. Because the values for total cost, total revenue, and total profit depend upon the value of this decision variable, we have placed a border around cell B12 and lightly screened the cell for emphasis. Based upon the value in cell B12, the cell formulas in cells B14, B16, and B18 are used to compute values for total cost, total revenue, and total profit (loss), respectively. First, recall that the value of total cost is the sum of the fixed cost (cell B3) and the total variable cost. Since the total variable cost is the product of the variable cost per unit (cell B5) and the production volume (cell B12), it is given by B5*B12. Thus, to compute the value of total cost we entered the formula =B3+B5*B12 in cell B14. Next, since total revenue is the product of the selling price per unit (cell B7) and the number of units produced (cell B12), in cell B16 we have entered the formula =B7*B12. Finally, the total profit (or loss) is the difference between the total revenue (cell B16) and the total cost (cell B14). Thus, in cell B18 we have entered the formula =B16−B14. The spreadsheet shown in Figure 1.7 shows the formulas used to make these computations; we refer to it as a formula spreadsheet.

Figure 1.7	FORMULA SPREADSHEET FOR THE NOWLIN PLASTICS PRODUCTION EXAMPLE

	A	B
1	**Nowlin Plastics**	
2		
3	**Fixed Cost**	3000
4		
5	**Variable Cost Per Unit**	2
6		
7	**Selling Price Per Unit**	5
8		
9		
10	**Models**	
11		
12	**Production Volume**	800
13		
14	**Total Cost**	=B3+B5*B12
15		
16	**Total Revenue**	=B7*B12
17		
18	**Total Profit (Loss)**	=B16-B14

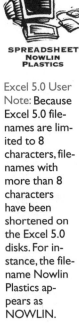

**SPREADSHEET
NOWLIN
PLASTICS**

Excel 5.0 User Note: Because Excel 5.0 file-names are limited to 8 characters, file-names with more than 8 characters have been shortened on the Excel 5.0 disks. For instance, the file-name Nowlin Plastics appears as NOWLIN.

To examine the effect of selecting a particular value for the production volume, we have entered a value of 800 in cell B12. The spreadsheet shown in Figure 1.8 shows the values obtained by the formulas; a production volume of 800 units results in total cost of $4600, total revenue of $4000, and a loss of $600. To examine the effect of other production volumes, we only need to enter a different value into cell B12. To examine the effect of different costs and selling prices, we simply enter the appropriate values in the data portion of the spreadsheet; the results will be displayed in the model section of the spreadsheet.

In Section 1.4 we illustrated break-even analysis. Let us now see how a spreadsheet approach can be used to compute the break-even point for the Nowlin Plastics production example. We begin by considering a trial-and-error approach.

Determining the Break-Even Point Using Excel's Table Command

The break-even point is the production volume that results in total revenue equal to total cost and hence a profit of $0. One way to determine the break-even point is to use a trial-and-error approach. For example, in Figure 1.8 we saw that a trial production volume of 800 units resulted in a loss of $600. Since this trial solution resulted in a loss, a production volume of 800 units cannot be the break-even point. We could continue to experiment with other production volumes by simply entering different values into cell B12 and observing the resulting profit or loss in cell B18. A better approach is to use Excel's Table command for doing this type of what-if analysis.

Figure 1.8   SPREADSHEET SOLUTION USING A PRODUCTION VOLUME OF 800 UNITS FOR THE NOWLIN PLASTICS PRODUCTION EXAMPLE

SPREADSHEET
NOWLIN
PLASTICS

	A	B
1	**Nowlin Plastics**	
2		
3	**Fixed Cost**	$3,000
4		
5	**Variable Cost Per Unit**	$2
6		
7	**Selling Price Per Unit**	$5
8		
9		
10	**Models**	
11		
12	**Production Volume**	800
13		
14	**Total Cost**	$4,600
15		
16	**Total Revenue**	$4,000
17		
18	**Total Profit (Loss)**	-$600

Suppose that we wanted to compute the profit or loss associated with production quantities ranging in value from 200 units to 2000 units, in increments of 200. We begin by entering these trial production values into a row or column of the spreadsheet. Note that we have entered these values into cells D13:D22 of the spreadsheet shown in Figure 1.9. Next, we enter the formula for profit into cell E12. Since the formula for profit has already been entered into cell B18, we entered the formula =B18 into cell E12. The following steps use Excel's Table command to compute profit and loss projections for each trial production value.

Step 1 Select cells D12:E22
Step 2 Select the **Data** pull-down menu
Step 3 Select the **Table** option
Step 4 When the **Table** dialog box appears
          Enter B12 in the **Column Input Cell**
          Select **OK**

The profit and loss values corresponding to each of the trial production values are displayed in cells E13:E22. Thus, we see that a production quantity of 200 units results in a loss of $2,400, a production quantity of 400 results in a loss of $1,800, and so on. Since a production quantity of 1000 results in a profit of $0, this is the break-even point for Nowlin Plastics.

Determining the Break-Even Point Using Goal Seek

Another way to find a break-even point using a spreadsheet is to use the Goal Seek tool. The Goal Seek tool in Microsoft Excel allows the user to determine the value for an input

		USING EXCEL'S TABLE COMMAND TO COMPUTE THE
Figure 1.9		BREAK-EVEN POINT FOR THE NOWLIN PLASTICS
		PRODUCTION EXAMPLE

**SPREADSHEET
NOWLIN
PLASTICS**

	A	B	C	D	E
1	**Nowlin Plastics**				
2					
3	Fixed Cost	$3,000			
4					
5	Variable Cost Per Unit	$2			
6					
7	Selling Price Per Unit	$5			
8					
9					
10	**Models**				
11					
12	**Production Volume**	800			-$600
13				200	-$2,400
14	Total Cost	$4,600		400	-$1,800
15				600	-$1,200
16	Total Revenue	$4,000		800	-$600
17				1000	$0
18	Total Profit (Loss)	-$600		1200	$600
19				1400	$1,200
20				1600	$1,800
21				1800	$2,400
22				2000	$3,000

cell that will cause the value of a related output cell to equal some specified value (called the *goal*). In the case of break-even analysis, the "goal" is to set Total Profit to zero by "seeking" an appropriate value for Production Volume. Goal Seek will allow us to find the value of production volume that will set Nowlin Plastic's total profit to zero. The following steps describe how to use Goal Seek to find the break-even point for Nowlin Plastics:

Step 1   Select the **Tools** pull-down menu
Step 2   Choose the **Goal Seek** option
Step 3   When the **Goal Seek dialog box** appears:
     Enter B18 in the **Set cell** box
     Enter 0 in the **To value** box
     Enter B12 in the **By changing cell** box
     Click **OK**

The completed **Goal Seek dialog box** is shown in Figure 1.10 and the spreadsheet obtained after selecting **OK** is shown in Figure 1.11. The Total Profit in cell B18 is zero and the Production Volume in cell B12 has been set to the break-even point of 1000.

Figure 1.10   GOAL SEEK DIALOG BOX FOR THE NOWLIN PLASTICS
PRODUCTION EXAMPLE

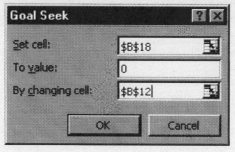

Figure 1.11   BREAK-EVEN POINT FOUND USING GOAL SEEK FOR THE
NOWLIN PLASTICS PRODUCTION EXAMPLE

SPREADSHEET
NOWLIN
PLASTICS

	A	B
1	**Nowlin Plastics**	
2		
3	**Fixed Cost**	$3,000
4		
5	**Variable Cost Per Unit**	$2
6		
7	**Selling Price Per Unit**	$5
8		
9		
10	**Models**	
11		
12	**Production Volume**	1000
13		
14	**Total Cost**	5000
15		
16	**Total Revenue**	5000
17		
18	**Total Profit (Loss)**	0

Throughout this text, we will encounter problems of much greater size and complexity than the Nowlin Plastics production example. We will see that a computer procedure is usually required to obtain a solution. Although many different types of software packages can be used to solve the problems introduced, we will illustrate how the Microsoft Excel spreadsheet package can be used to organize the problem data, develop an appropriate spreadsheet model, and solve the problem.

..../ /...........

SUMMARY

This book is about how quantitative methods may be used to help managers make better decisions. The focus of this text is on the decision-making process and on the role of quantitative methods in that process. We have discussed the problem orientation of this process and, in an overview, have shown how mathematical models can be used in this type of analysis.

The difference between the model and the situation or managerial problem it represents is an important point. Mathematical models are abstractions of real-world situations and, as such, cannot capture all aspects of a real situation. However, if a model can capture the major relevant aspects of the problem and can then provide a solution recommendation, it can be a valuable aid to decision making.

One of the characteristics of quantitative analysis that will become increasingly apparent as we proceed through the text is the search for a best solution to the problem. In carrying out the quantitative analysis, we shall be attempting to develop procedures for finding the "best" or optimal solution.

..../ /...........

GLOSSARY

Problem solving The process of identifying a difference between the actual and the desired state of affairs and then taking action to resolve the difference.

Decision making The process of defining the problem, identifying the alternatives, determining the criteria, evaluating the alternatives, and choosing an alternative.

Single-criterion decision problem A problem in which the objective is to find the "best" solution with respect to just one criterion.

Multicriteria decision problem A problem that involves more than one criterion; the objective is to find the "best" solution, taking into account all the criteria.

Decision The alternative selected.

Model A representation of a real object or situation.

Iconic model A physical replica, or representation, of a real object.

Analog model Although in physical form, an analog model does not have a physical appearance similar to the real object or situation it represents.

Mathematical model Mathematical symbols and expressions used to represent a real situation.

Constraints Restrictions or limitations imposed on a problem.

Objective function A mathematical expression used to represent the criterion for evaluating solutions to a problem.

Uncontrollable input The environmental factors or inputs that cannot be controlled by the decision maker.

Controllable input The decision alternatives or inputs that can be specified by the decision maker.

Decision variable Another term for controllable input.

Deterministic model A model in which all uncontrollable inputs are known and cannot vary.

Stochastic model A model in which at least one uncontrollable input is uncertain and subject to variation; stochastic models are also referred to as *probabilistic models.*

Optimal solution The specific decision variable value or values that provide the "best" output for the model.

Infeasible solution A decision alternative or solution that violates one or more constraints.

Feasible solution A decision alternative or solution that satisfies all constraints.

Fixed cost The portion of the total cost that does not depend on the volume; this cost remains the same no matter how much is produced.

Variable cost The portion of the total cost that is dependent on and varies with the volume.

Marginal cost The rate of change of the total cost with respect to production volume.

Marginal revenue The rate of change of total revenue with respect to sales volume.

Break-even point The volume at which total revenue equals total cost.

PROBLEMS

1. Define the terms *management science* and *operations research.*

2. Describe the major reasons for the growth in the use of quantitative methods since World War II.

3. Discuss the different roles played by the qualitative and quantitative approaches to managerial decision making. Why is having a good understanding of both approaches to decision making important for a manager or decision maker?

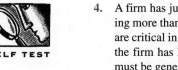

SELF TEST

4. A firm has just completed a new plant that will produce more than 500 different products, using more than 50 different production lines and machines. The production scheduling decisions are critical in that sales will be lost if customer demands are not met on time. If no individual in the firm has had experience with this production operation, and if new production schedules must be generated each week, why should the firm consider a quantitative approach to the production scheduling problem?

5. List and discuss the steps of the decision-making process.

6. Give an example of each type of model discussed in this chapter: iconic, analog, and mathematical.

7. What are the advantages of analyzing and experimenting with a model as opposed to analyzing and experimenting with a real object or situation?

SELF TEST

8. Recall the production model from Section 1.3:

$$\text{Max} \quad 10x$$
$$\text{s.t.}$$
$$5x \leq 40$$
$$x \geq 0$$

Suppose that the firm in this example considers producing a second product that has a unit profit of $5 and requires 2 hours for each unit produced. Use y as the number of units of product 2 produced.

a. Show the mathematical model when both products are considered simultaneously.

b. Identify the controllable and uncontrollable inputs for this model.

    c.   Draw the flowchart of the input-output process for this model (see Figure 1.5).

    d.   What are the optimal solution values of x and $y?$

9.   Is the model developed in Problem 8 a deterministic or a stochastic model? Explain.

10.   Suppose that we modify the model in Section 1.3 to obtain the following mathematical model:

$$\text{Max} \quad 10x$$

$$\text{s.t.}$$

$$ax \le 40$$

$$x \ge 0$$

where a is the number of hours required for each unit produced. With $a = 5$, the optimal solution is $x = 8$. If we have a stochastic model with $a = 3$, $a = 4$, $a = 5$, or $a = 6$ as the possible values for the number of hours required per unit, what is the optimal value for $x?$ What problems does this stochastic model cause?

11.   A retail store in Des Moines, Iowa, receives shipments of a particular product from Kansas City and Minneapolis. Let

$$x = \text{units of product received from Kansas City}$$

$$y = \text{units of product received from Minneapolis}$$

    a.   Write an expression for the total units of product received by the retail store in Des Moines.

    b.   Shipments from Kansas City cost $0.20 per unit, and shipments from Minneapolis cost $0.25 per unit. Develop an objective function representing the total cost of shipments to Des Moines.

    c.   Assuming that the monthly demand at the retail store is 5000 units, develop a constraint that requires 5000 units to be shipped to Des Moines.

    d.   No more than 4000 units can be shipped from Kansas City, and no more than 3000 units can be shipped from Minneapolis in a month. Develop constraints to model this situation.

    e.   Of course, negative amounts cannot be shipped. Combine the objective function and constraints developed to state a mathematical model for satisfying the demand at the Des Moines retail store at minimum cost.

12.   Suppose that you are going on a weekend trip to a city that is d miles away. Develop a model that determines your round-trip gasoline costs. What assumptions or approximations are necessary to treat this model as a deterministic model? Are these assumptions or approximations acceptable to you?

13.   For most products, higher prices result in a decreased demand, whereas lower prices result in an increased demand. Let

$$d = \text{annual demand for a product in units}$$

$$p = \text{price per unit}$$

Assume that a firm accepts the following price-demand relationship as being realistic:

$$d = 800 - 10p$$

where p must be between $20 and $70.

    a.   How many units can the firm sell at the $20 per-unit price? At the $70 per-unit price?

    b.   Show the mathematical model for the total revenue (TR), which is the annual demand multiplied by the unit price.

    c.   Based on other considerations, the firm's management will only consider price alternatives of $30, $40, and $50. Use your model from part (b) to determine the price alternative that will maximize the total revenue.

    d.   What are the expected annual demand and the total revenue according to your recommended price?

14. Suppose that a manager has a choice between the following two mathematical models of a given situation: (a) a relatively simple model that is a reasonable approximation of the real situation and (b) a thorough and complex model that is the most accurate mathematical representation of the real situation possible. Why might the model described in part (a) be preferred by the manager?

SELF TEST

15. The O'Neill Shoe Manufacturing Company will produce a special-style shoe if the order size is large enough to provide a reasonable profit. For each special-style order, the company incurs a fixed cost of $1000 for the production setup. The variable cost is $30 per pair, and each pair sells for $40.
    a. Let x indicate the number of pairs of shoes produced. Develop a mathematical model for the total cost of producing x pairs of shoes.
    b. Let P indicate the total profit. Develop a mathematical model for the total profit realized from an order for x pairs of shoes.
    c. How large must the shoe order be before O'Neill will break even?

16. Refer to the O'Neill Shoe Manufacturing Company situation in Problem 15.
    a. Develop spreadsheet models for total cost, total revenue, and total profit.
    b. Use Excel's Table command to determine the break-even point.
    c. Use Excel's Goal Seek tool to determine the break-even point.

17. Eastman Publishing Company is considering publishing a paperback textbook on spreadsheet applications for business. The fixed cost of manuscript preparation, textbook design, and production setup is estimated to be $80,000. Variable production and material costs are estimated to be $3 per book. Demand over the life of the book is estimated to be 4000 copies. The publisher plans to sell the text to college and university bookstores for $20 each.
    a. What is the break-even point?
    b. What profit or loss can be anticipated with a demand of 4000 copies?
    c. With a demand of 4000 copies, what is the minimum price per copy that the publisher must charge to break even?
    d. If the publisher believes that the price per copy could be increased to $25.95 and not affect the anticipated demand of 4000 copies, what action would you recommend? What profit or loss can be anticipated?

18. Refer to the Eastman Publishing Company situation in Problem 17.
    a. Develop spreadsheet models for total cost, total revenue, and total profit.
    b. Suppose that each book sells for $20. Use Excel's Goal Seek tool to determine the value of demand that will enable Eastman Publishing Company to break even.
    c. Management believes that if the price of the book is increased to $25.95, the lowest demand will be 3500 books. By considering values for demand ranging from 3500 books to 4500 books, in increments of 100 books, investigate the effect that the increased price may have on profits. Do you think Eastman should increase the price to $25.95?

19. Preliminary plans are underway for the construction of a new stadium for a major league baseball team. City officials have questioned the number and profitability of the luxury corporate boxes planned for the upper deck of the stadium. Corporations and selected individuals may buy the boxes for $100,000 each. The fixed construction cost for the upper-deck area is estimated to be $1,500,000, with a variable cost of $50,000 for each box constructed.
    a. What is the break-even point for the number of luxury boxes in the new stadium?
    b. Preliminary drawings for the stadium show that space is available for the construction of up to 50 luxury boxes. Promoters indicate that buyers are available and that all 50 could be sold if constructed. What is your recommendation concerning the construction of luxury boxes? What profit is anticipated?

20. Refer to Problem 19.
    a. Develop spreadsheet models for total cost, total revenue, and total profit.
    b. Use Excel's Table command to determine the break-even point for the number of luxury boxes in the new stadium.
    c. Use Excel's Goal Seek tool to determine the break-even point.

21. Financial Analysts, Inc., is an investment firm that manages stock portfolios for a number of clients. A new client has just requested that the firm handle an $80,000 portfolio. As an initial investment strategy, the client would like to restrict the portfolio to a mix of the following two stocks:

Stock	Price/ Share	Estimated Annual Return/Share	Maximum Possible Investment
Oil Alaska	$50	$6	$50,000
Southwest Petroleum	$30	$4	$45,000

Let

$$x = \text{number of shares of Oil Alaska}$$
$$y = \text{number of shares of Southwest Petroleum}$$

a. Develop the objective function, assuming that the client desires to maximize the total annual return.
b. Show the mathematical expression for each of the following three constraints:
   (1) Total investment funds available are $80,000.
   (2) Maximum Oil Alaska investment is $50,000.
   (3) Maximum Southwest Petroleum investment is $45,000.
   Note: Adding the $x \geq 0$ and $y \geq 0$ constraints provides a linear programming model for the investment problem. A solution procedure for this model is discussed in Chapter 2.

22. Models of inventory systems frequently consider the relationships among a beginning inventory, a production quantity, a demand or sales, and an ending inventory. For a given production period j, let

$$s_{j-1} = \text{ending inventory from the previous period (beginning inventory for period } j)$$
$$x_j = \text{production quantity in period } j$$
$$d_j = \text{demand in period } j$$
$$s_j = \text{ending inventory for period } j$$

a. Write the mathematical relationship or model that describes how these four variables are related.
b. What constraint should be added if production capacity for period j is given by C_j?
c. What constraint should be added if safety stock requirements for period j mandate an ending inventory of at least I_j?

··/ /··········

MANAGEMENT SCIENCE IN PRACTICE FEATURE

Management Science in Practice write-ups prepared by practitioners are presented at the end of 6 chapters. We feel these provide a meaningful extension to the text material. The purpose of these application write-ups is to provide the reader with a better appreciation for the types of companies that use Management Science and the types of problems these companies are able to solve.

Each Management Science in Practice write-up begins with a description of the company involved and continues with a discussion of the areas where the company has successfully applied management science. The remainder of the write-up deals with an application that is closely related to the preceding chapter and/or part of the book. An effort has been made to avoid unnecessary technical detail and to focus on the managerial aspects and the value of the results to the company.

Since Chapter 1 is designed to provide an introduction to management science, we have not emphasized any particular solution methodology. Thus, we have placed the Mead Corporation write-up at the end of this first chapter because it provides an overview of several areas in which management science can be used effectively. It is evidence of the impact quantitative approaches to decision making are having at some companies.

MANAGEMENT SCIENCE IN PRACTICE

MEAD CORPORATION*

DAYTON, OHIO

Mead is a major producer of papers for premium periodicals, books, commercial printing, and business forms, with special expertise in coating technologies. The company and its affiliates also produce pulp and lumber, a variety of specialty papers, and converted wood and paper products. Mead is a leader in the design and manufacture of packaging systems for beverage and other consumable markets. The company is a world leader in the production of coated board, and manufactures shipping containers and corrugating medium. Mead is a major manufacturer of paper-based school and office products, and operates a nationwide network of distribution centers for paper, packaging, and supplies.

Management Science at Mead Corporation

Management Science applications at Mead are developed and implemented by the company's Decision Analysis (DA) Department. The DA Department provides timely, efficient internal consulting services to the operating groups and corporate staff in the functional areas of operations, finance, marketing, and human resources. The department assists decision makers by providing them with analytical tools of management science as well as personal analysis and recommendations. Through conversations and observations, the department recognizes needs where management science techniques are applicable, and it then recommends appropriate projects. In addition, the department provides a resource reservoir for information and assistance on quantitative methodology and assumes responsibility for keeping

---

*The authors are indebted to Dr. Edward P. Winkofsky, Mead Corporation, Dayton, Ohio, for providing this application.

current in management science techniques that could produce efficiencies at Mead. This charter results in a variety of projects and applications that span the corporation. Four examples of management science applications at Mead are described here.

A Corporate Planning System

The DA Department built and maintains a corporate planning system. This system allows business units to create and evaluate their five-year plans in an interactive computer environment.

Once the individual business units have finished their planning, the system consolidates the information at a group level. The assumptions of the units and the group are evaluated and reconciled. The use of this computer model facilitates the process by ensuring uniformity of calculations and reporting by all the planning units. Ultimately, the information is consolidated and evaluated at a corporate level.

A Timberland Financing Model

Another example of a management science application involves the development of a timberland financing model. Working directly with financial management, analysts assisted in the creation of a deterministic model that considered the major factors in a timberland financing arrangement. The model was used to examine the liability and profitability of timberland acquisition under various assumptions concerning forest growth rates, the inflation rate, and other financial considerations. By using the model, management was able to examine fully the acquisition and modify the financial arrangement as operating conditions warranted. The model is currently operated and modified by financial management and is considered a major tool in the examination of timberland financing.

Inventory Analysis

Inventory analysis is an area in which more sophisticated tools of management science have been used. Simulation models have been used to describe the major factors (e.g., demand or usage rates, lead times, and production rates) in an inventory system. Typically, an inventory model includes purchase, storage, ordering, stockout, and degradation costs. The simulation model is used to evaluate reorder points, safety stocks, customer service levels, review periods, and the response time of the inventory system to extraordinary events.

Once developed and in place, the model can be updated as economic and operating conditions change. Thus, the model can be used by management to evaluate its inventory system on an ongoing basis and to ensure that it is operating in a cost-efficient manner. These inventory simulation models are user friendly and can be operated and maintained by management with little formal computer training.

A Timber Harvesting Model

Mead also uses models to assist with the long-range management of the company's timberland. Through the use of large-scale linear programs, timber harvesting plans have been developed to cover a substantial time horizon. These models consider wood market conditions, mill pulpwood requirements, harvesting capacities, and general forest management principles.Within these constraints, the model develops an optimal harvesting and purchasing schedule based on discounted cash flow. Alternative schedules are developed to reflect various assumptions concerning forest growth, wood availability, and general economic conditions.

Quantitative methods are also used in the development of the inputs for the linear programming models already described. Timber prices and supplies as well as mill requirements must be forecast over the time horizon. Advanced sampling techniques are used to evaluate land holdings and to project forest growth. The harvest schedule is developed through the use of a number of management science techniques.

Summary

The applications briefly described here—although only a few of the many management science projects at Mead—convey the breadth of the activities currently in use within the company. The management scientist at Mead must be able to work in a number of different environments and be proficient in a wide range of quantitative methods. In addition, the analyst must possess exceptional oral and written communication skills. Only with this background will the analyst be able to achieve the major objective of quantitative analysis at Mead—the development and implementation of user-friendly quantitative models that will support and enhance management decision making throughout the organization.

Questions

1. Which Mead applications use a deterministic model, and which use a stochastic model? What conditions in the applications indicate a stochastic model is necessary?
2. Discuss how quantitative analysis described in Section 1.3 occurs in Mead's inventory analysis application.
3. Discuss the benefits associated with the management science applications at Mead.

2

AN INTRODUCTION TO

LINEAR PROGRAMMING

Linear programming is a problem-solving approach that has been developed to help managers make decisions. The following applications are typical of linear programming.

Linear programming was initially referred to as "programming in a linear structure. In 1948 Tjalling Koopmans suggested to George Dantzig that the name was much too long; Koopman's suggestion was to shorten it to linear programming. George Dantzig agreed, and the field we now know as *linear programming* was named.

1. A manufacturer wants to develop a production schedule and an inventory policy that will satisfy sales demand in future periods. Ideally the schedule and policy will enable the company to satisfy demand and at the same time *minimize* the total production and inventory costs.
2. A financial analyst must select an investment portfolio from a variety of stock and bond investment alternatives. The analyst would like to establish the portfolio that *maximizes* the return on investment.
3. A marketing manager wants to determine how best to allocate a fixed advertising budget among alternative advertising media such as radio, television, newspaper, and magazines. The manager would like to determine the media mix that *maximizes* advertising effectiveness.
4. A company has warehouses in a number of locations throughout the United States. For a set of customer demands, the company would like to determine how much each warehouse should ship to each customer so that the total transportation costs are *minimized*.

These are only a few examples of situations in which linear programming has been used successfully, but the examples illustrate the diversity of linear programming applications. A close scrutiny reveals one basic property that all these examples have in common. In each example we were concerned with *maximizing* or *minimizing* some quantity. In example 1 the manufacturer wanted to minimize costs; in example 2 the financial analyst wanted to maximize return on investment; in example 3 the marketing manager wanted to maximize advertising effectiveness; and in example 4 the company wanted to minimize total transportation costs. *In all linear programming problems, the maximization or minimization of some quantity is the objective.*

All linear programming problems also have a second property: restrictions or **constraints** that limit the degree to which the objective can be pursued. In example 1 the manufacturer is restricted by constraints requiring product demand to be satisfied and by the constraints limiting production capacity. The financial analyst's portfolio problem is constrained by the total amount of investment funds available and the maximum amounts that can be invested in each stock or bond. The marketing manager's media selection decision is constrained by a fixed advertising budget and the availability of the various media. In the transportation problem, the minimum cost shipping schedule is constrained by the supply of product available at each warehouse. *Thus constraints are another general feature of every linear programming problem.*

2.1   A SIMPLE MAXIMIZATION PROBLEM

RMC, Inc., is a small firm that produces a variety of chemical-based products. In a particular production process, three raw materials are used to produce two products: a fuel additive and a solvent base. The fuel additive is sold to oil companies and is used in the production of gasoline and related fuels. The solvent base is sold to a variety of chemical firms and is used in both home and industrial cleaning products. The three raw materials are blended to form the fuel additive and solvent base as indicated in Table 2.1. It shows that a ton of fuel additive is a mixture of $\frac{2}{5}$ ton of material 1 and $\frac{3}{5}$ ton of material 3. A ton of solvent base is a mixture of $\frac{1}{2}$ ton of material 1, $\frac{1}{5}$ ton of material 2, and $\frac{3}{10}$ ton of material 3.

RMC's production is constrained by a limited availability of the three raw materials. For the current period, RMC has available 20 tons of material 1, 5 tons of material 2, and 21 tons of material 3. Because of spoilage and the nature of the production process, any materials not used for current production are useless and must be discarded.

The accounting department has reviewed the relevant costs and prices for both products and calculated a profit contribution[1] of $40 for every ton of fuel additive produced and

Table 2.1	MATERIAL REQUIREMENTS PER TON FOR THE RMC PROBLEM

	Product	
	Fuel Additive	**Solvent Base**
Material 1	$\frac{2}{5}$	$\frac{1}{2}$
Material 2	0	$\frac{1}{5}$
Material 3	$\frac{3}{5}$	$\frac{3}{10}$

3/5 ton of material 3 is used in each ton of fuel additive

---

1. From an accounting perspective, profit contribution is more correctly described as the contribution margin per ton; overhead and other shared costs have not been allocated.

$30 for every ton of solvent base produced. RMC's management, after an analysis of potential demand, has concluded that the prices established will ensure the sale of all the fuel additive and solvent base produced. How many tons of each product should be produced in order to maximize total profit contribution?

Problem Formulation

Problem formulation or **modeling** is the process of translating a verbal statement of a problem into a mathematical statement. The process of formulating models is an art that can only be mastered with practice and experience. Although every problem has *some* unique features, most problems also have common features. As a result, some general guidelines for model formulation can be helpful, especially for beginners. We will illustrate these general guidelines by developing a mathematical model for the RMC problem.

Understand the problem thoroughly.   We selected the RMC problem to introduce linear programming because it is easy to understand. However, more complex problems will require much more thinking in order to identify the items that need to be included in the model. In such cases, read the problem description quickly to get a feel for what is involved. Taking notes will help you focus on the key issues and facts.

Write a verbal statement of the objective and each constraint.   Objective: Maximize the total contribution to profit. Constraints: Three constraints relate to the amount of raw materials available; they restrict the number of tons of fuel additive and solvent base that can be produced.

Constraint 1:   Amount of material 1 used has to be less than or equal to the amount of material 1 available.

Constraint 2:   Amount of material 2 used has to be less than or equal to the amount of material 2 available.

Constraint 3:   Amount of material 3 used has to be less than or equal to the amount of material 3 available.

Define the decision variables.   The two decision variables are: number of tons of fuel additive produced and number of tons of solvent base produced. Let

$$F = \text{tons of fuel additive produced}$$

$$S = \text{tons of solvent base produced}$$

In linear programming terminology, F and S are referred to as the *decision variables.*

Write the objective in terms of the decision variables.   RMC's profit contribution comes from two sources: (1) the profit contribution made by producing F tons of fuel additive; and (2) the profit contribution made by producing S tons of solvent base. Since RMC makes $40 for every ton of fuel additive produced, the company will make $40F$ if F tons of fuel additive are produced. Also, since RMC makes $30 for every ton of solvent base produced, the company will make $30S$ if S tons of solvent base are produced. Deleting the dollar signs, we have

$$\text{Total Profit Contribution} = 40F + 30S \qquad (2.1)$$

Since the objective—maximize total profit contribution—is a *function* of the decision variables F and S, we refer to $40F + 30S$ as the **objective function.** Using "Max" as an abbreviation for maximize, we write RMC's objective as follows:

$$\text{Max } 40F + 30S \tag{2.2}$$

Write the constraints in terms of the decision variables.   Constraint 1:

$$\begin{pmatrix} \text{Amount of} \\ \text{Material 1 Used} \end{pmatrix} \leq \begin{pmatrix} \text{Amount of} \\ \text{Material 1 Available} \end{pmatrix}$$

Since every ton of fuel additive produced will use ⅖ ton of material 1, the total number of tons of material 1 used in the production of F tons of fuel additive is ⅖ F. In addition, every ton of solvent base produced uses ½ ton of material 1, so the total number of tons of material 1 used in the production of S tons of solvent base is ½ S. Thus, the total tons of material 1 used to produce F tons of fuel additive and S tons of solvent base is given by

$$\text{Amount of Material 1 Used} = ⅖F + ½S$$

Because RMC has a maximum of 20 tons of material 1 available, the production combination we select must satisfy the requirement

$$\frac{2}{5}F + \frac{1}{2}S \leq 20 \tag{2.3}$$

Constraint 2:

$$\begin{pmatrix} \text{Amount of} \\ \text{Material 2 Used} \end{pmatrix} \leq \begin{pmatrix} \text{Amount of} \\ \text{Material 2 Available} \end{pmatrix}$$

The production of fuel additive does not use any material 2, and each ton of solvent base uses ⅕ ton of material 2. Because 5 tons of material 2 are available,

$$0F + \frac{1}{5}S \leq 5$$

or, simply,

$$\frac{1}{5}S \leq 5 \tag{2.4}$$

Constraint 3:

$$\begin{pmatrix} \text{Amount of} \\ \text{Material 3 Used} \end{pmatrix} \leq \begin{pmatrix} \text{Amount of} \\ \text{Material 3 Available} \end{pmatrix}$$

Each ton of fuel additive produced uses ⅗ ton of material 3, and each ton of solvent base uses ³⁄₁₀ ton of material 3. Because 21 tons of material 3 are available,

$$\frac{3}{5}F + \frac{3}{10}S \leq 21 \tag{2.5}$$

We have now specified the mathematical relationships for the constraints associated with the three materials. Have we forgotten any other constraints? Can RMC produce a negative number of tons of fuel additive or solvent base? Clearly, the answer is no. Thus, to prevent the decision variables from having negative values, two constraints

$$F \geq 0 \text{ and } S \geq 0 \tag{2.6}$$

must be added. These constraints ensure that the solution to the problem will contain nonnegative values for the decision variables and are thus referred to as the **nonnegativity constraints.** Nonnegativity constraints are a general feature of all linear programming problems and may be written in the abbreviated form

$$F, S \geq 0$$

A Mathematical Model of the RMC Problem

The mathematical statement, or mathematical formulation, of the RMC problem is now complete. We have translated the objective and constraints of the real-world problem into a set of mathematical relationships referred to as a mathematical model. The complete mathematical model for the RMC problem is

$$\text{Max} \quad\quad 40F + 30S$$
$$\text{subject to (s.t.)}$$
$$\frac{2}{5}F + \frac{1}{2}S \leq 20 \quad \text{Material 1}$$
$$\frac{1}{5}S \leq 5 \quad \text{Material 2}$$
$$\frac{3}{5}F + \frac{3}{10}S \leq 21 \quad \text{Material 3}$$
$$F, S \geq 0$$

Our job now is to find the product mix (i.e., the combination of F and S) that satisfies all the constraints and, at the same time, yields a value for the objective function that is greater than or equal to the value given by any other feasible solution. In doing so, we will find the optimal solution to the problem.

The mathematical model of the RMC problem is a **linear program.** It has the objective and constraints that, as we said earlier, are common properties of all *linear* programs. But, what is the special feature of this mathematical model that makes it a "linear" program? The special feature that makes it a linear program is that the objective function and all **constraint functions** (the left-hand sides of the constraint inequalities) are linear functions of the decision variables.

Mathematical functions in which each variable appears in a separate term and is raised to the first power are called **linear functions.** The objective function ($40F + 30S$) is a linear function because each decision variable appears in a separate term and has an exponent of 1. The amount of material 1 used ($\frac{2}{5}F + \frac{1}{2}S$) is also a linear function of the decision variables for the same reason. Similarly, the functions on the left-hand side of constraints 2 and 3 are also linear functions. Thus, the mathematical model of the RMC problem is referred to as a *linear program.*

Linear *programming* has nothing to do with computer programming. The use of the word *programming* here means "choosing a course of action." Linear programming involves choosing a course of action when the mathematical model of the problem contains only linear functions.

N O T E S
and Comments

1. The three assumptions necessary for a linear programming model to be appropriate are proportionality, additivity, and divisibility. *Proportionality* means that the contribution to the objective function and the amount of resources used are proportional to the value of each decision variable. *Additivity* means that the value of the objective function and the total resources used can be found by summing the objective function contribution and the resources used for all decision variables. *Divisibility* means that the decision variables are continuous. The divisibility assumption plus the nonnegativity constraints means that decision variables can take on any value greater than or equal to zero.

2. Quantitative analysts formulate and solve a variety of mathematical models that contain an objective function and a set of constraints. Models of this type are referred to as *mathematical programming models.* Linear programming models are a special type of mathematical programming model in that the objective function and all constraint functions are linear.

2.2 GRAPHICAL SOLUTION PROCEDURE

In the RMC problem, any particular production combination of fuel additive and solvent base is referred to as a **solution** to the problem. However, only those solutions that satisfy *all* the constraints are referred to as **feasible solutions.** The particular feasible production combination or feasible solution that results in the largest profit contribution is referred to as the *optimal* production combination or, equivalently, the **optimal solution.** At this point, however, we have no idea what the optimal solution will be. In fact, we have not even developed a procedure for identifying feasible solutions. In this section, we will show how a graphical solution procedure can be used to identify the feasible solutions and the optimal solution for a linear programming problem involving two decision variables.

We begin the graphical solution procedure by developing a graph that displays the possible solutions (F and S values) for the RMC problem. The graph shown in Figure 2.1 has values of F on the horizontal axis and values of S on the vertical axis. Every point (F, S) corresponds to a possible solution, so every point on the graph is called a *solution*. The solution where $F = 0$ and $S = 0$ is referred to as the *origin*. Because F and S must be nonnegative, the graph in Figure 2.1 only displays solutions where $F \geq 0$ and $S \geq 0$.

Earlier we determined that the inequality representing the material 1 constraint was

$$\tfrac{2}{5}F + \tfrac{1}{2}S \leq 20$$

To show all solution points that satisfy this relationship, we start by graphing the line corresponding to the equation

$$\tfrac{2}{5}F + \tfrac{1}{2}S = 20$$

We graph this equation by identifying two points and then drawing a line through the points. Setting $F = 0$ and solving for S gives $\tfrac{1}{2}S = 20$ or $S = 40$; hence the point $(F = 0, S = 40)$ satisfies the preceding equation. To find a second point satisfying this equation, we set $S = 0$ and solve for F. Doing so, we obtain $\tfrac{2}{5}F = 20$, or $F = 50$. Thus a second point satisfying the equation is $(F = 50, S = 0)$. With these two points, we can now graph the line. This line, called the *material 1 constraint line,* is shown in Figure 2.2.

Recall that the inequality representing the material 1 constraint is

$$\tfrac{2}{5}F + \tfrac{1}{2}S \leq 20$$

Figure 2.1   GRAPH OF SOLUTION POINTS FOR THE TWO-VARIABLE RMC PROBLEM

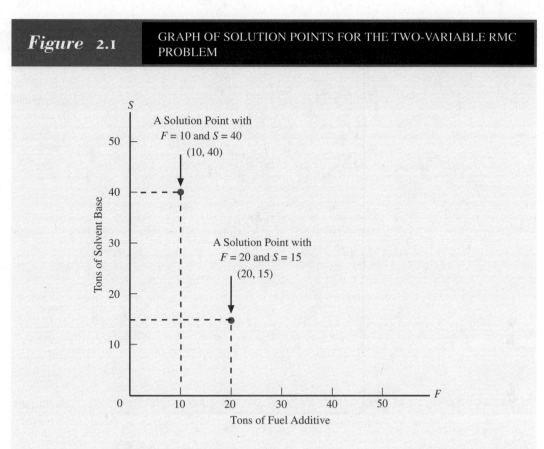

Can you identify all solutions that satisfy this constraint? First, note that any point on the line $\frac{2}{5}F + \frac{1}{2}S = 20$ must satisfy the constraint. But where are the solutions satisfying $\frac{2}{5}F + \frac{1}{2}S < 20$? Consider two solution points ($F = 10$, $S = 10$) and ($F = 40$, $S = 30$). Figure 2.2 shows that the first solution is below the constraint line and that the second is above the constraint line. Which of these solutions satisfies the material 1 constraint? For the point ($F = 10$, $S = 10$) we have

$$\tfrac{2}{5}F + \tfrac{1}{2}S = \tfrac{2}{5}(10) + \tfrac{1}{2}(10) = 9$$

Since 9 tons is less than the 20 tons of material 1 available, the $F = 10$, $S = 10$ production combination, or solution, satisfies the constraint. For $F = 40$ and $S = 30$ we have

$$\tfrac{2}{5}F + \tfrac{1}{2}S = \tfrac{2}{5}(40) + \tfrac{1}{2}(30) = 31$$

The 31 tons is greater than the 20 tons available, so the $F = 40$, $S = 30$ solution does not satisfy the constraint and thus is not feasible.

You should now be able to graph a constraint line and find the solution points that are feasible. Try Problem 2.

If a particular solution isn't feasible, all other solutions on the same side of the constraint line are not feasible. If a particular solution is feasible, all other solutions on the same side of the constraint line are feasible. Thus, you need to evaluate only one solution point to determine which side of a constraint line provides feasible solutions. In Figure 2.3 we show all points that satisfy the material 1 constraint by shading the feasible area.

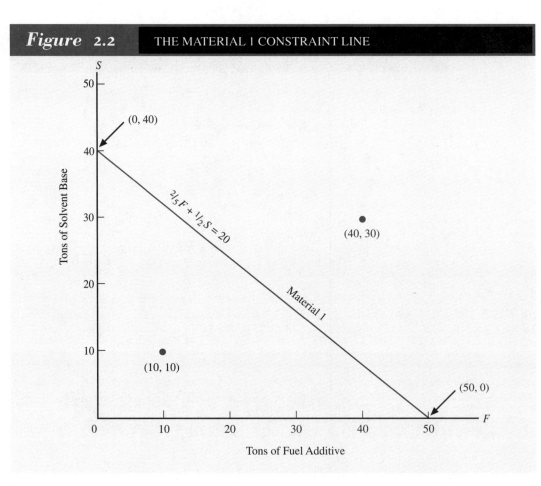

Figure 2.2 THE MATERIAL 1 CONSTRAINT LINE

Next let us identify all solution points that satisfy the material 2 constraint:

$$\frac{1}{5}S \le 5$$

We start by drawing the constraint line corresponding to the equation $\frac{1}{5}S = 5$. Since this equation is equivalent to the equation $S = 25$, we simply draw a line whose S value is 25 for every value of F; this line is parallel to and 25 units above the horizontal axis. In Figure 2.4 we have drawn the line corresponding to the material 2 constraint. Following the approach we used for the material 1 constraint, we realize that only points on or below the line will satisfy the material 2 constraint. Thus, in Figure 2.4 the shaded region corresponds to all feasible production combinations or feasible solutions for the material 2 constraint.

Similarly, we can determine the set of all feasible solutions for the material 3 constraint. Figure 2.5 shows the result. For practice, try to graph the feasible region for the material 3 constraint and determine whether your result agrees with that shown in Figure 2.5.

We now have three separate graphs showing the feasible solutions for each constraint. In a linear programming problem, we need to identify the solutions that satisfy *all* the constraints *simultaneously*. To find these solutions, we can draw the three constraints on one graph and observe the region containing the points that do in fact satisfy all the constraints simultaneously.

The graphs in Figures 2.3–2.5 can be superimposed to obtain one graph with all three constraints. Figure 2.6 shows this combined constraint graph. The shaded region in this fig-

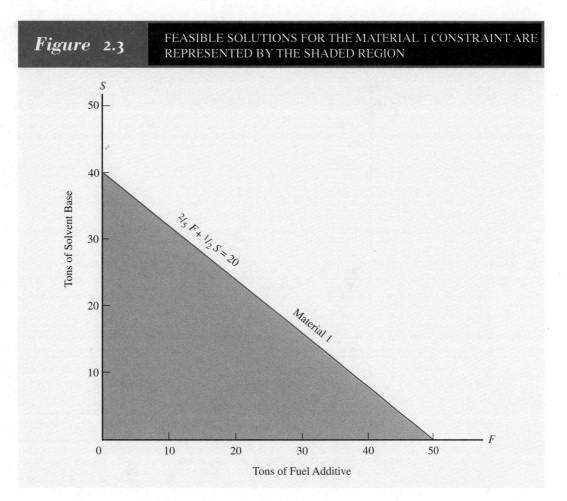

Figure 2.3 FEASIBLE SOLUTIONS FOR THE MATERIAL 1 CONSTRAINT ARE REPRESENTED BY THE SHADED REGION

You should now be able to find the feasible region given several constraints. Try Problem 6.

ure includes every solution point that satisfies all constraints simultaneously. Since solutions that satisfy all constraints simultaneously are termed *feasible solutions,* the shaded region is called the *feasible solution region,* or simply the **feasible region.** Any point on the boundary of the feasible region, or within the feasible region, is a *feasible solution point.*

Now that we have identified the feasible region, we are ready to proceed with the graphical solution method and find the optimal solution to the RMC problem. Recall that the optimal solution for a linear programming problem is the feasible solution that provides the best possible value of the objective function. Let us start the optimizing step of the graphical solution procedure by redrawing the feasible region on a separate graph. Figure 2.7 shows the graph.

One approach to finding the optimal solution would be to evaluate the objective function for each feasible solution; the optimal solution would then be the one yielding the largest value. The difficulty with this approach is that too many feasible solutions are possible (actually infinitely many); thus, evaluating all feasible solutions would not be possible. Hence, this trial-and-error procedure cannot be used to identify the optimal solution.

Rather than trying to compute the profit contribution for each feasible solution, we select an arbitrary value for profit contribution and identify all feasible solutions (F, S) that yield the selected value. For example, what feasible solutions provide a profit contribution

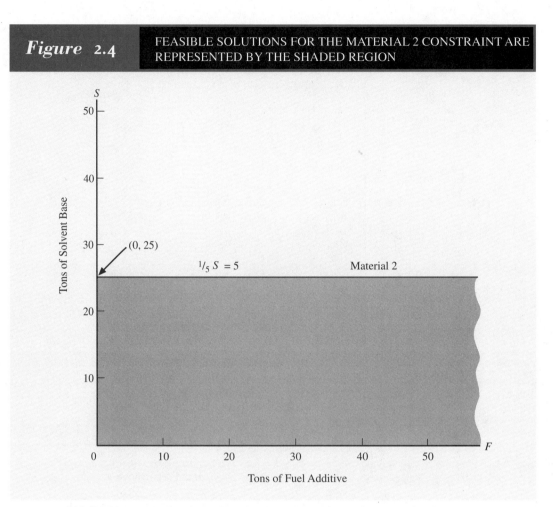

Figure 2.4   FEASIBLE SOLUTIONS FOR THE MATERIAL 2 CONSTRAINT ARE REPRESENTED BY THE SHADED REGION

of $240? These solutions are given by the values of F and S in the feasible region that will make the objective function

$$40F + 30S = 240$$

This expression is simply the equation of a line. Thus all feasible solutions (F, S) yielding a profit contribution of $240 must be on the line. We learned earlier in this section how to graph a constraint line. The procedure for graphing the profit or objective function line is the same. Letting $F = 0$, we see that S must be 8; thus the solution point $(F = 0, S = 8)$ is on the line. Similarly, by letting $S = 0$ we see that the solution point $(F = 6, S = 0)$ is also on the line. Drawing the line through these two points identifies all solutions that have a profit contribution of $240. A graph of this profit line is presented in Figure 2.8. It shows that an infinite number of feasible production combinations will provide a $240 profit contribution.

The objective is to find the feasible solution yielding the highest profit contribution, so we proceed by selecting higher profit contributions and finding solutions that yield the stated values. For example, what solutions provide a profit contribution of $720? What solutions provide a profit contribution of $1,200? To answer these questions, we must find the F and S values that are on the profit lines

$$40F + 30S = 720 \qquad \text{and} \qquad 40F + 30S = 1200$$

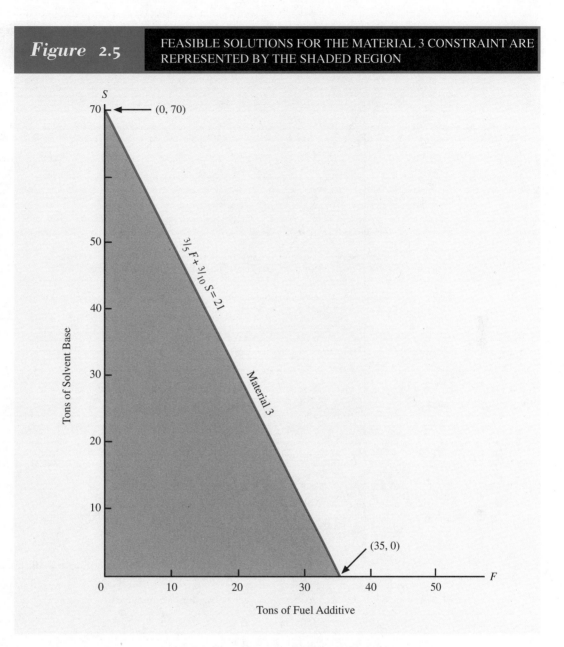

Figure 2.5 FEASIBLE SOLUTIONS FOR THE MATERIAL 3 CONSTRAINT ARE REPRESENTED BY THE SHADED REGION

Using the previous procedure for graphing profit and constraint lines, we graphed the $720 and $1,200 profit lines as shown in Figure 2.9. Not all solution points on the $1,200 profit line are in the feasible region, but at least some points on the line are; thus, we can obtain a feasible solution that provides a $1,200 profit contribution.

Can we find a feasible solution yielding an even higher profit contribution? Look at Figure 2.9 and make some general observations about the profit lines. You should be able to identify the following properties: (1) the profit lines are *parallel* to each other; and (2) profit lines with higher profit contributions are farther from the origin. Algebraically, with P representing total profit contribution, the objective function is

$$P = 40F + 30S$$

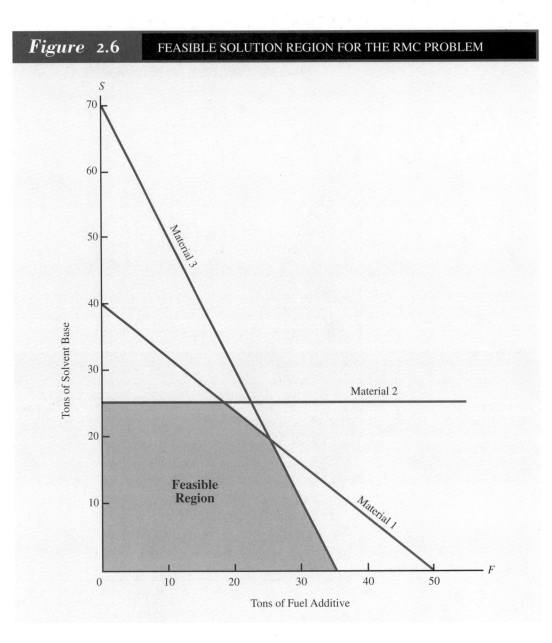

Figure 2.6   FEASIBLE SOLUTION REGION FOR THE RMC PROBLEM

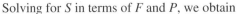

Solving for S in terms of F and P, we obtain

$$30S = -40F + P \qquad (2.7)$$

$$S = -\frac{40}{30}F + \frac{1}{30}P$$

Equation (2.7) is the *slope-intercept form* of the linear equation relating F and S. The coefficient of F, $-\frac{40}{30}$, is the slope of the line, and the term $\frac{1}{30}P$ is the S intercept (that is, the value of S where the graph of equation (2.7) crosses the S axis). Substituting the profit contributions of $P = 240$, $P = 720$, and $P = 1200$ into equation (2.7) yields the slope–intercept equations for the profit lines shown in Figure 2.9:

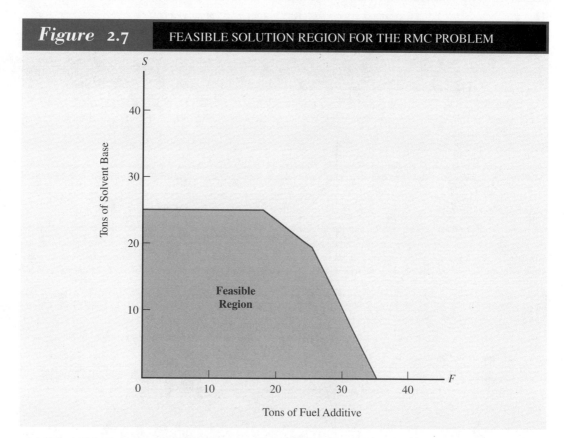

Figure 2.7 FEASIBLE SOLUTION REGION FOR THE RMC PROBLEM

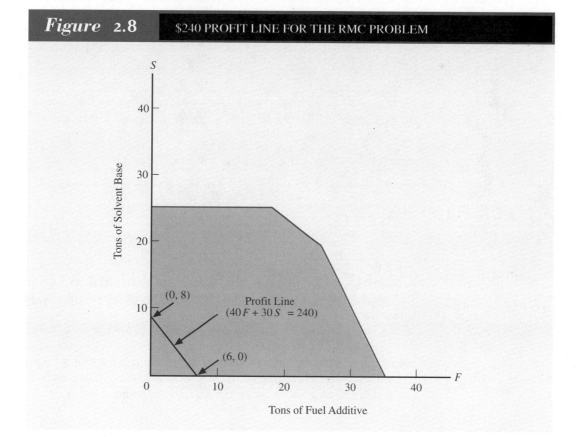

Figure 2.8 $240 PROFIT LINE FOR THE RMC PROBLEM

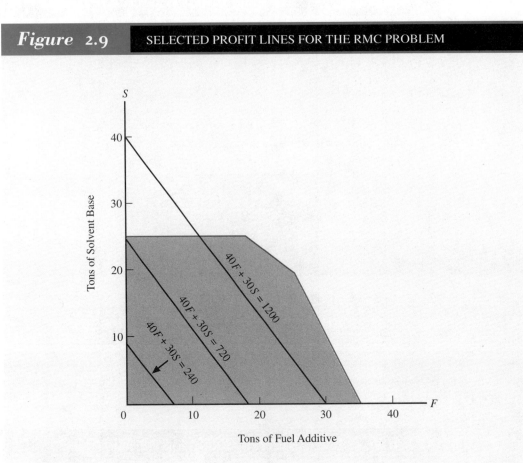

Figure 2.9   SELECTED PROFIT LINES FOR THE RMC PROBLEM

For $P = 240$,

$$S = -\frac{40}{30}F + 8$$

For $P = 720$,

$$S = -\frac{40}{30}F + 24$$

For $P = 1200$,

$$S = -\frac{40}{30}F + 40$$

Because the slope ($-\frac{40}{30}$) is the same for each profit line, the profit lines are parallel. Moreover, the S intercept increases with higher profit contributions. Thus, higher profit lines are farther from the origin.

Because the profit lines are parallel and higher profit lines are farther from the origin, we can obtain solutions that yield increasingly higher values for the objective function by continuing to move the profit line farther from the origin but keeping it parallel to the other profit lines. However, at some point any further outward movement will place the profit line entirely outside the feasible region. Because points outside the feasible region are unacceptable, the point in the feasible region that lies on the highest profit line is an optimal solution to the linear program.

You should now be able to identify the optimal solution point for the RMC problem. Use a ruler and move the profit line as far from the origin as you can. What is the last point in the feasible region? This point, which is the optimal solution, is shown graphically in Figure 2.10. The optimal values for the decision variables are the F and S values at this point.

Depending on the accuracy of your graph, you may or may not be able to determine the exact optimal values of F and S directly from the graph. However, refer to Figure 2.6 and note that the optimal solution point for the RMC example is at the *intersection* of the material 1 and material 3 constraint lines. That is, the optimal solution is on both the material 1 constraint line,

$$\tfrac{2}{5}F + \tfrac{1}{2}S = 20 \tag{2.8}$$

and the material 3 constraint line,

$$\tfrac{3}{5}F + \tfrac{3}{10}S = 21 \tag{2.9}$$

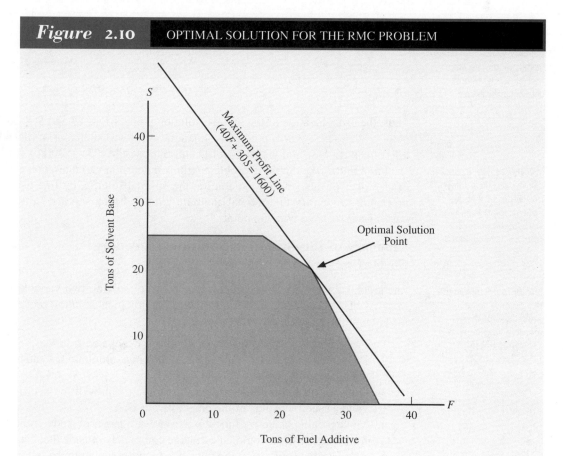

Figure 2.10   OPTIMAL SOLUTION FOR THE RMC PROBLEM

Thus, the values of the decision variables F and S must satisfy both equations (2.8) and (2.9) simultaneously. Using (2.8) and solving for F gives

$$\frac{2}{5}F = 20 - \frac{1}{2}S$$

or

$$F = 50 - \frac{5}{4}S \qquad\qquad (2.10)$$

Substituting this expression for F into equation (2.9) and solving for S yields

$$\frac{3}{5}(50 - \frac{5}{4}S) + \frac{3}{10}S = 21$$

$$30 - \frac{3}{4}S + \frac{3}{10}S = 21$$

$$30 - \frac{30}{40}S + \frac{12}{40}S = 21$$

$$-\frac{18}{40}S = -9$$

$$S = \left(\frac{40}{18}\right)(9) = 20$$

Substituting $S = 20$ in equation (2.10) and solving for F provides

$$F = 50 - \frac{5}{4}(20)$$

$$= 50 - 25 = 25$$

Although the optimal solution to the RMC problem consists of integer values for the decision variables, this will not always be the case.

Thus, the exact location of the optimal solution point is $F = 25$ and $S = 20$. This solution point provides the optimal production quantities for RMC at 25 tons of fuel additive and 20 tons of solvent base and yields a profit contribution of $40(25) + 30(20) = \$1600$.

For a linear programming problem with two decision variables, you can determine the exact values of the decision variables at the optimal solution by first using the graphical procedure to identify the optimal solution point and then solving the two simultaneous equations associated with the point.

You should now be able to use the graphical solution procedure to find the optimal solution and the value of the optimal solution. Try Problem 8.

Summary of the Graphical Solution Procedure for Maximization Problems

For more practice in using the graphical solution procedure for maximization problems, try Problem 16(b)–(d).

The graphical solution procedure is one method of solving two-variable linear programming problems, such as the RMC problem. The graphical solution procedure for a maximization problem involves the following steps.

1. Prepare a graph of the feasible solutions for each constraint.
2. Determine the feasible region by identifying solutions that satisfy all constraints simultaneously.
3. Draw an objective function line showing all values of the decision variables that yield a specified value of the objective function.
4. Move parallel objective function lines toward larger objective function values until further movement would take the line completely outside the feasible region.
5. Any feasible solution on the objective function line with the largest value is an optimal solution.

Slack Variables

In addition to the optimal solution and its associated profit contribution, the management of RMC will want information about the production requirements for the three materials. We can determine this information by substituting the optimal solution values ($F = 25$, $S = 20$) into the constraints of the linear program.

Constraint	Tons Required for $F = 25$, $S = 20$ Tons	Tons Available	Unused Tons
Material 1	$\frac{2}{5}(25) + \frac{1}{2}(20) = 20$	20	0
Material 2	$0(25) + \frac{1}{5}(20) = 4$	5	1
Material 3	$\frac{3}{5}(25) + \frac{3}{10}(20) = 21$	21	0

Can you identify the slack associated with a constraint? Try Problem 16(e).

Thus, the complete solution tells management that the production of 25 tons of fuel additive and 20 tons of solvent base will require all available material 1 and material 3 but only 4 of the 5 tons of material 2. The 1 ton of unused material 2 is referred to as *slack*. In linear programming terminology, any unused or idle capacity for a $\leq$ constraint is referred to as the *slack associated with the constraint*. Thus, the material 2 constraint has a slack of 1 ton.

Often variables, called **slack variables,** are added to the formulation of a linear programming problem to represent the slack, or idle capacity. Unused capacity makes no contribution to profit, so slack variables have coefficients of zero in the objective function. More generally, slack variables represent the difference between the right-hand side and the left-hand side of a $\leq$ constraint. After the addition of slack variables to the mathematical statement of the RMC problem, the mathematical model becomes

$$\text{Max} \quad 40F + 30S + 0S_1 + 0S_2 + 0S_3$$
$$\text{s.t.}$$
$$\frac{2}{5}F + \frac{1}{2}S + 1S_1 \qquad\qquad = 20$$
$$\frac{1}{5}S \qquad + 1S_2 \qquad = 5$$
$$\frac{3}{5}F + \frac{3}{10}S \qquad\qquad + 1S_3 = 21$$
$$F, S, S_1, S_2, S_3 \geq 0$$

Whenever all constraints in a linear program are expressed as equalities, the linear program is said to be written in **standard form.**

Referring to the standard form of the RMC problem, we see that at the optimal solution ($F = 25$, $S = 20$) the values for the slack variables are

Constraint	Value of Slack Variable
Material 1	$S_1 = 0$
Material 2	$S_2 = 1$
Material 3	$S_3 = 0$

Could we have used the graphical analysis to provide some of the previous information? The answer is yes. By finding the optimal solution in Figure 2.6, we see that the material 1 constraint and the material 3 constraint restrict, or *bind,* the feasible region at this point. Thus, the optimal solution requires the use of all of these two resources. In other words, the graph shows that at the optimal solution material 1 and material 3 will have zero slack. But, since the material 2 constraint is not binding the feasible region at the optimal solution, we can expect some slack for this resource.

Finally, some linear programs may have one or more constraints that do not affect the feasible region. That is, the feasible region remains the same whether the constraint is included in the problem or not. Because such a constraint does not affect the feasible region and thus cannot affect the optimal solution, it is called a **redundant constraint.** Redundant constraints can be dropped from the problem without having any effect on the optimal solution. However, in most linear programming problems, redundant constraints are not discarded because they are not immediately recognizable as being redundant. The RMC problem had no redundant constraints because each constraint had an effect on the feasible region.

Recognizing redundant constraints is easy with the graphical solution method. In problems with more than two decision variables, however, redundant constraints usually will not be apparent.

EXTREME POINTS AND THE OPTIMAL SOLUTION

Suppose that the profit contribution for 1 ton of solvent base increases from $30 to $60 while the profit contribution for 1 ton of fuel additive and all constraints remain unchanged. The complete linear programming model of this new problem is identical to the mathematical model in Section 2.1, except for the revised objective function:

$$\text{Max} \quad 40F + 60S$$

How does this change in the objective function affect the optimal solution to the RMC problem? Figure 2.11 shows the graphical solution of the RMC problem with the revised objective function. Note that because the constraints have not changed, the feasible region has not changed. However, the profit lines have been altered to reflect the new objective function.

By moving the profit line in a parallel manner away from the origin, we find the optimal solution as shown in Figure 2.11. The values of the decision variables at this point are $F = 18.75$ and $S = 25$. The increased profit for the solvent base has caused a change in the optimal solution. In fact, as you may have suspected, we are cutting back the production of the lower profit fuel additive and increasing the production of the higher profit solvent base.

What have you noticed about the location of the optimal solutions in the linear programming problems that we have solved thus far? Look closely at the graphical solutions in Figures 2.10 and 2.11. An important observation that you should be able to make is that the optimal solutions occur at one of the vertices or "corners" of the feasible region. In linear programming terminology these vertices are referred to as the **extreme points** of the feasible region. Thus, the RMC problem has five vertices or five extreme points (Figure 2.12). We can now state our observation about the location of optimal solutions[2]:

The optimal solution to a linear programming problem can be found at an extreme point of the feasible region for the problem.

---

2. In Section 2.6 we show that two special cases (infeasibility and unbounded) in linear programming have no optimal solution. The observation stated does not apply to these cases.

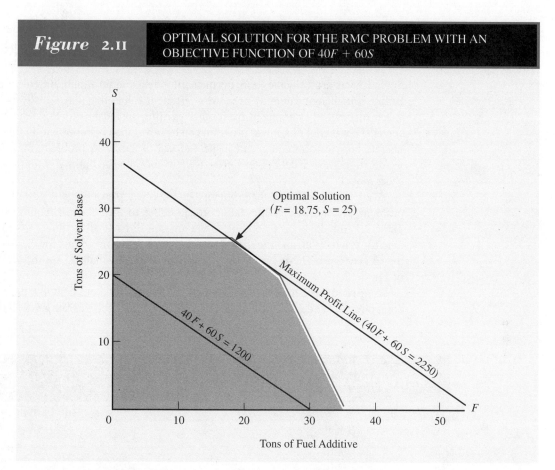

Figure 2.11   OPTIMAL SOLUTION FOR THE RMC PROBLEM WITH AN OBJECTIVE FUNCTION OF $40F + 60S$

You should be able to identify the extreme points of the feasible region and determine the optimal solution by computing and comparing the objective function value at each extreme point. Try Problem 10.

This observation about the location of optimal solutions means that, if you are looking for the optimal solution to a linear programming problem, you do not have to evaluate all feasible solution points. In fact, you have to consider *only* feasible solutions that occur at the extreme points of the feasible region. Thus, for the RMC problem, instead of computing and comparing the profit for all feasible solutions, we can find the optimal solution by evaluating the five extreme-point solutions and selecting the one that provides the highest profit. Actually, the graphical solution procedure is nothing more than a convenient way of identifying an optimal extreme point for two-variable problems.

NOTES and Comments

1. In the standard form representation of a linear program, the objective function coefficients for slack variables are zero. This condition implies that slack variables, which represent unused resources, do not affect the value of the objective function. However, in some applications, some or all unused resources can be sold and contribute to profit. In such cases the corresponding slack variables become decision variables representing the amount of resources to be sold. For each such variable, a nonzero coefficient in the objective function would reflect the profit associated with selling a unit of the corresponding resource.

2. Redundant constraints do not affect the feasible region; as a result they can be removed from a linear programming model without affecting the optimal solution. However, if the linear programming model is to be resolved later, changes in some of the data might change a previously redundant constraint into a binding constraint. Thus, we recommend keeping all constraints in the linear programming model even though one or more of the constraints may be redundant.

2.3   FORMULATING A SPREADSHEET MODEL OF THE RMC PROBLEM

Spreadsheets are valuable tools for managing data and information in most organizations. Because mathematical models require coefficient values that may already exist in a spreadsheet, or be easily computed from other existing spreadsheet data, understanding how a spreadsheet model of a linear program can be developed is important. In this section we illustrate how to formulate a spreadsheet model of the RMC problem; then, in Section 2.4 we illustrate how Excel Solver can be used to determine an optimal solution for this spreadsheet model.

We begin by entering the problem data into the top part of a spreadsheet. For the RMC problem, we must enter the data corresponding to the material requirements shown in Table 2.1, the data corresponding to the amount of each of the three raw materials available for production, and the data showing the profit contributions for the fuel additive and the solvent base. These data, with appropriate descriptive labels, are shown in cells A1:D8 of Figure 2.13.

A **spreadsheet model** of a linear programming problem contains the following four components: (1) cells for the decision variables; (2) a cell containing a formula for com-

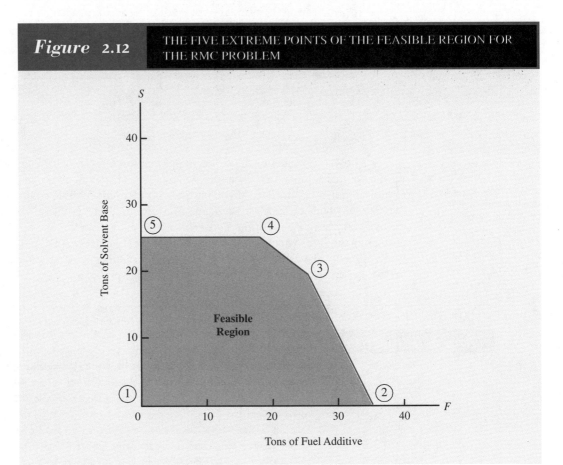

Figure 2.12   THE FIVE EXTREME POINTS OF THE FEASIBLE REGION FOR THE RMC PROBLEM

Figure 2.13	FORMULA SPREADSHEET FOR THE RMC PROBLEM

	A	B	C	D
1	**RMC Chapter 2**			
2				
3		**Material Requirements**		
4	**Material**	**Fuel Additive**	**Solvent Base**	**Amount Available**
5	Material 1	0.4	0.5	20
6	Material 2	0	0.2	5
7	Material 3	0.6	0.3	21
8	**Profit Per Ton**	40	30	
9				
10				
11	**Model**			
12				
13		**Decision Variables**		
14		**Fuel Additive**	**Solvent Base**	
15	**Tons Produced**			
16				
17	**Maximize Total Profit**	=B8*B15+C8*C15		
18				
19	**Constraints**	**Amount Used (LHS)**		**Amount Available (RHS)**
20	Material 1	=B5*B15+C5*C15	<=	=D5
21	Material 2	=B6*B15+C6*C15	<=	=D6
22	Material 3	=B7*B15+C7*C15	<=	=D7

puting the value of the objective function; (3) cells containing formulas for computing the left-hand sides of the constraints; and (4) cells containing the values of the right-hand sides of the constraints or cells containing formulas for computing the values of the right-hand sides. We will enter these four components of the spreadsheet model directly below the problem data.

Steps in a Spreadsheet Model Formulation

Throughout our discussion of linear programming models, whenever we formulate a spreadsheet model of a problem, we will perform the following five steps:

Step 1   Enter the problem data into the spreadsheet.
Step 2   Specify cell locations for all decision variables.
Step 3   Select a cell and enter a formula for computing the value of the objective function.
Step 4   Select a cell and enter a formula for computing the left-hand side of each constraint.
Step 5   Select a cell and enter a formula for computing the value of the right-hand side of each constraint.

The formula spreadsheet shown in Figure 2.13 was developed using the preceding five-step procedure. Note that the spreadsheet consists of two sections: a data section and a model section. One advantage to separating the data from the model is that once a decision has been made as to what cells will contain the problem data, the analyst can develop the model independently of the actual collection of the data. A second advantage is that once the model has been developed, we can study the effect of changing various inputs to the model by making changes only in the data section of the spreadsheet. Let us now describe in detail how the entries in each of these two sections were created for the RMC problem.

Step 1: Enter all problem data.   Problem data appears in the top part of the spreadsheet. The fractional values for the material requirements for each ton of fuel additive and each ton of solvent base have been converted to decimal form and are shown in cells B5:C7. The value of 0.4 in cell B5 shows that each ton of fuel additive produced uses 0.4 tons of material 1, the value of 0.5 in cell C5 shows that each ton of solvent base produced uses 0.5 tons of material 1, and so on. The number of tons available for each material is shown in cells D5:D7; 20 tons of material 1, 5 tons of material 2, and 21 tons of material 3. Finally, the profit contributions for each product are shown in cells B8 and C8; note that the profit contribution for each ton of fuel additive produced is $40, and the profit contribution for each ton of solvent base produced is $30.

Step 2: Specify cell locations for all decision variables.   Cell B15 will contain the value for the number of tons of fuel additive produced and cell C15 will contain the value for number of tons of solvent base produced. Note that currently no values are entered into these cells.

Step 3: Select a cell and enter a formula for computing the value of the objective function.   Cell B17 contains a formula for computing the value of the objective function. Since the value of the objective function is 40 (cell B8) times the number of tons of fuel additive produced (cell B15) plus 30 (cell C8) times the number of tons of solvent base produced (cell C15), we entered the following formula in cell B17:

$$=B8*B15+C8*C15$$

Step 4: Select a cell and enter a formula for computing left-hand-side function of each constraint. [These cells are referred to as the *left-hand-side cells* (LHS).]   Cells B20:B22 contain formulas showing how to compute the left-hand-side functions for the constraints. Let us demonstrate the logic of these formulas by showing how to compute the left-hand-side function for the material 1 constraint. First, note that the value in cell B5, 0.4, is the number of tons of material 1 used to produce one ton of fuel additive. Because cell B15 contains the number of tons of fuel additive produced, the total number of tons of material 1 used to produce fuel additive is B5*B15. The value in cell C5, 0.5, is the number of tons of material 1 used to produce one ton of solvent base. Because cell C15 contains the number of tons of solvent base produced, the total number of tons of material 1 used to produce solvent base is C5*C15. Thus, in cell B20 we entered the following formula for the total number of tons of material 1 used in the production of fuel additive and solvent base:

$$=B5*B15+C5*C15$$

The cell formulas shown in cells B21 and B22 were developed in a similar fashion.

Step 5: Select a cell and enter a formula for computing the value of the right-hand side of each constraint. [These cells are referred to as the right-hand-side cells (RHS).]   In the RMC problem, the values of the right-hand sides of the constraints represent the amount of material available. These values were provided in the problem description and originally entered into the data section of the input. Thus, for the material 1 constraint we entered the formula =D5 in cell D20 to indicate that the value of the right-hand side of the material 1 constraint is the value in cell D5 of the data section. Similarly, the formula =D6 in cell D21 shows that the right-hand side of the material 2 constraint is the value in cell D6, and the formula =D7 in cell D22 shows that the right-hand side of the material 3 constraint is the value in cell D7.

As we indicated previously, the spreadsheet model contains the following four components: (1) cells for the decision variables; (2) a cell containing a formula for computing the value of the objective function; (3) cells containing formulas for computing the left-hand sides of the constraints; and (4) cells containing the values of the right-hand sides of the constraints or cells containing formulas for computing the values of the right-hand sides. To make identifying these components in the spreadsheet easier, we always screen each component. In addition we place a border around cells that contain the decision variables.

In the model section of the RMC spreadsheet, we also entered the label "Maximize Total Profit" into cell A17 to indicate that the objective in the RMC problem is to maximize the total contribution to profit. In addition, we entered "<=" into cells C20:C22 to show the relationship that exists between the left-hand-side cells and the right-hand-side cells. Although these descriptive labels are not necessary to solve the RMC problem using Excel Solver, including them in the model section of the spreadsheet makes it easier to see the underlying structure of the problem.

Relationship Between the Mathematical Model and the Spreadsheet Model

Looking at the model section of the spreadsheet, we see that the spreadsheet model provides the same information as the mathematical model of the RMC problem (see Section 2.1). In fact, if we think of B15 and C15 as names for the decision variables, we can rewrite the mathematical model of the RMC problem in terms of the spreadsheet entries in the model section of the formula spreadsheet, as shown below:

$$\text{Max } B8*B15+C8*C15 \qquad \text{Profit}$$

s.t.

$$B5*B15+C5*C15 \le D5 \quad \text{Material 1}$$
$$B6*B15+C6*C15 \le D6 \quad \text{Material 2}$$
$$B7*B15+C7*C15 \le D7 \quad \text{Material 3}$$

Thus, the spreadsheet model of the RMC problem is simply another way to represent a linear programming model.[3] One advantage, however, is that if one or more values in the data section of the spreadsheet are changed, the values in the model section of the spreadsheet will automatically be updated to reflect these changes. In addition, the widespread availability and use of spreadsheet packages such as Excel, Lotus 1-2-3®, and Quattro Pro® means that linear programs can be developed and solved by increasing numbers of practitioners that do not have access to specialized linear programming solution procedures.

3. The nonnegativity constraints in the mathematical model are not shown here. We discuss how they are handled shortly.

2.4   SPREADSHEET SOLUTION OF THE RMC PROBLEM

In Section 2.2 we showed how the graphical solution procedure can be used to identify an optimal solution for the RMC problem. Because the graphical solution procedure is only practical for problems involving two decision variables, a computer procedure is needed to solve real linear programming problems. In this section we show how spreadsheet solvers can be used to identify an optimal solution for a spreadsheet model.

Trial-and-Error Approach

A trial-and-error approach can be used to generate solutions for a linear program in a spreadsheet. One iteratively selects trial values for the decision variables and observes the resulting values for the objective function and constraints. For instance, suppose that RMC produced 10 tons of fuel additive and 15 tons of solvent base. To see what happens, we simply enter a value of 10 into cell B15 and a value of 15 into cell C15 of the RMC spreadsheet; the results are shown in Figure 2.14. We see that this trial solution results in a total contribution to profit of $850 (cell B17). The number of tons of material 1 used is 11.5 (cell B20), the number of tons of material 2 used is 3 (cell B21), and the number of tons of material 3 used is 10.5 (cell B22). Because the number of tons of materials used is less than the number of tons available (20, 5, and 21), this trial solution is feasible for the RMC problem.

After reviewing this solution, we might decide to increase production of both products by, say, 5 tons each. Doing so increases total profit to $1200. The number of tons of materials 1, 2, and 3 used are 16, 4, and 15, respectively. Clearly, this is a better solution, and it is also feasible. However, it may not be the best solution.

We could continue with more trial solutions and observe the impact on profit as well as the amount of each material used. With this approach, we should be able to identify a feasible solution that also provides a good value for total profit. However, we probably will not be lucky enough to select the optimal production combination. Fortunately, another approach is better. We now show how the Excel Solver can be used to find an optimal solution directly.

Using Excel Solver to Identify an Optimal Solution

Spreadsheet packages such as Excel, Lotus 1-2-3, and Quattro Pro have built-in linear programming solvers. The Excel Solver is a general optimization and resource allocation tool. The following steps describe how to use Excel Solver to obtain the optimal solution to the RMC linear programming problem.

Step 1 Select the **Tools** pull-down menu
Step 2 Select the **Solver** option
Step 3 When the **Solver Parameters** dialog box appears
       Enter B17 into the **Set Target Cell** box
       Select the **Max** option
       Enter B15:C15 into the **By Changing Cells** box
       Choose **Add**
Step 4 When the **Add Constraint** dialog box appears
       Enter B20:B22 in the **Cell Reference** box
       Select <=
       Enter D20:D22 into the **Constraint** box
       Choose **OK**

Figure 2.14	TRIAL SOLUTION FOR THE RMC PROBLEM

	A	B	C	D
1	**RMC Chapter 2**			
2				
3		**Material Requirements**		
4	**Material**	**Fuel Additive**	**Solvent Base**	**Amount Available**
5	Material 1	0.4	0.5	20
6	Material 2	0	0.2	5
7	Material 3	0.6	0.3	21
8	**Profit Per Ton**	40	30	
9				
10				
11	**Model**			
12				
13		**Decision Variables**		
14		**Fuel Additive**	**Solvent Base**	
15	**Tons Produced**	10	15	
16				
17	**Maximize Total Profit**	850		
18				
19	**Constraints**	**Amount Used (LHS)**		**Amount Available (RHS)**
20	Material 1	11.5	<=	20
21	Material 2	3	<=	5
22	Material 3	10.5	<=	21

Step 5 When the **Solver Parameters** dialog box reappears
Choose **Options**

Step 6 When the **Solver Options** dialog box appears
Select **Assume Linear Model**
Select **Assume Non-Negative**
Choose **OK**

Step 7 When the **Solver Parameters** dialog box reappears
Choose **Solve**

Step 8 When the **Solver Results** dialog box appears
Select **Keep Solver Solution**
Choose **OK** to produce the optimal solution output

Figure 2.15 shows the completed **Solver Parameters** dialog box, and Figure 2.16 shows the optimal solution in the spreadsheet. Note that the optimal solution of 25 tons of fuel additive and 20 tons of solvent base is the same as we obtained using the graphical

Figure 2.15   SOLVER PARAMETERS DIALOG BOX FOR THE RMC PROBLEM

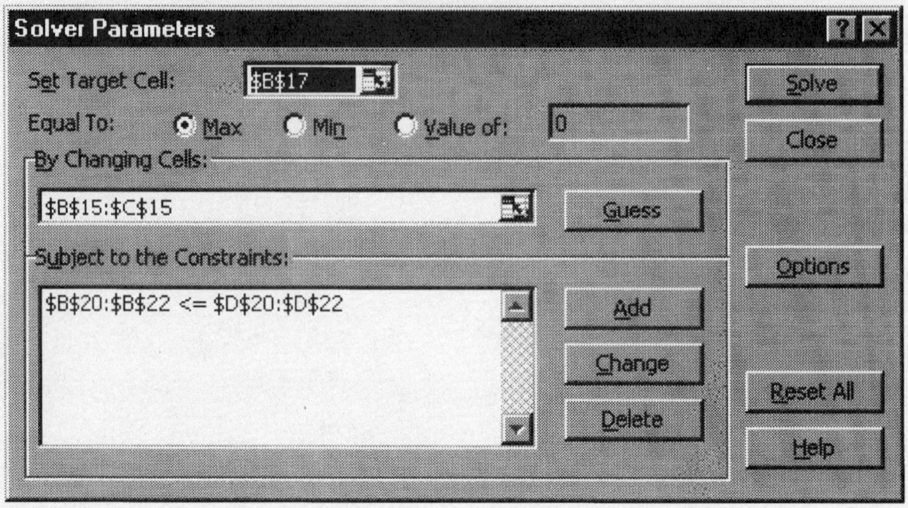

solution procedure. In addition to the output information shown in Figure 2.16, Solver has an option to provide sensitivity analysis information. We discuss sensitivity analysis in Chapter 3.

In Step 6 we selected the **Assume Non-Negative** option in the **Solver Options** dialog box. We did this to avoid having to enter nonnegativity constraints for the decision variables. In general, whenever we want to solve a linear programming model in which the decision variables are all restricted to be nonnegative, we will select this option. In addition, in Step 4 we entered all three less-than-or-equal-to constraints simultaneously by entering B20:B22 into the **Cell Reference** box, selecting <=, and entering D20:D22 into the **Constraint** box. Alternatively, we could have entered the three constraints in a one-at-a-time fashion by replacing the description in Step 4 as follows:

Enter B20 into the **Cell Reference** box

Select <=

Enter D20 into the **Constraint** box

Choose **Add**

Enter B21 into the **Cell Reference** box

Select <=

Enter D21 into the **Constraint** box

Choose **Add**

Enter B22 into the **Cell Reference** box

Select <=

Enter D22 into the **Constraint** box

Choose **Add**

Choose **OK**

Excel 5.0 User Note: The Solver in Excel 5.0 does not have the **Assume Non-Negative** option. Instead, the user must add additional constraints to restrict the decision variables to nonnegative values. For the RMC problem, this can be done by choosing **Add** in the **Solver Parameters** dialog box. When the **Add Constraint** dialog box appears, enter B15:C15 into the **Cell Reference** box, select >=, enter 0 into the **Constraint** box, and choose **OK**.

Figure 2.16   SPREADSHEET SOLUTION FOR THE RMC PROBLEM

SPREADSHEET
RMC CHAPTER 2

	A	B	C	D	E
1	**RMC Chapter 2**				
2					
3		**Material Requirements**			
4	**Material**	**Fuel Additive**	**Solvent Base**	**Amount Available**	
5	Material 1	0.4	0.5	20	
6	Material 2	0	0.2	5	
7	Material 3	0.6	0.3	21	
8	**Profit Per Ton**	40	30		
9					
10					
11	**Model**				
12					
13		**Decision Variables**			
14		**Fuel Additive**	**Solvent Base**		
15	**Tons Produced**	25	20		
16					
17	**Maximize Total Profit**	1600			
18					
19	**Constraints**	**Amount Used (LHS)**		**Amount Available (RHS)**	
20	Material 1	20	<=	20	
21	Material 2	4	<=	5	
22	Material 3	21	<=	21	

The approach you use is simply a matter of personal preference. However, as we start to solve more complex types of problems that include a combination of less-than-or-equal-to, equal to, and greater-than-or-equal-to constraints, you can often reduce the amount of effort required to enter the constraints by grouping them according to type (<=, =, >=), and then entering groups of constraints by each type using a procedure similar to that used for the three less-than-or-equal-to constraints in the RMC problem.

2.5   A SIMPLE MINIMIZATION PROBLEM

Innis Investments manages funds for companies and wealthy clients. The investment strategy is tailored to each client's needs. For a new client, Innis has been authorized to invest up to $1.2 million in two investment funds: a stock fund and a money market fund. Each unit of the stock fund costs $50 and provides an annual rate of return of 10%; each unit of the money market fund costs $100 and provides an annual rate of return of 4%.

The client wants to minimize risk but earn an annual income from the investment of at least $60,000. According to Innis's risk measurement system, each unit purchased in the stock fund has a risk index of 8, and each unit purchased in the money market fund has a risk index of 3; the higher risk index associated with the stock fund simply indicates that it is the riskier investment. Innis's client also has specified that at least $300,000 be invested in the money market fund. How many units of each fund should Innis purchase for the client if the objective is to minimize the total risk index for the portfolio?

Problem Formulation

To find the best allocation of funds between the stock and money market funds, we will formulate the Innis Investments problem as a linear program. We begin by defining the decision variables for the problem. Let

$$S = \text{number of units purchased in the stock fund}$$
$$M = \text{number of units purchased in the money market fund}$$

Since the risk index is 8 for each unit purchased in the stock fund and 3 for each unit purchased in the money market fund, the objective function that will minimize the total risk index for the portfolio is

$$\text{Min} \quad 8S + 3M$$

Next, consider the constraints associated with the problem. First, we recognize that Innis can invest up to $1,200,000. Since each unit of the stock fund costs $50 and each unit of the money market fund costs $100, the constraint needed on funds available is

$$50S + 100M \leq 1,200,000$$

In addition, the investment must result in an annual income of at least $60,000. With a 10% annual rate of return for the stock fund, each unit purchased in the stock fund will earn 0.10($50) = $5; similarly, the 4% annual rate of return for the money market fund results in earnings per unit of 0.04($100) = $4. Thus, the constraint required to ensure an annual income of at least $60,000 is

$$5S + 4M \geq 60,000$$

Finally, since each unit purchased in the money market fund costs $100, the requirement that at least $300,000 be invested in the money market fund means that at least 3000 units of the money market fund must be purchased; thus, we must add the constraint

$$M \geq 3000$$

After adding the nonnegativity constraints ($S, M \geq 0$), we obtain the linear programming model of the Innis Investments problem:

$$\text{Min} \quad 8S + 3M \qquad\qquad\qquad \text{Risk}$$

s.t.

$$
\begin{aligned}
50S + 100M &\leq 1{,}200{,}000 \quad &&\text{Funds available}\\
5S + 4M &\geq 60{,}000 \quad &&\text{Annual income}\\
M &\geq 3{,}000 \quad &&\text{Minimum units in money market}
\end{aligned}
$$

$$S, M \geq 0$$

Because the linear programming model has only two decision variables, we can use the graphical solution procedure to find the optimal investment plan. The graphical method for this problem, as in the RMC problem, requires us first to graph the constraint lines to find the feasible region. By graphing each constraint line separately and then checking points on either side of the constraint line, we can identify the feasible solutions for each constraint. By combining the feasible solutions for each constraint on the same graph, we obtain the feasible region shown in Figure 2.17.

To find the optimal solution (the one that will minimize the total risk index for the portfolio), we now draw the objective function line corresponding to a particular value for the total risk index. For example, we might start by drawing the line $8S + 3M = 120{,}000$, as

Figure 2.17   FEASIBLE REGION FOR INNIS INVESTMENTS PROBLEM

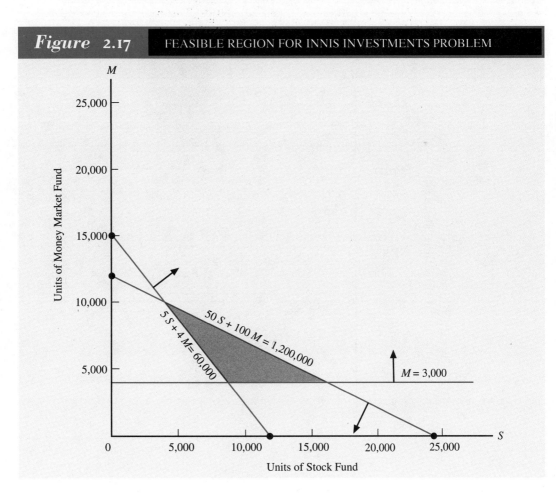

shown in Figure 2.18. Clearly, some points in the feasible region would provide a total risk index of 120,000. To find the values of S and M that provide a smaller total portfolio risk index, we move the objective function line down and to the left until, if we moved it any farther, it would be outside the feasible region. The objective function line $8S + 3M = 62,000$ intersects the feasible region at the extreme point $S = 4000$ and $M = 10,000$. This extreme point provides the minimum portfolio risk index with an objective function value of 62,000. Figures 2.17 and 2.18 show that the funds available and the annual income constraints are binding.

Summary of the Graphical Solution Procedure for Minimization Problems

Can you use the graphical solution procedure to determine the optimal solution for a minimization problem? Try Problem 11.

The graphical solution procedure for a minimization problem involves the following steps.

1. Prepare a graph of the feasible solution region for each constraint.
2. Determine the feasible solution region by identifying the solutions that satisfy all constraints simultaneously.
3. Draw an objective function line showing all values of the decision variables that yield a specified value of the objective function.

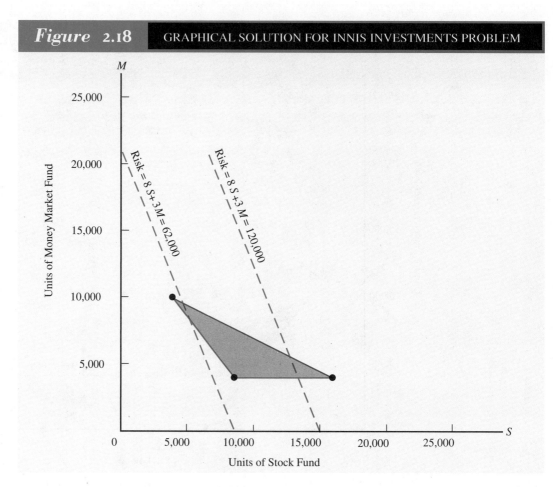

Figure 2.18   GRAPHICAL SOLUTION FOR INNIS INVESTMENTS PROBLEM

4. Move parallel objective function lines toward smaller objective function values until further movement would take the line completely outside the feasible region.
5. Any feasible solution on the objective function line with the smallest value is an optimal solution.

Surplus Variables

A complete analysis of the optimal solution to the Innis Investments problem shows that the total risk index for the optimal portfolio, $8S + 3M = 8(4000) + 3(10,000) = 62,000$, is achieved by using all available funds. That is, $50S + 100M = 50(4000) + 100(10,000) = 1,200,000$. The required annual income is achieved exactly: $5(4,000) + 4(10,000) = 60,000$. Note, however, that the purchase of 10,000 units of the money market fund exceeds the minimum requirement of 3000 by 7000 units. In linear programming terminology, any such excess quantity corresponding to a $\geq$ constraint is referred to as *surplus*.

Recall that with a $\leq$ constraint, a slack variable can be added to the left-hand side of the constraint in order to convert the constraint to equality form. With a $\geq$ constraint, a **surplus variable** can be subtracted from the left-hand side to convert the constraint to equality form. As with slack variables, surplus variables are given a coefficient of zero in the objective function because they have no effect on its value. After including one slack variable for the $\leq$ constraint and two surplus variables for the $\geq$ constraints, the linear programming model of the Innis Investments problem becomes

$$
\begin{aligned}
\text{Min} \quad & 8S + 3M + 0S_1 + 0S_2 + 0S_3 \\
\text{s.t.} \quad & \\
& 50S + 100M + 1S_1 \qquad\qquad\qquad = 1,200,000 \\
& 5S + 4M \qquad\quad - 1S_2 \qquad\qquad = 60,000 \\
& 1M \qquad\qquad\qquad - 1S_3 = 3,000 \\
& S, M, S_1, S_2, S_3 \geq 0
\end{aligned}
$$

All constraints are now equalities. Hence, the preceding formulation is the standard form representation of the Innis Investments problem. At the optimal solution, $S = 4000$ and $M = 10,000$, the values of the slack and surplus variables are

Constraint	Value of Slack or Surplus Variable
Funds available	$S_1 = 0$
Annual income	$S_2 = 0$
Minimum units in money market	$S_3 = 7000$

Refer to Figures 2.17 and 2.18. Note that the zero slack and surplus variables are associated with constraints that are binding at the optimal solution; that is, the constraints on funds available and annual income. The surplus of 7000 units is associated with the non-binding constraint on the minimum allowable investment in the money market fund.

Note that in the RMC problem all the constraints were of the ≤ type and that in the Innis Investments problem the constraints were a mixture of ≤ and ≥ types. In general, linear programming problems may have some ≤ constraints, some ≥ constraints, and some = constraints. For an equality constraint, feasible solutions must lie directly on the constraint line.

When solving linear programs graphically, you do not have to rewrite the problem in its standard form. Nevertheless, you should be able to compute the values of the slack and surplus variables and understand what they mean. Managers are often interested in the slack or surplus associated with constraints.

A final point: The standard form of the linear programming problem is equivalent to the original formulation of the problem. That is, the optimal solution to any linear programming problem is the same as the optimal solution to the standard form of the problem. The standard form has not changed the basic problem; it has only changed how we write the constraints for the problem.

Spreadsheet Formulation

In Section 2.3 we showed how to formulate a spreadsheet model of the RMC problem using the following five-step procedure:

Step 1 Enter the problem data into the spreadsheet.
Step 2 Specify cell locations for all decision variables.
Step 3 Select a cell and enter a formula for computing the value of the objective function.
Step 4 Select a cell and enter a formula for computing the left-hand side of each constraint.
Step 5 Select a cell and enter a formula for computing the value of the right-hand side of each constraint.

We now follow this procedure to develop a spreadsheet model of the Innis Investments problem.

Step 1:   Figure 2.19 shows a formula spreadsheet for the Innis Investment problem. The problem data are shown in the top section of the spreadsheet. The cost per unit data are shown in cells B4:C4, and the annual rate of return data[4] are shown in cells B5:C5. The earnings per unit formulas in cells B6:C6 are based on multiplying the annual rate of return and the cost per unit values. The earnings per unit for the stock fund is computed using the cell formula =B5*B4, and the earnings per unit for the money market fund is computed using the cell formula =C5*C4. The risk indexes per unit, 8 for the stock fund and 3 for the money market fund, are shown in cells B7:C7. The funds available for investment, the minimum annual income expected from the investment, and the minimum amount of money that the client wants invested in the money market fund are shown in cells B9:B11, respectively.

Step 2:   Cell B18 will contain the value of the number of units purchased in the stock fund and cell C18 will contain the value of the number of units purchased in the money market fund. These are the values of the decision variables.

---

4. The annual rate of return data for the stock fund and the money market fund were originally entered as 10% (cell B5) and 4% (cell C5), respectively; when Excel displays the formula spreadsheet, the cell values are automatically displayed in decimal form.

	A	B	C	D
1	**Innis Investments**			
2				
3		**Stock Fund**	**Money Market Fund**	
4	**Cost Per Unit**	50	100	
5	**Annual Rate of Return**	0.1	0.04	
6	**Earnings Per Unit**	=B5*B4	=C5*C4	
7	**Risk Index Per Unit**	8	3	
8				
9	**Funds Available**	1200000		
10	**Minimum Annual Income**	60000		
11	**Minimum $ in Money Market Fund**	300000		
12				
13				
14	**Model**			
15				
16			**Decision Variables**	
17		**Stock Fund**	**Money Market Fund**	
18	**Units Purchased**			
19				
20	**Minimize Total Risk**	=B7*B18+C7*C18		
21				
22	**Constraints**	**LHS**		**RHS**
23	Funds Available	=B4*B18+C4*C18	<=	=B9
24	Minimum Annual Income	=B6*B18+C6*C18	>=	=B10
25	Minimum Units in Money Market	=C18	>=	=B11/C4

**SPREADSHEET
INNIS
CHAPTER 2**

Figure 2.19 FORMULA SPREADSHEET FOR THE INNIS INVESTMENTS PROBLEM

Step 3: We have selected cell B20 for the objective function. The total risk index for the portfolio is the sum of the risk index for the stock fund and the risk index for the money market fund. The risk index for the stock fund investment is the product of the risk index per unit for the stock fund (cell B7) and the number of units purchased in the stock fund (cell B18). Similarly, the risk index for the money market fund is the product of the risk index per unit for the money market fund (cell C7) and the number of units purchased in the money market fund (cell C18). Thus, we have entered the following formula into cell B20:

$$=B7*B18+C7*C18$$

Step 4: The funds available constraint limits the total amount invested to at most $1,200,000. Because the total amount invested is the sum of the cost per unit for the stock fund (cell B4) times the number of units purchased in the stock fund (cell B18) and the cost per unit for the money market fund (cell C4) times the number of units purchased in the money market fund (cell C18), we entered the following formula for the LHS value of constraint 1 into cell B23:

$$=B4*B18+C4*C18$$

Since the LHS value for the second constraint represents the annual income from the investment, we entered the formula $=B6*B18+C6*C18$ into cell B24. The LHS of the third constraint is simply the number of units in the money market fund; thus, we entered the formula $=C18$ into cell B25.

Step 5: The RHS value for the first constraint is $1,200,000, the funds available for the investment; thus, in cell D23 we entered the formula $=B9$. Similarly, since the RHS value for the second constraint is $60,000, the minimum annual income the investment must earn, we entered the formula $=B10$ into cell D24. Finally, the RHS for the third constraint represents the minimum number of units that must be invested in the money market fund in order to provide a minimum investment of $300,000 (cell B11). Since each unit invested in the money market fund costs $100 (cell C4), we entered the formula $=B11/C4$ into cell D25.

Relationship Between the Mathematical Model and the Spreadsheet Model

Looking at the model section of the spreadsheet, we see that the spreadsheet model provides the same information as the mathematical model of the problem. In fact, if we think of B18 and C18 as names for the decision variables, we can rewrite the mathematical model of the Innis Investments problem in terms of the spreadsheet entries in the model section of the formula spreadsheet, as shown below:

Min	$B7*B18+C7*C18$	Risk
s.t.		
	$B4*B18+C4*C18 \le B9$	Funds Available
	$B6*B18+C6*C18 \ge B10$	Minimum Annual Income
	$C18 \ge B11/C4$	Minimum Units in Money Market

A Trial Solution

Before using Excel's Solver to find the optimal solution for the Innis Investments spreadsheet model, let us select a set of trial values for the decision variables. For instance, suppose that Innis purchased 10,000 units of the stock fund and 5000 units of the money market fund. To see the model result, we simply enter a value of 10,000 into cell B18 and a value of 5,000 into cell C18; the results for the objective function and LHS cells are shown in Figure 2.20. We see that this trial solution results in a total risk index of 95,000. Note also that this solution uses $1,000,000 of the $1,200,000 available for investment, results in an annual income of $70,000, and purchases 5000 units of the money market fund. All constraints are satisfied with this solution, so we have a feasible solution to the problem. Let us now see how to use Excel Solver to identify an optimal solution.

Figure 2.20   TRIAL SOLUTION FOR THE INNIS INVESTMENTS PROBLEM

SPREADSHEET
INNIS
CHAPTER 2

	A	B	C	D
1	**Innis Investments**			
2				
3		**Stock Fund**	**Money Market Fund**	
4	**Cost Per Unit**	$50	$100	
5	**Annual Rate of Return**	10%	4%	
6	**Earnings Per Unit**	$5	$4	
7	**Risk Index Per Unit**	8	3	
8				
9	**Funds Available**	$1,200,000		
10	**Minimum Annual Income**	$60,000		
11	**Minimum $ in Money Market Fund**	$300,000		
12				
13				
14	**Model**			
15				
16			**Decision Variables**	
17		**Stock Fund**	**Money Market Fund**	
18	**Units Purchased**	10,000	5,000	
19				
20	**Minimize Total Risk**	95,000		
21				
22	**Constraints**	**LHS**		**RHS**
23	Funds Available	$1,000,000	<=	$1,200,000
24	Minimum Annual Income	$70,000	>=	$60,000
25	Minimum Units in Money Market	5,000	>=	3,000

Using Excel Solver to Identify an Optimal Solution

The following steps describe how to use Excel Solver to obtain an optimal solution for the Innis Investments problem.

Step 1   Select the **Tools** pull-down menu

Step 2   Select the **Solver** option

Step 3   When the **Solver Parameters** dialog box appears
   Enter B20 into the **Set Target Cell** box
   Select the **Min** option
   Enter B18:C18 into the **By Changing Cells** box
   Choose **Add**

Step 4   When the **Add Constraint** dialog box appears
   Enter B23 into the **Cell Reference** box
   Select <=
   Enter D23 into the **Constraint** box
   Choose **Add**
   Enter B24:B25 into the **Cell Reference** box
   Select >=
   Enter D24:D25 into the **Constraint** box
   Choose **OK**

Step 5   When the **Solver Parameters** dialog box reappears
         Choose **Options**
Step 6   When the **Solver Options** dialog box appears
         Select **Assume Linear Model**
         Select **Assume Non-Negative**
         Choose **OK**
Step 7   When the **Solver Parameters** dialog box reappears
         Choose **Solve**
Step 8   When the **Solver Results** dialog box appears
         Select **Keep Solver Solution**
         Choose **OK** to produce the optimal solution output

Figure 2.21 shows the **Solver Parameters** dialog box that you will see in Step 7, and
Figure 2.22 shows the optimal solution output. Note that the optimal solution, consisting
of 4000 units of the stock fund and 10,000 units of the money market fund, is the same
as we obtained using the graphical solution procedure. Comparing cell B23 with cell D23,
we see that the funds available constraint is binding. Comparing cell B24 with cell D24,
we see that the annual income constraint is binding. Finally, comparing cell B25 with cell
D25, we see that the optimal solution provides a surplus of 7000 units in the money market fund.

2.6   SPECIAL CASES

In this section we discuss three special situations that can arise when we attempt to solve
linear programming problems.

Figure 2.21   SOLVER PARAMETERS DIALOG BOX FOR THE INNIS
INVESTMENTS PROBLEM

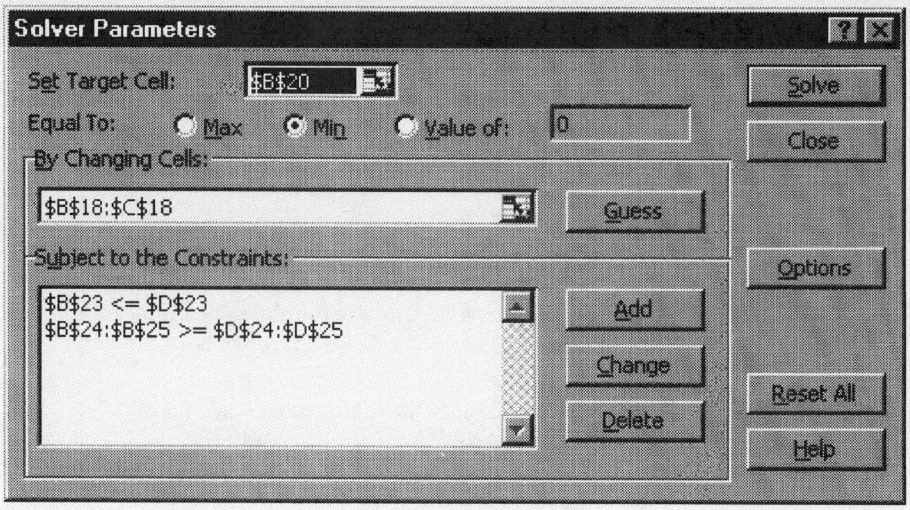

Figure 2.22	SPREADSHEET SOLUTION FOR THE INNIS INVESTMENTS PROBLEM		

SPREADSHEET
INNIS
CHAPTER 2

	A	B	C	D
1	**Innis Investments**			
2				
3		**Stock Fund**	**Money Market Fund**	
4	**Cost Per Unit**	$50	$100	
5	**Annual Rate of Return**	10%	4%	
6	**Earnings Per Unit**	$5	$4	
7	**Risk Index Per Unit**	8	3	
8				
9	**Funds Available**	$1,200,000		
10	**Minimum Annual Income**	$60,000		
11	**Minimum $ in Money Market Fund**	$300,000		
12				
13				
14	**Model**			
15				
16			**Decision Variables**	
17		**Stock Fund**	**Money Market Fund**	
18	**Units Purchased**	4,000	10,000	
19				
20	**Minimize Total Risk**	62,000		
21				
22	**Constraints**	**LHS**		**RHS**
23	Funds Available	$1,200,000	<=	$1,200,000
24	Minimum Annual Income	$60,000	>=	$60,000
25	Minimum Units in Money Market	10,000	>=	3,000

Alternative Optimal Solutions

From our discussion of the graphical solution procedure, we know that optimal solutions can be found at the extreme points of the feasible region. Now let us consider the special case where the optimal objective function line coincides with one of the binding constraint lines. It can lead to **alternative optimal solutions**; a case where more than one solution provides the optimal value for the objective function.

To illustrate the case of alternative optimal solutions, we return to the RMC, Inc., problem. However, let us assume that the profit contribution for the solvent base (F) has increased to $50. The revised objective function is $40F + 50S$. Figure 2.23 shows the graphical solution to this problem. Note that the optimal solution still occurs at an extreme point. In fact, it occurs at two extreme points: extreme point ③ ($F = 25$, $S = 20$) and extreme point ④ ($F = 18.75$, $S = 25$).

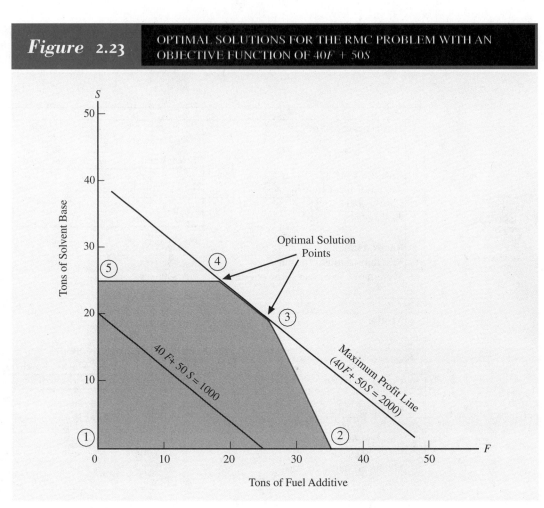

Figure 2.23   OPTIMAL SOLUTIONS FOR THE RMC PROBLEM WITH AN OBJECTIVE FUNCTION OF $40F + 50S$

The objective function values at these two extreme points are identical; that is,

$$40F + 50S = 40(25) + 50(20) = 2000$$

and

$$40F + 50S = 40(18.75) + 50(25) = 2000$$

Furthermore, any point on the line connecting the two optimal extreme points also provides an optimal solution. For example, the solution point ($F = 21.875$, $S = 22.5$), which is halfway between the two extreme points, also provides the optimal objective function value of

$$40F + 50S = 40(21.875) + 50(22.5) = 2000$$

A linear programming problem with alternative optimal solutions is generally a good situation for the manager or decision maker. It means that several combinations of the decision variables are optimal and that the manager can select the most desirable optimal solution.

Determining whether a problem has alternative optimal solutions is not a simple matter. For instance, if you solved the revised RMC problem using Excel Solver, you would obtain the optimal solution consisting of 18.75 tons of fuel additive and 25 tons of solvent base, with an objective function value of $2,000. However, none of the information provided indicates that other optimal solutions exist for this problem. If you were to use another linear programming software package to solve the same problem, you may find that you obtain the other optimal extreme point solution ($F = 25$, $S = 20$).

Infeasibility

Infeasibility means that no solution to the linear programming problem satisfies all constraints, including the nonnegativity conditions. Graphically, infeasibility means that a feasible region does not exist; that is, no points satisfy all constraint equations and nonnegativity conditions simultaneously. To illustrate this situation, let us return to the problem facing RMC.

Suppose that management had specified that at least 30 tons of fuel additive and at least 15 tons of solvent base must be produced. Figure 2.24 shows the graph of the solution region that reflects these requirements. The shaded area in the lower left portion of the graph

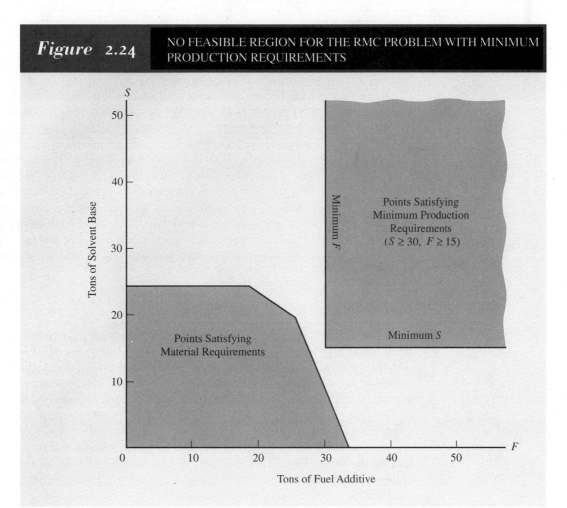

Figure 2.24   NO FEASIBLE REGION FOR THE RMC PROBLEM WITH MINIMUM PRODUCTION REQUIREMENTS

Problems with no feasible
solution do arise in
practice. Most often it's
because management's
expectations are too high
or because too many
restrictions have been
placed on the problem.

depicts those points satisfying the less-than-or-equal-to constraints on the amount of materials available. The shaded area in the upper right portion depicts those points satisfying the minimum production requirements of 30 tons of fuel additive and 15 tons of solvent base. But none of the points satisfy both sets of constraints. Thus, if management imposes these minimum production requirements, the linear programming problem will have no feasible solution.

How should we interpret this infeasibility in terms of the current problem? First, we should tell management that, for the available amounts of the three materials, producing 30 tons of fuel additive and 15 tons of solvent base isn't possible. Moreover, we can tell management exactly how much more of each material is needed.

Material	Minimum Tons Required for $F = 30, S = 15$	Tons Available	Additional Tons Required
Material 1	$^2/_5(30) + ^1/_2(15) = 19.5$	20	—
Material 2	$0(30) + ^1/_5(15) = 3$	5	—
Material 3	$^3/_5(30) + ^3/_{10}(15) = 22.5$	21	1.5

RMC has a sufficient supply of materials 1 and 2 but will need 1.5 additional tons of material 3 to meet management's production requirements of 30 tons of fuel additive and 15 tons of solvent base. If, after reviewing the above analysis, management still wants this level of production for the two products, RMC will somehow have to obtain the additional 1.5 tons of material 3.

Whenever you attempt to solve a problem that is infeasible using Excel Solver, you will obtain a **Solver Results** dialog box that contains the message, "Solver could not find a feasible solution." In this case you know that no solution to the linear programming problem will satisfy all constraints, including the nonnegativity conditions. Careful inspection of your formulation is necessary to try to identify why the problem is infeasible. In some situations, the only reasonable approach is to drop one or more constraints and resolve the problem. If you are able to find an optimal solution for this revised problem, you will know that the constraint(s) that were omitted, in conjunction with the others, are causing the problem to be infeasible.

Unbounded

The solution to a maximization linear programming problem is **unbounded** if the value of the solution may be made infinitely large without violating any constraints. For a minimization problem, the solution is unbounded if the value may be made infinitely small. This condition might be termed *managerial utopia.* For example, if this condition were to occur in a profit maximization problem, the manager could achieve unlimited profit.

In linear programming models of real-world problems, the occurrence of an unbounded solution means that the problem has been improperly formulated. We know that profits cannot increase indefinitely. Therefore, we must conclude that if a profit maximization problem results in an unbounded solution, the mathematical model doesn't represent the real-world problem sufficiently. Usually what has happened is that a constraint has been inadvertently omitted during problem formulation.

To illustrate how a missing constraint can result in an unbounded solution, recall the Innis Investments problem introduced in Section 2.5. In that problem the objective was to determine the allocation of funds between a stock and a money market fund that would minimize risk, subject to a funds available constraint, an annual income requirement, and a minimum investment in the money market fund. With S denoting the number of units purchased in the stock fund and M denoting the number of units purchased in the money market fund, we obtained the following linear programming model:

$$
\begin{array}{lll}
\text{Min} & 8S + 3M & \\
\text{s.t.} & & \\
& 50S + 100M \leq 1{,}200{,}000 & \text{Funds available} \\
& 5S + 4M \geq 60{,}000 & \text{Annual income} \\
& M \geq 3{,}000 & \text{Minimum units in money market} \\
& S, M \geq 0 &
\end{array}
$$

The optimal solution for this model was to purchase 4000 units in the stock fund and 10,000 units in the money market fund.

Suppose, however, that the objective in the problem is to maximize return, subject to the funds available constraint and the minimum investment in the money market fund. Because every unit in the stock fund provides an annual return of $5 and every unit invested in the money market fund provides an annual return of $4, the objective function for the revised problem is $5S + 4M$. In other words, the objective function for the revised problem is just the left-hand side of the annual income constraint in the original problem. The linear programming model for the revised problem is

$$
\begin{array}{lll}
\text{Max} & 5S + 4M & \\
\text{s.t.} & & \\
& 50S + 100M \leq 1{,}200{,}000 & \text{Funds available} \\
& M \geq 3{,}000 & \text{Minimum units in money market} \\
& S, M \geq 0 &
\end{array}
$$

Figure 2.25 shows the graphical solution for the revised Innis Investments problem. Note that the optimal solution is to purchase 18,000 units in the stock fund and 3000 units in the money market fund for a total revenue of $102,000.

Suppose, however, that in formulating the problem, the funds available constraint was inadvertently omitted during problem formulation. In Figure 2.26, we see that this would result in a feasible region that extended from the horizontal line $M = 3000$ to infinity. Looking at the objective function $5S + 4M$, we see that no matter what solution we pick, another feasible solution with a larger value will always be possible. Thus, the solution to this linear program is unbounded.

You should now be able to recognize whether a linear program involves alternative optimal solutions or infeasibility, or is unbounded. Try Problems 33 and 34.

Whenever you attempt to solve a problem that is unbounded using Excel Solver, you will obtain a **Solver Results** dialog box that contains the message, "The set of cell values do not converge." This message is Excel Solver's way of saying the problem that you are trying to solve is unbounded. Because unbounded solutions cannot occur in real problems, the first thing you should do is to review your model to determine whether you have incorrectly formulated the problem. As we demonstrated above, this error is often the result of inadvertently omitting a constraint during problem formulation.

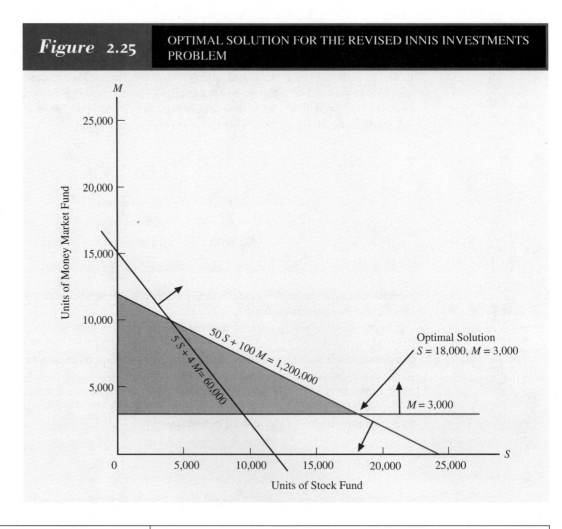

Figure 2.25 OPTIMAL SOLUTION FOR THE REVISED INNIS INVESTMENTS PROBLEM

N O T E S
and Comments

1. Infeasibility is independent of the objective function. It exists because the constraints are so restrictive that no feasible region for the linear programming model exists. Thus, when you encounter infeasibility, making changes in the coefficients of the objective function will not help; the problem will remain infeasible.

2. An unbounded solution often is the result of a missing constraint. However, a change in the objective function may cause a previously unbounded problem to become bounded with an optimal solution.

2.7 GENERAL LINEAR PROGRAMMING NOTATION

In this chapter we showed how to formulate mathematical and spreadsheet models for the RMC and Innis Investments linear programming problems. To formulate a mathematical model of the RMC problem we began by defining two decision variables: F = tons of fuel additive produced and S = tons of solvent base produced. In the Innis Investments problem, the two decision variables were defined as S = number of units purchased in the stock fund and M = number of units purchased in the money market fund. We selected decision variable names of F and S in the RMC problem and S and M in the Innis investments prob-

Figure 2.26   UNBOUNDED SOLUTION FOR THE REVISED INNIS INVESTMENTS PROBLEM

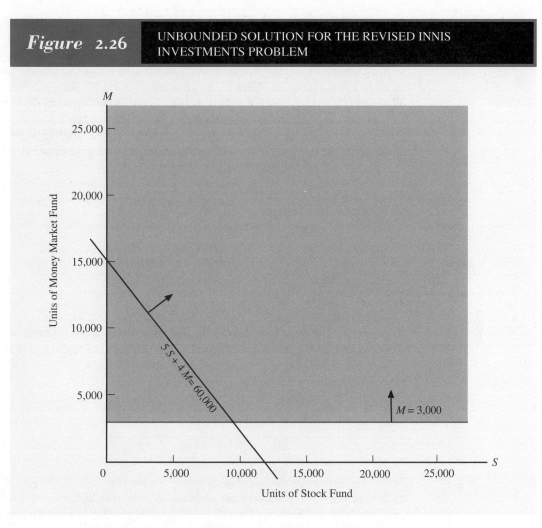

lem to make easier recalling what these decision variables represented in the problem. Although this approach works very well for linear programs involving a small number of decision variables, it can become difficult to use when dealing with problems involving a large number of decision variables.

A more general notation that is often used for linear programs uses the letter x with a subscript. For instance, in the RMC problem, we could have defined the decision variables as follows:

$$x_1 = \text{tons of fuel additive produced}$$
$$x_2 = \text{tons of solvent base produced}$$

In the Innis Investments problem, the same variable names would be used, but their definitions would change, as shown below:

$$x_1 = \text{number of units purchased in the stock fund}$$
$$x_2 = \text{number of units purchased in the money market fund}$$

A disadvantage of using general notation for decision variables is that we are no longer able to easily identify what the decision variables actually represent in the mathematical model.

However, the advantage of general notation is that formulating a mathematical model for a problem that involves a large number of decision variables is much easier. For instance, for a linear programming problem with three decision variables, we would use variable names of x_1 x_2, and x_3; for a problem with four decision variables, we would use variable names of x_1 x_2, x_3, and x_4, and so on. Clearly, if a problem involved 1000 decision variables, trying to identify 1000 unique names would be very difficult. However, using the general linear programming notation, the decision variables would be defined as x_1 x_2, x_3, . . . , x_{1000}.

To illustrate the graphical solution procedure for a linear program written using general linear programming notation, consider the following mathematical model for a maximization problem involving two decision variables:

$$
\begin{aligned}
\text{Max} \quad & 3x_1 + 2x_2 \\
\text{s.t.} \quad & \\
& 2x_1 + 2x_2 \le 8 \\
& 1x_1 + 0.5x_2 \le 3 \\
& x_1 \, x_2 \ge 0
\end{aligned}
$$

We must first develop a graph that displays the possible solutions (x_1 and x_2 values) for the problem. The usual convention is to plot values of x_1 along the horizontal axis and values of x_2 along the vertical axis. Figure 2.27 shows the graphical solution for this two variable problem. Note that for this problem the optimal solution is $x_1 = 2$ and $x_2 = 2$, with an objective function value of 10.

SUMMARY

We formulated mathematical models and spreadsheet models for two linear programming problems: the RMC maximization problem and the Innis Investments minimization problem. For both problems we showed how a graphical solution procedure and Excel Solver can be used to identify an optimal solution. In formulating a mathematical model of these problems, we developed a general definition of a linear program.

A linear program is a mathematical model that has

1. a linear objective function that is to be maximized or minimized,
2. a set of linear constraints, and
3. variables that are all restricted to nonnegative values.

Slack variables may be used to write less-than-or-equal-to constraints in equality form, and surplus variables may be used to write greater-than-or-equal-to constraints in equality form. The value of a slack variable usually can be interpreted as the amount of unused resource, and the value of a surplus variable indicates the amount by which a minimum requirement is exceeded. When all constraints are written as equalities, the linear program is in its standard form.

If the solution to a linear program is infeasible or unbounded, no optimal solution to the problem can be found. In the case of infeasibility, no feasible solutions are possible; whereas, in the case of an unbounded solution, the objective function can be made infinitely large for a maximization problem or infinitely small for a minimization problem.

| **Figure 2.27** | GRAPHICAL SOLUTION OF A TWO VARIABLE LINEAR PROGRAM WITH GENERAL NOTATION |

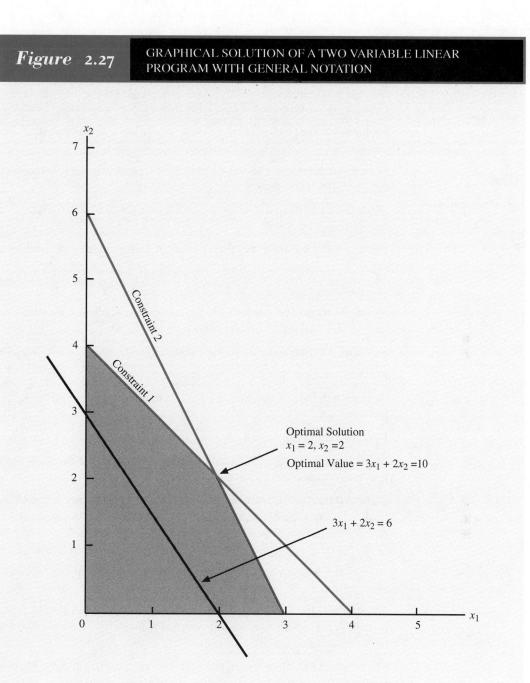

In the case of alternative optimal solutions, two or more optimal extreme points exist, and all points on the line segment connecting them also are optimal.

The chapter concluded with a section showing how to write a mathematical model using a general linear programming notation.

GLOSSARY

Constraint An equation or inequality that restricts the values of the decision variables.

Problem formulation The process of translating a verbal statement of a problem into a mathematical statement called a *mathematical model*.

Constraint function The left-hand side of a constraint (i.e., the portion of the constraint containing the variables).

Objective function All linear programs have a linear objective function that is either to be maximized or minimized.

Nonnegativity constraints A set of constraints that requires all variables to be nonnegative.

Linear program A mathematical model with a linear objective function, a set of linear constraints, and nonnegative variables.

Linear functions Mathematical expressions in which the variables appear in separate terms and are raised to the first power.

Solution Any set of values for the variables.

Feasible solution A solution that satisfies all constraints.

Optimal solution A feasible solution that maximizes or minimizes the value of the objective function.

Feasible region The set of solutions that satisfy all constraints simultaneously.

Slack variable A variable added to the left-hand side of a less-than-or-equal-to constraint to convert the constraint into an equality.

Standard form A linear program in which all constraints are written as equalities. The optimal solution of the standard form of a linear program is the same as the optimal solution of the original formulation of the linear program.

Redundant constraint A constraint that does not affect the feasible region. If a constraint is redundant, it could be removed from the problem without affecting the feasible region.

Extreme points The feasible solution points occurring at the vertices or "corners" of the feasible region. With two variables, extreme points are determined by the intersection of the constraint lines.

Spreadsheet model A representation of a linear programming problem containing the following four components: (1) cells for the decision variables; (2) a cell containing a formula for computing the value of the objective function; (3) cells containing formulas for computing the left-hand sides of the constraints; and (4) cells containing the values of the right-hand sides of the constraints or cells containing formulas for computing the values of the right-hand sides.

Surplus variable A variable subtracted from the left-hand side of a greater-than-or-equal-to constraint to convert the constraint into an equality.

Alternative optimal solutions A situation in which a linear program has more than one solution that provides the optimal value for the objective function.

Infeasibility A situation in which no solution to the linear programming problem satisfies all constraints.

Unbounded A maximization linear programming problem in which the value of the solution may be made infinitely large without violating any constraints; or, a minimization problem in which the value of the solution may be made infinitely small.

PROBLEMS

SELF TEST

1. Which of the following mathematical relationships could be found in a linear programming model, and which could not? For the relationships that are unacceptable for linear programs, state the reason for your answer.

   a. $-1x_1 + 2x_2 - 1x_3 \leq 70$

   b. $2x_1 - 2x_3 = 50$

   c. $1x_1 - 2x_2^2 + 4x_3 \leq 10$

   d. $3\sqrt{x_1} + 2x_2 - 1x_3 \geq 15$

   e. $1x_1 + 1x_2 + 1x_3 = 6$

   f. $2x_1 + 5x_2 + 1x_1x_2 \leq 25$

SELF TEST

2. Show a separate graph of the constraint lines and feasible solutions for each of the following constraints.

   a. $4x_1 + 2x_2 \leq 16$

   b. $4x_1 + 2x_2 \geq 16$

   c. $4x_1 + 2x_2 = 16$

3. Show a separate graph of the constraint lines and feasible solutions for each of the following constraints.

   a. $3x_1 + 2x_2 \leq 18$

   b. $12x_1 + 8x_2 \geq 480$

   c. $5x_1 + 10x_2 = 200$

4. Show a separate graph of the constraint lines and feasible solutions for each of the following constraints.

   a. $x_1 \geq 0.25 (x_1 + x_2)$

   b. $x_2 \leq 0.10 (x_1 + x_2)$

   c. $x_1 \leq 0.50 (x_1 + x_2)$

SELF TEST

5. Three objective functions for linear programming problems are $7x_1 + 10x_2$, $6x_1 + 4x_2$, and $-4x_1 + 7x_2$. Determine the slope of each objective function. Show the graph of each for objective function values equal to 420.

SELF TEST

6. Identify the feasible region for the following set of constraints.

$$\tfrac{1}{2}x_1 + \tfrac{1}{4}x_2 \geq 30$$

$$1x_1 + 5x_2 \geq 250$$

$$\tfrac{1}{4}x_1 + \tfrac{1}{2}x_2 \leq 50$$

$$x_1, x_2 \geq 0$$

7. Identify the feasible region for the following set of constraints.

$$3x_1 - 2x_2 \geq 0$$
$$2x_1 - 1x_2 \leq 200$$
$$1x_1 \leq 150$$
$$x_1, x_2 \geq 0$$

SELF TEST

8. For the linear program

$$\text{Max} \quad 2x_1 + 3x_2$$

s.t.

$$1x_1 + 2x_2 \leq 6$$
$$5x_1 + 3x_2 \leq 15$$
$$x_1, x_2 \geq 0$$

find the optimal solution using the graphical solution procedure. What is the value of the objective function at the optimal solution?

9. Solve the linear program using the graphical solution procedure.

$$\text{Max} \quad 5x_1 + 5x_2$$

s.t.

$$1x_1 \qquad \leq 100$$
$$1x_2 \leq 80$$
$$2x_1 + 4x_2 \leq 400$$
$$x_1, x_2 \geq 0$$

10. Consider the linear programming problem:

$$\text{Max} \quad 3x_1 + 3x_2$$

s.t.

$$2x_1 + 4x_2 \leq 12$$
$$6x_1 + 4x_2 \leq 24$$
$$x_1, x_2 \geq 0$$

a. Find the optimal solution using the graphical solution procedure.
b. If the objective function is changed to $2x_1 + 6x_2$, what will be the optimal solution?
c. How many extreme points are there? What are the values of x_1 and x_2 at each extreme point?

11. For the linear program

$$\text{Min} \quad 6x_1 + 4x_2$$

s.t.

$$2x_1 + 1x_2 \geq 12$$
$$1x_1 + 1x_2 \geq 10$$
$$1x_2 \leq 4$$
$$x_1, x_2 \geq 0$$

a. Solve the problem using the graphical solution procedure.
b. What are the values of the slack and surplus variables?

12. Consider the linear program:

$$\begin{aligned}
\text{Min} \quad & x_1 + 2x_2 \\
\text{s.t.} \quad & \\
& x_1 + 4x_2 \le 21 \\
& 2x_1 + x_2 \ge 7 \\
& 3x_1 + 1.5x_2 \le 21 \\
& -2x_1 + 6x_2 \ge 0 \\
& x_1, x_2 \ge 0
\end{aligned}$$

    a. Using the graphical solution procedure, find the optimal solution and the value of the objective function.

    b. Determine the amount of slack or surplus for each constraint.

    c. Suppose that the objective function is changed to max $5x_1 + 2x_2$. Find the optimal solution and the value of the objective function.

13. Par, Inc., is a small manufacturer of golf equipment and supplies. Par has been convinced by its distributor that markets for both a medium-priced golf bag, referred to as a standard model, and a high-priced golf bag, referred to as a deluxe model currently exist. The distributor is so confident of the market that, if Par can make the bags at a competitive price, the distributor has agreed to purchase all the bags that Par can manufacture over the next three months. A careful analysis of the manufacturing requirements resulted in the following table, which shows the production time requirements for the four required manufacturing operations and the accounting department's estimate of the profit contribution per bag.

	Production Time (hours)				
Product	Cutting and Dyeing	Sewing	Finishing	Inspection and Packaging	**Profit per Bag**
Standard	7/10	1/2	1	1/10	$10
Deluxe	1	5/6	2/3	1/4	$ 9

The director of manufacturing estimates that 630 hours of cutting and dyeing time, 600 hours of sewing time, 708 hours of finishing time, and 135 hours of inspection and packaging time will be available for the production of golf bags during the next 3 months. Assuming that the company wants to maximize total profit contribution, answer the following.

    a. Formulate a mathematical model for this problem.

    b. Use the graphical solution procedure to identify how many bags of each model to produce.

    c. What profit contribution can Par earn on those production quantities?

    d. How many hours of production time will be scheduled for each operation?

    e. What is the slack time in each operation?

14. Suppose that Par's management (Problem 13) encounters the following situations.
   a. The accounting department revises its estimate of the profit contribution for the deluxe bag to $18 per bag.
   b. A new low-cost material is available for the standard bag, and the profit contribution per standard bag can be increased to $20 per bag. (Assume that the profit contribution of the deluxe bag is the original $9 value.)
   c. New sewing equipment is available that would increase the sewing operation capacity to 750 hours. (Assume that $10x_1 + 9x_2$ is the appropriate objective function.)
   If each of these situations is encountered separately, what are the optimal solution and the total profit contribution? Use the graphical solution procedure.

15. Refer to the feasible region for the Par, Inc., situation in Problem 13.
   a. Develop an objective function that will make extreme point (0,540) the optimal extreme point.
   b. What is the optimal solution for the objective function you selected in part (a)?
   c. What are the values of the slack variables associated with this solution?

SELF TEST

16. Kelson Sporting Equipment, Inc., makes two different models of baseball gloves: a regular glove and a catcher's mitt. The firm has 900 hours of production time available in its cutting and sewing department, 300 hours available in its finishing department, and 100 hours available in its packaging and shipping department. The production time requirements and the profit contribution for each product are

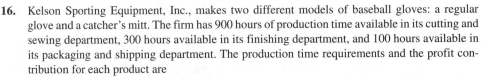

| | **Production Time (hours)** | | | |
Model	Cutting and Sewing	Finishing	Packaging and Shipping	Profit/Glove
Regular glove	1	1/2	1/8	$5
Catcher's mitt	3/2	1/3	1/4	$8

Assume that the company is interested in maximizing the total profit contribution.
   a. Formulate a mathematical model for this problem.
   b. Find the optimal solution using the graphical solution procedure. How many gloves of each model should Kelson manufacture?
   c. What is the total profit contribution Kelson can earn with the above production quantities?
   d. How many hours of production time will be scheduled in each department?
   e. What is the slack time in each department?

17. Investment Advisors, Inc., is a brokerage firm that manages stock portfolios for clients. A new client has requested that the firm handle an $80,000 investment portfolio. As an initial investment strategy, the client wants to restrict the portfolio to a mix of the following stocks.

Stock	Price/Share	Estimated Annual Return/Share	Risk Index/Share
U.S. Oil	$25	$3	0.50
Hub Properties	$50	$5	0.25

The risk index for the stock is a rating of the relative risk of the two investment alternatives. For the data given, U.S. Oil is judged to be the riskier investment. By constraining the total risk for the portfolio, the investment firm avoids placing excessive amounts of the portfolio in potentially high-return, high-risk investments. For the current portfolio, an upper limit of 700 has been set for the total risk index of all investments. The firm also has set an upper limit of 1000 shares for the more risky U.S. Oil stock.

a. Formulate a mathematical model that can be used to determine how many shares of each stock should be purchased to maximize the total annual return.

b. Find the optimal solution using the graphical solution procedure.

18. Healthtech Foods managers are considering developing a new low-fat snack food. It is to be a blend of two types of cereals, each of which has different fiber, fat, and protein characteristics. The following table shows these nutrition characteristics for one ounce of each type of cereal.

Cereal	Dietary Fiber (grams)	Fat (grams)	Protein (grams)
A	2	2	4
B	1.5	3	3

Note that each ounce of cereal A provides 2 grams of dietary fiber and that each ounce of cereal B provides 1.5 grams of dietary fiber. Thus, if Healthtech were to develop the new product using a mix consisting of 50% cereal A and 50% cereal B, 1 ounce of the snack food would contain 1.75 grams of dietary fiber. Healthtech's nutrition requirements call for each ounce of the new food to have at least 1.7 grams of dietary fiber, no more than 2.8 grams of fat, and no more than 3.6 grams of protein. The cost of cereal A is $0.02 per ounce, and the cost of cereal B is $0.025 per ounce. Healthtech wants to determine how much of each cereal is needed to produce 1 ounce of the new food product at the lowest possible cost.

a. Formulate a mathematical model for this situation.

b. Solve the problem using the graphical solution procedure.

c. What are the values of the slack and surplus variables?

d. If Healthtech markets the new snack food in an 8-ounce package, what is the cost per package?

19. Refer to the formula spreadsheet for the RMC problem in Figure 2.13. Suppose that RMC's management encounters the following situations. Revise the original spreadsheet and use Excel Solver to determine the optimal solution and the value of the optimal solution. Assume that each situation is encountered separately.

a. The accounting department revises its estimate of the profit contribution for the solvent base to $35 per ton. (Assume that the profit contribution of the fuel additive is the original $40 per ton.)

b. Only 18 tons of material 3 are available.

c. Suppose that 24 tons of material 1 are available for production.

d. The original problem data showed that each ton of solvent base required 0.5 tons of material 1, 0.2 tons of material 2, and 0.3 tons of material 3. Suppose that the correct values are 0.5 tons of material 1, 0.25 tons of material 2, and 0.3 tons of material 3.

20. Refer to the formula spreadsheet for the Innis Investments problem in Figure 2.19. Suppose that management encounters the following situations. Revise the original spreadsheet and use Excel Solver to determine the optimal solution and the value of the optimal solution. Assume that each situation is encountered separately.

a. The client is now willing to invest up to $1.5 million.

b. The client wants to minimize risk but earn an annual income from the investment of at least $75,000.

c. Suppose that each unit purchased in the stock fund has a risk index of 10 and that each unit purchased in the money market has a risk index of 3.

d. Suppose that each unit of the stock fund cost $55 and that each unit of the money market fund costs $96.

21. In Problem 13 you were required to formulate a mathematical model for the Par, Inc., problem. Figure 2.28 shows a spreadsheet layout for this problem.
    a. Enter the Excel formula that can be used to compute the value of total profit into cell B18.
    b. Enter the Excel formulas that can be used to compute the values of the number of hours used for each operation into cells B21:B24.
    c. Enter the Excel formulas that can be used to compute the values of the number of hours available for each operation into cells D21:D24.
    d. Use Excel Solver to determine the optimal solution.

22. In Problem 16 you were required to formulate a mathematical model for the Kelson Sporting Equipment, Inc., problem. Figure 2.29 shows a spreadsheet layout for this problem.
    a. Enter the Excel formula that can be used to compute the value of total profit into cell B17.

Figure 2.28   SPREADSHEET FOR PAR, INC. (PROBLEM 21)

SPREADSHEET
PAR, INC.

	A	B	C	D
1	**Par, Inc.**			
2				
3		**Production Time**		
4	**Operation**	**Standard**	**Deluxe**	**Time Available**
5	Cutting and Dyeing	0.7	1	630
6	Sewing	0.5	0.83333	600
7	Finishing	1	0.66667	708
8	Inspection and Packaging	0.1	0.25	135
9	**Profit Per Bag**	10	9	
10				
11				
12	**Model**			
13				
14		**Decision Variables**		
15		**Standard**	**Deluxe**	
16	**Bags Produced**			
17				
18	**Maximize Total Profit**			
19				
20	**Constraints**	**Hours Used (LHS)**		**Hours Available (RHS)**
21	Cutting and Dyeing		<=	
22	Sewing		<=	
23	Finishing		<=	
24	Inspection and Packaging		<=	

      b. Enter the Excel formulas that can be used to compute the values of the number of hours used for each department into cells B20:B22.

      c. Enter the Excel formulas that can be used to compute the values of the number of hours available for each department into cells D20:D22.

      d. Use Excel Solver to determine the optimal solution.

23. In Problem 18 you were required to formulate a mathematical model for the Healthtech Foods problem. Figure 2.30 shows a spreadsheet layout for this problem.

      a. Enter the Excel formula that can be used to compute the value of total cost into cell B20.

      b. Enter the Excel formulas that can be used to compute the values of the left sides of the constraints into cells B23:B26.

      c. Enter the Excel formulas that can be used to compute the values of the right sides of the constraints into cells D23:D26.

      d. Use Excel Solver to determine the optimal solution.

Figure 2.29   SPREADSHEET FOR KELSON (PROBLEM 22)

SPREADSHEET
KELSON
CHAPTER 2

	A	B	C	D
1	**Kelson Chapter 2**			
2				
3		**Production Time (hours)**		
4	**Department**	**Regular Glove**	**Catcher's Mitt**	**Time Available**
5	Cutting and Sewing	1	1.5	900
6	Finishing	0.5	0.33333	300
7	Packaging and Shipping	0.125	0.25	100
8	**Profit Per Glove**	5	8	
9				
10				
11	**Model**			
12				
13		**Decision Variables**		
14		**Regular Glove**	**Catcher's Mitt**	
15	**Number Produced**			
16				
17	**Maximize Total Profit**			
18				
19	**Constraints**	**Hours Used (LHS)**		**Hours Available (RHS)**
20	Cutting and Sewing		<=	
21	Finishing		<=	
22	Packaging and Shipping		<=	

24. George Johnson recently inherited a large sum of money; he wants to use a portion of this money to set up a trust fund for his two children. The trust fund has two investment options: (1) a bond fund and (2) a stock fund. The projected returns over the life of the investments are 6% for the bond fund and 10% for the stock fund. Whatever portion of the inheritance that he finally decides to commit to the trust fund, he wants to invest at least 30% of that amount in the bond fund. In addition, he wants to select a mix that will enable him to obtain a total return of at least 7.5%.

    a. Formulate a mathematical model that can be used to determine the percentage that should be allocated to each of the possible investment alternatives.
    b. Develop a spreadsheet formulation and solve.

25. The owner of the Sea Wharf Restaurant would like to determine the best way to allocate a monthly advertising budget of $1000 between newspaper advertising and radio advertising. Management has decided that at least 25% of the budget must be spent on each type of

SPREADSHEET
HEALTHTECH

| | *Figure* **2.30** | SPREADSHEET FOR HEALTHTECH (PROBLEM 23) |

	A	B	C	D	E
1	**Healthtech**				
2					
3		**Nutrition Characteristic (grams)**			**Cost per**
4	**Cereal**	**Fiber**	**Fat**	**Protein**	**Ounce (cents)**
5	**A**	2	2	4	2
6	**B**	1.5	3	3	3
7					
8	**Characteristic**	**Requirement (grams)**			
9	**Fiber**	at least	1.7		
10	**Fat**	no more than	2.8		
11	**Protein**	no more than	3.6		
12					
13					
14	**Model**				
15					
16		**Decision Variables**			
17		**Cereal A**	**Cereal B**		
18	**Percentage**				
19					
20	**Minimize Total Cost**				
21					
22	**Constraints**	**LHS**		**RHS**	
23	Minimum Fiber		>=		
24	Maximum Fat		<=		
25	Maximum Protein		<=		
26	Percentage Requirement		=		

media, and that the amount of money spent on local newspaper advertising must be at least twice the amount spent on radio advertising. A marketing consultant has developed an index that measures audience exposure per dollar of advertising on a scale from 0 to 100, with higher values implying greater audience exposure. If the value of the index for local newspaper advertising is 50 and the value of the index for spot radio advertising is 80, how should management allocate the advertising budget to maximize the value of total audience exposure?

    a. Formulate a linear programming model that can be used to determine how management should allocate the advertising budget to maximize the value of total audience exposure.

    b. Develop a spreadsheet formulation and solve.

26. Tom's Inc., produces various Mexican food products and sells them to Western Foods, a chain of grocery stores located in Texas and New Mexico. Tom's, Inc., makes two salsa products: Western Foods Salsa and Mexico City Salsa. Essentially, the two products have different blends of whole tomatoes, tomato sauce, and tomato paste. The Western Foods Salsa is a blend of 50% whole tomatoes, 30% tomato sauce, and 20% tomato paste. The Mexico City Salsa, which has a thicker and chunkier consistency, consists of 70% whole tomatoes, 10% tomato sauce, and 20% tomato paste. Each jar of salsa produced weighs 10 ounces. For the current production period Tom's, Inc., can purchase up to 280 pounds of whole tomatoes, 130 pounds of tomato sauce, and 100 pounds of tomato paste; the price per pound for these ingredients is $0.96, $0.64, and $0.56, respectively. The cost of the spices and the other ingredients is approximately $0.10 per jar. Tom's, Inc., buys empty glass jars for $0.02 each, and labeling and filling costs are estimated to be $0.03 for each jar of salsa produced. Tom's contract with Western Foods results in sales revenue of $1.64 for each jar of Western Foods Salsa and $1.93 for each jar of Mexico City Salsa.

    a. Formulate a mathematical model that will enable Tom's to determine the mix of salsa products that will maximize the total profit contribution.

    b. Develop a spreadsheet formulation and solve.

27. The production editor for Rayburn Publishing Company has 1800 pages of manuscript that must be copyedited. Because of the short time frame involved, only two copyeditors are available: Erhan Mergen and Sue Smith. Erhan has 10 days available, and Sue has 12 days available. Erhan can process 100 pages of manuscript per day, and Sue can process 150 pages of manuscript per day. Rayburn Publishing has developed an index used to measure the overall quality of a copyeditor on a scale from 1 (worst) to 10 (best). Erhan's quality rating is 9, and Sue's quality rating is 6. In addition, Erhan charges $3 per page of copyedited manuscript; Sue charges $2 per page. A budget of $4800 has been allocated for copyediting.

    a. Formulate a mathematical model that can be used to determine how many pages should be assigned to each copyeditor to complete the project with the highest possible quality.

    b. Develop a spreadsheet formulation and solve.

28. Car Phones, Inc., sells two models of car telephones: model X and model Y. Records show that 3 hours of sales time are used for each model X telephone that is sold and 5 hours of sales time for each model Y telephone. A total of 600 hours of sales time is available for the next 4-week period. In addition, management planning policies call for minimum sales goals of 25 units for both model X and model Y. The company makes a $40 profit contribution for each model X sold and a $50 profit contribution for each model Y sold.

    a. Formulate a mathematical model that can be used to determine the optimal sales goal for the company for the next 4-week period.

    b. Develop a spreadsheet formulation and solve.

    c. Suppose that management adds the restriction that Car Phones must sell at least as many model Y telephones as model X telephones. What is the new optimal solution?

29. The New England Cheese Company produces two cheese spreads by blending mild cheddar cheese with extra sharp cheddar cheese. The cheese spreads are packaged in 12-ounce containers, which are then sold to distributors throughout the Northeast. The Regular blend contains 80% mild cheddar and 20% extra sharp, and the Zesty blend contains 60% mild cheddar and 40%

extra sharp. This year, a local dairy cooperative has offered to provide up to 8100 pounds of mild cheddar cheese for $1.20 per pound and up to 3000 pounds of extra sharp cheddar cheese for $1.40 per pound. The cost to blend and package the cheese spreads, excluding the cost of the cheese, is $0.20 per container. Each container of Regular is sold for $1.95 and each container of Zesty is sold for $2.20.

    a. Formulate a mathematical model that can be used to determine how many containers of Regular and Zesty New England Cheese should produce.

    b. Develop a spreadsheet formulation and solve.

30. M&D Chemicals produces two products that are sold as raw materials to companies manufacturing bath soaps, laundry detergents, and other soap products. Based on an analysis of current inventory levels and potential demand for the coming month, M&D's management has specified that the total production for products 1 and 2 combined must be at least 350 gallons. Also, a major customer's order for 125 gallons of product 1 must be satisfied. Product 1 requires 2 hours of processing time per gallon and product 2 requires 1 hour of processing time per gallon; for the coming month, 600 hours of processing time are available. Production costs are $2 per gallon for product 1 and $3 per gallon for product 2.

    a. Formulate a mathematical model that can be used to determine the production quantities that will satisfy the requirements specified at minimum cost.

    b. Develop a spreadsheet formulation and solve. What is the total product cost?

    c. Identify the amount of any surplus production.

31. Photo Chemicals produces two types of photographic developing fluids. Both products cost Photo Chemicals $1 per gallon to produce. Based on an analysis of current inventory levels and outstanding orders for the next month, Photo Chemicals' management has specified that at least 30 gallons of product 1 and at least 20 gallons of product 2 must be produced during the next 2 weeks. Management also has stated that an existing inventory of highly perishable raw material required in the production of both fluids must be used within the next 2 weeks. The current inventory of the perishable raw material is 80 pounds. Although more of this raw material can be ordered if necessary, any of the current inventory that is not used within the next 2 weeks will spoil—hence, the management requirement that at least 80 pounds be used in the next 2 weeks. Furthermore, product 1 requires 1 pound of this perishable raw material per gallon and product 2 requires 2 pounds of the raw material per gallon. Since management's objective is to keep production costs at the minimum possible level, they are looking for a minimum-cost production plan that uses all 80 pounds of perishable raw material and provides at least 30 gallons of product 1 and at least 20 gallons of product 2.

    a. Formulate a mathematical model that can be used to determine the minimum-cost solution.

    b. Develop a spreadsheet formulation and solve.

32. Bryant's Pizza, Inc., is a producer of frozen pizza products. The company makes a profit of $1.00 for each regular pizza it produces and $1.50 for each deluxe pizza produced. Each pizza includes a combination of dough mix and topping mix. The firm currently has 150 pounds of dough mix and 50 pounds of topping mix. Each regular pizza uses 1 pound of dough mix and 4 ounces of topping mix. Each deluxe pizza uses 1 pound of dough mix and 8 ounces of topping mix. Based on past demand, Bryant can sell at least 50 regular pizzas and at least 25 deluxe pizzas. How many regular and deluxe pizzas should the company make to maximize profits?

    a. Formulate a mathematical model for this problem.

    b. Develop a spreadsheet formulation and solve.

33. Determine if the following linear program involves alternative optimal solutions, infeasibility, or is unbounded. Explain

SELF TEST

$$\text{Max} \quad 4x_1 + 8x_2$$
$$\text{s.t.}$$
$$2x_1 + 2x_2 \le 10$$
$$-1x_1 + 1x_2 \ge 8$$
$$x_1, x_2 \ge 0$$

34. Determine if the following linear program involves alternative optimal solutions infeasibility, or is unbounded.

$$\text{Max} \quad 1x_1 + 1x_2$$
$$\text{s.t.}$$
$$8x_1 + 6x_2 \geq 24$$
$$4x_1 + 6x_2 \geq -12$$
$$2x_2 \geq 4$$
$$x_1, x_2 \geq 0$$

35. Consider the linear program:

$$\text{Max} \quad 1x_1 + 1x_2$$
$$\text{s.t.}$$
$$5x_1 + 3x_2 \leq 15$$
$$3x_1 + 5x_2 \leq 15$$
$$x_1, x_2 \geq 0$$

a. Find the optimal solution.
b. Suppose that the objective function is changed to $1x_1 + 2x_2$. Find the new optimal solution.
c. By adjusting the coefficient of x_2 in the objective function, develop a new objective function that will make the solutions found in parts (a) and (b) alternative optimal solutions.

36. Consider the linear program:

$$\text{Max} \quad 1x_1 - 2x_2$$
$$\text{s.t.}$$
$$-4x_1 + 3x_2 \leq 3$$
$$1x_1 - 1x_2 \leq 3$$
$$x_1, x_2 \geq 0$$

a. Graph the feasible region for the problem.
b. Is the feasible region unbounded? Explain.
c. Find the optimal solution.
d. Does an unbounded feasible region imply that the optimal solution to the linear program will be unbounded?

37. Expedition Outfitters manufactures specialty clothing for hiking, skiing, and mountain climbing. Company management has decided to begin production on two new parkas designed for use in extremely cold weather; the names selected for the two models are the Mount Everest Parka and the Rocky Mountain Parka. The manufacturing plant has 120 hours of cutting time and 120 hours of sewing time available for producing these two parkas. Each Mount Everest Parka requires 30 minutes of cutting time and 45 minutes of sewing time, and each Rocky Mountain Parka requires 20 minutes of cutting time and 15 minutes of sewing time. The labor and material cost is $150 for each Mount Everest Parka and $50 for each Rocky Mountain Parka, and the retail prices through the firm's mail-order catalog are $250 for the Mount Everest Parka and $200 for the Rocky Mountain Parka. Because management believes that the Mount Everest Parka is a unique coat that will enhance the image of the firm, they have specified that at least 20% of the total production must consist of this model. Assuming that Expedition Outfitters can sell as many coats of each type as it can produce, how many units of each model should it manufacture to maximize the total profit contribution?

38. English Motors, Ltd, (EML), has developed a new all-wheel-drive sports utility vehicle. As part of the marketing campaign, EML has developed a videotape sales presentation that will be sent to both owners of current EML four-wheel-drive vehicles as well as to owners of four-wheel-drive sports utility vehicles offered by competitors; EML refers to these two target markets as

the current customer market and the new customer market. Individuals who receive the new promotion video will also receive a coupon for a test drive of the new EML model for one weekend. A key factor in the success of the new promotion is the response rate, the percentage of individuals that receives the new promotion and test drives the new model. EML estimates that the response rate for the current customer market is 25%, and the response rate for the new customer market is 20%. For the customers that test drive the new model, the sales rate is the percentage of individuals that makes a purchase. Marketing research studies indicate that the sales rate is 12% for the current customer market and 20% for the new customer market. The cost for each promotion, excluding the test drive costs, are $4 for each promotion sent to the current customer market and $6 for each promotion sent to the new customer market. Management has also specified that a minimum of 30,000 current customers should test drive the new model and a minimum of 10,000 new customers should test drive the new model. In addition, the number of current customers that test drives the new vehicle must be at least twice the number of new customers that test drives the new vehicle. If the marketing budget, excluding test drive costs, is $1,200,000, how many promotions should be sent to each group of customers to maximize total sales?

39. Creative Sports Designs (CSD) manufactures a standard-size racket and an oversize racket. The firm's rackets are extremely light due to the use of a magnesium-graphite alloy that was invented by the firm's founder. Each standard-size racket uses 0.125 kilograms of the alloy and each oversize racket uses 0.4 kilograms; over the next 2-week production period only 80 kilograms of the alloy are available. Each standard-size racket uses 10 minutes of manufacturing time and each oversize racket uses 12 minutes. The profit contributions are $10 for each standard-size racket and $15 for each oversize racket, and 40 hours of manufacturing time are available each week. Management has specified that at least 20% of the total production must be the standard-size racket. How many rackets of each type should CSD manufacture over the next 2 weeks to maximize the total profit contribution? Assume that because of the unique nature of their products, CSD can sell as many rackets as it can produce.

40. Management of High Tech Services (HTS) wants to develop a model that will help allocate its technicians' time between service calls to regular contract customers and new customers. A maximum of 80 hours of technician time is available over the 2-week planning period. To satisfy cash flow requirements, at least $800 in revenue (per technician) must be generated during the 2-week period. Technician time for regular customers generates $25 per hour. However, technician time for new customers only generates an average of $8 per hour because in many cases a new customer contact does not provide billable services. To ensure that new customer contacts are being maintained, the technician time spent on new customer contacts must be at least 60% of the time spent on regular customer contacts. For the revenue and policy requirements stated, HTS would like to determine how to allocate technician time between regular customers and new customers to maximize the total number of customers contacted during the 2-week period. Technicians require an average of 50 minutes for each regular customer contact and 1 hour for each new customer contact.
    a. Develop a linear programming model that will enable HTS to allocate technician time between regular customers and new customers.
    b. Find the optimal solution.

41. Jackson Hole Manufacturing is a small manufacturer of plastic products used in the automotive and computer industries. One major contract is with a large computer company and involves the production of plastic printer cases for the computer company's portable printers. The printer cases are produced on two injection molding machines. The M-100 machine has a production capacity of 25 printer cases per hour, and the M-200 machine has a production capacity of 40 cases per hour. Both machines use the same chemical material to produce the printer cases; the M-100 uses 40 pounds of the raw material per hour, and the M-200 uses 50 pounds per hour. The computer company has asked Jackson Hole to produce as many of the cases during the upcoming week as possible and has said that it will pay $18 for each case Jackson Hole can deliver. However, next week is a regularly scheduled vacation period for most of Jackson Hole's production employees; during this time, annual maintenance is performed for all equipment in the

plant. Because of the downtime for maintenance, the M-100 will be available for no more than 15 hours, and the M-200 will be available for no more than 10 hours. However, because of the high setup cost involved with both machines, management has a requirement that, if production is scheduled on either machine, the machine must be operated for at least 5 hours. The supplier of the chemical material used in the production process has informed Jackson Hole that a maximum of 1000 pounds of the chemical material will be available for next week's production; the cost for this raw material is $6 per pound. In addition to the raw material cost, Jackson Hole estimates that the hourly cost of operating the M-100 and the M-200 are $50 and $75, respectively.

a. Formulate a linear programming model that can be used to maximize the contribution to profit.

b. Find the optimal solution.

Case Problem   ADVERTISING STRATEGY

Midtown Motors, Inc., has hired a marketing services firm to develop an advertising strategy for promoting Midtown's used car sales. The marketing firm has recommended that Midtown use spot announcements on both television and radio as the advertising media for the proposed promotional campaign. Advertising strategy guidelines are expressed as follows:

1. Use at least 30 announcements for combined television and radio coverage.
2. Do not use more than 25 radio announcements.
3. The number of radio announcements cannot be less than the number of television announcements.

The television station has quoted a cost of $1200 per spot announcement, and the radio station has quoted a cost of $300 per spot announcement. Midtown's advertising budget has been set at $25,500. The marketing services firm has rated the various advertising media in terms of audience coverage and recall power of the advertisement. For Midtown's media alternatives, the television announcement is rated at 600 and the radio announcement is rated at 200. Midtown's president would like to know how many television and how many radio spot announcements should be used to maximize the overall rating of the advertising campaign.

Midtown's president believes that the television station will consider running the Midtown spot announcement on its highly rated evening news program (at the same cost) if Midtown will consider using additional television announcements.

Managerial Report

Perform an analysis of advertising strategy for Midtown Motors and prepare a report to Midtown's president presenting your findings and recommendations. Include (but do not limit your discussion to) a consideration of the following items.

1. The recommended number of television and radio spot announcements.
2. The relative merits of each advertising medium.
3. The rating that would be necessary for the news program before it would make sense to increase the number of television spots.
4. The number of television spots that should be purchased if the news program is rated highly enough to make increasing the number of television spots advisable.
5. The restrictions placed on the advertising strategy that Midtown might want to consider relaxing or altering.

6. The best use of any possible increase in the advertising budget.
7. Any other information that may help Midtown's president make the advertising strategy decision.

Case Problem   PRODUCTION STRATEGY

Better Fitness, Inc. (BFI) manufactures exercise equipment at its plant in Freeport, Long Island. It recently designed two universal weight machines for the home exercise market. Both machines use BFI-patented technology that provides the user with an extremely wide range of motion capability for each type of exercise performed. Until now, such capabilities have been available only on very expensive weight machines used primarily by physical therapists.

At a recent trade show, demonstrations of the machines resulted in significant dealer interest. In fact, the number of orders that BFI received at the trade show far exceeded its manufacturing capabilities for the current production period. As a result, management decided to begin production of the two machines. The two machines, which BFI has named the BodyPlus 100 and the BodyPlus 200, require different amounts of resources to produce.

The BodyPlus 100 consists of a frame unit, a press station, and a pec-dec station. Each frame produced uses 4 hours of machining and welding time and 2 hours of painting and finishing time. Each press station requires 2 hours of machining and welding time and 1 hour of painting and finishing time, and each pec-dec station uses 2 hours of machining and welding time and 2 hours of painting and finishing time. In addition, 2 hours are spent assembling, testing, and packaging each BodyPlus 100. The raw material costs are $450 for each frame, $300 for each press station, and $250 for each pec-dec station; packaging costs are estimated to be $50 per unit.

The BodyPlus 200 consists of a frame unit, a press station, a pec-dec station, and a leg-press station. Each frame produced uses 5 hours of machining and welding time and 4 hours of painting and finishing time. Each press station requires 3 hours of machining and welding time and 2 hours of painting and finishing time, each pec-dec station uses 2 hours of machining and welding time and 2 hours of painting and finishing time, and each leg-press station requires 2 hours of machining and welding time and 2 hours of painting and finishing time. In addition, 2 hours are spent assembling, testing, and packaging each BodyPlus 200. The raw material costs are $650 for each frame, $400 for each press station, $250 for each pec-dec station, and $200 for each leg-press station; packaging costs are estimated to be $75 per unit.

For the next production period, management estimates that 600 hours of machining and welding time, 450 hours of painting and finishing time, and 140 hours of assembly, testing, and packaging time will be available. Current labor costs are $20 per hour for machining and welding time, $15 per hour for painting and finishing time, and $12 per hour for assembly, testing, and packaging time. The market in which the two machines must compete suggests a retail price of $2400 for the BodyPlus 100 and $3500 for the BodyPlus 200, although some flexibility may be available to BFI because of the unique capabilities of the new machines. Authorized BFI dealers can purchase machines for 70% of the suggested retail price.

BFI's president believes that the unique capabilities of the BodyPlus 200 can help position BFI as one of the leaders in high-end exercise equipment. Consequently, he has stated that the number of units of the BodyPlus 200 produced must be at least 25% of the total production.

Managerial Report

Analyze Better Fitness, Inc.'s production problem and prepare a report to BFI's president presenting your findings and recommendations. Include (but do not limit your discussion to) a consideration of the following items.

1. The recommended number of BodyPlus 100 and BodyPlus 200 machines to produce.
2. The effect on profits of the requirement that the number of units of the BodyPlus 200 produced must be at least 25% of the total production.
3. Where efforts should be expended in order to increase profits.

3

LINEAR PROGRAMMING: SENSITIVITY

ANALYSIS AND INTERPRETATION OF SOLUTION

Sensitivity analysis is the study of how the changes in the coefficients of a linear program affect the optimal solution. Using sensitivity analysis, we can answer questions such as the following:

1. How will a change *in a coefficient of the objective function* affect the optimal solution?
2. How will a change in the *right-hand side value for a constraint* affect the optimal solution?

Because sensitivity analysis is concerned with how the above changes affect the optimal solution, the analysis does not begin until the optimal solution to the original linear programming problem has been obtained. For that reason, sensitivity analysis is often referred to as *postoptimality analysis*.

Our approach to sensitivity analysis parallels the approach used to introduce linear programming in Chapter 2. We begin by showing how a graphical method can be used to perform sensitivity analysis for linear programming problems with two decision variables. Then, we show how Excel Solver provides sensitivity analysis information.

We extend the discussion of problem formulation started in Chapter 2 by formulating and solving two slightly larger problems with three decision variables. In discussing the spreadsheet solution for each of these problems, we focus on managerial interpretation of the optimal solution and sensitivity analysis information. The final section of the chapter provides further practice in the formulation, solution, and interpretation of output for a larger problem involving four decision variables and various types of constraints.

3.1   INTRODUCTION TO SENSITIVITY ANALYSIS

Sensitivity analysis is important to decision makers because real-world problems exist in a changing environment. Prices of raw materials change, product demand changes, companies purchase new machinery, stock prices fluctuate, employee turnover occurs, and so on. If a linear programming model has been used in such an environment, we can expect some of the coefficients to change over time. We will then want to determine how these changes affect the optimal solution to the original linear programming problem. Sensitivity analysis provides us with the information needed to respond to such changes without requiring the complete solution of a revised linear program.

Recall the RMC problem:

$$\text{Max} \quad 40F + 30S$$

s.t.

$$\frac{2}{5}F + \frac{1}{2}S \le 20 \quad \text{Material 1}$$

$$\frac{1}{5}S \le 5 \quad \text{Material 2}$$

$$\frac{3}{5}F + \frac{3}{10}S \le 21 \quad \text{Material 3}$$

$$F, S \ge 0$$

The optimal solution, $F = 25$ tons of fuel additive and $S = 20$ tons of solvent base was based on profit contribution figures of $40 per ton of fuel additive and $30 per ton of solvent base. Suppose that we later learn that a price reduction causes the profit contribution for the fuel additive to fall from $40 to $35 per ton. Sensitivity analysis can be used to determine whether the production schedule calling for 25 tons of fuel additive and 20 tons of solvent base is still best. If it is, solving a modified linear programming problem with $35F + 30S$ as the new objective function will not be necessary.

Sensitivity analysis can also be used to determine which coefficients in a linear programming model are crucial. For example, suppose that management believes that the $30 per ton profit contribution for the solvent base is only a rough estimate of the profit contribution that will actually be obtained. If sensitivity analysis shows that 25 tons of fuel additive and 20 tons of solvent base will be the optimal solution as long as the profit contribution for the solvent base is between $20 and $40, management should feel comfortable with the $30 per ton estimate and the recommended production quantities. However, if sensitivity analysis shows that 25 tons of fuel additive and 20 tons of solvent base will be the optimal solution only if the profit contribution for the solvent base is between $29.90 and $32.00 per ton, management may want to review the accuracy of the $30 per ton estimate. Management would especially want to consider how the optimal production quantities should be revised if the profit contribution per ton for the solvent base were to drop.

Another aspect of sensitivity analysis concerns changes in the right-hand-side values of the constraints. Recall that in the RMC problem the optimal solution used all available material 1 and material 3. What would happen to the optimal solution and total profit contribution if RMC could obtain additional quantities of either of these resources? Sensitivity analysis can help determine how much each added ton of material is worth and how many tons can be added before diminishing returns set in.

3.2 GRAPHICAL SENSITIVITY ANALYSIS

For linear programming problems with two decision variables, graphical methods can be used to perform sensitivity analysis on the objective function coefficients and the right-hand-side values for the constraints.

Objective Function Coefficients

Let us consider how changes in the objective function coefficients might affect the optimal solution to the RMC problem. The current contribution to profit is $40 per ton of fuel additive and $30 per ton of solvent base. An increase in the profit contribution for one of the products might lead management to increase the production of that product, and a decrease in the profit contribution for one of the products might lead management to decrease production of that product. But how much the profit contribution would have to change before management would want to change the production quantities is not obvious.

The current optimal solution to the RMC problem calls for producing 25 tons of fuel additive and 20 tons of solvent base. The **range of optimality** for each objective function coefficient provides the range of values for the coefficient over which the current solution will remain optimal. Managerial attention should be focused on those objective function coefficients that have a narrow range of optimality and coefficients near the endpoints of the range. A small change in these coefficients can necessitate modifying the optimal solution. Let us now compute the ranges of optimality for the RMC problem.

Figure 3.1 shows the graphical solution to the RMC problem. Careful inspection of this graph shows that, as long as the slope of the objective function is between the slope of line A (which coincides with the material 1 constraint line) and the slope of line B (which coincides with the material 3 constraint line), extreme point ③ with $F = 25$ and $S = 20$ will be optimal. Changing an objective function coefficient for F or S will cause the slope of the objective function to change. Figure 3.1 shows that such a change causes the objective function line to rotate about extreme point ③. However, as long as the objective function line stays within the shaded region, extreme point ③ will remain optimal.

Rotating the objective function line *counterclockwise* increases the slope. Thus when the objective function line has been rotated counterclockwise (slope increased) enough to coincide with line A, we obtain alternative optimal solutions between extreme points ③ and ④. Any further counterclockwise rotation of the objective function line will cause extreme point ③ to be nonoptimal. Hence, the slope of line A provides an upper limit for the slope of the objective function line.

Rotating the objective function line *clockwise* decreases the slope. Thus, when the objective function line has been rotated clockwise (slope decreased) enough to coincide with line B, we obtain alternative optimal solutions between extreme points ③ and ②. Any further clockwise rotation of the objective function line will cause extreme point ③ to be nonoptimal. Hence, the slope of line B provides a lower limit for the slope of the objective function line.

Thus, extreme point ③ will be the optimal solution as long as

Slope of line $B \leq$ slope of objective function line $\leq$ slope of line A

In Figure 3.1 the equation for line A, the material 1 constraint line, is

$$\tfrac{2}{5}F + \tfrac{1}{2}S = 20$$

The slope of the objective function line usually is negative; hence, rotating the objective function line clockwise makes the line steeper even though the slope is getting smaller (more negative).

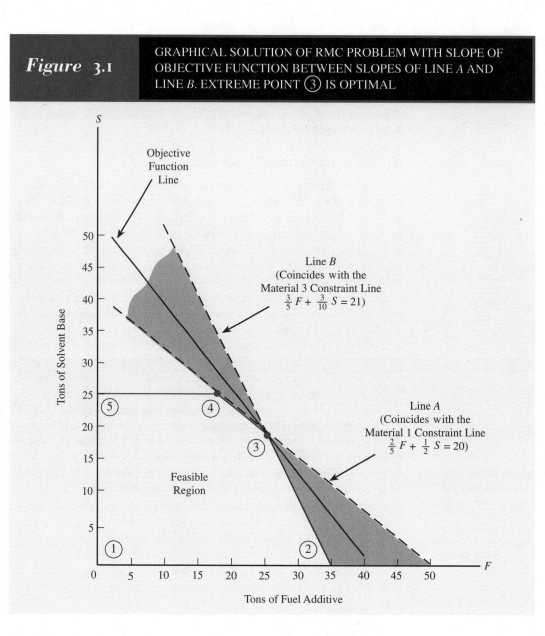

Figure 3.1 GRAPHICAL SOLUTION OF RMC PROBLEM WITH SLOPE OF OBJECTIVE FUNCTION BETWEEN SLOPES OF LINE *A* AND LINE *B*. EXTREME POINT ③ IS OPTIMAL

By solving this equation for *S*, we can write the equation for line *A* in its slope-intercept form:

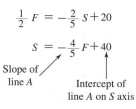

$$\tfrac{1}{2} F = -\tfrac{2}{5} S + 20$$

$$S = -\tfrac{4}{5} F + 40$$

Slope of line *A*

Intercept of line *A* on *S* axis

Thus, the slope for line *A* is $-\tfrac{4}{5}$ and its intercept on the *S* axis is 40.

Figure 3.1 also shows that the equation for line B, the material 3 constraint line, is

$$\frac{3}{5}F + \frac{3}{10}S = 21$$

Solving for S provides the slope-intercept form for line B:

$$\frac{3}{10}S = -\frac{3}{5}F + 21$$

$$S = -2F + 70$$

Thus, the slope for line B is -2 and its intercept on the S axis is 70.

Now that we have computed the slopes of lines A and B, for extreme point ③ to be optimal, we must have

$$-2 \leq \text{slope of the objective function line} \leq -\frac{4}{5} \tag{3.1}$$

We now consider the general form of the slope of the objective function line. Let C_F denote the profit contribution per ton of fuel additive, C_S the profit contribution per ton of solvent base, and P the value of the objective function. Using this notation, we can write the objective function as

$$P = C_F F + C_S S$$

Solving for S provides the slope-intercept form for the objective function line:

$$S = -\left(\frac{C_F}{C_S}\right)F + \frac{P}{C_S}$$

Thus, in general, the slope of the objective function line is $-C_F/C_S$. Substituting $-C_F/C_S$ into expression (3.1) shows that extreme point ③ will be optimal as long as

$$-2 \leq -\frac{C_F}{C_S} \leq -\frac{4}{5} \tag{3.2}$$

To compute the range of optimality for C_F, the fuel additive coefficient, we hold C_S, the coefficient for the solvent base, at its initial value, $C_S = 30$. Doing so, we obtain

$$-2 \leq -\frac{C_F}{30} \leq -\frac{4}{5}$$

From the left-hand inequality, we have

$$-2 \leq -\frac{C_F}{30}$$

Thus,

$$-60 \leq -C_F \qquad \text{or} \qquad C_F \leq 60$$

From the right-hand inequality, we have

$$-\frac{C_F}{30} \leq -\frac{4}{5}$$

Thus,

$$-C_F \leq -\frac{120}{5} = -24 \qquad \text{or} \qquad C_F \geq 24$$

You should now be able to compute the range of optimality using the graphical solution procedure. Try Problem 3.

Combining these limits for C_F provides the range of optimality for the fuel additive profit coefficient:

$$24 \leq C_F \leq 60$$

In the original RMC problem, the fuel additive had a profit contribution of $40 per ton. The resulting optimal solution was 25 tons of fuel additive and 20 tons of solvent base. The range of optimality for C_F tells RMC's management that, with other coefficients unchanged, the profit contribution for the fuel additive can be anywhere between $24 per ton and $60 per ton, and the production quantities of 25 tons of fuel additive and 20 tons of solvent base will remain optimal. Note here that, although the production quantities will not change, the total profit contribution will vary because of the change in the profit contribution per ton of fuel additive.

We can repeat the preceding computations holding the profit contribution per ton of fuel additive constant at $C_F = 40$. The range of optimality for C_S can then be determined. Verify that this range is $20 \leq C_S \leq 50$.

Right-Hand Sides

Let us now consider how a change in the right-hand-side value for a constraint may affect the feasible region and perhaps cause a change in the optimal solution to the problem. To illustrate this aspect of sensitivity analysis, we look at what happens if an additional 3 tons of material 3 become available. In this case, the right-hand side of the third constraint is changed from a 21 to 24, and the constraint is

$$\frac{3}{5}F + \frac{3}{10}S \leq 24$$

By obtaining an additional 3 tons of material 3, we have expanded the feasible region for the RMC problem; the new feasible region is shown in Figure 3.2. Since the feasible region has been enlarged, we now want to determine whether one of the new feasible solutions provides an improvement in the value of the objective function. Application of the graphical solution procedure to the problem with the enlarged feasible region shows that the extreme point with $F = {}^{100}\!/_3$ and $S = {}^{40}\!/_3$ now provides the optimal solution. The new value for the objective function is $40({}^{100}\!/_3) + 30({}^{40}\!/_3) = 1733.33$, providing an increase in

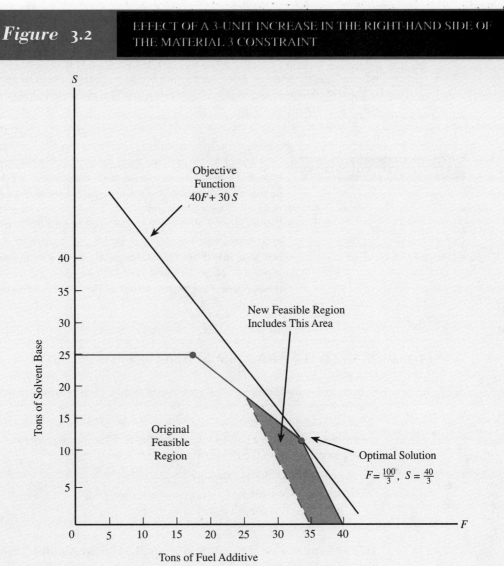

Figure 3.2   EFFECT OF A 3-UNIT INCREASE IN THE RIGHT-HAND SIDE OF THE MATERIAL 3 CONSTRAINT

profit of $1733.33 - $1600 = $133.33. Thus, the increased profit occurs at a rate of $133.33/3 = $44.44 per ton of material 3 added.

Can you compute and interpret the shadow price for a constraint? Try Problem 4.

The *change* in the value of the optimal solution per unit increase in the right-hand side of the constraint is called the **shadow price.** Here, the shadow price for the material 3 constraint is $44.44 per ton; in other words, if we increase the right-hand side of the material 3 constraint by 1 ton, the value of the objective function will increase by $44.44. Conversely, if we decrease the right-hand side of the material 3 constraint by 1 ton, the objective function will decrease by $44.44. Generally, the shadow price may be used to determine what will happen to the value of the objective function for a 1 unit change in the right-hand side of a constraint.

The value of the shadow price may only be applicable for small changes in the right-hand side. As more and more resources are obtained and the right-hand-side value continues to increase, other constraints will become binding and limit the change in the value of the objective function. For example, in the RMC problem we would eventually reach a point where more material 3 would be of no value. This result would occur when the material 3 constraint becomes nonbinding. Clearly, at that point the shadow price would equal zero. In the next section we show how to determine the range of values for a right-hand side over which the shadow price will accurately predict the change in the objective function. Finally, we note that the shadow price for any nonbinding constraint will be zero because a change in the right-hand side of such a constraint will affect only the value of the slack or surplus variable for that constraint.

1. If two objective function coefficients change simultaneously, both may move outside their respective ranges of optimality and not affect the optimal solution. For instance, in a two-variable linear program, the slope of the objective function will not change if both coefficients are changed by the same percentage.

2. Some texts associate the term *dual price* with each constraint. The concept of a dual price is closely related to the concept of a shadow price. The dual price associated with a constraint is the improvement in the value of the optimal solution per unit increase in the right-hand side of the constraint. In general, the dual price and the shadow price are the *same* for all *maximization* linear programs. In *minimization* linear programs, the dual price is the *negative* of the corresponding shadow price.

3.3   SENSITIVITY ANALYSIS: SPREADSHEET SOLUTION

In Section 2.4 we showed how Excel Solver can be used to solve the spreadsheet model of a linear program. Let us now see how it can be used to provide sensitivity analysis.

Recall that in order to use Excel Solver to identify an optimal solution for a linear programming problem, we had to select **Solver** from the **Tools** menu and then enter the following information in the **Solver Parameters** dialog box:

1. cell location for the objective function
2. type of problem: maximization or minimization
3. cell locations for the decision variables
4 all constraint relationships

After entering this information, specifying the options **Assume Linear Model** and **Assume Non-Negative,** and choosing **Solve,** Excel displays the **Solver Results** dialog box as shown in Figure 3.3. Previously, after solving the RMC problem in Section 2.4, we selected **Keep Solver Solution** to obtain the solution shown in Figure 3.4. To also obtain sensitivity analysis information, we must select **Sensitivity** in the **Reports** box as shown in Figure 3.3. Figure 3.5 shows the Excel Sensitivity Report provided after selecting **OK.**

Interpretation of Excel Sensitivity Report

In the Adjustable Cells section of the Sensitivity Report, the column labelled Final Value contains the optimal values of the decision variables. For the RMC problem the optimal solution is 25 tons of fuel additive and 20 tons of solvent base. Next, let us consider the values in the Reduced Cost column. For each decision variable, the absolute value of the **reduced cost** indicates how much the objective function coefficient of each decision variable would have to improve[1] before that variable could assume a positive value in the

---

1. For a maximization problem, *improve* means get bigger; for a minimization problem, *improve* means get smaller.

Figure 3.3 — EXCEL SOLVER RESULTS DIALOG BOX

Solver Results

Solver found a solution. All constraints and optimality conditions are satisfied.

Reports:
- Answer
- Sensitivity
- Limits

○ Keep Solver Solution
○ Restore Original Values

[OK] [Cancel] [Save Scenario...] [Help]

Figure 3.4 — SPREADSHEET SOLUTION FOR THE RMC PROBLEM

SPREADSHEET RMC CHAPTER 3

	A	B	C	D	E
1	**RMC Chapter 3**				
2					
3		**Material Requirements**			
4	**Material**	**Fuel Additive**	**Solvent Base**	**Amount Available**	
5	Material 1	0.4	0.5	20	
6	Material 2	0	0.2	5	
7	Material 3	0.6	0.3	21	
8	**Profit Per Ton**	40	30		
9					
10					
11	**Model**				
12					
13		**Decision Variables**			
14		**Fuel Additive**	**Solvent Base**		
15	**Tons Produced**	25	20		
16					
17	**Maximize Total Profit**	1600			
18					
19	**Constraints**	**Amount Used (LHS)**		**Amount Available (RHS)**	
20	Material 1	20	<=	20	
21	Material 2	4	<=	5	
22	Material 3	21	<=	21	

Figure 3.5 — SENSITIVITY REPORT FOR THE RMC PROBLEM

SPREADSHEET RMC CHAPTER 3

Adjustable Cells

Cell	Name	Final Value	Reduced Cost	Objective Coefficient	Allowable Increase	Allowable Decrease
$B$15	Tons Produced Fuel Additive	25	0	40	20	16
$C$15	Tons Produced Solvent Base	20	0	30	20	10

Constraints

Cell	Name	Final Value	Shadow Price	Constraint R.H. Side	Allowable Increase	Allowable Decrease
$B$20	Material 1 Amount Used (LHS)	20	33.33333333	20	1.5	6
$B$21	Material 2 Amount Used (LHS)	4	0	5	1E+30	1
$B$22	Material 3 Amount Used (LHS)	21	44.44444444	21	9	2.25

optimal solution. Some computer packages for solving linear programs use different sign conventions for the reduced cost values; but in every case, the absolute value of the reduced cost is the amount by which the coefficient would have to improve before the corresponding variable could become positive in the optimal solution. If a decision variable is already positive in the optimal solution, its reduced cost is zero. For the RMC problem, both decision variables already have positive values; thus, their reduced costs are zero. In Section 3.4 we interpret the reduced cost for a decision variable that does not have a positive value in the optimal solution.

To the right of the Reduced Cost column in Figure 3.5, we find three columns labeled Objective Coefficient, Allowable Increase, and Allowable Decrease. Note that for the fuel additive decision variable, the objective coefficient value is 40, the allowable increase value is 20, and the allowable decrease value is 16. Adding 20 to and subtracting 16 from the current coefficient of 40 provides the range of optimality for C_F:

$$24 \leq C_F \leq 60$$

This range tells us that as long as the profit contribution associated with the fuel additive is between \$24 and \$60, the production of 25 tons of fuel additive and 20 tons of solvent base will remain the optimal solution. Note that this is the same range of optimality that we obtained by performing graphical sensitivity analysis for C_F in Section 3.2. Similarly, the range of optimality for C_S is

$$20 \leq C_S \leq 50$$

This range tells us that as long as the profit contribution associated with the solvent base is between \$20 and \$50, the production of 25 tons of fuel additive and 20 tons of solvent base will remain the optimal solution.

Next, consider the information in the Constraints section of the report. The entries in the Final Value column are the number of tons of each material required to produce the optimal production combination of 25 tons of fuel additive and 20 tons of solvent base. Thus, at the optimal solution, 20 tons of material 1, 4 tons of material 2, and 21 tons of material 3 are required. The values in Constraint R.H. Side column are just the original right-hand-side values: 20 tons of material 1, 5 tons of material 2, and 21 tons of material 3.

For the RMC problem, the values of the slack variables for each constraint are simply the difference between the entries in the Final Value column and the corresponding entries in the Constraint R.H. Side column. The slack associated with the material 1 constraint is $20 - 20 = 0$ tons, the slack associated with the material 2 constraint is $5 - 4 = 1$ ton, and the slack associated with the material 3 constraint is $21 - 21 = 0$ tons. Since the material 1 and material 3 constraints have 0 slack, these constraints are binding constraints. The material 2 constraint has a slack or unused capacity of 1 ton; it is a nonbinding constraint. Thus, in terms of material availability, higher levels of profit might be achieved if additional amounts of material 1 and/or material 3 were available. To determine what additional amounts of these two materials would be worth, we need to look at the values in the Shadow Price column.

The nonzero shadow price of 33.33 for the material 1 constraint indicates that an additional ton of material 1 will increase profits by \$33.33. Thus, if the number of tons of material 1 is increased from 20 to 21, with all other coefficients in the problem remaining the same, RMC's profit would be increased by \$33.33 from \$1600 to \$1600 + \$33.33 = \$1633.33. Similarly, the nonzero shadow price of 44.44 for the material 3 constraint indicates that an additional ton of material 3 will increase profits by \$44.44. In other words, an increase from 21 to 22 tons of material 3, with all other coefficients in the problem remaining the same, would increase RMC's profit to

$1600 + $44.44 = $1644.44. Since the material 2 constraint has slack or unused capacity available, the shadow price of zero shows that additional units of this resource will not increase the value of the objective function.

The final three columns of the Sensitivity Report contain ranging information for the constraint right-hand sides. For example, consider the material 1 constraint with a constraint R.H. side value of 20, and allowable increase value of 1.5, and an allowable decrease value of 6. We know that with a shadow price of $33.33, additional tons of material 1 will increase the objective function by $33.33 per ton, and a reduction in the tons available will reduce the value of the objective function by $33.33. per ton. The values in the Allowable Increase and Allowable Decrease columns indicate that the shadow price of $33.33 is valid for increases of up to 1.5 tons and decreases of up to 6 tons. Thus, the shadow price of $33.33 is applicable for increases up to $20 + 1.5 = 21.5$ tons and decreases down to $20 - 6 = 14$ tons. We call the range over which the shadow price is applicable the **range of feasibility.** Thus, the range up feasibility for the material 1 constraint is 14 to 21.5 tons. For changes outside the range, the problem must be resolved to find the new shadow price.

Since the shadow price tells us how much the objective function will increase if one additional ton of raw material is available, it also tells us how much the objective function will decrease if one ton less is available. For example, suppose that instead of having 20 tons of material 1 available for production, we had only 19 tons available. Since the range of feasibility for the material 1 constraint is 14 to 21.5 tons, a right-hand-side value of 19 tons means that the shadow price of $33.33 is still applicable. In other words, a decrease from 20 tons to 19 tons of material 3, with all other coefficients in the problem remaining the same, would decrease RMC's profit to $1600 - $33.33 = $1566.67.

For the material 2 constraint, the allowable increase is 1E+30. This type of number format referred to as *scientific notation,* is frequently used to represent very large or very small numbers in the sensitivity report. The allowable increase value of 1E+30 for the material 1 constraint represents a number of consisting of a 1 followed by thirty zeros! Because this is such a large number, we can interpret the value as evidence that no upper limit exists on the range of feasibility for the material 2 constraint. In other words, the conclusion that additional amounts of material 2 will not increase the value of the objective function will hold true, no matter how much material 2 is available. The allowable decrease value of 1, indicates that the lower limit for the range of feasibility is $5 - 1 = 4$ tons. Thus, if only 4.5 tons of material 2 were available for production, the value of the objective function would not decrease. However, if less than 4 tons of material 2 were available, we would have to resolve the problem to determine a new optimal solution and shadow price.

For the material 3 constraint, the allowable increase value is 9 and the allowable decrease value is 2.25. Thus, the upper limit on the range of feasibility for the material 3 constraint is $21 + 9 = 30$ tons and the lower limit is $21 - 2.25 = 18.75$ tons. This means that the shadow price of 44.44 is applicable as long as the right-hand side of the constraint takes on values between 18.75 tons and 30 tons.

In summary, the right-hand-side ranges provide limits within which the shadow prices are applicable. For changes outside the range, the problem must be resolved to find the new optimal solution and the new shadow price. The ranges of feasibility for the RMC problem are

Constraint	Min RHS	Max RHS
Material 1	14	21.5
Material 2	4	No upper limit
Material 3	18.75	30

The sensitivity analysis information in computer output is based on the assumption that only one coefficient changes and that all other coefficients will remain as originally stated. Thus, the ranges for the objective function coefficients and the constraint right-hand sides are applicable only for changes in a single coefficient.

Interpretation of Computer Output—A Second Example

Recall the Innis Investments minimization problem introduced in Section 2.5. For a new client Innis has been authorized to invest up to $1.2 million in two investment funds: a stock fund and a money market fund. The objective is to minimize the total risk index for the portfolio. The linear programming model for this problem is restated below, where S = units purchased in the stock fund and M = units purchased in the money market fund.

$$
\begin{aligned}
\text{Min} \quad & 8S + 3M \\
\text{s.t.} \quad & \\
50S + 100M & \leq 1{,}200{,}000 \quad \text{Funds available} \\
5S + 4M & \geq 60{,}000 \quad \text{Annual income} \\
M & \geq 3{,}000 \quad \text{Minimum units in money market} \\
S, M & \geq 0
\end{aligned}
$$

In Section 2.5 we developed a spreadsheet solution for the Innis Investments problem. A copy of the Innis Investment spreadsheet showing the optimal solution is shown in Figure 3.6; the sensitivity report is shown in Figure 3.7. The solution shows that 4,000 units of the stock fund and 10,000 units of the money market fund provides the minimum total risk index portfolio. Let us now discuss the information provided in the sensitivity report.

SPREADSHEET
INNIS
CHAPTER 3

Figure 3.6 — SPREADSHEET SOLUTION FOR THE INNIS INVESTMENTS PROBLEM

	A	B	C	D
1	**Innis Investments**			
2				
3		**Stock Fund**	**Money Market Fund**	
4	**Cost Per Unit**	$50	$100	
5	**Annual Rate of Return**	10%	4%	
6	**Earnings Per Unit**	$5	$4	
7	**Risk Index Per Unit**	8	3	
8				
9	**Funds Available**	$1,200,000		
10	**Minimum Annual Income**	$60,000		
11	**Minimum $ in Money Market Fund**	$300,000		
12				
13				
14	**Model**			
15				
16			**Decision Variables**	
17		**Stock Fund**	**Money Market Fund**	
18	**Units Purchased**	4,000	10,000	
19				
20	**Minimize Total Risk**	62,000		
21				
22	**Constraints**	**LHS**		**RHS**
23	Funds Available	$1,200,000	<=	$1,200,000
24	Minimum Annual Income	$60,000	>=	$60,000
25	Minimum Units in Money Market	10,000	>=	3,000

Figure 3.7   SENSITIVITY REPORT FOR THE INNIS INVESTMENTS PROBLEM

Adjustable Cells

Cell	Name	Final Value	Reduced Cost	Objective Coefficient	Allowable Increase	Allowable Decrease
$B$18	Units Purchased Stock Fund	4,000	0	8	1E+30	4.25
$C$18	Units Purchased Money Market Fund	10,000	0	3	3.4	1E+30

Constraints

Cell	Name	Final Value	Shadow Price	Constraint R.H. Side	Allowable Increase	Allowable Decrease
$B$23	Funds Available LHS	$1,200,000	-0.057	1200000	300000	420000
$B$24	Minum Annual Income LHS	$60,000	2.167	60000	42000	12000
$B$25	Minimum Units in Money Market LHS	10,000	0.000	3000	7000	1E+30

SPREADSHEET
INNIS
CHAPTER 3

We begin with the Adjustable Cells section. In the Final Value column, we find the optimal values for the two decision variables. Since both decision variables have positive values, both values in the Reduced Cost column are zero. To develop the range of optimality for the objective function coefficients of the decision variables, we add the allowable increase and subtract the allowable decrease from the objective coefficient value. Since the allowable increase for the stock fund objective function coefficient is 1E+30, a number equal to 1 followed by thirty zeros, we can conclude that no upper limit exists on the range of optimality. With an allowable decrease of 4.25, the lower limit on the range of optimality is $8 - 4.25 = 3.75$. Thus, as long as the objective function coefficient for the stock fund decision variable is 3.75 or greater, the optimal solution, consisting of 4,000 units in the stock fund and 10,000 units in the money market fund, will not change.

For the money market decision variable, the allowable increase is 3.4. Thus, the upper limit on the range of optimality is $3 + 3.4 = 6.4$. Since the allowable decrease is 1E+30, we can conclude that no lower limit exists on the range of optimality. Thus, as long as the objective function coefficient for the money market fund decision variable does not exceed 6.4, the optimal solution will not change.

The Shadow Price column, in the Constraints section, shows the increase in the value of the optimal solution per-unit increase in the right-hand side of the constraints. Focusing first on the shadow price of -0.057 for the funds available constraint, we see that if we increase the funds available by $1, the objective function value will decrease by 0.057 risk-index units. Since the objective is to minimize the total risk index, if we increase the funds available by $1, the value of the optimal solution will improve to $62,000 - 0.057 = 61,999.943$. The funds available constraint shows an allowable increase of 300,000, which means that the upper limit on the range of feasibility is $1,200,000 + $300,000 = $1,500,000. Thus, the shadow price of -0.057 per unit would be applicable for every additional dollar up to a total of $1,500,000.

Let us now consider the shadow price for the annual income constraint. The shadow price of 2.167 tells us that if the right-hand side of the annual income constraint is increased from $60,000 to $60,001, the value of the optimal solution will increase by the amount of 2.167. Since the objective is to minimize the total risk index, increasing the right-hand side of this constraint will not help us. However, if we decrease the right-hand side by $1, the value of the optimal solution will decrease by 2.167. Thus, the value of the optimal solution will improve if we decrease the right-hand side of the constraint. Note that there is an allowable decrease of 12,000 for the annual income constraint. The lower limit for the range of feasibility is $60,000 - $12,000 = $48,000. Thus, the shadow price of 2.167 is applicable for decreases down to a value of $48,000.

Finally, we note that the shadow price for the money market constraint is 0. Recall that the money market constraint requires purchasing a minimum of 3000 units of the money market fund. Since the optimal solution calls for the purchase of 10,000 units, there is a surplus of 7000 units. Because there is a surplus, the constraint is not binding, and thus the shadow price must be 0.

Cautionary Note on the Interpretation of Shadow Prices

As stated previously, the shadow price is the change in the value of the optimal solution per-unit increase in the right-hand side of a constraint. When the right-hand side of the constraint represents the amount of a resource available, the associated shadow price often is interpreted as the maximum amount someone should be willing to pay for 1 additional unit of the resource. However, such an interpretation isn't always correct. To see why, we need to understand the difference between sunk and relevant costs. A **sunk cost** is one that is not affected by the decision made. It will be incurred regardless of the values the decision variables assume. A **relevant cost** is one that depends on the decision made. The amount of a relevant cost will vary, depending on the values of the decision variables.

Let us reconsider the RMC problem. The amount of material 1 available is 20 tons. The cost of material 1 is a sunk cost if it must be paid regardless of the number of tons of fuel additive and solvent base produced. It would be a relevant cost if RMC only had to pay for the number of tons of material 1 actually used to produce fuel additive and solvent base. All relevant costs should be reflected in the objective function of a linear program. Sunk costs should not be reflected in the objective function. For RMC, we have been assuming that the company has already paid for materials 1, 2, and 3. Therefore the cost of the raw materials for RMC is a sunk cost and has not been reflected in the objective function.

Only relevant costs should be included in the objective function.

When the cost of a resource is *sunk,* the shadow price can be interpreted as the maximum amount the company should be willing to pay for 1 additional unit of the resource. When the cost of a resource used is relevant, the shadow price can be interpreted as the amount by which the value of the resource exceeds its cost. Thus, when the resource cost is relevant, the shadow price can be interpreted as the maximum premium over the normal cost that the company should be willing to pay for 1 additional unit of the resource.

NOTES and Comments

1. Computer software packages for solving linear programs are readily available. Most provide the optimal solution, shadow price information, the range of optimality for the objective function coefficients, and the range of feasibility for the right-hand sides. The labels used for the ranges of optimality and feasibility may vary, but the meaning is the same as that used here.

2. Whenever one of the right-hand sides is at an end point of its range of feasibility, the shadow prices provide only one-sided information. In this case, they only predict the change in the optimal value of the objective function for changes toward the interior of the range.

3. A condition called *degeneracy* can cause a subtle difference in how we interpret changes in the objective function coefficients beyond the end points of the range of optimality. Degeneracy occurs when the shadow price equals zero for one of the binding constraints. Degeneracy does not affect the interpretation of changes toward the interior of the range of optimality. However, when degeneracy is present, changes beyond the end points of the range do not necessarily mean a different solution will be optimal. From a practical point of view, changes beyond the end points of the range of optimality necessitate resolving the problem.

4. Managers are frequently called on to provide an economic justification for new technology. Often the new technology is developed, or purchased, to conserve resources. The shadow price can be helpful in such cases because it can be used to determine the savings attributable to the new technology by showing the savings per unit of resource conserved.

3.4   LINEAR PROGRAMS WITH MORE THAN TWO DECISION VARIABLES

In this section we discuss the formulation and solution of two slightly larger linear programs. In doing so, we further interpret sensitivity analysis and show how to use constraints involving ratios, or percentages.

The Modified RMC Problem

The original RMC mathematical model with decimal coefficients follows:

$$\text{Max} \quad 40F + 30S$$

s.t.

$$
\begin{aligned}
0.4F + 0.5S &\leq 20 \quad \text{Material 1}\\
0.2S &\leq 5 \quad \text{Material 2}\\
0.6F + 0.3S &\leq 21 \quad \text{Material 3}\\
F, S &\geq 0
\end{aligned}
$$

Recall that F is the number of tons of fuel additive produced and that S is the number of tons of solvent base produced. Suppose that management is now considering producing a carpet cleaning fluid. Estimates are that each ton of carpet cleaning fluid will require 0.6 tons of material 1, 0.1 tons of material 2, and 0.3 tons of material 3. Because of the unique capabilities of the new product, RMC's management believes that the company will realize a profit contribution of $50 for each ton of carpet cleaning fluid produced during the current production period.

Let us consider the modifications in the original linear programming model that are needed to incorporate the effect of this additional decision variable. We let C denote the number of tons of carpet cleaning fluid produced. After adding additional terms involving C to the objective function and to each of the three constraints, we obtain a model for the modified problem:

$$\text{Max} \quad 40F + 30S + 50C$$

s.t.

$$
\begin{aligned}
0.4F + 0.5S + 0.6C &\leq 20\\
0.2S + 0.1C &\leq 5\\
0.6F + 0.3S + 0.3C &\leq 21\\
F, S, C &\geq 0
\end{aligned}
$$

The spreadsheet formulation and solution of the modified RMC problem is shown in Figure 3.8. The data and descriptive labels are in cells A1:E8. The screened cells in the model section contain the information required by Excel Solver.

Decision Variables   Cells B15:D15 are reserved for the decision variables. The optimal values are shown to be $F = 27.5$, $S = 0$, and $C = 15$.

Objective Function   The formula $=B8*B15+C8*C15+D8*D15$ has been placed into cell B17 to reflect the total profit obtained with the solution shown. The optimal solution provides a total profit of $1,850.

Left-Hand Sides   The left-hand sides for the three constraints are placed into cells B20:B22.

Cell B20   =B5*B15+C5*C15+D5*D15
Cell B21   =B6*B15+C6*C15+D6*D15
Cell B22   =B7*B15+C7*C15+D7*D15

Right-Hand Sides   The right-hand sides for the three constraints are placed into cells D 20:D22.

Cell D20   =E5   (Copy to cells D21:D22)

The solution was obtained by selecting **Solver** from the **Tools** menu, entering the proper values into the **Solver Parameters** dialog box, and specifying the options **Assume Linear Model** and **Assume Non-Negative.** The information entered in the **Solver Parameters** dialog box is shown in Figure 3.9. After solving, we requested the sensitivity report shown in Figure 3.10.

The optimal solution calls for the production of 27.5 tons of fuel additive, 0 tons of solvent base, and 15 tons of carpet cleaning fluid. The value of the optimal solution is $1,850. Let us now consider the information contained in the Reduced Cost column of the sensitivity report. Recall that the absolute value of a reduced cost indicates how much an objective function coefficient would have to improve before the corresponding decision variable *could* assume a positive value in the optimal solution. First, note that the reduced costs for the fuel additive and carpet cleaning decision variables are zero because these variables already have positive values in the optimal solution. Since the value in the Reduced Cost col-

Figure 3.8   SPREADSHEET SOLUTION FOR THE MODIFIED RMC PROBLEM

SPREADSHEET MODIFIED RMC

	A	B	C	D	E
1	**Modified RMC**				
2					
3			**Material Requirements**		
4	**Material**	**Fuel Additive**	**Solvent Base**	**Cleaning Fluid**	**Amount Available**
5	Material 1	0.4	0.5	0.6	20
6	Material 2	0	0.2	0.1	5
7	Material 3	0.6	0.3	0.3	21
8	**Profit Per Ton**	40	30	50	
9					
10					
11	**Model**				
12					
13			**Decision Variables**		
14		**Fuel Additive**	**Solvent Base**	**Cleaning Fluid**	
15	**Tons Produced**	27.5	0	15	
16					
17	**Maximize Total Profit**	1850			
18					
19	**Constraints**	**Amount Used (LHS)**		**Amount Available (RHS)**	
20	Material 1	20	<=	20	
21	Material 2	1.5	<=	5	
22	Material 3	21	<=	21	

Figure 3.9	SOLVER PARAMETERS DIALOG BOX FOR THE MODIFIED RMC PROBLEM

umn for the solvent base is −12.50, the absolute value of the reduced cost for the solvent base objective function coefficient is 12.50. This cost tells us that the profit contribution of the solvent base would have to increase to at least $30 + $12.50 = $42.50 before the solvent base decision variable *could* [2] assume a positive value in the optimal solution. In other words, unless the profit contribution for solvent base increases by at least $12.50, the optimal solution will not call for the production of any solvent base. You can verify this result by increasing the profit coefficient of the solvent base by $12.501 and then resolving the problem using Excel Solver; the new optimal solution calls for the production of 25 tons of fuel additive and 20 tons of solvent base.

Figure 3.10 also shows that the shadow prices for the material 1 and material 3 constraints are 75.000 and 16.667, respectively, indicating that these two constraints are binding in the optimal solution. Thus, each additional ton of material 1 would increase the value of the optimal solution by $75 and each additional ton of material 3 would increase the value of the optimal solution by $16.667.

Suppose that after reviewing the optimal solution shown in Figure 3.8, management states that it will not consider any solution that doesn't include the production of some solvent base. Management then decides to add the requirement that the number of tons of solvent base produced must be at least 25% of the number of tons of fuel additive produced. Writing this requirement using the decision variables, F and S, we obtain

$$S \geq 0.25F$$

Adding this new constraint to the modified RMC spreadsheet formulation and resolving the problem using Excel Solver, we obtain the optimal solution shown in Figure 3.11; the

---

2. In the case of degeneracy, a variable may not assume a positive value in the optimal solution even when the improvement in the profit contributions exceeds the value of the reduced cost. Our definition of reduced costs, stated as " . . . *could* assume a positive value . . . ," provides for such special cases. More advanced texts on mathematical programming discuss these special types of situations.

Figure 3.10   SENSITIVITY REPORT FOR THE MODIFIED RMC PROBLEM

Adjustable Cells

Cell	Name	Final Value	Reduced Cost	Objective Coefficient	Allowable Increase	Allowable Decrease
$B$15	Tons Produced Fuel Additive	27.5	0	40	60	6.666666667
$C$15	Tons Produced Solvent Base	0	-12.5	30	12.5	1E+30
$D$15	Tons Produced Cleaning Fluid	15	0	50	10	16.66666667

Constraints

Cell	Name	Final Value	Shadow Price	Constraint R.H. Side	Allowable Increase	Allowable Decrease
$B$20	Material 1 Amount Used (LHS)	20	75	20	14	6
$B$21	Material 2 Amount Used (LHS)	1.5	0	5	1E+30	3.5
$B$22	Material 3 Amount Used (LHS)	21	16.66666667	21	9	11

SPREADSHEET MODIFIED RMC

corresponding sensitivity report is shown in Figure 3.12. Before interpreting this output, let us briefly consider the changes to the modified RMC spreadsheet formulation shown in Figure 3.8 that are needed to account for this new constraint.

Figure 3.11   SPREADSHEET SOLUTION FOR THE MODIFIED RMC PROBLEM WITH 25% SOLVENT BASE REQUIREMENT

SPREADSHEET MODIFIED RMC VERSION 2

	A	B	C	D	E
1	**Modified RMC with 25% Solvent Base Requirement**				
2					
3		**Material Requirements**			
4	**Material**	**Fuel Additive**	**Solvent Base**	**Cleaning Fluid**	**Amount Available**
5	Material 1	0.4	0.5	0.6	20
6	Material 2	0	0.2	0.1	5
7	Material 3	0.6	0.3	0.3	21
8	**Profit Per Ton**	40	30	50	
9					
10	**Min Solvent Base**	25%			
11					
12	**Model**				
13					
14		**Decision Variables**			
15		**Fuel Additive**	**Solvent Base**	**Cleaning Fluid**	
16	**Tons Produced**	26.66666667	6.666666667	10	
17					
18	**Maximize Total Profit**	1767			
19					
20	**Constraints**	**Amount Used (LHS)**		**Amount Available (RHS)**	
21	Material 1	20	<=	20	
22	Material 2	2.333333333	<=	5	
23	Material 3	21	<=	21	
24	Min Solvent Base	6.666666667	>=	6.666666667	

Refer to Figure 3.11. Note that cell B10 contains the minimum percentage of 25%. With the addition of this new data value, we see that each cell in the model section has been shifted down one row; however, this has no effect on the formulas we previously created because Excel automatically adjusts each formula to account for the addition of the new row. Thus, all we have to do to add the new constraint is to enter the left-hand side and right-hand side formulas for the new constraint. The left-hand side of the new constraint is S; therefore, we entered the formula =C16 into cell B24. To account for the right-hand side of the constraint, $0.25F$, we entered the formula =B10*B16 into cell D24. Resolving the problem using Excel Solver we obtained the optimal solution consisting of 26.67 tons of fuel additive, 6.67 tons of solvent base, and 10 tons of cleaning fluid, with a corresponding total profit of $1,767. Let us now continue by discussing the sensitivity report shown in Figure 3.12.

The shadow price for constraint 4, the requirement that the number of tons of solvent base produced must be at least 25% of the number of tons of fuel additive produced, is -12.121. Thus, a 1-unit increase in the right-hand side of the constraint will lower profits by $12.121. In other words, the shadow price of -12.121 is telling us what will happen to the value of the optimal solution if the constraint is changed to

$$S \geq 0.25F + 1$$

The correct interpretation of the shadow price of -12.121 can now be stated as follows: If we are forced to produce 1 ton of solvent base over and above the minimum 25% requirement, total profits will decrease by $12.121. Conversely, if we relax the minimum 25% requirement by 1 ton ($S \geq 0.25F - 1$), total profits will increase by $12.121.

The shadow price for a percentage (or ratio) constraint, such as this, will not directly provide answers to questions concerning a percentage increase or decrease in the right-hand side of the constraint. For example, what would happen to the value of the optimal solution if the number of tons of solvent base produced has to be at least 26% of the number of standard bags? To answer such a question, we would have to resolve the problem using the constraint $S \geq 0.26F$.

Because percentage (or ratio) constraints frequently occur in linear programming models, we need to consider another example. For instance, suppose that RMC's management

---

Figure 3.12   SENSITIVITY REPORT FOR THE MODIFIED RMC PROBLEM WITH 25% SOLVENT BASE REQUIREMENT

Adjustable Cells

Cell	Name	Final Value	Reduced Cost	Objective Coefficient	Allowable Increase	Allowable Decrease
$B$16	Tons Produced Fuel Additive	26.66666667	0	40	65	3.75
$C$16	Tons Produced Solvent Base	6.666666667	0	30	12.5	15
$D$16	Tons Produced Cleaning Fluid	10	0	50	4.285714286	16.66666667

Constraints

Cell	Name	Final Value	Shadow Price	Constraint R.H. Side	Allowable Increase	Allowable Decrease
$B$21	Material 1 Amount Used (LHS)	20	78.78787879	20	12.57142857	3.666666667
$B$22	Material 2 Amount Used (LHS)	2.333333333	0	5	1E+30	2.666666667
$B$23	Material 3 Amount Used (LHS)	21	9.090909091	21	4.714285714	11
$B$24	Min Solvent Base Amount Used (LHS)	6.666666667	-12.12121212	0	13.75	6.875

SPREADSHEET
MODIFIED RMC
VERSION 2

states that the number of tons of carpet cleaning fluid produced may not exceed 20% of total production. Since total production is $F + S + C$, we can write this constraint as

$$C \leq 0.2(F + S + C)$$

The solution obtained using Excel Solver for the model that incorporates both the effects of this new percentage requirement and the previous requirement ($S \geq 0.25F$) is shown in Figure 3.13; the corresponding sensitivity report is shown in Figure 3.14.

Refer to Figure 3.13. The value in cell B11, 20%, is the upper limit on the percentage of carpet cleaning fluid that can be produced. Total production ($F + S + C$) can be expressed in Excel using the SUM function; that is, total production is SUM(B17:D17). Since the right-hand-side value for the new percentage requirement is $0.2(F + S + C)$, we entered the formula = B11*SUM(B17:D17) into cell D26. Note that the new optimal solution calls for the production of 26.452 tons of fuel additive, 8.387 tons of solvent base, and 8.710 tons of solvent base, and the value of the optimal solution is $1,745.

**SPREADSHEET
MODIFIED RMC
VERSION 3**

	Figure 3.13	SPREADSHEET SOLUTION FOR THE MODIFIED RMC PROBLEM WITH 25% SOLVENT BASE AND 20% CLEANING FLUID REQUIREMENTS

	A	B	C	D	E
1	**Modified RMC with 25% Solvent Base and 20% Cleaning Fluid Requirements**				
2					
3			**Material Requirements**		
4	**Material**	**Fuel Additive**	**Solvent Base**	**Cleaning Fluid**	**Amount Available**
5	Material 1	0.4	0.5	0.6	20
6	Material 2	0	0.2	0.1	5
7	Material 3	0.6	0.3	0.3	21
8	**Profit Per Ton**	40	30	50	
9					
10	**Min Solvent Base**	25%			
11	**Max Cleaning Fluid**	20%			
12					
13	**Model**				
14					
15			**Decision Variables**		
16		**Fuel Additive**	**Solvent Base**	**Cleaning Fluid**	
17	**Tons Produced**	26.4516129	8.387096774	8.709677419	
18					
19	**Maximize Total Profit**	1745			
20					
21	**Constraints**	**Amount Used (LHS)**		**Amount Available (RHS)**	
22	Material 1	20	<=	20	
23	Material 2	2.548387097	<=	5	
24	Material 3	21	<=	21	
25	Min Solvent Base	8.387096774	>=	6.612903226	
26	Max Cleaning Fluid	8.709677419	<=	8.709677419	

**SPREADSHEET
MODIFIED RMC
VERSION 3**

	SENSITIVITY REPORT FOR THE MODIFIED RMC PROBLEM WITH 25% SOLVENT BASE AND 20% CLEANING FLUID REQUIREMENTS
Figure 3.14	

Adjustable Cells

Cell	Name	Final Value	Reduced Cost	Objective Coefficient	Allowable Increase	Allowable Decrease
$B$17	Tons Produced Fuel Additive	26.4516129	0	40	24	16.53846154
$C$17	Tons Produced Solvent Base	8.387096774	0	30	12.5	13.33333333
$D$17	Tons Produced Cleaning Fluid	8.709677419	0	50	1E+30	16.66666667

Constraints

Cell	Name	Final Value	Shadow Price	Constraint R.H. Side	Allowable Increase	Allowable Decrease
$B$22	Material 1 Amount Used (LHS)	20	38.70967742	20	4	0.536585366
$B$23	Material 2 Amount Used (LHS)	2.548387097	0	5	1E+30	2.451612903
$B$24	Material 3 Amount Used (LHS)	21	46.23655914	21	0.578947368	5.302325581
$B$25	Min Solvent Base Amount Used (LHS)	8.387096774	0	0	1.774193548	1E+30
$B$26	Max Cleaning Fluid Amount Used (LHS)	8.709677419	16.12903226	0	1.333333333	9

Refer to Figure 3.14. After rounding, the shadow price for the new maximum cleaning fluid constraint is 16.13. Thus, every additional ton of carpet cleaning fluid that we produce over the current 20% limit will increase the value of the objective function by $16.13; moreover, the right-hand-side range for this constraint shows that this interpretation is valid for increases of up to 1.333 tons.

The Bluegrass Farms Problem

To provide additional practice in formulating and interpreting the computer solution for linear programs involving more than two decision variables, we consider a minimization problem involving three decision variables. Bluegrass Farms, located in Lexington, Kentucky, has been experimenting with a special diet for its racehorses. The feed components available for the diet are a standard horse feed product, a vitamin-enriched oat product, and a new vitamin and mineral feed additive. The nutritional values in units per pound and the costs for the three feed components are summarized in Table 3.1; for example, each pound of the standard feed component contains 0.8 unit of ingredient A, 1 unit of ingredient B, and 0.1 unit of ingredient C. The minimum daily diet requirements for each horse are three units of ingredient A, six units of ingredient B, and four units of ingredient C. In addition, to control the weight of the horses, the total daily feed for a horse should not exceed 6 pounds. Bluegrass Farms wants to determine the minimum-cost mix that will satisfy the daily diet requirements.

To formulate a linear programming model for the Bluegrass Farms problem, we introduce three decision variables:

S = number of pounds of the standard horse feed product

E = number of pounds of the enriched oat product

A = number of pounds of the vitamin and mineral feed additive

Using the data in Table 3.1, we write the objective function for minimizing the total cost associated with the daily feed as follows:

	Feed Component		
	Standard	**Enriched Oat**	**Additive**
Ingredient A	0.8	0.2	0.0
Ingredient B	1.0	1.5	3.0
Ingredient C	0.1	0.6	2.0
Cost per pound	$0.25	$0.50	$3.00

Table 3.1 — NUTRITIONAL VALUE AND COST DATA FOR THE BLUEGRASS FARMS PROBLEM

$$\text{Min} \quad 0.25S + 0.50E + 3A$$

For the minimum daily requirement for ingredient A of 3 units, we obtain the constraint

$$0.8S + 0.2E \geq 3$$

The constraint for ingredient B is

$$1.0S + 1.5E + 3.0A \geq 6$$

and the constraint for ingredient C is

$$0.1S + 0.6E + 2.0A \geq 4$$

Finally, the constraint that restricts the mix to no more than 6 pounds is

$$S + E + A \leq 6$$

Combining all constraints with the nonnegativity requirements enables us to write the complete linear programming model for the Bluegrass Farms problem as follows:

$$\text{Min} \quad 0.25S + 0.50E + 3A$$
$$\text{s.t.}$$
$$
\begin{array}{llll}
0.8S + 0.2E & & \geq 3 & \text{Ingredient A} \\
1.0S + 1.5E & + 3.0A & \geq 6 & \text{Ingredient B} \\
0.1S + 0.6E & + 2.0A & \geq 4 & \text{Ingredient C} \\
S + \quad E + & A & \leq 6 & \text{Weight} \\
S, E, A & \geq 0
\end{array}
$$

The spreadsheet formulation and solution of the Bluegrass Farms problem is shown in Figure 3.15. The data and descriptive labels are in cells A1:E10. The screened cells in the model section contain the information required by Excel Solver.

Decision Variables   Cells B17:D17 are reserved for the decision variables. The optimal values (after rounding) are shown to be $S = 3.52$, $E = 0.95$, and $A = 1.54$.

**SPREADSHEET
BLUEGRASS
FARMS**

Figure 3.15   SPREADSHEET SOLUTION FOR THE BLUEGRASS FARMS PROBLEM

	A	B	C	D	E
1	**Bluegrass Farms**				
2					
3			**Feed Component**		**Minimum**
4	**Ingredient**	**Standard**	**Enriched Oat**	**Additive**	**Daily Amount**
5	Ingredient A	0.8	0.2	0	3
6	Ingredient B	1	1.5	3	6
7	Ingredient C	0.1	0.6	2	4
8	**Cost Per Pound**	$0.25	$0.50	$3.00	
9					
10	**Max Weight**	6			
11					
12					
13	**Model**				
14					
15			**Decision Variables**		
16		**Standard**	**Enriched Oat**	**Additive**	
17	**Number of Pounds**	3.513513514	0.945945946	1.540540541	
18					
19	**Minimize Total Cost**	5.972972973			
20					
21					
22	**Constraint**	**LHS**		**RHS**	
23	Ingredient A	3	>=	3	
24	Ingredient B	9.554054054	>=	6	
25	Ingredient C	4	>=	4	
26	Weight	6	<=	6	

Objective Function   The formula =B8*B17+C8*C17+D8*D17 has been placed into cell B19 to reflect the total cost obtained with the solution shown. The optimal solution provides a total cost of $5.97.

Left-Hand Sides   The left-hand sides for the four constraints are placed into cells[3] B23:B26.

Cell B23   =SUMPRODUCT(B5:D5,B17:D17)
Cell B24   =SUMPRODUCT(B6:D6,B17:D17)
Cell B25   =SUMPRODUCT(B7:D7,B17:D17)
Cell B26   =B17+C17+D17

---

3. The SUMPRODUCT function is used here for the first time. It is useful for multiplying and summing two ranges of numbers with the same number of cells in each range. It sums the term-by-term product of the cells in each range. This function is very useful in the spreadsheet formulation of linear programs. The SUMPRODUCT formula in cell B23 is equivalent to =B5*B17+C5*C17+D5*D17.

Right-Hand Sides: The right-hand sides for the four constraints are placed into cells D23:D26.

Cell D23 =E5
Cell D23 =E6
Cell D23 =E7
Cell D23 =B10

The solution was obtained by selecting **Solver** from the **Tools** menu, entering the proper values into the **Solver Parameters** dialog box, and specifying the options **Assume Linear Model** and **Assume Non-Negative.** The information entered in the **Solver Parameters** dialog box is shown in Figure 3.16. After solving, we requested the sensitivity report shown in Figure 3.17.

Figure 3.16 SOLVER PARAMETERS DIALOG BOX FOR THE BLUEGRASS FARMS PROBLEM

Solver Parameters

Set Target Cell: $B$19

Equal To: ○ Max ● Min ○ Value of: 0

By Changing Cells:

$B$17:$D$17   [Guess]

Subject to the Constraints:

$B$23:$B$25 >= $D$23:$D$25
$B$26 <= $D$26

[Add] [Change] [Delete]

[Solve] [Close] [Options] [Reset All] [Help]

Figure 3.17 SENSITIVITY REPORT FOR THE BLUEGRASS FARMS PROBLEM

Adjustable Cells

Cell	Name	Final Value	Reduced Cost	Objective Coefficient	Allowable Increase	Allowable Decrease
$B$17	Number of Pounds Standard	3.513513514	0	0.25	1E+30	0.642857143
$C$17	Number of Pounds Enriched Oat	0.945945946	0	0.5	0.425	1E+30
$D$17	Number of Pounds Additive	1.540540541	0	3	1E+30	1.47826087

Constraints

Cell	Name	Final Value	Shadow Price	Constraint R.H. Side	Allowable Increase	Allowable Decrease
$B$23	Ingredient A LHS	3	1.216216216	3	0.368421053	1.857142857
$B$24	Ingredient B LHS	9.554054054	0	6	3.554054054	1E+30
$B$25	Ingredient C LHS	4	1.959459459	4	0.875	1.9
$B$26	Weight LHS	6	-0.918918919	6	2.47826087	0.4375

SPREADSHEET BLUEGRASS FARMS

The optimal solution (after rounding) calls for a daily diet consisting of 3.51 pounds of the standard horse feed product, 0.95 pounds of the enriched oat product, and 1.54 pounds of the vitamin and mineral feed additive. Thus, with feed component costs of $0.25, $0.50, and $3.00, the total cost of the optimal diet is

$$
\begin{array}{ll}
3.51 \text{ @ } \$0.25 \text{ per pound} = & \$0.878 \\
0.95 \text{ @ } \$0.50 \text{ per pound} = & 0.475 \\
1.54 \text{ @ } \$3.00 \text{ per pound} = & \underline{4.620} \\
\text{Total cost} \qquad\qquad = & \$5.973
\end{array}
$$

Note that, after rounding, this total is the same as the objective function value in the spreadsheet (cell B19).

Since the LHS value for the Ingredient B constraint (9.554) exceeds the RHS value (6), the optimal solution exceeds the minimum daily requirement for ingredient B by 3.554. In other words, there is a surplus of ingredient B. However, since the LHS value and RHS value for the ingredient A and ingredient C constraints are the same, the optimal diet just meets the minimum requirements for ingredients A and C; in other words, the surplus values for both these constraints are zero. Moreover, since the LHS of the weight constraint is the same as the RHS value, the optimal solution provides a total daily feed weight of 6 pounds; thus, the slack value associated with this constraint is zero.

Refer to Figure 3.17. The shadow price (after rounding) for the ingredient A constraint is 1.22. Thus, increasing the right-hand side of this constraint by 1 will increase total costs by $1.22. Conversely, a decrease in the right-hand side of the ingredient A constraint will decrease the total cost by $1.22. Looking at the allowable increase and allowable decrease values, we see that these interpretations are correct as long as the right-hand side is between $3 - 1.857 = 1.143$ and $3 + 3.368 = 6.368$.

Suppose that the Bluegrass management is willing to reconsider its position regarding the maximum weight of the daily diet. The shadow price of −0.92 (after rounding) for the weight constraint shows that a 1-unit increase in the right-hand side of this constraint will reduce total cost by $0.92. The allowable increase value shows that this interpretation is correct for increases of up to $6 + 2.478 = 8.478$ pounds. Thus, the effect of increasing the right-hand side of the weight constraint from 6 to 8 pounds is a decrease in the total daily cost of $2 \times \$0.92$ or $1.84. Keep in mind that if this change were made, the feasible region would change, and we would obtain a new optimal solution.

The Adjustable Cells section of the sensitivity report shows an allowable decrease value of 0.643 for S. Since the objective function coefficient of S is 0.25, the lower limit for the range of optimality is $0.25 - 0.643 = -0.393$. Clearly, in a real-world problem, the objective function coefficient of S (the cost of the standard horse feed product) cannot take on a negative value. So, from a practical point of view, we can think of the lower limit for the objective function coefficient of S as being zero. We can thus conclude that no matter how much the cost of the standard mix were to decrease, the optimal solution would not change. Even if Bluegrass Farms could obtain the standard horse feed product for free, the optimal solution would still specify a daily diet of 3.51 pounds of the standard horse feed product, 0.95 pound of the enriched oat product, and 1.54 pounds of the vitamin and mineral feed additive. However, any decrease in the per-unit cost of the standard feed would result in a decrease in the total cost for the optimal daily diet.

Note that the allowable increase values for the objective function coefficient values for S and A are 1E+30; thus, these coefficients have no upper limit. Even if the cost of A were to increase, for example, from $3.00 to $13.00 per pound, the optimal solution would not change; the total cost of the solution, however, would increase by $10 (the amount of the increase) times 1.541 or \$15.41. The interpretations that we have made using the sensitivity analysis information in the computer output are appropriate only if all other coefficient in the problem do not change.

N O T E S *and Comments*	1. Although Excel Solver allows the right-hand side of a constraint to be a function of the decision variables, many software packages for solving linear programs require the right-hand side of each constraint to be a constant. Using these types of packages to solve a problem with a constraint such as $S \geq 0.25F$, we would first have to take the value of $0.25F$ to the left-hand side. Thus, the constraint would be written as

$$-0.25F + S \geq 0$$

Although $S \geq 0.25F$ and $-0.25F + S \geq 0$ are identical mathematically, the convenience of being able to write the constraint in its original form can be a significant advantage when constructing the model as well as when interpreting the shadow price for the constraint.

2. The Management Science in Action: An Optimal Wood Procurement Policy describes how Wellborn Cabinet, Inc., realized projected annual savings of \$412,000 by using a linear programming model to determine an optimal wood procurement policy.

MANAGEMENT SCIENCE IN ACTION

AN OPTIMAL WOOD PROCUREMENT POLICY*

Wellborn Cabinet, Inc., operates an integrated sawmill and cabinet manufacturing system in Alabama. Its manufacturing facility consists of a sawmill, four dry kilns, and a wood cabinet assembly plant; the assembly plant includes a rough mill for producing cabinet components that are referred to as blanks. Because of the pressure to market quality products at competitive prices, a major concern for Wellborn Cabinet is to maintain consistency in product quality. A key factor in maintaining this quality depends on controlling the quality and costs of raw materials.

To produce blanks, Wellborn Cabinet purchases #1 and #2 grade hardwood logs, as well as #1 and #2 dry or green common grade lumber (note: higher numbers denote higher quality). During a typical five-day week of operation, the sawmill can process up to 1550 logs with a small-end diameter from 9 to 22 inches. Usually, the lumber is purchased in bundles containing random sizes. Both the logs processed by the sawmill and the green lumber purchased from outside suppliers are dried at the kilns to an average moisture content of 7%; the dried material is then planed and converted into about 130 different sizes of blanks at the rough mill.

Wellborn developed a linear programming model of the blank production system. The objective was to determine a procurement plan that would minimize the total cost of producing blanks for a five-day work week. Constraints included capacities of the sawmill and dry kilns, the demand for blanks at the manufacturing plant, and the available supply of raw materials. The initial results indicate that the company can minimize the total cost of producing blanks by purchasing only #2 grade logs and #2 common green lumber; approximately 88% of the rough mill dry lumber requirements should come from #2 grade logs and the rest from purchased #2 common green lumber. The projected annual savings in raw material costs were \$412,000.

*Based on H. F. Carino, and C. H. LeNoir, Jr., "Optimizing Wood Procurement in Cabinet Manufacturing." *Interfaces* (March–April 1988,) pp. 10–19.

3.5   THE ELECTRONIC COMMUNICATIONS PROBLEM

The Electronic Communications problem introduced in this section is a maximization problem involving four decision variables, two less-than-or-equal-to constraints, one equality constraint, and one greater-than-or-equal-to constraint. Our objective is to provide a summary of the material covered involving the process of formulating a mathematical model, developing a spreadsheet formulation, using Excel solver to obtain an optimal solution, and interpreting the spreadsheet solution and sensitivity report information.

Electronic Communications manufactures portable radio systems that can be used for two-way communications. The company's new product, which has a range of up to 25 miles, is suitable for a variety of business and personal uses. The distribution channels for the new radio are

1. marine equipment distributors,
2. business equipment distributors,
3. national chain of retail stores, and
4. direct mail.

Because of differing distribution and promotional costs, the profitability of the product will vary with the distribution channel. In addition, the advertising cost and the personal sales effort required will vary with the distribution channels. Table 3.2 summarizes the contribution to profit, advertising cost, and personal sales effort data pertaining to the Electronic Communications problem. The firm has set the advertising budget at $5,000, and a maximum of 1800 hours of sales force time is available for allocation to the sales effort. Management also decided to produce 600 units for the current production period. Finally, an ongoing contract with the national chain of retail stores requires that at least 150 units be distributed through this distribution channel.

Electronic Communications now faces the problem of establishing a distribution strategy for the radios that will maximize overall profitability of the new radio production. Decisions must be made about how many units should be allocated to each of the four distribution channels, as well as how to allocate the advertising budget and sales force effort to each of the four distribution channels.

Problem Formulation

A written statement of the problem has been presented. Let us now attempt to write a verbal statement of the objective function and each constraint. For the objective function, we can write

Objective function: Maximize profit

Four constraints appear to be necessary for this problem because of (1) a limited advertising budget, (2) a limited sales force availability, (3) a production requirement, and (4) a retail stores distribution requirement.

| *Table* 3.2 | PROFIT, ADVERTISING COST, AND PERSONAL SALES TIME DATA FOR THE ELECTRONIC COMMUNICATIONS PROBLEM |

Distribution Channel	Profit per Unit Sold	Advertising Cost per Unit Sold	Personal Sales Effort per Unit Sold
Marine distributors	$90	$10	2 hours
Business distributors	$84	$ 8	3 hours
National retail stores	$70	$ 9	3 hours
Direct Mail	$60	$15	None

> Constraint 1: Advertising expenditures $\leq$ Budget
>
> Constraint 2: Sales time used $\leq$ Time available
>
> Constraint 3: Radios produced $=$ Management requirement
>
> Constraint 4: Retail distribution $\geq$ Contract requirement

With this verbal description of the objective function and the constraints, we are now ready to define the decision variables representing the decisions that the manager must make. For the Electronic Communications problem, we introduce four decision variables.

M = the number of units produced for the marine equipment distribution channel

B = the number of units produced for the business equipment distribution channel

R = the number of units produced for the national retail chain distribution channel

D = the number of units produced for the direct-mail distribution channel

Using the data in Table 3.2, we write the objective function for maximizing the total contribution to profit associated with the radios as

$$\text{Max} \quad 90M + 84B + 70R + 60D$$

We now develop a mathematical statement of the constraints for the problem. With an advertising budget of $5,000, the constraint that limits the amount of advertising expenditure is

$$10M + 8B + 9R + 15D \leq 5000$$

Similarly, for the sales time limit of 1800 hours,

$$2M + 3B + 3R \leq 1800$$

Management's decision to produce 600 units during the current production period yields

$$1M + 1B + 1R + 1D = 600$$

Finally, to account for the 150 or more units that must be distributed by the national chain of retail stores, we add the constraint

$$1R \geq 150$$

Combining all constraints with the nonnegativity requirements enables us to write the complete linear programming model for the Electronic Communications problem:

$$
\begin{aligned}
\text{Max} \quad & 90M + 84B + 70R + 60D \\
\text{s.t.} \quad & \\
& 10M + 8B + 9R + 15D \leq 5000 \quad \text{Advertising budget} \\
& 2M + 3B + 3R \leq 1800 \quad \text{Salesforce availability} \\
& 1M + 1B + 1R + 1D = 600 \quad \text{Production level} \\
& 1R \geq 150 \quad \text{Retail stores requirement} \\
& M, B, R, D \geq 0
\end{aligned}
$$

Spreadsheet Solution and Interpretation

The spreadsheet formulation and solution of the Electronic Communications problem is shown in Figure 3.18. The data and descriptive labels are in cells A1:E12. The screened cells in the model section contain the information required by Excel Solver.

Decision Variables   Cells B19:E19 are reserved for the decision variables. The optimal values are shown to be $M = 25$, $B = 425$, $R = 150$, and $D = 0$.

Objective Function   The formula =SUMPRODUCT(B5:E5,B19:E19) has been placed into cell B21 to reflect the total profit obtained with the solution shown. The optimal solution provides a total cost of $48,450.

Left-Hand Sides   The left-hand sides for the four constraints are placed into cells B24:B27.

Cell B24   =SUMPRODUCT(B6:E6,B19:E19)
Cell B25   =SUMPRODUCT(B7:E7,B19:E19)

SPREADSHEET
ELECTRONIC
COMMUNICATIONS

Figure 3.18   SPREADSHEET SOLUTION FOR THE ELECTRONIC COMMUNICATIONS PROBLEM

	A	B	C	D	E
1	**Electronic Communications**				
2					
3			**Distribution Channel**		
4		**Marine**	**Business**	**Retail**	**Direct Mail**
5	**Profit Per Unit Sold**	$90	$84	$70	$60
6	**Advertising Cost Per Unit Sold**	$10	$8	$9	$15
7	**Sales Effort Per Unit Sold (hours)**	2	3	3	0
8					
9	**Advertising Budget**	$5,000			
10	**Salesforce Availability (hours)**	1800			
11	**Production Level**	600			
12	**Retail Stores Requirement**	150			
13					
14					
15	**Model**				
16					
17			**Decision Variables**		
18		**Marine**	**Business**	**Retail**	**Direct Mail**
19	**Number of Units Produced**	25	425	150	0
20					
21	**Maximize Total Profit**	48450			
22					
23		**LHS**		**RHS**	
24	**Advertising Budget**	5000	<=	$5,000	
25	**Salesforce Availability (hours)**	1775	<=	1800	
26	**Production Level**	600	=	600	
27	**Retail Stores Requirement**	150	>=	150	

Cell B26   =SUM(B19:E19)
Cell B27   =D19

Right-Hand Sides   The right-hand sides for the four constraints are placed into cells D24:D27.

Cell D24   =B9   (Copy to cells D25:D27)

The solution was obtained by selecting **Solver** from the **Tools** menu, entering the proper values into the **Solver Parameters** dialog box, and specifying the options **Assume Linear Model** and **Assume Non-Negative.** The information entered in the **Solver Parameters** dialog box is shown in Figure 3.19. After solving, we requested the sensitivity report shown in Figure 3.20.

In reviewing the output from Excel Solver, we first note that the optimal solution to the problem will provide a maximum profit of $48,450. The optimal values of the decision variables are given by $M = 25$, $B = 425$, $R = 150$, and $D = 0$. Thus, the optimal strategy for Electronic Communications is to concentrate on the business equipment distribution channel with $B = 425$ units. In addition, the firm should allocate 25 units to the marine distribution channel ($M = 25$) and meet its 150-unit commitment to the national retail chain store distribution channel ($R = 150$). With $D = 0$, the optimal solution indicates that the firm should not use the direct mail distribution channel.

Now consider the information contained in the Reduced Costs column of the sensitivity report (Figure 3.20). Recall that the absolute value of the reduced cost indicates how much each objective function coefficient would have to improve before the corresponding decision variable could assume a positive value in the optimal solution. As the sensitivity report output shows, the first three reduced costs are zero because the corresponding decision variables already have positive values in the optimal solution. However, the absolute value of the reduced cost (45.000) for the direct mail decision variables tells us that the profit for the new radios distributed via the direct-mail channel would have to increase from

Figure **3.19**   SOLVER PARAMETERS DIALOG BOX FOR THE ELECTRONIC COMMUNICATIONS PROBLEM

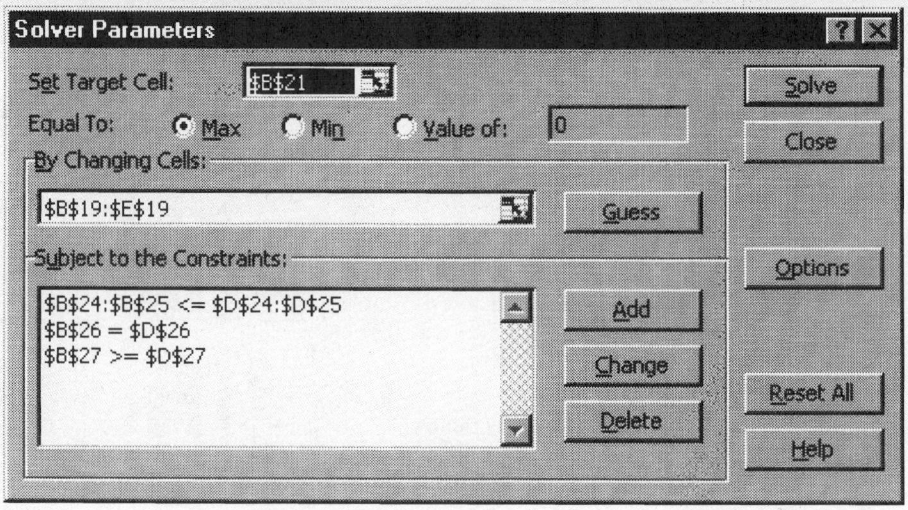

Figure 3.20	SENSITIVITY REPORT FOR THE ELECTRONIC COMMUNICATIONS PROBLEM

Adjustable Cells

Cell	Name	Final Value	Reduced Cost	Objective Coefficient	Allowable Increase	Allowable Decrease
$B$19	Number of Units Produced Marine	25	0	90	1E+30	6.000000001
$C$19	Number of Units Produced Business	425	0	84	6.000000002	33.99999999
$D$19	Number of Units Produced Retail	150	0	70	17	1E+30
$E$19	Number of Units Produced Direct Mail	0	-45	60	45	1E+30

SPREADSHEET
ELECTRONIC
COMMUNICATIONS

Constraints

Cell	Name	Final Value	Shadow Price	Constraint R.H. Side	Allowable Increase	Allowable Decrease
$B$24	Advertising Budget LHS	5000	3	5000	850.0000002	50.00000001
$B$25	Salesforce Availability (hours) LHS	1775	0	1800	1E+30	25
$B$26	Production Level LHS	600	60	600	3.571428572	85.00000002
$B$27	Retail Stores Requirement LHS	150	-17	150	50.00000001	150

its current value of $60 per unit to at least $60 + $45 = $105 per unit before using the direct-mail distribution channel would be profitable.

At the optimal solution, the LHS value of the advertising budget constraint is the same as the RHS value; thus, the advertising budget constraint has a slack of zero, indicating that the entire budget of $5,000 has been used. The corresponding shadow price of 3 tells us that an additional dollar added to the advertising budget will increase profit by $3. Since the allowable increase for this right-hand side is 850, this statement about the value of increasing the advertising budget is appropriate up to $5,850. Increases above this level would not necessarily be beneficial. Nonetheless, the firm should seriously consider the possibility of increasing the advertising budget.

The optimal solution also shows that only 1775 hours (LHS value) of the 1800 hours (RHS) of salesforce availability has been used, which creates a slack of 25 hours. Hence, the shadow price for this constraint is zero. Note also that a shadow price of 60 for the production level constraint indicates that if the firm were to consider increasing the production level for the radios, profit would increase at the rate of $60 per unit produced. Finally, since the value of the LHS (150 units) and the value of the RHS (150 units) of the retail stores requirement are equal at the optimal solution, there is a surplus of zero associated with this constraint, and thus the constraint is binding. The shadow price of −17 for this constraint shows that increasing the right-hand side of the constraint from 150 to 151 units will actually decrease profits by $17. Thus, Electronic Communications may want to consider reducing its commitment to the retail store distribution channel since a decrease in this commitment will actually increase profits at the rate of $17 per unit. With an allowable decrease value of 150 for this right-hand side, the lower limit on the range of feasibility shows that the commitment would be reduced to zero and the value of the reduction would be at the rate of $17 per unit.

We now consider the ranges of optimality for the objective function coefficients. Recall that these ranges can be computed by adding and subtracting the allowable increase and allowable decrease values in the Adjustable Cells section of the sensitivity report from the objective function coefficient. Since the allowable increase value for the marine objective function coefficient is 1E+30, we can conclude that there is no upper limit. With an allowable decrease value of 6, the lower limit is $90 - 6 = 84$. Thus, we can write the range of optimality as

$$84 \leq C_M < \text{No upper limit}$$

The ranges of optimality for the remaining three objective function coefficients are

$$50 \leq C_B \leq 90$$
$$\text{No lower limit} < C_R \leq 87$$
$$\text{No lower limit} < C_D \leq 105$$

Note in particular the range of optimality associated with the direct-mail distribution channel coefficient, C_D. This information is consistent with the earlier observation for the reduced costs. In both instances, the profit per unit would have to increase to \$105 before the direct mail distribution channel could be in the optimal solution with a positive value.

Finally, recall that the complete solution to the Electronic Communications problem requested information not only on the number of units to be distributed over each channel but also on the allocation of the advertising budget and the salesforce effort to each distribution channel. Since the optimal solution is $M = 25$, $B = 425$, $R = 150$, and $D = 0$, we can simply evaluate each term in a given constraint to determine how much of the constraint resource is allocated to each distribution channel. For example, the advertising budget constraint of

$$10M + 8B + 9R + 15D \leq 5000$$

shows $10M = 10(25) = \$250$, $8B = 8(425) = \$3400$, $9R = 9(150) = \$1350$, and $15D = 15(0) = \$0$. Thus, the advertising budget allocations are, respectively, \$250, \$3,400, \$1,350, and \$0 for each of the four distribution channels. Note that it would be a simple matter to enter cell formulas for these calculations into the spreadsheet shown in Figure 3.18, and thus make this information part of the Excel output. Making a similar calculation for the salesforce constraint results in the managerial summary of the Electronics Communications optimal solution shown in Table 3.3.

Table 3.3	PROFIT-MAXIMIZING STRATEGY FOR THE ELECTRONIC COMMUNICATIONS PROBLEM		
Distribution Channel	**Volume**	**Advertising Allocation**	**Salesforce Allocation (hours)**
Marine distributors	25	$ 250	50
Business distributors	425	3400	1275
National retail stores	150	1350	450
Direct mail	0	0	0
Total	600	$5000	1775

Projected total profit contribution = $48,450

............/ /..............

SUMMARY

We began the chapter with a discussion of sensitivity analysis: The study of how changes in the coefficients of a linear program affect the optimal solution. First, we showed how a graphical method can be used to determine how a change in one of the objective function coefficients or a change in the right-hand-side-value for a constraint will affect the optimal solution to the problem. Since graphical sensitivity analysis is limited to linear programs with two decision variables, we then showed how Excel Solver can be used to produce a sensitivity report containing the same information.

We continued our discussion of problem formulation, sensitivity analysis, and the interpretation of the solution by introducing several modifications of the RMC problem. They involved an additional decision variable and several types of percentage, or ratio, constraints. Then, in order to provide additional practice in formulating and interpreting the solution for linear programs involving more than two decision variables, we introduced the Bluegrass Farms problem, a maximization problem involving three decision variables. In the last section we summarized all the work to date using the Electronic Communications problem, a maximization problem with four decision variables, two less-than-or-equal-to constraints, one equality constraint, and one greater-than-or-equal-to constraint.

The Management Science in Action: Using Linear Programming for Traffic Control provides another example of the widespread use of linear programming. It is being used all over the world for a wide variety of problems. In the next chapter we will see many more applications of linear programming.

............/ /..............

GLOSSARY

Sensitivity analysis The study of how the changes in the coefficients of a linear program affect the optimal solution.

Range of optimality The range of values over which an objective function coefficient may vary without causing any change in the values of the decision variables in the optimal solution.

Shadow price The change in the value of the objective function per unit increase in a constraint right-hand side.

Reduced cost The absolute value of the reduced cost is the amount by which an objective function coefficient would have to improve (increase for a maximization problem, decrease for a minimization problem), before it would be possible for the corresponding variable to assume a positive value in the optimal solution.

Range of feasibility The range of values over which a right-hand side may vary without changing the value and interpretation of the shadow price.

Sunk cost A cost that is not affected by the decision made. It will be incurred regardless of the values the decision variables assume.

Relevant cost A cost that depends upon the decision made. The amount of a relevant cost will vary depending on the values of the decision variables.

MANAGEMENT SCIENCE IN ACTION

USING LINEAR PROGRAMMING FOR TRAFFIC CONTROL*

The Hanshin Expressway was the first urban toll expressway in Osaka, Japan. Although in 1964 its length was only 2.3 kilometers, today it is a large-scale urban expressway network of 200 kilometers. The Hanshin Expressway provides service for the Hanshin (Osaka-Kobe) area, the second-most populated area in Japan. An average of 828,000 vehicles use the expressway each day, with daily traffic sometimes exceeding 1,000,000 vehicles. In 1970, the Hanshin Expressway Public Corporation started using an automated traffic-control system in order to maximize the number of vehicles flowing into the expressway network.

The automated traffic-control system relies on two control methods: (1) limiting the number of cars that enter the expressway at each entrance ramp; and (2) providing drivers with up-to-date and accurate traffic information, including expected travel times and information about accidents. The approach used to limit the number of vehicles depends upon whether the expressway is in a normal or steady state of operation, or whether some type of unusual event, such as an accident or a breakdown, has occurred.

In the first phase of the steady-state case, the Hanshin system uses a linear programming model to maximize the total number of vehicles entering the system, while preventing traffic congestion and adverse effects on surrounding road networks. The data that drives the linear programming model is collected from detectors installed every 500 meters along the expressway and at all entrance and exit ramps. Every five minutes the real-time data collected from the detectors is used to update the model coefficients and a new linear program computes the maximum number of vehicles the expressway can accommodate.

The automated traffic control system has been very successful. According to surveys, traffic control has decreased the length of congested portions of the expressway by 30 percent and the duration by 20 percent. It has been shown to be extremely cost effective, and drivers consider it an indispensable service.

*Based on Yoshino, T., T. Sasaki, and T. Hasegawa, "The Traffic-Control System on the Hanshin Expressway." *Interfaces* January–February 1995, pp. 94–108.

PROBLEMS

1. Recall the Par, Inc., problem (Chapter 2, Problem 13) Letting

    S = number of standard bags produced
    D = number of deluxe bags produced

    leads to the formulation

    $$\text{Max} \quad 10S + 9D$$

    s.t.

    $$\frac{7}{10}S + 1D \leq 630 \quad \text{Cutting and dyeing time}$$
    $$\frac{1}{2}S + \frac{5}{6}D \leq 600 \quad \text{Sewing time}$$
    $$1S + \frac{2}{3}D \leq 708 \quad \text{Finishing time}$$
    $$\frac{1}{10}S + \frac{1}{4}D \leq 135 \quad \text{Inspection and packaging time}$$
    $$S, D \geq 0$$

    Use the graphical sensitivity analysis approach to determine the range of optimality for the objective function coefficients.

2. For Problem 1 use the graphical sensitivity analysis approach to determine what happens if an additional 10 hours of cutting and dyeing time become available. What is the corresponding shadow price for the constraint?

SELF TEST

3. Consider the linear program given below.

$$\text{Max} \quad 2x_1 + 3x_2$$

s.t.

$$x_1 + x_2 \leq 10$$
$$2x_1 + x_2 \geq 4$$
$$x_1 + 3x_2 \leq 24$$
$$2x_1 + x_2 \leq 16$$
$$x_1, x_2 \geq 0$$

a. Solve this problem using the graphical solution procedure.
b. Compute the range of optimality for the objective function coefficient of x_1.
c. Compute the range of optimality for the objective function coefficient of x_2.
d. Suppose that the objective function coefficient of x_1 is increased from 2 to 2.5. What is the new optimal solution?
e. Suppose that the objective function coefficient of x_2 is decreased from 3 to 1. What is the new optimal solution?

4. Refer to Problem 3. Compute the shadow prices for constraints 1 and 2 and interpret them.

5. Consider the linear program given below.

SELF TEST

$$\text{Min} \quad x_1 + x_2$$

s.t.

$$x_1 + 2x_2 \geq 7$$
$$2x_1 + x_2 \geq 5$$
$$x_1 + 6x_2 \geq 11$$
$$x_1, x_2 \geq 0$$

a. Solve this problem using the graphical solution procedure.
b. Compute the range of optimality for the objective function coefficient of x_1.
c. Compute the range of optimality for the objective function coefficient of x_2.
d. Suppose that the objective function coefficient of x_1 is increased to 1.5. Find the new optimal solution.
e. Suppose that the objective function coefficient of x_2 is decreased to $\frac{1}{3}$. Find the new optimal solution.

6. Refer to Problem 5. Compute and interpret the shadow prices for the constraints.

7. Consider the linear program given below.

$$\text{Max} \quad 5x_1 + 7x_2$$

s.t.

$$2x_1 + x_2 \geq 3$$
$$-x_1 + 5x_2 \geq 4$$
$$2x_1 - 3x_2 \leq 6$$
$$3x_1 + 2x_2 \leq 35$$
$$\tfrac{3}{4}x_1 + x_2 \leq 10$$
$$x_1, x_2 \geq 0$$

a. Solve this problem using the graphical solution procedure.
b. Compute the range of optimality for the objective function coefficient of x_1.
c. Compute the range of optimality for the objective function coefficient of x_2.
d. Suppose that the objective function coefficient of x_1 is decreased to 2. What is the new optimal solution?
e. Suppose that the objective function coefficient of x_2 is increased to 10. What is the new optimal solution?

8. Refer to Problem 7. Suppose that the objective function coefficient for x_2 is reduced to 3.
   a. Resolve using the graphical solution procedure.
   b. Compute the shadow prices for constraints 2 and 3.

9. Refer again to Problem 3.
   a. Suppose that the objective function coefficient of x_1 is increased to 3 and that the objective function coefficient of x_2 is increased to 4. Find the new optimal solution.
   b. Suppose that the objective function coefficient of x_1 is increased to 3 and that the objective function coefficient of x_2 is decreased to 2. Find the new optimal solution.

10. Refer again to Problem 7.
   a. Suppose that the objective function coefficient of x_1 is decreased to 4 and that the objective function coefficient of x_2 is increased to 10. Find the new optimal solution.
   b. Suppose that the objective function coefficient of x_1 is decreased to 4 and that the objective function coefficient of x_2 is increased to 8. Find the new optimal solution.

11. Recall the Kelson Sporting Equipment problem (Chapter 2, Problem 16). Letting

$$R = \text{number of regular gloves}$$
$$C = \text{number of catcher's mitts}$$

leads to the formulation:

$$
\begin{aligned}
\text{Max} \quad & 5R + 8C \\
\text{s.t.} \quad & \\
& R + \tfrac{3}{2}C \le 900 \quad \text{Cutting and sewing} \\
& \tfrac{1}{2}R + \tfrac{1}{3}C \le 300 \quad \text{Finishing} \\
& \tfrac{1}{8}R + \tfrac{1}{4}C \le 100 \quad \text{Packaging and shipping} \\
& R, C \ge 0
\end{aligned}
$$

The spreadsheet solution and sensitivity report are shown in Figure 3.21.
   a. What is the optimal solution and what is the value of the total profit contribution?
   b. Which constraints are binding?
   c. What are the shadow prices for the resources? Interpret each.
   d. If overtime can be scheduled in one of the departments, where would you recommend doing so?

12. Refer to the spreadsheet solution and sensitivity report for the Kelson Sporting Equipment problem shown in Figure 3.21 (see Problem 11).
   a. What are the ranges of optimality for the objective function coefficients.
   b. Interpret the ranges in part (a).
   c. Interpret the range of feasibility for the right-hand sides.
   d. How much will the value of the optimal solution improve if 20 extra hours of packaging and shipping time are made available?

13. Recall the Investment Advisors problem (Chapter 2, Problem 17). Letting

$$U = \text{shares of U.S. Oil}$$
$$H = \text{shares of Hub Properties}$$

leads to the formulation:

$$
\begin{aligned}
\text{Max} \quad 3U + \quad 5H \qquad\qquad & \text{Maximize total annual return} \\
\text{s.t.} \quad\quad\quad & \\
25U + \quad 50H \le 80{,}000 \quad & \text{Funds available} \\
0.50U + 0.25H \le \quad 700 \quad & \text{Risk maximum} \\
1U \qquad\quad \le \quad 1000 \quad & \text{U.S. Oil maximum} \\
U, H \ge 0 \qquad\qquad &
\end{aligned}
$$

Figure 3.21	SPREADSHEET SOLUTION AND SENSITIVITY REPORT FOR THE KELSON SPORTING EQUIPMENT PROBLEM

	A	B	C	D	E
1	**Kelson Chapter 3**				
2					
3		**Production Time (hours)**			
4	**Department**	**Regular Glove**	**Catcher's Mitt**	**Time Available**	
5	Cutting and Sewing	1	1.5	900	
6	Finishing	0.5	0.33333	300	
7	Packaging and Shipping	0.125	0.25	100	
8	**Profit Per Glove**	5	8		
9					
10					
11	**Model**				
12					
13		**Decision Variables**			
14		**Regular Glove**	**Catcher's Mitt**		
15	**Number Produced**	500.0015	149.99925		
16					
17	**Maximize Total Profit**	3700			
18					
19	**Constraints**	**Amount Used (LHS)**		**Amount Available (RHS)**	
20	Cutting and Sewing	725.000375	<=	900	
21	Finishing	300	<=	300	
22	Packaging and Shipping	100	<=	100	

SPREADSHEET
KELSON
CHAPTER 3

Adjustable Cells

Cell	Name	Final Value	Reduced Cost	Objective Coefficient	Allowable Increase	Allowable Decrease
$B$15	Number Produced Regular Glove	500.0015	0	5	7.000120001	1
$C$15	Number Produced Catcher's Mitt	149.99925	0	8	2	4.6667

Constraints

Cell	Name	Final Value	Shadow Price	Constraint R.H. Side	Allowable Increase	Allowable Decrease
$B$20	Cutting and Sewing Amount Used (LHS)	725.000375	0	900	1E+30	174.999625
$B$21	Finishing Amount Used (LHS)	300	2.999985	300	100	166.668
$B$22	Packaging and Shipping Amount Used (LHS)	100	28.00006	100	34.99982	25

The spreadsheet solution and sensitivity report for this problem are shown in Figure 3.22.

a. What is the optimal solution and what is the value of the total estimated annual return?

b. Which constraints are binding? What is your interpretation of this condition in terms of the problem?

c. What are the shadow prices for the constraints? Interpret each.

d. Would relaxing the constraint on the amount invested in U.S. Oil be beneficial? Why or why not?

14. Refer to Figure 3.22, which shows the spreadsheet solution and sensitivity report for Problem 13.

    a. How much would the estimated return per share for U.S. Oil have to increase before increasing the investment in this stock would be beneficial?

SPREADSHEET
INVESTMENT
ADVISORS

Figure 3.22	SPREADSHEET SOLUTION AND SENSITIVITY REPORT FOR THE INVESTMENT ADVISORS PROBLEM

	A	B	C	D
1	**Investment Advisors**			
2				
3	**Stock**	**Price/Share**	**Annual Return/Share**	**Risk Index/Share**
4	**U.S. Oil**	$25.00	$3.00	0.50
5	**Hub Properties**	$50.00	$5.00	0.25
6				
7	**Funds Available**	$80,000		
8	**Maximum Total Risk Index**	700		
9	**Maximum U.S. Oil Stock (shares)**	1,000		
10				
11				
12				
13	**Model**			
14				
15			**Decision Variables**	
16		**U.S. Oil**	**Hub Properties**	
17	**Shares Purchased**	800	1,200	
18				
19	**Maximize Total Return**	$8,400.00		
20				
21	**Constraints**	**LHS**		**RHS**
22	**Funds Available**	$80,000	<=	$80,000
23	**Maximum Total Risk Index**	700	<=	700
24	**Maximum U.S. Oil Stock (shares)**	800	<=	1,000

Adjustable Cells

Cell	Name	Final Value	Reduced Cost	Objective Coefficient	Allowable Increase	Allowable Decrease
$B$17	Units Purchased U.S. Oil	800	0	3	7	0.5
$C$17	Units Purchased Hub Properties	1,200	0	5	1	3.5

Constraints

Cell	Name	Final Value	Shadow Price	Constraint R.H. Side	Allowable Increase	Allowable Decrease
$B$22	Funds Available LHS	$80,000	$0.093	80000	60000	15000
$B$23	Maximum Total Risk Index LHS	700	$1.333	700	75	300
$B$24	Maximum U.S. Oil Stock (shares) LHS	800	$0.000	1000	1E+30	200

    b. How much would the estimated return per share for Hub Properties have to decrease before reducing the investment in this stock would be beneficial?

    c. How much would the total annual return be reduced if the U.S. Oil maximum were reduced to 900 shares?

15. Recall the M&D Chemicals problem (Chapter 2, Problem 30). Letting

$$P_1 = \text{gallons of product 1 produced}$$
$$P_2 = \text{gallons of product 2 produced}$$

leads to the formulation:

$$\text{Min} \quad 2P_1 + 3P_2$$

s.t.

$1P_1$		≥ 125	Demand for product 1
$1P_1 + 1P_2$		≥ 350	Total production requirement
$2P_1 + 1P_2$		≤ 600	Processing time limitation
	$P_1, P_2 \geq 0$		

The spreadsheet solution and sensitivity report are shown in Figure 3.23.

    a. What is the optimal solution and what is the minimum production cost?

    b. Specify the range of optimality for the objective function coefficients.

    c. What are the shadow prices for each constraint? Interpret each.

    d. If the total production requirement were increased from 350 to 450 gallons, how would the value of the optimal solution change?

    e. Identify the range of feasibility for the right-hand-side values.

16. Recall the Photo Chemicals problem (Chapter 2, Problem 31). Letting

$$P_1 = \text{gallons of product 1 produced}$$
$$P_2 = \text{gallons of product 2 produced}$$

SELF TEST

leads to the formulation:

$$\text{Min} \quad 1P_1 + 1P_2 \qquad \text{Minimize production cost}$$

s.t.

$1P_1 + 2P_2$	≥ 80	Raw material
$1P_1$	≥ 30	Product 1 minimum
$1P_2$	≥ 20	Product 2 minimum
$P_1, P_2 \geq 0$		

The spreadsheet solution and sensitivity report are shown in Figure 3.24.

    a. What is the optimal solution and what is minimum production cost?

    b. Specify the range of optimality for the objective function coefficients.

    c. What are the shadow prices for each constraint? Interpret each.

    d. If the amount of raw material to be processed were increased from 80 to 85 gallons, how would the optimal solution change?

    e. Identify the range of feasibility for each right-hand-side value.

17. Recall the Tom's, Inc., problem (Chapter 2, Problem 26). Letting

$$W = \text{jars of Western Foods Salsa produced}$$
$$M = \text{jars of Mexico City Salsa produced}$$

Figure 3.23   SPREADSHEET SOLUTION AND SENSITIVITY REPORT FOR THE M&D CHEMICALS PROBLEM

SPREADSHEET
M&D CHEMICALS

	A	B	C	D	E
1	**M&D Chemical**				
2					
3					
4		**Product 1**	**Product 2**	**Time Available**	
5	**Processing Time (hours)**	2	1	600	
6	**Production Cost**	$2.00	$3.00		
7					
8	**Minimum Total Production**	350			
9	**Product 1 Minimum**	125			
10					
11					
12	**Model**				
13					
14			**Decision Variables**		
15		**Product 1**	**Product 2**		
16	**Gallons Produced**	250	100		
17					
18	**Minimize Total Cost**	800			
19					
20	**Constraints**	**LHS**		**RHS**	
21	Processing Time	600	<=	600	
22	Minimum Total Production	350	>=	350	
23	Product 1 Minimum	250	>=	125	

Adjustable Cells

Cell	Name	Final Value	Reduced Cost	Objective Coefficient	Allowable Increase	Allowable Decrease
$B$15	Gallons Produced Product 1	250	0	2	1	1E+30
$C$15	Gallons Produced Product 2	100	0	3	1E+30	1

Constraints

Cell	Name	Final Value	Shadow Price	Constraint R.H. Side	Allowable Increase	Allowable Decrease
$B$20	Processing Time LHS	600	-1	600	100	125
$B$21	Minimum Total Production LHS	350	4	350	125	50
$B$22	Product 1 Minimum LHS	250	0	125	125	1E+30

leads to the formulation:

$$\text{Max} \quad 1W + 1.25M$$

s.t.

$$5W + 7M \leq 4480 \quad \text{Whole tomatoes}$$
$$3W + 1M \leq 2080 \quad \text{Tomato sauce}$$
$$2W + 2M \leq 1600 \quad \text{Tomato paste}$$
$$W, M \geq 0$$

Figure 3.24	SPREADSHEET SOLUTION AND SENSITIVITY REPORT FOR THE PHOTO CHEMICALS PROBLEM

SPREADSHEET
PHOTO
CHEMICALS

	A	B	C	D	E
1	**Photo Chemicals**				
2					
3					
4		**Product 1**	**Product 2**	**Material Available**	
5	**Raw Material (pounds)**	1	2	80	
6	**Production Cost**	$1.00	$1.00		
7					
8	**Product 1 Minimum (gallons)**	30			
9	**Product 2 Minimum (gallons)**	20			
10					
11	**Model**				
12					
13		**Decision Variables**			
14		**Product 1**	**Product 2**		
15	**Gallons Produced**	30	25		
16					
17	**Minimize Total Cost**	55			
18					
19	**Constraints**	**LHS**		**RHS**	
20	Raw Material	80	>=	80	
21	Product 1 Minimum	30	>=	30	
22	Product 2 Minimum	25	>=	20	

Adjustable Cells

Cell	Name	Final Value	Reduced Cost	Objective Coefficient	Allowable Increase	Allowable Decrease
$B$15	Gallons Produced Product 1	30	0	1	1E+30	0.5
$C$15	Gallons Produced Product 2	25	0	1	1	1

Constraints

Cell	Name	Final Value	Shadow Price	Constraint R.H. Side	Allowable Increase	Allowable Decrease
$B$21	Product 1 Minimum LHS	30	0.5	30	10	30
$B$22	Product 2 Minimum LHS	25	0	20	5	1E+30
$B$20	Raw Material LHS	80	0.5	80	1E+30	10

The spreadsheet solution and sensitivity report are shown in Figure 3.25.

a. What is the optimal solution and what are the optimal production quantities?

b. Specify the range of optimality for the objective function coefficients.

c. What are the shadow prices for each constraint? Interpret each.

d. Identify the range of feasibility for each right-hand-side value.

Figure 3.25 SPREADSHEET SOLUTION AND SENSITIVITY REPORT FOR THE TOM'S INC.. PROBLEM

SPREADSHEET
TOM'S, INC.

	A	B	C	D	E
1	Tom's Inc.				
2			Percentage Data		
3	Product	Whole Tomatoes	Tomato Sauce	Tomato Paste	
4	Western Foods Salsa	50%	30%	20%	
5	Mexico City Salsa	70%	10%	20%	
6	Price per Pound	$0.96	$0.64	$0.56	
7	Price per Ounce	$0.06	$0.04	$0.04	
8	Pounds Available	280	130	100	
9	Ounces Available	4480	2080	1600	
10					
11	Weight of Each Jar (ounces)	10			
12					
13	Cost of Jar	$0.02			
14	Spices and Other Ingredients	$0.10			
15	Labeling and Filling	$0.03			
16	Total Misc. Cost	$0.15			
17			Ounces Required		
18	Product	Whole Tomatoes	Tomato Sauce	Tomato Paste	Tomato Cost
19	Western Foods Salsa	5	3	2	0.49
20	Mexico City Salsa	7	1	2	0.53
21					
22	Product	Sales Revenue	Misc. Cost	Tomato Cost	Profit
23	Western Foods Salsa	$1.64	$0.15	$0.49	$1.00
24	Mexico City Salsa	$1.93	$0.15	$0.53	$1.25
25					
26					
27	Model				
28					
29			Decision Variables		
30		Western Foods Salsa	Mexico City Salsa		
31	Number of Jars Produced	560	240		
32					
33	Maximize Total Return	$860.00			
34					
35	Constraints	LHS		RHS	
36	Whole Tomatoes	4,480	<=	4,480	
37	Tomato Sauce	1,920	<=	2,080	
38	Tomato Paste	1,600	<=	1,600	

Adjustable Cells

Cell	Name	Final Value	Reduced Cost	Objective Coefficient	Allowable Increase	Allowable Decrease
$B$27	Number of Jars Produced Western Foods Salsa	560	0	1	0.25	0.107142857
$C$27	Number of Jars Produced Mexico City Salsa	240	0	1.25	0.15	0.25

Constraints

Cell	Name	Final Value	Shadow Price	Constraint R.H. Side	Allowable Increase	Allowable Decrease
$B$32	Whole Tomatoes LHS	4,480	0.125	4480	1120	160
$B$33	Tomato Sauce LHS	1,920	0.000	2080	1E+30	160
$B$34	Tomato Paste LHS	1,600	0.188	1600	40	320

SELF TEST

18. Suppose that in a product-mix problem x_1, x_2, x_3, and x_4 indicate the units of products 1, 2, 3, and 4, respectively, and the linear program is

$$\text{Max} \quad 4x_1 + 6x_2 + 3x_3 + 1x_4$$
$$\text{s.t.}$$
$$1.5x_1 + 2x_2 + 4x_3 + 3x_4 \leq 550 \quad \text{Machine 1 hours}$$
$$4x_1 + 1x_2 + 2x_3 + 1x_4 \leq 700 \quad \text{Machine 2 hours}$$
$$2x_1 + 3x_2 + 1x_3 + 2x_4 \leq 200 \quad \text{Machine 3 hours}$$
$$x_1, x_2, x_3, x_4 \geq 0$$

SPREADSHEET PROBLEM 18

| **Figure 3.26** | SPREADSHEET SOLUTION AND SENSITIVITY REPORT FOR PROBLEM 18 |

	A	B	C	D	E	F
1	**Problem 18**					
2						
3			**Machine Requirements**			
4	**Machine**	**Product 1**	**Product 2**	**Product 3**	**Product 4**	**Hours Available**
5	Machine 1	1.5	2	4	3	550
6	Machine 2	4	1	2	1	700
7	Machine 3	2	3	1	2	200
8	**Profit Per Unit**	4	6	3	1	
9						
10						
11	**Model**					
12						
13			**Decision Variables**			
14		**Product 1**	**Product 2**	**Product 3**	**Product 4**	
15	**Units Produced**	0	25	125	0	
16						
17	**Maximize Total Profit**	525				
18						
19	**Constraints**	**Amount Used (LHS)**		**Amount Available (RHS)**		
20	Machine 1	550	<=	550		
21	Machine 2	275	<=	700		
22	Machine 3	200	<=	200		

Adjustable Cells

Cell	Name	Final Value	Reduced Cost	Objective Coefficient	Allowable Increase	Allowable Decrease
$B$15	Units Produced Product 1	0	-0.05	4	0.05	1E+30
$C$15	Units Produced Product 2	25	0	6	2.999999999	0.076923077
$D$15	Units Produced Product 3	125	0	3	9.000000001	1
$E$15	Units Produced Product 4	0	-3.5	1	3.5	1E+30

Constraints

Cell	Name	Final Value	Shadow Price	Constraint R.H. Side	Allowable Increase	Allowable Decrease
$B$20	Machine 1 Amount Used (LHS)	550	0.3	550	250	416.6666667
$B$21	Machine 2 Amount Used (LHS)	275	0	700	1E+30	425
$B$22	Machine 3 Amount Used (LHS)	200	1.8	200	625	62.5

The spreadsheet solution and sensitivity report are shown in Figure 3.26.
a. What is the optimal solution and what is the value of the objective function?
b. Which constraints are binding?
c. Which machines have excess capacity available? How much?
d. If the objective function coefficient of x_1 is increased by 0.50, will the optimal solution change?

SELF TEST

19. Refer to the spreadsheet solution and sensitivity report for Problem 18 in Figure 3.26.
a. Identify the range of optimality for each objective function coefficient.
b. Identify the range of feasibility for the right-hand-side values.
c. If the number of hours available on machine 1 is increased by 300, will the shadow price for that constraint change?

20. Consider the following linear program and the spreadsheet solution and sensitivity report shown in Figure 3.27.

$$\text{Min} \quad 15x_1 + 15x_2 + 16x_3$$

s.t.

$$1x_1 \qquad + 1x_3 \leq 30$$
$$0.5x_1 - 1x_2 + 6x_3 \geq 15$$
$$3x_1 + 4x_2 - 1x_3 \geq 20$$
$$x_1, x_2, x_3 \geq 0$$

a. What is the optimal solution and what is the optimal value for the objective function?
b. Which constraints are binding?
c. What are the shadow prices? Interpret each.
d. If you could change the right-hand side of one constraint by one unit, which one would you choose? What would be the new value of the right-hand side?

21. Refer to the spreadsheet solution of Problem 20 in Figure 3.27.
a. Interpret the ranges of optimality for the objective function coefficients.
b. Suppose that the objective function coefficient of x_1 is increased by 0.25. What is the new optimal solution?

22. Supersport Footballs, Inc., has to determine the best number of All-Pro (A), College (C), and High School (H) types of footballs to produce to maximize profits. Constraints include production capacity limitations (time available in minutes) in each of three departments (cutting and dyeing, sewing, and inspection and packaging) as well as a constraint that requires the production of at least 1000 All-Pro footballs. The linear programming model of Supersport's problem is

$$\text{Max} \quad 3A + 5C + 4H$$

s.t.

$$12A + 10C + 8H \leq 18,000 \quad \text{Cutting and dyeing}$$
$$15A + 15C + 12H \leq 18,000 \quad \text{Sewing}$$
$$3A + 4C + 2H \leq 9,000 \quad \text{Inspection and packaging}$$
$$1A \qquad\qquad\qquad \geq 1,000 \quad \text{All-Pro model}$$
$$A, C, H \geq 0$$

Figure 3.27	SPREADSHEET SOLUTION AND SENSITIVITY REPORT FOR PROBLEM 20

	A	B	C	D	E
1	**Problem 20**				
2					
3		**Left-Hand Side Requirements**			
4	**Constraint**	**Variable 1**	**Variable 2**	**Variable 3**	
5	Constraint 1	1		1	30
6	Constraint 2	0.5	-1	6	15
7	Constraint 3	3	4	-1	20
8	**Profit Per Unit**	15	15	16	
9					
10					
11	**Model**				
12		**Decision Variables**			
13		**Variable 1**	**Variable 2**	**Variable 3**	
14	**Units Produced**	7.297297297	0	1.891891892	
15					
16	**Maximize Total Profit**	140			
17					
18	**Constraints**	**Amount Used (LHS)**		**Amount Available (RHS)**	
19	Machine 1	9.189189189	<=	30	
20	Machine 2	15	>=	15	
21	Machine 3	20	>=	20	

SPREADSHEET
PROBLEM 20

Adjustable Cells

Cell	Name	Final Value	Reduced Cost	Objective Coefficient	Allowable Increase	Allowable Decrease
$B$14	Units Produced Variable 1	7.297297297	0	15	0.543478261	13.66666667
$C$14	Units Produced Variable 2	0	0.675675676	15	1E+30	0.675675676
$D$14	Units Produced Variable 3	1.891891892	0	16	164	2.5

Constraints

Cell	Name	Final Value	Shadow Price	Constraint R.H. Side	Allowable Increase	Allowable Decrease
$B$19	Machine 1 Amount Used (LHS)	9.189189189	0	30	1E+30	20.81081081
$B$20	Machine 2 Amount Used (LHS)	15	3.405405405	15	96.25	11.66666667
$B$21	Machine 3 Amount Used (LHS)	20	4.432432432	20	70	22.5

The spreadsheet solution and sensitivity report for the Supersport problem are shown in Figure 3.28.

a. How many footballs of each type should Supersport produce to maximize the total profit contribution?

b. Which constraints are binding?

c. Interpret the slack and/or surplus in each constraint.

d. Interpret the ranges of optimality for the profit contributions of the three types of football.

Figure 3.28	SPREADSHEET SOLUTION AND SENSITIVITY REPORT FOR THE SUPERSPORT FOOTBALLS PROBLEM

SPREADSHEET
SUPERSPORT

	A	B	C	D	E	F
1	**Supersport**					
2						
3			**Production Requirements**			
4	**Department**	**All-Pro**	**College**	**High School**	**Time Available (min.)**	
5	Cutting and dyeing	12	10	8	18,000	
6	Sewing	15	15	12	18,000	
7	Inspection and packaging	3	4	2	9,000	
8	**Profit Per Unit**	$3	$5	$4		
9						
10	**All-Pro Minimum**	1000				
11						
12						
13	**Model**					
14						
15			**Decision Variables**			
16		**All-Pro**	**College**	**High School**		
17	**Units Produced**	1000	200	0		
18						
19	**Maximize Total Profit**	4000				
20						
21	**Constraints**	**LHS**		**RHS**		
22	Cutting and dyeing	14000	<=	18000		
23	Sewing	18000	<=	18000		
24	Inspection and packaging	3800	<=	9000		
25	All-Pro Minimum	1000	>=	1000		

Adjustable Cells

Cell	Name	Final Value	Reduced Cost	Objective Coefficient	Allowable Increase	Allowable Decrease
$B$16	Units Produced All-Pro	1000	0	3	2	1E+30
$C$16	Units Produced College	200	0	5	1E+30	0
$D$16	Units Produced High School	0	0	4	0	1E+30

Constraints

Cell	Name	Final Value	Shadow Price	Constraint R.H. Side	Allowable Increase	Allowable Decrease
$B$21	Cutting and dyeing LHS	14000	0	18000	1E+30	4000
$B$22	Sewing LHS	18000	0.333333333	18000	6000	3000
$B$23	Inspection and packaging LHS	3800	0	9000	1E+30	5200
$B$24	All-Pro Minimum LHS	1000	-2	1000	200	1000

23. Refer to the spreadsheet solution and sensitivity report for Problem 22 (see Figure 3.28).
   a. Overtime rates in the sewing department are $12 per hour. Would you recommend that the company consider using overtime in that department? Explain.
   b. What is the shadow price for the fourth constraint? Interpret its value for management.
   c. Note that the reduced cost for H, the High-School football, is zero, but H is not in the solution at a positive value. What is your interpretation?
   d. Suppose that the profit contribution of the College ball is increased by $1. How do you expect the solution to change?

Note: Problems 24–32 and the case problems require computer solution and interpretation of the results.

24. Better Products, Inc., manufactures three products on two machines. In a typical week, 40 hours are available on each machine. The profit contribution and production time in hours per unit are

Category	Product 1	Product 2	Product 3
Profit/unit	$30	$50	$20
Machine 1 hours/unit	0.5	2.0	0.75
Machine 2 hours/unit	1.0	1.0	0.5

Two operators are required for machine 1; thus, 2 hours of labor must be scheduled for each hour of machine 1 time. Only one operator is required for machine 2. A maximum of 100 labor hours is available for assignment to the machines during the coming week. Other production requirements are that product 1 cannot account for more than 50% of the units produced and that product 3 must account for at least 20% of the units produced.

a. How many units of each product should be produced to maximize the total profit contribution? What is the projected weekly profit contribution associated with your solution?

b. How many hours of production time will be scheduled on each machine?

c. What is the value of an additional hour of labor?

d. Assume that labor capacity can be increased to 120 hours. Would you be interested in using the additional 20 hours available for this resource? Develop the optimal product mix assuming that the extra hours are made available.

25. Vollmer Manufacturing makes three components for sale to refrigeration companies. The components are processed on two machines: a shaper and a grinder. The times (in minutes) required on each machine are shown below.

	Machine	
Component	Shaper	Grinder
1	6	4
2	4	5
3	4	2

The shaper is available for 120 hours, and the grinder is available for 110 hours. No more than 200 units of component 3 can be sold, but up to 1000 units of each of the other components can be sold. In fact, the company already has orders for 600 units of component 1 that must be satisfied. The profit contributions for components 1, 2, and 3 are $8, $6, and $9, respectively.

a. Formulate and solve for the recommended production quantities.

b. What are the ranges of optimality for the profit contributions of the three components? Interpret these ranges for company management.

c. What are the ranges of feasibility for the right-hand sides? Interpret these ranges for company management.

d. If more time could be made available on the grinder, how much would it be worth?

e. If more units of component 3 can be sold by reducing the sales price by $4, should the company reduce the price?

26. National Insurance Associates carries an investment portfolio of stocks, bonds, and other investment alternatives. Currently $200,000 of funds are available and must be considered for new investment opportunities. The four stock options National is considering and the relevant financial data are as follows:

	Stock			
Financial Data	A	B	C	D
Price per share	$100	$50	$80	$40
Annual rate of return	0.12	0.08	0.06	0.10
Risk measure per dollar invested	0.10	0.07	0.05	0.08

The risk measure indicates the relative uncertainty associated with the stock in terms of its realizing the projected annual return; higher values indicate greater risk. The risk measures are provided by the firm's top financial advisor.

National's top management has stipulated the following investment guidelines.

- The annual rate of return for the portfolio must be at least 9%.

- No one stock can account for more than 50% of the total dollar investment.
  a. Use linear programming to develop an investment portfolio that minimizes risk.
  b. If the firm ignores risk and uses a maximum return-on-investment strategy, what is the investment portfolio?
  c. What is the dollar difference between the portfolios in parts (a) and (b)? Why might the company prefer the solution developed in part (a)?

27. The management of Carson Stapler Manufacturing Company forecasts a 5000-unit demand for its Sure-Hold model during the next quarter. This stapler is assembled from three major components: base, staple cartridge, and handle. Until now Carson has manufactured all three components. However, the forecast of 5000 units is a new high in sales volume, and the firm may not have sufficient production capacity to make all the components. Management is considering contracting with a local firm to produce at least some of the components. The production time requirements per unit are as follows:

	Production Time (hours)			**Time Available**
Department	Base	Cartridge	Handle	**(hours)**
A	0.03	0.02	0.05	400
B	0.04	0.02	0.04	400
C	0.02	0.03	0.01	400

Note that each component manufactured by Carson uses manufacturing time in each of three departments.

After considering the firm's overhead, material, and labor costs, the accounting department has determined the unit manufacturing cost for each component. These data, along with the purchase price quotations by the contracting firm, are as follows:

Component	Manufacturing Cost	Purchase Cost
Base	$0.75	$0.95
Cartridge	$0.40	$0.55
Handle	$1.10	$1.40

a. Determine the make-or-buy decision for Carson that will meet the 5000-unit demand at a minimum total cost. How many units of each component should be made and how many purchased?

b. Which departments are limiting the manufacturing volume? If overtime could be considered at the additional cost of $3 per hour, which department(s) should be allocated the overtime? Explain.

c. Suppose that up to 80 hours of overtime could be scheduled in department A. What would you recommend?

28. Golf Shafts, Inc. (GSI), produces graphite shafts for several manufacturers of golf clubs. Two GSI manufacturing facilities, one located in San Diego and the other in Tampa, have the capability to produce shafts in varying degrees of stiffness, ranging from regular models used primarily by average golfers to extra stiff models used primarily by low-handicap and professional golfers. GSI has just received a contract for the production of 200,000 regular shafts and 75,000 stiff shafts. Since both plants are currently producing shafts for previous orders, neither plant has sufficient capacity by itself to fill the new order. The San Diego plant can produce up to a total of 120,000 shafts, and the Tampa plant can produce up to a total of 180,000 shafts. Because of equipment differences at each of the plants and differing labor costs, the per-unit production costs vary as shown here:

	San Diego Cost	Tampa Cost
Regular shaft	$5.25	$4.95
Stiff shaft	$5.45	$5.70

a. Formulate a linear programming model to determine how GSI should schedule production for the new order in order to minimize the total production cost.

b. Solve the model that you developed in part (a).

c. Suppose that some of the previous orders at the Tampa plant could be rescheduled in order to free up additional capacity for the new order. Would this change be worthwhile? Explain.

d. Suppose that the cost to produce a stiff shaft in Tampa had been incorrectly computed and that the correct cost is $5.30 per shaft. What effect, if any, would this cost have on the optimal solution developed in part (b)? What effect would this decrease have on total production cost?

29. The Pfeiffer Company manages approximately $15 million for clients. For each client, Pfeiffer chooses a mix of three types of investments: a growth stock fund, an income fund, and a money market fund. Each client has different investment objectives and different tolerances for risk. To accommodate these differences, Pfeiffer places limits on the percentage of each portfolio that may be invested in the three funds and assigns a portfolio risk index to each client.

Here's how the system works for Dennis Hartmann, one of Pfeiffer's clients. Based on an evaluation of Hartmann's risk tolerance, Pfeiffer has assigned Hartmann's portfolio a risk index of 0.05. Furthermore, to maintain diversity, the fraction of Hartmann's portfolio invested in the growth and income funds must be at least 10% in each, and at least 20% must be invested in the money market fund.

The risk ratings for the growth, income, and money market funds are 0.10, 0.05, and 0.01, respectively. A portfolio risk index is computed as a weighted average of the risk ratings for the three funds where the weights are the fraction of the portfolio invested in each fund. Hartmann has given Pfeiffer $300,000 to manage. Pfeiffer is currently forecasting a yield of 20% on the growth fund, 10% on the income fund, and 6% on the money market fund.

a. Develop a linear programming model to select the best mix of investments for Hartmann's portfolio.

b. Solve the model you developed in part (a).

c. How much may the yields on the three funds vary before Pfeiffer has to modify Hartmann's portfolio?

d. If Hartmann were more risk tolerant, how much of a yield increase could he expect? For instance, what if his portfolio risk index is increased to 0.06?

e. If Pfeiffer revised its yield estimate for the growth fund downward to 10%, how would you recommend modifying Hartmann's portfolio?

f. What information must Pfeiffer maintain on each client to use this system to manage client portfolios?

g. On a weekly basis Pfeiffer revises the yield estimates for the three funds. Suppose that Pfeiffer has 50 clients. Describe how Pfeiffer could make weekly modifications in each client's portfolio and allocate the total funds managed among the three investment funds.

30. La Jolla Beverage Products is considering producing a wine cooler that would be a blend of a white wine, a rosé wine, and fruit juice. To meet taste specifications, the wine cooler must consist of at least 50% white wine, at least 20% and no more than 30% rosé, and 20% fruit juice. La Jolla purchases the wine from local wineries and the fruit juice from a processing plant in San Francisco. For the current production period, 10,000 gallons of white wine and 8000 gallons of rosé wine can be purchased; the amount of fruit juice that can be ordered is unlimited. The costs for the wine are $1.00 per gallon for the white and $1.50 per gallon for the rosé; the fruit juice can be purchased for $0.50 per gallon. La Jolla Beverage Products can sell all the wine cooler it can produce for $2.50 per gallon.

a. Is the cost of the wine and fruit juice a sunk cost or a relevant cost in this situation? Explain.

b. Formulate a linear program to determine the blend of the three ingredients that will maximize the total profit contribution. Solve the linear program to determine the number of gallons of each ingredient La Jolla should purchase and the total profit contribution they will realize from this blend.

c. If La Jolla could obtain additional amounts of the white wine, should they do so? If so, how much should they be willing to pay for each additional gallon, and how many additional gallons would they want to purchase?

d. If La Jolla Beverage Products could obtain additional amounts of the rosé wine, should they do so? If so, how much should they be willing to pay for each additional gallon, and how many additional gallons would they want to purchase?

e. Interpret the shadow price for the constraint corresponding to the requirement that the wine cooler must contain at least 50% white wine. What is your advice to management given this shadow price?

f. Interpret the shadow price for the constraint corresponding to the requirement that the wine cooler must contain exactly 20% fruit juice. What is your advice to management given this shadow price?

31. The program manager for Channel 10 wants to determine the best way to allocate the time for the 11:00–11:30 evening news broadcast. Specifically, she would like to determine the number of minutes of broadcast time to devote to local news, national news, weather, and sports. Over the 30-minute broadcast, 10 minutes are set aside for advertising. The station's broadcast policy states that at least 15% of the time available should be devoted to local news coverage; the time devoted to local news or national news must be at least 50% of the total broadcast time; the time devoted to the weather segment must be less than or equal to the time devoted to the sports segment; the time devoted to the sports segment should be no longer than the total time spent on the local and national news; and at least 20% of the time should be devoted to the weather segment. The production costs per minute are $300 for local news, $200 for national news, $100 for weather, and $100 for sports.

a. Formulate and solve a linear program that can determine how the 20 available minutes should be used to minimize the total cost of producing the program.

b. Interpret the shadow price for the constraint corresponding to the available time. What advice would you give the station manager given this shadow price?

c. Interpret the shadow price for the constraint corresponding to the requirement that at least 15% of the available time should be devoted to local coverage. What advice would you give the station manager given this shadow price?

d. Interpret the shadow price for the constraint corresponding to the requirement that the time devoted to the local and the national news must be at least 50% of the total broadcast time. What advice would you give the station manager given this shadow price?

e. Interpret the shadow price for the constraint corresponding to the requirement that the time devoted to the weather segment must be less than or equal to the time devoted to the sports segment. What advice would you give the station manager given this shadow price?

32. Gulf Coast Electronics is ready to award contracts for printing its annual report. For the past several years, the four-color annual report has been printed by Johnson Printing and Lakeside Litho. A new firm, Benson Printing, has inquired into the possibility of doing a portion of the printing. The quality and service level provided by Lakeside Litho has been extremely high; in fact, only 0.5% of their reports have had to be discarded because of quality problems. Johnson Printing also has had a high quality level historically, producing an average of only 1% unacceptable reports. Since Gulf Coast Electronics has had no experience with Benson Printing, they have estimated its defective rate to be 10%. Gulf Coast would like to determine how many reports should be printed by each firm to obtain 75,000 reports of acceptable quality. To ensure that Benson Printing will receive some of the contract, management has specified that the number of reports awarded to Benson Printing must be at least 10% of the volume given to Johnson Printing. In addition, the total volume assigned to Benson Printing, Johnson Printing, and Lakeside Litho should not exceed 30,000, 50,000, and 50,000 copies, respectively. Because of the long-term relationship that has developed with Lakeside Litho, management also has specified that at least 30,000 reports should be awarded to Lakeside Litho. The cost per copy is $2.45 for Benson Printing, $2.50 for Johnson Printing, and $2.75 for Lakeside Litho.

a. Formulate and solve a linear program for determining how many copies should be assigned to each printing firm to minimize the total cost of obtaining 75,000 reports of acceptable quality.

b. Suppose that the quality level for Benson Printing is much better than estimated. What effect, if any, would this have?

c. Suppose that management is willing to reconsider its requirement that Lakeside Litho be awarded at least 30,000 reports. What effect, if any, would this have?

Case Problem   PRODUCT MIX

TJ's, Inc., makes three nut mixes for sale to grocery chains located in the Southeast. The three mixes, referred to as the Regular Mix, the Deluxe Mix, and the Holiday Mix, are made by mixing different percentages of five types of nuts.

In preparation for the fall season, TJ's has just purchased the following shipments of nuts (in pounds) at the prices shown.

Type of Nut	Shipment Amount	Cost per Shipment
Almond	6000	$7500
Brazil	7500	$7125
Filbert	7500	$6750
Pecan	6000	$7200
Walnut	7500	$7875

The Regular Mix consists of 15% almonds, 25% Brazil nuts, 25% filberts, 10% pecans, and 25% walnuts. The Deluxe Mix consists of 20% of each type of nut, and the Holiday Mix consists of 25% almonds, 15% Brazil nuts, 15% filberts, 25% pecans, and 20% walnuts.

TJ's accountant has analyzed the cost of packaging materials, sales price per pound, and other factors and has determined that the profit contribution per pound is $1.65 for the Regular Mix, $2.00 for the Deluxe Mix, and $2.25 for the Holiday Mix. These figures do not include the cost of specific types of nuts in the different mixes because that cost can vary greatly in the commodity markets.

Customer orders (in pounds) already received are summarized below:

Type of Mix	Orders
Regular	10,000
Deluxe	3,000
Holiday	5,000

Because demand is running high, TJ's expects to receive many more orders than it can satisfy.

TJ's is committed to using the available nuts to maximize total profit contribution over the fall season; nuts not used will be given to the Free Store. Even if it is not profitable to do so, TJ's president has indicated that the orders already received must be satisfied.

Managerial Report

Perform an analysis of TJ's product-mix problem, and prepare a report for TJ's president that summarizes your findings. Be sure to include information on and analysis of the following items.

1. The cost per pound of the nuts included in the Regular, Deluxe, and Holiday mixes.
2. The optimal product mix and the total profit contribution.
3. Recommendations regarding how the total profit contribution can be increased if additional quantities of nuts can be purchased.
4. A recommendation as to whether TJ's should purchase an additional 1000 pounds of almonds for $1000 from a supplier who overbought.
5. Recommendations on how profit contribution could be increased (if at all) if TJ's does not satisfy all existing orders.

..../ /.............

Case Problem   TRUCK LEASING STRATEGY

Reep Construction has recently won a contract for the excavation and site preparation of a new rest area on the Pennsylvania turnpike. In preparing his bid for the job, Bob Reep, founder and president of Reep Construction, estimated that it would take 4 months to perform the work and that 10, 12, 14, and 8 trucks would be needed in months 1 through 4, respectively.

The firm currently has 20 trucks of the type needed to perform the work on the new project. These trucks were obtained last year when Bob signed a long-term lease with PennState Leasing. Although most of these trucks are currently being used on existing jobs, Bob estimates that one truck will be available for use on the new project in month 1, two trucks will be available in month 2, three trucks will be available in month 3, and one truck will be available in month 4. Thus, to complete the project, Bob will have to lease additional trucks.

The long-term leasing contract with PennState has a monthly cost of $600 per truck. Reep Construction pays its truck drivers $20 an hour, and daily fuel costs are approximately $100 per truck. All maintenance costs are paid by PennState Leasing. For planning purposes, Bob estimates that each truck used on the new project will be operating 8 hours a day, 5 days a week for approximately 4 weeks each month.

Bob does not believe that current business conditions justify committing the firm to additional long-term leases. In discussing the short-term leasing possibilities with PennState Leasing, Bob has learned that he can obtain short-term leases of 1–4 months. Short-term leases differ from long-term leases in that the short-term leasing plans include the cost of both a truck and a driver. Maintenance costs for short-term leases also are paid by PennState Leasing. The following costs for each of the 4 months cover the lease of a truck and driver

Length of Lease	Cost per Month
1	$4000
2	$3700
3	$3225
4	$3040

Bob Reep would like to acquire a lease that would minimize the cost of meeting the monthly trucking requirements for his new project, but he also takes great pride in the fact that his company has never laid off employees. Bob is committed to maintaining his no-layoff policy; that is, he will use his own drivers even if costs are higher.

Managerial Report

Perform an analysis of Reep Construction's leasing problem and prepare a report for Bob Reep that summarizes your findings. Be sure to include information on and analysis of the following items

1. The optimal leasing plan.
2. The costs associated with the optimal leasing plan.
3. The cost for Reep Construction to maintain its current policy of no layoffs.

EASTMAN KODAK*

ROCHESTER, NEW YORK

In 1880 entrepreneur/inventor George Eastman formed the Eastman Dry Plate Company with a vision that it would become a worldwide manufacturer and marketer of photographic goods. Today, Eastman Kodak has manufacturing operations on four continents and customers in over 150 countries. Headquartered in Rochester, New York, Kodak's imaging products include amateur roll film, photographic paper, medical and industrial X-ray film, motion picture film, and graphic arts materials. In addition, Kodak is a manufacturer of imaging equipment and chemicals.

Management Science at Kodak

Management science applications at Kodak can be traced back to pioneering efforts in the 1950s. Since then, management science has been employed to solve a variety of problems involving most of the operational areas of the company. Today, the majority of the applications are conducted by the Management Services Division, while a small group called Distribution Operations Research focuses on applying management science to worldwide logistics issues.

Assigning Products to Worldwide Facilities

The sensitizing operation is the heart of the manufacturing process for photographic paper and film. In this operation, a light-sensitive emulsion is coated on a base to produce a sensitized master roll. The sensitized master rolls are then sent to a finishing operation where they are cut into proper dimensions. The sensitizing operation,

by virtue of its centrality to the overall process and the peculiarity of the manufacturing technologies required, receives a great deal of managerial attention, both at the operational and strategic levels.

One of Kodak's major planning issues involves the allocation of product to the various sensitizing facilities located throughout the world. The assignment of product to facilities is called the "world load." In determining the world load, Kodak is confronted with a number of interesting trade-offs. For instance, in terms of manufacturing costs, not all sensitizing facilities are equally efficient for all products. Some facilities tend to be more cost efficient over a broad range of products, but the margins by which they are better varies from product to product. However, many product–facility combinations are essentially impossible because of unique product specifications and machine capabilities. Nonetheless, there is a choice of facilities for practically every product.

The product-facility manufacturing costs are only part of the picture. The least expensive location to sensitize a particular product might, for example, be Australia. But, if most of the customers for that product are in Europe, then Australia becomes less favorable because of the high transportation costs involved. Transportation costs are therefore among the costs considered in determining the world load.

Another cost that must be considered involves the duties and duty drawbacks for the various countries throughout the world. Duty drawback is the "forgiving" of duty for a manufacturer who brings a semifinished product into a country, adds value to it, and then ships it out of that country. The effects of duty and duty drawback can significantly affect the allocation decision.

---

*The authors are indebted to Greg Sampson of Eastman Kodak for providing this application.

To assist in determining the world load, Kodak developed a linear programming model that accounts for the physical nature of the distribution problem and the various cost elements described above. More specifically, the program's objective is to minimize total cost (manufacturing, transportation, and duties) subject to "natural" constraints such as satisfying demand and capacity constraints for each facility.

Sensitivity Analysis and Interpretation

The linear programming model is a static representation of the problem situation, and the real world is always changing. Thus, Kodak cannot simply solve the linear program and implement the optimal solution; the static linear programming model must be used in a dynamic way. For instance, when demand expectations change, the model can be used to determine the effect the change will have on the world load. Or, suppose that country A and country B tear down duty barriers between them; what effect will this have on the world load? Suppose that the currency of country A rises compared to the currency of country B; how should the world load be modified? These examples show a few situations in which the world load must be reevaluated based on the impact of external stimuli.

In addition to using the linear programming model in a "how-to-react" mode, the model is useful in a more active mode by considering questions such as the following: Is it worthwhile for facility F to spend D dollars to lower the unit manufacturing cost of product P from X to Y? If such an investment is made, the effect may go well beyond the simple first-order impact at facility F. In fact, the change at facility F will likely result in a reshuffling of the world load. The linear programming model helps evaluate the overall effect of possible changes at any facility.

Managerial Use

The world-load model gives excellent directional advice and integrates the complex interaction of many factors. However, many aspects of the world-load problem do not fall neatly into the cost categories discussed previously. Although constructing a model that would account for almost every aspect of the real-world situation might be possible, the time and cost needed to develop it would be prohibitive. Kodak has chosen to use a simpler world-load model; sensitivity analysis is then used to explore many of the questions that management may want to address. In the final analysis, managers recognize that they cannot use the model by simply turning it on, reading the results, and executing the solution. The model's recommendations combined with managerial judgment provide the final decisions and actions for world-load allocation.

Questions

1. What are some of the trade-offs associated with allocating the products to the various sensitizing facilities?
2. What costs are included in the objective function of the world-load model?
3. Briefly describe the role of sensitivity analysis in this application.
4. The world-load model does not account for all the various issues involved in assigning products to sensitizing facilities. What reason did Kodak have for not addressing *all* the issues, and what implications does this have for management?

4

LINEAR PROGRAMMING APPLICATIONS

Linear programming has proven to be one of the most successful quantitative approaches to managerial decision making. Applications have been reported in almost every industry. Problems studied include production scheduling, media selection, financial planning, capital budgeting, transportation, distribution system design, product mix, staffing, blending, and many others. As the variety of applications suggests, linear programming is a flexible problem-solving tool. In this chapter we present a variety of applications including several from the traditional business areas of marketing, finance, and operations management. Modeling, computer solution, and interpretation of output are emphasized.

A mathematical model is developed for each problem studied. These models can be solved using a variety of computer packages including LINDO®, The Management Scientist®, and Excel's Solver. In the chapter we show how to set up and solve the problems using the Excel Spreadsheet Solver. We then interpret the solution in the context of the managerial problem.

Before starting, let us comment briefly on the spreadsheet formulations developed. One advantage of using spreadsheets is their flexibility. A linear program can be set up and solved in a spreadsheet in many different ways. Indeed, this flexibility sometimes makes setting up a spreadsheet model and identifying the key elements difficult for beginners. In the previous two chapters, we have attempted to establish a consistent approach to spreadsheet formulation by keeping the data for a problem separate from the linear programming model and by screening the key elements of the model. We continue with that approach here.

The data for the problem will be organized in the top portion of the spreadsheet; the model will be contained in the bottom portion. All data that may change in subsequent solutions of the same problem are thus kept separate from the model portion of the spreadsheet.

..../ /............

4.1   MARKETING APPLICATIONS

Applications of linear programming in marketing are numerous. In this section we discuss applications in media selection and marketing research.

Media Selection

In Section 2.1 we provided some general guidelines for modeling linear programming problems. You may want to review Section 2.1 before proceeding with the linear programming applications in this chapter.

Media selection applications of linear programming are designed to help marketing managers allocate a fixed advertising budget to various media. Potential media include newspapers, magazines, radio, television, and direct mail. In these applications, the objective is to maximize reach, frequency, and quality of exposure. Restrictions on the allowable allocation usually arise during consideration of company policy, contract requirements, and media availability. In the application that follows, we illustrate how a media selection problem might be formulated and solved using a linear programming model.

Relax-and-Enjoy Lake Development Corporation is developing a lakeside community. The primary market for the lakeside lots and homes includes all middle- and upper-income families within approximately 100 miles of the development. Relax-and-Enjoy has employed the advertising firm of Boone, Phillips and Jackson (BP&J) to design the promotional campaign.

After considering possible advertising media and the market to be covered, BP&J has recommended that the first month's advertising be restricted to five media. At the end of the month, BP&J will then reevaluate its strategy. BP&J has collected data on the number of potential customers reached, the cost per advertisement, the maximum number of times each is available, and the exposure quality rating for each of the five media. The quality rating is measured in terms of an exposure quality unit, a measure of the relative value of one advertisement in each of the media. This measure, based on BP&J's experience in the advertising business, takes into account factors such as audience demographics (age, income, and education of the audience reached), image presented, and quality of the advertisement. The information collected is presented in Table 4.1.

Table **4.1**	ADVERTISING MEDIA ALTERNATIVES FOR THE RELAX-AND-ENJOY LAKE DEVELOPMENT CORPORATION

Advertising Media	Number of Potential Customers Reached	Cost per Advertisement	Maximum Times Available per Month*	Exposure Quality Units
1. Daytime TV (1 min), station WKLA	1000	$1500	15	65
2. Evening TV (30 sec), station WKLA	2000	$3000	10	90
3. Daily newspaper (full page), *The Morning Journal*	1500	$ 400	25	40
4. Sunday newspaper magazine (½ page color), *The Sunday Press*	2500	$1000	4	60
5. Radio, 8:00 A.M. or 5:00 P.M. news (30 sec), station KNOP	300	$ 100	30	20

*The maximum number of times the medium is available is either the maximum number of times the advertising medium occurs (e.g., four Sundays per month) or the maximum number of times BP&J recommends that the medium be used.

Relax-and-Enjoy provided BP&J with an advertising budget of $30,000 for the first month's campaign. In addition, Relax-and-Enjoy imposed the following restrictions on how BP&J may allocate these funds: at least 10 television commercials must be used, at least 50,000 potential customers must be reached, and no more than $18,000 may be spent on television advertisements. What advertising media selection plan should be recommended?

The decision to be made is how many times to use each medium. We begin by defining the decision variables:

$$DTV = \text{number of times daytime TV is used}$$
$$ETV = \text{number of times evening TV is used}$$
$$DN = \text{number of times daily newspaper is used}$$
$$SN = \text{number of times Sunday newspaper is used}$$
$$R = \text{number of times radio is used}$$

The data on quality of exposure in Table 4.1 show that each daytime TV (DTV) advertisement is rated at 65 exposure quality units. Thus, an advertising plan with DTV advertisements will provide a total of $65DTV$ exposure quality units. Continuing with the data in Table 4.1, we find evening TV (ETV) rated at 90 exposure quality units, daily newspaper (DN) rated at 40 exposure quality units, Sunday newspaper (SN) rated at 60 exposure quality units, and radio (R) rated at 20 exposure quality units. With the objective of maximizing the total exposure quality units for the overall media selection plan, the objective function becomes

$$\text{Max} \quad 65DTV + 90ETV + 40DN + 60SN + 20R \qquad \text{Exposure quality}$$

We now formulate the constraints for the model from the information given:

Care must be taken to ensure the linear programming formulation accurately reflects the problem being analyzed. You should review your formulation thoroughly before attempting to solve the problem.

$$1000DTV + 2000ETV + 1500DN + 2500SN + 300R \geq 50{,}000 \quad \text{Customers reached}$$

$$\left.\begin{array}{rcl} DTV + \quad ETV & \geq & 10 \\ 1500DTV + 3000ETV & \leq & 18{,}000 \end{array}\right\} \begin{array}{l} \text{Television} \\ \text{restrictions} \end{array}$$

$$1500DTV + 3000ETV + \quad 400DN + 1000SN + 100R \leq 30{,}000 \qquad \text{Budget}$$

$$\left.\begin{array}{rcl} DTV & \leq & 15 \\ ETV & \leq & 10 \\ DN & \leq & 25 \\ SN & \leq & 4 \\ R \leq & & 30 \end{array}\right\} \begin{array}{l} \text{Availability} \\ \text{of media} \end{array}$$

$$DTV, ETV, DN, SN, R \geq 0$$

The spreadsheet formulation and solution of the Relax-and-Enjoy problem is shown in Figure 4.1. We first describe the key elements of the spreadsheet formulation and solution, then interpret the results.

Spreadsheet Formulation.   The data and descriptive labels are in cells A1:I8. The screened cells in the spreadsheet contain the information required by the Excel Solver.

Figure 4.1 — SPREADSHEET SOLUTION FOR THE RELAX-AND-ENJOY LAKE DEVELOPMENT CORPORATION PROBLEM

**SPREADSHEET
RELAX-AND-ENJOY**

	A	B	C	D	E	F	G	H	I
1	Relax-and-Enjoy Lake Development Corporation								
2									
3				Media					
4		DTV	ETV	DN	SN	R			
5	Cust Rch	1000	2000	1500	2500	300		Min Cust Rch	50000
6	Cost/Ad	1500	3000	400	1000	100		Min TV Ads.	10
7	Availability	15	10	25	4	30		Max TV. Budget	18000
8	Exp./Ad	65	90	40	60	20		Budget	30000
9									
10	Model								
11									
12		DTV	ETV	DN	SN	R			
13	Ads Placed	10	0	25	2	30			
14									
15	Max Exposure	2370							
16									
17	Constraints	LHS		RHS					
18	Reach	61500	>=	50000					
19	Num TV Ads	10	>=	10					
20	TV Budget	15000	<=	18000					
21	Budget	30000	<=	30000					

Decision Variables   Cells B13:F13 are reserved for the decision variables. The optimal values are shown to be DTV = 10, ETV = 0, DN = 25, SN = 2, and R = 30.

Objective Function   The formula =SUMPRODUCT(B8:F8,B13:F13) has been placed into cell B15 to relect the exposure quality units obtained with the solution shown. The optimal solution provides 2370 exposure quality units.

Left-Hand Sides   The left-hand sides for the first 4 constraints are placed into cells B18:B21.
   Cell B18 =SUMPRODUCT(B5:F5,B13:F13)
   Cell B19 =B13+C13
   Cell B20 =SUMPRODUCT(B6:C6,B13:C13)
   Cell B21 =SUMPRODUCT(B6:F6,B13:F13)

Right-Hand Sides   The right-hand sides for the first 4 constraints are placed into cells D18:D21.
   Cell D18 =I5   (Copy to D19:D21)

Note that the last 5 constraints in the mathematical model define the upper bounds on the decision variables. We will specify these constraints directly in the **solver** dialog box. Cells B7:F7, in the data section, have been screened to indicate that they contain the right-hand sides of these upper bound constraints.

Spreadsheet Solution.   The solution can be obtained by selecting **Solver** from the **Tools** menu, entering the proper values into the **Solver Parameters** dialog box, and specifying the options **Assume Linear Model** and **Assume Non-Negative.** The information entered

Problem I provides practice at formulating a similar media selection model.

into the **Solver Parameters** dialog box is shown in Figure 4.2. After solving, we requested the sensitivity report shown in Figure 4.3.

Discussion.   The optimal solution calls for advertisements to be distributed among daytime TV, daily newspaper, Sunday newspaper, and radio. The maximum number of exposure quality units is 2,370, and the total number of customers reached is 61,500. The

---

Figure 4.2   SOLVER PARAMETERS DIALOG BOX FOR THE RELAX-AND-ENJOY LAKE DEVELOPMENT CORPORATION PROBLEM

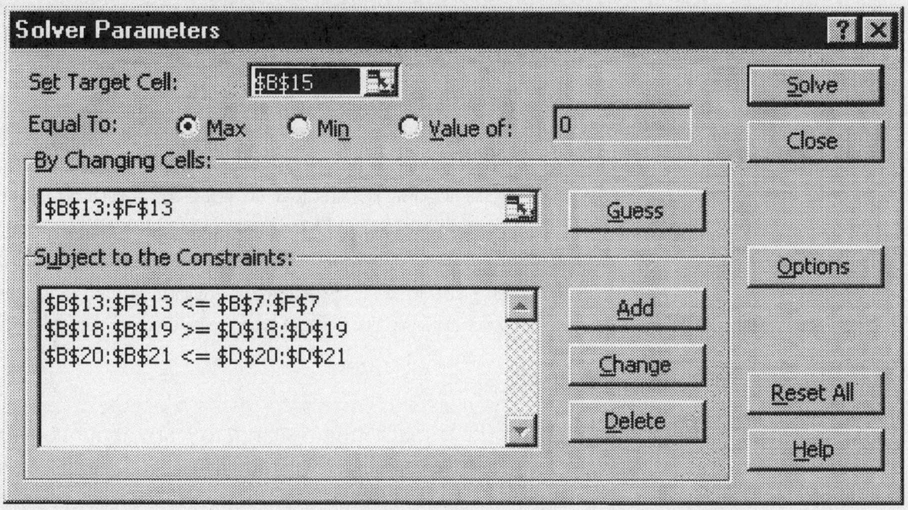

Figure 4.3   SENSITIVITY REPORT FOR THE RELAX-AND-ENJOY LAKE DEVELOPMENT CORPORATION PROBLEM

Adjustable Cells

Cell	Name	Final Value	Reduced Cost	Objective Coefficient	Allowable Increase	Allowable Decrease
$B$13	Ads Placed DTV	10	0	65	25	65
$C$13	Ads Placed ETV	0	-65	90	65	1.00E+30
$D$13	Ads Placed DN	25	16	40	1.00E+30	16
$E$13	Ads Placed SN	2	0	60	40	16.6666667
$F$13	Ads Placed R	30	14	20	1.00E+30	14

Constraints

Cell	Name	Final Value	Shadow Price	Constraint R.H. Side	Allowable Increase	Allowable Decrease
$B$18	Reach LHS	61500	0	50000	11500	1.00E+30
$B$19	Num TV Ads LHS	10	-25	10	1.33333333	1.33333333
$B$20	TV Budget LHS	15000	0	18000	1.00E+30	3000
$B$21	Budget LHS	30000	0.06	30000	2000	2000

More complex media selection models may include considerations such as reduced exposure quality value for repeat media usage, cost discounts for repeat media usage, audience overlap by different media, and/or timing recommendations for the advertisements.

Reduced Cost column in the upper portion of Figure 4.3 indicates that the number of exposure quality units for evening TV would have to increase by at least 65 before this media alternative could appear in the optimal solution. Note that the budget constraint (see the Constraints section of Figure 4.3) has a shadow price of 0.06 exposure quality units. The shadow price of -25 for constraint 2 indicates that reducing the number of television commercials will increase the exposure quality of the advertising plan. Thus, Relax-and-Enjoy should consider reducing the requirement of having at least 10 television commercials.

A possible shortcoming of this model is that, even if the exposure quality measure were not subject to error, there is no guarantee that maximization of total exposure quality will lead to a maximization of profit or of sales (a common surrogate for profit). However, this shortcoming is not a shortcoming of linear programming; rather, it is a shortcoming of the use of exposure quality as a criterion. If we were able to measure directly the effect of an advertisement on profit, we could use total profit as the objective to be maximized.

NOTES and Comments

1. The media selection model required subjective evaluations of the exposure quality for the media alternatives. Marketing managers may have substantial data concerning exposure quality, but the final coefficients used in the objective function may also include considerations based primarily on managerial judgment. Judgment is an acceptable way of obtaining input for a linear programming model.

2. The media selection model presented in this section uses exposure quality as the objective function and places a constraint on the number of customers reached. An alternative formulation of this problem would be to use the number of customers reached as the objective function and add a constraint indicating the minimum total exposure quality required for the media plan.

Marketing Research

An organization conducts marketing research to learn about consumer characteristics, attitudes, and preferences. Marketing research firms that specialize in providing such information often do the actual research for client organizations. Typical services offered by a marketing research firm include designing the study, conducting market surveys, analyzing the data collected, and providing summary reports and recommendations for the client. In the research design phase, targets or quotas may be established for the number and types of respondents to be surveyed. The marketing research firm's objective is to conduct the survey so as to meet the client's needs at a minimum cost.

Market Survey, Inc. (MSI), specializes in evaluating consumer reaction to new products, services, and advertising campaigns. A client firm has requested MSI's assistance in assessing consumer reaction to a recently marketed household product. During meetings with the client, MSI agreed to conduct door-to-door personal interviews to obtain responses from households with children and households without children. In addition, MSI agreed to conduct both day and evening interviews. Specifically, the client's contract called for MSI to conduct 1000 interviews under the following quota guidelines.

1. At least 400 households with children would be interviewed.
2. At least 400 households without children would be interviewed.
3. The total number of households interviewed during the evening would be at least as great as the number of households interviewed during the day.
4. At least 40% of the interviews for households with children would be conducted during the evening.
5. At least 60% of the interviews for households without children would be conducted during the evening.

Because the interviews for households with children take additional interviewer time and because evening interviewers are paid more than daytime interviewers, the cost varies with the type of interview. Based on previous research studies, estimates of the interview costs are as follows:

	Interview Cost	
Household	**Day**	**Evening**
Children	$20	$25
No children	$18	$20

What is the household, time-of-day interview plan that will satisfy the contract requirements at a minimum total interviewing cost?

In formulating the linear programming model for the MSI problem, we use the following decision-variable notation:

$$DC = \text{the number of daytime interviews of households with children}$$
$$EC = \text{the number of evening interviews of households with children}$$
$$DNC = \text{the number of daytime interviews of households without children}$$
$$ENC = \text{the number of evening interviews of households without children}$$

We begin the linear programming model formulation by using the cost-per-interview data to develop the objective function:

$$\text{Min} \quad 20DC + 25EC + 18DNC + 20ENC$$

The constraint requiring a total of 1000 interviews is

$$DC + EC + DNC + ENC = 1000$$

The five specifications concerning the types of interviews are as follows.

- Households with children:

$$DC + EC \geq 400$$

- Households without children:

$$DNC + ENC \geq 400$$

- At least as many evening interviews as day interviews:

$$EC + ENC \geq DC + DNC$$

- At least 40% of interviews for households with children during the evening:

$$EC \geq 0.4(DC + EC)$$

- At least 60% of interviews for households without children during the evening:

$$ENC \geq 0.6(DNC + ENC)$$

When we add the nonnegativity requirements, the four-variable and six-constraint linear programming model becomes[1]

Min $\quad 20DC + 25EC + 18DNC + 20ENC$
s.t.

$DC +$	$EC +$	$DNC +$	$ENC = 1000$		Total interviews
$DC +$	EC		≥ 400		Households with children
		$DNC +$	$ENC \geq 400$		Households without children
	$EC +$	$ENC \geq DC + DNC$			Evening interviews
	EC		$\geq .4(DC + EC)$		Evening households with children
		$ENC \geq .6(DNC + ENC)$			Evening households without children

$$DC, EC, DNC, ENC \geq 0$$

The spreadsheet formulation and solution of the Market Survey problem is shown in Figure 4.4. We describe the key elements of the spreadsheet formulation and solution, then interpret the results.

Spreadsheet Formulation.   The data and descriptive labels are in cells A1:I8. The screened cells contain the information required by the Excel Solver.

Decision Variables   Cells B14:C15 are reserved for the decision variables. The optimal values are shown to be $DC = 240$, $EC = 160$, $DNC = 240$, and $ENC = 360$.

Objective Function   The formula =SUMPRODUCT(B5:C6,B14:C15) has been placed into cell G13 to reflect the cost of the interview plan shown. The optimal solution has a cost of $20,320.

Left-Hand Sides   The left-hand sides for the 6 constraints are placed into cells H16:H21.
   Cell H16 =D16
   Cell H17 =D14
   Cell H18 =D15
   Cell H19 =C16
   Cell H20 =C14
   Cell H21 =C15

---

1. The traditional format for linear programming model formulation and computer input places all decision variables on the left-hand side of the constraints and a constant (possibly zero) on the right-hand side. Doing so here would require algebraic manipulation of the last three constraints. Such manipulation makes the constraints less intuitively understandable and is not required by the Excel Spreadsheet Solver.

Figure 4.4   SPREADSHEET SOLUTION FOR THE MARKET SURVEY PROBLEM

	A	B	C	D	E	F	G	H	I	J
1	**MSI Market Survey**									
2										
3		**Interview Cost ($)**								
4	**Household**	Day	Evening			**Total Interviews Required**			1000	
5	Children	20	25			**Minimum with Children**			400	
6	No Children	18	20			**Minimum without Children**			400	
7						**Min Eve. with Children**			40%	
8						**Min Eve. without Children**			60%	
9										
10	**Model**									
11										
12		**Number of Interviews**								
13	**Household**	Day	Evening	**Total**		**Min Cost**	20320			
14	Children	240	160	400						
15	No Children	240	360	600		**Constraints**		**LHS**		**RHS**
16	**Total**	480	520	1000		Total Int.		1000	=	1000
17						Children		400	>=	400
18						No Children		600	>=	400
19						Eve. Interviews		520	>=	480
20						Eve. Children		160	>=	160
21						Eve. No Children		360	>=	360

For this problem, some of the left-hand-side cells in column H reference other cells that contain formulas. These referenced cells and their formulas are as follows:

Cell D16 =SUM(D14:D15)
Cell D14 =SUM(B14:C14)
Cell D15 =SUM(B15:C15)
Cell C16 =SUM(C14:C15)

Right-Hand Sides   The right-hand sides for the 6 constraints are placed into cells J16:J21.
Cell J16 =I4   (Copy to J17:J18)
Cell J19 =B16
Cell J20 =I7*D14
Cell J21 =I8*D15

Spreadsheet Solution.   The solution can be obtained by selecting **Solver** from the **Tools** menu, entering the proper values into the **Solver Parameters** dialog box, and specifying the options **Assume Linear Model** and **Assume Non-Negative.** The information entered into the **Solver Parameters** dialog box is shown in Figure 4.5. After solving, we requested the sensitivity report shown in Figure 4.6.

Discussion.   The optimal interview schedule, as shown in Figure 4.4, calls for 480 daytime interviews and 520 evening interviews. The daytime interviews are evenly split (240 each) between households with children and households without children. The evening interviews include 160 households with children and 360 households without children.

Selected sensitivity analysis information from Figure 4.6 shows a shadow price of 19.2 for the total interviews constraint. This price means that the objective function will go up

Figure 4.5   SOLVER PARAMETERS DIALOG BOX FOR THE MARKET SURVEY PROBLEM

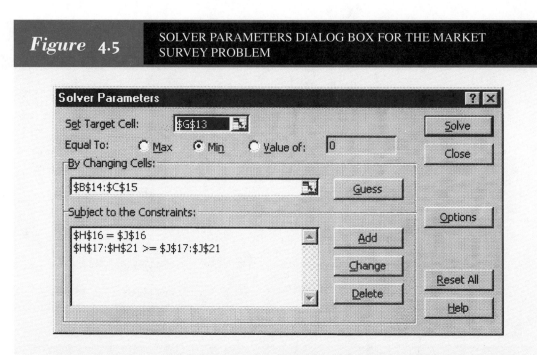

Figure 4.6   SENSITIVITY REPORT FOR THE MARKET SURVEY PROBLEM

Adjustable Cells

Cell	Name	Final Value	Reduced Cost	Objective Coefficient	Allowable Increase	Allowable Decrease
$B$14	Children Day	240	0	20	5	4.66666667
$C$14	Children Evening	160	0	25	1.00E+30	5
$B$15	No Children Day	240	0	18	2	1.00E+30
$C$15	No Children Evening	360	0	20	4.66666667	2

Constraints

Cell	Name	Final Value	Shadow Price	Constraint R.H. Side	Allowable Increase	Allowable Decrease
$H$16	Total Int. LHS	1000	19.2	1000	1.00E+30	200
$H$17	Children LHS	400	2.8	0	100	400
$H$18	No Children LHS	600	0	0	200	1.00E+30
$H$19	Eve. Interviews LHS	520	0	0	40	1.00E+30
$H$20	Eve. Children LHS	160	5	0	240	20
$H$21	Eve. No Children LHS	360	2	0	240	20

by 19.20 (a cost increase) if the number of required interviews is increased from 1000 to 1001. Thus, $19.20 is the marginal cost of obtaining additional interviews. It also is the savings that could be realized by reducing the number of interviews from 1000 to 999.

The "No Children" constraint (see row 18 of Figure 4.4) shows that 200 more households without children will be interviewed than required. Similarly, the "Eve. Interviews" constraint (see row 19 of Figure 4.4) shows that the number of evening interviews exceeds the number of daytime interviews by 40. The fact that the last 2 constraints are satisfied as equalities (see rows 20 and 21 of Figure 4.4) shows that the more expensive evening interviews are being held at a minimum. Indeed, the shadow price of 5 for the 5th constraint (see Figure 4.6) indicates that if one more household with children than the minimum requirement must be interviewed during the evening, the total interviewing cost will go up by $5.00. Similarly, the shadow price for the 6th constraint shows that requiring one more household without children to be interviewed during the evening will increase costs by $2.00.

4.2   FINANCIAL APPLICATIONS

Financial applications of linear programming include capital budgeting, make-or-buy decisions, asset allocation, portfolio selection, financial planning, and many more. In this section, we describe a portfolio selection problem and a problem involving funding of an early retirement program.

Portfolio Selection

Portfolio selection problems involve situations in which a financial manager must select specific investments—for example, stocks and bonds—from a variety of investment alternatives. Managers of mutual funds, credit unions, insurance companies, and banks frequently encounter this type of problem. The objective function for portfolio selection problems usually is maximization of expected return or minimization of risk. The constraints usually take the form of restrictions on the type of permissible investments, state laws, company policy, maximum permissible risk, and so on. Problems of this type have been formulated and solved using a variety of mathematical programming techniques. In this section we show how to formulate and solve a portfolio selection problem as a linear program.

Consider the case of Welte Mutual Funds, Inc., located in New York City. Welte has just obtained $100,000 by converting industrial bonds to cash and is now looking for other investment opportunities for these funds. Based on Welte's current investments, the firm's top financial analyst recommends that all new investments be made in the oil industry, steel industry, or in government bonds. Specifically, the analyst has identified five investment opportunities and projected their annual rates of return. The investments and rates of return are shown in Table 4.2.

Table 4.2	INVESTMENT OPPORTUNITIES FOR WELTE MUTUAL FUNDS

Investment	Projected Rate of Return (%)
Atlantic Oil	7.3
Pacific Oil	10.3
Midwest Steel	6.4
Huber Steel	7.5
Government bonds	4.5

Management of Welte has imposed the following investment guidelines.

1. Neither industry (oil or steel) should receive more than $50,000.
2. The investment in Pacific Oil, the high-return but high-risk investment, cannot be more than 60% of the total oil industry investment.
3. Government bonds should be at least 25% of the steel industry investments.

What portfolio recommendations—investments and amounts—should be made for the available $100,000? Given the objective of maximizing projected return subject to the budgetary and managerially imposed constraints, we answer this question by formulating a linear programming model of the problem. The solution will provide investment recommendations for the management of Welte Mutual Funds.

Let

$$A = \text{dollars invested in Atlantic Oil}$$
$$P = \text{dollars invested in Pacific Oil}$$
$$M = \text{dollars invested in Midwest Steel}$$
$$H = \text{dollars invested in Huber Steel}$$
$$G = \text{dollars invested in government bonds}$$

Using the projected rates of return shown in Table 4.2, we write the objective function for maximizing the total return for the portfolio as

$$\text{Max} \quad 0.073A + 0.103P + 0.064M + 0.075H + 0.045G$$

The constraint specifying investment of the available $100,000 is

$$A + P + M + H + G = 100{,}000$$

The requirements that neither the oil nor the steel industry should receive more than $50,000 are

$$A + P \le 50{,}000$$
$$M + H \le 50{,}000$$

The constraint that Pacific Oil cannot be more than 60% of the total oil industry investment is

$$P \le 0.60(A + P)$$

Finally, the requirement that government bonds be at least 25% of the steel industry investment is expressed as

$$G \ge 0.25(M + H)$$

By adding the nonnegativity restrictions, we obtain the complete linear programming model for the Welte Mutual Fund investment problem:

Max $0.073A + 0.103P + 0.064M + 0.075H + 0.045G$

s.t.

$$
\begin{array}{lllllll}
A + & P + & M + & H + & G & = 100{,}000 & \text{Available funds} \\
A + & P & & & & \leq 50{,}000 & \text{Oil industry maximum} \\
& & M + & H & & \leq 50{,}000 & \text{Steel industry maximum} \\
& P & & & & \leq 0.60\,(A + P) & \text{Pacific Oil restriction} \\
& & & & G & \geq 0.25(M + H) & \text{Government bond minimum}
\end{array}
$$

$A, P, M, H, G \geq 0$

The spreadsheet formulation and solution of the Welte Mutual Funds problem are shown in Figure 4.7.

Spreadsheet Formulation.   The data and descriptive labels are contained in cells A1:F9. As usual, the screened cells in the figure contain the key elements of the linear programming model. They contain the information needed by the Excel Solver.

Figure 4.7   SPREADSHEET SOLUTION FOR THE WELTE MUTUAL FUNDS PROBLEM

SPREADSHEET
WELTE

	A	B	C	D	E	F	G
1	**Welte Mutual Funds Problem**						
2							
3							
4	**Investment**	**Projected Rate of Return**					
5	Atlantic Oil	0.073		**Available Funds**		100000	
6	Pacific Oil	0.103		**Oil Max**		50000	
7	Midwest Steel	0.064		**Steel Max**		50000	
8	Huber Steel	0.075		**Pacific Oil Max**		0.6	
9	Gov't Bonds	0.045		**Gov't Bonds Min**		0.25	
10							
11	**Model**						
12							
13	**Investment**	**Amount Invested**		**Constraints**	**LHS**		**RHS**
14	Atlantic Oil	20000		Avl. Funds	100000	=	100000
15	Pacific Oil	30000		Oil Max	50000	<=	50000
16	Midwest Steel	0		Steel Max	40000	<=	50000
17	Huber Steel	40000		Pacific Oil	30000	<=	30000
18	Gov't Bonds	10000		Gov't Bonds	10000	>=	10000
19							
20	**Max Total Return**	8000					

Decision Variables Cells B14:B18 are reserved for the decision variables. The optimal values are shown to be $A = 20000$, $P = 30000$, $M = 0$, $H = 40000$, and $G = 10000$.

Objective Function The formula =SUMPRODUCT(B5:B9,B14:B18) has been placed into cell B20 to reflect the total earnings on the portfolio shown. The optimal solution provides annual earnings of $8000.

Left-Hand Sides The left-hand sides for the 5 constraints are placed into cells E14:E18.
　　　　　　　Cell E14 =SUM(B14:B18)
　　　　　　　Cell E15 =SUM(B14:B15)
　　　　　　　Cell E16 =SUM(B16:B17)
　　　　　　　Cell E17 =B15
　　　　　　　Cell E18 =B18

Right-Hand Sides The right-hand sides for the 5 constraints are placed into cells G14:G18.
　　　　　　　Cell G14 =F5　　　(Copy to G15:G16)
　　　　　　　Cell G17 =F8*(B14+B15)
　　　　　　　Cell G18 =F9*(B16+B17)

Spreadsheet Solution.　The solution can be obtained by selecting **Solver** from the **Tools** menu, entering the proper values in the **Solver Parameters** dialog box and specifying the options **Assume Linear Model** and **Assume Non-Negative.** The information entered into the **Solver Parameters** dialog box is shown in Figure 4.8. After solving, we requested the sensitivity report shown in Figure 4.9.

Discussion.　As shown in Figure 4.7, the optimal solution indicates that the portfolio should be diversified among all investment opportunities except Midwest Steel. The projected annual return for this portfolio is $8000, which is an overall return of 8%.

Figure 4.8　SOLVER PARAMETERS DIALOG BOX FOR THE WELTE MUTUAL FUNDS PROBLEM

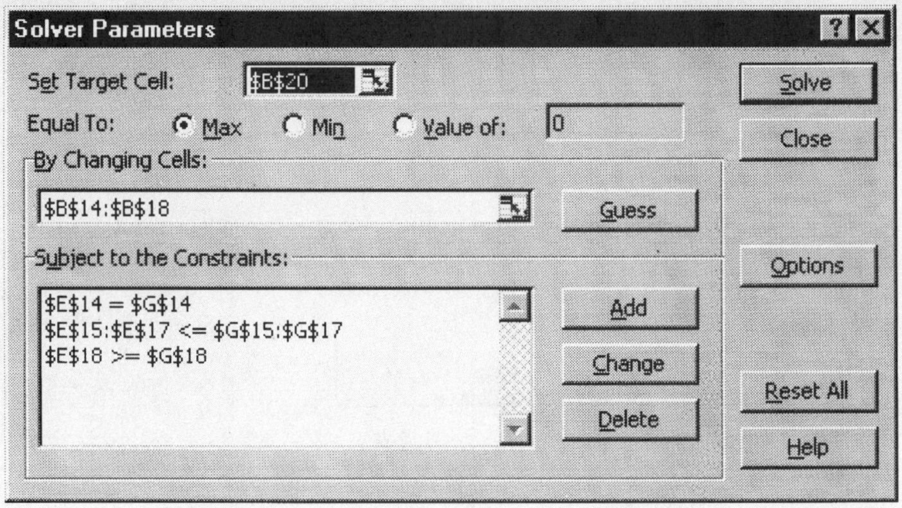

Figure 4.9	SENSITIVITY REPORT FOR THE WELTE MUTUAL FUNDS PROBLEM

Adjustable Cells

Cell	Name	Final Value	Reduced Cost	Objective Coefficient	Allowable Increase	Allowable Decrease
$B$14	Atlantic Oil Amount Invested	20000	0	0.073	0.03	0.055
$B$15	Pacific Oil Amount Invested	30000	0	0.103	1.00E+30	0.03
$B$16	Midwest Steel Amount Invested	0	-0.011	0.064	0.011	1.00E+30
$B$17	Huber Steel Amount Invested	40000	0	0.075	0.0275	0.011
$B$18	Gov't Bonds Amount Invested	10000	0	0.045	0.03	1.00E+30

Constraints

Cell	Name	Final Value	Shadow Price	Constraint R.H. Side	Allowable Increase	Allowable Decrease
$E$14	Avl. Funds LHS	100000	0.069	100000	12500	50000
$E$15	Oil Max LHS	50000	0.022	0	50000	12500
$E$16	Steel Max LHS	40000	0	0	1.00E+30	10000
$E$17	Pacific Oil LHS	30000	0.03	0	20000	30000
$E$18	Gov't Bonds LHS	10000	-0.024	0	50000	12500

The sensitivity report (see Constraints section of Figure 4.9) shows a shadow price of zero for the steel industry maximum. The reason is that the steel industry maximum isn't a binding constraint; increases in the steel industry limit of $50,000 will not improve the value of the objective function. Indeed, the left-hand side for this constraint (see Figure 4.7) shows that the current steel industry investment is only $40,000. The shadow prices for the other constraints are nonzero, indicating that these constraints are binding.

The shadow price for the available funds constraint provides information on the rate of return from additional investment funds.

The shadow price of 0.069 for the available funds constraint shows that the objective function can be increased by 0.069 if one more dollar can be made available for investment. If more funds can be obtained at a cost of less than 6.9%, management should consider obtaining them. However, if a return in excess of 6.9% can be obtained by investing funds elsewhere (other than in these five securities), management should question the wisdom of investing the entire $100,000 in this portfolio.

Similar interpretations can be given to the other shadow prices. Note that the shadow price for the government bond minimum is −0.024. This means that requiring one more dollar to be invested in government bonds can be expected to lower the objective function value by $0.024. To see why, note from the shadow price for the available funds constraint that the marginal return on the portfolio is 6.9% (the average return is 8%). The rate of return on government bonds is 4.5%. Thus, the cost of investing one more dollar in government bonds is the difference between the marginal return on the portfolio and the marginal return on government bonds: 6.9% − 4.5% = 2.4%.

Note that the optimal solution shows that Midwest Steel should not be included in the portfolio. The associated reduced cost of −0.011 (see the Adjustable Cells section in Figure 4.9) tells us that the objective function coefficient for Midwest Steel would have to increase by 0.011 before considering the Midwest Steel investment alternative would be advisable. With such an increase the Midwest Steel return would be 0.064 + 0.011 = 0.075, making this investment just as desirable as the currently used Huber Steel investment alternative.

Practice formulating a variation of the Welte problem by working Problem 9.

Finally, a simple modification of the Welte linear programming model permits determining the fraction of available funds invested in each security. That is, divide the right-hand sides of the first 3 constraints by 100,000. Then the optimal values for the variables will give the fraction of funds that should be invested in each security for a portfolio of any size.

N O T E S and Comments

1. The optimal solution to the Welte Mutual Funds problem indicates that $20,000 is to be spent on the Atlantic Oil stock. If Atlantic Oil sells for $75 per share, we would have to purchase exactly $266^2/_3$ shares in order to spend exactly $20,000. The difficulty of purchasing fractional shares is usually handled by purchasing the largest possible integer number of shares with the allotted funds (e.g., 266 shares of Atlantic Oil). This approach guarantees that the budget constraint will not be violated. This approach, of course, introduces the possibility that the solution will no longer be optimal, but the danger is slight if a large number of securities are involved. In cases where the analyst believes that the decision variables *must* have integer values, the problem must be formulated as an integer linear programming model. Integer linear programming is the topic of Chapter 6.

2. Financial portfolio theory stresses obtaining a proper balance between risk and return. In the Welte problem, we explicitly considered return in the objective function. Risk is controlled by choosing constraints that ensure diversity among oil and steel stocks and a balance between government bonds and the steel industry investment.

MANAGEMENT SCIENCE IN ACTION

USING LINEAR PROGRAMMING FOR OPTIMAL LEASE STRUCTURING*

GE Capital is a $70-billion subsidiary of General Electric. As one of the nation's largest and most diverse financial services companies, GE Capital arranges leases in both domestic and international markets, including leases for telecommunications, data processing, construction, and fleets of cars, trucks, and commercial aircraft. To help allocate and schedule the rental and debt payments of a leveraged lease, GE Capital analysts have developed an optimization model, which is available as an optional component of the company's lease analysis proprietary software.

Leveraged leases are designed to provide financing for assets with economic lives of at least five years, which require large capital outlays. A leveraged lease represents an agreement among the lessor (the owner of the asset), the lessee (the user of the asset), and the lender who provides a nonrecourse loan of 50% to 80% of the lessor's purchase price. In a nonrecourse loan, the lenders cannot turn to the lessor for repayment in the event of default. As the lessor in such arrangements, GE Capital is able to claim ownership and realize income tax benefits, such as depreciation and interest deductions. These deductions usually produce tax losses during the early years of the lease, which reduces the total tax liability. Approximately 85% of all financial leases in the United States are leveraged leases.

In its simplest form, the leveraged lease structuring problem can be formulated as a linear program. The linear program models the after-tax cash flow for the lessor, taking into consideration rental receipts, borrowing and repaying of the loan, and income taxes. Constraints are formulated to ensure compliance with IRS guidelines and to enable customizing of leases to meet lessee and lessor requirements. The objective function can be entered in a custom fashion or selected from a predefined list. Typically, the objective is to minimize the lessee's cost, expressed as the net present value of rental payments, or to maximize the lessor's after-tax yield.

GE Capital developed an optimization approach that could be applied to single-investor lease structuring. In a study with the department most involved with these transactions, the optimization approach yielded substantial benefits. The approach has been used on a limited basis and has helped GE Capital win some single-investor transactions ranging in size from $1 million to $20 million.

*Based on C.J. Litty, "Optimal Lease Structuring at GE Capital," *Interfaces* (May–June 1994): 34–45.

Financial Planning

Linear programming has been used for a variety of financial planning applications. The Management Science in Action: Using Linear Programming for Optimal Lease Structuring describes how GE Capital used linear programming to optimize the structure of a leveraged lease.

Hewlitt Corporation has established an early retirement program as part of its corporate restructuring. At the close of the voluntary sign-up period, 68 employees had elected early retirement. As a result of these early retirements, the company has incurred the following obligations over the next 8 years. Cash requirements (in thousands of dollars) are due at the beginning of each year.

Year	1	2	3	4	5	6	7	8
Cash Requirement	430	210	222	231	240	195	225	255

The corporate treasurer must determine how much money has to be set aside today to meet the 8-year financial obligations as they come due. The financing plan for the retirement program includes investments in government bonds as well as savings. The investments in government bonds are limited to three choices:

Bond	Price	Rate	Years to Maturity
1	$1150	8.875	5
2	1000	5.500	6
3	1350	11.750	7

The government bonds have a par value of $1000, which means that even with different purchase prices each bond pays $1000 at maturity. The rates shown are based on the par value. For purposes of planning, the treasurer has assumed that any funds not invested in bonds will be placed into savings and earn interest at an annual rate of 4%.

We define the decision variables as follows:

F = total dollars required to meet the retirement plan's 8-year obligation

B_1 = units of bond 1 purchased (par value $1000)

B_2 = units of bond 2 purchased (par value $1000)

B_3 = units of bond 3 purchased (par value $1000)

S_i = investment in savings at the beginning of the year i for $i = 1, \ldots, 8$

The objective function is to minimize the total dollars that must be set aside now to meet the retirement plan's 8-year obligation, or

$$\text{Min} \quad F$$

A key feature of this type of financial planning problem is that there is a constraint for each year of the planning horizon. In general, each constraint takes the form:

$$\begin{pmatrix} \text{Funds avaliable at} \\ \text{the beginning of the year} \end{pmatrix} - \begin{pmatrix} \text{Funds invested in bonds} \\ \text{and saved} \end{pmatrix} = \begin{pmatrix} \text{Cash obligation for} \\ \text{the current year} \end{pmatrix}$$

We defined F to be the funds available at the beginning of year 1. With a current price of $1150 for bond 1 and investments expressed in thousands of dollars, the total investment for B_1 units of bond 1 would be $1.15B_1$. Similarly, the total investment in bonds 2 and

3 would be $1B_2$ and $1.35B_3$ respectively. The investment in savings for year 1 is S_1. Using these results and the first-year obligation of 430, we obtain the constraint for year 1:

$$F - 1.15B_1 - 1B_2 - 1.35B_3 - S_1 = 430 \qquad \text{Year 1}$$

Investments in bonds can take place only in this first year, and the bonds will be held until maturity.

The funds available at the beginning of year 2 include the investment returns of 8.875% on the par value of bond 1, 5.5% on the par value of bond 2, 11.75% on the par value of bond 3, and 4% on savings. The new amount to be invested in savings for year 2 is S_2. With an obligation of 210, the constraint for year 2 is

$$0.08875B_1 + 0.055B_2 + 0.1175B_3 + 1.04S_1 - S_2 = 210 \quad \text{Year 2}$$

Similarly, the constraints for years 3 to 8 are

$$0.08875B_1 + 0.055B_2 + 0.1175B_3 + 1.04S_2 - S_3 = 222 \quad \text{Year 3}$$
$$0.08875B_1 + 0.055B_2 + 0.1175B_3 + 1.04S_3 - S_4 = 231 \quad \text{Year 4}$$
$$0.08875B_1 + 0.055B_2 + 0.1175B_3 + 1.04S_4 - S_5 = 240 \quad \text{Year 5}$$
$$1.08875B_1 + 0.055B_2 + 0.1175B_3 + 1.04S_5 - S_6 = 195 \quad \text{Year 6}$$
$$1.055B_2 + 0.1175B_3 + 1.04S_6 - S_7 = 225 \quad \text{Year 7}$$
$$1.1175B_3 + 1.04S_7 - S_8 = 255 \quad \text{Year 8}$$

Note that the constraint for year 6 shows that funds available from bond 1 are $1.08875B_1$. The coefficient of 1.08875 reflects the fact that bond 1 matures at the end of year 5. As a result, the par value plus the interest from bond 1 during year 5 are available at the beginning of year 6. Also, because bond 1 matures in year 5 and its principal is used at the beginning of year 6, the variable B_1 does not appear in the constraints for years 7 and 8. Note the similar interpretation for bond 2, which matures at the end of year 6 and has the par value plus interest available at the beginning of year 7. In addition, bond 3 matures at the end of year 7 and has the par value plus interest available at the beginning of year 8.

Finally, note that a variable S_8 appears in the constraint for year 8. The retirement fund obligation will be completed at the beginning of year 8, so we anticipate that S_8 will be zero and that no funds will be put into savings. However, the formulation includes S_8 in the event that the bond income plus interest from the savings in year 7 exceed the 255 cash requirement for year 8. Thus, S_8 is a surplus variable that shows any funds remaining after the 8-year cash requirements have been satisfied.

The spreadsheet formulation and solution of the Hewlitt Corporation problem are shown in Figure 4.10.

Spreadsheet Formulation. The data and descriptive labels are contained in cells A1:G12. The screened cells in the bottom portion of the spreadsheet contain the information required by the Excel Solver.

Decision Variables   Cells A17:L17 are reserved for the decision variables. The optimal values, rounded to 3 places) are shown to be $F = 1728.794$, $B_1 = 144.988$, $B_2 = 187.856$, $B_3 = 228.188$, $S_1 = 636.148$, $S_2 = 501.606$, $S_3 = 349.682$, $S_4 = 182.681$, and $S_5 = S_6 = S_7 = S_8 = 0$.

Figure 4.10	SPREADSHEET SOLUTION FOR THE HEWLITT CORPORATION PROBLEM

SPREADSHEET HEWLITT

	A	B	C	D	E	F	G	H	I	J	K	L
1	**Hewlitt Corporation Cash Requirements**											
2												
3		**Cash**										
4	**Year**	**Rqmt.**				**Bond**						
5	1	430			1	2	3					
6	2	210		Price ($1000)	1.15	1	1.35					
7	3	222		Rate	0.08875	0.055	0.1175					
8	4	231		Years to Maturity	5	6	7					
9	5	240										
10	6	195		Annual Savings Multiple	1.04							
11	7	225										
12	8	255										
13												
14	**Model**											
15												
16	F	B1	B2	B3	S1	S2	S3	S4	S5	S6	S7	S8
17	1728.79385	144.9881	187.8558	228.1879195	636.1479	501.6057	349.68179	182.6809	0	0	0	0
18												
19					**Cash Flow**		**Net Cash**		**Cash**			
20	**Min Funds**	1728.794		Constraints	In	Out	**Flow**		**Rqmt.**			
21				Year 1	1728.794	1298.794	430	=	430			
22				Year 2	711.6057	501.6057	240	=	210			
23				Year 3	571.6818	349.6818	222	=	222			
24				Year 4	413.6809	182.6809	231	=	231			
25				Year 5	240	0	240	=	240			
26				Year 6	195	0	195	=	195			
27				Year 7	225	0	225	=	225			
28				Year 8	255	0	255	=	255			

Objective Function   The formula =A17 has been placed into cell B20 to reflect the total funds required. It is simply the value of the decision variable, *F*. The total funds required by the optimal solution is shown to be $1,728,794.

Left-Hand Sides   The left-hand sides for the 8 constraints represent the annual net cash flow. They are placed into cells G21:G28.

Cell G21 =E21−F21   (Copy to G22:G28)

For this problem, some of the above left-hand side cells reference other cells that contain formulas. These referenced cells provide Hewlitt's cash flow in and cash flow out for each of the eight years.[2] The cells and their formulas are as follows:

Cell E21 =A17
Cell E22 =SUMPRODUCT($E$7:$G$7,$B$17:$D$17)
          +$F$10*E17
Cell E23 =SUMPRODUCT($E$7:$G$7,$B$17:$D$17)
          +$F$10*F17

---

2. The cash flow in is the sum of the positive terms in each constraint equation in the mathematical model, and the cash flow out is the sum of the negative terms in each constraint equation.

Cell E24   =SUMPRODUCT($E$7:$G$7,$B$17:$D$17)
                +$F$10*G17
Cell E25   =SUMPRODUCT($E$7:$G$7,$B$17:$D$17)
                +$F$10*H17
Cell E26   =(1+E7)*B17+F7*C17+G7*D17+F10*I17
Cell E27   =(1+F7)*C17+G7*D17+F10*J17
Cell E28   =(1+G7)*D17+F10*K17
Cell F21   =SUMPRODUCT(E6:G6,B17:D17) + E17
Cell F22   =F17
Cell F23   =G17
Cell F24   =H17
Cell F25   =I17
Cell F26   =J17
Cell F27   =K17
Cell F28   =L17

Right-Hand Sides   The right-hand sides for the 8 constraints represent the annual cash requirements. They are placed into cells I21:I28.
Cell I21   =B5   (Copy to I22:I28)

Spreadsheet Solution.   The solution can be obtained by selecting **Solver** from the **Tools**
menu, entering the proper values into the **Solver Parameters** dialog box and specifying the
options **Assume Linear Model** and **Assume Non-Negative.** The information entered into
the **Solver Parameters** dialog box is shown in Figure 4.11. After solving, we requested the
sensitivity report shown in Figure 4.12.

Figure **4.11**   SOLVER PARAMETERS DIALOG BOX FOR THE HEWLITT
CORPORATION PROBLEM

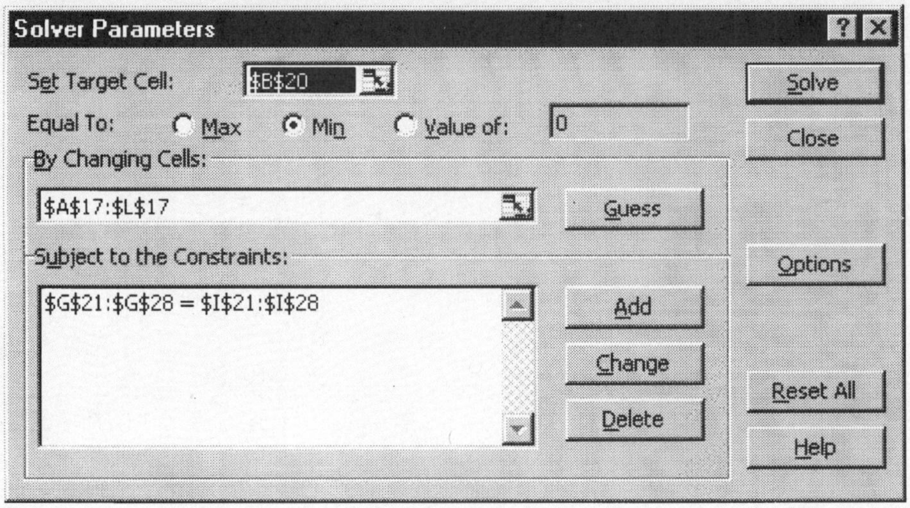

Figure 4.12 — CONSTRAINTS SECTION OF THE SENSITIVITY REPORT FOR THE HEWLITT CORPORATION PROBLEM

Constraints

Cell	Name	Final Value	Shadow Price	Constraint R.H. Side	Allowable Increase	Allowable Decrease
$G$21	Year 1 Flow	430	1	430	1E+30	1728.793855
$G$22	Year 2 Flow	210	0.961538462	210	1E+30	661.5938616
$G$23	Year 3 Flow	222	0.924556213	222	1E+30	521.6699405
$G$24	Year 4 Flow	231	0.888996359	231	1E+30	363.6690626
$G$25	Year 5 Flow	240	0.854804191	240	1E+30	189.9881496
$G$26	Year 6 Flow	195	0.760364454	195	2149.927647	157.8558478
$G$27	Year 7 Flow	225	0.718991202	225	3027.962172	198.1879195
$G$28	Year 8 Flow	255	0.670839393	255	1583.881915	255

Discussion. The total funds required to meet the retirement plan's 8-year obligation is $1,728,794. Using the current prices of $1150, $1000, and $1350 for each bond respectively, we can summarize the initial investments in the three bonds as follows:

Bond	Decision Variable Value	Investment Amount
1	$B_1 = 144.988$	$1150(144.988) = \$166,736$
2	$B_2 = 187.856$	$1000(187.856) = \$187,856$
3	$B_3 = 228.188$	$1350(228.188) = \$308,054$

The solution also shows that $636,148 (see S_1) will be placed into savings at the beginning of the first year. By starting with $1,728,794, the company can make the specified bond and savings investments and have enough left over to meet the retirement program's first-year cash requirement of $430,000.

The optimal solution in Figure 4.10 shows that the decision variables S_1, S_2, S_3, and S_4 all are greater than zero, indicating investments in savings are required in each of the first four years. However, interest from the bonds plus the bond maturity incomes will be sufficient to cover the retirement program's cash requirements in years 6 through 8.

The shadow prices have an interesting interpretation in this application. Each right-hand-side value corresponds to the payment that must be made in that year. Note that the shadow prices are positive, indicating that reducing the payment in any year would be beneficial because the total funds required for the retirement program's obligation would be less. Also note that the shadow prices show that reductions are more beneficial in the early years, with decreasing benefits in subsequent years. As a result, Hewlitt would benefit by reducing cash requirements in the early years even if it had to make equivalently larger cash payments in later years.

In this application, the shadow price can be thought of as the present value of each dollar in the cash requirement. For example, each dollar that must be paid in year 8 has a present value of $0.67084.

1. The optimal solution for the Hewlitt Corporation problem shows fractional numbers of government bonds at 144.988, 187.856, and 228.188 units, respectively. However, fractional bond units usually are not available. If we were conservative and rounded up to 145, 188, and 229 units, respectively, the total funds required for the 8-year retirement program obligation would be approximately $1254 more than the total funds indicated by the objective function. Because of the magnitude of the funds involved, rounding up probably would provide a very workable solution. If an optimal integer solution were required, the methods of integer linear programming covered in Chapter 6 would have to be used.

2. We implicitly assumed that interest from the government bonds is paid annually. Investments such as treasury notes actually provide interest payments every 6 months. In such cases, the model can be reformulated with 6-month periods; interest and/or cash payments would occur every 6 months.

4.3   PRODUCTION MANAGEMENT APPLICATIONS

Many linear programming applications have been developed for production and operations management, including scheduling, staffing, inventory control, and capacity planning. In this section we describe examples with make-or-buy decisions, production scheduling, and workforce assignments.

A Make-or-Buy Decision

We illustrate the use of a linear programming model to determine how much of each of several component parts a company should manufacture and how much it should purchase from an outside supplier. Such a decision is referred to as a **make-or-buy decision.**

The Janders Company markets various business and engineering products. Currently, Janders is preparing to introduce two new calculators: one for the business market called the Financial Manager and one for the engineering market called the Technician. Each calculator has three components: a base, an electronic cartridge, and a face plate or top. The same base is used for both calculators, but the cartridges and tops are different. All components can be manufactured by the company or purchased from outside suppliers. The manufacturing costs and purchase prices for the components are summarized in Table 4.3.

Janders' forecasters indicate that 3000 Financial Manager calculators and 2000 Technician calculators will be needed. However, manufacturing capacity is limited. The company has 200 hours of regular manufacturing time and 50 hours of overtime that can be

Table 4.3	MANUFACTURING COSTS AND PURCHASE PRICES FOR JANDERS' CALCULATOR COMPONENTS

	Cost Per Unit	
Component	Manufacture (Regular Time)	Purchase
Base	$0.50	$0.60
Financial cartridge	3.75	4.00
Technician cartridge	3.30	3.90
Financial top	0.60	0.65
Technician top	0.75	0.78

scheduled for the calculators. Overtime involves a premium at the additional cost of $9 per hour. Table 4.4 shows manufacturing times (in minutes) for the components.

The problem for Janders is to determine how many units of each component to manufacture and how many units of each component to purchase. We define the decision variables as follows:

$$BM = \text{number of bases manufactured}$$
$$BP = \text{number of bases purchased}$$
$$FCM = \text{number of Financial cartridges manufactured}$$
$$FCP = \text{number of Financial cartridges purchased}$$
$$TCM = \text{number of Technician cartridges manufactured}$$
$$TCP = \text{number of Technician cartridges purchased}$$
$$FTM = \text{number of Financial tops manufactured}$$
$$FTP = \text{number of Financial tops purchased}$$
$$TTM = \text{number of Technician tops manufactured}$$
$$TTP = \text{number of Technician tops purchased}$$

One additional decision variable is needed to determine the hours of overtime that must be scheduled:

$$OT = \text{number of hours of overtime to be scheduled}$$

The objective function is to minimize the total cost, including manufacturing costs, purchase costs, and overtime costs. Using the cost per unit data in Table 4.3 and the overtime premium cost rate of $9 per hour, we write the objective function as

$$\text{Min}\quad 0.5BM + 0.6BP + 3.75FCM + 4FCP + 3.3TCM + 3.9TCP + 0.6FTM$$
$$+ 0.65FTP + 0.75TTM + 0.78TTP + 9OT$$

The first five constraints specify the number of each component that must be obtained to satisfy the demand for 3000 Financial Manager calculators and 2000 Technician calculators. A total of 5000 base components are needed, with the number of other components depending on the demand for the particular calculator. The five demand constraints are

$$BM + BP = 5000 \quad \text{Bases}$$
$$FCM + FCP = 3000 \quad \text{Financial cartridges}$$
$$TCM + TCP = 2000 \quad \text{Technician cartridges}$$
$$FTM + FTP = 3000 \quad \text{Financial tops}$$
$$TTM + TTP = 2000 \quad \text{Technician tops}$$

Table 4.4 — MANUFACTURING TIMES IN MINUTES PER UNIT FOR JANDERS' CALCULATOR COMPONENTS

Component	Manufacturing Time
Base	1.0
Financial cartridge	3.0
Technician cartridge	2.5
Financial top	1.0
Technician top	1.5

Two constraints are needed to guarantee that the manufacturing capacities for regular time and overtime cannot be exceeded. The first constraint limits overtime capacity to 50 hours.

$$OT \leq 50$$

The second constraint states that the total manufacturing time required for all components must be less than or equal to the total manufacturing capacity, including regular time plus overtime. The manufacturing times for the components are expressed in minutes, so we state the total manufacturing capacity constraint in minutes, with the 200 hours of regular time capacity becoming $60(200) = 12,000$ minutes. The actual overtime required is unknown at this point, so we write the overtime as $60OT$ minutes. Using the manufacturing times from Table 4.4, we have

The same units of measure must be used for both the left-hand side and right-hand side of the constraint. In this case, minutes are used.

$$BM + 3FCM + 2.5TCM + FTM + 1.5TTM \leq 12,000 + 60OT$$

The complete formulation of Janders' make-or-buy problem with all decision variables greater than or equal to zero is

$$\text{Min} \quad 0.5BM + 0.6BP + 3.75FCM + 4FCP + 3.3TCM + 3.9TCP$$
$$+ 0.6FTM + 0.65FTP + 0.75TTM + 0.78TTP + 9OT$$

s.t.

BM				$+ BP =$	5000	Bases
	FCM			$+ FCP =$	3000	Financial cartridges
		TCM		$+ TCP =$	2000	Technician cartridges
			FTM	$+ FTP =$	3000	Financial tops
				$TTM + TTP =$	2000	Technician tops
				$OT \leq$	50	Overtime hours
$BM + 3FCM + 2.5TCM + FTM + 1.5TTM$				$\leq 12,000 + 60OT$		Manufacturing capacity

The spreadsheet formulation and solution of the Janders' problem are shown in Figure 4.13.

Spreadsheet Formulation. The data and descriptive labels are contained in cells A1:G12. The screened cells in the bottom portion of the spreadsheet contain the information required by the Excel Solver.

Decision Variables   Cells B21:C25 and B27 are reserved for the decision variables. The optimal values (rounded to 3 places) are shown to be $BM = 5000$, $FCM = 666.667$, $TCM = 2000$, $FCP = 2333.333$, $FTP = 3000$ and $TTP = 2000$. All other decision variables $= 0$.

Objective Function   The formula =SUMPRODUCT(B5:C9,B21:C25)+G12*B27 has been placed into cell C17 to reflect the total cost. The total cost associated with the optimal solution is shown to be $24,443.33.

Left-Hand Sides   The left-hand sides for the 7 constraints are placed into cells D21:D25 and D30:D31.
     Cell D21 =B21+C21   (Copy to D22:D25)
     Cell D30 =B27
     Cell D31 =SUMPRODUCT(D5:D9,B21:B25)

Figure 4.13	SPREADSHEET SOLUTION FOR THE JANDERS COMPANY PROBLEM

SPREADSHEET
JANDERS

	A	B	C	D	E	F	G
1	**Janders Make-or-Buy**						
2							
3		**Cost per Unit**		**Mfg. Time**			
4	**Component**	Make	Buy	in Minutes		Calculator	Demand
5	Base	$0.50	$0.60	1.0		Financial	3000
6	Fin. Cart.	$3.75	$4.00	3.0		Technician	2000
7	Tech. Cart.	$3.30	$3.90	2.5			
8	Fin. Top	$0.60	$0.65	1.0		**Time Available (Hours)**	
9	Tech.Top	$0.75	$0.78	1.5		Regular	Overtime
10						200	50
11							
12						**Overtime Cost per Hour:**	9
13							
14	**Model**						
15							
16							
17		**Min Cost**	24443.33333				
18							
19				**Number**		**Number**	
20	**Component**	Make	Buy	**Available**		**Required**	
21	Base	5000	0	5000	=	5000	
22	Fin. Cart.	666.666667	2333.333333	3000	=	3000	
23	Tech. Cart.	2000	0	2000	=	2000	
24	Fin. Top	0	3000	3000	=	3000	
25	Tech.Top	0	2000	2000	=	2000	
26							
27	**Overtime Used**	0					
28							
29				**Time Used**		**Time Avl.**	
30			**Overtime**	0	<=	50	
31			**Mfg. Time**	12000	<=	12000	

Right-Hand Sides   The right-hand sides for the 7 constraints are placed into cells F21:F25 and F30:F31.

Cell F21 =G5+G6
Cell F22 =G5
Cell F23 =G6
Cell F24 =G5
Cell F25 =G6
Cell F30 =G10
Cell F31 =60*(F10+B27)

Spreadsheet Solution.   The solution can be obtained by selecting **Solver** from the **Tools** menu, entering the proper values into the **Solver Parameters** dialog box and specifying the options **Assume Linear Model** and **Assume Non-Negative.** The information entered into the **Solver Parameters** dialog box is shown in Figure 4.14. After solving, we requested the sensitivity report shown in Figure 4.15.

Discussion.   The optimal solution indicates that all 5000 bases (*BM*), 667 Financial Manager cartridges (*FCM*), and 2000 Technician cartridges (*TCM*) should be manufactured. The remaining 2333 Financial Manager cartridges (*FCP*), all the Financial Manager tops (*FTP*), and all Technician tops (*TTP*) should be purchased. No overtime manufacturing is necessary, and the total cost associated with the optimal make-or-buy plan is $24,443.33.

Sensitivity analysis provides some additional information about the unused overtime capacity. The Reduced Cost column (see the Adjustable Cells section of Figure 4.15) shows that the overtime (*OT*) premium would have to decrease by $4 per hour before overtime production should be considered. That is, if the overtime premium is $9 − $4 = $5 or less, Janders should replace some of the purchased components with components manufactured on overtime. Problem 12 at the end of the chapter asks you to reconsider the Janders problem with a lower overtime premium to show how the optimal make-or-buy solution changes.

The shadow price for the manufacturing capacity constraint 7 is −0.083. This number indicates that additional manufacturing capacity is worth $0.083 per minute or ($0.083)(60) = $5 per hour. The allowable increase for the manufacturing time constraint shows that this conclusion is valid until the amount of regular time increases to 19,000 minutes, or 316.7 hours.

Sensitivity analysis also indicates that a change in prices charged by the outside suppliers can affect the optimal solution. For instance, the allowable decrease for the objective function coefficient for *BP* is 0.017. If the purchase price for bases remains at $0.583 or more, the number of bases purchased (*BP*) will remain at zero. However, if the purchase price drops below $0.583, Janders should begin to purchase rather than manufacture the base component. Similar sensitivity analysis conclusions about the purchase price ranges can be drawn for the other components.

Try Problem 12 for practice with a variation of the Janders make-or-buy problem.

Figure 4.14   SOLVER PARAMETERS DIALOG BOX FOR THE JANDERS COMPANY PROBLEM

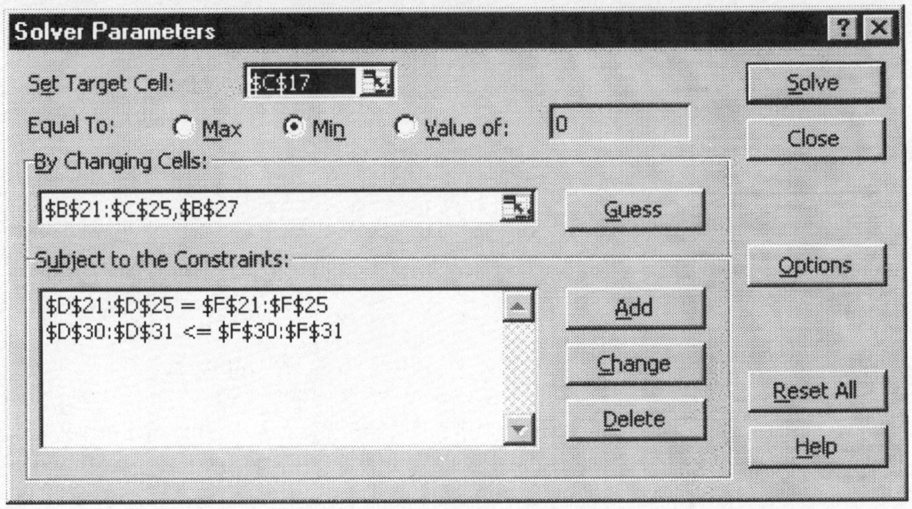

Figure 4.15   SENSITIVITY REPORT FOR THE JANDERS COMPANY PROBLEM

Adjustable Cells

Cell	Name	Final Value	Reduced Cost	Objective Coefficient	Allowable Increase	Allowable Decrease
$B$21	Base Make	5000	0	0.5	0.016666667	1.00E+30
$C$21	Base Buy	0	0.016666667	0.6	1.00E+30	0.016666667
$B$22	Fin. Cart. Make	666.6666667	0	3.75	0.1	0.05
$C$22	Fin. Cart. Buy	2333.333333	0	4	0.05	0.1
$B$23	Tech. Cart. Make	2000	0	3.3	0.391666667	1.00E+30
$C$23	Tech. Cart. Buy	0	0.391666667	3.9	1.00E+30	0.391666667
$B$24	Fin. Top Make	0	0.033333333	0.6	1.00E+30	0.033333333
$C$24	Fin. Top Buy	3000	0	0.65	0.033333333	1.00E+30
$B$25	Tech.Top Make	0	0.095	0.75	1.00E+30	0.095
$C$25	Tech.Top Buy	2000	0	0.78	0.095	1.00E+30
$B$27	Overtime Used Make	0	4	9	1.00E+30	4

Constraints

Cell	Name	Final Value	Shadow Price	Constraint R.H. Side	Allowable Increase	Allowable Decrease
$D$21	Base Available	5000	0.583333333	5000	2000	5000
$D$22	Fin. Cart. Available	3000	4	3000	1.00E+30	2333.333333
$D$23	Tech. Cart. Available	2000	3.508333333	2000	800	2000
$D$24	Fin. Top Available	3000	0.65	3000	1.00E+30	3000
$D$25	Tech.Top Available	2000	0.78	2000	1.00E+30	2000
$D$30	Overtime Time Used	0	0	0	1.00E+30	50
$D$31	Mfg. Time Time Used	12000	-0.083333333	0	7000	2000

NOTES and Comments

The proper interpretation of the shadow price for manufacturing capacity (constraint 7) in the Janders problem is that an additional hour of manufacturing capacity is worth ($0.083)(60) = $5 per hour. Thus, the company should be willing to pay a premium of $5 per hour over and above the current regular time cost per hour, which is already included in the manufacturing cost of the product. Thus, if the regular time cost is $18 per hour, Janders should be willing to pay up to $18 + $5 = $23 per hour to obtain additional manufacturing capacity.

Production Scheduling

One of the most important applications of linear programming deals with multiperiod planning such as production scheduling. The solution to a production scheduling problem enables the manager to establish an efficient low-cost production schedule for one or more products over several time periods (weeks or months). Essentially, a production scheduling problem can be viewed as a product-mix problem for each of several periods in the future. The manager must determine the production levels that will allow the company to meet product demand requirements, given limitations on production capacity, labor capacity, and storage space, while minimizing total production costs.

One advantage of using linear programming for production scheduling problems is that they recur. A production schedule must be established for the current month, then again for the next month, for the month after that, and so on. When looking at the problem each month, the production manager will find that, although demand for the products has changed, production times, production capacities, storage space limitations, and so on are roughly the same. Thus, the production manager is basically resolving the same problem handled in previous months, and a general linear programming model of the production scheduling procedure may be frequently applied. Once the model has been formulated, the manager can simply supply the data—demand, capacities, and so on—for the given production period and use the linear programming model repeatedly to develop the production schedule.

Let us consider the case of the Bollinger Electronics Company, which produces two different electronic components for a major airplane engine manufacturer. The airplane engine manufacturer notifies the Bollinger sales office each quarter of its monthly requirements for components for each of the next 3 months. The monthly requirements for the components may vary considerably, depending on the type of engine the airplane engine manufacturer is producing. The order shown in Table 4.5 has just been received for the next 3-month period.

After the order is processed, a demand statement is sent to the production control department. The production control department must then develop a 3-month production plan for the components. In arriving at the desired schedule, the production manager will want to identify

1. total production cost,
2. inventory holding cost, and
3. change-in-production-level costs.

In the remainder of this section we show how to formulate a linear programming model of the production and inventory process for Bollinger Electronics to minimize the total cost.

To develop the model, we let x_{im} denote the production volume in units for product i in month m. Here $i = 1, 2$, and $m = 1, 2, 3$; $i = 1$ refers to component 322A, $i = 2$ refers to component 802B, $m = 1$ refers to April, $m = 2$ refers to May, and $m = 3$ refers to June. The purpose of the double subscript is to provide a more descriptive notation. We could simply use x_6 to represent the number of units of product 2 produced in month 3, but x_{23} is more descriptive, identifying directly the product and month represented by the variable.

If component 322A costs $20 per unit produced and component 802B costs $10 per unit produced, the total production cost part of the objective function is

$$\text{Total production cost} = 20x_{11} + 20x_{12} + 20x_{13} + 10x_{21} + 10x_{22} + 10x_{23}$$

However, the production cost per unit is the same each month, so we don't need to include the production costs in the objective function; that is, regardless of the production schedule selected, the total production cost will remain the same. In other words, production costs are not relevant costs for the production scheduling decision under consideration. In cases where the production cost per unit is expected to change each month, the variable production costs per unit per month must be included in the objective function. Since the solution for the Bollinger Electronics problem will be the same whether these costs are included or not, we included them so that the value of the linear programming objective function will include all the costs associated with the problem.

Table 4.5	THREE-MONTH ORDER FOR BOLLINGER ELECTRONICS COMPANY		
Component	**April**	**May**	**June**
322A	1000	3000	5000
802B	1000	500	3000

To incorporate the relevant inventory holding costs into the model, we let s_{im} denote the inventory level for product i at the end of month m. Bollinger has determined that on a monthly basis inventory holding costs are 1.5% of the cost of the product; that is, $(0.015)(\$20) = \$0.30$ per unit for component 322A and $(0.015)(\$10) = \$0.15$ per unit for component 802B. A common assumption made in using the linear programming approach to production scheduling is that monthly ending inventories are an acceptable approximation to the average inventory levels throughout the month. Making this assumption, we write the inventory holding cost portion of the objective function as

$$\text{Inventory holding cost} = 0.30s_{11} + 0.30s_{12} + 0.30s_{13} + 0.15s_{21} + 0.15s_{22} + 0.15s_{23}$$

To incorporate the costs of fluctuations in production levels from month to month, we need to define two additional variables:

$$I_m = \text{increase in the total production level necessary during month } m$$
$$D_m = \text{decrease in the total production level necessary during month } m$$

After estimating the effects of employee layoffs, turnovers, reassignment training costs, and other costs associated with fluctuating production levels, Bollinger estimates that the cost associated with increasing the production level for any month is $0.50 per unit increase. A similar cost associated with decreasing the production level for any month is $0.20 per unit. Thus, we write the third portion of the objective function as

$$\text{Change-in-production-level costs} = 0.50I_1 + 0.50I_2 + 0.50I_3$$
$$+ 0.20D_1 + 0.20D_2 + 0.20D_3$$

Note that the cost associated with changes in production level is a function of the change in the total number of units produced in month m compared to the total number of units produced in month $m - 1$. In other production scheduling applications, fluctuations in production level might be measured in terms of machine hours or labor-hours required rather than in terms of the total number of units produced.

Combining all three costs, the complete objective function becomes

$$\begin{aligned}
\text{Min} \quad &20x_{11} + 20x_{12} + 20x_{13} + 10x_{21} + 10x_{22} + 10x_{23} + 0.30s_{11} \\
&+ 0.30s_{12} + 0.30s_{13} + 0.15s_{21} + 0.15s_{22} + 0.15s_{23} + 0.50I_1 \\
&+ 0.50I_2 + 0.50I_3 + 0.20D_1 + 0.20D_2 + 0.20D_3
\end{aligned}$$

We now consider the constraints. First, we must guarantee that the schedule meets customer demand. Since the units shipped can come from the current month's production or from inventory carried over from previous months, the demand requirement takes the form

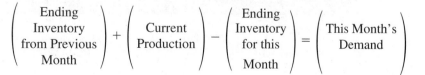

Suppose that the inventories at the beginning of the 3-month scheduling period were 500 units for component 322A and 200 units for component 802B. The demand for each

product in the first month (April) was 1000 units, so the constraints for meeting demand in the first month become

$$500 + x_{11} - s_{11} = 1000$$
$$200 + x_{21} - s_{21} = 1000$$

Similarly, we need demand constraints for both products in the second and third months. We write them as follows.

Month 2

$$s_{11} + x_{12} - s_{12} = 3000$$
$$s_{21} + x_{22} - s_{22} = 500$$

Month 3

$$s_{12} + x_{13} - s_{13} = 5000$$
$$s_{22} + x_{23} - s_{23} = 3000$$

If the company specifies a minimum inventory level at the end of the 3-month period of at least 400 units of component 322A and at least 200 units of component 802B, we can add the constraints

$$s_{13} \geq 400$$
$$s_{23} \geq 200$$

Suppose that we have the additional information on machine, labor, and storage capacity shown in Table 4.6. Machine, labor, and storage space requirements are given in Table 4.7. To reflect these limitations, additional constraints are necessary.

Table 4.6 — MACHINE, LABOR, AND STORAGE CAPACITIES FOR BOLLINGER ELECTRONICS

Month	Machine Capacity (hours)	Labor Capacity (hours)	Storage Capacity (square feet)
April	400	300	10,000
May	500	300	10,000
June	600	300	10,000

Table 4.7 — MACHINE, LABOR, AND STORAGE REQUIREMENTS FOR COMPONENTS 322A AND 802B

Component	Machine (hours/unit)	Labor (hours/unit)	Storage (square feet/unit)
322A	0.10	0.05	2
802B	0.08	0.07	3

Machine Capacity

$$0.10x_{11} + 0.08x_{21} \le 400 \qquad \text{Month 1}$$
$$0.10x_{12} + 0.08x_{22} \le 500 \qquad \text{Month 2}$$
$$0.10x_{13} + 0.08x_{23} \le 600 \qquad \text{Month 3}$$

Labor Capacity

$$0.05x_{11} + 0.07x_{21} \le 300 \qquad \text{Month 1}$$
$$0.05x_{12} + 0.07x_{22} \le 300 \qquad \text{Month 2}$$
$$0.05x_{13} + 0.07x_{23} \le 300 \qquad \text{Month 3}$$

Storage Capacity

$$2s_{11} + 3s_{21} \quad \le 10,000 \quad \text{Month 1}$$
$$2s_{12} + 3s_{22} \quad \le 10,000 \quad \text{Month 2}$$
$$2s_{13} + 3s_{23} \quad \le 10,000 \quad \text{Month 3}$$

One final set of constraints must be added to guarantee that I_m and D_m will reflect the increase or decrease in the total production level for month m. Suppose that the production levels for March, the month before the start of the current production scheduling period, had been 1500 units of component 322A and 1000 units of component 802B for a total production level of $1500 + 1000 = 2500$ units. We can find the amount of the change in production for April from the relationship

$$\text{April production} - \text{March production} = \text{Change}$$

Using the April production variables, x_{11} and x_{21}, and the March production of 2500 units, we have

$$(x_{11} + x_{21}) - 2500 = \text{Change}$$

Note that the change can be positive or negative. A positive change reflects an increase in the total production level, and a negative change reflects a decrease in the total production level. We can use the increase in production for April, I_1, and the decrease in production for April, D_1, to specify the constraint for the change in total production for the month of April:

$$(x_{11} + x_{21}) - 2500 = I_1 - D_1$$

Of course, we cannot have an increase in production and a decrease in production during the same 1-month period; thus, either I_1 or D_1 will be zero. If April requires 3000 units of production, $I_1 = 500$ and $D_1 = 0$. If April requires 2200 units of production, $I_1 = 0$ and $D_1 = 300$. This approach of denoting the change in production level as the difference between two nonnegative variables, I_1 and D_1, permits both positive and negative changes in the total production level. If a single variable (say, c_m) had been used to represent the change in production level, only positive changes would be possible because of the nonnegativity requirement.

Using the same approach in May and June (always subtracting the previous month's total production from the current month's total production), we obtain the constraints for the second and third months of the production scheduling period:

$$(x_{12} + x_{22}) - (x_{11} + x_{21}) = I_2 - D_2$$
$$(x_{13} + x_{23}) - (x_{12} + x_{22}) = I_3 - D_3$$

The initially rather small, 2-product, 3-month scheduling problem has now developed into an 18-variable, 20-constraint linear programming problem. Note that in this problem we were concerned only with one type of machine process, one type of labor, and one type of storage area. Actual production scheduling problems usually involve several machine types, several labor grades, and/or several storage areas, requiring large-scale linear programs. For instance, a problem involving 100 products over a 12-month period could have over 1000 variables and constraints.

The spreadsheet formulation and solution of the Bollinger Electronics problem are shown in Figure 4.16.

**SPREADSHEET
BOLLINGER**

Figure 4.16   SPREADSHEET SOLUTION FOR THE BOLLINGER ELECTRONICS PROBLEM

	A	B	C	D	E	F	G	H	I	J	K	L	M
1	**Bollinger Electronics**												
2													
3			**Production Cost**			**Inventory Cost**				**Change in Production Level Cost**			
4		April	May	June	April	May	June			April	May	June	
5	322A	20	20	20	0.30	0.30	0.30		**Increase**	0.5	0.5	0.5	
6	802B	10	10	10	0.15	0.15	0.15		**Decrease**	0.2	0.2	0.2	
7													
8			**Demand**			**Beginning**		**Ending**		**Production Level-March**		2500	
9		April	May	June		**Inventory**		**Inventory**					
10	322A	1000	3000	5000		500		400					
11	802B	1000	500	3000		200		200					
12													
13													
14		**Machine**	**Labor**	**Storage**				**Capacity**					
15		**(hrs/unit)**	**(hrs/unit)**	**(sq. ft./unit)**			Machine Hrs.	Labor Hrs.	Storage (sq.ft.)				
16	322A	0.1	0.05	2		**April**	400	300	10000				
17	802B	0.08	0.07	3		**May**	500	300	10000				
18						**June**	600	300	10000				
19													
20													
21													
22	**Model**												
23													
24			**Production**			**Ending Inventory**				**Change in Production Level**			
25		April	May	June	April	May	June			April	May	June	
26	322A	500	3200	5200	0	200	400		**Increase**	500	2200	9.76386E-13	
27	802B	2500	2000	0	1700	3200	200		**Decrease**	0	0	0	
28													
29													
30	**Min Cost**	225295											
31								**Capacity Constraints**			**Change in Production Level**		
32		**Beg. Inv. + Prod. - End. Inv.**			**Demand**			**Used**		**Available**	**Cur.Mo.- Prev. Mo.**		**I - D**
33	322A/April	1000	=	1000		Mach/Apr	250	<=	400	**April**	500	=	500
34	802B/April	1000	=	1000		Mach/May	480	<=	500	**May**	2200	=	2200
35	322A/May	3000	=	3000		Mach/June	520	<=	600	**June**	0	=	9.76E-13
36	802B/May	500	=	500		Labor/Apr	200	<=	300				
37	322A/June	5000	=	5000		labor/May	300	<=	300				
38	802B/June	3000	=	3000		Labor/June	260	<=	300				
39						Stor/Apr	5100	<=	10000				
40				**End. Inv.**		Stor/May	10000	<=	10000				
41		**End. Inv.**		**Rqmt.**		Stor/June	1400	<=	10000				
42	322A	400	>=	400									
43	802B	200	>=	200									

Spreadsheet Formulation. The Bollinger Electronics problem is the largest problem we have tackled, and the spreadsheet may appear complex. However, as usual, we have organized the data in the top portion of the spreadsheet (cells A1:L18) and the key elements of the model are screened in the bottom portion of the spreadsheet.

Decision Variables   Cells B26:G27 and J26:L27 are reserved for the 18 decision variables. The production variables are in cells B26:D27, the inventory variables are in cells E26:G27, and variables representing the change in production levels are in cells J26:L27. The optimal values are shown. Note that the entry in cell L26 is 9.76386E-13. This is scientific notation for a very small number with 12 zeros to the right of the decimal point prior to 976386. It can be treated as zero.

Objective Function   The formula =SUMPRODUCT(B5:G6,B26:G27)+SUMPRODUCT (J5:L6,J26:L27) has been placed into cell B30 to reflect the total cost (production + inventory + change in production level). The minimum total cost is \$225,295.

Left-Hand Sides   The left-hand sides for the 20 constraints are placed into cells B33:B38, B42:B43, G33:G41, and K33:K35.

    Cell B33 =F10+B26−E26   (Copy to B34)
    Cell B35 =E26+C26−F26   (Copy to B36)
    Cell B37 =F26+D26−G26   (Copy to B38)
    Cell B42 =G26   (Copy to B43)
    Cell G33 =SUMPRODUCT(B16:B17,B26:B27)
    Cell G34 =SUMPRODUCT(B16:B17,C26:C27)
    Cell G35 =SUMPRODUCT(B16:B17,D26:D27)
    Cell G36 =SUMPRODUCT(C16:C17,B26:B27)
    Cell G37 =SUMPRODUCT(C16:C17,C26:C27)
    Cell G38 =SUMPRODUCT(C16:C17,D26:D27)
    Cell G39 =SUMPRODUCT(D16:D17,E26:E27)
    Cell G40 =SUMPRODUCT(D16:D17,F26:F27)
    Cell G41 =SUMPRODUCT(D16:D17,G26:G27)
    Cell K33 =B26+B27−L8
    Cell K34 =C26+C27−B26−B27
    Cell K35 =D26+D27−C26−C27

Right-Hand Sides   The right-hand sides for the 20 constraints are placed into cells D33:D38, D42:D43, I33:I41, and M33:M35.

    Cell D33   =B10   (Copy to D34)
    Cell D35   =C10   (Copy to D36)
    Cell D37   =D10   (Copy to D38)
    Cell D42   =H10   (Copy to D43)
    Cell I33   =G16   (Copy to I34:I35)
    Cell I36   =H16   (Copy to I37:I38)
    Cell I39   =I16   (Copy to I40:I41)
    Cell M33 =J26−J27
    Cell M34 =K26−K27
    Cell M35 =L26−L27

Spreadsheet Solution.   The solution can be obtained by selecting **Solver** from the **Tools** menu, entering the proper values into the **Solver Parameters** dialog box, and specifying the options **Assume Linear Model** and **Assume Non-Negative.** The information entered into the **Solver Parameters** dialog box is shown in Figure 4.17. After solving, we requested the sensitivity report shown in Figure 4.18.

Figure 4.17	SOLVER PARAMETERS DIALOG BOX FOR THE BOLLINGER ELECTRONICS PROBLEM

Figure 4.18	CONSTRAINTS SECTION OF THE SENSITIVITY REPORT FOR THE BOLLINGER ELECTRONICS PROBLEM

Constraints

Cell	Name	Final Value	Shadow Price	Constraint R.H. Side	Allowable Increase	Allowable Decrease
$B$33	322A/April Beg. Inv. + Prod. - End. Inv.	1000	20	1000	1500	500
$B$34	802B/April Beg. Inv. + Prod. - End. Inv.	1000	10	1000	1428.57143	500
$B$35	322A/May Beg. Inv. + Prod. - End. Inv.	3000	20.1071429	3000	3.42E-12	700
$B$36	802B/May Beg. Inv. + Prod. - End. Inv.	500	10.15	500	1428.57143	500
$B$37	322A/June Beg. Inv. + Prod. - End. Inv.	5000	20.5	5000	800	9.76E-13
$B$38	802B/June Beg. Inv. + Prod. - End. Inv.	3000	10.4392857	3000	133.333333	5.06E-13
$B$42	322A End. Inv.	400	20.8	400	800	9.76E-13
$B$43	802B End. Inv.	200	10.5892857	200	133.333333	5.06E-13
$G$33	Mach/Apr Used	250	0	400	1.00E+30	150
$G$34	Mach/May Used	480	0	500	1.00E+30	20
$G$35	Mach/June Used	520	0	600	1.00E+30	80
$G$36	Labor/Apr Used	200	0	300	1.00E+30	100
$G$37	labor/May Used	300	-2.14285714	300	6.83E-14	77
$G$38	Labor/June Used	260	0	300	1.00E+30	40
$G$39	Stor/Apr Used	5100	0	10000	1.00E+30	4900
$G$40	Stor/May Used	10000	-0.04642857	10000	1.52E-12	400
$G$41	Stor/June Used	1400	0	10000	1.00E+30	8600
$K$33	April Cur.Mo.- Prev. Mo.	500	-0.5	0	500	1.00E+30
$K$34	May Cur.Mo.- Prev. Mo.	2200	-0.5	0	2200	1.00E+30
$K$35	June Cur.Mo.- Prev. Mo.	0	-0.5	0	9.76E-13	1.00E+30

Problem 19 involves a production scheduling application with labor-smoothing constraints.

Discussion.   Figure 4.16 shows the solution of the Bollinger Electronics problem in the spreadsheet. The spreadsheet solution could actually be used as a managerial report. However, we have prepared another summary of the solution, containing a few extra details, in Table 4.8.

Consider the monthly variation in the production and inventory schedule shown in Table 4.8. Recall that the inventory cost for component 802B is one-half the inventory cost for component 322A. Therefore, as might be expected, component 802B is produced heavily in the first month (April) and then held in inventory for the demand that will occur in future months. Component 322A tends to be produced when needed, and only small amounts are carried in inventory.

Linear programming models for production scheduling are often very large. Thousands of decision variables and constraints are necessary when the problem involves numerous products, machines, and time periods. Data collection for large-scale models can be more time-consuming than either the formulation of the model or the development of the computer solution.

The costs of increasing and decreasing the total production volume tend to smooth the monthly variations. In fact, the minimum-cost schedule calls for a 500-unit increase in total production in April and a 2200-unit increase in total production in May. The May production level of 5200 units is then maintained during June.

The machine usage section of the report shows ample machine capacity in all 3 months. However, labor capacity is at full utilization (slack = 0 for labor constraint in Figure 4.16) in the month of May. The shadow price shows that an additional hour of labor capacity in May will improve the objective function (lower cost) by approximately $2.14.

A linear programming model of a 2-product, 3-month production system can provide valuable information in terms of identifying a minimum-cost production schedule. In larger production systems, where the number of variables and constraints is too large to track manually, linear programming models can provide a significant advantage in developing cost-saving production schedules. The Management Science in Action: Libbey-Owens-Ford shows just how large linear programming models can be for applications involving production scheduling.

Table 4.8 — MINIMUM-COST PRODUCTION SCHEDULE FOR THE BOLLINGER ELECTRONICS PROBLEM

Activity	April	May	June
Production			
Component 322A	500	3200	5200
Component 802B	2500	2000	0
Totals	3000	5200	5200
Ending inventory			
Component 322A	0	200	400
Component 802B	1700	3200	200
Machine usage			
Scheduled hours	250	480	520
Slack capacity hours	150	20	80
Labor usage			
Scheduled hours	200	300	260
Slack capacity hours	100	0	40
Storage usage			
Scheduled storage	5100	10,000	1400
Slack capacity	4900	0	8600

Total production, inventory, and production-smoothing cost = $225,295

MANAGEMENT SCIENCE IN ACTION

LIBBEY-OWENS-FORD*

Libbey-Owens-Ford uses a large-scale linear programming model to achieve integrated production, distribution, and inventory planning for its flat glass products. The linear programming model is called FLAGPOL. Schedulers and planners in the flat-glass products group must coordinate production schedules for more than 200 different glass products. The products are made in 4 colors (clear, gray, bronze, and blue-green) and 26 thicknesses. Other options include 3 quality levels, 2 cutting classifications, 4 packaging modes, and various fabrication methods, including tempered glass and/or coated glass.

To integrate production, distribution, and inventory planning, company analysts developed a linear programming model that optimizes operations for all products over a 12-month planning horizon. The model

is applied monthly, and its output helps planners react to unexpected changes in the operating environment and deal with strategic issues such as adding new plants and expanding capacity. A typical linear programming model has approximately 100,000 variables and 26,000 constraints. The computer solution for problems of this size can take 3 to 4 hours. The company estimates that the FLAGPOL model provides an annual savings of more than $2 million.

*Based on Clarence H. Martin, Denver C. Dent, and James C. Eckhart, "Integrated Production, Distribution and Inventory Planning at Libbey-Owens-Ford," *Interfaces* (May–June 1993): 68–78.

Workforce Assignment

Workforce assignment problems frequently occur when operations managers must make decisions involving staffing requirements for a given planning period. Workforce assignments often have some flexibility, and at least some personnel can be assigned to more than one department or work center. Such is the case when employees have been cross-trained on two or more jobs or, for instance, when sales personnel can be transferred between stores. In the following application we show how linear programming can be used to determine not only an optimal product mix but also an optimal workforce assignment.

McCormick Manufacturing Company produces two products with contributions to profit per unit of $10 and $9, respectively. The labor requirements per unit produced and the total hours of labor available from personnel assigned to each of four departments are shown in Table 4.9. Assuming that the number of hours available in each department is

Table 4.9	DEPARTMENTAL LABOR-HOURS PER UNIT AND TOTAL HOURS AVAILABLE FOR THE McCORMICK MANUFACTURING COMPANY

| | **Labor-Hours per Unit** | | |
Department	**Product 1**	**Product 2**	**Total Hours Available**
1	0.65	0.95	6500
2	0.45	0.85	6000
3	1.00	0.70	7000
4	0.15	0.30	1400

fixed, we can formulate McCormick's problem as a standard product-mix linear program with the following decision variables:

$$P_1 = \text{units of product 1}$$
$$P_2 = \text{units of product 2}$$

A profit maximizing linear programming model of the McCormick problem is given below.

$$\text{Max} \quad 10P_1 + 9P_2$$
$$\text{s.t.}$$
$$0.65P_1 + 0.95P_2 \leq 6500$$
$$0.45P_1 + 0.85P_2 \leq 6000$$
$$1.00P_1 + 0.70P_2 \leq 7000$$
$$0.15P_1 + 0.30P_2 \leq 1400$$
$$P_1, P_2 \geq 0$$

The spreadsheet formulation and solution of the McCormick Manufacturing Company problem are shown in Figure 4.19.

SPREADSHEET
MCCORMICK

Figure 4.19   SPREADSHEET SOLUTION FOR THE MCCORMICK MANUFACTURING COMPANY PROBLEM—NO TRANSFERS PERMITTED

	A	B	C	D	E	F	G	H	I	J
1	**McCormick Manufacturing Company**									
2										
3		**Labor Hrs. per Unit**								
4	**Dept.**	**P1**	**P2**	**Hrs. Avail.**						
5	**1**	0.65	0.95	6500.00						
6	**2**	0.45	0.85	6000.00						
7	**3**	1.00	0.70	7000.00						
8	**4**	0.15	0.30	1400.00						
9										
10	**Profit/Unit**	10.00	9.00							
11										
12										
13	**Model**									
14										
15										
16	**Production Schedule**						**Labor Hours**			
17	**P1**	**P2**					Used		Available	**Slack**
18	5743.59	1794.87		**Max Profit**	73589.74		5438.46	<=	6500.00	1061.54
19							4110.26	<=	6000.00	1889.74
20							7000.00	<=	7000.00	0.00
21							1400.00	<=	1400.00	0.00

Spreadsheet Formulation.   As usual, the data are in the top portion of the spreadsheet (cells A1:D10). The screened cells in the bottom portion contain the key elements of the model required by the Excel Solver.

Decision Variables   Cells A18:B18 are reserved for the two decision variables. The optimal solution calls for production of 5743.59 units of product 1 and 1794.87 units of product 2.

Objective Function   The formula =SUMPRODUCT(B10:C10,A18:B18) has been placed into cell E18 to reflect the profit. The optimal solution is shown to provide a profit of $73,589.74.

Left-Hand Sides   The left-hand sides for the 4 constraints are placed into cells G18:G21.
                     Cell G18 =SUMPRODUCT(B5:C5,$A$18:$B$18)
                              (Copy to G19:G21)

Right-Hand Sides   The right-hand sides for the 4 constraints are placed into cells I18:I21.
                     Cell I18   =D5   (Copy to I19:I21)

Spreadsheet Solution.   The solution can be obtained by selecting **Solver** from the **Tools** menu, entering the proper values into the **Solver Parameters** dialog box, and specifying the options **Assume Linear Model** and **Assume Non-Negative.** The information entered into the **Solver Parameters** dialog box is shown in Figure 4.20.

Discussion.   After rounding, the optimal solution calls for 5744 units of product 1, 1795 units of product 2, and provides a total profit of $73,590. With this solution, departments 3 and 4 are operating at capacity; departments 1 and 2 have a slack of approximately 1062 and 1890 hours, respectively. (See cells J18:J21 of Figure 4.19.) We would anticipate that the product mix would change and that the total profit would increase if the workforce as-

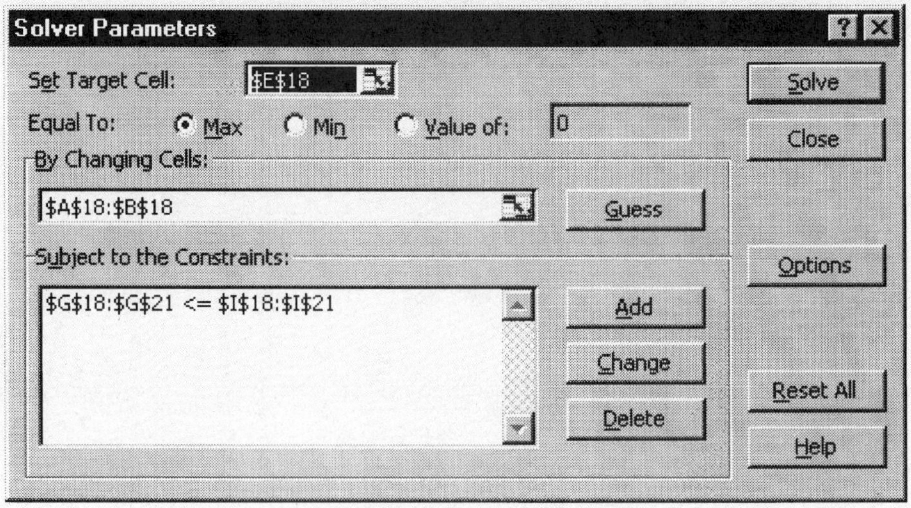

Figure 4.20   SOLVER PARAMETERS DIALOG BOX FOR THE MCCORMICK MANUFACTURING COMPANY PROBLEM—NO TRANSFERS PERMITTED

signment could be revised so that the slack, or unused hours, in departments 1 and 2 could be transferred to the departments currently working at capacity. However, the operations manager may be uncertain as to how the workforce should be reallocated among the four departments. Let us expand the linear programming model to include decision variables that will help determine the optimal workforce assignment in addition to the profit-maximizing product mix.

Suppose that McCormick has a cross-training program that enables some employees to be transferred between departments. By taking advantage of the cross-training skills, a limited number of employees and labor-hours may be transferred from one department to another. For example, suppose that the cross-training permits transfers as shown in Table 4.10. Row 1 of this table shows that some employees assigned to department 1 have cross-training skills that permit them to be transferred to department 2 or 3. The right-hand column shows that, for the current production planning period, a maximum of 400 hours can be transferred from department 1. Similar cross-training transfer capabilities and capacities are shown for departments 2, 3, and 4.

When workforce assignments are flexible, we do not automatically know how many hours of labor should be assigned to or transferred from each department. We will account for such changes by letting

b_i = the labor-hours allocated to department i for i = 1, 2, 3, and 4

t_{ij} = the labor-hours transferred from department i to department j

We can now write the capacity restrictions for the four departments as follows:

$$0.65P_1 + 0.95P_2 \leq b_1$$
$$0.45P_1 + 0.85P_2 \leq b_2$$
$$1.00P_1 + 0.70P_2 \leq b_3$$
$$0.15P_1 + 0.30P_2 \leq b_4$$

The labor-hours ultimately allocated to each department must be determined by a series of labor balance equations, or constraints, that include the number of hours initially assigned to each department plus the number of hours transferred into the department minus

Table **4.10**	CROSS-TRAINING ABILITY AND CAPACITY INFORMATION				
From Department	**Cross-Training Transfers Permitted to Department**				**Maximum Hours Transferable**
	1	**2**	**3**	**4**	
1	—	yes	yes	—	400
2	—	—	yes	yes	800
3	—	—	—	yes	100
4	yes	yes	—	—	200

the number of hours transferred out of the department. Using department 1 as an example, we determine the workforce allocation as follows:

$$b_1 = \begin{pmatrix} \text{Hours} \\ \text{Initially In} \\ \text{Department 1} \end{pmatrix} + \begin{pmatrix} \text{Hours} \\ \text{Transferred Into} \\ \text{Department 1} \end{pmatrix} - \begin{pmatrix} \text{Hours} \\ \text{Transferred Out of} \\ \text{Department 1} \end{pmatrix}$$

Table 4.9 shows 6500 hours initially assigned to department 1. We use the transfer decision variables t_{i1} to denote transfers into department 1 and t_{1j} to denote transfers from department 1. Table 4.10 shows that the cross-training capabilities involving department 1 are restricted to transfers from department 4 (variable t_{41}) and transfers to either department 2 or department 3 (variables t_{12} and t_{13}). Thus, we can express the total workforce allocation for department 1 as

$$b_1 = 6500 + t_{41} - t_{12} - t_{13}$$

This form of constraint will be needed for each of the four departments. Thus, the following labor balance equations are necessary to express the total workforce allocation to departments 2, 3, and 4.

$$b_2 = 6000 + t_{12} + t_{42} - t_{23} - t_{24}$$
$$b_3 = 7000 + t_{13} + t_{23} - t_{34}$$
$$b_4 = 1400 + t_{24} + t_{34} - t_{41} - t_{42}$$

Finally, since Table 4.10 shows that the number of hours that may be transferred from each department is limited, a transfer capacity constraint must be added for each of the four departments. The additional constraints are

$$t_{12} + t_{13} \le 400$$
$$t_{23} + t_{24} \le 800$$
$$t_{34} \qquad \le 100$$
$$t_{41} + t_{42} \le 200$$

The complete linear programming model now has 2 product decision variables (P_1 and P_2), 7 transfer decision variables, and 8 constraints. The spreadsheet formulation and solution of the McCormick Manufacturing Company problem with transfers permitted are shown in Figure 4.21.

Spreadsheet Formulation.   We have added the maximum hours transferable to the data section of the spreadsheet. The data and descriptive labels are contained in cells A1:H10. The screened cells in the bottom portion of the spreadsheet contain the key elements of the model required by the Excel Solver.

Decision Variables   Cells A18:B18, C25:D25, D26:E26, E27, and B28:C28 are reserved for the 2 production and 7 transfer variables. The optimal values are shown to be $P_1 = 6824.86$, $P_2 = 1751.41$, $t_{13} = 400$, $t_{23} = 650.85$, $t_{24} = 149.15$, and $t_{12} = t_{34} = t_{41} = t_{42} = 0$.

Figure 4.21 SPREADSHEET SOLUTION FOR THE MCCORMICK MANUFACTURING COMPANY PROBLEM—LABOR TRANSFERS PERMITTED

SPREADSHEET
McCormick

	A	B	C	D	E	F	G	H	I	J	K
1	McCormick Manufacturing Company										
2											
3		Labor Hrs. per Unit						Max Hrs.			
4	Dept.	P1	P2	Hrs. Avail.			Dept.	Transferable			
5	1	0.65	0.95	6500.00			1	400.00			
6	2	0.45	0.85	6000.00			2	800.00			
7	3	1.00	0.70	7000.00			3	100.00			
8	4	0.15	0.30	1400.00			4	200.00			
9											
10	Profit/Unit	10.00	9.00								
11											
12											
13	Model										
14											
15											
16	Production Schedule							Labor Hours			
17	P1	P2						Used		Available	Slack
18	6824.86	1751.41		Max Profit	84011.30			6100.00	<=	6100.00	0.00
19								4559.89	<=	5200.00	640.11
20								8050.85	<=	8050.85	0.00
21								1549.15	<=	1549.15	0.00
22											
23			TRANSFER MATRIX					Max			
24	From/To	1	2	3	4	Total		Transfer			
25	1		0.00	400.00		400.00	<=	400.00			
26	2			650.85	149.15	800.00	<=	800.00			
27	3				0.00	0.00	<=	100.00			
28	4	0.00	0.00			0.00	<=	200.00			
29	Total	0.00	0.00	1050.85	149.15						

Objective Function   The formula =SUMPRODUCT(B10:C10,A18:B18) has been placed into cell E18 to reflect the profit. The optimal solution is shown to provide a profit of $84,011.30.

Left-Hand Sides   The left-hand sides for the 8 constraints are placed into cells H18:H21 and F25:F28.

      Cell H18 =SUMPRODUCT(B5:C5,$A$18:$B$18)
              (Copy to H19:H21)
      Cell F25 =SUM(C25:D25)
      Cell F26 =SUM(D26:E26)
      Cell F27 =E27
      Cell F28 =SUM(B28:C28)

Right-Hand Sides   The right-hand sides for the 8 constraints are placed into cells J18:J21 and H25:H28.

      Cell J18 =D5+B29−F25
      Cell J19 =D6+C29−F26
      Cell J20 =D7+D29−F27
      Cell J21 =D8+E29−F28
      Cell H25 =H5   (Copy to H26:H28)

Spreadsheet Solution.   The solution can be obtained by selecting **Solver** from the **Tools** menu, entering the proper values into the **Solver Parameters** dialog box, and specifying the options **Assume Linear Model** and **Assume Non-Negative.** The information entered into the **Solver Parameters** dialog box is shown in Figure 4.22.

Discussion.   Comparing the solutions shown in Figures 4.19 and 4.21, we see that McCormick's profit can be increased by $10,421 to $84,011 by taking advantage of cross-training and workforce transfers. The optimal product mix (rounded) of 6825 units of product 1 and 1751 units of product 2 can be achieved if $t_{13} = 400$ hours are transferred from department 1 to department 3; $t_{23} = 651$ hours are transferred from department 2 to department 3; and $t_{24} = 149$ hours are transferred from department 2 to department 4. The resulting workforce assignments for departments 1–4 provide 6100, 5200, 8051, and 1549 hours, respectively.

Variations in the workforce assignment model could be used in situations such as allocating raw material resources to products, allocating machine time to products, and allocating salesforce time to stores or sales territories.

If a manager has the flexibility to assign personnel to different departments, reduced workforce idle time, improved workforce utilization, and improved profit should result. The linear programming model in this section automatically assigns employees and labor-hours to the departments in the most profitable manner.

4.4   BLENDING PROBLEMS

Blending problems arise whenever a manager must decide how to blend two or more resources to produce one or more products. In these situations, the resources contain one or more essential ingredients that must be blended into final products that will contain specific percentages of each. In most of these applications, then, management must decide how

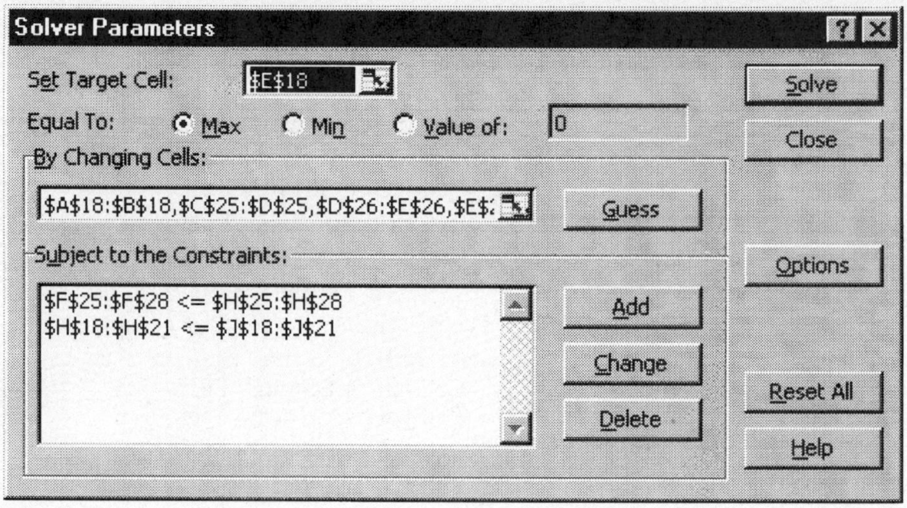

Figure **4.22** SOLVER PARAMETERS DIALOG BOX FOR THE MCCORMICK MANUFACTURING COMPANY PROBLEM—LABOR TRANSFERS PERMITTED

much of each resource to purchase to satisfy product specifications and product demands at minimum cost.

Blending problems occur frequently in the petroleum industry (e.g., blending crude oil to produce different-octane gasolines), chemical industry (e.g., blending chemicals to produce fertilizers and weed killers), and food industry (e.g., blending ingredients to produce soft drinks and soups). In this section we illustrate how to apply linear programming to a blending problem in the petroleum industry.

The Grand Strand Oil Company produces regular and premium gasoline for independent service stations in the southeastern United States. The Grand Strand refinery manufactures the gasoline products by blending three petroleum components. The gasolines are sold at different prices, and the petroleum components have different costs. The firm wants to determine how to mix or blend the three components into the two gasoline products and maximize profits.

Data available show that regular gasoline can be sold for $1.00 per gallon and premium gasoline for $1.08 per gallon. For the current production planning period, Grand Strand can obtain the three petroleum components at the cost per gallon and in the quantities shown in Table 4.11.

Product specifications for the regular and premium gasolines restrict the amounts of each component that can be used in each gasoline product. Table 4.12 lists the product specifications. Current commitments to distributors require Grand Strand to produce at least 10,000 gallons of regular gasoline.

The Grand Strand blending problem is to determine how many gallons of each component should be used in the regular gasoline blend and how many gallons should be used in the premium gasoline blend. The optimal blending solution should maximize the firm's profit, subject to the constraints on the available petroleum supplies shown in Table 4.11,

Table 4.11 PETROLEUM COST AND SUPPLY FOR THE GRAND STRAND BLENDING PROBLEM

Petroleum Component	Cost/Gallon	Maximum Available
1	$0.50	5,000 gallons
2	$0.60	10,000 gallons
3	$0.84	10,000 gallons

Table 4.12 PRODUCT SPECIFICATIONS FOR THE GRAND STRAND BLENDING PROBLEM

Product	Specifications
Regular gasoline	At most 30% component 1
	At most 20% component 3
	At least 40% component 2
Premium gasoline	At least 25% component 1
	At least 30% component 3
	At most 40% component 2

the product specifications shown in Table 4.12, and the required 10,000 gallons of regular gasoline.

We define the decision variables as

$$x_{ij} = \text{gallons of component } i \text{ used in gasoline } j,$$
$$\text{where } i = 1, 2, \text{ or } 3 \text{ for components 1, 2, or 3,}$$
$$\text{and } j = r \text{ if regular or } j = p \text{ if premium}$$

The six decision variables are

$$x_{1r} = \text{gallons of component 1 in regular gasoline}$$
$$x_{2r} = \text{gallons of component 2 in regular gasoline}$$
$$x_{3r} = \text{gallons of component 3 in regular gasoline}$$
$$x_{1p} = \text{gallons of component 1 in premium gasoline}$$
$$x_{2p} = \text{gallons of component 2 in premium gasoline}$$
$$x_{3p} = \text{gallons of component 3 in premium gasoline}$$

The total number of gallons of each type of gasoline produced is the sum of the number of gallons produced using each of the three petroleum components.

Total Gallons Produced

$$\text{Regular gasoline} = x_{1r} + x_{2r} + x_{3r}$$
$$\text{Premium gasoline} = x_{1p} + x_{2p} + x_{3p}$$

Similarly, the total gallons of each petroleum component used are provided by

Total Petroleum Component Use

$$\text{Component 1} = x_{1r} + x_{1p}$$
$$\text{Component 2} = x_{2r} + x_{2p}$$
$$\text{Component 3} = x_{3r} + x_{3p}$$

We develop the objective function of maximizing the profit contribution by identifying the difference between the total revenue from both gasolines and the total cost of the three petroleum components. By multiplying the $1.00 per gallon price by the total gallons of regular gasoline, the $1.08 per gallon price by the total gallons of premium gasoline, and the component cost per gallon figures in Table 4.11 by the total gallons of each component used, we obtain the objective function:

$$\text{Max} \quad 1.00(x_{1r} + x_{2r} + x_{3r}) + 1.08(x_{1p} + x_{2p} + x_{3p})$$
$$- 0.50(x_{1r} + x_{1p}) - 0.60(x_{2r} + x_{2p}) - 0.84(x_{3r} + x_{3p})$$

The limitations on the availability of the three petroleum components are

$$x_{1r} + x_{1p} \leq 5{,}000 \quad \text{Component 1}$$
$$x_{2r} + x_{2p} \leq 10{,}000 \quad \text{Component 2}$$
$$x_{3r} + x_{3p} \leq 10{,}000 \quad \text{Component 3}$$

The constraint requiring production of at least 10,000 gallons of regular gasoline is

$$x_{1r} + x_{2r} + x_{3r} \geq 10{,}000$$

Six constraints are now required to meet the product specifications stated in Table 4.12. The first specification states that component 1 can account for no more than 30% of the total gallons of regular gasoline produced. That is,

$$x_{1r} \leq 0.30(x_{1r} + x_{2r} + x_{3r})$$

The second product specification for regular gasoline results in the following constraint:

$$x_{3r} \leq .2(x_{1r} + x_{2r} + x_{3r})$$

The third product specification for regular gasoline leads to the following constraint:

$$x_{2r} \geq 0.40(x_{1r} + x_{2r} + x_{3r})$$

Similarly, the 3 product specifications for premium gasoline (see Table 4.12) lead to the following constraints:

$$x_{1p} \geq 0.25(x_{1p} + x_{2p} + x_{3p})$$
$$x_{3p} \geq 0.30(x_{1p} + x_{2p} + x_{3p})$$
$$x_{2p} \leq 0.40(x_{1p} + x_{2p} + x_{3p})$$

The complete linear programming model has 6 decision variables and 10 constraints. The spreadsheet formulation and solution are shown in Figure 4.23.

Spreadsheet Formulation.   The data and descriptive labels are contained in cells A1:L11 in the top portion of the spreadsheet. The screened cells in the bottom portion of the spreadsheet contain the key elements of the model required by the Excel Solver.

Decision Variables   Cells B20:D21 are reserved for the decision variables—the amount of each component used in each type of gasoline. The optimal values are shown to be $x_{1r} = 0$, $x_{2r} = 8000$, $x_{3r} = 2000$, $x_{1p} = 5000$, $x_{2p} = 2000$, $x_{3p} = 8000$.

Objective Function   The formula =SUMPRODUCT(B4:B5,E20:E21)−SUMPRODUCT (B9:D9,B22:D22) has been placed into cell C16 to reflect the profit. The optimal solution is shown to provide a profit of $9300.

Left-Hand Sides   The left-hand sides for the 10 constraints are placed into cells B22:D22, E20, J19:J21, and J24:J26.
    Cell B22 =SUM(B20:B21)   (Copy to C22:D22)
    Cell E20 =SUM(B20:D20)
    Cell J19 =B20
    Cell J20 =D20
    Cell J21 =C20

					SPREADSHEET SOLUTION FOR THE GRAND STRAND OIL
	Figure 4.23				COMPANY PROBLEM

Figure 4.23 SPREADSHEET SOLUTION FOR THE GRAND STRAND OIL COMPANY PROBLEM

	A	B	C	D	E	F	G	H	I	J	K	L
1	**Grand Strand Blending**											
2												
3		**Sales Price**				**Regular**						
4	**Regular**	1.00				Max Comp 1	30%					
5	**Premium**	1.08				Max Comp 3	20%		**Min Production - Regular**			10000
6						Min Comp 2	40%					
7			**Component**									
8		1	2	3		**Premium**						
9	**Cost/Gal**	0.50	0.60	0.84		Min Comp 1	25%					
10	**Gal/Avl**	5000	10000	10000		Min Comp 3	30%					
11						Max Comp 2	40%					
12												
13												
14	**Model**											
15												
16		**Max Profit**	9300									
17												
18			**Component**						**Regular**			
19		1	2	3	**Total**		**Demand**		Max Comp 1	0	<=	3000
20	**Regular**	0	8000	2000	10000	>=	10000		Max Comp 3	2000	<=	2000
21	**Premium**	5000	2000	8000	15000				Min Comp 2	8000	>=	4000
22	**Total**	5000	10000	10000								
23		<=	<=	<=					**Premium**			
24		5000	10000	10000					Min Comp 1	5000	>=	3750
25									Min Comp 3	8000	>=	4500
26									Max Comp 2	2000	<=	6000

Cell J24 =B21
Cell J25 =D21
Cell J26 =C21

Right-Hand Sides   The right-hand sides for the 10 constraints are placed into cells B24:D24, G20, L19:L21, and L24:L26.

Cell B24 =B10   (Copy to C24:C25)
Cell G20 =L5
Cell L19 =G4*$E$20   (Copy to L20:L21)
Cell L24 =G9*$E$21   (Copy to L25:L26)

Try Problem 15 as another example of a blending model.

Spreadsheet Solution.   The solution can be obtained by selecting **Solver** from the **Tools** menu, entering the proper values into the **Solver Parameters** dialog box and specifying the options **Assume Linear Model** and **Assume Non-Negative.** The information entered into the **Solver Parameters** dialog box is shown in Figure 4.24.

Discussion.   The optimal solution provides a profit of $9,300. A summary showing the percentage of each component in the 2 types of gasolines is shown in Table 4.13. Ten-thousand gallons of regular gasoline should be produced as a blend of 80% component 2 and 20% component 3. Fifteen-thousand gallons of premium gasoline should be produced as a blend of 33.3% component 1, 13.3% component 2, and 53.3% component 3.

From Figure 4.23 we see that all component ingredients are used (compare cells B22:D22 with B24:D24). In terms of the product specifications, the only binding constraint is the maximum amount of component 3 that may be used in regular gasoline (compare cells J20 and L20).

Figure 4.24   SOLVER PARAMETERS DIALOG BOX FOR THE GRAND STRAND OIL COMPANY

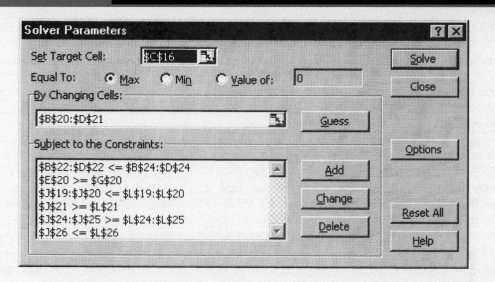

Table 4.13   GRAND STRAND GASOLINE BLENDING SOLUTION

	Gallons of Component (percentage)			
Gasoline	**Component 1**	**Component 2**	**Component 3**	**Total**
Regular	0 (0%)	8000 (80%)	2000 (20%)	10,000
Premium	5000 (33$1/3$%)	2000 (13$1/3$%)	8000 (53$1/3$%)	15,000

N O T E S
and Comments

The product specifications in a blending problem (see Table 4.12) can be thought of as providing the recipe for the final products. The recipe tells how to blend the ingredients to make the final product. In cases where the product specification constraints are inequalities, some latitude in how the ingredients are blended to meet the objective is allowed.

4.5   DATA ENVELOPMENT ANALYSIS

Data envelopment analysis (DEA) is an application of linear programming that has been used to measure the relative efficiency of operating units with the same goals and objectives. For example, DEA has been used to compare fast-food outlets in the same chain. In this case, the goal of DEA was to identify the inefficient outlets that should be targeted for further study and, if necessary, corrective action. Other applications of DEA have measured the relative efficiencies of hospitals, banks, courts, schools, and so on. In these applications, the performance of each institution or organization was measured relative to the performance of all operating units in the same system. The Management Science in Action: Managing Bank Productivity describes how a large northeastern bank used DEA to determine which branches were operating inefficiently.

MANAGEMENT SCIENCE IN ACTION

MANAGING BANK PRODUCTIVITY*

A large northeastern bank wanted to expand its existing 33 branch system to cover a wider geographic region. To help finance the expansion, management wanted to identify ways in which they could streamline existing operations in order to obtain substantial savings but at the same time avoid sacrificing quality of service. As the first step in reviewing productivity of the branches, data envelopment analysis (DEA) was used to indicate which branches were operating inefficiently.

The DEA model developed compared the actual operating results of each branch with those of all other branches in order to identify the less-productive branches. A less-productive branch is one that requires more resources to produce the same output as the best-practice branches. The best-practice branches are identified by a DEA productivity rating of 100 percent ($E = 1.00$), and the inefficient or less-productive branches are identified by a productivity rating of less than 100 percent ($E < 1.00$).

Five key resources used by each branch were used, including the number of teller and manager personnel full-time equivalents (FTEs), branch operating expenses, and square feet of office space. In addition, 15 services that were performed by each branch were combined into five categories of service. For instance, the deposits, withdrawals, and checks cashed category was formed by treating each deposit, withdrawal, or check cashed as one transaction. For this service category, the output measure was the number of deposits, withdrawals, or checks cashed. Other service categories included measures of the number of bank checks, traveler checks, night deposits, and loans made by the branch.

For each branch, data were collected for these resource and service measures for the previous year.

The solution to the DEA linear programming model using these data showed that 10 of the 33 branches had a DEA productivity rating of 100 percent and that 23 branches had a rating of less than 100 percent; in other words, 23 branches were less productive. For instance, one branch had a DEA rating of 37 percent, indicating that it was using about 63 percent excess resources. Overall, the findings indicated that the bank could make substantial productivity improvements and realize significant cost reductions by improving performance at the 23 less-productive branches.

Focusing on the less-productive branches, the bank was able to identify ways in which these branches could significantly reduce their resource requirement without reducing quality of service and while maintaining or even increasing the volume of services provided. The total potential savings were determined to be approximately $9 million. However, some changes required square feet reductions at certain branches, something that could not be done in the short run. For the next year, management concluded and reported to the board of directors that savings of over $6 million of the $30 million operating costs for the less-productive branches could be realized.

*Based on H. David Sherman and George Ladino, "Managing Bank Productivity Using Data Envelopment Analysis (DEA)," *Interfaces* (March-April 1995): 60–73.

The operating units of most organizations have multiple inputs, such as staff size, salaries, hours of operation, and advertising budget, as well as multiple outputs, such as profit, market share, and growth rate. In these situations, a manager often has difficulty determining which operating units are inefficient in converting their multiple inputs into multiple outputs. This particular area is where data envelopment analysis has proven to be a helpful managerial tool. We illustrate the application of data envelopment analysis by evaluating the performance of a group of four hospitals.

Evaluating the Performance of Hospitals

The hospital administrators at General Hospital, University Hospital, County Hospital, and State Hospital have been meeting to discuss ways in which they can help one another improve the performance at each of their hospitals. A consultant has suggested that they consider using DEA to measure the performance of each hospital relative to the performance of all four hospitals. In discussing how this could be done, the following three input measures and four output measures were identified:

Input Measures

1. The number of full-time equivalent (FTE) nonphysician personnel
2. The amount spent on supplies
3. The number of bed-days available

Output Measures

1. Patient-days of service under Medicare
2. Patient-days of service not under Medicare
3. Number of nurses trained
4. Number of interns trained

Summaries of the input and output measures for a 1-year period at each of the four hospitals are shown in Tables 4.14 and 4.15. Let us show how DEA can use these data to identify relatively inefficient hospitals.

An Overview of the DEA Approach

In this application of DEA, a linear programming model is developed for each hospital whose efficiency is to be evaluated. To illustrate the modeling process, we formulate a linear program that can be used to determine the relative efficiency of County Hospital.

Problem 26 asks you to formulate and solve a linear program to assess the relative efficiency of General Hospital.

First, using a linear programming model, we construct a hypothetical composite hospital based on the outputs and inputs for all four hospitals. For each of the four output measures, the output for the composite hospital is determined by computing a weighted average of the corresponding outputs for all four hospitals. For each of the three input measures, the input for the composite hospital is determined by using the same weights

Table **4.14**	ANNUAL RESOURCES CONSUMED (INPUTS) FOR THE FOUR HOSPITALS			
	Hospital			
Input Measure	**General**	**University**	**County**	**State**
Full-time equivalent nonphysicians	285.20	162.30	275.70	210.40
Supply expense ($1000s)	123.80	128.70	348.50	154.10
Bed-days available (1000s)	106.72	64.21	104.10	104.04

Table **4.15**	ANNUAL SERVICES PROVIDED (OUTPUTS) FOR THE FOUR HOSPITALS			
	Hospital			
Output Measure	**General**	**University**	**County**	**State**
Medicare patient-days (1000s)	48.14	34.62	36.72	33.16
Non-Medicare patient-days (1000s)	43.10	27.11	45.98	56.46
Nurses trained	253	148	175	160
Interns trained	41	27	23	84

to compute a weighted average of the corresponding inputs for all four hospitals. Constraints in the linear programming model require all outputs for the composite hospital to be *greater than or equal to* the outputs of County Hospital, the hospital being evaluated. If the inputs for the composite unit can be shown to be *less than* the inputs for County Hospital, the composite hospital will be shown to have the same, or more, output for *less input*. In this case, the model shows that the composite hospital is more efficient than County Hospital. In other words, the hospital being evaluated is *less efficient* than the composite hospital. Since the composite hospital is based on all four hospitals, the hospital being evaluated can be judged *relatively inefficient* when compared to the other hospitals in the group.

The DEA Linear Programming Model

To determine the weight that each hospital will have in computing the outputs and inputs for the composite hospital, we use the following decision variables:

$$wg = \text{weight applied to inputs and outputs for General Hospital}$$
$$wu = \text{weight applied to inputs and outputs for University Hospital}$$
$$wc = \text{weight applied to inputs and outputs for County Hospital}$$
$$ws = \text{weight applied to inputs and outputs for State Hospital}$$

The DEA approach requires that the sum of these weights equal 1. Thus, the first constraint is

$$wg + wu + wc + ws = 1$$

In general, every DEA linear programming model will include a constraint that requires the weights for the operating units to sum to 1.

As we stated previously, for each output measure, the output for the composite hospital is determined by computing a weighted average of the corresponding outputs for all four hospitals. For instance, for output measure 1, the number of patient days of service under Medicare, the output for the composite hospital is

$$\begin{pmatrix} \text{Medicare Patient-Days} \\ \text{for Composite Hospital} \end{pmatrix} = \begin{pmatrix} \text{Medicare Patient-Days} \\ \text{for General Hospital} \end{pmatrix}wg + \begin{pmatrix} \text{Medicare Patient-Days} \\ \text{for University Hospital} \end{pmatrix}wu$$
$$+ \begin{pmatrix} \text{Medicare Patient-Days} \\ \text{for County Hospital} \end{pmatrix}wc + \begin{pmatrix} \text{Medicare Patient-Days} \\ \text{for State Hospital} \end{pmatrix}ws$$

Substituting the number of medicare patient-days for each hospital as shown in Table 4.15, we obtain the following expression:

$$\begin{matrix} \text{Medicare Patient-Days} \\ \text{for Composite Hospital} \end{matrix} = 48.14wg + 34.62wu + 36.72wc + 33.16ws$$

The other output measures for the composite hospital are computed in a similar fashion. Figure 4.25 provides a summary of the results.

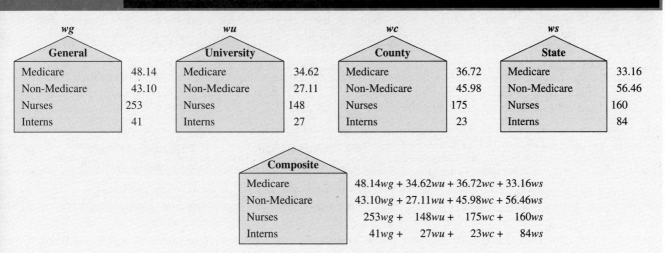

Figure 4.25 RELATIONSHIP BETWEEN THE OUTPUT MEASURES FOR THE FOUR HOSPITALS AND THE OUTPUT MEASURES FOR THE COMPOSITE HOSPITAL

For each of the four output measures, we need to write a constraint that requires the output for the composite hospital to be greater than or equal to the output for County Hospital. Thus, the general form of the output constraints is

$$\text{Output for the Composite Hospital} \geq \text{Output for County Hospital}$$

Since the number of medicare patient-days for County Hospital is 36.72, the output constraint corresponding to the number of medicare patient-days is

$$48.14wg + 34.62wu + 36.72wc + 33.16ws \geq 36.72$$

In a similar fashion, we formulated a constraint for each of the other three output measures, with the results as shown:

$$43.10wg + 27.11wu + 45.98wc + 56.46ws \geq 45.98 \quad \text{Non-Medicare}$$
$$253wg + 148wu + 175wc + 160ws \geq 175 \quad \text{Nurses}$$
$$41wg + 27wu + 23wc + 84ws \geq 23 \quad \text{Interns}$$

The four output constraints require the linear programming solution to provide weights that will make each output measure for the composite hospital greater than or equal to the corresponding output measure for County Hospital. Thus, if a solution satisfying the output constraints can be found, the composite hospital will have produced at least as much of each output as County Hospital.

Next, we need to consider the constraints needed to model the relationship between the inputs for the composite hospital and the resources available to the composite hospital. A constraint is required for each of the three input measures. The general form for the input constraints is as follows:

$$\text{Input for the Composite Hospital} \leq \text{Resources Available to the Composite Hospital}$$

For each input measure, the input for the composite hospital is a weighted average of the corresponding input for each of the four hospitals. Thus, for input measure 1, the number of full-time equivalent nonphysicians, the input for the composite hospital is

$$\begin{pmatrix} \text{FTE Nonphysicians} \\ \text{for Composite} \\ \text{Hospital} \end{pmatrix} = \begin{pmatrix} \text{FTE Nonphysicians} \\ \text{for General Hospital} \end{pmatrix} wg + \begin{pmatrix} \text{FTE Nonphysicians} \\ \text{for University Hospital} \end{pmatrix} wu$$
$$+ \begin{pmatrix} \text{FTE Nonphysicians} \\ \text{for County Hospital} \end{pmatrix} wc + \begin{pmatrix} \text{FTE Nonphysicians} \\ \text{for State Hospital} \end{pmatrix} ws$$

Substituting the values for the number of full-time equivalent nonphysicians for each hospital as shown in Table 4.14, we obtain the following expression for the number of full-time equivalent nonphysicians for the composite hospital:

$$285.20wg + 162.30wu + 275.70wc + 210.40ws$$

In a similar manner, we can write expressions for each of the other two input measures as shown in Figure 4.26.

To complete the formulation of the input constraints, we must write expressions for the right-hand-side values for each constraint. First, note that the right-hand-side values are

Figure 4.26   RELATIONSHIP BETWEEN THE INPUT MEASURES FOR THE FOUR HOSPITALS AND THE INPUT MEASURES FOR THE COMPOSITE HOSPITAL

	wg		wu		wc		ws
	General		**University**		**County**		**State**
285.20	FTE Nonphysicians	162.30	FTE Nonphysicians	275.70	FTE Nonphysicians	210.40	FTE Nonphysicians
123.80	Supply Expense	128.70	Supply Expense	348.50	Supply Expense	154.10	Supply Expense
106.72	Bed-Days	64.21	Bed-Days	104.10	Bed-Days	104.04	Bed-Days

Composite

$285.20wg + 162.30wu + 275.70wc + 210.40ws$	FTE Nonphysicians
$123.80wg + 128.70wu + 348.50wc + 154.10ws$	Supply Expense
$106.72wg + 64.21wu + 104.10wc + 104.04ws$	Bed-Days

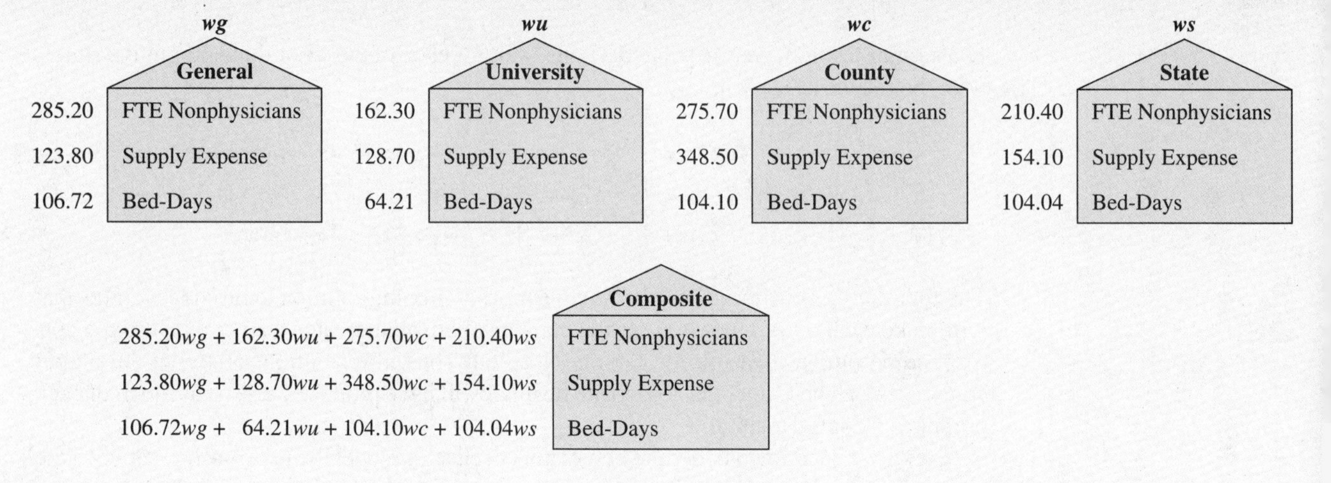

the resources available to the composite hospital. In the DEA approach, these right-hand-side values are a percentage of the input values for County Hospital. Thus, we must introduce the following decision variables:

$$E = \text{the fraction of County Hospital's input available to the composite hospital}$$

The logic of a DEA model is to determine whether a composite facility can achieve the *same or more output* as the test facility *while requiring less input.* If more output with less input can be achieved, the test facility is judged to be relatively inefficient.

In order to illustrate the important role that E plays in the DEA approach, we show how to write the expression for the number of FTE nonphysicians available to the composite hospital. Table 4.14 shows that the number of FTE nonphysicians used by County Hospital was 275.70; thus, 275.70E is the number of FTE nonphysicians available to the composite hospital. If $E = 1$, the number of FTE nonphysicians available to the composite hospital is 275.70, the same as the number of FTE nonphysicians used by County Hospital. However, if E is greater than 1, the composite hospital would have available proportionally more FTE nonphysicians, while if E is less than 1, the composite hospital would have available proportionally fewer FTE nonphysicians. Because of the effect that E has in determining the resources available to the composite hospital, E is referred to as the **efficiency index.**

We can now write the input constraint corresponding to the number of FTE nonphysicians available to the composite hospital:

$$285.20wg + 162.30wu + 275.70wc + 210.40ws \leq 275.70E$$

In a similar manner, we can write the input constraints for the supplies and bed-days available to the composite hospital. First, using the data in Table 4.14, we note that for each resource, the amount that is available to the composite hospital is 348.50E and 104.10E, respectively. Thus, the input constraints for the supplies and bed-days are written as follows:

$$123.80wg + 128.70wu + 348.50wc + 154.10ws \leq 348.50E \quad \text{Supplies}$$
$$106.72wg + 64.21wu + 104.10wc + 104.04ws \leq 104.10E \quad \text{Bed-days}$$

If a solution with $E < 1$ can be found, the composite hospital does not need as many resources as County Hospital needs to produce the same level of output.

The objective function in a DEA model is always Min E. The facility being analyzed (County Hospital in this example) can be judged relatively inefficient if the optimal solution provides E less than 1, indicating that the composite facility requires less input resources.

The objective function for the DEA model is to minimize the value of E, which is equivalent to minimizing the input resources available to the composite hospital. Thus, the objective function is written as

$$\text{Min } E$$

The DEA efficiency conclusion is based on the optimal objective function value for E. The decision rule is as follows:

If $E = 1$, the composite hospital requires *as much input* as County Hospital does. There is no evidence that County Hospital is inefficient.

If $E < 1$, the composite hospital requires *less input* to obtain the output achieved by County Hospital. The composite hospital is more efficient; thus, County Hospital can be judged relatively inefficient.

The DEA linear programming model for the efficiency evaluation of County Hospital has five decision variables and eight constraints. The complete model is rewritten below:

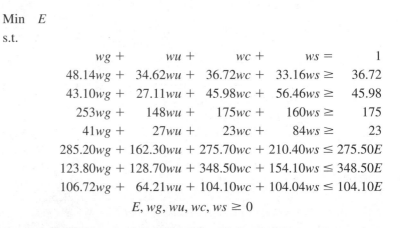

Min E

s.t.

$$
\begin{aligned}
wg + wu + wc + ws &= 1 \\
48.14wg + 34.62wu + 36.72wc + 33.16ws &\geq 36.72 \\
43.10wg + 27.11wu + 45.98wc + 56.46ws &\geq 45.98 \\
253wg + 148wu + 175wc + 160ws &\geq 175 \\
41wg + 27wu + 23wc + 84ws &\geq 23 \\
285.20wg + 162.30wu + 275.70wc + 210.40ws &\leq 275.50E \\
123.80wg + 128.70wu + 348.50wc + 154.10ws &\leq 348.50E \\
106.72wg + 64.21wu + 104.10wc + 104.04ws &\leq 104.10E \\
E, wg, wu, wc, ws &\geq 0
\end{aligned}
$$

The spreadsheet formulation and solution are shown in Figure 4.27.

SPREADSHEET
COUNTY
HOSPITAL

Figure 4.27   SPREADSHEET SOLUTION FOR THE COUNTY HOSPITAL PROBLEM

	A	B	C	D	E	F	G
1	**County Hospital**						
2							
3				**Hospital**			
4	**Input Measure**	General	University	County	State		
5	FTE nonphys.	285.20	162.30	275.70	210.40		
6	Supply Expense($1000s)	123.80	128.70	348.50	154.10		
7	Bed Days Available (1000s)	106.72	64.21	104.10	104.04		
8							
9				**Hospital**			
10	**Output Measure**	General	University	County	State		
11	Med. Pat. Days (1000s)	48.14	34.62	36.72	33.16		
12	Non-Med. Pat. Days (1000s)	43.10	27.11	45.98	56.46		
13	Nurses Trained	253	148	175	160		
14	Interns Trained	41	27	23	84		
15							
16							
17	**Model**						
18							
19				**Weights**		**Efficiency**	
20		WG	WU	WC	WS	E	
21	Optimal Solution	0.2122662	0.260447	0	0.527287	0.905237878	
22							
23		**LHS**		**RHS**		**Min E**	0.905238
24	Sum	1	=	1			
25	Med. Pat. Days (1000s)	36.72	>=	36.72			
26	Non-Med. Pat. Days (1000s)	45.98	>=	45.98			
27	Nurses Trained	176.61539	>=	175.00			
28	Interns Trained	60.027067	>=	23.00			
29	FTE nonphys.	213.75	<=	249.574			
30	Supply Expense($1000s)	141.05298	<=	315.475			
31	Bed Days Available (1000s)	94.235263	<=	94.2353			

Spreadsheet Formulation.   The data and descriptive labels are contained in cells A1:E14 in the top portion of the spreadsheet. The screened cells in the bottom portion of the spreadsheet contain the key elements of the model required by the Excel Solver.

Decision Variables   Cells B21:F21 are reserved for the 5 decision variables. The optimal values are shown to be $wg = 0.212$, $wu = 0.260$, $wc = 0$, $ws = 0.527$, and $E = 0.90524$.

Objective Function   The formula =F21 has been placed into cell G23 to reflect the efficiency score for County Hospital. Note that it is the same as the decision variable E contained in cell F21.

Left-Hand Sides   The left-hand sides for the 8 constraints are placed into cells B24:B31.

> Cell B24 =SUM(B21:E21)
>
> Cell B25 =SUMPRODUCT(B11:E11,$B$21:$E$21)
> (Copy to B26:B28)
>
> Cell B29 =SUMPRODUCT(B5:E5,$B$21:$E$21)
> (Copy to B30:B31)

Right-Hand Sides   The right-hand sides for the 8 constraints are placed into cells D24:D31.
> Cell D24 1
> Cell D25 =D11   (Copy to D26:D28)
> Cell D29 =D5*$F$21   (Copy to D30:D31)

Spreadsheet Solution.   The solution can be obtained by selecting **Solver** from the **Tools** menu, entering the proper values into the **Solver Parameters** dialog box, and specifying the options **Assume Linear Model** and **Assume Non-Negative.** The information entered into the **Solver Parameters** dialog box is shown in Figure 4.28.

Figure 4.28   SOLVER PARAMETERS DIALOG BOX FOR THE COUNTY HOSPITAL PROBLEM

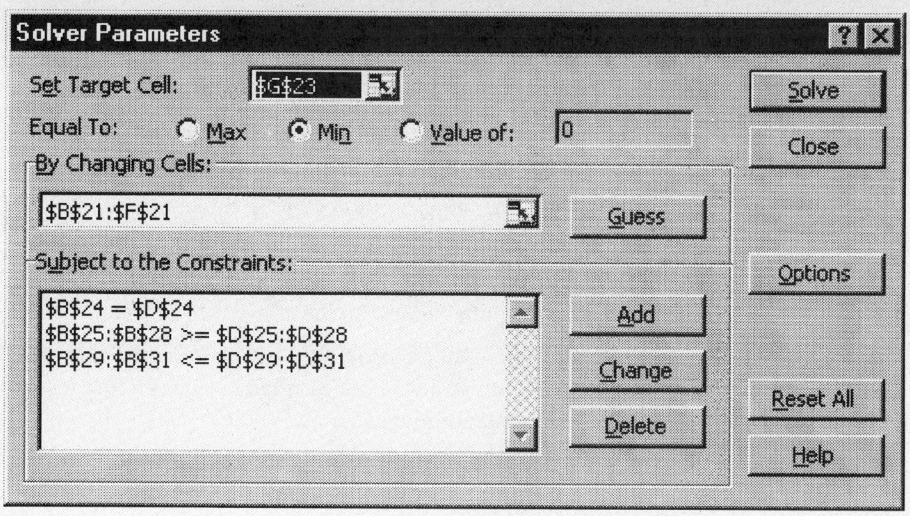

Discussion.   Reviewing the optimal solution (see Figure 4.27), we note that the objective function shows that the efficiency score for County Hospital is 0.905. This result tells us that the composite hospital can obtain at least the level of each output that County Hospital obtains by having available no more than 90.5% of the input resources required by County Hospital. Thus, the composite hospital is more efficient, and the DEA analysis has identified County Hospital as being relatively inefficient.

From the solution in Figure 4.27, we see that the composite hospital is formed from the weighted average of General Hospital ($wg = 0.212$), University Hospital ($wu = 0.260$), and State Hospital ($ws = 0.527$). Each input and output of the composite hospital is determined by the same weighted average of the inputs and outputs of these three hospitals.

Analysis of the constraints provides some additional information about the efficiency of County Hospital compared to the composite hospital. The composite hospital provides at least as much of each output as County Hospital (compare cells B25:B28 with cells D25:D28). Indeed, the composite hospital is capable of training 1.6 more nurses and 37 more interns with less resources than County Hospital. From the "Bed-Days" constraint we see that the composite hospital uses approximately 90.5% of the bed-days used by County Hospital (compare cells B31 and D31 of Figure 4.27). Furthermore, comparing cells B29:B30 with D29:D30, we see that the composite hospital uses much less than 90.5% of the County Hospital resources involving FTE nonphysician and supply expenses.

Clearly, the composite hospital is more efficient than County Hospital, and we are justified in concluding that County Hospital is relatively inefficient compared to the hospitals in the group. Given the results of the DEA analysis, hospital administrators should examine operations to determine how County Hospital resources can be more effectively utilized.

Summary of the DEA Approach

To use data envelopment analysis to measure the relative efficiency of County Hospital, we used a linear programming model to construct a hypothetical composite hospital based on the outputs and inputs for the four hospitals in the problem. The approach to solving other types of problems using DEA is similar. That is, for each operating unit that we want to measure the efficiency of, we must formulate and solve a linear programming model similar to the linear program we solved to measure the relative efficiency of County Hospital. The following step-by-step procedure should help you in formulating a linear programming model for other types of DEA applications. Note that the operating unit that we want to measure the relative efficiency of is referred to as the jth operating unit.

Step 1:   Define decision variables or weights (one for each operating unit) that can be used to determine the inputs and outputs for the composite operating unit.

Step 2:   Write a constraint that requires the weights to sum to 1.

Step 3:   For each output measure write a constraint that requires the output for the composite operating unit to be greater than or equal to the corresponding output for the jth operating unit.

Step 4:   Define a decision variable, E, which determines the fraction of the jth operating unit's input available to the composite hospital.

Step 5:   For each input measure write a constraint that requires the input for the composite operating unit to be less than or equal to the resources available to the composite operating unit.

Step 6:   Write the objective function as Min E.

N O T E S
and Comments

1. Remember that the goal of data envelopment analysis is to identify operating units that are relatively inefficient. The method *does not* necessarily identify the operating units that are *relatively efficient*. Just because the efficiency index is $E = 1$, we cannot conclude that the unit being analyzed is relatively efficient. Indeed, any unit that has the largest output on any one of the output measures cannot be judged relatively inefficient.

2. DEA could show all but one unit to be relatively inefficient. Such would be the case if a unit producing the most of every output also consumes the least of every input. Such cases are extremely rare in practice.

3. In applying data envelopment analysis to problems involving a large group of operating units, practitioners have found that roughly 50% of the operating units can be identified as inefficient. Comparing each relatively inefficient unit to the units contributing to the composite unit may be helpful in understanding how the operation of each relatively inefficient unit can be improved.

SUMMARY

In this chapter we presented a broad range of applications that demonstrate how linear programming can be used in decision-making. We formulated and solved problems from marketing, finance, operations management, and illustrated how linear programming can be applied to blending problems and data envelopment analysis.

Many of the illustrations presented in this chapter are scaled-down versions of actual situations in which linear programming has been applied. In real-world applications, the problem is usually not so concisely stated, the data for the problem is usually not as readily available, and the problem often involves more variables and constraints. However, a thorough study of the applications in this chapter is a good place to begin in applying linear programming to real problems.

We close with a few comments on using spreadsheets to solve linear programming problems in practice. Practitioners generally recognize three steps in using linear programming methodology: matrix generation, solution, and report writing. *Matrix generation* involves taking the raw data and putting it into a form that is acceptable to the linear programing solver. *Solution* simply means using the solver to get the optimal solution. We have used Excel's solver in this chapter, but many other solvers are available. *Report writing* is the process of using the optimal solution to prepare managerial reports. In addition to the many solvers that are available, software packages are available to handle the matrix generation and report writing functions.

For the applications described in this chapter matrix generation, solution, and report writing were all accomplished with one spreadsheet. We organized the raw data in the top portion of the spreadsheet and the model in the bottom portion of the spreadsheet. The key elements of the model can be thought of as the output of the matrix generator. Essentially the spreadsheet formulas accomplish the matrix generation task. After the spreadsheet solver has been used to find an optimal solution, the bottom portion of the spreadsheet constitutes a managerial report. In this chapter, we have made an effort to layout the spreadsheets so that a manager could readily interpret the optimal solution. One advantage of using spreadsheets is that, within limits, each user can design the model section to suit her/his own needs. However, the key elements of the model that are required by the solver (decision variables, objective function, left-hand sides, and right-hand sides) must be present in the spreadsheet.

We have successfully employed spreadsheets to solve moderate-sized linear programs in practice. However, in many of these applications using three separate worksheets within the same Excel workbook is advantageous. One worksheet is used for the raw data—this worksheet is usually prepared by company management. A second worksheet is used for the model. We have used Visual Basic for Applications (a feature of Excel) to write a short program that creates the key elements of the model worksheet from the raw data. Then, we have used another Visual Basic program (module) to create a managerial report on a third worksheet.

Using spreadsheets for large-scale applications has a downside. First, the basic spreadsheet solvers are not designed for large problems. The standard solver available with Excel 97® will only solve problems with up to 200 variables. However, add ins are available from third party vendors that overcome size limitations.[3] Probably the biggest shortcoming of spreadsheets is their limited ability to accommodate structural changes in a model. For instance, as variables are added many of the formulas may have to be modified to accommodate the new problem. Also, accommodating problems in which only a few of the variables appear in most of the constraints is not necessarily easy. Such problems are called *sparse problems.* Unless the user is very knowledgeable, much spreadsheet space is wasted and large, sparse problems become unsolvable. In the next chapter, we show how to use spreadsheet space efficiently for a sparse transshipment problem.

··/ /···········

GLOSSARY

Make-or-buy decision A decision concerning whether to make a product inhouse or to purchase it outside.

Data envelopment analysis (DEA) An application of linear programming used to evaluate the relative efficiency of operating units.

Efficiency index An efficiency measure used in DEA. If the efficiency index for a unit is less than one, the unit is judged to be relatively inefficient.

··/ /···········

PROBLEMS

Note: The following problems have been designed to give you an understanding and appreciation of the broad range of problems that can be formulated as linear programs. You should be able to formulate a linear programming model for each problem. However, you will need access to a spreadsheet solver or another linear programming computer package to develop the solutions and make the requested interpretations.

---

3. Frontline Systems, Incline Village, Nevada, markets solver add ins for Excel, Lotus, and Quattro Pro that will solve problems with almost any number of variables.

1. The Westchester Chamber of Commerce periodically sponsors public service seminars and programs. Currently, promotional plans are under way for this year's program. Advertising alternatives include television, radio, and newspaper. Audience estimates, costs, and maximum media usage limitations are as shown.

Constraint	Television	Radio	Newspaper
Audience per advertisement	100,000	18,000	40,000
Cost per advertisement	$2,000	$300	$600
Maximum media usage	10	20	10

To ensure a balanced use of advertising media, radio advertisements must not exceed 50% of the total number of advertisements authorized. In addition, television should account for at least 10% of the total number of advertisements authorized.

a. If the promotional budget is limited to $18,200, how many commercial messages should be run on each medium to maximize total audience contact? What is the allocation of the budget among the three media, and what is the total audience reached?

b. By how much would audience contact increase if an extra $100 were allocated to the advertising budget?

2. The Hartman Company is trying to determine how much of each of two products to produce over the coming planning period. The following information concerns labor availability, labor utilization, and product profitability.

Department	Product (hours/unit)		Labor-Hours Available
	1	2	
A	1.00	0.35	100
B	0.30	0.20	36
C	0.20	0.50	50
Profit contribution/unit	$30.00	$15.00	—

a. Develop a linear programming model of the Hartman Company problem. Solve the model to determine the optimal production quantities of products 1 and 2.

b. In computing the profit contribution per unit, Hartman doesn't deduct labor costs because they are considered fixed for the upcoming planning period. However, suppose that overtime can be scheduled in some of the departments. Which departments would you recommend scheduling for overtime? How much would you be willing to pay per hour of overtime in each department?

c. Suppose that 10, 6, and 8 hours of overtime may be scheduled in departments A, B, and C, respectively. The cost per hour of overtime is $18 in department A, $22.50 in department B, and $12 in department C. Formulate a linear programming model that can be used to determine the optimal production quantities if overtime is made available. What are the optimal production quantities and what is the revised total contribution to profit? How much overtime do you recommend using in each department? What is the increase in the total contribution to profit if overtime is used?

3. The employee credit union at State University is planning the allocation of funds for the coming year. The credit union makes four types of loans to its members. In addition, the credit union

invests in risk-free securities to stabilize income. The various revenue-producing investments together with annual rates of return are as follows.

Type of Loan/Investment	Annual Rate of Return (%)
Automobile loans	8
Furniture loans	10
Other secured loans	11
Signature loans	12
Risk-free securities	9

The credit union will have $2,000,000 available for investment during the coming year. State laws and credit union policies impose the following restrictions on the composition of the loans and investments.

- Risk-free securities may not exceed 30% of the total funds available for investment.
- Signature loans may not exceed 10% of the funds invested in all loans (automobile, furniture, and other secured and signature loans).
- Furniture loans plus other secured loans may not exceed the automobile loans.
- Other secured loans plus signature loans may not exceed the funds invested in risk-free securities.

How should the $2,000,000 be allocated to each of the loan/investment alternatives to maximize total annual return? What is the projected total annual return?

4. Hilltop Coffee manufactures a coffee product by blending three types of coffee beans. The cost per pound and the available pounds of each bean are as follows.

Bean	Cost per Pound	Available Pounds
1	$0.50	500
2	$0.70	600
3	$0.45	400

Consumer tests with coffee products were used to provide ratings on a scale of 0–100, with higher ratings indicating higher quality. Product quality standards for the blended coffee require a consumer rating for aroma to be at least 75 and a consumer rating for taste to be at least 80. The individual ratings of the aroma and taste for coffee made from 100% of each bean are as follows.

Bean	Aroma Rating	Taste Rating
1	75	86
2	85	88
3	60	75

Assume that the aroma and taste attributes of the coffee blend will be a weighted average of the attributes of the beans used in the blend.

a. What is the minimum-cost blend that will meet the quality standards and provide 1000 pounds of the blended coffee product?

b. What is the cost per pound for the coffee blend?

    c.   Determine the aroma and taste ratings for the coffee blend.

    d.   If additional coffee were to be produced, what would be the expected cost per pound?

5. Ajax Fuels, Inc., is developing a new additive for airplane fuels. The additive is a mixture of three ingredients: A, B, and C. For proper performance, the total amount of additive (amount of A + amount of B + amount of C) must be at least 10 ounces per gallon of fuel. However, because of safety reasons, the amount of additive must not exceed 15 ounces per gallon of fuel. The mix or blend of the three ingredients is critical. At least 1 ounce of ingredient A must be used for every ounce of ingredient B. The amount of ingredient C must be greater than one-half the amount of ingredient A. If the costs per ounce for ingredients A, B, and C are $0.10, $0.03, and $0.09, respectively, find the minimum-cost mixture of A, B, and C for each gallon of airplane fuel.

6. G. Kunz and Sons, Inc., manufactures two products used in the heavy equipment industry. Both products require manufacturing operations in two departments. The following are the production time (in hours) and profit contribution figures for the two products.

		Labor-Hours	
Product	**Profit per Unit**	**Dept. A**	**Dept. B**
1	$25	6	12
2	$20	8	10

For the coming production period, Kunz has available a total of 900 hours of labor that can be allocated to either of the two departments. Find the production plan and labor allocation (hours assigned in each department) that will maximize the total contribution to profit.

7. As part of the settlement for a class action lawsuit, Hoxworth Corporation must provide sufficient cash to make the following annual payments (in thousands of dollars).

Year	1	2	3	4	5	6
Payment	190	215	240	285	315	460

The annual payments must be made at the beginning of each year. The judge will approve an amount that, along with earnings on its investment, will cover the annual payments. Investment of the funds will be limited to savings (at 4% annually) and government securities, at prices and rates currently quoted in *The Wall Street Journal.*

    Hoxworth wants to develop a plan for making the annual payments by investing in the following securities (par value = $1000). Funds not invested in these securities will be placed in savings.

Security	**Current Price**	**Rate (%)**	**Years to Maturity**
1	$1055	6.750	3
2	$1000	5.125	4

Assume that interest is paid annually. The plan will be submitted to the judge and, if approved, Hoxworth will be required to pay a trustee the amount that will be required to fund the plan.

    a.   Use linear programming to find the minimum cash settlement necessary to fund the annual payments.

    b.   Use the shadow price to determine how much more Hoxworth should be willing to pay now to reduce the payment at the beginning of year 6 to $400,000.

    c. Use the shadow price to determine how much more Hoxworth should be willing to pay to reduce the year 1 payment to $150,000?

    d. Suppose that the annual payments are to be made at the end of each year. Reformulate the model to accommodate this change. How much would Hoxworth save if this change could be negotiated?

8. The Clark County Sheriff's Department schedules police officers for 8-hour shifts. The beginning times for the shifts are 8:00 A.M., noon, 4:00 P.M., 8:00 P.M., midnight, and 4:00 A.M. An officer beginning a shift at one of the these times works for the next 8 hours. During normal weekday operations, the number of officers needed varies depending on the time of day. The department staffing guidelines require the following minimum number of officers on duty;

Time of Day	Minimum Officers on Duty
8:00 A.M.–noon	5
Noon–4:00 P.M.	6
4:00 P.M.–8:00 P.M.	10
8:00 P.M.–midnight	7
Midnight–4:00 A.M.	4
4:00 A.M.–8:00 A.M.	6

Determine the number of police officers that should be scheduled to begin the 8-hour shifts at each of the six times (8:00 A.M., noon, 4:00 P.M., 8:00 P.M., midnight, and 4:00 A.M.) to minimize the total number of officers required. (Hint: Let x_1 = the number of officers beginning work at 8:00 A.M., x_2 = the number of officers beginning work at noon, and so on.)

SELF TEST

9. Reconsider the Welte Mutual Funds problem from Section 4.2. Define your decision variables as the fraction of funds invested in each security. Also, modify the constraints limiting investments in the oil and steel industries as follows: No more than 50% of the total funds invested in stock (oil and steel) may be invested in the oil industry, and no more than 50% of the funds invested in stock (oil and steel) may be invested in the steel industry.

    a. Solve the revised linear programming model. What fraction of the portfolio should be invested in each type of security?

    b. How much should be invested in each type of security?

    c. What are the total earnings for the portfolio?

    d. What is the marginal rate of return on the portfolio? That is, how much more could be earned by investing one more dollar in the portfolio?

10. Lurix Electronics manufactures two products that can be produced on two different production lines. Both products have their lowest production costs when produced on the newer of the two production lines. However, the newer production line does not have the capacity to handle the total production. As a result, some production will have to be routed to the older production line. The following data show total production requirements, production line capacities, and production costs.

Product	Production Cost/Unit		Minimum Production Requirements
	New Line	Old Line	
1	$ 3.00	$ 5.00	500 units
2	$ 2.50	$ 4.00	700 units
Production line capacities	800	600	

Formulate a linear programming model that can be used to make the production routing decision. What is the recommended decision and the total cost?

11. Edwards Manufacturing Company purchases two component parts from three different suppliers. The suppliers have limited capacity, and no one supplier can meet all the company's needs. In addition, the suppliers charge different prices for the components. Component price data (in price/unit) are as follows.

| | Supplier | | |
Component	1	2	3
1	$12	$13	$14
2	$10	$11	$10

Each supplier has a limited capacity in terms of the total number of components it can supply. However, as long as Edwards provides sufficient advance orders, each supplier can devote its capacity to component 1, component 2, or any combination of the two components. Supplier capacities are as follows.

Supplier	1	2	3
Capacity	600	1000	800

If the Edwards production plan for the next period calls for 1000 units of component 1 and 800 units of component 2, what purchases do you recommend? That is, how many units of each component should be ordered from each supplier? What is the total purchase cost for the components?

SELF TEST

12. Refer to the Janders application in Section 4.3. Consider each of the following variations of the original problem separately. Modify the Janders' file on the disk accompanying the text to answer the questions.
    a. Suppose that Janders' supplier lowers the price for the bases to $0.55 per unit. What is the new optimal solution and its value?
    b. Suppose that the supplier of the tops for the Technician calculator raises the unit price to $0.82. What is the new optimal solution and its value?
    c. If Janders' employees were willing to work overtime for an overtime premium of only $2 per hour, should Janders schedule overtime? Why or why not? What is the new optimal solution and its value?

13. Reconsider the McCormick Company Manufacturing problem in Section 4.3. Each of the following parts presents a variation of the original problem. Consider each question separately.
    a. Suppose that no more than 600 hours can be transferred from department 2. Based on the shadow price information, how does the value of the optimal solution change?
    b. Modify the linear programming model to reflect the change described in part (a). Use a computer solution of the revised formulation to verify your conclusion in part (a). What transfers are recommended?
    c. Suppose that the employees transferred from department 1 to department 3 are only 80% as productive in department 3 as the employees originally assigned to that department. Reformulate the original model in Section 4.3 accordingly and solve. What is the new optimal solution? (Hint: Modify the labor balance equation for department 3.)

14. The production manager for the Classic Boat Corporation must determine how many units of the Classic 21 model to produce over the next four quarters. The company has a beginning inventory of 100 Classic 21 boats, and demand for the four quarters is 2000 units in quarter 1, 4000 units in quarter 2, 3000 units in quarter 3, and 1500 units in quarter 4. The firm has limited production capacity in each quarter. That is, up to 4000 units can be produced in quarter 1, 3000 units in quarter 2, 2000 units in quarter 3, and 4000 units in quarter 4. Each boat held in inventory in quarters 1 and 2 incurs an inventory holding cost of $250 per unit; the holding cost for quarters 3 and 4 is $300 per unit. The production costs for the first quarter are $10,000 per unit; these costs are expected to increase by 10% each quarter because of increases in labor

and material costs. Management has specified that the ending inventory for quarter 4 must be at least 500 boats.

   a. Formulate a linear programming model that can be used to determine the production schedule that will minimize the total cost of meeting demand in each quarter subject to the production capacities in each quarter and also to the required ending inventory in quarter 4.

   b. Solve the linear program formulated in part (a).

   c. Interpret each shadow price corresponding to the constraints developed to meet demand in each quarter. Based on these shadow prices what advice would you give the production manager?

   d. Interpret each shadow price corresponding to the production capacity in each quarter. Based on each of these shadow prices what advice would you give the production manager?

SELF TEST

15. Seastrand Oil Company produces two grades of gasoline: regular and high octane. Both gasolines are produced by blending two types of crude oil. Although both types of crude oil contain the two important ingredients required to produce both gasolines, the percentage of important ingredients in each type of crude oil differs, as does the cost per gallon. The percentage of ingredients A and B in each type of crude oil and the cost per gallon are shown.

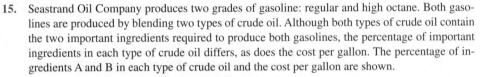

Crude Oil	Cost	Ingredient A	Ingredient B	
1	$0.10	20%	60%	Crude oil 1 is 60% ingredient B
2	$0.15	50%	30%	

Each gallon of regular gasoline must contain at least 40% of ingredient A, whereas each gallon of high octane can contain at most 50% of ingredient B. Daily demand for regular and high-octane gasoline is 800,000 and 500,000 gallons, respectively. How many gallons of each type of crude oil should be used in the two gasolines to satisfy daily demand at a minimum cost?

16. The Ferguson Paper Company produces rolls of paper for use in adding machines, desk calculators, and cash registers. The rolls, which are 200 feet long, are produced in widths of 1½, 2½, and 3½ inches. The production process provides 200-foot rolls in 10-inch widths only. The firm must therefore cut the rolls to the desired final product sizes. The seven cutting alternatives and the amount of waste generated by each are as follows.

Cutting Alternative	Number of Rolls			Waste (inches)
	1½ in.	2½ in.	3½ in.	
1	6	0	0	1
2	0	4	0	0
3	2	0	2	0
4	0	1	2	½
5	1	3	0	1
6	1	2	1	0
7	4	0	1	½

The minimum requirements for the three products are

Roll Width (inches)	1½	2½	3½
Units	1000	2000	4000

   a. If the company wants to minimize the number of 10-inch rolls that must be manufactured, how many 10-inch rolls will be processed on each cutting alternative? How many rolls are required, and what is the total waste (inches)?

b. If the company wants to minimize the waste generated, how many 10-inch units will be processed on each cutting alternative? How many rolls are required, and what is the total waste (inches)?

c. What are the differences in approaches (a) and (b) to this problem? In this case, which objective do you prefer? Explain. What types of situations would make the other objective more desirable?

17. Frandec Company manufactures, assembles, and rebuilds material handling equipment used in warehouses and distribution centers. One product, called a Liftmaster, is assembled from four components: a frame, a motor, two supports, and a metal strap. Frandec's production schedule calls for 5000 Liftmasters to be made next month. Frandec purchases the motors from an outside supplier, but the frames, supports, and straps may either be manufactured by the company or purchased from an outside supplier. Manufacturing and purchase costs per unit are shown.

Component	Manufacturing Cost	Purchase Cost
Frame	$38.00	$51.00
Support	11.50	15.00
Strap	6.50	7.50

Three departments are involved in the production of these components. The time (in minutes per unit) required to process each component in each department is given, along with the available capacity (in hours) for the three departments.

	Department		
Component	Cutting	Milling	Shaping
Frame	3.5	2.2	3.1
Support	1.3	1.7	2.6
Strap	0.8	—	1.7
Capacity (hours)	350	420	680

a. Formulate and solve a linear programming model for this make-or-buy application. How many of each component should be manufactured and how many should be purchased?

b. What is the total cost of the manufacturing and purchasing plan?

c. How many hours of production time are used in each department?

d. How much should Frandec be willing to pay for an additional hour of time in the shaping department?

e. Another manufacturer has offered to sell frames to Frandec for $45.00 each. Could Frandec improve its position by pursuing this opportunity? Why or why not?

18. The Two-Rivers Oil Company near Pittsburgh transports gasoline to its distributors by truck. The company has recently contracted to supply gasoline distributors in southern Ohio, and it has $600,000 available to spend on the necessary expansion of its fleet of gasoline tank trucks. Three models of gasoline tank trucks are available.

Truck Model	Capacity (gallons)	Purchase Cost	Monthly Operating Cost, Including Depreciation
Super Tanker	5000	$67,000	$550
Regular Line	2500	$55,000	$425
Econo-Tanker	1000	$46,000	$350

The company estimates that the monthly demand for the region will be 550,000 gallons of gasoline. Because of the size and speed differences of the trucks, the number of deliveries or round trips possible per month for each truck model will vary. Trip capacities are estimated at 15 trips per month for the Super Tanker, 20 trips per month for the Regular Line, and 25 trips per month for the Econo-Tanker. Based on maintenance and driver availability, the firm does not want to add more than 15 new vehicles to its fleet. In addition, the company has decided to purchase at least three of the new Econo-Tankers for use on short-run, low-demand routes. As a final constraint, the company does not want more than half the new models to be Super Tankers.

a. If the company wishes to satisfy the gasoline demand with a minimum monthly operating expense, how many models of each truck should be purchased?

b. If the company did not require at least three Econo-Tankers and did not limit the number of Super Tankers to at most half the new models, how many models of each truck should be purchased?

SELF TEST

19. The Silver Star Bicycle Company will be manufacturing both men's and women's models for its Easy-Pedal 10-speed bicycles during the next 2 months. The company wants to develop a production schedule indicating how many bicycles of each model should be produced in each month. Current demand forecasts call for 150 men's and 125 women's models to be shipped during the first month and 200 men's and 150 women's models to be shipped during the second month. Additional data are shown.

Model	Production Costs	Labor Requirements (hours)		Current Inventory
		Manufacturing	Assembly	
Men's	$120	2.0	1.5	20
Women's	$ 90	1.6	1.0	30

Last month the company used a total of 1000 hours of labor. The company's labor relations policy will not allow the combined total hours of labor (manufacturing plus assembly) to increase or decrease by more than 100 hours from month to month. In addition, the company charges monthly inventory at the rate of 2% of the production cost based on the inventory levels at the end of the month. The company would like to have at least 25 units of each model in inventory at the end of the 2 months.

a. Establish a production schedule that minimizes production and inventory costs and satisfies the labor-smoothing, demand, and inventory requirements. What inventories will be maintained and what are the monthly labor requirements?

b. If the company changed the constraints so that monthly labor increases and decreases could not exceed 50 hours, what would happen to the production schedule? How much will the cost increase? What would you recommend?

20. Filtron Corporation produces filtration containers used in water treatment systems. Although business has been growing, the demand each month varies considerably. As a result, the company uses a mix of part-time and full-time employees to meet production demands. Although this approach provides Filtron with great flexibility, it has resulted in increased costs and morale problems among employees. For instance, if Filtron needs to increase production from one month to the next, additional part-time employees have to be hired and trained, and costs go up. If Filtron has to decrease production, the workforce has to be reduced and Filtron incurs additional costs in terms of unemployment benefits and decreased morale. Best estimates are that increasing the number of units produced from one month to the next will increase production costs by $1.25 per unit, and that decreasing the number of units produced will increase production costs by $1.00 per unit. In February Filtron produced 10,000 filtration containers but only sold 7500 units; 2500 units are currently in inventory. The sales forecasts for March, April, and May are for 12,000 units, 8,000 units, and 15,000 units, respectively. In addition, Filtron has the capacity to store up to 3000 filtration containers at the end of any month. Determine the num-

ber of units to be produced in March, April, and May that will minimize the total cost of the monthly production increases and decreases.

21. Greenville Cabinets has received a contract to produce speaker cabinets for a major speaker manufacturer. The contract calls for the production of 3300 bookshelf speakers and 4100 floor speakers over the next two months, with the following delivery schedule.

Model	Month 1	Month 2
Bookshelf	2100	1200
Floor	1500	2600

Greenville estimates that the production time for each bookshelf model is .7 hour and the production time for each floor model is 1 hour. The raw material costs are $10 for each bookshelf model and $12 for each floor model. Labor costs are $22 per hour using regular production time and $33 using overtime. Greenville has up to 2400 hours of regular production time available each month, and up to 1000 additional hours of overtime available each month. If production for either cabinet exceeds demand in month 1, the cabinets can be stored at a cost of $5 per cabinet. For each product, determine the number of units that should be manufactured each month on regular time and on overtime in order to minimize total production and storage costs.

22. The Williams Calculator Company manufactures two kinds of calculators: the TW100 and the TW200. The assembly process requires three people. The assembly times are as follows.

| | Calculator | | Maximum Labor Available |
Assembler	TW100	TW200	(hours/day)
1	4 min	3 min	8
2	2 min	4 min	8
3	$3^1/_2$ min	3 min	8

The company policy is to balance workloads on all assembly jobs. In fact, management wants to schedule work so that no assembler will have more than 30 minutes more work per day than other assemblers. That is, in a regular 8-hour shift, all assemblers will be assigned at least $7\frac{1}{2}$ hours of work. If the firm makes a $2.50 profit for each TW100 and a $3.50 profit for each TW200, how many units of each calculator should be produced per day? How much time will each assembler be assigned per day?

23. Multiperiod production and inventory planning models determine a production schedule and an ending inventory schedule for each of several periods that will maximize profit or minimize cost. Considering selling price, regular production costs, overtime costs, inventory carrying costs, and lost sales costs, develop a three-period production and inventory planning model for Allen Manufacturing Company. Use the following relevant information.

Period	Selling Price per Unit	Production Cost per Unit	Demand	Ending Inventory Cost per Unit
1	$5.00	$2.80	500	$0.50
2	$5.00	$2.90	300	$0.50
3	$5.50	$3.00	400	$0.55

	Production Capacity (units)	
Period	Regular	Overtime
1	250	100
2	300	100
3	300	125

The overtime cost per unit in each period is 20% greater than the production cost per unit shown. The lost sales cost, which is $4 per unit in any period, accounts for lost customer goodwill, but it does not account for the cost associated with the lost revenue. The beginning inventory for period 1 is 100 units. In addition, the firm wants to have at least 50 units in ending inventory for period 3 to prepare for period 4.

To account for the multiperiod aspects of the problem, each period t will require balance equations or constraints based on two relationships:

$$\text{Lost sales } (t) = \text{demand } (t) - \text{sales } (t)$$
$$\text{Ending inventory } (t) = \text{beginning inventory } (t) + \text{production } (t) - \text{sales } (t)$$

Develop a linear program that can be used to determine the optimal production and inventory schedule for Allen Manufacturing. Determine the sales, regular production, overtime production, ending inventory, and lost sales for each of the three periods. What is the net profit associated with your solution?

24. The Morton Financial Institution must decide on the percentage of available funds to commit to each of two investments, referred to as A and B, over the next four periods. The following table shows the amount of new funds available for each of the four periods, as well as the cash expenditure required for each investment (negative values) or the cash income from the investment (positive values). The data shown (in thousands of dollars) reflect the amount of expenditure or income if 100% of the funds available in any period are invested in either A or B. For example, if Morton decides to invest 100% of the funds available in any period in investment A, it will incur cash expenditures of $1000 in period 1, $800 in period 2, $200 in period 3, and income of $200 in period 4. Note, however, if Morton made the decision to invest 80% in investment A, the cash expenditures or income would be 80% of the values shown.

	New Investment	Investment	
Period	Funds Available	A	B
1	1500	−1000	−800
2	400	−800	−500
3	500	−200	−300
4	100	200	300

The amount of funds available in any period is the sum of the new investment funds for the period, the new loan funds, the savings from the previous period, the cash income from investment A, and the cash income from investment B. The funds available in any period can be used to pay the loan and interest from the previous period, placed in savings, used to pay the cash expenditures for investment A, or used to pay the cash expenditures for investment B.

Assume an interest rate of 10% per period for savings and an interest rate of 18% per period on borrowed funds. Let

$$S(t) = \text{the savings for period } t$$
$$L(t) = \text{the new loan funds for period } t$$

Then, in any period t, the savings income from the previous period is $1.1S(t-1)$, and the loan and interest expenditure from the previous period is $1.18L(t-1)$.

At the end of period 4, investment A is expected to have a cash value of \$3200 (assuming a 100% investment in A), and investment B is expected to have a cash value of \$2500 (assuming a 100% investment in B). Additional income and expenses at the end of period 4 will be income from savings in period 4 less the repayment of the period 4 loan plus interest.

Suppose that the decision variables are defined as

$$x_1 = \text{the proportion of investment A undertaken}$$
$$x_2 = \text{the proportion of investment B undertaken}$$

For example, if $x_1 = 0.5$, \$500 would be invested in investment A during the first period, and all remaining cash flows and ending investment A values would be multiplied by 0.5. The same holds for investment B. The model must include constraints $x_1 \leq 1$ and $x_2 \leq 1$ to make sure that no more than 100% of the investments can be undertaken.

If no more than \$200 can be borrowed in any period, determine the proportions of investments A and B and the amount of savings and borrowing in each period that will maximize the cash value for the firm at the end of the four periods.

25. Western Family Steakhouse offers a variety of low-cost meals and quick service. Other than management, the steakhouse operates with two full-time employees who work 8 hours per day. The rest of the employees are part-time employees who are scheduled for 4-hour shifts during peak meal times. On Saturdays the steakhouse is open from 11:00 A.M. to 10:00 P.M. Management wants to develop a schedule for part-time employees that will minimize labor costs and still provide excellent customer service. The average wage rate for the part-time employees is \$4.60 per hour. The total number of full-time and part-time employees needed varies with the time of the day as shown as follows.

Time	Total Number of Employees Needed
11:00 A.M.–noon	9
Noon–1:00 P.M.	9
1:00 P.M.–2:00 P.M.	9
2:00 P.M.–3:00 P.M.	3
3:00 P.M.–4:00 P.M.	3
4:00 P.M.–5:00 P.M.	3
5:00 P.M.–6:00 P.M.	6
6:00 P.M.–7:00 P.M.	12
7:00 P.M.–8:00 P.M.	12
8:00 P.M.–9:00 P.M.	7
9:00 P.M.–10:00 P.M.	7

One full-time employee comes on duty at 11:00 A.M., works 4 hours, takes an hour off, and returns for another 4 hours. The other full-time employee comes to work at 1:00 P.M. and works the same 4-hours-on, 1-hour-off, 4-hours-on pattern.

a. Develop a minimum-cost schedule for part-time employees.

b. What is the total payroll for the part-time employees? How many part-time shifts are needed? Use the surplus employees to comment on the desirability of scheduling at least some of the part-time employees for 3-hour shifts.

c. Assume that part-time employees can be assigned either a 3-hour or 4-hour shift. Develop a minimum-cost schedule for the part-time employees. How many part-time shifts are needed and what is the cost savings compared to the previous schedule?

26. In Section 4.5 data envelopment analysis was used to evaluate the relative efficiencies of four hospitals. Data for three input measures and four output measures were provided in Tables 4.14 and 4.15.
    a. Use these data to develop a linear programming model that could be used to evaluate the performance of General Hospital.
    b. Which hospital or hospitals make up the composite unit used to evaluate General Hospital? State why this is true.

27. Data envelopment analysis has been used to measure the relative efficiency of a group of hospitals (H. David Sherman, "Hospital Efficiency Measurement and Evaluation," *Medical Care* (October 1984)). Sherman's study involved seven teaching hospitals; data on three input measures and four output measures are contained in the following tables.

	Input Measures		
Hospital	Full-Time Equivalent Nonphysicians	Supply Expense ($1000s)	Bed-Days Available ($1000s)
A	310.0	134.60	116.00
B	278.5	114.30	106.80
C	165.6	131.30	65.52
D	250.0	316.00	94.40
E	206.4	151.20	102.10
F	384.0	217.00	153.70
G	530.1	770.80	215.00

	Output Measures			
Hospital	Patient-Days (65 or older) (1000s)	Patient-Days (under 65) (1000s)	Nurses Trained	Interns Trained
A	55.31	49.52	291	47
B	37.64	55.63	156	3
C	32.91	25.77	141	26
D	33.53	41.99	160	21
E	32.48	55.30	157	82
F	48.78	81.92	285	92
G	58.41	119.70	111	89

a. Formulate a linear programming model so that data envelopment analysis can be used to evaluate the performance of hospital D.
b. Solve the model.
c. Is hospital D relatively inefficient? What is the interpretation of the value of the objective function?
d. How many patient-days of each type are produced by the composite hospital?
e. Which hospitals would you recommend hospital D consider emulating to improve the efficiency of its operation?

28. Refer again to the data presented in Problem 27.
    a. Formulate a linear programming model that can be used to perform data envelopment analysis for hospital E.
    b. Solve the model.

c. Is hospital E relatively inefficient? What is the interpretation of the value of the objective function?

d. Which hospitals are involved in making up the composite hospital? Can you make a general statement about which hospitals will make up the composite unit associated with a unit that is not inefficient?

29. The Ranch House, Inc., operates five fast-food restaurants. Input measures for the restaurants include weekly hours of operation, full-time equivalent staff, and weekly supply expenses. Output measures of performance include average weekly contribution to profit, market share, and annual growth rate. Data for the input and output measures are shown in the following tables.

	Input Measures		
Restaurant	Hours of Operation	FTE Staff	Supplies ($)
Bardstown	96	16	850
Clarksville	110	22	1400
Jeffersonville	100	18	1200
New Albany	125	25	1500
St. Matthews	120	24	1600

	Output Measures		
Restaurant	Weekly Profit	Market Share (%)	Growth Rate (%)
Bardstown	$3800	25	8.0
Clarksville	$4600	32	8.5
Jeffersonville	$4400	35	8.0
New Albany	$6500	30	10.0
St. Matthews	$6000	28	9.0

a. Develop a linear programming model that can be used to evaluate the performance of the Clarksville Ranch House restaurant.

b. Solve the model.

c. Is the Clarksville Ranch House restaurant relatively inefficient? Discuss.

d. Where does the composite restaurant have more output than the Clarksville restaurant? How much less of each input resource does the composite restaurant require when compared to the Clarksville restaurant?

e. What other restaurants should be studied to find suggested ways for the Clarksville restaurant to improve its efficiency?

Case Problem   ENVIRONMENTAL PROTECTION

Skillings Industrial Chemicals, Inc., operates a refinery in southwestern Ohio near the Ohio River. The company's primary product is manufactured from a chemical process that requires the use of two raw materials—material A and material B. The production of 1 pound of the primary product requires the use of 1 pound of material A and 2 pounds of material B. The output of the chemical process is 1 pound of the primary product, 1 pound of liquid waste material, and 1 pound of solid waste by-product. The solid waste by-product is given

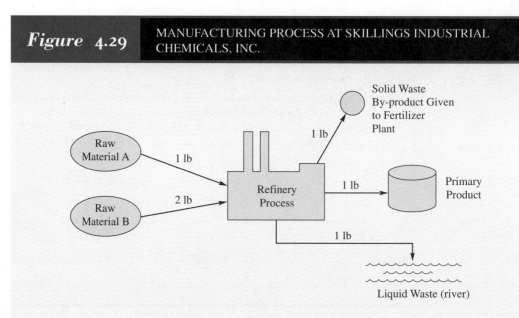

Figure 4.29 MANUFACTURING PROCESS AT SKILLINGS INDUSTRIAL CHEMICALS, INC.

to a local fertilizer plant as payment for picking it up and disposing of it. The liquid waste material has no market value, so the refinery has been dumping it directly into the Ohio River. The company's manufacturing process is shown schematically in Figure 4.29.

Government pollution guidelines established by the Environmental Protection Agency will no longer permit disposal of the liquid waste directly into the river. The refinery's research group has developed the following set of alternative uses for the liquid waste material.

1. Produce a secondary product K by adding 1 pound of raw material A to every pound of liquid waste.
2. Produce a secondary product M by adding 1 pound of raw material B to every pound of liquid waste.
3. Specially treat the liquid waste so that it meets pollution standards before dumping it into the river.

These three alternatives are depicted in Figure 4.30.

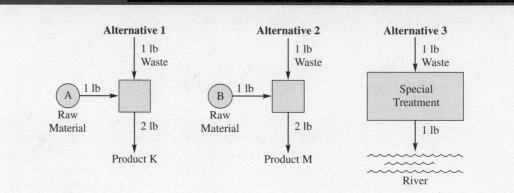

Figure 4.30 ALTERNATIVES FOR HANDLING THE REFINERY LIQUID WASTE

The company's management knows that the secondary products will be low in quality and may not be very profitable. However, management also recognizes that the special treatment alternative will be a relatively expensive operation. The company's problem is to determine how to satisfy the pollution regulations and still maintain the highest possible profit. How should the liquid waste material be handled? Should Skillings produce product K, produce product M, use the special treatment, or employ some combination of the three alternatives?

Last month 10,000 pounds of the company's primary product were produced. The accounting department has prepared a cost report showing the breakdown of fixed and variable expenses that were incurred during the month.

Cost Analysis for 10,000 Pounds of Primary Product

Fixed costs	
Administrative expenses	$12,000
Refinery overhead	4,000
Variable costs	
Raw material A	15,000
Raw material B	16,000
Direct labor	5,000
Total	$52,000

In this cost analysis, the fixed-cost portion of the expenses is the same every month regardless of production level. Direct labor costs are expected to run $0.20 per pound for product K and $0.10 per pound for product M.

The company's primary product sells for $5.70 per pound. Secondary products K and M sell for $0.85 and $0.65 per pound, respectively. The special treatment of the liquid waste will cost $0.25 per pound.

One of the company's accountants believes that product K is too expensive to manufacture and cannot be sold at a price that recovers its material and labor cost. The accountant's recommendation is to eliminate product K as an alternative.

For the upcoming production period, 5000 pounds of raw material A and 7000 pounds of raw material B will be available.

Managerial Report

Develop an approach to the problem that will allow the company to determine how much primary product to produce, given the limitations on the amounts of the raw material available. Include recommendations as to how the company should dispose of the liquid waste to satisfy the environmental protection guidelines. How many pounds of product K should be produced? How many pounds of product M should be produced? How many pounds of liquid waste should be specially treated and dumped into the river? Include a discussion and analysis of the following in your report.

1. A cost analysis showing the profit contribution per pound for the primary product, product K, and product M.
2. The optimal production quantities and waste disposal plan, including the projected profit.
3. A discussion of the value of additional pounds of each raw material.

4. A discussion of the sensitivity analysis of the objective function coefficients.
5. Comments on the accountant's recommendation to eliminate product K as an alternative. Does the recommendation appear reasonable? What is your reaction to the recommendation? How would the optimal solution change if product K were eliminated?

Case Problem   INVESTMENT STRATEGY

J. D. Williams, Inc., is an investment advisory firm that manages more than $120 million in funds for its numerous clients. The company uses an asset allocation model that recommends the portion of each client's portfolio to be invested in a growth stock fund, an income fund, and a money market fund. To maintain diversity in each client's portfolio, the firm places limits on the percentage of each portfolio that may be invested in each of the three funds. General guidelines indicate that the amount invested in the growth fund must be between 20% and 40% of the total portfolio value. Similar percentages for the other two funds stipulate that between 20% and 50% of the total portfolio value must be in the income fund and at least 30% of the total portfolio value must be in the money market fund.

In addition, the company attempts to assess the risk tolerance of each client and adjust the portfolio to meet the needs of the individual investor. For example, Williams has just contracted with a new client who has $800,000 to invest. Based on an evaluation of the client's risk tolerance, Williams has assigned a maximum risk index of 0.05 for the client. The firm's risk indicators show the risk of the growth fund at 0.10, the income fund at 0.07, and the money market fund at 0.01. An overall portfolio risk index is computed as a weighted average of the risk rating for the three funds where the weights are the fraction of the client's portfolio invested in each of the funds.

Additionally, Williams is currently forecasting annual yields of 18% for the growth fund, 12.5% for the income fund, and 7.5% for the money market fund. Based on the information provided, how should the new client be advised to allocate the $800,000 among the growth, income, and money market funds? Develop a linear programming model that will provide the maximum yield for the portfolio. Use your model to develop a managerial report as described next.

Managerial Report

1. Recommend how much of the $800,000 should be invested in each of the three funds. What is the annual yield you anticipate for the investment recommendation?
2. Assume that the client's risk index could be increased to 0.055. How much would the yield increase and how would the investment recommendation change?
3. Refer again to the original situation where the client's risk index was assessed to be 0.05. How would your investment recommendation change if the annual yield for the growth fund were revised downward to 16% or even to 14%?
4. Assume that the client has expressed some concern about having too much money in the growth fund. How would the original recommendation change if the amount invested in the growth fund is not allowed to exceed the amount invested in the income fund?
5. The asset allocation model you have developed may be useful in modifying the portfolios for all the firm's clients whenever the anticipated yields for the three funds are periodically revised. What is your recommendation as to whether this is possible?

Case Problem   TEXTILE MILL SCHEDULING

The Scottsville Textile Mill* produces five different fabrics. Each fabric can be woven on one or more of the mill's 38 looms. The sales department has forecast demand for the next month. The demand data are shown in Table 4.16, along with data on the selling price per yard, variable cost per yard, and purchase price per yard. The mill operates 24 hours per day and is scheduled for 30 days during the coming month.

The mill has two types of looms: dobbie and regular. The dobbie looms are more versatile and can be used for all five fabrics. The regular looms can produce only three of the fabrics. There are a total of 38 looms—8 dobbie and 30 regular. The rate of production for each fabric on each type of loom is given in Table 4.17. The time required to change over from producing one fabric to another is negligible and does not have to be considered.

The Scottsville Textile Mill satisfies all demand with either its own fabric or fabric purchased from another mill. That is, fabrics that cannot be woven at the Scottsville Mill because of limited loom capacity will be purchased from another mill. The purchase price of each fabric is also shown in Table 4.16.

Table 4.16	MONTHLY DEMAND, SELLING PRICE, VARIABLE COST, AND PURCHASE PRICE DATA FOR SCOTTSVILLE FABRICS			
Fabric	**Demand (yards)**	**Selling Price ($/yard)**	**Variable Cost ($/yard)**	**Purchase Price ($/yard)**
1	16,500	0.99	0.66	0.80
2	22,000	0.86	0.55	0.70
3	62,000	1.10	0.49	0.60
4	7,500	1.24	0.51	0.70
5	62,000	0.70	0.50	0.70

Table 4.17	LOOM PRODUCTION RATES FOR THE SCOTTSVILLE TEXTILE MILL	
	Loom Rate (yards/hour)	
Fabric	**Dobbie**	**Regular**
1	4.63	—
2	4.63	—
3	5.23	5.23
4	5.23	5.23
5	4.17	4.17

Note: Fabrics 1 and 2 can be manufactured only on the dobbie loom.

*This case is based on the Calhoun Textile Mill Case by Jeffrey D. Camm, P.M. Dearing, and Suresh K. Tadisnia.

Managerial Report

Develop a model that can be used to schedule production for the Scottsville Textile Mill, and at the same time, determine how many yards of each fabric must be purchased from another mill. Include a discussion and analysis of the following items in your report.

1. The final production schedule and loom assignments for each fabric.
2. The projected total contribution to profit.
3. A discussion of the value of additional loom time. The mill is considering purchasing a ninth dobbie loom. What is your estimate of the monthly profit contribution of this additional loom?
4. A discussion of the ranges for the objective function coefficients.
5. A discussion of how the objective of minimizing total costs would provide a different model than the objective of maximizing total profit contribution. How would the interpretation of the ranges for the objective function coefficients differ for these two models?

MARATHON OIL COMPANY*

FINDLAY, OHIO

Marathon Oil Company was founded in 1887 when 14 oilmen pooled their properties to organize an oil-producing company in the Trenton Rock oil fields of Ohio. In 1924 Marathon entered the refining and marketing phase of the petroleum industry. Today Marathon is a fully integrated oil company with significant international operations. In the United States the company markets petroleum products in 21 states, primarily in the Midwest and Southeast. Marathon is a unit of USX.

Management Science at Marathon Oil Company

Marathon Oil's Operations Research Department was formed in 1963 in order to aid problem solving and decision making in all areas of the company. Approximately 50% of the applications involve linear programming. Typical problems include refinery models, distribution models, gasoline and fuel oil blending models, and crude oil evaluation studies. Another 30% of the applications involve complex chemical engineering simulation models of process operations. The remaining applications involve solution techniques using nonlinear programming, network flow algorithms, and statistical techniques such as regression analysis.

A Marketing Planning Model

Marathon Oil Company has four refineries within the United States, operates 50 light products terminals, and has product demand at over 95 locations. The Supply and Transportation Division is faced with the problem of determining which refinery should supply which termi-

nal and, at the same time, determining which products should be transported via which pipeline, barge, or tanker in order to minimize cost. Product demand must be satisfied, and the supply capability of each refinery must not be exceeded. To help solve this difficult problem, Marathon's Operations Research Department developed a marketing planning model for the Operations Planning Department.

The marketing planning model is a large-scale linear programming model that takes into account sales not only at Marathon product terminals but also at all exchange locations. An exchange contract is an agreement with other oil product marketers that involves exchanging or trading Marathon's products for theirs at different locations. Thus, some geographic imbalance between supply and demand can be reduced. Both sides of the exchanges are represented since this not only affects the net requirements at a demand location, but in addition has important financial implications. All pipelines, barges, and tankers within Marathon's marketing area are also represented in the linear programming model. The objective of the linear programming model is to minimize the cost of meeting a given demand structure, taking into account sales price, pipeline tariffs, exchange contract costs, product demand, terminal operating costs, refining costs, and product purchases.

The marketing planning model is used to solve a wide variety of planning problems. These vary from evaluating gasoline blending economics to analyzing the economics of a new terminal or pipeline. Although the types of problems that can be solved are almost unlimited, the model is most effective in handling the following:

1. Evaluating additional product demand locations, pipelines, and exchange contracts

---

*The authors are indebted to Robert W. Wernert of Marathon Oil Company, Findlay, Ohio, for providing this application.

2. Determining profitability of shifting sales from one product demand location to another
3. Determining the effects on supply and distribution when a pipeline increases its tariff
4. Optimizing production of the grades at the five refineries based on distribution

The linear programming model not only solves these problems, but also gives the financial impact of each solution.

Benefits

With daily sales of about 10 million gallons of refined light product, a savings of even one-thousandth of a cent per gallon can result in significant long-term sav-ings. At the same time, what may appear to be a savings in one area, such as refining or transportation, may actually add to overall costs when the effects are fully realized throughout the system. The marketing planning model allows a simultaneous examination of this total effect.

Questions

1. What is the primary objective of Marathon's marketing planning model?
2. Describe the types of problems the marketing planning model is most effective in handling.
3. If daily savings using the model are one-tenth of a cent per gallon sold, what is the projected daily savings?

5

TRANSPORTATION, ASSIGNMENT,
AND TRANSSHIPMENT PROBLEMS

Transportation, assignment, and transshipment problems belong to a special class of linear programming problems called **network flow problems**. A separate chapter is devoted to these problems for two reasons. First, a wide variety of applications can be modeled as transportation, assignment, or transshipment problems. These models are the basic building blocks of models involving the distribution of goods and services. Second, a simplified graphical representation, called a **network**, can be used to help with the modeling process.

As usual, we take an applications approach to the material. We begin by introducing a typical application of the problem, then a graphical network model is developed to represent the problem. We show how to develop a linear programming model from the network and then show how to formulate and solve the problem on a spreadsheet. Of course, we use the same approach as in previous chapters for spreadsheet formulation and solution, so your major focus in this chapter should be on understanding the types of problem situations that can be modeled as networks and how to develop a network model.

We could go directly from the graphical network model to spreadsheet formulation and solution without first developing a linear programming model. We note how this process can be done after the fundamental relationships among network models, linear programming, and spreadsheet solution are clear. As a final point, we note that the network flow problems of this chapter have a special mathematical structure that has enabled management scientists to develop specialized solution procedures for solving them; as a result, even very large problems can be solved with just a few seconds of computer time. Current spreadsheet technology does not employ these methods; more advanced texts discuss the specialized solution procedures.

5.1   THE TRANSPORTATION PROBLEM

The **transportation problem** arises frequently in planning for the distribution of goods and services from several supply locations to several demand locations. Typically, the quantity of goods available at each supply location (origin) is limited, and the quantity of goods needed at each of several demand locations (destinations) is known. The usual objective in a transportation problem is to minimize the cost of shipping goods from the origins to the destinations.

Let us illustrate by considering a transportation problem faced by Foster Generators. This problem involves the transportation of a product from three plants to four distribution centers. Foster Generators has plants in Cleveland, Ohio; Bedford, Indiana; and York, Pennsylvania. Production capacities over the next 3-month planning period for one particular type of generator are as follows:

Origin	Plant	3-Month Production Capacity (units)
1	Cleveland	5,000
2	Bedford	6,000
3	York	2,500
	Total	13,500

The firm distributes its generators through four regional distribution centers located in Boston, Chicago, St. Louis, and Lexington; the 3-month forecast of demand for the distribution centers is as follows:

Destination	Distribution Center	3-Month Demand Forecast (units)
1	Boston	6,000
2	Chicago	4,000
3	St. Louis	2,000
4	Lexington	1,500
	Total	13,500

Management would like to determine how much of its production should be shipped from each plant to each distribution center. Figure 5.1 shows graphically the 12 distribution routes Foster can use. Such a graph is called a *network;* the circles are referred to as **nodes** and the lines connecting the nodes as **arcs.** Each origin and destination is represented by a node, and each possible shipping route is represented by an arc. The amount of the supply is written next to each origin node, and the amount of the demand is written next to each destination node. The goods shipped from the origins to the destinations represent the flow in the network. Note that the direction of flow (from origin to destination) is indicated by the arrows.

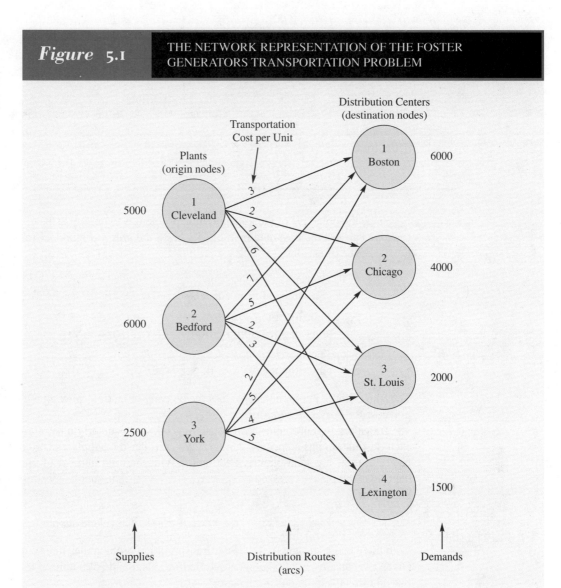

Figure 5.1   THE NETWORK REPRESENTATION OF THE FOSTER GENERATORS TRANSPORTATION PROBLEM

Try Problem 1 for practice in developing a network model of a transportation problem.

For Foster's transportation problem, the objective is to determine the routes to be used and the quantity to be shipped via each route that will provide the minimum total transportation cost. The cost for each unit shipped on each route is given in Table 5.1 and is shown on each arc in Figure 5.1.

A linear programming model can be used to solve this transportation problem. We use double-subscripted decision variables with the first subscript denoting the origin node and the second subscript denoting the destination node. Thus, x_{11} denotes the number of units shipped from origin 1 (Cleveland) to destination 1 (Boston), x_{12} denotes the number of units shipped from origin 1 (Cleveland) to destination 2 (Chicago), and so on. In general, the decision variables for a transportation problem having m origins and n destinations are written as follows:

The first subscript identifies the "from" node of the corresponding arc, and the second subscript identifies the "to" node of the arc.

$$x_{ij} = \text{number of units shipped from origin } i \text{ to destination } j$$
$$\text{where } i = 1, 2, \ldots, m \text{ and } j = 1, 2, \ldots, n$$

Table 5.1	TRANSPORTATION COST PER UNIT FOR THE FOSTER GENERATORS TRANSPORTATION PROBLEM

	Destination			
Origin	Boston	Chicago	St. Louis	Lexington
Cleveland	3	2	7	6
Bedford	7	5	2	3
York	2	5	4	5

Since the objective of the transportation problem is to minimize the total transportation cost, we can use the cost data in Table 5.1 or on the arcs in Figure 5.1 to develop the following cost expressions:

Transportation costs for
units shipped from Cleveland $= 3x_{11} + 2x_{12} + 7x_{13} + 6x_{14}$

Transportation costs for
units shipped from Bedford $= 7x_{21} + 5x_{22} + 2x_{23} + 3x_{24}$

Transportation costs for
units shipped from York $= 2x_{31} + 5x_{32} + 4x_{33} + 5x_{34}$

The sum of these expressions provides the objective function showing the total transportation cost for Foster Generators.

Transportation problems need constraints because each origin has a limited supply and each destination has a specific demand. We consider the supply constraints first. The capacity at the Cleveland plant is 5000 units. With the total number of units shipped from the Cleveland plant expressed as $x_{11} + x_{12} + x_{13} + x_{14}$, the supply constraint for the Cleveland plant is

$$x_{11} + x_{12} + x_{13} + x_{14} \leq 5000 \quad \text{Cleveland supply}$$

With three origins (plants), the Foster transportation problem has three supply constraints. Given the capacity of 6000 units at the Bedford plant and 2500 units at the York plant, the two additional supply constraints are

$$x_{21} + x_{22} + x_{23} + x_{24} \leq 6000 \quad \text{Bedford supply}$$
$$x_{31} + x_{32} + x_{33} + x_{34} \leq 2500 \quad \text{York supply}$$

With the four distribution centers as the destinations, four demand constraints are needed to ensure that destination demands will be satisfied:

To obtain a feasible solution, the total supply must be greater than or equal to the total demand.

$$x_{11} + x_{21} + x_{31} = 6000 \quad \text{Boston demand}$$
$$x_{12} + x_{22} + x_{32} = 4000 \quad \text{Chicago demand}$$
$$x_{13} + x_{23} + x_{33} = 2000 \quad \text{St. Louis demand}$$
$$x_{14} + x_{24} + x_{34} = 1500 \quad \text{Lexington demand}$$

Combining the objective function and constraints into one model provides a 12-variable, 7-constraint linear programming model of the Foster Generators transportation problem:

$$\text{Min} \quad 3x_{11} + 2x_{12} + 7x_{13} + 6x_{14} + 7x_{21} + 5x_{22} + 2x_{23} + 3x_{24} + 2x_{31} + 5x_{32} + 4x_{33} + 5x_{34}$$

s.t.

$$
\begin{array}{llll}
x_{11} + x_{12} + x_{13} + x_{14} & & & \leq 5000 \\
 & x_{21} + x_{22} + x_{23} + x_{24} & & \leq 6000 \\
 & & x_{31} + x_{32} + x_{33} + x_{34} & \leq 2500 \\
x_{11} \qquad\qquad + x_{21} \qquad\qquad + x_{31} & & & = 6000 \\
\quad x_{12} \qquad\qquad + x_{22} \qquad\qquad + x_{32} & & & = 4000 \\
\qquad x_{13} \qquad\qquad + x_{23} \qquad\qquad + x_{33} & & & = 2000 \\
\qquad\quad x_{14} \qquad\qquad + x_{24} \qquad\qquad + x_{34} & & & = 1500
\end{array}
$$

$$x_{ij} \geq 0 \quad \text{for } i = 1, 2, 3 \text{ and } j = 1, 2, 3, 4$$

Comparing the linear programming model to the network in Figure 5.1 leads to several observations. All the information needed for the linear programming formulation is on the network. Each node has one constraint, and each arc has one variable. The sum of the variables corresponding to arcs from an origin node must be less than or equal to the origin's supply, and the sum of the variables corresponding to the arcs into a destination node must be equal to the destination's demand.

The spreadsheet formulation and solution of the Foster Generators problem are shown in Figure 5.2. The data is in the top portion of the spreadsheet. The model appears in the bottom portion of the spreadsheet; the key elements are screened as usual.

You should now be able to develop a linear programming model of a transportation problem. Try Problem 2(a).

Spreadsheet Formulation.   The data and descriptive labels are contained in cells A1:F8. The shipping costs are in cells B5:E7. The origin supplies are in cells F5:F7, and the destination demands are in cells B8:E8. The key elements of the model required by the Excel Solver are the decision variables, the objective function, the constraint left-hand sides, and the constraint right-hand sides. These cells are screened.

Decision Variables   Cells B17:E19 are reserved for the decision variables. The optimal values are shown to be $x_{11} = 3500$, $x_{12} = 1500$, $x_{22} = 2500$, $x_{23} = 2000$, $x_{24} = 1500$, and $x_{41} = 2500$. All other decision variables equal zero indicating nothing will be shipped over the corresponding routes.

Objective Function   The formula =SUMPRODUCT(B5:E7,B17:E19) has been placed into cell C13 to reflect the cost of the solution. The minimum cost solution is shown to have a value of $39,500.

Left-Hand Sides   Cells F17:F19 contain the left-hand sides for the supply constraints, and cells B20:E20 contain the left-hand sides for the demand constraints.
    Cell F17   =SUM(B17:E17)   (Copy to F18:F19)
    Cell B20   =SUM(B17:B19)   (Copy to C20:E20)

Right-Hand Sides   Cells H17:H19 contain the right-hand sides for the supply constraints and Cells B22:E22 contain the right-hand sides for the demand constraints.
    Cell H17   =F5   (Copy to H18:H19)
    Cell B22   =B8   (Copy to C22:E22)

Spreadsheet Solution.   The solution can be obtained by selecting **Solver** from the **Tools** menu, entering the proper values into the **Solver Parameters** dialog box, and specifying the options **Assume Linear Model** and **Assume Non-Negative.** The information entered into the **Solver Parameters** dialog box is shown in Figure 5.3.

Figure 5.2   SPREADSHEET SOLUTION OF THE FOSTER GENERATORS PROBLEM

	A	B	C	D	E	F	G	H
1	**Foster Generators**							
2								
3			**Destination**					
4	**Origin**	Boston	Chicago	St. Louis	Lexington	**Supply**		
5	Cleveland	3	2	7	6	5000		
6	Bedford	7	5	2	3	6000		
7	York	2	5	4	5	2500		
8	**Demand**	6000	4000	2000	1500			
9								
10								
11	**Model**							
12								
13		**Min Cost**	39500					
14								
15			**Destination**					
16	**Origin**	Boston	Chicago	St. Louis	Lexington	**Total**		
17	Cleveland	3500	1500	0	0	5000	<=	5000
18	Bedford	0	2500	2000	1500	6000	<=	6000
19	York	2500	0	0	0	2500	<=	2500
20	**Total**	6000	4000	2000	1500			
21		=	=	=	=			
22		6000	4000	2000	1500			

You should now be able to solve a transportation problem. Try Problem 2(b).

Discussion.   The optimal solution (see Figure 5.2) shows that the minimum total transportation cost is $39,500. The values for the decision variables show the optimal amounts to ship over each route. For example, with $x_{11} = 3500$, 3500 units should be shipped from Cleveland to Boston, and with $x_{12} = 1500$, 1500 units should be shipped from Cleveland to Chicago. Other values of the decision variables indicate the remaining shipping quantities and routes. Table 5.2 shows the minimum-cost transportation schedule and Figure 5.4 summarizes the optimal solution on the network.

Problem Variations

The Foster Generators problem illustrates use of the basic transportation model. Variations of the basic transportation problem may involve one or more of the following situations:

1. Total supply not equal to total demand
2. Maximization objective function
3. Route capacities or route minimums
4. Unacceptable routes

With slight modifications in the linear programming model, you can easily accommodate these situations.

Figure 5.3 SOLVER PARAMETERS DIALOG BOX FOR FOSTER GENERATORS PROBLEM

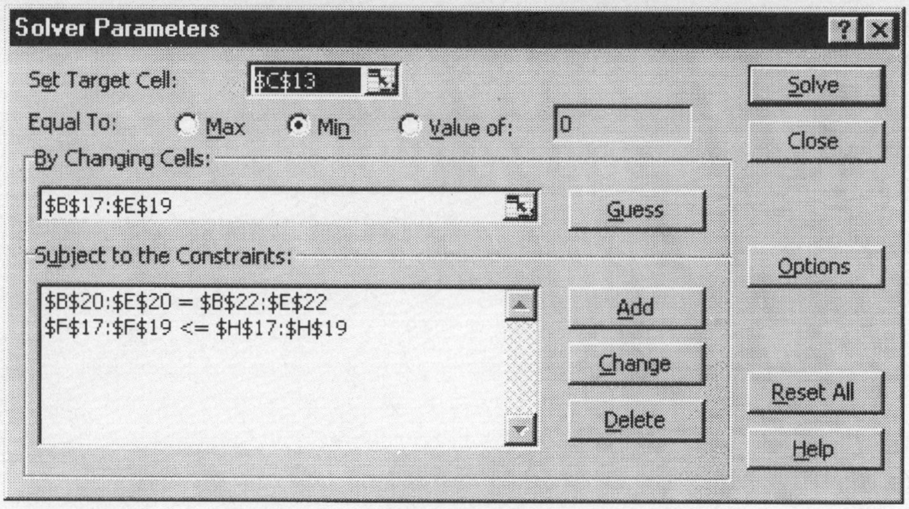

Total Supply Not Equal to Total Demand.   Often *the total supply is not equal to the total demand.* If total supply exceeds total demand, no modification in the linear programming formulation is necessary. Excess supply will appear as slack in the linear programming solution. Slack for any particular origin can be interpreted as the unused supply or amount not shipped from the origin.

If total supply is less than total demand, the linear programming model of a transportation problem will not have a feasible solution. In this case, we modify the network representation by adding a **dummy origin** with a supply equal to the difference between the total demand and the total supply. With the addition of the dummy origin, and an arc from the dummy origin to each destination, the linear programming model will have a feasible solution. A zero cost per unit is assigned to each arc leaving the dummy origin so that the value of the optimal solution for the revised problem will represent the shipping cost for the units actually shipped (no shipments actually will be made from the dummy origin). When the optimal solution is implemented, the destinations showing shipments being

Whenever total supply is less than total demand, the model does not determine how the unsatisfied demand is handled (e.g., backorders). The manager must handle this aspect of the problem.

Table 5.2 OPTIMAL SOLUTION TO THE FOSTER GENERATORS TRANSPORTATION PROBLEM

| Route | | Units | Cost | Total |
From	To	Shipped	per Unit	Cost
Cleveland	Boston	3500	$3	$10,500
Cleveland	Chicago	1500	$2	3,000
Bedford	Chicago	2500	$5	12,500
Bedford	St. Louis	2000	$2	4,000
Bedford	Lexington	1500	$3	4,500
York	Boston	2500	$2	5,000
				$39,500

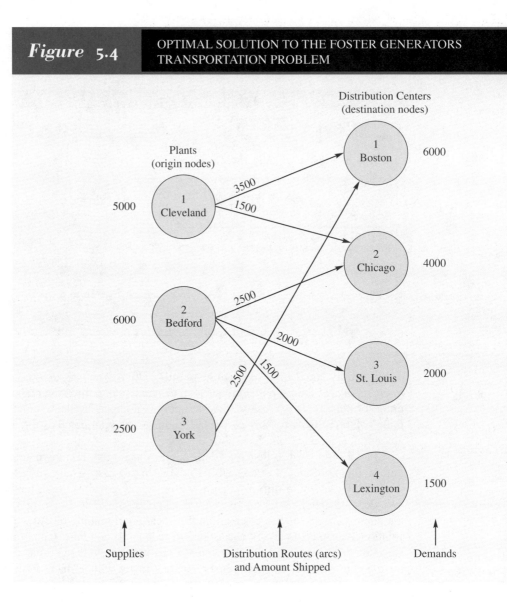

Figure 5.4   OPTIMAL SOLUTION TO THE FOSTER GENERATORS TRANSPORTATION PROBLEM

received from the dummy origin will be the destinations experiencing a shortfall or unsatisfied demand.

Try Problem 8 to see if you can handle a case where demand is greater than supply with a maximization objective.

Maximization Objective Function.   In some transportation problems, the objective is to find a solution that maximizes profit or revenue. Using the values for profit or revenue per unit as coefficients in the objective function, we simply solve a maximization rather than a minimization linear program. This change does not affect the constraints.

Route Capacities and/or Route Minimums.   The linear programming formulation of the transportation problem also can accommodate capacities and/or minimum quantities for one or more of the routes. For example, suppose that in the Foster Generators problem the York–Boston route (origin 3 to destination 1) had a capacity of 1000 units because of limited space availability on its normal mode of transportation. With x_{31} denoting the amount shipped from York to Boston, the route capacity constraint for the York–Boston route would be

$$x_{31} \leq 1000$$

Similarly, route minimums can be specified. For example,

$$x_{22} \geq 2000$$

would guarantee that a previously committed order for a Bedford–Chicago delivery of at least 2000 units would be maintained in the optimal solution.

Unacceptable Routes.   Finally, establishing a route from every origin to every destination may not be possible. To handle this situation, we simply drop the corresponding arc from the network and remove the corresponding variable from the linear programming formulation. For example, if the Cleveland–St. Louis route were unacceptable or unusable, the arc from Cleveland to St. Louis could be dropped in Figure 5.1, and x_{13} could be removed from the linear programming formulation. Solving the resulting 11-variable, 7-constraint model would provide the optimal solution while guaranteeing that the Cleveland–St. Louis route is not used.

The way this can be handled in the spreadsheet formulation we are using is to insert a very large cost for any route over which shipments cannot be made. If the cost is large enough, no shipments will be made over that route unless no other solutions are feasible. This alternative causes the least amount of change in a spreadsheet formulation.

A General Linear Programming Model of the Transportation Problem

To show the general linear programming model of the transportation problem, we use the notation:

$$i = \text{index for origins, } i = 1, 2, \ldots, m$$
$$j = \text{index for destinations, } j = 1, 2, \ldots, n$$
$$x_{ij} = \text{number of units shipped from origin } i \text{ to destination } j$$
$$c_{ij} = \text{cost per unit of shipping from origin } i \text{ to destination } j$$
$$s_i = \text{supply or capacity in units at origin } i$$
$$d_j = \text{demand in units at destination } j$$

The general linear programming model of the m-origin, n-destination transportation problem is

$$\text{Min} \quad \sum_{i=1}^{m} \sum_{j=1}^{n} c_{ij} x_{ij}$$

s.t.

$$\sum_{j=1}^{n} x_{ij} \leq s_i \qquad i = 1, 2, \ldots, m \quad \text{Supply}$$

$$\sum_{i=1}^{m} x_{ij} = d_j \qquad j = 1, 2, \ldots, n \quad \text{Demand}$$

$$x_{ij} \geq 0 \qquad \text{for all } i \text{ and } j$$

As mentioned previously, we can add additional constraints of the form $x_{ij} \leq L_{ij}$ if the route from origin i to destination j has capacity L_{ij}. A transportation problem that includes constraints of this type is called a **capacitated transportation problem.** Similarly, we can add route minimum constraints of the form $x_{ij} \geq M_{ij}$ if the route from origin i to destination j must handle at least M_{ij} units.

NOTES and Comments

1. Transportation problems encountered in practice usually lead to very large linear programs; problems with 100 origins and 100 destinations are not unusual. Such a problem would involve $(100)(100) = 10{,}000$ variables (assuming all arcs are feasible). For such a problem, special-purpose solution procedures are much more efficient than general-purpose linear programming or spreadsheet solvers. But if speed is not an issue, a general-purpose linear programming code that has the capability to solve large problems will solve most transportation problems.

2. The optimal solution to a transportation model will consist of integer values for the decision variables as long as all supply and demand values are integers. The reason is the special mathematical structure of the linear programming model. Each variable appears in exactly one supply and one demand constraint, and all coefficients in the constraint equations are 1's or 0's.

3. Although many transportation problems involve minimizing the cost of transporting goods between locations, other applications of the transportation model exist. The Management Science in Action: Marine Corps Mobilization illustrates the use of a transportation model to send Marine Corps officers to billets.

MANAGEMENT SCIENCE IN ACTION

MARINE CORPS MOBILIZATION*

The U.S. Marine Corps has developed a network model for mobilizing its officers in the event of a world crisis or war. The problem is to send officers to billets (duty assignments) as quickly as possible. The model developed to solve this problem is a transportation model much like the ones discussed in this chapter, only much larger. The origins or supply nodes represent the officers available, and the destinations or demand nodes represent the billets. A realistic implementation might involve as many as 40,000 officers and 25,000 billets. If all officer-to-billets arc combinations are permitted, the transportation problem would have 1 billion arcs. To reduce the problem size, officers with similar qualifications are aggregated into the same supply node and similar duty assignments are aggregated into the same demand nodes. Using this approach and methods for eliminating infeasible arcs, the Marine Corps has

solved problems involving 27,000 officers and 10,000 billets in 10 seconds on a personal computer.

Excellent results in sending officers of appropriate grade and job qualifications to the desired billets have been obtained. In a crisis, the availability and use of this system can make the difference between an appropriate response and disaster. The prior system required 2–4 days to produce a complete mobilization plan and provided a lower quality match between officer qualifications and billet needs. The Marine Corps is now using the mobilization model to enhance its peace-time capability.

*Based on D. O. Bausch, G. G. Brown, D. R. Hundley, S. H. Rapp, and R. E. Rosenthal, "Mobilizing Marine Corps Officers," *Interfaces* (July–August 1991): 26–38.

5.2   THE ASSIGNMENT PROBLEM

The **assignment problem** arises in a variety of decision-making situations; typical assignment problems involve assigning jobs to machines, agents to tasks, sales personnel to sales territories, contracts to bidders, and so on. A distinguishing feature of the assignment problem is that *one* agent is assigned to *one and only one* task. Specifically, we look for the set of assignments that will optimize a stated objective, such as minimize cost, minimize time, or maximize profits.

To illustrate the assignment problem, let us consider the case of Fowle Marketing Research, which has just received requests for market research studies from three new clients. The company faces the task of assigning a project leader (agent) to each client (task). Currently, three individuals have no other commitments and are available for the project leader assignments. Fowle's management realizes, however, that the time required to complete each study will depend on the experience and ability of the project leader assigned. The three projects have approximately the same priority, and the company wants to assign project leaders to minimize the total number of days required to complete all three projects. If a project leader is to be assigned to one client only, what assignments should be made?

To answer the assignment question, Fowle's management must first consider all possible project leader-client assignments and then estimate the corresponding project completion times. With three project leaders and three clients, nine assignment alternatives are possible. The alternatives and the estimated project completion times in days are summarized in Table 5.3.

Figure 5.5 shows the network representation of Fowle's assignment problem. The nodes correspond to the project leaders and clients, and the arcs represent the possible assignments of project leaders to clients. The supply at each origin node and the demand at each destination node are 1; the cost of assigning a project leader to a client is the time that project leader needs to complete the client's task. Note the similarity between the network models of the assignment problem (Figure 5.5) and the transportation problem (Figure 5.1). The assignment problem is a special case of the transportation problem in which all supply and demand values equal 1, and the amount shipped over each arc is either 0 or 1.

Try part (a) of Problem 12 to see if you can develop a network model for an assignment problem.

Since the assignment problem is a special case of the transportation problem, a linear programming formulation can be developed. Again, we need a constraint for each node and a variable for each arc. As in the transportation problem, we use double-subscripted decision variables, with x_{11} denoting the assignment of project leader 1 (Terry) to client 1, x_{12} denoting the assignment of project leader 1 (Terry) to client 2, and so on. Thus, we define the decision variables for Fowle's assignment problem as

$$x_{ij} = \begin{cases} 1 \text{ if project leader } i \text{ is assigned to client } j \\ 0 \text{ otherwise} \end{cases}$$

where $i = 1, 2, 3$, and $j = 1, 2, 3$

Using this notation and the completion time data in Table 5.3, we develop completion time expressions:

Days required for Terry's assignment	$= 10x_{11} + 15x_{12} + 9x_{13}$
Days required for Carle's assignment	$= 9x_{21} + 18x_{22} + 5x_{23}$
Days required for McClymonds's assignment	$= 6x_{31} + 14x_{32} + 3x_{33}$

Table 5.3   ESTIMATED PROJECT COMPLETION TIMES (DAYS) FOR THE FOWLE MARKETING RESEARCH ASSIGNMENT PROBLEM

	Client		
Project Leader	1	2	3
1. Terry	10	15	9
2. Carle	9	18	5
3. McClymonds	6	14	3

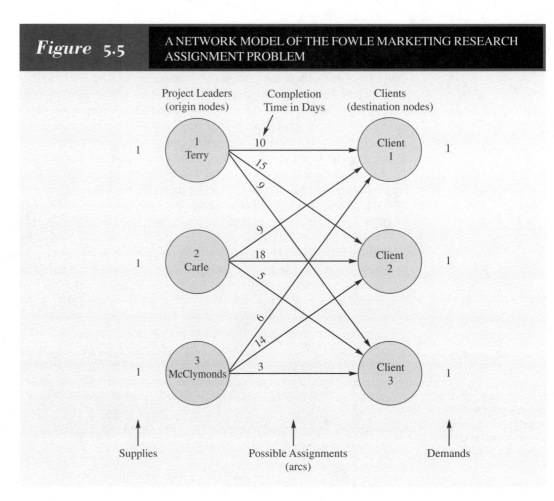

Figure 5.5 A NETWORK MODEL OF THE FOWLE MARKETING RESEARCH ASSIGNMENT PROBLEM

The sum of the completion times for the three project leaders will provide the total days required to complete the three assignments. Thus, the objective function is

$$\text{Min} \quad 10x_{11} + 15x_{12} + 9x_{13} + 9x_{21} + 18x_{22} + 5x_{23} + 6x_{31} + 14x_{32} + 3x_{33}$$

The constraints for the assignment problem reflect the conditions that each project leader can be assigned to at most one client and that each client must have one assigned project leader. These constraints are written as follows:

Since the number of project leaders equals the number of clients, all the constraints could be written as equalites. But when the number of project leaders exceeds the number of clients, less-than-or-equal-to constraints must be used for the project leader constraints.

$$x_{11} + x_{12} + x_{13} \le 1 \quad \text{Terry's assignment}$$
$$x_{21} + x_{22} + x_{23} \le 1 \quad \text{Carle's assignment}$$
$$x_{31} + x_{32} + x_{33} \le 1 \quad \text{McClymonds's assignment}$$
$$x_{11} + x_{21} + x_{31} = 1 \quad \text{Client 1}$$
$$x_{12} + x_{22} + x_{32} = 1 \quad \text{Client 2}$$
$$x_{13} + x_{23} + x_{33} = 1 \quad \text{Client 3}$$

Note that there is one constraint for each node in Figure 5.5.

Combining the objective function and constraints into one model provides the following 9-variable, 6-constraint linear programming model of the Fowle Marketing Research assignment problem.

$$\text{Min} \quad 10x_{11} + 15x_{12} + 9x_{13} + 9x_{21} + 18x_{22} + 5x_{23} + 6x_{31} + 14x_{32} + 3x_{33}$$

s.t.

$$
\begin{array}{lcr}
x_{11} + x_{12} + x_{13} & & \leq 1 \\
x_{21} + x_{22} + x_{23} & & \leq 1 \\
x_{31} + x_{32} + x_{33} & \leq 1 \\
x_{11} \quad\quad\quad + x_{21} \quad\quad\quad + x_{31} & & = 1 \\
x_{12} \quad\quad\quad + x_{22} \quad\quad\quad + x_{32} & & = 1 \\
x_{13} \quad\quad\quad + x_{23} \quad\quad\quad + x_{33} & = 1 \\
\end{array}
$$

$$x_{ij} \geq 0 \quad \text{for } i = 1, 2, 3; j = 1, 2, 3$$

The spreadsheet formulation and solution are shown in Figure 5.6.

Spreadsheet Formulation.   The data and descriptive labels are contained in cells A1:D7. Note that we have not inserted supply and demand values since they are always equal to 1 in an assignment problem. The model appears in the bottom portion of the spreadsheet with the key elements screened.

SPREADSHEET FOWLE MARKETING RESEARCH

Figure 5.6   SPREADSHEET SOLUTION OF THE FOWLE MARKETING RESEARCH PROBLEM

	A	B	C	D	E	F	G	H
1	**Fowle Marketing Research**							
2								
3			**Client**					
4	**Project Leader**	1	2	3				
5	Terry	10	15	9				
6	Carle	9	18	5				
7	McClymonds	6	14	3				
8								
9								
10	**Model**							
11								
12		**Min Time**	26					
13								
14			**Client**					
15	**Project Leader**	1	2	3	**Total**			
16	Terry	0	1	0	1	<=	1	
17	Carle	0	0	1	1	<=	1	
18	McClymonds	1	0	0	1	<=	1	
19	**Total**	1	1	1				
20		=	=	=				
21		1	1	1				

Decision Variables   Cells B16:D18 are reserved for the decision variables. The optimal values are shown to be $x_{12} = 1, x_{23} = 1$, and $x_{31} = 1$ with all other variables $= 0$.

Objective Function   The formula =SUMPRODUCT(B5:D7,B16:D18) has been placed into cell C12 to reflect the number of days required to complete all the jobs. The minimum time solution has a value of 26 days.

Left-Hand Sides   Cells E16:E18 contain the left-hand sides of the constraints for the number of clients each project leader can handle. Cells B19:D19 contain the left-hand sides of the constraints requiring that each client must be assigned a project leader.

         Cell E16 =SUM(B16:D16)   (Copy to E17:E18)
         Cell B19 =SUM(B16:B18)   (Copy to C19:D19)

Right-Hand Sides   Cells G16:G18 contain the right-hand sides for the project leader constraints and cells B21:D21 contain the right-hand sides for the client constraints. All right-hand side cells values are 1.

Spreadsheet Solution.   The solution can be obtained by selecting **Solver** from the **Tools** menu, entering the proper values into the **Solver Parameters** dialog box, and specifying the options **Assume Linear Model** and **Assume Non-Negative.** The information entered into the **Solver Parameters** dialog box is shown in Figure 5.7.

At this point, you should be able to formulate and solve an assignment problem. Try part (b) of Problem 12.

     Table 5.4 provides a summary of the optimal solution. Terry is assigned to client 2 $(x_{12} = 1)$, Carle is assigned to client 3 $(x_{23} = 1)$, and McClymonds is assigned to client 1 $(x_{31} = 1)$. The total completion time required is 26 days.

Problem Variations

Because the assignment problem can be viewed as a special case of the transportation problem, the problem variations that may arise in an assignment problem parallel those for the transportation problem. Specifically, we can handle

Figure 5.7   SOLVER PARAMETERS DIALOG BOX FOR FOWLE MARKETING RESEARCH PROBLEM

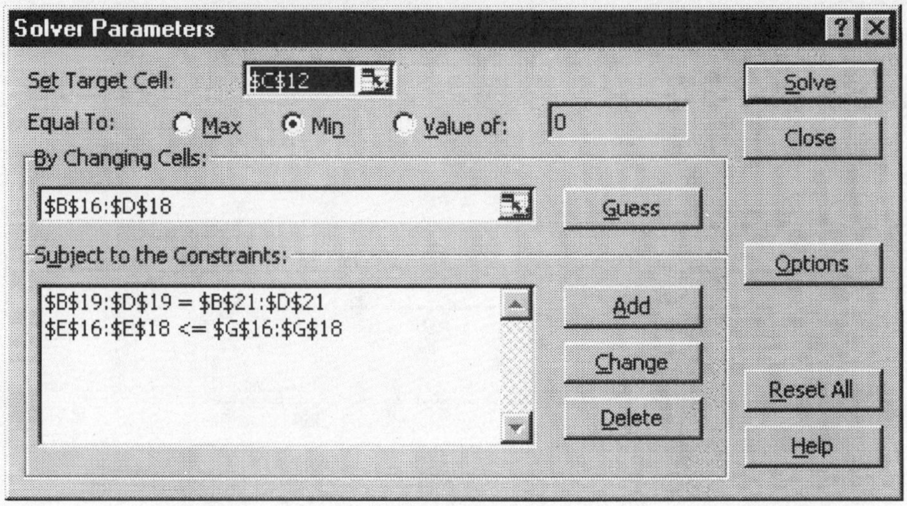

Table 5.4	OPTIMAL PROJECT LEADER ASSIGNMENTS FOR THE FOWLE MARKETING RESEARCH PROBLEM

Project Leader	Assigned Client	Days
Terry	2	15
Carle	3	5
McClymonds	1	6
	Total	26

1. Total number of agents (supply) not equal to the total number of tasks (demand)
2. A maximization objective function
3. Unacceptable assignments

The situation in which the number of agents does not equal the number of tasks is analogous to total supply not equaling total demand in a transportation problem. If the number of agents exceeds the number of tasks, the extra agents simply remain unassigned in the linear programming model. If the number of tasks exceeds the number of agents, the linear programming model will not have a feasible solution. In this situation, a simple modification is to add enough dummy agents to equalize the number of agents and the number of tasks. For instance, in the Fowle problem we might have had five clients (tasks) and only three project leaders (agents). By adding two dummy project leaders, we can create a new assignment problem with the number of project leaders equal to the number of clients. The objective function coefficients for the assignment of dummy project leaders would be zero so that the value of the optimal solution would represent the total number of days required by the assignments actually made (no assignments will actually be made to the clients receiving dummy project leaders).

In the linear programming formulation of a problem with five clients and only three project leaders, we could get by with one dummy project leader by placing a 2 on the right-hand side of the constraint for the dummy project leader.

If the assignment alternatives are evaluated in terms of revenue or profit rather than time or cost, the linear programming formulation can be solved as a maximization rather than a minimization problem. In addition, if one or more assignments are unacceptable, the corresponding decision variable can be removed from the linear programming formulation. This could happen, for example, if an agent did not have the experience necessary for one or more of the tasks. In the spreadsheet formulation, the easiest way to handle this situation is to assign a very large cost to any decision variable corresponding to an unacceptable assignment.

A General Linear Programming Model of the Assignment Problem

The general assignment problem involves m agents and n tasks. If we let $x_{ij} = 1$ or 0 according to whether agent i is assigned to task j or not, and if c_{ij} denotes the cost of assigning agent i to task j, we can write the general assignment model as

$$\text{Min} \quad \sum_{i=1}^{m} \sum_{j=1}^{n} c_{ij} x_{ij}$$

s.t.

$$\sum_{j=1}^{n} x_{ij} \leq 1 \qquad i = 1, 2, \ldots, m \qquad \text{Agents}$$

$$\sum_{i=1}^{m} x_{ij} = 1 \qquad j = 1, 2, \ldots, n \qquad \text{Tasks}$$

$$x_{ij} \geq 0 \qquad \text{for all } i \text{ and } j$$

Multiple Assignments

At the beginning of this section, we indicated that a distinguishing feature of the assignment problem is that *one* agent is assigned to *one and only one* task. In generalizations of the assignment problem where one agent can be assigned to two or more tasks, the linear programming formulation of the problem can be easily modified. For example, let us assume that in the Fowle Marketing Research problem Terry could be assigned up to two clients; in this case, the constraint representing Terry's assignment would be $x_{11} + x_{12} + x_{13} \leq 2$. In general, if a_i denotes the upper limit for the number of tasks to which agent i can be assigned, we write the agent constraints as

$$\sum_{j=1}^{n} x_{ij} \leq a_i \qquad i = 1, 2, \ldots, m$$

Thus, we see that one advantage of formulating and solving assignment problems as linear programs is that special cases such as the situation involving multiple assignments can be easily handled.

N O T E S
and Comments

1. As noted, the assignment model is a special case of the transportation model. We stated in the notes and comments at the end of the preceding section that the optimal solution to the transportation problem will consist of integer values for the decision variables as long as the supplies and demands are integers. For the assignment problem, all supplies and demands equal 1; thus, the optimal solution must be integer valued and the integer values must be 0 or 1.

2. Combining the method for handling multiple assignments with the notion of a dummy agent provides another means of dealing with situations when the number of tasks exceeds the number of agents. That is, we add one dummy agent, but provide the dummy agent with the capability to handle multiple tasks. The number of tasks the dummy agent can handle is equal to the difference between the number of tasks and the number of agents.

5.3   THE TRANSSHIPMENT PROBLEM

The **transshipment problem** is an extension of the transportation problem in which intermediate nodes, referred to as *transshipment nodes,* are added to account for locations such as warehouses. In this more general type of distribution problem, shipments may be made between any pair of the three general types of nodes: origin nodes, transshipment nodes, and destination nodes. Furthermore, some of the nodes allow both shipments in and shipments out (transshipments). For example, the transshipment problem permits shipments of goods from origins to transshipment nodes and on to destinations, from one origin to another origin, from one transshipment location to another, from one destination location to another, and directly from origins to destinations.

As was true for the transportation problem, the supply available at each origin is limited, and the demand at each destination is specified. The objective in the transshipment problem is to determine how many units should be shipped over each arc in the network so that all destination demands are satisfied with the minimum possible transportation cost.

Try part (a) of Problem 23 for practice in developing a network representation of a transshipment problem.

Let us consider the transshipment problem faced by Ryan Electronics. Ryan is an electronics company with production facilities in Denver and Atlanta. Components produced at either facility may be shipped to either of the firm's regional warehouses, which are located in Kansas City and Louisville. From the regional warehouses, the firm supplies retail outlets in Detroit, Miami, Dallas, and New Orleans. The key features of the problem are shown in the network model depicted in Figure 5.8. Note that the supply at each origin and demand at each destination are shown in the left and right margins, respectively. Nodes 1 and 2 are the origin nodes; nodes 3 and 4 are the transshipment nodes; and nodes 5, 6, 7, and 8 are the destination nodes. The transportation cost per unit for each distribution route is shown in Table 5.5 and on the arcs of the network model in Figure 5.8.

As with the transportation and assignment problems, we can formulate a linear programming model of the transshipment problem from a network representation. Again, we need a constraint for each node and a variable for each arc. Let x_{ij} denote the number of units shipped from node i to node j. For example, x_{13} denotes the number of units shipped from the Denver plant to the Kansas City warehouse, x_{14} denotes the number of units shipped from the Denver plant to the Louisville warehouse, and so on.

In developing the constraints for a transshipment problem, it is useful to think in terms of the net shipments from each node (there may be shipments in and shipments out) and the

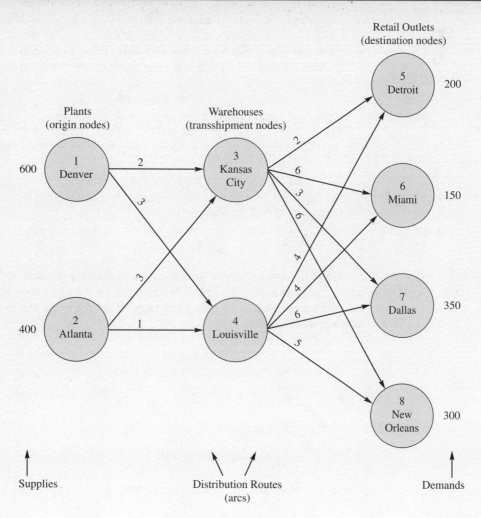

Figure 5.8   NETWORK REPRESENTATION OF THE RYAN ELECTRONICS TRANSSHIPMENT PROBLEM

Table 5.5	TRANSPORTATION COSTS PER UNIT FOR THE RYAN ELECTRONICS TRANSSHIPMENT PROBLEM

Warehouse

Plant	Kansas City	Louisville
Denver	2	3
Atlanta	3	1

Retail Outlet

Warehouse	Detroit	Miami	Dallas	New Orleans
Kansas City	2	6	3	6
Louisville	4	4	6	5

supply at each node. We define **net shipments** for a node as the amount shipped out minus the amount shipped in. Additionally, we define the **supply** at each node to be the amount by which shipments out may exceed shipments in. For origin nodes, the supply will be positive. For transshipment nodes, the supply will be zero. For destination nodes the supply will be negative because there is less shipped out than shipped in. For each supply node in a transshipment problem, we define a constraint of the following form:

$$\text{Net shipments} \leq \text{Supply}$$

The supply at the Denver plant is 600 units and, since there are no shipments in, the net shipments are given by $x_{13} + x_{14}$. So the constraint for the Denver plant is

$$x_{13} + x_{14} \leq 600$$

Similarly, for the Atlanta plant we have

$$x_{23} + x_{24} \leq 400$$

We now consider how to write the constraints corresponding to the two transshipment nodes. For node 3 (the Kansas City warehouse), we must guarantee that the number of units shipped out must equal the number of units shipped into the warehouse. That is, net shipments must equal zero.

$$\text{Number of units shipped out of node 3} = x_{35} + x_{36} + x_{37} + x_{38}$$

and

$$\text{Number of units shipped into node 3} = x_{13} + x_{23}$$

Therefore, net shipments for node 3 are given by

$$\text{Net shipments} = x_{35} + x_{36} + x_{37} + x_{38} - x_{13} - x_{23}$$

The constraint for node 3 (after rearranging the variables) is then

$$-x_{13} - x_{23} + x_{35} + x_{36} + x_{37} + x_{38} = 0$$

Similarly, the constraint corresponding to node 4 is

$$-x_{14} - x_{24} + x_{45} + x_{46} + x_{47} + x_{48} = 0$$

To develop the constraints associated with the destination nodes, we recognize that for the Ryan Electronics problem there are no shipments out. Turning to node 5 (the Detroit retail outlet), we see that net shipments are (shipments out) − (shipments in) = $-x_{35} - x_{45}$. With supply = −200, we obtain the following constraint:

$$-x_{35} - x_{45} = -200$$

Similarly, for nodes 6, 7, and 8 we have

$$-x_{36} - x_{46} = -150$$
$$-x_{37} - x_{47} = -350$$
$$-x_{38} - x_{48} = -300$$

As usual, the objective function reflects the total shipping cost over the 12 shipping routes. Combining the objective function and constraints leads to a 12-variable, 8-constraint linear programming model of the Ryan Electronics transshipment problem (see Figure 5.9).

The spreadsheet formulation and solution of the Ryan Electronics problem are shown in Figure 5.10. Note that we have deviated from our previous practice of maintaining a separation of the problem data and the model. We have grouped together all information concerning arcs in cells A3:D16 and all information concerning the nodes in cells F5:K14. This arrangement allows for a more compact spreadsheet and has other advantages that we mention later.

Spreadsheet Formulation.   The data for the problem consists of the cost per unit to ship over each arc and the supply at each node. The arc data, along with descriptive labels, are

Figure 5.9   LINEAR PROGRAMMING FORMULATION OF THE RYAN ELECTRONICS TRANSSHIPMENT PROBLEM

Min $2x_{13} + 3x_{14} + 3x_{23} + 1x_{24} + 2x_{35} + 6x_{36} + 3x_{37} + 6x_{38} + 4x_{45} + 4x_{46} + 6x_{47} + 5x_{48}$
s.t.

$$
\begin{array}{llll}
x_{13} + x_{14} & & \leq 600 & \left.\right\} \text{Origin node constraints} \\
\quad x_{23} + x_{24} & & \leq 400 & \\
-x_{13} \quad -x_{23} \quad +x_{35} + x_{36} + x_{37} + x_{38} & & = 0 & \left.\right\} \text{Transshipment node} \\
\quad -x_{14} \quad -x_{24} \quad +x_{45} + x_{46} + x_{47} + x_{48} & = 0 & & \text{constraints} \\
\quad -x_{35} \quad -x_{45} & & = -200 & \left.\right\} \\
\quad -x_{36} \quad -x_{46} & & = -150 & \left.\right\} \text{Destination node} \\
\quad -x_{37} \quad -x_{47} & & = -350 & \text{constraints} \\
\quad -x_{38} \quad -x_{48} & = -300 & &
\end{array}
$$

$x_{ij} \geq 0$ for all i and j

Figure 5.10	SPREADSHEET SOLUTION FOR THE RYAN ELECTRONICS PROBLEM

	A	B	C	D	E	F	G	H	I	J	K
1	**Ryan Electronics Transshipment**										
2											
3		**Route**			**Units**						
4	Start Node	End Node	Cost	Shipped							
5	Denver	Kansas City	2	550			**Units Shipped**		**Net**		
6	Denver	Louisville	3	50		**Node**	In	Out	**Shipments**		**Supply**
7	Atlanta	Kansas City	3	0		Denver		600	600	<=	600
8	Atlanta	Louisville	1	400		Atlanta		400	400	<=	400
9	Kansas City	Detroit	2	200		Kansas City	550	550	0	=	0
10	Kansas City	Miami	6	0		Louisville	450	450	0	=	0
11	Kansas City	Dallas	3	350		Detroit	200		-200	=	-200
12	Kansas City	New Orleans	6	0		Miami	150		-150	=	-150
13	Louisville	Detroit	4	0		Dallas	350		-350	=	-350
14	Louisville	Miami	4	150		New Orleans	300		-300	=	-300
15	Louisville	Dallas	6	0							
16	Louisville	New Orleans	5	300							
17											
18								**Total Cost**	5200		
19											
20											
21											

contained in cells A3:C16. The supply data along with a descriptive label for the nodes are contained in cells K6:K14. As in previous spreadsheet formulations, we have screened the key elements required by the Excel solver.

Decision Variables   Cells D5:D16 are reserved for the decision variables. The optimal number of units to ship over each route is shown.

Objective Function   The formula =SUMPRODUCT(C5:C16,D5:D16) is placed into cell I18 to show the total cost associated with the solution. As shown, the total cost is $5,200.

Left-Hand Sides   The left-hand sides of the constraints represent the net shipments for each node. Cells I7:I14 are reserved for these.
      Cell I7   =H7−G7   (Copy to I8:I14)

The above left-hand-side cells reference cells that contain additional formulas. These referenced cells provide the units shipped in and the units shipped out for each node in the network. The referenced cells and their formulas are as follows:

Units Shipped In
      Cell G9   =D5+D7
      Cell G10 =D6+D8
      Cell G11 =D9+D13
      Cell G12 =D10+D14
      Cell G13 =D11+D15
      Cell G14 =D12+D16

Units Shipped Out
      Cell H7   =SUM(D5:D6)
      Cell H8   =SUM(D7:D8)
      Cell H9   =SUM(D9:D12)
      Cell H10 =SUM(D13:D16)

Right-Hand Sides   The right-hand sides of the constraints represent the supply at each node. Cells K7:K14 are reserved for these. (Note the negative supply at the four demand nodes.)

Try parts (b) and (c) of Problem 23 for practice in developing the linear programming model and in solving a transshipment problem.

Spreadsheet Solution.   The solution can be obtained by selecting **Solver** from the **Tools** menu, entering the proper values into the **Solver Parameters** dialog box, and specifying the options **Assume Linear Model** and **Assume Non-Negative.** The information entered into the **Solver Parameters** dialog box is shown in Figure 5.11. Table 5.6 provides a summary of the optimal solution.

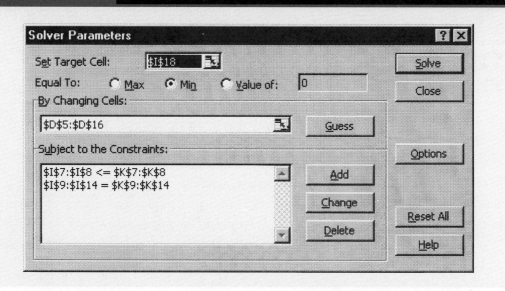

Figure 5.11   SOLVER PARAMETERS DIALOG BOX FOR THE RYAN ELECTRONICS PROBLEM

Table 5.6   OPTIMAL SOLUTION TO THE RYAN ELECTRONICS TRANSSHIPMENT PROBLEM

| Route | | | | |
From	To	Units Shipped	Cost Per Unit	Total Cost
Denver	Kansas City	550	$2	$1100
Denver	Louisville	50	$3	150
Atlanta	Louisville	400	$1	400
Kansas City	Detroit	200	$2	400
Kansas City	Dallas	350	$3	1050
Louisville	Miami	150	$4	600
Louisville	New Orleans	300	$5	1500
				$5200

A Modified Problem

As mentioned at the beginning of this section, arcs may connect any pair of nodes in a transshipment problem. The linear programming model still only requires one constraint per node, but the constraint must include a variable for every arc entering and every arc leaving the node. For origin nodes, the constraints take the form of net shipments (amount shipped out minus amount shipped in) less-than-or-equal-to supply. For transshipment and destination nodes, the constraints take the form of net shipments equal supply where supply is 0 for transshipment nodes and the negative of demand for destination nodes.

For an illustration of this more general type of transshipment problem, let us modify the Ryan Electronics problem. Suppose that Ryan can ship directly from Atlanta to New Orleans at $4 per unit and from Dallas to New Orleans at $1 per unit. The network model corresponding to this modified Ryan Electronics problem is shown in Figure 5.12, and the linear programming formulation is shown in Figure 5.13.

In Figure 5.12 we see that two new arcs have been added to the previous network model (see Figure 5.8). Thus, two new decision variables are necessary in the linear programming model. Figure 5.13 shows that the new variables x_{28} and x_{78} appear in the objective function and in the constraints corresponding to the nodes to which the new arcs are connected. Figure 5.14 shows the spreadsheet formulation and solution of the modified Ryan Electronics transshipment problem.

Try Problem 24 for practice working with transshipment problems with this more general structure.

Spreadsheet Formulation.   The input data concerning the arcs are contained in cells A3:C18, and the supply data for the nodes are contained in cells K6:K14. The key elements of the model required by the Excel Solver are screened.

Decision Variables   Cells D5:D18 are reserved for the decision variables. The optimal number of units to ship over each route is shown.

Objective Function   The formula =SUMPRODUCT(C5:C18,D5:D18) is placed into cell I18 to reflect the cost associated with the solution.

Left-Hand Sides   The left-hand sides of the constraints represent the net shipments from each node. Cells I7:I14 are reserved for these.
    Cell I7   =H7−G7   (Copy to I8:I14)

The above left-hand-side cells reference cells that contain additional formulas. These reference cells provide the units shipped in and the units shipped out for each node in the network. The referenced cells and their formulas are as follows:

Units Shipped In   Cell G9   =D5+D7
                     Cell G10 =D6+D8
                     Cell G11 =D10+D14
                     Cell G12 =D11+D15
                     Cell G13 =D12+D16
                     Cell G14 =D9+D13+D17+D18

Units Shipped Out   Cell H7   =SUM(D5:D6)
                     Cell H8   =SUM(D7:D9)
                     Cell H9   =SUM(D10:D13)
                     Cell H10 =SUM(D14:D17)
                     Cell H13 =D18

Right-Hand Sides   The right-hand sides of the constraints represent the supply at each node. Cells K7:K14 are reserved for these. (Note the negative supply at demand nodes).

Figure 5.12   NETWORK REPRESENTATION OF THE MODIFIED RYAN ELECTRONICS TRANSSHIPMENT PROBLEM

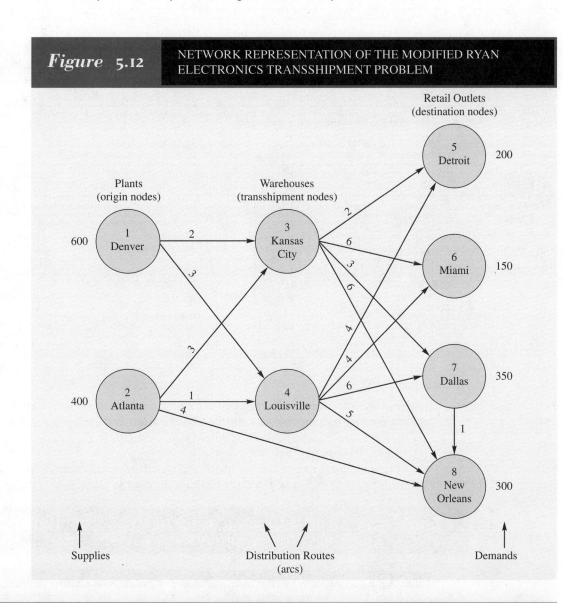

Figure 5.13   LINEAR PROGRAMMING FORMULATION OF THE MODIFIED RYAN ELECTRONICS TRANSSHIPMENT PROBLEM

$$\text{Min}\quad 2x_{13} + 3x_{14} + 3x_{23} + 1x_{24} + 2x_{35} + 6x_{36} + 3x_{37} + 6x_{38} + 4x_{45} + 4x_{46} + 6x_{47} + 5x_{48} + 4x_{28} + 1x_{78}$$

s.t.

$$
\begin{array}{lr}
x_{13} + x_{14} & \leq 600 \\
\quad x_{23} + x_{24} \qquad\qquad\qquad\qquad\qquad\qquad + x_{28} & \leq 400 \\
-x_{13} \quad - x_{23} \quad + x_{35} + x_{36} + x_{37} + x_{38} & = 0 \\
\quad - x_{14} \quad - x_{24} \qquad\qquad + x_{45} + x_{46} + x_{47} + x_{48} & = 0 \\
\quad - x_{35} \qquad\qquad\qquad - x_{45} & = -200 \\
\quad - x_{36} \qquad\qquad\qquad - x_{46} & = -150 \\
\quad - x_{37} \qquad\qquad\qquad - x_{47} \qquad + x_{78} & = -350 \\
\quad - x_{38} \qquad\qquad\qquad - x_{48} - x_{28} - x_{78} & = -300
\end{array}
$$

Origin node constraints

Transshipment node constraints

Destination node constraints

$x_{ij} \geq 0$ for all i and j

Figure 5.14   SPREADSHEET SOLUTION FOR THE MODIFIED RYAN ELECTRONICS PROBLEM

	A	B	C	D	E	F	G	H	I	J	K
1	**Modified Ryan Electronics Transshipment**										
2											
3		**Route**		**Units**							
4	Start Node	End Node	**Cost**	**Shipped**							
5	Denver	Kansas City	2	550			**Units Shipped**		**Net**		
6	Denver	Louisville	3	50		**Node**	In	Out	**Shipments**		**Supply**
7	Atlanta	Kansas City	3	0		Denver		600	600	<=	600
8	Atlanta	Louisville	1	100		Atlanta		400	400	<=	400
9	Atlanta	New Orleans	4	300		Kansas City	550	550	0	=	0
10	Kansas City	Detroit	2	200		Louisville	150	150	0	=	0
11	Kansas City	Miami	6	0		Detroit	200		-200	=	-200
12	Kansas City	Dallas	3	350		Miami	150		-150	=	-150
13	Kansas City	New Orleans	6	0		Dallas	350	0	-350	=	-350
14	Louisville	Detroit	4	0		New Orleans	300		-300	=	-300
15	Louisville	Miami	4	150							
16	Louisville	Dallas	6	0							
17	Louisville	New Orleans	5	0							
18	Dallas	New Orleans	4	0				**Total Cost**	**4600**		
19											
20											
21											

SPREADSHEET MODIFIED RYAN ELECTRONICS

Spreadsheet Solution. The solution can be obtained by selecting **Solver** from the **Tools** menu, entering the proper values into the **Solver Parameters** dialog box, and specifying the options **Assume Linear Model** and **Assume Non-Negative.** The information entered into the **Solver Parameters** dialog box is shown in Figure 5.15.

From Figure 5.14 we see that the optimal solution to the modified Ryan Electronics problem has a total cost of $4,600—a savings of $600 over the previous solution. Three-

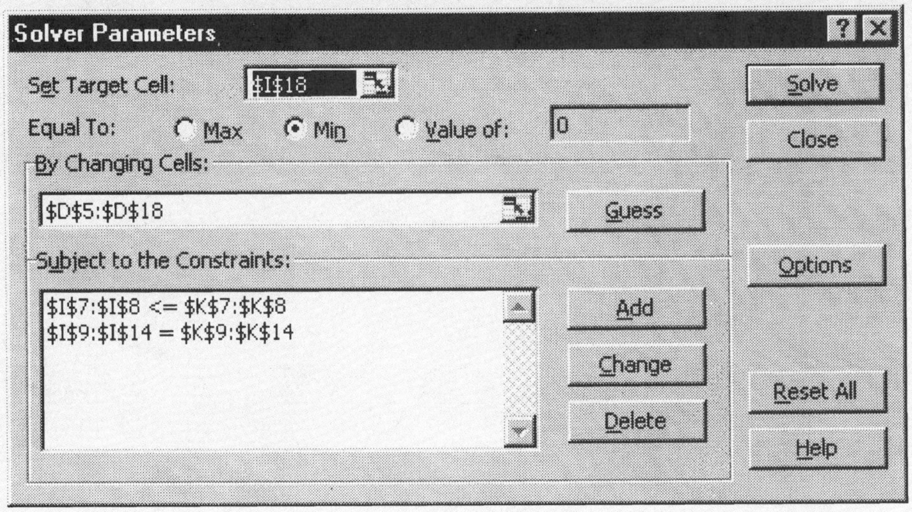

Figure 5.15   SOLVER PARAMETERS DIALOG BOX FOR THE MODIFIED RYAN ELECTRONICS PROBLEM

hundred units are shipped directly over the new route from Atlanta to New Orleans. Nothing is shipped over the new route from Dallas to New Orleans.

Problem Variations

As with transportation and assignment problems, transshipment problems may be formulated with several variations, including

1. Total supply not equal to total demand
2. Maximization objective function
3. Route capacities or route minimums
4. Unacceptable routes

The linear programming model modifications required to accommodate these variations are identical to the modifications required for the transportation problem described in Section 5.1. When we add one or more constraints of the form $x_{ij} \leq L_{ij}$ to show that the route from node i to node j has capacity L_{ij}, we refer to the transshipment problem as a **capacitated transshipment problem.**

A General Linear Programming Model of the Transshipment Problem

The general linear programming model of the transshipment problem is

$$\text{Min} \quad \sum_{\text{all arcs}} c_{ij} x_{ij}$$

s.t.

$$\sum_{\text{arcs out}} x_{ij} - \sum_{\text{arcs in}} x_{ij} \leq s_i \qquad \text{Origin nodes } i$$

$$\sum_{\text{arcs out}} x_{ij} - \sum_{\text{arcs in}} x_{ij} = 0 \qquad \text{Transshipment nodes}$$

$$\sum_{\text{arcs out}} x_{ij} - \sum_{\text{arcs in}} x_{ij} = -d_j \qquad \text{Destination nodes } j$$

$$x_{ij} \geq 0 \text{ for all } i \text{ and } j$$

where

x_{ij} = number of units shipped from node i to node j

c_{ij} = cost per unit of shipping from node i to node j

s_i = supply at origin node i

d_j = demand at destination node j

N O T E S
and Comments

1. In more advanced treatments of linear programming and network flow problems, the capacitated transshipment problem is called the *pure network flow problem*. Efficient special-purpose solution procedures are available for network flow problems and their special cases.

2. The spreadsheet formulation we have used for the transshipment problem has an arc section and a node section. Only arcs that are actually present in the problem need be considered. Thus, if numerous arcs are unacceptable, we simply don't include them. Because the transportation problem is a special case of the transshipment problem, this formulation may also be used for transportation problems. Most large transportation and transshipment problems encountered in practice have only a small fraction of all possible arcs present. In such cases, this formulation provides a much more efficient use of spreadsheet space and a smaller problem (fewer decision variables) to solve.

..../ /.............

5.4 A PRODUCTION AND INVENTORY APPLICATION

The introduction to the transportation and transshipment problems in Sections 5.1 and 5.3 involved applications for the shipment of goods from several supply locations or origins to several demand sites or destinations. Although the shipment of goods is the subject of many transportation and transshipment problems, transportation and/or transshipment models can be developed for applications that have nothing to do with the physical shipment of goods from origins to destinations. In this section we show how to use a transshipment model to solve a production scheduling and inventory problem.

Contois Carpets is a small manufacturer of carpeting for home and office installations. Production capacity, demand, production cost per square yard, and inventory holding cost per square yard for the next four quarters are shown in Table 5.7. Note that production capacity, demand, and production costs vary by quarter, whereas the cost of carrying inventory from one quarter to the next is constant at $0.25 per yard. Contois wants to determine how many yards of carpeting to manufacture each quarter to minimize the total production and inventory cost for the four-quarter period.

The fact that the network shows flows into and out of demand nodes is what makes the model a transshipment model.

We begin by developing a network representation of the problem. First, we create four nodes corresponding to the production in each quarter and four nodes corresponding to the demand in each quarter. Each production node is connected by an outgoing arc to the demand node for the same period. The flow on the arc represents the number of square yards of carpet manufactured for the period. For each demand node, an outgoing arc represents the amount of inventory (square yards of carpet) carried over to the demand node for the next period. Figure 5.16 shows the network model. Note that nodes 1–4 represent the production for each quarter and that nodes 5–8 represent the demand for each quarter. The quarterly production capacities are shown in the left margin, and the quarterly demands are shown in the right margin.

The objective is to determine a production scheduling and inventory policy that will minimize the total production and inventory cost for the four quarters. Constraints involve production capacity and demand in each quarter. As usual, a linear programming model can be developed from the network by establishing a constraint for each node and a variable for each arc.

Let x_{15} denote the number of square yards of carpet manufactured in quarter 1. The capacity of the facility is 600 square yards in quarter 1, so the production capacity constraint is

$$x_{15} \leq 600$$

Table 5.7		PRODUCTION, DEMAND, AND COST ESTIMATES FOR CONTOIS CARPETS		
Quarter	Production Capacity (square yards)	Demand (square yards)	Production Cost ($/square yard)	Inventory Cost ($/square yard)
1	600	400	2	0.25
2	300	500	5	0.25
3	500	400	3	0.25
4	400	400	3	0.25

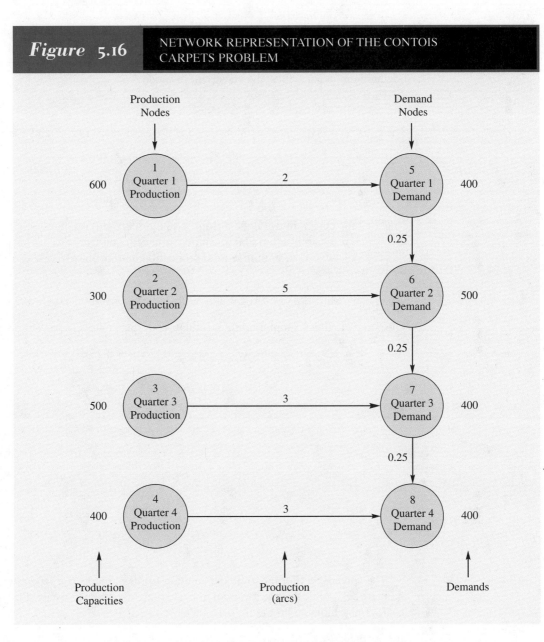

Figure 5.16 NETWORK REPRESENTATION OF THE CONTOIS CARPETS PROBLEM

We now consider the development of the constraints for each demand node. For node 5, one arc enters the node, which represents the number of square yards of carpet produced in quarter 1, and one arc leaves the node, which represents the number of square yards of carpet that will not be sold in quarter 1 and will be carried over for possible sale in quarter 2. The general format for transshipment node constraints is amount shipped out minus

Using similar decision variables, we obtain the production capacities for quarters 2–4:

$$x_{26} \leq 300$$
$$x_{37} \leq 500$$
$$x_{48} \leq 400$$

amount shipped in (net shipments) equals supply. For each demand node, the amount shipped out is the ending inventory for the period; the amount shipped in is the beginning inventory plus production. The supply is the negative of demand. However, for quarter 1 there is no beginning inventory; thus, the constraint for node 5 is

$$x_{56} - x_{15} = -400$$

The constraints associated with the demand nodes in quarters 2, 3, and 4 are

$$x_{67} - x_{56} - x_{26} = -500$$
$$x_{78} - x_{67} - x_{37} = -400$$
$$-x_{78} - x_{48} = -400$$

Note that the constraint for node 8 (fourth-quarter demand) involves only two variables as there is no provision for holding inventory for a fifth quarter.

The objective is to minimize total production and inventory cost, so we write the objective function as

$$\text{Min} \quad 2x_{15} + 5x_{26} + 3x_{37} + 3x_{48} + 0.25x_{56} + 0.25x_{67} + 0.25x_{78}$$

The complete linear programming formulation of the Contois Carpets problem is

$$\text{Min} \quad 2x_{15} + 5x_{26} + 3x_{37} + 3x_{48} + 0.25x_{56} + 0.25x_{67} + 0.25x_{78}$$

s.t.

$$
\begin{array}{rcrcrcrclr}
x_{15} & & & & & & & & \leq & 600 \\
& x_{26} & & & & & & & \leq & 300 \\
& & x_{37} & & & & & & \leq & 500 \\
& & & x_{48} & & & & & \leq & 400 \\
-x_{15} & & & & + & x_{56} & & & = & -400 \\
& -x_{26} & & & - & x_{56} & + & x_{67} & = & -500 \\
& & -x_{37} & & & & - & x_{67} & + & x_{78} & = & -400 \\
& & & -x_{48} & & & & & - & x_{78} & = & -400 \\
\end{array}
$$

$$x_{ij} \geq 0 \quad \text{for all } i \text{ and } j$$

The spreadsheet formulation and solution for the Contois Carpets problem are shown in Figure 5.17. Note that the same column labels are used here as we used for the Ryan Electronics transshipment problem.

Spreadsheet Formulation.   The input data concerning the arcs are contained in cells A3:C11, and the supply data for the nodes are contained in cells K6:K14. The key elements of the model required by the Excel Solver are screened.

Decision Variables   Cells D5:D11 are reserved for the decision variables. The optimal number of units to produce and to hold in inventory are shown.

Objective Function   The formula =SUMPRODUCT(C5:C11,D5:D11) is placed into cell I18 to show the total production and inventory cost associated with the solution. The total cost is $5,150.

Left-Hand Sides   The left-hand sides of the constraints represent the net shipments for each node. Cells I7:I14 are reserved for these.

       Cell I7   =H7−G7   (Copy to I8:I14)

	SPREADSHEET SOLUTION FOR THE CONTOIS
Figure **5.17**	CARPETS PROBLEM

	A	B	C	D	E	F	G	H	I	J	K
1	**Contois Carpets**										
2											
3		**Route**		**Units**							
4	Start Node	End Node	Cost	Shipped							
5	Production 1	Demand 1	2	600			**Units Shipped**		**Net**		
6	Production 2	Demand 2	5	300		**Node**	In	Out	**Shipments**		**Supply**
7	Production 3	Demand 3	3	400		Production 1		600	600	<=	600
8	Production 4	Demand 4	3	400		Production 2		300	300	<=	300
9	Demand 1	Demand 2	0.25	200		Production 3		400	400	<=	500
10	Demand 2	Demand 3	0.25	0		Production 4		400	400	<=	400
11	Demand 3	Demand 4	0.25	0		Demand 1	600	200	-400	=	-400
12						Demand 2	500	0	-500	=	-500
13						Demand 3	400	0	-400	=	-400
14						Demand 4	400		-400	=	-400
15											
16											
17											
18							**Total Cost**		5150		

SPREADSHEET CONTOIS CARPETS

The left-hand-side cells reference cells that contain additional formulas. These referenced cells provide the units shipped in and the units shipped out for each node in the network. The referenced cells and their formulas are as follows:

Units Shipped In	Cell G11	=D5
	Cell G12	=D6+D9
	Cell G13	=D7+D10
	Cell G14	=D8+D11

Units Shipped Out	Cell H7	=D5
	Cell H8	=D6
	Cell H9	=D7
	Cell H10	=D8
	Cell H11	=D9
	Cell H12	=D10
	Cell H13	=D11

Right-Hand Sides   The right-hand sides of the constraints represent the supply at each node (note the negative supply at the demand nodes). Cells K7:K14 are reserved for these. The values in these cells are the supply data for the problem.

Spreadsheet Solution.   The solution can be obtained by selecting **Solver** from the **Tools** menu, entering the proper values into the **Solver Parameters** dialog box, and specifying the options **Assume Linear Model** and **Assume Non-Negative.** The information entered into the **Solver Parameters** dialog box is shown in Figure 5.18.

Discussion.   From Figure 5.17, we see that Contois Carpets should manufacture 600 square yards of carpet in quarter 1, 300 square yards in quarter 2, 400 square yards in

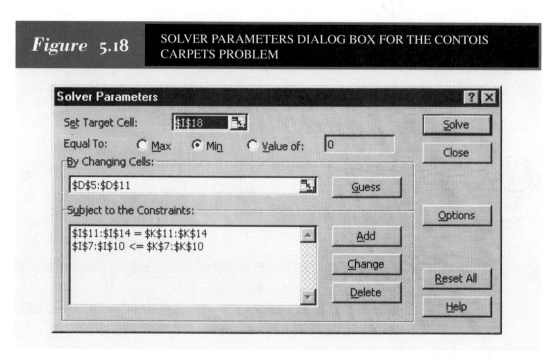

Figure 5.18 SOLVER PARAMETERS DIALOG BOX FOR THE CONTOIS CARPETS PROBLEM

quarter 3, and 400 square yards in quarter 4 (see cells D5:D8). Note also that 200 square yards will be carried over from quarter 1 to quarter 2 (see cell D9). Comparing cell I9 with K9 we see an excess production capacity of 100 square yards in quarter 3. The total production and inventory cost, shown in cell I18 is $5,150.

In the network model we developed for the transshipment problem, the amount leaving the starting node for an arc is always equal to the amount entering the ending node for that arc. An extension of such a network model is the case where a gain or a loss occurs as an arc is traversed. The amount entering the destination node may be greater or smaller than the amount leaving the origin node. For instance, if cash is the commodity flowing across an arc, the cash earns interest from one period to the next. Thus, the amount of cash entering the next period is greater than the amount leaving the previous period by the amount of interest earned. Networks with gains or losses are treated in more advanced texts on network flow programming.

SUMMARY

In this chapter we introduced transportation, assignment, and transshipment problems. All three types of problems belong to the special category of linear programs called *network flow problems*. The network model of a transportation problem consists of nodes representing a set of origins and a set of destinations. In the basic model, an arc is used to represent the route from each origin to each destination. Each origin has a supply and each destination has a demand. The problem is to determine the optimal amount to ship from each origin to each destination.

The assignment model is a special case of the transportation model in which all supply and all demand values are equal to 1. We represent each agent as an origin node and each task as a destination node. The transshipment model is an extension of the transportation model to distribution problems involving transfer points referred to as *transshipment nodes*. In this more general model, we allow arcs between any pair of nodes. A variation of the transshipment problem allows for placing capacities on the arcs. This variation, called the *capacitated transshipment problem,* is also known in the network flow literature as the *pure network problem.*

We showed how each of these network flow problems could be modeled as a linear program, and showed how to develop a spreadsheet formulation and solution. In network flow problems, the optimal solution will be integral as long as all supplies and demands are integral. Therefore, when solving any transportation, assignment, or transshipment problem in which the supplies and demands are integral, we can expect to obtain an integer-valued solution.

GLOSSARY

Network   A graphical representation of a problem consisting of numbered circles (nodes) interconnected by a series of lines (arcs); arrowheads on the arcs show the direction of flow. Transportation, assignment, and transshipment problems are network flow problems.

Transportation problem   A network flow problem that often involves minimizing the cost of shipping goods from a set of origins to a set of destinations; it can be formulated and solved as a linear program by including a variable for each arc and a constraint for each node.

Nodes   The intersection or junction points of a network.

Arcs   The lines connecting the nodes in a network.

Dummy origin   An origin added to a transportation problem in order to make the total supply equal to the total demand. The supply assigned to the dummy origin is the difference between the total demand and the total supply.

Capacitated transportation problem   A variation of the basic transportation problem in which there are capacities on some or all arcs.

Assignment problem   A network flow problem that often involves the assignment of agents to tasks; it can be formulated as a linear program and is a special case of the transportation problem.

Transshipment problem   An extension of the transportation problem to distribution problems involving transfer points and possible shipments between any pair of nodes.

Net shipments   The amount shipped out of a node in a transshipment problem minus the amount shipped in.

Capacitated transshipment problem   A variation of the transshipment problem in which there are capacities on some or all arcs.

Supply   The amount at each node by which shipments out may exceed shipments in.

··/ /··········

PROBLEMS

Note: In most of the problems that follow, we ask you to formulate and solve the problem as a linear program. You may use a spreadsheet to fomulate and solve the problem or any other computer package at your disposal.

SELF TEST

1. A company imports goods at two ports: Philadelphia and New Orleans. Shipments of one of its products are made to customers in Atlanta, Dallas, Columbus, and Boston. For the next planning period, the supplies at each port, customer demands, and shipping costs per case from each port to each customer are as follows:

	Customers				Port
Port	Atlanta	Dallas	Columbus	Boston	**Supply**
Philadelphia	2	6	6	2	5000
New Orleans	1	2	5	7	3000
Demand	1400	3200	2000	1400	

Develop a network model of the distribution system (transportation problem).

SELF TEST

2. Consider the following network representation of a transportation problem:

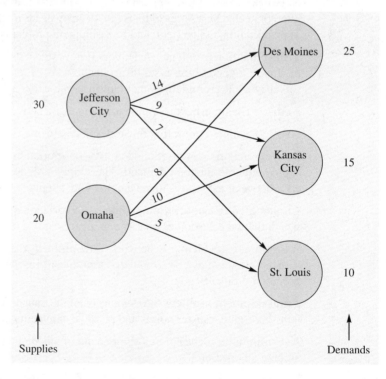

The supplies, demands, and transportation costs per unit are shown on the network.

a. Develop a linear programming model for this problem; be sure to define the variables in your model.

b. Solve the linear program to determine the optimal solution.

3. Reconsider the distribution system described in Problem 1.
   a. Develop a linear programming model that can be solved to minimize transportation cost.
   b. Solve the linear program to determine the minimum-cost shipping schedule.

4. A product is produced at three plants and shipped to three warehouses (the transportation costs per unit are shown in the following table).

Plant	Warehouse			Plant Capacity
	W_1	W_2	W_3	
P_1	20	16	24	300
P_2	10	10	8	500
P_3	12	18	10	100
Warehouse demand	200	400	300	

   a. Show a network representation of the problem.
   b. Develop a linear programming model for minimizing transportation costs; solve this model to determine the minimum-cost solution.
   c. Suppose that the entries in the table represent profit per unit produced at plant i and sold to warehouse j. How does the model formulation change from that in part (b)?

5. Tri-County Utilities, Inc., supplies natural gas to customers in a three-county area. The company purchases natural gas from two companies: Southern Gas and Northwest Gas. Demand forecasts for the coming winter season are Hamilton County, 400 units; Butler County, 200 units; and Clermont County, 300 units. Contracts have been written to provide the following quantities: Southern Gas, 500 units; and Northwest Gas, 400 units. Distribution costs for the counties vary, depending upon the location of the suppliers. The distribution costs per unit (in thousands of dollars) are as follows:

	To		
From	Hamilton	Butler	Clermont
Southern Gas	10	20	15
Northwest Gas	12	15	18

   a. Develop a network representation of this problem.
   b. Develop a linear programming model that can be used to determine the plan that will minimize total distribution costs.
   c. Describe the distribution plan and show the total distribution cost.
   d. Recent residential and industrial growth in Butler County has the potential for increasing demand by as much as 100 units. Which supplier should Tri-County contract with to supply the additional capacity?

6. Arnoff Enterprises manufactures the central processing unit (CPU) for a line of personal computers. The CPUs are manufactured in Seattle, Columbus, and New York and shipped to warehouses in Pittsburgh, Mobile, Denver, Los Angeles, and Washington, D.C., for further distribution. The following table shows the number of CPUs available at each plant and the number of CPUs required by each warehouse. The shipping costs (dollars per unit) are also shown.
   a. Develop a network representation of this problem.
   b. Determine the amount that should be shipped from each plant to each warehouse to minimize the total shipping cost.
   c. The Pittsburgh warehouse has just increased its order by 1000 units, and Arnoff has authorized the Columbus plant to increase its production by 1000 units. Will this lead to an increase or decrease in total shipping costs? Solve for the new optimal solution.

				Warehouse		
Plant	Pittsburgh	Mobile	Denver	Los Angeles	Washington	CPUs Available
Seattle	10	20	5	9	10	9000
Columbus	2	10	8	30	6	4000
New York	1	20	7	10	4	8000
CPUs Required	3000	5000	4000	6000	3000	21,000

7. Premier Consulting has two consultants, Avery and Baker, who can be scheduled to work for clients up to a maximum of 160 hours each over the next four weeks. A third consultant, Campbell, has some administrative assignments already planned and is available for clients up to a maximum of 140 hours over the next four weeks. The company has four clients with projects in process. The estimated hourly requirements for each client over the four-week period are

Client	Hours
A	180
B	75
C	100
D	85

Hourly rates vary for the consultant-client combination and are based on several factors, including project type and the consultant's experience. The rates (dollars per hour) for each consultant-client combination are

Consultant	Client A	Client B	Client C	Client D
Avery	100	125	115	100
Baker	120	135	115	120
Campbell	155	150	140	130

  a. Develop a network representation of the problem.
  b. Formulate the problem as a linear program, with the optimal solution providing the hours each consultant should be scheduled for each client to maximize the consulting firm's billings. What is the schedule and what is the total billing?
  c. New information shows that Avery doesn't have the experience to be scheduled for client B. If this consulting assignment is not permitted, what impact does it have on total billings? What is the revised schedule?

SELF TEST

8. Klein Chemicals, Inc., produces a special oil-base material that is currently in short supply. Four of Klein's customers have already placed orders that together exceed the combined capacity of Klein's two plants. Klein's management faces the problem of deciding how many units it should supply to each customer. Since the four customers are in different industries, different prices can be charged because of the various industry pricing structures. However, slightly different production costs at the two plants and varying transportation costs between the plants and customers make a "sell to the highest bidder" strategy unacceptable. After considering price, production costs, and transportation costs, Klein has established the following profit per unit for each plant-customer alternative.

	Customer			
Plant	D_1	D_2	D_3	D_4
Clifton Springs	$32	$34	$32	$40
Danville	$34	$30	$28	$38

The plant capacities and customer orders are as follows:

Plant Capacity (units)		Distributor Orders (units)	
Clifton Springs	5000	D_1	2000
		D_2	5000
Danville	3000	D_3	3000
		D_4	2000

How many units should each plant produce for each customer to maximize profits? Which customer demands will not be met? Show your network model and linear programming formulation.

9. Sound Electronics, Inc., produces a battery-operated tape recorder at plants located in Martinsville, North Carolina; Plymouth, New York; and Franklin, Missouri. The unit transportation cost for shipments from the three plants to distribution centers in Chicago, Dallas, and New York are as follows:

	To		
From	Chicago	Dallas	New York
Martinsville	$1.45	$1.60	$1.40
Plymouth	$1.10	$2.25	$0.60
Franklin	$1.20	$1.20	$1.80

After considering transportation costs, management has decided that under no circumstances will it use the Plymouth-Dallas route. The plant capacities and distributor orders for the next month are as follows:

Plant	Capacity (units)		Distributor	Orders (units)
Martinsville	400		Chicago	400
Plymouth	600		Dallas	400
Franklin	300		New York	400

Because of different wage scales at the three plants, the unit production cost varies from plant to plant. Assuming that the costs are $29.50 per unit at Martinsville, $31.20 per unit at Plymouth, and $30.35 per unit at Franklin, find the production and distribution plan that minimizes production and transportation costs.

10. The Ace Manufacturing Company has orders for three similar products:

Product	Orders (units)
A	2000
B	500
C	1200

Three machines are available for the manufacturing operations. All three machines can produce all products at the same production rate. However, due to varying defect percentages of each product on each machine, the unit costs of the products vary depending on the machine used. Machine capacities for the next week, and the unit costs, are as follows:

Machine	Capacity (units)
1	1500
2	1500
3	1000

Machine	Product A	Product B	Product C
1	$1.00	$1.20	$0.90
2	$1.30	$1.40	$1.20
3	$1.10	$1.00	$1.20

Use the transportation model to develop the minimum-cost production schedule for the products and machines.

11. Forbelt Corporation has a one-year contract to supply motors for all refrigerators produced by the Ice Age Corporation. Ice Age manufactures the refrigerators at four locations around the country: Boston, Dallas, Los Angeles, and St. Paul. Plans call for the following number (in thousands) of refrigerators to be produced at each location.

Boston	50
Dallas	70
Los Angeles	60
St. Paul	80

Forbelt has three plants that are capable of producing the motors. The plants and production capacities (in thousands) are

Denver	100
Atlanta	100
Chicago	150

Because of varying production and transportation costs, the profit that Forbelt earns on each lot of 1000 units depends on which plant produced the lot and which destination it was shipped to. The following table gives the accounting department estimates of the profit per unit (shipments will be made in lots of 1000 units).

	Shipped To			
Produced At	Boston	Dallas	Los Angeles	St. Paul
Denver	7	11	8	13
Atlanta	20	17	12	10
Chicago	8	18	13	16

With profit maximization as a criterion, Forbelt wants to determine how many motors should be produced at each plant and how many motors should be shipped from each plant to each destination.
  a. Develop a network representation of this problem.
  b. Find the optimal solution.

SELF TEST

12. Scott and Associates, Inc., is an accounting firm that has three new clients. Project leaders will be assigned to the three clients. Based on the different backgrounds and experiences of the leaders, the various leader-client assignments differ in terms of projected completion times. The possible assignments and the estimated completion times in days are

Project	**Client**		
Leader	1	2	3
Jackson	10	16	32
Ellis	14	22	40
Smith	22	24	34

  a. Develop a network representation of this problem.
  b. Formulate the problem as a linear program, and solve. What is the total time required?

13. Assume that in Problem 12 an additional employee is available for possible assignment. The following table shows the assignment alternatives and the estimated completion times.

Project	**Client**		
Leader	1	2	3
Jackson	10	16	32
Ellis	14	22	40
Smith	22	24	34
Burton	14	18	36

    a. What is the optimal assignment?

    b. How did the assignment change compared to the best assignment possible in Problem 12? Were any savings associated with considering Burton as one of the possible project leaders?

    c. Which project leader remains unassigned?

14. Wilson Distributors, Inc., is opening two new sales territories in the western states. Three individuals currently selling in the Midwest and the East are being considered for promotion to regional sales manager positions in the new sales territories. Management has estimated total annual sales (in thousands of dollars) for the assignment of each individual to each sales territory. The management sales projections are as follows:

	Sales Region	
Regional Managers	Northwest	Southwest
Bostock	$100	$95
McMahon	$85	$80
Miller	$90	$75

    a. Develop a network representation of the problem.

    b. Obtain the optimal solution to this problem.

15. Fowle Marketing Research has four project leaders available for assignment to three clients. Find the assignment of project leaders to clients that will minimize the total time to complete all projects. The estimated project completion times in days are as follows:

Project	Client		
Leader	1	2	3
Terry	10	15	9
Carle	9	18	5
McClymonds	6	14	3
Higley	8	16	6

16. Salisbury Discounts has just leased a new store and is in the process of determining locations for the various departments. Only 4 locations are remaining, and the following 5 departments are being considered: shoes, toys, auto parts, housewares, and videos. After a careful study of the layout of the remainder of the store, the store manager has made estimates of the expected annual profit for each department in each location. The estimated annual profit ($1000s) for each department-location combination is shown. Which departments should be assigned to which location and which department should not be included? What is the expected annual profit?

	Location			
Department	1	2	3	4
Shoes	10	6	12	8
Toys	15	18	5	11
Auto parts	17	10	13	16
Housewares	14	12	13	10
Videos	14	16	6	12

17. Reconsider the Salisbury Discounts assignment problem in Problem 16. Suppose that the store manager believed (because of adjacent departments, size, etc.) that the toy department should not be considered for location 2 and that the auto parts department should not be considered for location 4. Which departments should now be assigned to the 4 store locations and what is the expected annual profit?

18. In a job shop operation, four jobs may be performed on any of four machines. The numbers of hours required for each job on each machine are summarized in the table. What is the minimum total time job-machine assignment?

		Machine		
Job	A	B	C	D
1	32	18	32	26
2	22	24	12	16
3	24	30	26	24
4	26	30	28	20

19. Mayfax Distributors, Inc., has four sales territories, each of which must be assigned a sales representative. From experience the firm's sales manager has estimated the annual sales volume (in thousands of dollars) for each sales representative in each sales territory. Find the sales representative-territory assignments that will maximize sales.

		Sales Territory		
Sales Representative	A	B	C	D
Washington	44	80	52	60
Benson	60	56	40	72
Fredricks	36	60	48	48
Hodson	52	76	36	40

20. The department head of a management science department at a major midwestern university will be scheduling faculty to teach courses during the coming autumn term. Four core courses need to be covered. The four courses are at the UG, MBA, MS, and Ph.D. levels. Four professors will be assigned to the courses, with each professor receiving one of the courses. Student evaluations of professors are available from previous terms. Based on a rating scale of 4 (excellent), 3 (very good), 2 (average), 1 (fair), and 0 (poor), the average student evaluations for each professor are shown. Professor D does not have a Ph.D. and cannot be assigned to teach the Ph.D.-level course. If the department head makes teaching assignments based on maximizing the student evaluation ratings over all four courses, what staffing assignments should be made?

		Course		
Professor	UG	MBA	MS	Ph.D.
A	2.8	2.2	3.3	3.0
B	3.2	3.0	3.6	3.6
C	3.3	3.2	3.5	3.5
D	3.2	2.8	2.5	—

21. A market research firm has three clients who have each requested that the firm conduct a sample survey. Four available statisticians can be assigned to these three projects; however, all four statisticians are busy, and therefore each can handle only one client. The following data show the number of hours required for each statistician to complete each job; the differences in time are based on experience and ability of the statisticians.

		Client	
Statistician	A	B	C
1	150	210	270
2	170	230	220
3	180	230	225
4	160	240	230

a. Formulate and solve this problem.

b. Suppose that the time statistician 4 needs to complete the job for client A is increased from 160 to 165 hours. What effect will this increase have on the solution?

c. Suppose that the time statistician 4 needs to complete the job for client A is decreased to 140 hours. What effect will this decrease have on the solution?

d. Suppose that the time statistician 3 needs to complete the job for client B increases to 250 hours. What effect will this increase have on the solution?

22. Hatcher Enterprises uses a chemical called Rbase in production operations at five divisions. Only six suppliers of Rbase meet Hatcher's quality control standards. All six suppliers can produce Rbase in sufficient quantities to accommodate the needs of each division. The quantity of Rbase needed by each of Hatcher's divisions and the price per gallon charged by each supplier are as follows:

Division	Demand (1000s of gallons)
1	40
2	45
3	50
4	35
5	45

Supplier	Price per Gallon ($)
1	12.60
2	14.00
3	10.20
4	14.20
5	12.00
6	13.00

The cost per gallon ($) for shipping from each supplier to each division is provided in the following table.

			Division		
Supplier	1	2	3	4	5
1	2.75	0.80	4.70	2.60	3.40
2	2.50	0.20	2.60	1.80	0.40
3	3.15	5.40	5.30	4.40	5.00
4	2.80	1.20	2.80	2.40	1.20
5	2.75	3.40	6.00	5.00	2.60
6	2.75	1.00	5.60	2.80	3.60

Hatcher believes in spreading its business among suppliers so that the company will be less affected by supplier problems (e.g., labor strikes or resource availability). Company policy requires that each division have a separate supplier.

a. For each supplier-division combination, compute the total cost of supplying the division's demand.

b. Determine the optimal assignment of suppliers to divisions.

SELF TEST

23. The distribution system for the Herman Company consists of three plants, two warehouses, and four customers. Plant capacities and shipping costs (in $) from each plant to each warehouse are

	Warehouse		
Plant	1	2	Capacity
1	4	7	450
2	8	5	600
3	5	6	380

Customer demand and shipping costs per unit (in $) from each warehouse to each customer are

	Customer			
Warehouse	1	2	3	4
1	6	4	8	4
2	3	6	7	7
Demand	300	300	300	400

a. Develop a network representation of this problem.

b. Formulate a linear programming model of the problem.

c. Find the optimal shipping plan.

24. Refer to Problem 23. Suppose that shipments between the two warehouses are permitted at $2 per unit and that direct shipments can be made from plant 3 to customer 4 at a cost of $7 per unit.

a. Develop a network representation of this problem.

b. Formulate a linear programming model of this problem.

c. Find the optimal shipping plan.

25. A company has two plants (P_1 and P_2), one regional warehouse (W), and two retail outlets (R_1 and R_2). The plant capacities, retail outlet demands, and per-unit shipping costs are shown in the network at the top of page 266.

a. Find optimal shipping plan for this transshipment network.

b. What change would have to be made if the maximum amount of goods that can be shipped from W to R_1 is 500? How would this limitation change the optimal solution?

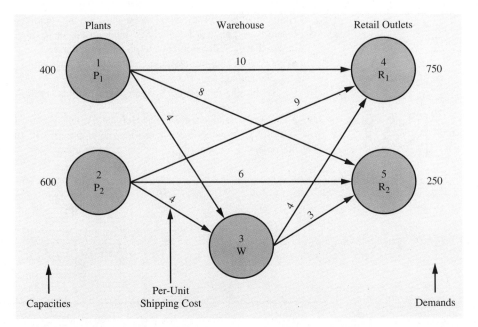

26. Adirondack Paper Mills, Inc., has paper plants in Augusta, Maine, and Tupper Lake, New York. Warehouse facilities are located in Albany, New York, and Portsmouth, New Hampshire. Distributors are located in Boston, New York, and Philadelphia. The plant capacities and distributor demands for the next month are as follows:

Plant	Capacity (units)
Augusta	300
Tupper Lake	100

Distributor	Demand (units)
Boston	150
New York	100
Philadelphia	150

The unit transportation costs ($) for shipments from the two plants to the two warehouses and from the two warehouses to the three distributors are as follows:

	Warehouse	
Plant	Albany	Portsmouth
Augusta	7	5
Tupper Lake	3	4

	Distributor		
Warehouse	Boston	New York	Philadelphia
Albany	8	5	7
Portsmouth	5	6	10

a. Draw the network representation of the Adirondack Paper Mills problem.
b. Formulate the Adirondack Paper Mills problem as a linear programming problem.
c. Determine the minimum-cost shipping schedule for the problem.

27. Consider a transshipment problem consisting of three origin nodes, two transshipment nodes, and four destination nodes. The supplies at the origin nodes and the demands at the destination nodes are as follows:

Origin	Supply
1	400
2	450
3	350

Destination	Demand
1	200
2	500
3	300
4	200

The shipping costs per unit are provided in the following table.

From			Transshipment		To Destination			
			1	2	1	2	3	4
Origin	1		6	8	—	—	—	—
	2		8	12	—	—	—	—
	3		10	5	—	—	—	—
Transshipment	1		—	—	9	7	6	10
	2		—	—	7	9	6	8

a. Draw the network representation of this problem.
b. Solve for the optimal solution.

28. The Moore & Harman Company is in the business of buying and selling grain. An important aspect of the company's business is arranging for the purchased grain to be shipped to customers. If the company can keep freight costs low, profitability will be improved.

Currently, the company has purchased three rail cars of grain at Muncie, Indiana; six rail cars at Brazil, Indiana; and five rail cars at Xenia, Ohio. Twelve carloads of grain have been sold. The locations and the amount sold at each location are as follows:

Location	Number of Rail Car Loads
Macon, Ga.	2
Greenwood, S.C.	4
Concord, S.C.	3
Chatham, N.C.	3

All shipments must be routed through either Louisville or Cincinnati. Shown are the shipping costs per bushel (in cents) from the origins to Louisville and Cincinnati and the costs per bushel to ship from Louisville and Cincinnati to the destinations.

	To		
From	Louisville	Cincinnati	
Muncie	8	6	← Cost per bushel from Muncie to Cincinnati is 6¢
Brazil	3	8	
Xenia	9	3	

	To			
From	Macon	Greenwood	Concord	Chatham
Louisville	44	34	34	32
Cincinnati	57	35	28	24

Cost per bushel from Cincinnati to Greenwood is 35¢

Determine a shipping schedule that will minimize the freight costs necessary to satisfy demand. Which (if any) rail cars of grain must be held at the origin until buyers can be found?

29. A rental car company has an imbalance of cars at seven of its locations. The following network shows the locations of concern (the nodes) and the cost to move a car between locations. A positive number by a node indicates an excess supply at the node, and a negative number indicates an excess demand.

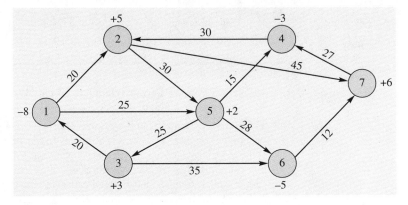

a. Develop a linear programming model of this problem.
b. Solve the model formulated in part (a) to determine how the cars should be redistributed among the locations.

30. The following linear programming formulation is for a transshipment problem.

$$\text{Min} \quad 11x_{13} + 12x_{14} + 10x_{21} + 8x_{34} + 10x_{35} + 11x_{42} + 9x_{45} + 12x_{52}$$

s.t.

$$
\begin{aligned}
x_{13} + x_{14} - x_{21} && \le 5 \\
x_{21} && - x_{42} - x_{52} \le 3 \\
x_{13} - x_{34} - x_{35} && = 6 \\
- x_{14} - x_{34} + x_{42} + x_{45} && \le 2 \\
x_{35} + x_{45} - x_{52} && = 4
\end{aligned}
$$

$$x_{ij} \ge 0 \quad \text{for all } i, j$$

Show the network representation of this problem.

31. Refer to the Contois Carpets problem for which the network representation is shown in Figure 5.16. Suppose that Contois has a beginning inventory of 50 yards of carpet and requires an inventory of 100 yards at the end of quarter 4.

    a. Develop a network representation of this modified problem.

    b. Solve for the optimal solution.

32. Sanders Fishing Supply of Naples, Florida, manufactures a variety of fishing equipment, which it sells throughout the United States. For the next three months, Sanders estimates demand for a particular product at 150, 250, and 300 units, respectively. Sanders can supply this demand by producing on regular time or overtime. Because of other commitments and anticipated cost increases in month 3, the production capacities in units and the production costs per unit are as follows:

Production	Capacity (units)	Cost per Unit
Month 1—Regular	275	$50
Month 1—Overtime	100	80
Month 2—Regular	200	50
Month 2—Overtime	50	80
Month 3—Regular	100	60
Month 3—Overtime	50	100

Inventory may be carried from one month to the next, but the cost is $20 per unit per month. For example, regular production from month 1 used to meet demand in month 2 would cost Sanders $50 + $20 = $70 per unit. This same month 1 production used to meet demand in month 3 would cost Sanders $50 + 2($20) = $90 per unit.

    a. Develop a network representation of this production scheduling problem as a transshipment problem. (Hint: Use six origin nodes; the supply for origin node 1 is the maximum that can be produced in month 1 on regular time, and so on.)

    b. What is the production schedule, how many units are carried in inventory each month, and what is the total cost?

    c. Is there any unused production capacity? If so, where?

Case Problem   ASSIGNING UMPIRE CREWS*

The American Baseball League consists of 14 professional baseball teams organized into 3 divisions: the West Division with Seattle, Oakland, California, and Texas; the Central Division with Kansas City, Minnesota, Chicago, Milwaukee, and Cleveland; and the East Division with Detroit, Toronto, Baltimore, New York, and Boston.[†]

In addition to the schedules for each team, the American League must determine the best way to assign the umpire crews to the various games played throughout the league. Umpire crews are assigned to specific home-team cities for the two-, three-, or four-game series in that city, but they are not assigned on an individual-game basis. Since there are 14 American League teams, as many as seven games can be played at the same time (doubleheaders count as one game in assigning crews); hence, seven umpire crews must be assigned.

Several considerations are important in making the umpire crew assignments. Because of the amount of travel required, airline costs can be substantial. Thus, from a cost point of view, umpire crew assignments with minimum travel distances are desirable. However, a

---

*The authors are indebted to James R. Evans, consultant to the American League, New York, N.Y., for providing this case problem.

†This case is based on the American League organization prior to the 1998 realignment.

second consideration in the assignment of the umpire crews is that there should be a balance such that each crew works approximately the same number of games with each team and in each city. The considerations of minimizing travel distances and, at the same time, balancing the crew assignments among the teams and cities are in conflict.

In addition to these considerations, a number of requirements must be satisfied. The most important of these are

1. A crew cannot travel from city A to city B if the last game in city A is a night game and the first game in city B is an afternoon game on the next day.
2. A crew cannot travel from a West Coast location (Seattle, Oakland, or California) to Chicago, Milwaukee, Cleveland, or any East Division city without a day off.
3. Because of flight scheduling difficulties, a crew traveling into or out of Toronto must have a day off unless coming from or going to New York, Boston, Detroit, or Cleveland.
4. Any crew traveling from a night game in Seattle, Oakland, or California cannot be assigned to Kansas City or Texas for a game on the next day.
5. No crew should be assigned to the same team for more than two series in a row.

The umpire crews have already been scheduled for the first four series of the five-series schedule shown in Table 5.8. Table 5.9 summarizes the crew assignments for the first four series in the schedule and shows the pairings for the fifth series. The superscript next to each team identification indicates the umpire crew assigned for that pairing. For exam-

Table 5.8 — SEGMENT OF THE AMERICAN LEAGUE SCHEDULE SHOWING FIVE SERIES

Home Team

Series	Date	SEA	OAK	CAL	TEX	KC	MIN	CHI	MKE	DET	CLE	TOR	BAL	NY	BOS
1	Mon.		CAL*		BOS*		SEA		TOR*	NY*			CHI*		
	Tues.		CAL*		BOS*		SEA		TOR*	NY*	KC*		CHI*		
	Wed.		CAL		BOS*		SEA		TOR*	NY	KC*		CHI*		
2	Thurs.	DET*		MKE*	KC*						CHI*		TOR*		MIN*
	Fri.	DET*	NY*	MKE*	KC*						CHI*		TOR*		MIN*
	Sat.	DET*	NY	MKE*	KC*						CHI		TOR*		MIN*
	Sun.	DET	NY(2)	MKE	KC*						CHI		TOR		MIN*
3	Mon.	MKE*			NY*		BOS*						MIN*		
	Tues.	MKE*	DET*		NY*	CHI*	BOS*					CLE*	MIN*		
	Wed.	MKE*	DET*		NY*	CHI*	BOS*					CLE*	MIN*		
	Thurs.	MKE*	DET		NY*	CHI*						CLE*			
4	Fri.	NY*	MKE*	DET*	BAL*		CLE*	KC*					BOS*		
	Sat.	NY*	MKE	DET*	BAL*		CLE*	KC*					BOS		
	Sun.	NY*	MKE	DET	BAL*		CLE	KC					BOS		
5	Mon.					TEX*		CLE*					BOS*		
	Tues.					TEX*	BOS*	CLE*	CAL*	SEA*			BAL*	OAK*	
	Wed.					TEX*	BOS*	CLE*	CAL*	SEA*			BAL*	OAK*	
	Thurs.					TEX*	BOS		CAL	SEA*			BAL*	OAK*	

*Denotes night game or early-evening start. (2)Denotes doubleheader (two games in one day).

Table 5.9 — UMPIRE CREW ASSIGNMENTS FOR THE FIRST FOUR SERIES ARE SHOWN AS SUPERSCRIPTS

Home Team

Series	SEA	OAK	CAL	TEX	KC	MIN	CHI	MKE	DET	CLE	TOR	BAL	NY	BOS
1		CAL⁵		BOS³		SEA⁷		TOR⁴	NY¹	KC⁶		CHI²		
2	DET³	NY²	MKE⁷	KC⁵						CHI⁶		TOR⁴		MIN¹
3	MKE²	DET⁷	NY³	CHI⁶	BOS⁵						CLE¹	MIN⁴		
4	NY⁷	MKE³	DET²	BAL⁶		CLE⁵	KC⁴				BOS¹			
5					TEX	BOS	CLE	CAL	SEA		BAL		OAK	

For the fourth series, umpire crew 1 is assigned to the Boston at Toronto series

ple, for the fourth series, crew 1 is assigned to the Boston-Toronto games, crew 2 is assigned to the Detroit-California games, and so on.

Table 5.10 shows the distances from the cities where the fourth series is being played to the cities where the fifth series is being played. League management would like to consider some other issues in assigning crews to the next series. Over the past nine series, crew 4 has umpired three series with Kansas City and three series with Milwaukee. Also, crew 5 has not been assigned to any games with New York, Toronto, or Detroit over the past month.

Managerial Report

Prepare a written recommendation to league management concerning the assignment of umpire crews to the fifth series that will minimize the distance traveled.

Table 5.10 — DISTANCE COST MATRIX FOR UMPIRE CREW ASSIGNMENTS (SERIES 5)

Crew From	KC	MIN	CHI	MKE	DET	TOR	NY
SEA(7)	1825	1399	2007	1694	1939	2124	2421
OAK(3)	1498	1589	2125	1845	2079	2286	2586
CAL(2)	1363	1536	2035	1756	1979	2175	2475
TEX(6)	506	853	798	843	982	1186	1383
MIN(5)	394	0	334	297	528	780	1028
CHI(4)	403	334	0	74	235	430	740
TOR(1)	968	897	497	583	206	0	366

Note: The numbers in parentheses reference umpire crews.

Case Problem   DISTRIBUTION SYSTEM DESIGN

The Darby Company manufactures and distributes meters used to measure electric power consumption. The company started with a small production plant in El Paso and gradually built a customer base throughout Texas. A distribution center was established in Ft. Worth, Texas, and later, as business expanded, a second distribution center was established in Santa Fe, New Mexico.

The El Paso plant was expanded when the company began marketing its meters in Arizona, California, Nevada, and Utah. With the growth of the West Coast business, the Darby Company opened a third distribution center in Las Vegas and just two years ago opened a second production plant in San Bernardino, California.

Manufacturing costs differ between the company's production plants. The cost of each meter produced at the El Paso plant is $10.50. The San Bernardino plant uses newer and more efficient equipment; as a result, manufacturing costs are $0.50 per meter less than at the El Paso plant.

Due to the company's rapid growth, not much attention had been paid to the efficiency of the distribution system, but Darby's management has decided that it is time to address this issue. The cost of shipping a meter from each of the two plants to each of the three distribution centers is shown in Table 5.11.

The quarterly production capacity is 30,000 meters at the older El Paso plant and 20,000 meters at the San Bernardino plant. Note that no shipments are allowed from the San Bernardino plant to the Ft. Worth distribution center.

The company serves nine customer zones from the three distribution centers. The forecast of the number of meters needed in each customer zone for the next quarter is shown in Table 5.12.

The cost per unit of shipping from each distribution center to each customer zone is given in Table 5.13; note that some distribution centers cannot serve certain customer zones.

Table 5.11　SHIPPING COST PER UNIT FROM PRODUCTION PLANTS TO DISTRIBUTION CENTERS (IN $)

	Distribution Center		
Plant	Ft. Worth	Santa Fe	Las Vegas
El Paso	3.20	2.20	4.20
San Bernardino	—	3.90	1.20

Table 5.12　QUARTERLY DEMAND FORECAST

Customer Zone	Demand (meters)
Dallas	6300
San Antonio	4880
Wichita	2130
Kansas City	1210
Denver	6120
Salt Lake City	4830
Phoenix	2750
Los Angeles	8580
San Diego	4460

Table 5.13	SHIPPING COST FROM THE DISTRIBUTION CENTERS TO THE CUSTOMER ZONES

Distribution Center	Customer Zone								
	Dallas	San Antonio	Wichita	Kansas City	Denver	Salt Lake City	Phoenix	Los Angeles	San Diego
Ft. Worth	0.3	2.1	3.1	4.4	6.0	—	—	—	—
Santa Fe	5.2	5.4	4.5	6.0	2.7	4.7	3.4	3.3	2.7
Las Vegas	—	—	—	—	5.4	3.3	2.4	2.1	2.5

In the current distribution system, demand at the Dallas, San Antonio, Wichita, and Kansas City customer zones is satisfied by shipments from the Ft. Worth distribution center. In a similar manner, the Denver, Salt Lake City, and Phoenix customer zones are served by the Santa Fe distribution center, and the Los Angeles and San Diego customer zones are served by the Las Vegas distribution center. To determine how many units to ship from each plant, the quarterly customer demand forecasts are aggregated at the distribution centers, and a transportation model is used to minimize the cost of shipping from the production plants to the distribution centers.

Managerial Report

You have been called in to make recommendations for improving the distribution system. Your report should address, but not be limited to, the following issues.

1. If the company does not change its current distribution strategy, what will its distribution costs be for the following quarter?
2. Suppose that the company is willing to consider dropping the distribution center limitations; that is, customers could be served by any of the distribution centers for which costs are available. Can costs be reduced? By how much?
3. The company wants to explore the possibility of satisfying some of the customer demand directly from the production plants. In particular, the shipping cost is $0.30 per unit from San Bernardino to Los Angeles and $0.70 from San Bernardino to San Diego. The cost for direct shipments from El Paso to San Antonio is $3.50 per unit. Can distribution costs be further reduced by considering these direct plant-customer shipments?
4. Over the next five years, Darby is anticipating moderate growth (5000 meters) to the North and West. Would you recommend that they consider plant expansion at this time?

PROCTER & GAMBLE*

CINCINNATI, OHIO

Procter & Gamble (P&G) is in the consumer-products business worldwide. P&G produces and markets such products as detergents, disposable diapers, coffee, over-the-counter pharmaceuticals, dentifrices, bar soaps, mouthwashes, and paper towels. It has the leading brand in more categories than any other consumer-products company in the United States.

In order to maintain its leadership position in its many markets, P&G makes extensive use of management science. Some of the methodologies employed include probability and risk analysis, linear and integer programming, network flow analysis, and simulation. The individuals employing these methodologies are scattered throughout P&G's numerous divisions with perhaps the largest concentration being in the management systems division. P&G employs engineers, operations researchers, computer scientists, and businesspeople who are skilled in employing quantitative methodologies.

Recently P&G embarked on a major strategic planning initiative: the North American Product Sourcing Study. P&G was interested in consolidating its product sources and optimizing its distribution system design throughout North America. One of the decision support systems that proved to be a great aid in this project was called the Product Sourcing Heuristic (PSH). This heuristic was based on a transshipment model much like the ones described in this chapter.

In a preprocessing phase, the many P&G products were aggregated into groups that shared the same technology and could be made at the same plant. The PSH was used by product strategy teams that had responsibility for developing product sourcing options for the separate product groups. The various plants that could produce the

product group were source nodes, the company's regional distribution centers were the transshipment nodes, and P&G's customer zones were the destinations. Direct shipments to customer zones as well as shipments through distribution centers were employed.

The product strategy teams used the heuristic interactively to explore a variety of questions concerning product sourcing and distribution. For instance, the team might be interested in the impact of closing two plants and consolidating production in three remaining plants. The product sourcing heuristic would then delete the source nodes corresponding to the two closed plants, make any capacity modifications recommended to the sources corresponding to the remaining three plants, and resolve the transshipment problem. The product strategy team could then examine the new solution, make some more modifications, solve again, and so on.

The Product Sourcing Heuristic was viewed as a valuable decision support system by all who used it. Probably the most valuable feature was that the model permitted a rapid evaluation of a variety of strategic options. A feature that was viewed as a big plus by all who used it was that solutions provided by the PSH were displayed on a map of North America using a geographic information system. This map enabled strategic planners to review immediately the impact of their sourcing decisions across North America. The PSH has proven so successful that P&G is considering using it in other markets around the world.

*The authors are indebted to Mr. Franz Dill and Mr. Tom Chorman of Proctor & Gamble for providing this application.

6

INTEGER LINEAR PROGRAMMING

In this chapter we discuss a class of problems that are modeled as linear programs with the additional requirement that one or more variables must be integer. Such problems are called **integer linear programs.** If all variables must be integer, we have an **all-integer linear program.** If some, but not all, variables must be integer, we have a **mixed-integer linear program.** In many applications of integer linear programming, one or more integer variables are required to equal either 0 or 1. Such variables are called *0–1 or binary variables*. If all variables are 0–1 variables, we have a **0–1 integer linear program.**

Integer variables—especially 0–1 variables—provide substantial modeling flexibility. As a result, the number of applications that can be addressed with linear programming methodology is expanded. The cost of the added modeling flexibility is that problems involving integer variables are often much more difficult to solve. A linear programming problem with several thousand continuous variables can be solved with any of several commercial linear programming solvers. However, an all-integer linear programming problem with less than 100 variables may be extremely difficult to solve. Experienced management scientists can help identify the types of integer linear programs that are easy, or at least reasonable, to solve. Commercial computer software packages, such as MPSX-MIP®, OSL®, CPLEX®, and LINDO®, have extensive integer programming capability. Spreadsheet packages, such as Excel, have the capability for solving smaller integer linear programs.

The objective of this chapter is to provide an applications-oriented introduction to integer linear programming. First, we discuss the different types of integer linear programming models. Then we show the formulation, graphical solution, and spreadsheet solution of an all-integer linear program. In Section 6.3, we discuss four applications of integer linear programming that make use of

0–1 variables: capital budgeting, fixed cost, distribution system design, and bank location problems. In Section 6.4, we provide additional illustrations of the modeling flexibility provided by 0–1 variables.

N O T E S
and Comments

1. Because integer linear programs are harder to solve than linear programs, one should not try to solve a problem as an integer program if simply rounding the linear programming solution is adequate. In many linear programming problems, such as those in previous chapters, rounding has very little economic consequence on the objective function and feasibility is not an issue. But, in problems such as determining how many jet engines to manufacture, the consequences of rounding can be substantial and integer programming methodology should be employed.

2. Some linear programming problems have a special structure which guarantees that the variables will have integer values. The assignment, transportation, and transshipment problems of Chapter 5 have such structures. If the supply and the demand for transportation and transshipment problems are integer, the optimal linear programming solution will provide integer amounts shipped. For the assignment problem, the optimal linear programming solution will consist of 0s and 1s. So, for these specially structured problems linear programming methodology can be used to find optimal integer solutions. Integer linear programming algorithms are not necessary.

6.1 TYPES OF INTEGER LINEAR PROGRAMMING MODELS

The only difference between the problems studied in this chapter and the ones studied in earlier chapters on linear programming is that one, or more, variables are required to be integer. If all variables are required to be integer, we have an *all-integer linear program*. The following is a two-variable, all-integer linear programming model.

$$\text{Max} \quad 2x_1 + 3x_2$$
$$\text{s.t.}$$
$$3x_1 + 3x_2 \le 12$$
$$\tfrac{2}{3}x_1 + 1x_2 \le 4$$
$$1x_1 + 2x_2 \le 6$$
$$x_1, x_2 \ge 0 \text{ and integer}$$

Note that if we drop the phrase "and integer" from this model, we have the familiar two-variable linear program. The linear program that results from dropping the integer requirements is called the **LP Relaxation** of the integer linear program.

If some, but not all, variables are required to be integer, we have a *mixed-integer linear program*. The following is a two-variable, mixed-integer linear program.

$$\text{Max} \quad 3x_1 + 4x_2$$
$$\text{s.t.}$$
$$-1x_1 + 2x_2 \le 8$$
$$1x_1 + 2x_2 \le 12$$
$$2x_1 + 1x_2 \le 16$$
$$x_1, x_2 \ge 0 \text{ and } x_2 \text{ integer}$$

We obtain the LP Relaxation of this mixed-integer linear program by dropping the requirement that x_2 be integer.

In many applications of integer programming, one or more integer variables are required to take on the values 0 or 1. As we see later in the chapter, 0–1 variables provide addition modeling capability. The Management Science in Action: Planning the Size of KLM's Aircraft Maintenance Teams describes how integer and 0–1 integer variables are used to determine the size of the engineering teams that perform maintenance on KLM's aircraft.

MANAGEMENT SCIENCE IN ACTION

PLANNING THE SIZE OF KLM'S AIRCRAFT MAINTENANCE TEAMS*

KLM Royal Dutch Airlines has been the major Dutch carrier since 1919. Currently, KLM owns 90 aircraft of 8 different types and operates flights to 150 cities in 79 countries. To guarantee safety, KLM has a high-quality aircraft maintenance program with a workforce that includes 250 engineers and 150 nontechnical employees.

Preventive maintenance on the aircraft consists of both major and minor inspections. Major inspections require several hours to several months to complete. Minor inspections are conducted during the ground time between aircraft arrival and departure at an airport. Engineers from KLM's aircraft maintenance group are organized into teams that carry out the maintenance tasks.

The engineers are highly skilled and well trained. A governmental rule specifies that maintenance engineers are allowed to carry out inspections on a specific aircraft type only if licensed for that aircraft type. KLM's internal safety rules further limit engineers to licenses on at most two aircraft types. When licensed for a particular aircraft, an individual engineer's skills are certified as being mechanical, electrical, or radio.

KLM's management strives to develop a good match between workload requirements and the abilities of the assigned workforce. Given a set of maintenance jobs, management attempts to minimize the number of engineers with appropriate license and skill combinations necessary to complete the jobs. An integer linear programming model helps with this task. The objective function is to minimize the number of engineers required per maintenance team. Integer decision variables are required because the number of engineers with each license and skill combination cannot be fractional. In addition, 0–1 integer variables are included in the model to guarantee that each maintenance job is carried out exactly once. Another integer programming model is used to determine the maximum number of maintenance jobs that can be scheduled given the size and composition of the maintenance workforce. KLM has found integer linear programming to be a valuable tool for solving problems dealing with personnel planning for aircraft maintenance.

*Based on M. C. Dijkstra, L. G. Kroon, M. Slomon, J. A. E. E. Van Nunen, and L. N. Van Wassenhove, "Planning the Size and Organization of KLM's Aircraft Maintenance Personnel," *Interfaces* (November–December 1994): 47–58.

6.2 GRAPHICAL AND SPREADSHEET SOLUTION FOR AN ALL-INTEGER LINEAR PROGRAM

Eastborne Realty has $2,000,000 available for the purchase of new rental property. After an initial screening, Eastborne has reduced the investment alternatives to townhouses and apartment buildings. Each townhouse can be purchased for $282,000, and five are available. Each apartment building can be purchased for $400,000, and the developer will construct as many buildings as Eastborne wants to purchase

Eastborne's property manager can devote up to 140 hours per month to these new properties; each townhouse is expected to require 4 hours per month, and each apartment building is expected to require 40 hours per month. The annual cash flow, after deducting mortgage payments and operating expenses, is estimated to be $10,000 per townhouse and $15,000 per apartment building. Eastborne's owner would like to determine the number of townhouses and the number of apartment buildings to purchase to maximize annual cash flow.

We begin by defining the decision variables as follows:

$$T = \text{number of townhouses purchased}$$
$$A = \text{number of apartment buildings purchased}$$

The objective function for cash flow ($1000s) is

$$\text{Max} \quad 10T + 15A$$

Three constraints must be satisfied:

$$282T + 400A \leq 2000 \quad \text{Funds Available}$$
$$4T + 40A \leq 140 \quad \text{Manager's time}$$
$$T \leq 5 \quad \text{Townhouses Available}$$

The variables T and A must be nonnegative. In addition, the purchase of a fractional number of townhouses and/or a fractional number of apartment buildings is unacceptable. Thus, T and A must be integer. The model for the Eastborne Realty problem is the following all-integer linear program.

$$\text{Max} \quad 10T + 15A$$
$$\text{s.t.}$$
$$282T + 400A \leq 2000$$
$$4T + 40A \leq 140$$
$$T \leq 5$$
$$T, A \geq 0 \text{ and integer}$$

Graphical Solution of the LP Relaxation

Suppose that we drop the integer requirements for T and A and solve the LP Relaxation of the Eastborne Realty Problem. Using the graphical solution procedure, as presented in Chapter 2, the optimal linear programming solution is shown in Figure 6.1. It is $T = 2.479$ townhouses and $A = 3.252$ apartment buildings. The optimal value of the objective function is 73.574, which indicates an annual cash flow of $73,574. Unfortunately, Eastborne cannot purchase fractional numbers of townhouses and apartment buildings; further analysis is necessary.

Rounding to Obtain an Integer Solution

In many cases, a non-integer solution can be rounded to obtain an acceptable integer solution. For instance, a linear programming solution to a production scheduling problem might call for the production of 15,132.4 cases of breakfast cereal. The rounded integer solution of 15,132 cases would probably have minimal impact on the value of the objective function and the feasibility of the solution. Rounding would be a sensible approach. Indeed, whenever rounding has a minimal impact on the objective function and constraints, most managers find it acceptable. A near-optimal solution is fine.

However, rounding may not always be a good strategy. When the decision variables take on small values that have a major impact on the value of the objective function and/or

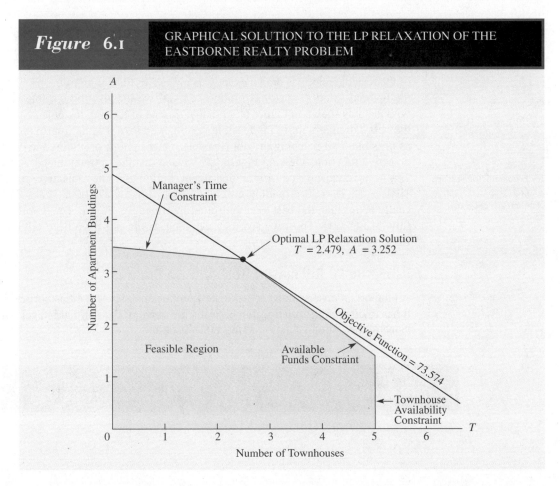

Figure 6.1   GRAPHICAL SOLUTION TO THE LP RELAXATION OF THE EASTBORNE REALTY PROBLEM

feasibility, an optimal integer solution is recommended. Let us return to the Eastborne Realty problem and examine the impact of rounding. The optimal solution to the LP Relaxation for Eastborne Realty resulted in $T = 2.479$ townhouses and $A = 3.252$ apartment buildings. Since each townhouse costs \$282,000 and each apartment building costs \$400,000, rounding to an integer solution can be expected to have a significant economic impact on the problem.

Suppose that we round the solution to the LP Relaxation to obtain the integer solution $T = 2$ and $A = 3$, with an objective function value of $10(2) + 15(3) = 65$. The annual cash flow of \$65,000 is substantially less than the annual cash flow of \$73,574 provided by the solution to the LP Relaxation. Do other rounding possibilities exist? Exploring other rounding alternatives shows that the integer solution $T = 3$ and $A = 3$ is infeasible because it requires more funds than the \$2,000,000 Eastborne has available. The rounded solution of $T = 2$ and $A = 4$ is also infeasible for the same reason. At this point, rounding has led to two townhouses and three apartment buildings with an annual cash flow of \$65,000 as the best feasible integer solution to the problem. However, is this the best integer solution to the problem?

Rounding to an integer solution is a trial-and-error approach. Each rounded solution must be evaluated for feasibility as well as for its impact on the value of the objective function. Even in cases where a rounded solution is feasible, we do not have a guarantee that we have found the optimal integer solution.

If a problem has only less-than-or-equal-to constraints with positive coefficients for the variables, rounding down will always provide a feasible integer solution.

Graphical Solution of the All-Integer Problem

Figure 6.2 shows the changes in the linear programming graphical solution procedure required to solve the Eastborne Realty integer linear programming problem. First, the graph of the feasible region is drawn exactly as in the LP Relaxation of the problem. Then, since the optimal solution must have integer values, we identify the feasible integer solutions with the dots shown in Figure 6.2. Finally, instead of moving the objective function line to the best extreme point in the feasible region, we move it in an improving direction as far as possible until reaching the dot (feasible integer point) providing the best value for the objective function. Viewing Figure 6.2, we see that the optimal integer solution occurs at $T = 4$ townhouses and $A = 2$ apartment buildings. The objective function value is $10(4) + 15(2) = 70$ providing an annual cash flow of \$70,000. This solution is significantly better than the best solution found by rounding: $T = 3$, $A = 3$ with an annual cash flow of \$65,000. Thus, we see that rounding would not have been the best strategy for Eastborne Realty.

Try Problem 2 for practice with the graphical solution of an integer program.

Using the LP Relaxation to Establish Bounds

An important observation can be made from the analysis of the Eastborne Realty problem. It has to do with the relationship between the value of the optimal integer solution and the value of the optimal solution to the LP Relaxation.

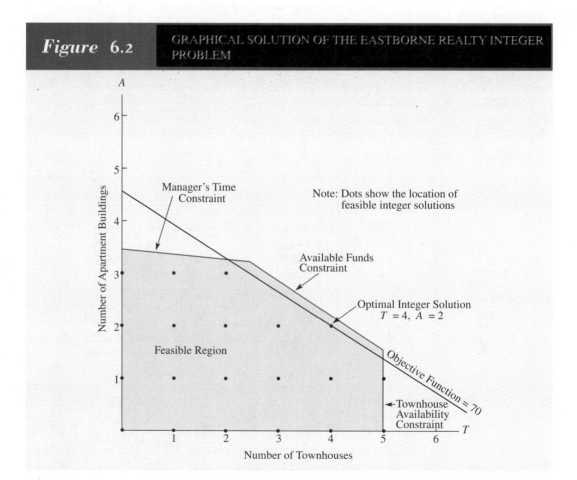

Figure 6.2   GRAPHICAL SOLUTION OF THE EASTBORNE REALTY INTEGER PROBLEM

For integer linear programs involving maximization, the value of the optimal solution to the LP Relaxation provides an upper bound on the value of the optimal integer solution. For integer linear programs involving minimization, the value of the optimal solution to the LP Relaxation provides a lower bound on the value of the optimal integer solution.

This observation is valid for the Eastborne Realty problem. The value of the optimal integer solution is $70,000, and the value of the optimal solution to the LP Relaxation is $73,574. Thus, we know from the LP Relaxation solution that the upper bound for the value of the objective function is $73,574.

The bounding property of the LP Relaxation allows us to conclude that if, by chance, the solution to an LP Relaxation turns out to be an integer solution, it is also optimal for the integer linear program. This bounding property can also be helpful in determining if a rounded solution is "good enough." If a rounded LP Relaxation solution is feasible and provides a value of the objective function that is "almost as good as" the value of the objective function for the LP Relaxation, we know the rounded solution is a near-optimal integer solution. When this happens, we can avoid having to solve the problem as an integer linear program.

Try Problem 5 for the graphical solution of a mixed integer program.

Spreadsheet Solution for the Eastborne Realty Problem

Let us demonstrate the spreadsheet solution of an integer linear program by showing how Excel can be used to solve the Eastborne Realty problem. The spreadsheet with the optimal solution is shown in Figure 6.3. We will describe the key elements of the spreadsheet and then interpret the solution.

Spreadsheet Formulation.   The data and descriptive labels appear in cells A1:G7 of the spreadsheet in Figure 6.3. The screened cells contain the information required by the Excel Solver (decision variables, objective function, constraint left-hand sides, and constraint right-hand sides).

Decision Variables   Cells B17:C17 are reserved for the decision variables. The optimal solution is to purchase 4 townhouses and 2 apartment buildings.

Objective Function   The formula =SUMPRODUCT(B7:C7,B17:C17) has been placed into cell B13 to reflect the annual cash flow associated with the solution. The optimal solution provides an annual cash flow of $70,000.

Left-Hand Sides   The left-hand sides for the 3 constraints are placed into cells F15:F17.
        Cell F15 =SUMPRODUCT(B4:C4,$B$17:$C$17)
                (Copy to cell F16)
        Cell F17 =B17

Right-Hand Sides   The right-hand sides for the 3 constraints are placed into cells H15:H17.
        Cell H15 =G4   (Copy to cells H16:H17)

Spreadsheet Solution.   Begin the solution procedure by selecting **Solver** from the **Tools** menu and entering the proper values into the **Solver Parameters** dialog box as shown in Figure 6.4. The first constraint shown is $B$17:$C$17 = integer. This constraint tells Solver that the decision variables in cell B17 and cell C17 must be integer. The integer requirement is created by using **Add-Constraint** procedure. $B$17:$C17 is entered as the **Cell Reference** and **"int"** rather than <=, = or => is selected as the form of the constraint. When **"int"** is selected, the term integer automatically appears as the right-hand

	A	B	C	D	E	F	G	H
1	**Eastborne Realty Problem**							
2								
3		Townhouse	Apt. Bldg.					
4	**Price($1000s)**	282	400		Funds Avl.($1000s)		2000	
5	**Mgr. Time**	4	40		Mgr. Time Avl.		140	
6					Townhouses Avl.		5	
7	**Ann. Cash Flow ($1000s)**	10	15					
8								
9								
10	**Model**							
11								
12								
13	**Max Cash Flow**	70						
14					**Constraints**	**LHS**		**RHS**
15		**Number of**			Funds	1928	<=	2000
16		Townhouses	Apt. Bldgs.		Time	96	<=	140
17	**Purchase Plan**	4	2		Twnhses	4	<=	5

SPREADSHEET
EASTBORNE
REALTY

Figure 6.3 — SPREADSHEET SOLUTION FOR THE EASTBORNE REALTY PROBLEM

Figure 6.4 — SOLVER PARAMETERS DIALOG BOX FOR THE EASTBORNE REALTY PROBLEM

Solver Parameters

Se_t Target Cell: $B$13

Equal To: ⦿ Ma_x ◯ Mi_n ◯ _Value of: 0

_By Changing Cells:

$B$17:$C$17

_Subject to the Constraints:

$B$17:$C$17 = integer
$F$15:$F$17 <= $H$15:$H$17

[Guess] [Add] [Change] [Delete]
[Solve] [Close] [Options] [Reset All] [Help]

---

side of the constraint. Figure 6.4 shows the additional information required to complete the **Solver Parameters** dialog box.

Next the **Options** button must be selected. As with linear programs, the options **Assume Linear Model** and **Assume Non-Negative** must be checked. Finally, 0 can be entered into the **Tolerance** box to replace the default setting of 5%. The tolerance of 5% means

Figure 6.5 SOLVER OPTIONS SELECTED FOR EASTBORNE REALTY PROBLEM. ASSUME LINEAR MODEL AND ASSUME NON-NEGATIVE BOXES ARE CHECKED AND TOLERANCE HAS BEEN SET TO ZERO

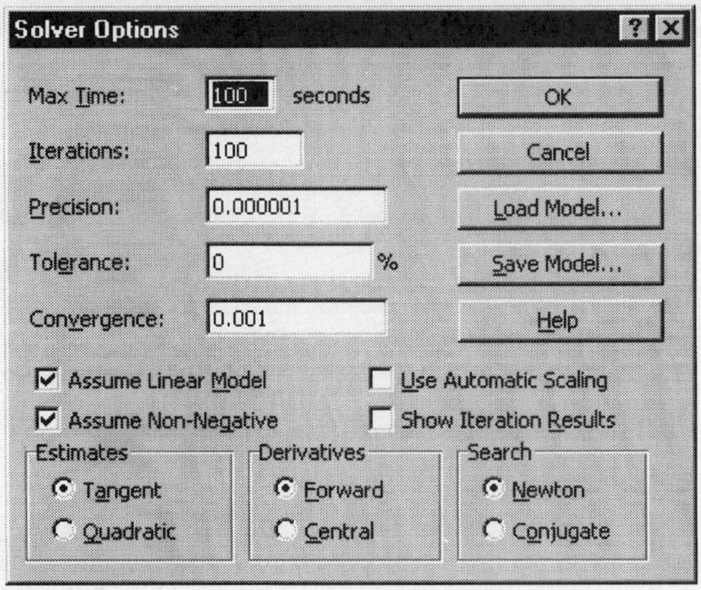

that Solver will stop the search for the optimal integer solution whenever it finds an integer solution that is within 5% of the value of the optimal solution (e.g., within 5% of the value of the optimal solution to the LP Relaxation). To guarantee that Solver will keep searching until an optimal integer solution is found, 0 must be entered into the **Tolerance** box. Figure 6.5 shows the completed **Solver Options** dialog box for the Eastborne Realty problem.[1] Selecting **OK** in the **Solver Options** dialog box and selecting **Solve** in the **Solver Parameters** dialog box will instruct Solver to compute the optimal integer solution. The spreadsheet in Figure 6.3 shows that the optimal solution is to purchase 4 townhouses and 2 apartment buildings. The annual cash flow is $70,000.

6.3   APPLICATIONS INVOLVING 0–1 VARIABLES

Much of the modeling flexibility provided by integer linear programming is due to the use of 0–1 variables. In many applications, 0–1 variables provide selections or choices with the value of the variable equal to 1 if a corresponding activity is undertaken and equal to 0 if the corresponding activity is not undertaken. The capital budgeting, fixed cost, distribution system design, and bank location applications presented in this section make use of 0–1 variables.

---

1. The time required to obtain an optimal solution can be highly variable for integer linear programs. If an optimal solution has not been found within a reasonable amount of time, the tolerance can be reset to 5% or some other non-zero value so that the search procedure may stop when a near-optimal integer solution has been found.

Capital Budgeting

The Ice-Cold Refrigerator Company is considering investing in several projects that have varying capital requirements over the next four years. Faced with limited capital each year, management would like to select the most profitable projects. The estimated net present value for each project,[2] the capital requirements, and the available capital over the four-year period are shown in Table 6.1.

The four 0–1 decision variables are as follows:

$$P = 1 \text{ if the plant expansion project is accepted; 0 if rejected}$$
$$W = 1 \text{ if the warehouse expansion project is accepted; 0 if rejected}$$
$$M = 1 \text{ if the new machinery project is accepted; 0 if rejected}$$
$$R = 1 \text{ if the new product research project is accepted; 0 if rejected}$$

The company's objective function is to maximize the net present value of the capital budgeting projects. The problem has four constraints: one for the funds available in each of the next four years.

A 0–1 integer linear programming model with dollars in thousands is as follows:

$$\text{Max} \quad 90P + 40W + 10M + 37R$$

s.t.

$$15P + 10W + 10M + 15R \le 40 \quad \text{(Year 1 capital available)}$$
$$20P + 15W \qquad\quad + 10R \le 50 \quad \text{(Year 2 capital available)}$$
$$20P + 20W \qquad\quad + 10R \le 40 \quad \text{(Year 3 capital available)}$$
$$15P + 5W + 4M + 10R \le 35 \quad \text{(Year 4 capital available)}$$
$$P, W, M, R = 0, 1$$

The spreadsheet formulation and solution for the Ice-Cold Refrigerator problem are shown in Figure 6.6.

Table **6.1**	PROJECT NET PRESENT VALUE, CAPITAL REQUIREMENTS, AND AVAILABLE CAPITAL FOR THE ICE-COLD REFRIGERATOR COMPANY

	Plant Expansion	Warehouse Expansion	New Machinery	New Product Research	
			Project		
Estimated Net Present Value	$90,000	$40,000	$10,000	$37,000	Total Capital Available
Year 1 Capital	$15,000	$10,000	$10,000	$15,000	$40,000
Year 2 Capital	$20,000	$15,000		$10,000	$50,000
Year 3 Capital	$20,000	$20,000		$10,000	$40,000
Year 4 Capital	$15,000	$5,000	$4,000	$10,000	$35,000

2. The estimated net present value is the net cash flow discounted back to the beginning of year 1.

Figure 6.6	SPREADSHEET SOLUTION FOR THE ICE-COLD REFRIGERATOR PROBLEM

SPREADSHEET ICE-COLD REFRIGERATOR

	A	B	C	D	E	F	G	H	I	J
1	Ice-Cold Refrigerator									
2										
3			**Financial Data ($1000s)**							
4			Plant	Warehouse	New	New Prod.				
5			Expansion	Expansion	Machinery	Research	**Capital**			
6	Net Present Value		90	40	10	37	**Available**			
7	Year 1 Capital		15	10	10	15	40			
8	Year 2 Capital		20	15		10	50			
9	Year 3 Capital		20	20		10	40			
10	Year 4 Capital		15	5	4	10	35			
11										
12										
13	Model									
14										
15										
16		Max Net Present Value	140					**LHS**		**RHS**
17								35	<=	40
18			Plant	Warehouse	New	New Prod.		35	<=	50
19			Expansion	Expansion	Machinery	Research		40	<=	40
20		Investment Plan	1	1	1	0		24	<=	35

Spreadsheet Formulation.   The data and descriptive labels are in cells A1:G10. The screened cells in the bottom portion of the spreadsheet contain the information required by the Excel Solver.

Decision Variables   Cells C20:F20 are reserved for the decision variables. The optimal solution is to invest in plant expansion (P=1), warehouse expansion (W=1), and new machinery (M=1).

Objective Function   The formula =SUMPRODUCT(C6:F6,C20:F20) has been placed into cell D16 to reflect the total net present value associated with the solution shown. The optimal solution is shown to provide a maximum net present value of $140,000.

Left-Hand Sides   The left-hand sides for the 4 constraints are placed into cells H17:H20.
        Cell H17 =SUMPRODUCT(C7:F7,$C$20:$F$20)
            (Copy to cells H18:H20)

Right-Hand Sides   The right-hand sides for the 4 constraints are placed into cells J17:J20.
        Cell J17   =G7   (Copy to cells J18:J20)

Spreadsheet Solution.   Begin the solution procedure by selecting **Solver** from the **Tools** menu and enter the proper values into the **Solver Parameters** dialog box as shown in Figure 6.7. The first constraint shown is $C$20:$F$20 = binary. This constraint tells Solver that the decision variables in cells C20:F20 must be 0−1 integer variables. The 0−1 integer requirement is created by using the **Add-Constraint** procedure. $C$20:$F$20 is entered as the **Cell Reference** and **"bin"** rather than <=, = or => is selected as the form of the constraint. When **"bin"** is selected, the term *binary* automatically appears as the right-hand side of the constraint. Figure 6.7 shows the additional information required in order to complete the **Solver Parameters** dialog box. Specifying the options **Assume**

Excel 5.0 User Note: Excel 5.0 does not have a separate capabliity for handling binary integer variables. In Excel 5.0, the constraint $C$20:$F$20 = binary is replaced with $C$20:$F$20 = integer and another constraint is added ($C$20:$F$20 ≤ 1) to guarantee the integer variables are less-than-or-equal-to one.

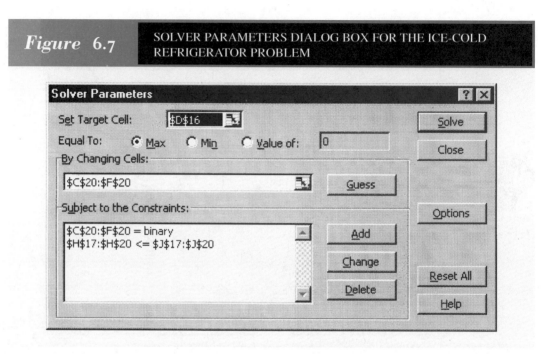

Figure 6.7   SOLVER PARAMETERS DIALOG BOX FOR THE ICE-COLD REFRIGERATOR PROBLEM

Linear Model, Assume Non-Negative, and a **Tolerance** of 0 enables Solver to compute the optimal solution.

Discussion.   Figure 6.6 shows that the optimal solution is to fund the plant expansion, the warehouse expansion, and the new machinery projects. The new product research project should not be initiated at this time unless additional capital funds become available. Comparing the left-hand-side cells and the right-hand-side cells, we see that the company will have $40,000 − $35,000 = $5,000 of unused funds in year 1, $50,000 − $35,000 = $15,000 of unused funds in year 2, and $35,000 − $24,000 = $11,000 of unused funds in year 4. Checking the capital requirements for the new product research project in Table 6.1, we see that the company has enough funds for the new product research project in years 2 and 4. However, additional capital funds of $10,000 would be needed in years 1 and 3 in order to accept the new product research project.

Fixed Cost

In many applications, the cost of production has two components: a setup cost, which is a fixed cost, and a variable cost, which is directly related to the production quantity. The use of 0–1 variables makes including the setup cost possible in a model for a production application.

Consider the modified RMC problem introduced in Section 3.4. In this example, RMC's objective is to maximize the profit associated with 3 products: a fuel additive, a solvent base, and a carpet cleaning fluid. The following decision variables are used.

$$F = \text{tons of fuel additive produced}$$
$$S = \text{tons of solvent base produced}$$
$$C = \text{tons of carpet cleaning fluid produced}$$

The profit contributions are $40 per ton for the fuel additive, $30 per ton for the solvent base, and $50 per ton for the carpet cleaning fluid. Each ton of fuel additive is a blend of 0.4

tons of material 1 and 0.6 tons of material 3. Each ton of solvent base is a blend of 0.5 tons of material 1, 0.2 tons of material 2, and 0.3 tons of material 3. Each ton of carpet cleaning fluid is a blend of 0.6 tons of material 1, 0.1 tons of material 2, and 0.3 tons of material 3. RMC has 20 tons of material 1, 5 tons of material 2, and 21 tons of material 3 and is interested in determining the optimal production quantities for the upcoming planning period.

The following linear programming model of this RMC problem was developed in Section 3.4.

$$\text{Max} \quad 40F + 30S + 50C$$

s.t.

$$0.4F + 0.5S + 0.6C \leq 20 \quad \text{Material 1}$$
$$0.2S + 0.1C \leq 5 \quad \text{Material 2}$$
$$0.6F + 0.3S + 0.3C \leq 21 \quad \text{Material 3}$$
$$F, S, C \geq 0$$

This linear programming formulation does not include a fixed cost to setup for production of the products. Suppose that the following data are available concerning the setup cost and the maximum production quantity for each of the 3 products.

Product	Setup Cost	Maximum Production
Fuel additive	$200	50 tons
Solvent base	$ 50	25 tons
Carpet cleaning fluid	$400	40 tons

The modeling flexibility provided by 0–1 variables can now be used to incorporate the fixed setup costs into the production model. The 0–1 variables are defined as follows:

$$SF = 1 \text{ if the fuel additive is produced; 0 if not}$$
$$SS = 1 \text{ if the solvent base is produced; 0 if not}$$
$$SC = 1 \text{ if the carpet cleaning fluid is produced; 0 if not}$$

Using these setup variables, the total setup cost is

$$200SF + 50SS + 400SC$$

We can now rewrite the objective function to include the setup cost. Thus, the net profit objective function becomes

$$\text{Max} \quad 40F + 30S + 50C - 200SF - 50SS - 400SC$$

Next, we must write production capacity constraints so that if a setup variable equals 0, production of the corresponding product is not permitted and, if a setup variable equals 1, production is permitted up to the maximum quantity. For the fuel additive, we do so by adding the following constraint:

$$F \leq 50SF$$

Note that, with this constraint present, production of the fuel additive is not permitted when $SF = 0$. When $SF = 1$, production of up to 50 tons of fuel additive is permitted. We can think of the setup variable as a switch. When it is off ($SF = 0$), production is not permitted; when it is on ($SF = 1$), production is permitted.

Similar production capacity constraints, using 0–1 variables, are added for the solvent base and carpet cleaning products

$$S \leq 25SS$$
$$C \leq 40SC$$

The complete model for the problem is as follows:

Max $40F + 30S + 50C - 200SF - 50SS - 400SC$
s.t.

$$
\begin{array}{lll}
0.4F + 0.5S + 0.6C & \leq 20 & \text{Material 1} \\
0.2S + 0.1C & \leq 5 & \text{Material 2} \\
0.6F + 0.3S + 0.3C & \leq 21 & \text{Material 3} \\
F & \leq 50SF & \text{Maximum } F \\
S & \leq 25SS & \text{Maximum } S \\
C & \leq 40SC & \text{Maximum } C
\end{array}
$$

$F, S, C \geq 0; \; SF, SS, SC = 0, 1$

The spreadsheet formulation and solution for this modified RMC problem are shown in Figure 6.8.

**SPREADSHEET
MODIFIED RMC**

Figure 6.8   SPREADSHEET SOLUTION FOR THE MODIFIED RMC PROBLEM WITH SETUP COSTS

	A	B	C	D	E	F	G	H	I
1	**Modified RMC with Setup Costs**								
2									
3			**Material Requirements(tons)**						
4			Fuel	Solvent	Cleaning	Tons			
5	**Materials**	Additive	Base	Fluid	**Available**				
6	Material 1	0.4	0.5	0.6	20				
7	Material 2		0.2	0.1	5				
8	Material 3	0.6	0.3	0.3	21				
9	**Profit per Ton**	40	30	50					
10	**Setup Cost**	200	50	400					
11	**Capacity (Tons)**	50	25	40					
12									
13									
14	**Model**								
15									
16									
17		**Max Net Profit**		1350		**Constraints**	**LHS**		**RHS**
18						Material 1	20	<=	20
19			Fuel	Solvent	Cleaning	Material 2	4	<=	5
20			Additive	Base	Fluid	Material 3	21	<=	21
21	**Tons Produced**	25	20	0	Max F	25	<=	50
22	**Setup**	1	1	0	Max S	20	<=	25
23						Max C	0	<=	0

Spreadsheet Formulation. The data and descriptive labels are in cells A1:E11. The screened cells in the bottom portion of the spreadsheet contain the information required by the Excel Solver.

Decision Variables   Cells B21:D22 are reserved for the decision variables. The optimal solution is to setup for production of the fuel additive and solvent base and to produce 25 tons of the fuel additive and 20 tons of the solvent base.

Objective Function   The formula =SUMPRODUCT(B9:D9,B21:D21)−SUMPRODUCT (B10:D10,B22:D22) has been placed into cell C17 to reflect the net profit associated with the solution shown. The optimal solution is shown to provide a net profit of $1,350.

Left-Hand Sides   The left-hand sides for the 6 constraints are placed into cells G18:G23.
    Cell G18 =SUMPRODUCT(B6:D6,$B$21:$D$21)
            (Copy to cells G19:G20)
    Cell G21 =B21
    Cell G22 =C21
    Cell G23 =D21

Right-Hand Sides   The right-hand sides for the 6 constraints are placed into cells I18:I23.
    Cell I18 =E6   (Copy to I19:I20)
    Cell I21 =B11*B22
    Cell I22 =C11*C22
    Cell I23 =D11*D22

Spreadsheet Solution. The solution can be obtained by selecting **Solver** from the **Tools** menu, entering the proper values into the **Solver Parameter** dialog box and specifying the options **Assume Linear Model, Assume Non-Negative,** and **Tolerance** equal to 0. The information entered into the **Solver Parameters** dialog box is shown in Figure 6.9. Note that the 0–1 decision variables in cells B22:D22 are required to be binary.

Figure **6.9**   SOLVER PARAMETERS DIALOG BOX FOR THE MODIFIED RMC PROBLEM WITH SETUP COSTS

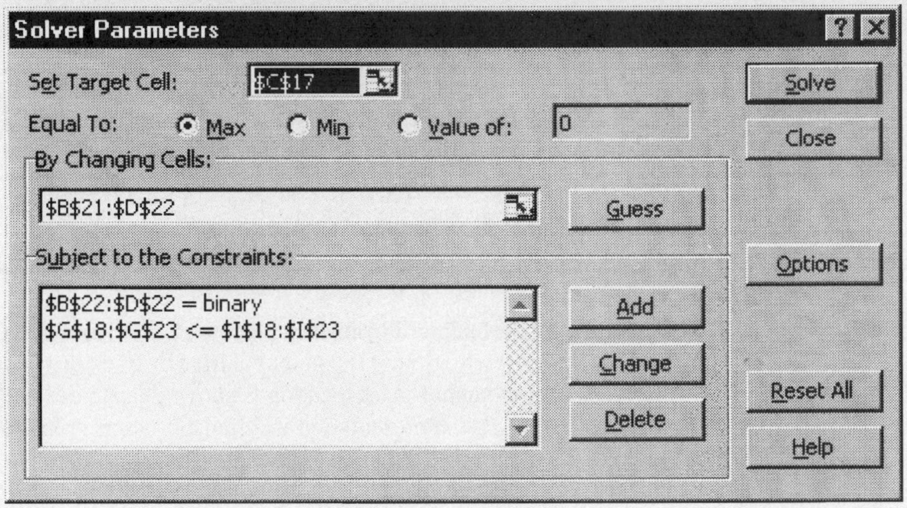

Discussion. As shown in Figure 6.8, the optimal solution shows 25 tons of fuel additive and 20 tons of solvent base. The value of the objective function including the set-up cost is $1,350. The setup cost for the fuel additive and the solvent base is $200 + $50 = $250. The optimal solution shows $SC = 0$, which indicates that the more expensive $400 setup cost for the carpet cleaning fluid should be avoided. Thus the carpet cleaning fluid is not produced.

The key to developing a fixed-charge model such as the modified RMC problem is the introduction of a 0–1 variable for each fixed charge and the specification of an upper bound for the corresponding production variable. For a production quantity x, a constraint of the form $x \leq My$ can then be used to allow production when the setup variable $y = 1$ and not to allow production when the setup variable $y = 0$. The value of the maximum production quantity M should be large enough to allow for all reasonable levels of production. Research has shown that choosing values of M too large will slow the solution procedure.

Distribution System Design

The Martin-Beck Company operates a plant in St. Louis which has an annual production capacity of 30,000 units. The final product is shipped to regional distribution centers located in Boston, Atlanta, and Houston. Because of an anticipated increase in demand, Martin-Beck plans to increase capacity by constructing a new plant in one or more of the following cities: Detroit, Toledo, Denver, and/or Kansas City. The estimated annual fixed cost and the annual capacity for the four proposed plants are as follows:

Proposed Plant	Annual Fixed Cost ($)	Annual Capacity (units)
Detroit	175,000	10,000
Toledo	300,000	20,000
Denver	375,000	30,000
Kansas City	500,000	40,000

The company's long-range planning group has developed the following forecasts of the anticipated annual demand at the distribution centers:

Distribution Center	Annual Demand (units)
Boston	30,000
Atlanta	20,000
Houston	20,000

The shipping cost per unit from each plant to each distribution center is shown in Table 6.2. A network representation of the potential Martin-Beck distribution system is shown in Figure 6.10. Each potential plant location is shown; capacities and demands are shown in thousands of units. This representation is a transportation problem with a plant at all four proposed sites. Of course, the decision has not yet been made as to which new plant, or plants, will be constructed.

Let us show how 0–1 variables can help us develop a model for choosing the best new plant location or locations and for determining how much should be shipped from each plant

Table 6.2	SHIPPING COST PER UNIT FOR THE MARTIN-BECK DISTRIBUTION SYSTEM		
	Distribution Centers		
Plant Site	**Boston**	**Atlanta**	**Houston**
Detroit	5	2	3
Toledo	4	3	4
Denver	9	7	5
Kansas City	10	4	2
St. Louis	8	4	3

Figure 6.10	THE NETWORK REPRESENTATION OF THE MARTIN-BECK COMPANY DISTRIBUTION SYSTEM PROBLEM

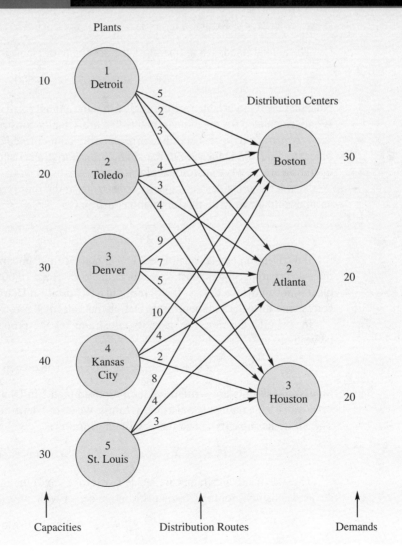

to each distribution center. The following 0–1 variables can be used to represent the plant construction decision.

$$y_1 = 1 \text{ if a plant is constructed in Detroit; 0 if not}$$
$$y_2 = 1 \text{ if a plant is constructed in Toledo; 0 if not}$$
$$y_3 = 1 \text{ if a plant is constructed in Denver; 0 if not}$$
$$y_4 = 1 \text{ if a plant is constructed in Kansas City; 0 if not}$$

The variables representing the amount shipped from each potential plant site to each distribution center are defined just as for a transportation problem.

$$x_{ij} = \text{the units shipped, in thousands, from plant } i \text{ to distribution center } j$$
$$i = 1, 2, 3, 4, 5 \quad \text{and} \quad j = 1, 2, 3$$

Using the shipping cost data in Table 6.2, the annual transportation cost in thousand of dollars is

$$5x_{11} + 2x_{12} + 3x_{13} + 4x_{21} + 3x_{22} + 4x_{23} + 9x_{31} + 7x_{32} + 5x_{33} + 10x_{41} + 4x_{42}$$
$$+ 2x_{43} + 8x_{51} + 4x_{52} + 3x_{53}$$

The annual fixed cost of operating the new plant or plants in thousand of dollars is

$$175y_1 + 300y_2 + 375y_3 + 500y_4$$

Note that the 0–1 variables are defined so that the annual fixed cost of operating a new plant is only calculated for the plant or plants that are actually constructed (i.e., $y_i = 1$). If a plant is not constructed, $y_i = 0$ and the corresponding annual fixed cost is \$0. The Martin-Beck objective function is the sum of the annual transportation cost plus the annual fixed cost of operating any newly constructed plants.

Now let us consider the capacity constraints at the four proposed plants. Using Detroit as an example, we write the following constraint:

$$x_{11} + x_{12} + x_{13} \leq 10y_1$$

If the Detroit plant is constructed, $y_1 = 1$ and the total amount shipped from Detroit to the three distribution centers must be less or equal to Detroit's 10,000 unit capacity. If the Detroit plant is not constructed, $y_1 = 0$ will result in a 0 capacity at Detroit. In this case, the variables corresponding to the shipments from Detroit must all equal zero: $x_{11} = 0, x_{12} = 0$, and $x_{13} = 0$.

In a similar fashion, the capacity constraint for the proposed plant in Toledo would be written

$$x_{21} + x_{22} + x_{23} \leq 20y_2 \quad \text{Toledo capacity}$$

Similar constraints are written for the proposed plants in Denver and Kansas City. However, since a plant already exists in St. Louis, we do not define a 0–1 variable for that plant. The St. Louis capacity constraint is written as follows:

$$x_{51} + x_{52} + x_{53} \leq 30 \quad \text{St. Louis capacity}$$

Three demand constraints are needed, one for each of the three distribution centers. The demand constraint for the Boston distribution center with units in thousands is written as

$$x_{11} + x_{21} + x_{31} + x_{41} + x_{51} = 30 \quad \text{Boston demand}$$

Similar constraints appear for the Atlanta and Houston distribution centers.

The complete mixed integer programming model for the Martin-Beck distribution system design problem is now stated.

$$\text{Min} \quad 5x_{11} + 2x_{12} + 3x_{13} + 4x_{21} + 3x_{22} + 4x_{23} + 9x_{31} + 7x_{32} + 5x_{33} + 10x_{41} + 4x_{42}$$
$$+ \; 2x_{43} + 8x_{51} + 4x_{52} + 3x_{53} + 175y_1 + 300y_2 + 375y_3 + 500y_4$$

s.t.

$$
\begin{array}{lll}
x_{11} + x_{12} + x_{13} & \leq 10y_1 & \text{Detroit capacity} \\
x_{21} + x_{22} + x_{23} & \leq 20y_2 & \text{Toledo capacity} \\
x_{31} + x_{32} + x_{33} & \leq 30y_3 & \text{Denver capacity} \\
x_{41} + x_{42} + x_{43} & \leq 40y_4 & \text{Kansas City capacity} \\
x_{51} + x_{52} + x_{53} & \leq 30 & \text{St. Louis capacity} \\
x_{11} + x_{21} + x_{31} + x_{41} + x_{51} & = 30 & \text{Boston demand} \\
x_{12} + x_{22} + x_{32} + x_{42} + x_{52} & = 20 & \text{Atlanta demand} \\
x_{13} + x_{23} + x_{33} + x_{43} + x_{53} & = 20 & \text{Houston demand} \\
\end{array}
$$
$$x_{ij} \geq 0 \text{ for all } i \text{ and } j; \; y_1, y_2, y_3, y_4 = 0, 1$$

The spreadsheet formulation and solution for the Martin-Beck Company problem are shown in Figure 6.11.

Spreadsheet Formulation.   The data and descriptive labels are in cells A1:F10. The screened cells in the bottom portion of the spreadsheet contain the information required by the Excel Solver.

Decision Variables   Cells B20:D24 and H20:H23 are reserved for the decision variables. From Cells H20:H23 we see that the optimal solution has $y_4 = 1$ and recommends construction of a new plant in Kansas City. The entries in cells B20:D24 show that all shipments are made from the 2 open plants: Kansas City and St. Louis.

Objective Function   The formula =SUMPRODUCT(B5:D9,B20:D24)+SUMPRODUCT (F5:F8,H20:H23) has been placed into cell C15 to reflect the total cost associated with the solution shown. The optimal solution provides a total cost of $860,000.

Left-Hand Sides   The left-hand sides for the 8 constraints are placed into cells E20:E24 and into cells B25:D25.

   Cell E20 =SUM(B20:D20)   (Copy to E21:E24)
   Cell B25 =SUM(B20:B24)   (Copy to C25:D25)

Right-Hand Sides   The right-hand sides for the 8 constraints are contained in cells G20:G24 and in cells B27:D27.

   Cell G20 =E5*H20   (Copy to G21:G23)
   Cell G24 =E9
   Cell B27 =B10   (Copy to C27:D27)

Spreadsheet Solution.   The solution can be obtained by selecting **Solver** from the **Tools** menu, entering the proper values into the **Solver Parameter** dialog box and specifying the options **Assume Linear Model, Assume Non-Negative,** and **Tolerance** equal to 0. The information entered into the **Solver Parameters** dialog box is shown in Figure 6.12. Note that the 0–1 decision variables in cells H20:H23 are required to be binary.

Figure 6.11 — SPREADSHEET SOLUTION FOR THE MARTIN-BECK COMPANY PROBLEM

SPREADSHEET MARTIN-BECK

	A	B	C	D	E	F	G	H
1	**Martin-Beck Company Distribution System Design**							
2								
3			**Distribution Center**			**Fixed**		
4	**Plant**	Boston	Atlanta	Houston	**Capacity**	**Cost($1000s)**		
5	Detroit	5	2	3	10000	175000		
6	Toledo	4	3	4	20000	300000		
7	Denver	9	7	5	30000	375000		
8	Kansas City	10	4	2	40000	500000		
9	St. Louis	8	4	3	30000			
10	**Demand**	30000	20000	20000				
11								
12								
13	**Model**							
14								
15		**Min Cost**	860000					
16								
17								
18			**Distribution Center**					**Open or**
19	**Plant**	Boston	Atlanta	Houston	**Total**		**Capacity**	**Closed**
20	Detroit	0	0	0	0	<=	0	0
21	Toledo	0	0	0	0	<=	0	0
22	Denver	0	0	0	0	<=	0	0
23	Kansas City	0	20000	20000	40000	<=	40000	1
24	St. Louis	30000	0	0	30000	<=	30000	
25	**Total**	30000	20000	20000				
26		=	=	=				
27	**Demand**	30000	20000	20000				

Discussion. The optimal solution recommends construction of a plant in Kansas City; 20,000 units to be shipped from Kansas City to Atlanta, 20,000 units to be shipped from Kansas City to Houston, and 30,000 units to be shipped from St. Louis to Boston. The total cost of this solution, including the fixed cost of $500,000 to construct the plant in Kansas City, is $860,000.

This model can be expanded to accommodate more complex distribution systems involving direct shipments from plants to warehouses, from plants to retail outlets, and of multiple products.[3] Using the special properties of 0–1 variables, the model can also be expanded to accommodate a variety of configuration constraints on the plant locations. For example, suppose that in another problem, site 1 was in Dallas and site 2 was in Fort Worth. A company might not want to locate plants in both Dallas and Fort Worth because

---

3. For computational reasons, it is usually preferable to replace the m plant capacity constraints with mn shipping route capacity constraints of the form $x_{ij} \le$ Min $\{s_i, d_j\}\, y_i$ for $i = 1, \ldots, m$ and $j = 1, \ldots, n$. The coefficient for y_i in each constraint is the smaller of the origin capacity (s_i) or the destination demand (d_j). These additional constraints often cause the solution of the LP Relaxation to be integer.

Figure 6.12	SOLVER PARAMETERS DIALOG BOX FOR THE MARTIN-BECK COMPANY PROBLEM

Solver Parameters [?] [X]

Se_t Target Cell: $C$15

Equal To: ○ _Max   ◉ Mi_n   ○ _Value of: 0

_By Changing Cells:

$B$20:$D$24,$H$20:$H$23

_Subject to the Constraints:

$B$25:$D$25 = $B$27:$D$27
$E$20:$E$24 <= $G$20:$G$24
$H$20:$H$23 = binary

[Solve] [Close] [Guess] [Options] [Add] [Change] [Delete] [Reset All] [Help]

the cities are so close together. To prevent this result, the following constraint can be added to the model:

$$y_1 + y_2 \leq 1$$

Problem 13, which is based on the Martin-Beck distribution system problem, provides additional practice involving 0–1 variables.

This constraint allows either y_1 or y_2 to equal 1 but not both. If we had written the constraint as an equality, it would require that a plant be located in either Dallas or Fort Worth.

Bank Location

The long-range planning department for the Ohio Trust Company is considering expanding its operation into a 20-county region in northeastern Ohio (see Figure 6.13). Currently, Ohio Trust does not have a principal place of business in any of the 20 counties. According to the banking laws in Ohio, if a bank establishes a principal place of business (PPB) in any county, branch banks can be established in that county and in any adjacent county. However, to establish a new principal place of business, Ohio Trust must either obtain approval for a new bank from the state's superintendent of banks or purchase an existing bank.

Table 6.3 lists the 20 counties in the region and adjacent counties. For example, Ashtabula County is adjacent to Lake, Geauga, and Trumbull counties; Lake County is adjacent to Ashtabula, Cuyahoga, and Geauga counties; and so on.

As an initial step in its planning, Ohio Trust would like to determine the minimum number of PPBs necessary to do business throughout the 20-county region. A 0–1

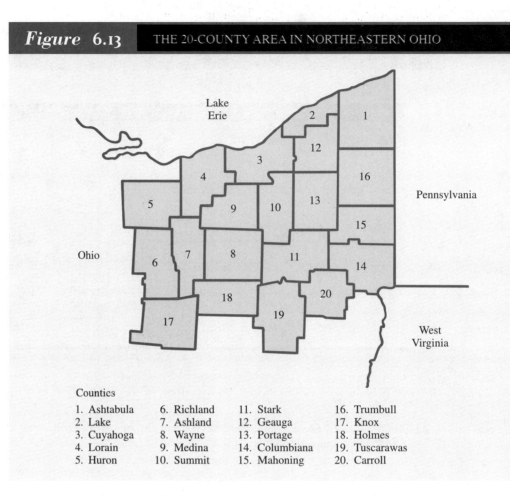

Figure **6.13**   THE 20-COUNTY AREA IN NORTHEASTERN OHIO

Counties

1. Ashtabula	6. Richland	11. Stark	16. Trumbull
2. Lake	7. Ashland	12. Geauga	17. Knox
3. Cuyahoga	8. Wayne	13. Portage	18. Holmes
4. Lorain	9. Medina	14. Columbiana	19. Tuscarawas
5. Huron	10. Summit	15. Mahoning	20. Carroll

integer programming model can be used to solve this problem for Ohio Trust. We define the variables as

$$x_i = 1 \text{ if a PPB is established in county } i; 0 \text{ otherwise}$$

To minimize the number of PPBs needed, we write the objective function as

$$\text{Min} \quad x_1 + x_2 + \cdots + x_{20}$$

The bank may locate branches in a county if the county contains a PPB or is adjacent to another county with a PPB. Thus, there will be one constraint for each county. For example, the constraint for Ashtabula County is

$$x_1 + x_2 + x_{12} + x_{16} \geq 1 \qquad \text{Ashtabula}$$

Note that satisfaction of this constraint ensures that a PPB will be placed in Ashtabula County *or* in one or more of the adjacent counties. This constraint thus guarantees that Ohio Trust will be able to place branch banks in Ashtabula County.

Table 6.3	COUNTIES IN THE OHIO TRUST EXPANSION REGION

Counties Under Consideration	Adjacent Counties (by Number)
1. Ashtabula	2, 12, 16
2. Lake	1, 3, 12
3. Cuyahoga	2, 4, 9, 10, 12, 13
4. Lorain	3, 5, 7, 9
5. Huron	4, 6, 7
6. Richland	5, 7, 17
7. Ashland	4, 5, 6, 8, 9, 17, 18
8. Wayne	7, 9, 10, 11, 18
9. Medina	3, 4, 7, 8, 10
10. Summit	3, 8, 9, 11, 12, 13
11. Stark	8, 10, 13, 14, 15, 18, 19, 20
12. Geauga	1, 2, 3, 10, 13, 16
13. Portage	3, 10, 11, 12, 15, 16
14. Columbiana	11, 15, 20
15. Mahoning	11, 13, 14, 16
16. Trumbull	1, 12, 13, 15
17. Knox	6, 7, 18
18. Holmes	7, 8, 11, 17, 19
19. Tuscarawas	11, 18, 20
20. Carroll	11, 14, 19

The complete statement of the bank location problem is

$$\text{Min} \quad x_1 + x_2 + \quad \cdots \quad + x_{20}$$

s.t.

$$x_1 + x_2 \qquad + x_{12} + x_{16} \qquad \geq 1 \quad \text{Ashtabula}$$
$$x_1 + x_2 + x_3 + x_{12} \qquad \qquad \geq 1 \quad \text{Lake}$$

$$\vdots \qquad\qquad\qquad \vdots$$

$$x_{11} + x_{14} + x_{19} + x_{20} \geq 1 \quad \text{Carroll}$$
$$x_i = 0, 1 \quad i = 1, 2, \ldots, 20$$

The spreadsheet formulation and solution for the Ohio Trust Bank Location problem are shown in Figure 6.14.

Spreadsheet Formulation.   A separate data section is not shown here. The data concern whether counties are adjacent to one another; this data is incorporated directly into the constraint left-hand sides as we describe below.

Decision Variables   Cells D6:D25 are reserved for the decision variables. A 1 is shown if a principal place of business is located in the associated county;

Figure 6.14 SPREADSHEET SOLUTION FOR THE BANK LOCATION PROBLEM

SPREADSHEET
OHIO TRUST

	A	B	C	D	E	F	G	H
1	**Ohio Trust Bank Location**							
2								
3								
4	**Min PPBs**	3		**PPB**		**Coverage**		**Coverage**
5				**Chosen**		**Provided**		**Required**
6			Ashtabula	0		1	>=	1
7			Lake	0		1	>=	1
8			Cuyahoga	0		1	>=	1
9			Lorain	0		1	>=	1
10			Huron	0		1	>=	1
11			Richland	0		1	>=	1
12			Ashland	1		1	>=	1
13			Wayne	0		2	>=	1
14			Medina	0		1	>=	1
15			Summit	0		2	>=	1
16			Stark	1		1	>=	1
17			Geauga	1		1	>=	1
18			Portage	0		2	>=	1
19			Columbiana	0		1	>=	1
20			Mahoning	0		1	>=	1
21			Trumbull	0		1	>=	1
22			Knox	0		1	>=	1
23			Holmes	0		2	>=	1
24			Tuscarawas	0		1	>=	1
25			Carroll	0		1	>=	1

otherwise a 0 is shown. As can be seen, the optimal solution is to open PPBs in Ashland, Stark, and Geauga counties.

Objective Function   The formula =SUM(D6:D25) is placed into cell B4 to reflect the number of PPBs needed to provide the desired coverage. The minimum number of PPBs required to provide complete coverage of all 20 counties is 3.

Left-Hand Sides   The left-hand sides for the 20 coverage constraints are placed into cells F6:F25.

Cell F6   =D6+D7+D17+D21
Cell F7   =D6+D7+D8+D17
⋮   ⋮
Cell F25   =D16+D19+D24+D25

Right-Hand Sides   The right-hand sides for the 20 constraints are placed into cells H6:H25. A 1 is placed into each of these cells to indicate that each county must be covered by at least one PPB.

Spreadsheet Solution.   The solution can be obtained by selecting **Solver** from the **Tools** menu, entering the proper values into the **Solver Parameters** dialog box and specifying the options **Assume Linear Model, Assume Non-Negative,** and **Tolerance** equal to 0. The information entered into the **Solver Parameters** dialog box is shown in Figure 6.15. Note that the decision variables (cells D6:D25) are required to be binary.

Discussion.   The optimal solution calls for principal places of business in Ashland, Stark, and Geauga counties. With PPBs in these three counties, Ohio Trust can place branch banks in all 20 counties (see Figure 6.16). All other decision variables have an optimal value of zero, indicating that a PPB should not be placed in these counties. Clearly the integer programming model could be enlarged to allow for expansion into a larger area or throughout the entire state.

N O T E S
and Comments

1. Most practical applications of integer linear programming involve only 0–1 integer variables. Indeed, some mixed-integer computer codes are designed to handle only integer variables with binary values. However, if a clever mathematical trick is employed, these codes can still be used for problems involving general integer variables. The trick is called *binary expansion* and requires that an upper bound be established for each integer variable. More advanced texts on integer programming show how this can be done.

2. The Management Science in Action: Analyzing Price Quotations Under Business Volume Discounts describes how 0–1 variables can be used in a model designed to take advantage of business volume discounts. Bellcore clients have saved millions of dollars by using a mixed-integer programming model.

3. General-purpose mixed-integer linear programming codes and spreadsheet packages can be used for linear programming problems, all-integer problems, and problems involving some continuous and some integer variables. General-purpose codes are seldom the fastest for solving problems with special structure (such as the transportation, assignment, and transshipment problems); however, unless the problems are very large, speed is usually not a critical issue.

MANAGEMENT SCIENCE IN ACTION

ANALYZING PRICE QUOTATIONS UNDER BUSINESS VOLUME DISCOUNTS*

Bellcore was formed in 1984 to provide various support services for the regional Bell operating telephone companies. To reduce the cost of buying goods and services, Bellcore client companies are increasingly requesting business volume discounts from suppliers in place of traditional quantity discounts. With traditional quantity discounts, the price of each item purchased is discounted on the basis of the amount of the item purchased. Business volume discounts differ from single-item quantity discounts in that the supplier discounts the price of each item by a percentage that is based on the total dollar volume of business over all items awarded to the supplier; whatever this percentage, it remains the same for each item. In general, a firm can realize lower overall purchasing costs with business volume discounts, and a supplier can increase total revenues by obtaining a larger volume of that firm's business. However, business volume discounts greatly increase the complexity of the procurement process because the discount obtained depends on the purchase quantities and prices of all products purchased.

To assist Bellcore client companies in using business volume discounts, Bellcore developed the procurement decision support-system (PDSS), a PC-based decision support program that uses a mixed-integer programming model to minimize the total cost of purchases. The model uses 0–1 integer variables to model the discount categories applicable to the problem and includes a variety of constraints involving factors such as supplier capacity and limits on the dollar amount awarded to a supplier. Since 1990, one Bellcore client company has reported two savings, one of $4.5 million and another of $15 million; these figures represent approximately 10% on the cost of purchases. Another client company has realized a reduction of approximately 80% in the cost of analyzing quotations, and users generally believe that PDSS is a useful tool in identifying opportunities in negotiations with suppliers.

*Based on P. Katz, A. Sadrian, and P. Tendick, "Telephone Companies Analyze Price Quotations with Bellcore's PDSS Software," *Interfaces* (January–February 1994): 50–63.

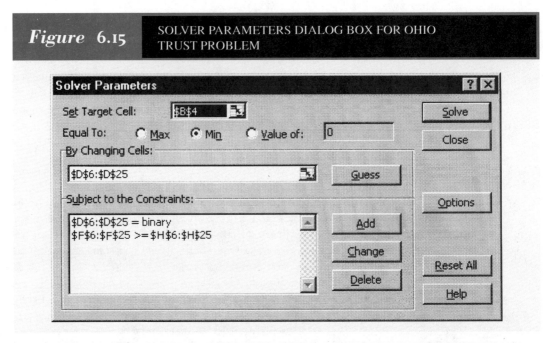

Figure 6.15   SOLVER PARAMETERS DIALOG BOX FOR OHIO TRUST PROBLEM

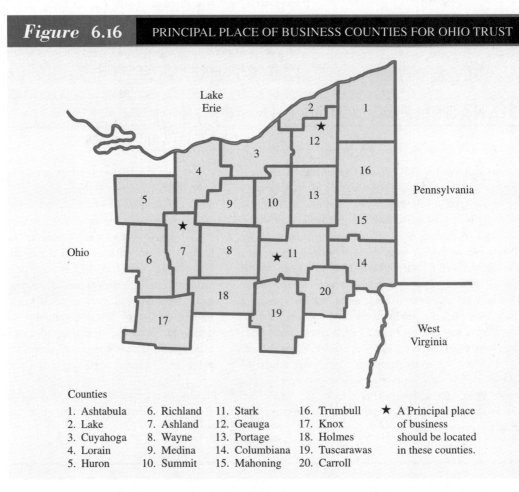

Figure 6.16   PRINCIPAL PLACE OF BUSINESS COUNTIES FOR OHIO TRUST

Counties

1. Ashtabula   6. Richland   11. Stark   16. Trumbull   ★ A Principal place
2. Lake   7. Ashland   12. Geauga   17. Knox   of business
3. Cuyahoga   8. Wayne   13. Portage   18. Holmes   should be located
4. Lorain   9. Medina   14. Columbiana   19. Tuscarawas   in these counties.
5. Huron   10. Summit   15. Mahoning   20. Carroll

..../ /.............

6.4   MODELING FLEXIBILITY PROVIDED BY 0–1 INTEGER VARIABLES

In Section 6.3 we presented four applications involving 0–1 integer variables. In this section we continue the discussion of the use of 0–1 integer variables in modeling. First, we show how 0–1 integer variables can be used to model multiple-choice and mutually exclusive constraints. Then, we show how 0–1 integer variables can be used to model situations in which k projects out of a set of n projects must be selected, as well as situations in which the acceptance of one project is conditional on the acceptance of another. We close the section with a cautionary note on the role of sensitivity analysis in integer linear programming.

Multiple-Choice and Mutually Exclusive Constraints

Recall the Ice-Cold Refrigerator capital budgeting problem introduced in Section 6.3. The decision variables were defined as

$P = 1$ if the plant expansion project is accepted; 0 if rejected
$W = 1$ if the warehouse expansion project is accepted; 0 if rejected
$M = 1$ if the new machinery project is accepted; 0 if rejected
$R = 1$ if the new product research project is accepted; 0 if rejected

Suppose that, instead of one warehouse expansion project, the Ice-Cold Refrigerator Company actually has three warehouse expansion projects under consideration. One of the warehouses *must* be expanded because of increasing product demand, but new demand isn't sufficient to make expansion of more than one warehouse necessary. The following variable definitions and **multiple-choice constraint** could be incorporated into the previous 0–1 integer linear programming model to reflect this situation. Let

$W_1 = 1$ if the original warehouse expansion project is accepted; 0 if rejected
$W_2 = 1$ if the second warehouse expansion project is accepted; 0 if rejected
$W_3 = 1$ if the third warehouse expansion project is accepted; 0 if rejected

The multiple-choice constraint reflecting the requirement that exactly one of these projects must be selected is

$$W_1 + W_2 + W_3 = 1$$

Since W_1, W_2, and W_3 are allowed to assume only the values 0 or 1, one and only one of these projects must be selected from among the three choices.

  If the requirement that one warehouse must be expanded did not exist, the multiple-choice constraint could be modified as follows:

$$W_1 + W_2 + W_3 \leq 1$$

This modification allows for the case of no warehouse expansion ($W_1 = W_2 = W_3 = 0$) but does not permit more than one warehouse to be expanded. This type of constraint is often called a **mutually exclusive constraint.**

k Out of n Alternatives Constraint

An extension of the notion of a multiple-choice constraint can be used to model situations in which k *out of a set of n* projects must be selected—a **k out of n alternatives constraint.** Suppose that W_1, W_2, W_3, W_4, and W_5 represent five potential warehouse expansion projects and that two of the five projects must be accepted. The constraint that satisfies this new requirement is

$$W_1 + W_2 + W_3 + W_4 + W_5 = 2$$

If no more than two of the projects are to be selected, we would use the following less-than-or-equal-to constraint:

$$W_1 + W_2 + W_3 + W_4 + W_5 \leq 2$$

Again, each of these variables must be restricted to 0–1 values.

Conditional and Corequisite Constraints

Sometimes the acceptance of one project is conditional on the acceptance of another. For example, suppose for the Ice-Cold Refrigerator Company that the warehouse expansion project was conditional on the plant expansion project. That is, management will not consider expanding the warehouse unless the plant is expanded. With P representing plant expansion and W representing warehouse expansion, a **conditional constraint** could be introduced to enforce this requirement:

$$W \leq P$$

As both P and W must be 0 or 1, whenever P is 0, W will be forced to 0. When P is 1, W is also allowed to be 1; thus, both the plant and the warehouse can be expanded. However, we note that the preceding constraint does not force the warehouse expansion project (W) to be accepted if the plant expansion project (P) is accepted.

If the warehouse expansion project had to be accepted whenever the plant expansion project was, and vice versa, we would say that P and W represented **corequisite constraint** projects. To model such a situation, we simply write the preceding constraint as an equality:

$$W = P$$

Try Problem 7 for practice with the modeling flexibility provided by 0–1 variables.

This constraint forces P and W to take on the same value.

A Cautionary Note About Sensitivity Analysis

Sensitivity analysis often is more crucial for integer linear programming problems than for linear programming problems. A very small change in one of the coefficients in the constraints can cause a relatively large change in the value of the optimal solution. To understand why, consider the following integer programming model of a simple capital budgeting problem involving four projects and a budgetary constraint for a single time period:

$$\text{Max} \quad 40x_1 + 60x_2 + 70x_3 + 160x_4$$

s.t.

$$16x_1 + 35x_2 + 45x_3 + 85x_4 \leq 100$$

$$x_1, x_2, x_3, x_4 = 0, 1$$

We obtain the optimal solution to this problem by enumerating the alternatives. It is $x_1 = 1$, $x_2 = 1$, $x_3 = 1$, and $x_4 = 0$, with an objective function value of $170. However, note that if the budget available is increased by $1 (from $100 to $101), the optimal solution changes to $x_1 = 1$, $x_2 = 0$, $x_3 = 0$, and $x_4 = 1$, with an objective function value of $200. That is, one additional dollar in the budget would lead to a $30 increase in the return. Surely management, when faced with such a situation, would increase the budget by $1. Because of the extreme sensitivity of the value of the optimal solution to the constraint coefficients, practitioners usually recommend resolving the integer linear program several times with slight variations in the coefficients before attempting to choose an optimal solution for implementation.

Shadow prices cannot be used for sensitivity analysis as they are for linear programs. Multiple computer runs usually are necessary for sensitivity analysis of integer linear programs.

SUMMARY

In this chapter, we introduced the important extension of linear programming referred to as *integer linear programming*. The only difference between the integer linear programming problems discussed in this chapter and the linear programming problems studied in previous chapters is that one or more of the variables must be integer. If all variables must be integer, we have an all-integer linear program. If some, but not all, variables must be integer, we have a mixed-integer linear program. If all variables are 0–1 or binary variables, we have a 0–1 integer linear program.

There are two major reasons for studying integer linear programming. First, integer linear programming may be helpful when fractional values for the variables are not permitted. Since rounding a linear programming solution may not provide an optimal integer solution, methods for finding optimal integer solutions are needed when the economic consequences of rounding are significant. A second reason for studying integer linear programming is the increased modeling flexibility provided through the use of 0–1 variables. We showed how 0–1 variables could be used to model important managerial considerations in capital budgeting, fixed cost, distribution system design, and bank location applications.

The number of applications of integer linear programming has been growing in recent years. This growth is due in part to the availability of commercial integer linear programming software packages. As researchers develop solution procedures capable of solving larger integer linear programs and as computer speed increases, a continuation of this growth of integer linear programming applications is expected.

GLOSSARY

Integer linear program   A linear program with the additional requirement that at least one of the variables must be integer.

All-integer linear program   An integer linear program in which all variables are required to be integer.

Mixed-integer linear program   An integer linear program in which some, but not all, variables are required to be integer.

0–1 integer linear program   An all-integer or mixed-integer linear program in which the integer variables are only permitted to assume the values 0 or 1. Also called *binary integer program*.

LP Relaxation The linear program that results from dropping the integer requirements for the variables.

Multiple-choice constraint A constraint requiring that the sum of two or more 0–1 variables equal 1. Thus, any feasible solution makes a choice of one of these variables to set equal to 1.

Mutually exclusive constraint A constraint requiring that the sum of two or more 0–1 variables be less than or equal to 1. Thus, if one of the variables equals 1, the others must equal 0. However, all variables could equal 0.

***k* out of *n* alternatives constraint** An extension of the multiple-choice constraint. This constraint requires that the sum of *n* 0–1 variables equal *k*.

Conditional constraint A constraint involving 0–1 variables that does not allow certain variables to equal 1 unless certain other variables are equal to 1.

Corequisite constraint A constraint requiring that two 0–1 variables be equal. Thus, they are both in or out of solution together.

PROBLEMS

1. Indicate which of the following is an all-integer linear program and which is a mixed-integer linear program. Write the LP Relaxation for the problem but do not attempt to solve.

   a. Max $30x_1 + 25x_2$

   s.t.

   $$3x_1 + 1.5x_2 \leq 400$$
   $$1.5x_1 + 2x_2 \leq 250$$
   $$1x_1 + 1x_2 \leq 150$$
   $$x_1, x_2 \geq 0 \text{ and } x_2 \text{ integer}$$

   b. Min $3x_1 + 4x_2$

   s.t.

   $$2x_1 + 4x_2 \geq 8$$
   $$2x_1 + 6x_2 \geq 12$$
   $$x_1, x_2 \geq 0 \text{ and integer}$$

2. Consider the following all-integer linear program.

   SELF TEST

   $$\text{Max} \quad 5x_1 + 8x_2$$

   s.t.

   $$6x_1 + 5x_2 \leq 30$$
   $$9x_1 + 4x_2 \leq 36$$
   $$1x_1 + 2x_2 \leq 10$$
   $$x_1, x_2 \geq 0 \text{ and integer}$$

   a. Graph the constraints for this problem. Use heavy dots to indicate all feasible integer solutions.

b. Find the optimal solution to the LP Relaxation. Round down to find a feasible integer solution.

c. Find the optimal integer solution. Is it the same as the solution obtained in part (b) by rounding down?

3. Consider the following all-integer linear program.

$$\text{Max} \quad 1x_1 + 1x_2$$
$$\text{s.t.}$$
$$4x_1 + 6x_2 \le 22$$
$$1x_1 + 5x_2 \le 15$$
$$2x_1 + 1x_2 \le 9$$
$$x_1, x_2 \ge 0 \text{ and integer}$$

a. Graph the constraints for this problem. Use heavy dots to indicate all feasible integer solutions.

b. Solve the LP Relaxation of this problem.

c. Find the optimal integer solution.

4. Consider the following all-integer linear program.

$$\text{Max} \quad 10x_1 + 3x_2$$
$$\text{s.t.}$$
$$6x_1 + 7x_2 \le 40$$
$$3x_1 + 1x_2 \le 11$$
$$x_1, x_2 \ge 0 \text{ and integer}$$

a. Formulate and solve the LP Relaxation of the problem. Solve it graphically, and round down to find a feasible solution. Specify an upper bound on the value of the optimal solution.

b. Solve the integer linear program graphically. Compare the value of this solution with the solution obtained in part (a).

c. Suppose that the objective function changes to Max $3x_1 + 6x_2$. Repeat parts (a) and (b).

SELF TEST

5. Consider the following mixed-integer linear program.

$$\text{Max} \quad 2x_1 + 3x_2$$
$$\text{s.t.}$$
$$4x_1 + 9x_2 \le 36$$
$$7x_1 + 5x_2 \le 35$$
$$x_1, x_2 \ge 0 \text{ and } x_1 \text{ integer}$$

a. Graph the constraints for this problem. Indicate on your graph all feasible mixed-integer solutions.

b. Find the optimal solution to the LP Relaxation. Round the value of x_1 down to find a feasible mixed-integer solution. Is this solution optimal? Why or why not?

c. Find the optimal solution for the mixed-integer linear program.

6. Consider the following mixed-integer linear program.

$$\text{Max} \quad 1x_1 + 1x_2$$

s.t.

$$7x_1 + 9x_2 \leq 63$$
$$9x_1 + 5x_2 \leq 45$$
$$3x_1 + 1x_2 \leq 12$$
$$x_1, x_2 \geq 0 \text{ and } x_2 \text{ integer}$$

a. Graph the constraints for this problem. Indicate on your graph all feasible mixed-integer solutions.
b. Find the optimal solution to the LP Relaxation. Round the value of x_2 down to find a feasible mixed-integer solution. Specify upper and lower bounds on the value of the optimal solution to the mixed-integer linear program.
c. Find the optimal solution to the mixed-integer linear program.

SELF TEST

7. The following questions refer to a capital budgeting problem with six projects represented by 0–1 variables $x_1, x_2, x_3, x_4, x_5,$ and x_6.
a. Write a constraint modeling a situation in which two of the projects 1, 3, 5, and 6 must be undertaken.
b. Write a constraint modeling a situation in which if projects 3 and 5 are undertaken, they must be undertaken simultaneously.
c. Write a constraint modeling a situation in which project 1 or 4 must be undertaken but not both.
d. Write constraints modeling a situation where project 4 cannot be undertaken unless projects 1 and 3 also are undertaken.
e. Revise the requirement in part (d) to accommodate the case in which, when projects 1 and 3 are undertaken, project 4 also must be undertaken.

8. Spencer Enterprises is attempting to choose among a series of new investment alternatives. The potential investment alternatives, the net present value of the future stream of returns, the capital requirements, and the available capital funds over the next 3 years are summarized as follows:

| | Project | | | | | | |
	Limited Warehouse Expansion	Extensive Warehouse Expansion	Test Market New Product	Advertising Campaign	Basic Research	Purchase New Equipment	**Capital Available**
Net Present Value	4000	6000	10500	4000	8000	3000	—
Year 1 Capital	3000	2500	6000	2000	5000	1000	10500
Year 2 Capital	1000	3500	4000	1500	1000	500	7000
Year 3 Capital	4000	3500	5000	1800	4000	900	8750

a. Develop and solve an integer programming model for maximizing the net present value.
b. Assume that only one of the warehouse expansion projects can be implemented. Modify your model of part (a).
c. Suppose that, if test marketing of the new product is carried out, the advertising campaign also must be conducted. Modify your formulation of part (b) to reflect this new situation.

9. Hawkins Manufacturing Company produces connecting rods for 4- and 6-cylinder automobile engines using the same production line. The cost required to set up the production line to produce the 4-cylinder connecting rods is $2,000, and the cost required to set up the production line for the 6-cylinder connecting rods is $3,500. Manufacturing costs are $15 for each 4-cylinder connecting rod and $18 for each 6-cylinder connecting rod. Hawkins makes a decision at the end of each week as to which product will be manufactured the following week. If there is a production changeover from one week to the next, the weekend is used to reconfigure the production line. Once the line has been set up, the weekly production capacities are 6000, 6-cylinder connecting rods and 8000, 4-cylinder connecting rods. Let

x_4 = the number of 4-cylinder connecting rods produced next week

x_6 = the number of 6-cylinder connecting rods produced next week

s_4 = 1 if the production line is set up to produce the 4-cylinder connecting rods; 0 otherwise

s_6 = 1 if the production line is set up to produce the 6-cylinder connecting rods; 0 otherwise

a. Using the decision variables x_4 and s_4, write a constraint that limits next week's production of the 4-cylinder connecting rods to either 0 or 8000 units.
b. Using the decision variables x_6 and s_6, write a constraint that limits next week's production of the 6-cylinder connecting rods to either 0 or 6000 units.
c. Write 3 constraints that, taken together, limit the production of connecting rods for next week.
d. Write an objective function for minimizing the cost of production for next week.

10. Grave City is considering the relocation of several police substations to obtain better enforcement in high-crime areas. The locations under consideration together with the areas that can be covered from these locations are given in the following table.

Potential Locations for Substations	Areas Covered
A	1, 5, 7
B	1, 2, 5, 7
C	1, 3, 5
D	2, 4, 5
E	3, 4, 6
F	4, 5, 6
G	1, 5, 6, 7

a. Formulate an integer programming model that could be used to find the minimum number of locations necessary to provide coverage to all areas.
b. Solve the problem in part (a).

11. Hart Manufacturing makes three products. Each product requires manufacturing operations in three departments: A, B, and C. The labor-hour requirements, by department, are

Department	Product 1	Product 2	Product 3
A	1.50	3.00	2.00
B	2.00	1.00	2.50
C	0.25	0.25	0.25

During the next production period, the labor-hours available are 450 in department A, 350 in department B, and 50 in department C. The profit contributions per unit are $25 for product 1, $28 for product 2, and $30 for product 3.

a. Formulate a linear programming model for maximizing total profit contribution.

b. Solve the linear program formulated in part (a). How much of each product should be produced and what is the projected total profit contribution?

c. After evaluating the solution obtained in part (b), a production supervisor noted that production setup costs had not been taken into account. She noted that setup costs are $400 for product 1, $550 for product 2, and $600 for product 3. If the solution developed in part (b) is to be used, what is the total profit contribution after taking into account the setup costs?

d. Management realized that the optimal product mix, taking setup costs into account, might be different from the one recommended in part (b). Formulate a mixed-integer linear program that takes setup costs into account.

e. Solve the mixed integer linear program formulated in part (d). How much of each product should be produced and what is the projected total profit contribution? Compare this profit contribution to that obtained in part (c).

12. Yates Company supplies road salt to county highway departments. The company has three trucks, and the dispatcher is trying to schedule tomorrow's deliveries to Polk, Dallas, and Jasper counties. Two trucks have 15-ton capacities, and the third truck has a 30-ton capacity. Based on these truck capacities, two counties will receive 15 tons and the third will receive 30 tons of road salt. The dispatcher wants to determine how much to ship to each county. Let

$$P = \text{amount shipped to Polk County}$$
$$D = \text{amount shipped to Dallas County}$$
$$J = \text{amount shipped to Jasper County}$$

and

$$Y_i = \begin{cases} 1 \text{ if the 30-ton truck is assigned to county } i \\ 0 \text{ otherwise} \end{cases}$$

a. Use these variable definitions and write constraints that appropriately restrict the amount shipped to each county.

b. The cost of assigning the 30-ton truck to the three counties is $100 to Polk, $85 to Dallas, and $50 to Jasper. Formulate and solve a mixed-integer linear program to determine how much to ship to each county.

SELF TEST

13. Recall the Martin-Beck Company distribution system problem in Section 6.3.

a. Modify the formulation shown in Section 6.3 to account for the policy restriction that one plant, but not two, must be located either in Detroit or in Toledo.

b. Modify the formulation shown in Section 6.3 to account for the policy restriction that no more than two plants can be located in Denver, Kansas City, and St. Louis.

14. An automobile manufacturer has five outdated plants: one each in Michigan, Ohio, and California and two in New York. Management is considering modernizing these plants to manufacture engine blocks and transmissions for a new model car. The cost to modernize each plant and the manufacturing capacity after modernization are as follows:

Plant	Cost (millions)	Engine Blocks (1000s)	Transmissions (1000s)
Michigan	25	500	300
New York	35	800	400
New York	35	400	800
Ohio	40	900	600
California	20	200	300

The projected needs are for total capacities of 900,000 engine blocks and 900,000 transmissions. Management wants to determine which plants to modernize to meet projected manufacturing needs and, at the same time, minimize the total cost of modernization.

a. Develop a table that lists every possible option available to management. As part of your table, indicate the total engine block capacity and transmission capacity for each possible option, whether the option is feasible based on the projected needs, and the total modernization cost for each option.

b. Based on your analysis in part (a), what recommendation would you provide management?

c. Formulate a 0–1 integer programming model that could be used to determine the optimal solution to the modernization question facing management.

d. Solve the model formulated in part (c) to provide a recommendation for management.

15. CHB, Inc., is a bank holding company that is evaluating the potential for expanding into a 13-county region in the southwestern part of the state. State law permits establishing branches in any county that is adjacent to a county in which a PPB (principal place of business) is located. The following map shows the 13-county region with the population of each county indicated.

a. Assume that only one PPB can be established in the region. Where should it be located to maximize the population served? (Hint: Review the Ohio Trust formulation in Section 6.3. Introduce the variable $y_i = 1$ if it is possible to establish a branch in county i, and $y_i = 0$ otherwise.)

b. Suppose that two PPBs can be established in the region. Where should they be located to maximize the population served?

c. Management has learned that a bank located in county 5 is considering selling. If CHB purchases this bank, the requisite PPB will be established in county 5, and a base for beginning expansion in the region will also be established. What advice would you give the management of CHB?

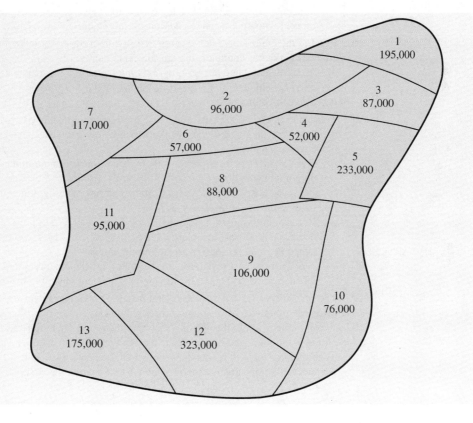

16. The Northshore Bank is working to develop an efficient work schedule for full-time and part-time tellers. The schedule must provide for efficient operation of the bank including adequate customer service, employee breaks, and so on. On Fridays the bank is open from 9:00 A.M. to 7:00 P.M. The number of tellers necessary to provide adequate customer service during each hour of operation is summarized here.

Time	Number of Tellers	Time	Number of Tellers
9:00 A.M.–10:00 A.M.	6	2:00 P.M.–3:00 P.M.	6
10:00 A.M.–11:00 A.M.	4	3:00 P.M.–4:00 P.M.	4
11:00 A.M.–Noon	8	4:00 P.M.–5:00 P.M.	7
Noon –1:00 P.M.	10	5:00 P.M.–6:00 P.M.	6
1:00 P.M.–2:00 P.M.	9	6:00 P.M.–7:00 P.M.	6

Each full-time employee starts on the hour and works a four-hour shift, followed by one hour for lunch, and then a three-hour shift. Part-time employees work one four-hour shift beginning on the hour. Considering salary and fringe benefits, full-time employees cost the bank $15 per hour ($105 a day), and part-time employees cost the bank $8 per hour ($32 a day).

   a. Formulate an integer programming model that can be used to develop a schedule that will satisfy customer service needs at a minimum employee cost. (Hint: Let x_i = number of full-time employees coming on duty at the beginning of hour i and y_i = number of part-time employees coming on duty at the beginning of hour i.)

   b. Solve the LP Relaxation of your model in part (a).

   c. Solve for the optimal schedule of tellers. Comment on the solution.

   d. After reviewing the solution to part (c), the bank manager has realized that some additional requirements must be specified. Specifically, she wants to ensure that one full-time employee is on duty at all times and that there is a staff of at least five full-time employees. Revise your model to incorporate these additional requirements and solve for the optimal solution.

17. Refer to the Ohio Trust bank location problem introduced in Section 6.3. Table 6.3 shows the counties under consideration and the adjacent counties.

   a. Write the complete integer programming model for expansion into the following counties only: Lorain, Huron, Richland, Ashland, Wayne, Medina, and Knox.

   b. Solve the problem in part (a).

18. Refer to Problem 14. Suppose that management determined that its cost estimates to modernize the New York plants were too low. Specifically, suppose that the actual cost is $40 million to modernize each plant.

   a. What changes in your previous 0–1 integer linear programming model are needed to incorporate these changes in costs?

   b. For these cost changes, what recommendations would you now provide management regarding the modernization plan?

   c. Reconsider the solution obtained using the revised cost figures. Suppose that management decides that at least one plant must be in New York. How could this policy restriction be added to your 0–1 integer programming model?

   d. Based on the cost revisions and the policy restrictions presented in part (c), what recommendations would you now provide management regarding the modernization plan?

19. The Bayside Art Gallery is considering installing a video camera security system to reduce its insurance premiums. A diagram of the eight display rooms that Bayside uses for exhibitions is shown in Figure 6.17; the openings between the rooms are numbered 1–13. A security firm has proposed that two-way cameras be installed at some room openings. Each camera has the ability to monitor the two rooms between which the camera is located. For example, if a camera were located at opening number 4, rooms 1 and 4 would be covered; if a camera were located at opening 11, rooms 7 and 8 would be covered; and so on. Management has decided not to

locate a camera system at the entrance to the display rooms. The objective is to provide security coverage for all eight rooms using the minimum number of two-way cameras.

a. Formulate a 0–1 integer linear programming model that will enable Bayside's management to determine the locations for the camera systems.

b. Solve the model formulated in part (a) to determine how many two-way systems to purchase and where they should be located.

c. Suppose that management wants to provide additional security coverage for room 7. Specifically, management wants room 7 to be covered by two cameras. How would your model formulated in part (a) have to change to accommodate this policy restriction?

d. With the policy restriction specified in part (c), determine how many two-way camera systems will need to be purchased and where they will be located.

Figure 6.17   DIAGRAM OF DISPLAY ROOMS FOR PROBLEM 19

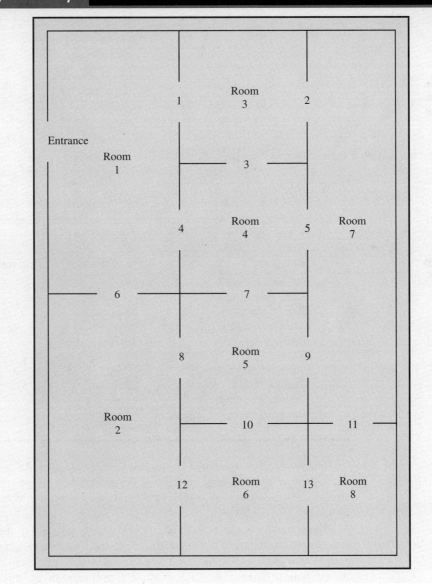

20. The Delta Group is a management consulting firm specializing in the health care industry. A team is being formed to study possible new markets, and a linear programming model has been developed for selecting team members. However, one constraint the president has imposed is a team size of three, five, or seven members. The staff can't figure out how to incorporate this requirement into the model. The current model requires that team members be selected from three departments and uses the following variable definitions.

$$x_1 = \text{the number of employees selected from department 1}$$
$$x_2 = \text{the number of employees selected from department 2}$$
$$x_3 = \text{the number of employees selected from department 3}$$

Show the staff how to write constraints that will ensure that the team will consist of three, five, or seven employees. The following integer variables should be helpful.

$$y_1 = \begin{cases} 1 & \text{if team size is 3} \\ 0 & \text{otherwise} \end{cases}$$

$$y_2 = \begin{cases} 1 & \text{if team size is 5} \\ 0 & \text{otherwise} \end{cases}$$

$$y_3 = \begin{cases} 1 & \text{if team size is 7} \\ 0 & \text{otherwise} \end{cases}$$

Case Problem   TEXTBOOK PUBLISHING

ASW Publishing, Inc., a small publisher of college textbooks, must make a decision regarding which books to publish next year. The books under consideration are listed in the following table, along with the projected three-year sales expected from each book.

Book Subject	Type of Book	Projected Sales (1000s)
Business calculus	New	20
Finite mathematics	Revision	30
General statistics	New	15
Mathematical statistics	New	10
Business statistics	Revision	25
Finance	New	18
Financial accounting	New	25
Managerial accounting	Revision	50
English literature	New	20
German	New	30

The books that are listed as revisions are texts that ASW already has under contract; these texts are being considered for publication as new editions. The books that are listed as new have been reviewed by the company, but contracts have not yet been signed.

The company has three individuals who can be assigned to these projects, all of whom have varying amounts of time available; John has 60 days available, and Susan and Monica both have 40 days available. The days required by each person to complete each project are shown in the following table. For instance, if the business calculus book is published, it will require 30 days of John's time and 40 days of Susan's time. An "X" indicates that the person will not be used on the project. Note that at least two staff members will be assigned to each project except the finance book.

Book Subject	John	Susan	Monica
Business calculus	30	40	X
Finite mathematics	16	24	X
General statistics	24	X	30
Mathematical statistics	20	X	24
Business statistics	10	X	16
Finance	X	X	14
Financial accounting	X	24	26
Managerial accounting	X	28	30
English literature	40	34	30
German	X	50	36

ASW will not publish more than two statistics books or more than one accounting text in a single year. In addition, management has decided that one of the mathematics books (business calculus or finite math) must be published, but not both.

Managerial Report

Prepare a report for the editorial director of ASW that describes your findings and recommendations regarding the best publication strategy for next year. In carrying out your analysis, assume that the fixed costs and the sales revenues per unit are approximately equal for all books; management is interested primarily in maximizing the total sales volume.

The editorial director has also asked that you include recommendations regarding the following possible changes.

1. If it would be advantageous to do so, Susan can be moved off another project to allow her to work 12 more days.
2. If it would be advantageous to do so, Monica can also be made available for another 10 days.
3. If one or more of the revisions could be postponed for another year, should they be? Clearly the company will risk losing market share by postponing a revision.

Include details of your analysis in an appendix to your report.

Case Problem   PRODUCTION SCHEDULING WITH CHANGEOVER COSTS

Buckeye Manufacturing produces heads for engines used in the manufacture of trucks. The production line is highly complex, and it measures 900 feet in length. Two types of engine heads are produced on this line: the P-Head and the H-Head. The P-Head is used in heavy-duty trucks, and the H-Head is used in smaller trucks. Because only one type of head can be produced at a time, the line is either set up to manufacture the P-Head or the H-Head, but not both. Changeovers are made over a weekend; costs are $500 in going from a setup for the P-Head to a setup for the H-Head, and vice-versa. When set up for the P-Head, the maximum production rate is 100 units per week and when set up for the H-Head, the maximum production rate is 80 units per week.

Buckeye has just shut down for the week; the line has been producing the P-Head. The manager wants to plan production and changeovers for the next eight weeks. Currently, Buckeye has an inventory of 125 P-Heads and 143 H-Heads. Inventory carrying costs are charged at an annual rate of 19.5% of the value of inventory. The production cost for the P-Head is $225, and the production cost for the H-Head is $310. The objective in developing a production schedule is to minimize the sum of production cost, plus inventory carrying cost, plus changeover cost.

Buckeye has received the following requirements schedule from its customer (an engine assembly plant) for the next nine weeks.

	Product Demand	
Week	P-Head	H-Head
1	55	38
2	55	38
3	44	30
4	0	0
5	45	48
6	45	48
7	36	58
8	35	57
9	35	58

Safety stock requirements are such that week-ending inventory must provide for at least 80% of the next week's demand.

Managerial Report

Prepare a report for Buckeye's management with a production and changeover schedule for the next eight weeks. Be sure to note how much of the total cost is due to production, how much is due to inventory, and how much is due to changeover.

KETRON*

ARLINGTON, VIRGINIA

Ketron Division of The Bionetics Corporation is an operations research organization with offices throughout the United States. An important part of Ketron's business involves work for local, state, and national governmental agencies.

The Ketron Management Science group is responsible for the development, enhancement, marketing, and support of MPSIII, a proprietary mathematical programming system that runs on a wide range of computers—from PCs to mainframes. Ketron Management Science provides consulting services for the design and implementation of mathematical programming applications. One such mixed-integer programming (MIP) application developed for a major sporting equipment company is outlined in the following sections.

A Customer Order Allocation Model

A major sporting equipment company satisfies demand for its products by making shipments from its factories and other locations around the country where inventories are maintained. The company markets approximately 300 products and has about 30 sources of supply (factory and warehouse locations). The problem of interest is to determine how best to allocate customer orders to the various sources of supply such that the total manufacturing cost is minimized. Although transportation cost is not directly considered, it can be accounted for indirectly by not including variables corresponding to shipments from distant locations. Figure 6.18 provides a graphical representation of this problem. Note in the figure that each customer can receive shipments from only a few of the various sources of supply. For

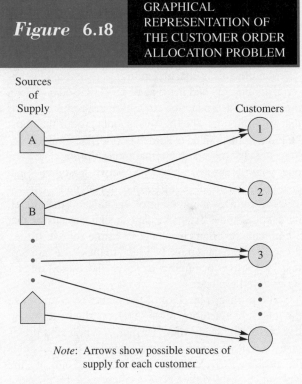

Figure 6.18 GRAPHICAL REPRESENTATION OF THE CUSTOMER ORDER ALLOCATION PROBLEM

Sources of Supply

Customers

Note: Arrows show possible sources of supply for each customer

example, we see that customer 1 may be supplied by source A or B, customer 2 may be supplied only by source A, and so on.

The customer order allocation problem is solved periodically. In a typical period, between 30 and 40 customers are to be supplied. Since most customers require several products, usually between 600 and 800 orders must be assigned to the sources of supply.

*The authors are indebted to J. A. Tomlin for providing this application.

The sporting equipment company classifies each customer order as either a "guaranteed" or a "secondary" order. Guaranteed orders are single-source orders in that they must be filled by a single supplier to ensure that the complete order will be delivered to the customer at one time. This single-source requirement necessitates the use of integer variables in the model. Approximately 80% of the company's orders are guaranteed orders.

Secondary orders can be split among the various sources of supply. These orders are made by customers restocking inventory, and receiving partial shipments from different sources at different times is not a problem. The total of all secondary orders for a given product is treated as a goal or target in the model formulation. Deviations below the goal are permitted, but a penalty cost is associated with these deviations in the objective function. When deviations occur in the optimal solution, the secondary orders will not be completely satisfied; the shortfall is spread among customers in specified proportions.

Manufacturing considerations are such that raw material availability and the type of process used constrain the amount of production. In addition, groups of items that are similar may belong to a "model group" that must be jointly constrained at some factories. Several restrictions are also placed on international shipping. For various policy reasons, shipments between sources and customers in certain countries may not be made. This restriction reduces the number of variables in the model, but it necessitates extensive data checking to ensure that all guaranteed orders have a permissible source. If they do not, some means must be found to make the problem feasible before beginning to solve the mixed-integer programming model.

The primary objective of the model is to minimize the total manufacturing costs subject to the requirement that the guaranteed orders be met. As indicated previously, the deviations below the secondary demand goals are dealt with by defining variables that indicate the amount of any shortage. The cost associated with these variables represents a penalty for not having the item in inventory when it is required.

A description of the constraints and the objective function for the model follows.

Constraints

- *Guaranteed orders:* Each customer's order for each product is assigned to a single supplier. (This is a multiple-choice constraint.)

- *Secondary orders:* For each product, the total amount of secondary demand assigned plus the shortfall must equal the total demand goal (target).
- *Raw material capacities:* The amount of each type of raw material used at a supply source cannot exceed the amount available.
- *Manufacturing capacities:* At each supply source, the capacity for each type of production process cannot be exceeded.
- *Individual product capacities:* The amount of product produced at a site cannot exceed that site's capacity for the product.
- *Group capacities:* The total production for a group of similar products at a site cannot exceed that site's capacity for the group of products.

Objective Function

The objective is to minimize the sum of (1) the manufacturing cost for guaranteed orders, (2) the manufacturing cost for secondary orders, and (3) the penalty cost for unsatisfied secondary demand.

Model Solution

Expecting to obtain an optimal solution for a problem of this complexity is unreasonable. Furthermore, the goal programming methodology for handling the secondary demand means that an "optimum" is of questionable interpretation. A "good" feasible mixed-integer solution is needed. If an integer solution is found whose value is within a few percent of the value of the LP Relaxation solution, the room for improvement is obviously small.

A fairly typical problem has about 800 constraints, 2000 0–1 assignment variables for the guaranteed orders, and 500 continuous variables associated with the secondary orders. This model is solved using Ketron's MPSIII system.

Implementation Notes

In large-scale applications such as this, considerable systems work is involved in generating the data for the model and the managerial reports. Special data processing languages are often available to ease the programming burden of these phases. The DATAFORM language facility of MPSIII is used to generate the data for this model and to prepare the reports.

In this application, making a completely separate preprocessing run is necessary to check for internal consistency and errors in the data. Only when the data appear logically error-free is the model generated and solved. Although tedious, this kind of preprocessing effort is critical for mixed-integer models since the cost of solving the wrong model can be significant. Furthermore, in some cases the data preprocessing step permits the size of the model to be reduced. Such a reduction is possible in this application when a demand for a product has only one legitimate source. The computational benefits of such reductions can be substantial.

Questions

1. Discuss the relationship between the method for handling secondary orders and feasibility.
2. Discuss what is meant by the statement, an "optimum" is of questionable interpretation. Does it mean that any feasible solution is acceptable?

7

WAITING LINE MODELS

Recall the last time that you had to wait at a supermarket checkout counter, for a teller at your local bank, or to be served at a fast-food restaurant. In these and many other waiting line situations, the time spent waiting is undesirable. Adding more checkout clerks, bank tellers, or servers is not always the most economical strategy for improving service, so businesses need to determine ways to keep waiting times within tolerable limits.

Models have been developed to help managers understand and make better decisions concerning the operation of waiting lines. In management science terminology, a waiting line is also known as a **queue,** and the body of knowledge dealing with waiting lines is known as **queuing theory.** In the early 1900s A. K. Erlang, a Danish telephone engineer, began a study of the congestion and waiting times occurring in the completion of telephone calls. Since then, queuing theory has grown far more sophisticated and has been applied to a wide variety of waiting line situations.

Waiting line models consist of mathematical formulas and relationships that can be used to determine the **operating characteristics** (performance measures) for a waiting line. Some of the operating characteristics of interest are

1. the probability that no units are in the system,
2. the average number of units in the waiting line,
3. the average number of units in the system (the number of units in the waiting line plus the number of units being served),
4. the average time a unit spends in the waiting line,
5. the average time a unit spends in the system (the waiting time plus the service time), and
6. the probability that an arriving unit has to wait for service.

Managers who have such information are better able to make decisions that balance desirable service levels against the cost of providing the service.

7.1   THE STRUCTURE OF A WAITING LINE SYSTEM

To illustrate the basic features of a waiting line model, we consider the waiting line at the Burger Dome fast-food restaurant. Burger Dome sells hamburgers, cheeseburgers, french fries, soft drinks, and milk shakes, as well as a limited number of specialty items and dessert selections. Although Burger Dome would like to serve each customer immediately, at times more customers arrive than can be handled by the Burger Dome food-service staff. Thus, customers wait in line to place and receive their orders.

Burger Dome is concerned that the methods they are currently using to serve customers are resulting in excessive waiting times. Management has asked that a waiting line study be performed to help determine the best approach to reducing waiting times and improving service.

The Single-Channel Waiting Line

In the current Burger Dome operation, a server takes a customer's order, determines the total cost of the order, takes the money from the customer, and then fills the order. Once the first customer's order is filled, the server takes the order of the next customer waiting for service. This operation is an example of a **single-channel waiting line.** By this, we mean that each customer entering the Burger Dome restaurant must pass through the *one* channel—one order-taking and order-filling station—to place an order, pay the bill, and receive the food. When more customers arrive than can be served immediately, they form a waiting line and wait for the order-taking and order-filling station to become available. A diagram of the Burger Dome single-channel waiting line is shown in Figure 7.1.

The Distribution of Arrivals

Defining the arrival process for a waiting line involves determining the probability distribution for the number of arrivals in a given period of time. For many waiting line situations, the arrivals occur *randomly and independently* of other arrivals, and we cannot predict when an arrival will occur. In such cases, management scientists have found that the **Poisson probability distribution** provides a good description of the arrival pattern.

The Poisson probability function provides the probability of x arrivals in a specific time period. The probability function is as follows.[1]

$$P(x) = \frac{\lambda^x e^{-\lambda}}{x!} \quad \text{for } x = 0, 1, 2, \ldots \tag{7.1}$$

where

$x =$ the number of arrivals in the time period

$\lambda =$ the mean number of arrivals per time period

$e =$ 2.71828

---

1. The term *x!, x factorial,* is defined as $x! = x(x - 1)(x - 2) \ldots (2)(1)$. For example, $4! = (4)(3)(2)(1) = 24$. For the special case of $x = 0, 0! = 1$ by definition.

Figure 7.1   THE BURGER DOME SINGLE-CHANNEL WAITING LINE

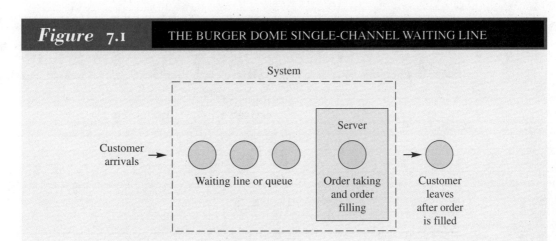

Suppose that Burger Dome has analyzed data on customer arrivals and has concluded that the mean arrival rate is 45 customers per hour. For a 1-minute period, the mean number of arrivals would be $\lambda = 45/60 = 0.75$ arrivals per minute. Thus, we can use the following Poisson probability function to compute the probability of x arrivals during a 1-minute period:

$$P(x) = \frac{\lambda^x e^{-\lambda}}{x!} = \frac{0.75^x e^{-0.75}}{x!} \qquad (7.2)$$

Thus, the probabilities of 0, 1, and 2 arrivals during a 1-minute period are

$$P(0) = \frac{(0.75)^0 e^{-0.75}}{0!} = e^{-0.75} = 0.4724$$

$$P(1) = \frac{(0.75)^1 e^{-0.75}}{1!} = 0.75 e^{-0.75} = 0.75(0.4724) = 0.3543$$

$$P(2) = \frac{(0.75)^2 e^{-0.75}}{2!} = \frac{(0.75)^2 e^{-0.75}}{2!} = \frac{(0.5625)(0.4724)}{2} = 0.1329$$

The probability of no arrivals in a 1-minute period is 0.4724, the probability of 1 arrival in a 1-minute period is 0.3543, and the probability of 2 arrivals in a 1-minute period is 0.1329. Table 7.1 shows the Poisson probability distribution of arrivals during a 1-minute period.

The waiting line models presented in Sections 7.2 and 7.3 use the Poisson probability distribution to describe the customer arrivals at Burger Dome. In practice, you should record the actual number of arrivals per time period for several days or weeks and compare the frequency distribution of the observed number of arrivals to the Poisson probability distribution to determine whether the Poisson probability distribution provides a reasonable approximation of the arrival distribution.

The Distribution of Service Times

The service time is the time a customer spends at the service facility once the service has started. At Burger Dome, the service time starts when a customer begins to place the order with the food server and continues until the customer has received the order. Service times are rarely constant. At Burger Dome, the number of items ordered and the mix of items ordered vary considerably from one customer to the next. Small orders can be handled in a matter of seconds, but large orders may require more than 2 minutes to process.

Table 7.1	POISSON PROBABILITIES FOR THE NUMBER OF ARRIVALS AT A BURGER DOME RESTAURANT DURING A 1-MINUTE PERIOD ($\lambda = 0.75$)

Number of Arrivals	Probability
0	0.4724
1	0.3543
2	0.1329
3	0.0332
4	0.0062
5 or more	0.0010

Management scientists have found that if the probability distribution for the service time can be assumed to follow an **exponential probability distribution,** formulas are available for providing useful information about the operation of the waiting line. Using an exponential probability distribution, the probability that the service time will be less than or equal to a time of length t is

$$P(\text{service time} \le t) = 1 - e^{-\mu t} \tag{7.3}$$

where

$$\mu = \text{the mean number of units that can be served per time period}$$

A property of the exponential probability distribution is that there is a 0.6321 probability that the random variable takes on a value less than the mean. In waiting line applications, the exponential probability distribution indicates that approximately 63% of the service times are less than the mean service time and approximately 37% of the service times are greater than the mean service time.

Suppose that Burger Dome has studied the order-taking and order-filling process and has found that the single food server can process an average of 60 customer orders per hour. On a 1-minute basis, the average or mean service rate would be $\mu = 60/60 = 1$ customer per minute. For example, with $\mu = 1$, we can use equation (7.3) to compute probabilities such as the probability an order can be processed in ½ minute or less, 1 minute or less, and 2 minutes or less. These computations are

$$P(\text{service time} \le 0.5 \text{ min.}) = 1 - e^{-1(0.5)} = 1 - 0.6065 = 0.3935$$
$$P(\text{service time} \le 1.0 \text{ min.}) = 1 - e^{-1(1.0)} = 1 - 0.3679 = 0.6321$$
$$P(\text{service time} \le 2.0 \text{ min.}) = 1 - e^{-1(2.0)} = 1 - 0.1353 = 0.8647$$

Thus, we would conclude that there is a 0.3935 probability that an order can be processed in ½ minute or less, a 0.6321 probability that it can be processed in 1 minute or less, and a 0.8647 probability that it can be processed in 2 minutes or less.

In several waiting line models presented in this chapter, we assume that the probability distributions for the service times follow an exponential probability distribution. In practice, you should collect data on actual service times to see whether the exponential probability distribution is a reasonable approximation of the service times for your application.

Queue Discipline

In describing a waiting line system, we must define the manner in which the waiting units are arranged for service. For the Burger Dome waiting line, and in general for most customer-oriented waiting lines, the units waiting for service are arranged on a **first-come, first-served** basis; this approach is referred to as an **FCFS** queue discipline. However, some situations call for different queue disciplines. For example, when people wait for an elevator, the last one on the elevator is usually the first one to complete service (i.e., the first to leave the elevator). Other types of queue disciplines assign priorities to the waiting units and then serve the unit with the highest priority first. In this chapter we consider only waiting lines based on a first-come, first-served queue discipline.

Steady-State Operation

When the Burger Dome restaurant opens in the morning, no customers are in the restaurant. Gradually, activity builds up to a normal or steady state. The beginning or start-up period is referred to as the **transient period.** The transient period ends when the system reaches the normal or **steady-state operation.** Waiting line models describe the steady-state operating characteristics of the waiting line.

7.2   THE SINGLE-CHANNEL WAITING LINE MODEL WITH POISSON ARRIVALS AND EXPONENTIAL SERVICE TIMES

Waiting line models are often based on assumptions such as Poisson arrivals and exponential service times. When applying any waiting line model, data should be collected on the actual system to ensure that the assumptions of the model are reasonable.

In this section we present formulas that can be used to determine the steady-state operating characteristics for a single-channel waiting line. The formulas are applicable if the arrivals follow a Poisson probability distribution and the service times follow an exponential probability distribution. As these assumptions apply to the Burger Dome waiting line problem introduced in Section 7.1, we show how formulas can be used to determine Burger Dome's operating characteristics and thus provide management with helpful decision-making information.

The mathematical methodology used to derive the formulas for the operating characteristics of waiting lines is rather complex. However, our purpose in this chapter is not to provide the theoretical development of waiting line models, but rather to show how the formulas that have been developed can provide information about operating characteristics of the waiting line. Readers interested in the mathematical development of the formulas can consult the specialized texts listed in the References and Bibliography section at the end of the text.

The Operating Characteristics

Equations (7.4) through (7.10) show that waiting line models do not provide formulas for *optimal* conditions. Rather, these equations provide information about the steady-state operating characteristics of the system.

The following formulas can be used to compute the steady-state operating characteristics for a single-channel waiting line with Poisson arrivals and exponential service times, where

λ = the mean number of arrivals per time period (the mean arrival rate)

μ = the mean number of services per time period (the mean service rate)

1. The probability that no units are in the system:

$$P_0 = 1 - \frac{\lambda}{\mu} \tag{7.4}$$

2. The average number of units in the waiting line:

$$L_q = \frac{\lambda^2}{\mu(\mu - \lambda)} \tag{7.5}$$

3. The average number of units in the system:

$$L = L_q + \frac{\lambda}{\mu} \qquad (7.6)$$

4. The average time a unit spends in the waiting line:

$$W_q = \frac{L_q}{\lambda} \qquad (7.7)$$

5. The average time a unit spends in the system:

$$W = W_q + \frac{1}{\mu} \qquad (7.8)$$

6. The probability that an arriving unit has to wait for service:

$$P_w = \frac{\lambda}{\mu} \qquad (7.9)$$

7. The probability of n units in the system:

$$P_n = \left(\frac{\lambda}{\mu}\right)^n P_0 \qquad (7.10)$$

The values of the **mean arrival rate** λ and the **mean service rate** μ are clearly important components in determining the operating characteristics. Equation (7.9) shows that the ratio of the mean arrival rate to the mean service rate, λ/μ, provides the probability that an arriving unit has to wait because the service facility is busy. Hence, λ/μ often is referred to as the *utilization factor* for the service facility.

The operating characteristics presented in equations (7.4) through (7.10) are applicable only when the mean service rate μ is *greater than* the mean arrival rate λ—in other words, when $\lambda/\mu < 1$. If this condition does not exist, the waiting line will continue to grow without limit because the service facility does not have sufficient capacity to handle the arriving units. Thus, in using equations (7.4) through (7.10), we must have $\mu > \lambda$.

Operating Characteristics for the Burger Dome Problem

Recall that for the Burger Dome problem we had a mean arrival rate of $\lambda = 0.75$ customers per minute and a mean service rate of $\mu = 1$ customer per minute. Thus, with $\mu > \lambda$, equations (7.4) through (7.10) can be used to provide operating characteristics for the Burger Dome single-channel waiting line:

$$P_0 = 1 - \frac{\lambda}{\mu} = 1 - \frac{0.75}{1} = 0.25$$

$$L_q = \frac{\lambda^2}{\mu(\mu - \lambda)} = \frac{0.75^2}{1(1 - 0.75)} = 2.25 \text{ customers}$$

$$L = L_q + \frac{\lambda}{\mu} = 2.25 + \frac{0.75}{1} = 3 \text{ customers}$$

$$W_q = \frac{L_q}{\lambda} = \frac{2.25}{0.75} = 3 \text{ minutes}$$

$$W = W_q + \frac{1}{\mu} = 3 + \frac{1}{1} = 4 \text{ minutes}$$

Problem 5 asks you to compute the operating characteristics for a single-channel waiting line application.

$$P_w = \frac{\lambda}{\mu} = \frac{0.75}{1} = 0.75$$

Equation (7.10) can be used to determine the probability of any number of customers in the system. Applying it provides the probability information summarized in Table 7.2.

Table 7.2	THE PROBABILITY OF n CUSTOMERS IN THE SYSTEM FOR THE BURGER DOME WAITING LINE PROBLEM

Number of Customers	Probability
0	0.2500
1	0.1875
2	0.1406
3	0.1055
4	0.0791
5	0.0593
6	0.0445
7 or more	0.1335

The Manager's Use of Waiting Line Models

The results of the single-channel waiting line for Burger Dome show several important things about the operation of the waiting line. In particular, customers wait an average of 3 minutes before beginning to place an order, which appears somewhat long for a business based on fast service. In addition, the facts that the average number of customers waiting in line is 2.25 and that 75% of the arriving customers have to wait for service are indicators that something should be done to improve the waiting line operation. Table 7.2 shows a 0.1335 probability that seven or more customers are in the Burger Dome system at one time. This condition indicates a fairly high probability that Burger Dome will experience some long waiting lines if it continues to use the single-channel operation.

If the operating characteristics are unsatisfactory in terms of meeting company standards for service, Burger Dome's management should consider alternative designs or plans for improving the waiting line operation.

Spreadsheet Solution for the Burger Dome Single-Channel Waiting Line

Spreadsheets provide a fast and easy way to compute the operating characteristics of a waiting line system. Figure 7.2 shows the spreadsheet for the Burger Dome single-channel waiting line system. Note that we have listed the assumptions of Poisson arrivals and exponential service times in cells A4 and A5 as a reminder that these are the assumptions for the waiting line model being used to analyze the Burger Dome system.

Only two input values are required: the mean arrival rate, $\lambda = 0.75$ customers per minute, shown in cell B7; and the mean service rate, $\mu = 1$ customer per minute, shown in cell B8. The operating characteristics provided by equations (7.4) through (7.9) are computed using the following cell formulas:

Cell C13	Probability that no customers are in the system, P_0	
	$=1-B7/B8$	
Cell C14	Average number of customers in the waiting line, L_q	
	$=B7\char94 2/(B8*(B8-B7))$	
Cell C15	Average number of customers in the system, L	
	$=C14+B7/B8$	

	A	B	C
1	**Burger Dome Single-Channel Waiting Line**		
2			
3	**Assumptions**		
4	**Poisson Arrivals**		
5	**Exponential Service Times**		
6			
7	Mean Arrival Rate	0.75	
8	Mean Service Rate	1	
9			
10			
11	**Operating Characteristics**		
12			
13	Probability that no customers are in the system, P_o		0.2500
14	Average number of customers in the waiting line, L_q		2.2500
15	Average number of customers in the system, L		3.0000
16	Average time a customer spends in the waiting line, W_q		3.0000
17	Average time a customer spends in the system, W		4.0000
18	Probability an arriving customer has to wait, P_w		0.7500

SPREADSHEET
BURGER DOME
SINGLE
CHANNEL

Cell C16   Average time a customer spends in the waiting line, W_q
=C14/B7

Cell C17   Average time a customer spends in the system, W
=C16+1/B8

Cell C18   Probability an arriving customer has to wait for service, P_w
=B7/B8

Improving the Waiting Line Operation

Waiting line models often indicate where improvements in operating characteristics are desirable. However, the decision of how to modify the waiting line configuration to improve the operating characteristics must be based on the insights and creativity of the analyst.

After reviewing the operating characteristics provided by the waiting line model, Burger Dome's management concluded that improvements designed to reduce waiting times are desirable. To make improvements in the waiting line operation, analysts often focus on ways to improve the service rate. Generally, service rate improvements are obtained by making either or both of the following changes:

1. Increase the mean service rate μ by making a creative design change or by using new technology.
2. Add service channels so that more customers can be served simultaneously.

Assume that in considering alternative 1, Burger Dome's management decides to employ an order filler who will assist the order taker at the cash register. The customer begins the service process by placing the order with the order taker. As the order is placed, the order taker announces the order over an intercom system, and the order filler begins filling the order. When the order is completed, the order taker handles the money, while the order filler continues to fill the order. With this design, Burger Dome's management estimates the mean service rate can be increased from the current service rate of 60 customers per hour to 75 customers per hour. Thus, the mean service rate for the revised system is $\mu = 75/60 = 1.25$ customers per minute. Entering a mean service rate of $\mu = 1.25$ into spreadsheet cell B8 provides the operating characteristics shown in Figure 7.3.

The revised spreadsheet shows that all the operating characteristics have improved because of the increased service rate. In particular, the average time a customer spends in the waiting line has been reduced from 3 to 1.2 minutes and the average time in the system has been reduced from 4 to 2 minutes. Are other alternatives possible for increasing the service rate? If so, and if the mean service rate μ can be identified for each alternative, the spreadsheet can be used to determine any improvements in the system. The added cost of any proposed change can be compared to the corresponding service improvements to help the manager determine whether the proposed service improvements are worthwhile.

As mentioned previously, another option that is usually available is to provide one or more additional service channels so that more than one customer may be served at the same time. The extension of the single-channel waiting line model to the multiple-channel waiting line model is the topic of the next section.

Problem 11 asks you to determine whether a change in the mean service rate will meet the company's service guideline for its customers.

Figure 7.3	SPREADSHEET SOLUTION FOR THE BURGER DOME SINGLE-CHANNEL PROBLEM WITH SERVICE RATE $\mu = 1.25$

SPREADSHEET BURGER DOME SINGLE CHANNEL

	A	B	C
1	**Burger Dome Single-Channel Waiting Line**		
2			
3	**Assumptions**		
4	**Poisson Arrivals**		
5	**Exponential Service Times**		
6			
7	Mean Arrival Rate	0.75	
8	Mean Service Rate	1.25	
9			
10			
11	**Operating Characteristics**		
12			
13	Probability that no customers are in the system, P_o		0.4000
14	Average number of customers in the waiting line, L_q		0.9000
15	Average number of customers in the system, L		1.5000
16	Average time a customer spends in the waiting line, W_q		1.2000
17	Average time a customer spends in the system, W		2.0000
18	Probability an arriving customer has to wait, P_w		0.6000

The assumption that arrivals follow a Poisson probability distribution is equivalent to the assumption that the time between arrivals has an exponential probability distribution. For example, if the arrivals for a waiting line follow a Poisson probability distribution with a mean of 20 arrivals per hour, the time between arrivals will follow an exponential probability distribution, with a mean time between arrivals of $1/20$ or 0.05 hour.

Many individuals believe that whenever the mean service rate μ is greater than the mean arrival rate λ, the system should be able to handle or serve all arivals. However, as the Burger Done example shows, the variability of arrival times and service times may result in long waiting times even when the mean service rate exceeds the mean arrival rate. A contribution of waiting line models is that they can point out undesirable waiting line operating characteristics even when the $\mu > \lambda$ condition appears satisfactory.

7.3 THE MULTIPLE-CHANNEL WAITING LINE MODEL WITH POISSON ARRIVALS AND EXPONENTIAL SERVICE TIMES

A **multiple-channel waiting line** consists of two or more channels or service locations that are assumed to be identical in terms of service capability. In the multiple-channel system, arriving units wait in a single waiting line and then move to the first available channel to be served.

The single-channel Burger Dome operation could be expanded to a two-channel system by opening a second service channel. Figure 7.4 shows a diagram of the Burger Dome two-channel waiting line.

In this section we present formulas that can be used to determine the steady-state operating characteristics for a multiple-channel waiting line. These formulas are applicable if

1. the arrivals follow a Poisson probability distribution,
2. the service time for each channel follows an exponential probability distribution,
3. the mean service rate μ is the same for each channel,
4. the arrivals wait in a single waiting line and then move to the first open channel for service.

You may be familiar with multiple-channel systems that also have multiple waiting lines. The waiting line model in this section has multiple channels, but only a single waiting line. Operating characteristics for a multiple-channel system are better when a single waiting line, rather than multiple waiting lines, is used.

The Operating Characteristics

The following formulas can be used to compute the steady-state operating characteristics for multiple-channel waiting lines, where

$$\lambda = \text{the mean arrival rate for the system}$$

$$\mu = \text{the mean service rate for } each \text{ channel}$$

$$k = \text{the number of channels}$$

1. The probability that no units are in the system:

$$P_0 = \frac{1}{\displaystyle\sum_{n=0}^{k-1} \frac{(\lambda/\mu)^n}{n!} + \frac{(\lambda/\mu)^k}{k!}\left(\frac{k\mu}{k\mu - \lambda}\right)} \tag{7.11}$$

2. The average number of units in the waiting line:

$$L_q = \frac{(\lambda/\mu)^k \lambda \mu}{(k-1)!(k\mu - \lambda)^2} P_0 \tag{7.12}$$

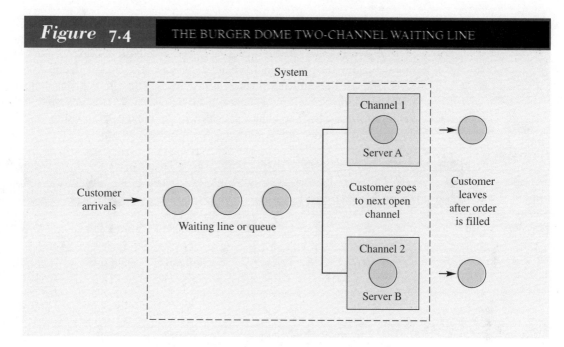

Figure 7.4   THE BURGER DOME TWO-CHANNEL WAITING LINE

3. The average number of units in the system:

$$L = L_q + \frac{\lambda}{\mu} \tag{7.13}$$

4. The average time a unit spends in the waiting line:

$$W_q = \frac{L_q}{\lambda} \tag{7.14}$$

5. The average time a unit spends in the system:

$$W = W_q + \frac{1}{\mu} \tag{7.15}$$

6. The probability that an arriving unit has to wait for service:

$$P_w = \frac{1}{k!} \left(\frac{\lambda}{\mu} \right)^k \left(\frac{k\mu}{k\mu - \lambda} \right) P_0 \tag{7.16}$$

7. The probability of n units in the system:

$$P_n = \frac{(\lambda/\mu)^n}{n!} P_0 \quad \text{for } n \leq k \tag{7.17}$$

$$P_n = \frac{(\lambda/\mu)^n}{k!k^{(n-k)}} P_0 \quad \text{for } n > k \tag{7.18}$$

Because μ is the mean service rate for each channel, $k\mu$ is the mean service rate for the multiple-channel system. As was true for the single-channel waiting line model, the formulas for the operating characteristics of multiple-channel waiting lines can be applied only in situations where the mean service rate for the system is greater than the mean arrival rate for the system; in other words, the formulas are applicable only if $k\mu$ is greater than λ.

Some expressions for the operating characteristics of multiple-channel waiting lines are more complex than their single-channel counterparts. However, equations (7.11) through (7.18) provide the same information as provided by the single-channel model. To help simplify the use of the multiple-channel equations, Table 7.3 contains values of P_0 for selected values of λ/μ and k. The values provided in the table correspond to cases where $k\mu > \lambda$, and hence the service rate is sufficient to process all arrivals.

Table 7.3	VALUES OF P_0 FOR MULTIPLE-CHANNEL WAITING LINES WITH POISSON ARRIVALS AND EXPONENTIAL SERVICE TIMES

| | Number of Channels (k) | | | |
Ratio λ/μ	2	3	4	5
0.15	0.8605	0.8607	0.8607	0.8607
0.20	0.8182	0.8187	0.8187	0.8187
0.25	0.7778	0.7788	0.7788	0.7788
0.30	0.7391	0.7407	0.7408	0.7408
0.35	0.7021	0.7046	0.7047	0.7047
0.40	0.6667	0.6701	0.6703	0.6703
0.45	0.6327	0.6373	0.6376	0.6376
0.50	0.6000	0.6061	0.6065	0.6065
0.55	0.5686	0.5763	0.5769	0.5769
0.60	0.5385	0.5479	0.5487	0.5488
0.65	0.5094	0.5209	0.5219	0.5220
0.70	0.4815	0.4952	0.4965	0.4966
0.75	0.4545	0.4706	0.4722	0.4724
0.80	0.4286	0.4472	0.4491	0.4493
0.85	0.4035	0.4248	0.4271	0.4274
0.90	0.3793	0.4035	0.4062	0.4065
0.95	0.3559	0.3831	0.3863	0.3867
1.00	0.3333	0.3636	0.3673	0.3678
1.20	0.2500	0.2941	0.3002	0.3011
1.40	0.1765	0.2360	0.2449	0.2463
1.60	0.1111	0.1872	0.1993	0.2014
1.80	0.0526	0.1460	0.1616	0.1646
2.00		0.1111	0.1304	0.1343
2.20		0.0815	0.1046	0.1094
2.40		0.0562	0.0831	0.0889
2.60		0.0345	0.0651	0.0721
2.80		0.0160	0.0521	0.0581
3.00			0.0377	0.0466
3.20			0.0273	0.0372
3.40			0.0186	0.0293
3.60			0.0113	0.0228
3.80			0.0051	0.0174
4.00				0.0130
4.20				0.0093
4.40				0.0063
4.60				0.0038
4.80				0.0017

Operating Characteristics for the Burger Dome Problem

To illustrate the multiple-channel waiting line model, we return to the Burger Dome fast-food restaurant waiting line problem. Suppose that management wants to evaluate the desirability of opening a second order-processing station so that two customers can be served simultaneously. Assume a single waiting line with the first customer in line moving to the first available server. Let us evaluate the operating characteristics for this two-channel system.

We use equations (7.12) through (7.18) for the $k = 2$ channel system. For a mean arrival rate of $\lambda = 0.75$ customers per minute and mean service rate of $\mu = 1$ customer per minute for each channel, we obtain the operating characteristics:

$$P_0 = 0.4545 \quad \text{(from Table 7.3 with } \lambda/\mu = 0.75\text{)}$$

$$L_q = \frac{(0.75/1)^2(0.75)(1)}{(2 - 1)![2(1) - 0.75]^2}(0.4545) = 0.1227 \text{ customer}$$

$$L = L_q + \frac{\lambda}{\mu} = 0.1227 + \frac{0.75}{1} = 0.8727 \text{ customer}$$

$$W_q = \frac{L_q}{\lambda} = \frac{0.1227}{0.75} = 0.1636 \text{ minute}$$

$$W = W_q + \frac{1}{\mu} = 0.1636 + \frac{1}{1} = 1.1636 \text{ minutes}$$

$$P_w = \frac{1}{2!}\left(\frac{0.75}{1}\right)^2\left[\frac{2(1)}{2(1) - 0.75}\right](0.4545) = 0.2045$$

Using equations (7.17) and (7.18), we can compute the probabilities of n customers in the system. The results from these computations are summarized in Table 7.4.

Try Problem 19, which will give you practice in determining the operating characteristics for a two-channel waiting line.

Spreadsheet Solution for the Burger Dome Multiple-Channel Waiting Line

To show how a spreadsheet can be used to compute the operating characteristics of a multiple-channel waiting line with Poisson arrivals and exponential service times, we use the same spreadsheet format that we used for the single-channel waiting line model in Figures 7.2 and 7.3. The only difference is that we use equations (7.11) through (7.16) to

Table 7.4	THE PROBABILITY OF n CUSTOMERS IN THE SYSTEM FOR THE BURGER DOME TWO-CHANNEL WAITING LINE

Number of Customers	Probability
0	0.4545
1	0.3409
2	0.1278
3	0.0479
4	0.0180
5 or more	0.0109

compute the desired operating characteristics. Figure 7.5 shows the spreadsheet for the Burger Dome multiple-channel waiting line system. The assumptions of Poisson arrivals and exponential service times are shown in cells A4 and A5. The three required inputs and their cell locations are as follows: the number of channels, $k = 2$, shown in cell B7; the mean arrival rate, $\lambda = 0.75$ customers per minute, shown in cell B8; and the mean service rate, $\mu = 1$ customer per minute, shown in cell B9. The six operating characteristics in Figure 7.5 are based upon the values of k, λ and μ.

In some cases, the equations used to compute the operating characteristics for a multiple-channel waiting line are more complex than the equations used for a single-channel waiting line. Note in particular equation (7.11), which provides the probability that no units are in the system, P_0. This equation is substantially more complex than the equation for P_0 shown in equation (7.4). In fact, equation (7.11) is so complex that we will develop a special Excel function to evaluate it. The details of developing a special Excel function to compute P_0 are discussed in the appendix of this chapter. Since the value of P_0 is based on the number of channels k, the mean arrival rate λ and the mean service rate μ, the format of the function is $P_0(k, \lambda, \mu)$; we will refer to this function as the P_0 function. Since the values of k, λ, and μ are in cells B7, B8, and B9, respectively, we can enter the newly created P_0 function in the spreadsheet as follows:

Cell C14   Probability that no customers are in the system, P_0

$$=P0(B7,B8,B9)$$

SPREADSHEET
BURGER DOME
MULTIPLE
CHANNEL

Figure 7.5   SPREADSHEET SOLUTION FOR THE BURGER DOME TWO-CHANNEL PROBLEM

	A	B	C
1	**Burger Dome Multiple-Channel Waiting Line**		
2			
3	**Assumptions**		
4	**Poisson Arrivals**		
5	**Exponential Service Times**		
6			
7	Number of Channels	2	
8	Mean Arrival Rate	0.75	
9	Mean Service Rate Per Channel	1	
10			
11			
12	**Operating Characteristics**		
13			
14	Probability that no customers are in the system, P_0		0.4545
15	Average number of customers in the waiting line, L_q		0.1227
16	Average number of customers in the system, L		0.8727
17	Average time a customer spends in the waiting line, W_q		0.1636
18	Average time a customer spends in the system, W		1.1636
19	Probability an arriving customer has to wait, P_w		0.2045

As shown in Figure 7.5, this function provides the probability of no customers in the system, $P_0 = 0.4545$.

The operating characteristics provided by equations (7.12) through (7.16) are computed using the following cell formulas:[2]

Cell C15	Average number of customers in the waiting line, L_q
	$=(((B8/B9)^{\wedge}B7*B8*B9)/(FACT (B7-1)*(B7*B9-B8)^{\wedge}2))*C14$
Cell C16	Average number of customers in the system, L
	$=C15+B8/B9$
Cell C17	Average time a customer spends in the waiting line, W_q
	$=C15/B8$
Cell C18	Average time a customer spends in the system, W
	$=C17+1/B9$
Cell C19	Probability an arriving customer has to wait for service, P_w
	$=(1/FACT(B7))*(B8/B9)^{\wedge}B7*(B7*B9/(B7*B9-B8))*C14$

The spreadsheet shown in Figure 7.5 can be used to compute the operating characteristics for both single-channel and multiple-channel waiting lines with Poisson arrivals and exponential service times. For example, entering 1 for the number of channels into cell B7 will provide the Burger Dome single-channel operating characteristics shown previously in Figure 7.2. In fact, the spreadsheet in Figure 7.5 is a general spreadsheet that can be used for any waiting line where the assumptions of Poisson arrivals and exponential service times are appropriate. Entering the number of channels, the mean arrival rate and the mean service rate is all that is necessary to compute the desired operating characteristic information. Thus, the spreadsheet provides a quick and easy way to determine how alternative designs affect the operating characteristics of the waiting line.

Clearly the two-channel system will significantly improve the operating characteristics of the waiting line. However, adding an order filler at each service station would further increase the mean service rate and improve the operating characteristics. The final decision regarding the staffing policy at Burger Dome rests with the Burger Dome management. The waiting line study has simply provided the operating characteristics that can be anticipated under three configurations: a single-channel system with one employee, a single-channel system with two employees, and a two-channel system with an employee for each channel. After considering these results, what action would you recommend? In this case, Burger Dome adopted the following policy statement: For periods when customer arrivals are expected to average 45 customers per hour, Burger Dome will open two order-processing channels with one employee assigned to each.

By changing the mean arrival rate λ to reflect arrival rates at different times of the day, and then computing the operating characteristics, Burger Dome's management can establish guidelines and policies that tell the store managers when they should schedule service operations with a single channel, two channels, or perhaps even three or more channels. The Management Science in Action article for Lourdes Hospital shows how a multiple-channel waiting line model has been used to help make hospital staffing decisions.

---

2. Cell formulas C15 and C19 use Excel's FACT worksheet function to compute the factorial of a number. For instance, FACT (B7 − 1) in cell formula C15 is used to compute the value of $(k − 1)!$ in equation (7.12).

The multiple-channel waiting line model is based on a single waiting line. You may have also encountered situations where each of the k channels has its own waiting line. Management scientists have shown that the operating characteristics of multiple-channel systems are better if a single waiting line is used. People like them better also; no one who comes in after you can be served ahead of you. Thus, when possible, banks, airline reservation counters, food-service establishments, and other businesses typically use a single waiting line for a multiple-channel system.

MANAGEMENT SCIENCE IN ACTION

HOSPITAL STAFFING BASED ON A MULTIPLE-CHANNEL WAITING LINE MODEL*

Lourdes Hospital in Binghamton, New York, uses a centralized staff to schedule appointments for the hospital's outpatient, inpatient, and ambulance services. Physicians, their staffs, hospital personnel, and patients contact the centralized scheduling office by telephone to establish desired appointment times.

Efficiency of the scheduling process depends on the department's staff being able to process incoming telephone calls in a timely manner. Periodically, incoming requests for services overload the staff's ability to answer the telephone and process the appointments. As a result, users reported undesirable delays and lengthy waiting times. Management used a waiting line model to study the operation and suggest staffing changes that could improve the efficiency of the centralized scheduling process.

Data were collected on the number of telephone calls that arrived during each 15-minute period. The calls were random, not depending on the day of the week. A Poisson probability distribution was a good description of the random arrivals, with peak arrival times occurring between 9:00 A.M. and 11:30 A.M. and between 2:00 P.M. and 3:45 P.M. each day. An investigation of service times found that, although service times were not exactly exponential, the exponential probability distribution provided a reasonable approximation.

In effect, the hospital's scheduling service was viewed as a multiple-channel waiting line with Poisson arrivals and exponential service times. The number of channels was simply the number of individuals on the scheduling staff. With the mean arrival rate adjusted for the different periods of the day, a waiting line model with k channels was used to estimate the probability that an arriving call would have to wait for service. The staff size was determined by selecting the number of channels that kept the steady state probability of waiting to no more than 10%. Staff schedules and workloads were adjusted, efficiency improved, and the number of complaints about waiting for service declined.

*Based on S. R. Agnihothri and P. F. Taylor, "Staffing a Centralized Appointment Scheduling Department in Lourdes Hospital," *Interfaces* 21, no. 5 (September–October 1991): 1–11.

7.4 SOME GENERAL RELATIONSHIPS FOR WAITING LINE MODELS

In Sections 7.2 and 7.3 we presented formulas for computing the operating characteristics for single-channel and multiple-channel waiting lines with Poisson arrivals and exponential service times. The operating characteristics of interest included

L_q = the average number of units in the waiting line

L = the average number of units in the system

W_q = the average time a unit spends in the waiting line

W = the average time a unit spends in the system

John D. C. Little showed that several relationships exist among these four characteristics and that these relationships apply to a variety of different waiting line systems. Two of the relationships, referred to as *Little's flow equations,* are

$$L = \lambda W \tag{7.19}$$

$$L_q = \lambda W_q \tag{7.20}$$

Equation (7.19) shows that the average number of units in the system, L, can be found by multiplying the mean arrival rate, λ, by the average time a unit spends in the system, W. Equation (7.20) shows that the same relationship holds between the average number of units in the waiting line, L_q, and the average time a unit spends in the waiting line, W_q.

Using equation (7.20) and solving for W_q, we obtain

$$W_q = \frac{L_q}{\lambda} \tag{7.21}$$

Equation (7.21) follows directly from Little's second flow equation. We used it for the single-channel waiting line model in Section 7.2 and the multiple-channel waiting line model in Section 7.3 [see equations (7.7) and (7.14)]. Once L_q is computed for either of these models, equation (7.21) can then be used to compute W_q.

Another general expression that applies to waiting line models is that the average time in the system, W, is equal to the average time in the waiting line, W_q, plus the average service time. For a system with a mean service rate μ, the mean service time is $1/\mu$. Thus, we have the general relationship

$$W = W_q + \frac{1}{\mu} \tag{7.22}$$

Recall that we used equation (7.22) to provide the average time in the system for both the single- and multiple-channel waiting line models [see equations (7.8) and (7.15)].

The advantage of Little's flow equations is that they show how operating characteristics L, L_q, W, and W_q are related in any waiting line system. Arrivals and service times do not have to follow specific probability distributions for the flow equations to be applicable.

The importance of Little's flow equations is that they apply to *any waiting line model* regardless of whether arrivals follow the Poisson probability distribution and regardless of whether service times follow the exponential probability distribution. For example, in a study of the grocery checkout counters at Murphy's Foodliner, an analyst concluded that arrivals follow the Poisson probability distribution with the mean arrival rate of 24 customers per hour or $\lambda = 24/60 = 0.40$ customers per minute. However, the analyst found that service times follow a normal probability distribution rather than an exponential probability distribution. The mean service rate was found to be 30 customers per hour or $\mu = 30/60 = 0.50$ customers per minute. A time study of actual customer waiting times showed that, on average, a customer spends 4.5 minutes in the system (waiting time plus checkout time); that is, $W = 4.5$. Using the waiting line relationships discussed in this section, we can now compute other operating characteristics for this waiting line.

First, using equation (7.22) and solving for W_q, we have

$$W_q = W - \frac{1}{\mu} = 4.5 - \frac{1}{0.50} = 2.5 \text{ minutes}$$

The application of Little's flow equations are demonstrated in Problem 25.

With both W and W_q known, we can use Little's flow equations, (7.19) and (7.20), to compute

$$L = \lambda W = 0.40(4.5) = 1.8 \text{ customers}$$
$$L_q = \lambda W_q = 0.40(2.5) = 1 \text{ customer}$$

The manager of Murphy's Foodliner can now review these operating characteristics to see whether action should be taken to improve the service and to reduce the waiting time and the length of the waiting line.

7.5   ECONOMIC ANALYSIS OF WAITING LINES

Frequently, decisions involving the design of waiting lines will be based on a subjective evaluation of the operating characteristics of the waiting line. For example, a manager may decide that an average waiting time of one minute or less and an average of two customers or less in the system are reasonable goals. The waiting line models presented in the preceding sections can be used to determine the number of channels that will meet the manager's waiting line performance goals.

On the other hand, a manager may want to identify the cost of operating the waiting line system and then base the decision regarding system design on a minimum hourly or daily operating cost. Before an economic analysis of a waiting line can be conducted, a total-cost model, which includes the cost of waiting and the cost of service, must be developed.

To develop a total-cost model for a waiting line, we begin by defining the notation to be used:

> Generally, c_s is easier to estimate than c_w. The reason is that the cost of customer waiting, c_w, is more subjective in that it often includes the cost of lost goodwill owing to customer waiting time.

$$c_w = \text{the waiting cost per time period for each unit}$$
$$L = \text{the average number of units in the system}$$
$$c_s = \text{the service cost per time period for each channel}$$
$$k = \text{the number of channels}$$
$$TC = \text{the total cost per time period}$$

> Waiting cost is based on average number of units in the system. It includes the time spent waiting in line plus the time spent waiting while being served.

The total cost is the sum of the waiting cost and the service cost; that is,

$$TC = c_w L + c_s k \tag{7.23}$$

To conduct an economic analysis of a waiting line, we must obtain reasonable estimates of the waiting cost and the service cost. Of these two costs, the waiting cost is usually the more difficult to evaluate. In the Burger Dome restaurant problem, the waiting cost would be the cost per minute for a customer waiting for service. This cost is not a direct cost to Burger Dome. However, if Burger Dome ignores this cost and allows long waiting lines, customers ultimately will take their business elsewhere. Thus, Burger Dome will experience lost sales and, in effect, incur a cost.

> Adding more channels always improves the operating characteristics of the waiting line and reduces the waiting cost. However, additional channels increases the service cost. An economic analysis of waiting lines attempts to find the number of channels that will minimize total cost by balancing the waiting cost and the service cost.

The service cost is generally easier to determine. This cost is the relevant cost associated with operating each service channel. In the Burger Dome problem, this cost would include the server's wages, benefits, and any other direct costs associated with operating the service channel. At Burger Dome, this cost is estimated to be $7 per hour.

To demonstrate the use of equation (7.23), we assume that Burger Dome is willing to assign a cost of $10 per hour for customer waiting time. We use the average number of units in the system, L, as computed in Sections 7.2 and 7.3 to obtain the total hourly cost for the single-channel and two-channel systems:

Single-channel system ($L = 3$ customers)

$$TC = c_w L + c_s k$$
$$= \$10(3) + \$7(1) = \$37.00 \text{ per hour}$$

Two-channel system ($L = 0.8727$ customer)

$$TC = c_w L + c_s k$$
$$= \$10(0.8727) + \$7(2) = \$22.73 \text{ per hour}$$

Problem 21 will test your ability to conduct an economic analysis of proposed single-channel and two-channel waiting line systems.

Thus, based on the cost data provided by Burger Dome, the two-channel system provides the most economical operation.

Figure 7.6 shows that an economic analysis of waiting lines can be easily handled using a spreadsheet. The total cost per time period is computed in cell C26 using the cell

Figure 7.6   SPREADSHEET SOLUTION FOR THE BURGER DOME TWO-CHANNEL PROBLEM INCLUDING TOTAL COST

SPREADSHEET
BURGER DOME
MULTIPLE
CHANNEL

	A	B	C
1	**Burger Dome Multiple-Channel Waiting Line**		
2			
3	**Assumptions**		
4	**Poisson Arrivals**		
5	**Exponential Service Times**		
6			
7	Number of Channels	2	
8	Mean Arrival Rate	0.75	
9	Mean Service Rate Per Channel	1	
10			
11			
12	**Operating Characteristics**		
13			
14	Probability that no customers are in the system, P_0		0.4545
15	Average number of customers in the waiting line, L_q		0.1227
16	Average number of customers in the system, L		0.8727
17	Average time a customer spends in the waiting line, W_q		0.1636
18	Average time a customer spends in the system, W		1.1636
19	Probability an arriving customer has to wait, P_w		0.2045
20			
21	**Total Cost per Time Period (Optional)**		
22			
23	The waiting cost per unit	10	
24	The service cost per channel	7	
25			
26	Total cost per time period		$ 22.73

formula =B23*C16+B24*B7. Since an economic analysis of a waiting line is not always requested, the total cost section of the spreadsheet is labeled optional.

Figure 7.7 shows the general shapes of the cost curves in the economic analysis of waiting lines. The service cost increases as the number of channels is increased. However, with more channels, the service is better. As a result, waiting time and cost decrease as the number of channels is increased. The number of channels that will provide a good approximation of the minimum total-cost design can be found by evaluating the total cost for several design alternatives.

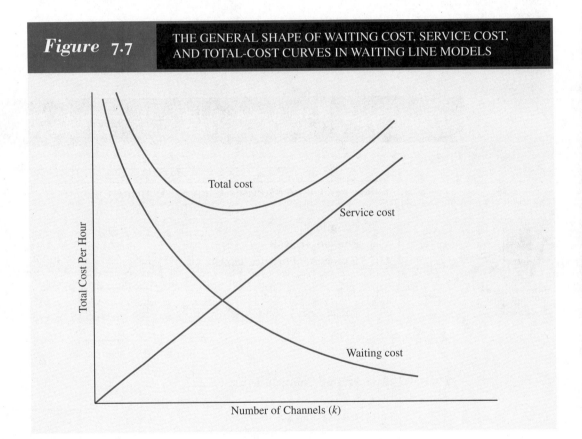

Figure 7·7   THE GENERAL SHAPE OF WAITING COST, SERVICE COST, AND TOTAL-COST CURVES IN WAITING LINE MODELS

Total cost

Service cost

Waiting cost

Total Cost Per Hour

Number of Channels (k)

N O T E S

and Comments

1. In dealing with government agencies and utility companies, customers may not be able to take their business elsewhere. In these situations, no lost business occurs when long waiting times are encountered. This condition is one reason that service in such organizations may be poor and that customers in such situations may experience long waiting times.

2. In some instances, the organization providing the service also employs the units waiting for the service. For example, consider the case of a company that owns and operates the trucks used to deliver goods to and from its manufacturing plant. In addition to the costs associated with the trucks waiting to be loaded or unloaded, the firm also pays the wages of the truck loaders and unloaders who operate the service channel. In this case, the cost of having the trucks wait and the cost of operating the service channel are direct expenses to the firm. An economic analysis of the waiting line system is highly recommended for these types of situations.

···/ /············

7.6   OTHER WAITING LINE MODELS

D. G. Kendall suggested a notation that is helpful in classifying the wide variety of different waiting line models that have been developed. The three-symbol Kendall notation is as follows:

$$A/B/k$$

where

A   denotes the probability distribution for the arrivals

B   denotes the probability distribution for the service time

k   denotes the number of channels

Depending on the letter appearing in the A or B position, a wide variety of waiting line systems can be described. The letters that are commonly used are as follows:

M   designates a Poisson probability distribution for the arrivals
or an exponential probability distribution for service time

D   designates that the arrivals or the service time is
deterministic or constant

G   designates that the arrivals or the service time has a general
probability distribution with a known mean and variance

Using the Kendall notation, the single-channel waiting line model with Poisson arrivals and exponential service times is classified as an M/M/1 model. The 2-channel waiting line model with Poisson arrivals and exponential service times presented in Section 7.3 would be classified as an M/M/2 model.

N O T E S
and Comments

In some cases, the Kendall notation is extended to five symbols. The fourth symbol indicates the largest number of units that can be in the system, and the fifth symbol indicates the size of the population. The fourth symbol is used in situations where the waiting line can hold a finite or maximum number of units, and the fifth symbol is necessary when the population of arriving units or customers is finite. When the fourth and fifth symbols of the Kendall notation are omitted, the waiting line system is assumed to have infinite capacity, and the population is assumed to be infinite.

···/ /············

7.7   THE SINGLE-CHANNEL WAITING LINE MODEL WITH POISSON ARRIVALS AND ARBITRARY SERVICE TIMES

Let us return to the single-channel waiting line model where arrivals are described by a Poisson probability distribution. However, we now assume that the probability distribution for the service times is not an exponential probability distribution. Thus, using the Kendall notation, the waiting line model that is appropriate is an M/G/1 model, where G denotes a general or unspecified probability distribution.

Operating Characteristics for the *M/G/*1 Model

When providing input to the *M/G/*1 model, you should be consistent in terms of the time period. For example, if λ and μ are expressed in terms of the number of units per *hour,* the standard deviation of the service time should be expressed in *hours.* The example that follows uses minutes as the time period for the arrival and service data.

The notation used to describe the operating characteristics for the *M/G/*1 model is

$$\lambda = \text{the mean arrival rate}$$
$$\mu = \text{the mean service rate}$$
$$\sigma = \text{the standard deviation of the service time}$$

Some of the steady-state operating characteristics of the *M/G/*1 waiting line model are as follows:

1. The probability that no units are in the system:

$$P_0 = 1 - \frac{\lambda}{\mu} \tag{7.24}$$

2. The average number of units in the waiting line:

$$L_q = \frac{\lambda^2 \sigma^2 + (\lambda/\mu)^2}{2(1 - \lambda/\mu)} \tag{7.25}$$

3. The average number of units in the system:

$$L = L_q + \frac{\lambda}{\mu} \tag{7.26}$$

4. The average time a unit spends in the waiting line:

$$W_q = \frac{L_q}{\lambda} \tag{7.27}$$

5. The average time a unit spends in the system:

$$W = W_q + \frac{1}{\mu} \tag{7.28}$$

6. The probability that an arriving unit has to wait for service:

$$P_w = \frac{\lambda}{\mu} \tag{7.29}$$

Note that the relationships for L, W_q, and W are the same as the relationships used for the waiting line models in Sections 7.2 and 7.3. They are the same as Little's flow equations.

An Example. Retail sales at Hartlage's Seafood Supply are handled by one clerk. Customer arrivals are random, and the average arrival rate is 21 customers per hour or $\lambda = 21/60 = 0.35$ customers per minute. A study of the service process shows that the average or mean service time is 2 minutes per customer, with a standard deviation of $\sigma = 1.2$ minutes. The mean time of 2 minutes per customer shows that the clerk has a mean service rate of $\mu = \frac{1}{2} = 0.50$ customers per minute. The operating characteristics of this *M/G/*1 waiting line system are

Problem 27 provides another application of a single-channel waiting line with Poisson arrivals and arbitrary service times.

$$P_0 = 1 - \frac{\lambda}{\mu} = 1 - \frac{0.35}{0.50} = 0.30$$

$$L_q = \frac{(0.35)^2(1.2)^2 + (0.35/0.50)^2}{2(1 - 0.35/0.50)} = 1.1107 \text{ customers}$$

$$L = L_q + \frac{\lambda}{\mu} = 1.1107 + \frac{0.35}{0.50} = 1.8107 \text{ customers}$$

$$W_q = \frac{L_q}{\lambda} = \frac{1.1107}{0.35} = 3.1733 \text{ minutes}$$

$$W = W_q + \frac{1}{\mu} = 3.1733 + \frac{1}{0.50} = 5.1733 \text{ minutes}$$

$$P_w = \frac{\lambda}{\mu} = \frac{0.35}{0.50} = 0.70$$

Hartlage's manager can review these operating characteristics to determine whether scheduling a second clerk appears to be worthwhile.

Spreadsheet Solution for the Hartlage Seafood Supply $M/G/1$ Waiting Line

Figure 7.8 shows the spreadsheet for the Hartlage Seafood Supply $M/G/1$ waiting line system. We have listed the assumptions of Poisson arrivals and arbitrary service times in cells A4 and A5 as a reminder that these are the assumptions for the waiting line model being

Figure 7.8   SPREADSHEET SOLUTION FOR THE HARTLAGE SEAFOOD PROBLEM

SPREADSHEET
HARTLAGE
SEAFOOD

	A	B	C
1	**Hartlage Seafood**		
2			
3	**Assumptions**		
4	**Poisson Arrivals**		
5	**Arbitrary Service Times**		
6			
7	Mean Arrival Rate	0.35	
8	Mean Service Rate	0.5	
9	Standard Deviation of Service Time	1.2	
10			
11			
12	**Operating Characteristics**		
13			
14	Probability that no customers are in the system, P_o		0.3000
15	Average number of customers in the waiting line, L_q		1.1107
16	Average number of customers in the system, L		1.8107
17	Average time a customer spends in the waiting line, W_q		3.1733
18	Average time a customer spends in the system, W		5.1733
19	Probability an arriving customer has to wait, P_w		0.7000

used to analyze the waiting line system. Three inputs are required: the mean arrival rate, $\lambda = 0.35$ customers per minute, shown in cell B7; the mean service rate, $\mu = 0.5$ customers per minute, shown in cell B8; and the standard deviation of service times, $\sigma = 1.2$ minutes, shown in cell B9. The operating characteristics provided by equations (7.24) through (7.29) are computed using the following cell formulas:

> Cell C14   Probability that no customers are in the system, P_0
>
> $=1-B7/B8$
>
> Cell C15   Average number of customers in the waiting line, L_q
>
> $=(B7^2*B9^2+(B7/B8)^2)/(2*(1-B7/B8))$
>
> Cell C16   Average number of customers in the system, L
>
> $=C15+B7/B8$
>
> Cell C17   Average time a customer spends in the waiting line, W_q
>
> $=C15/B7$
>
> Cell C18   Average time a customer spends in the system, W
>
> $=C17+1/B8$
>
> Cell C19   Probability an arriving customer has to wait, P_w
> $=B7/B8$

Constant Service Times

We want to comment briefly on the single-channel waiting line model that assumes random arrivals but constant service times. Such a waiting line can occur in production and manufacturing environments where machine-controlled service times are constant. This waiting line is described by the $M/D/1$ model, with the D referring to the deterministic service times. With the $M/D/1$ model, the average number of units in the waiting line, L_q, can be found by using equation (7.25) with the condition that the standard deviation of the constant service time is $\sigma = 0$. Thus, the expression for the average number of units in the waiting line for the $M/D/1$ waiting line becomes

$$L_q = \frac{(\lambda/\mu)^2}{2(1 - \lambda/\mu)} \tag{7.30}$$

The spreadsheet in Figure 7.8 can be used to accommodate the constant service time model by entering 0 in cell B9 for the standard deviation of service time. The other expressions presented earlier in this section can be used to determine additional operating characteristics of the $M/D/1$ system.

N O T E S
and Comments

Whenever the operating characteristics of a waiting line are unacceptable, managers often try to improve service by increasing the mean service rate μ. This decision is a good idea, but equation (7.25) shows that the variation in the service times also affects the operating characteristics of the waiting line. Because the standard deviation of service times, σ, appears in the numerator of equation (7.25), a larger variation in service times results in a larger average number of units in the waiting line. Hence, another alternative for improving the service capabilities of a waiting line is to reduce the variation in the service times. Thus, even when the mean service rate of the service facility cannot be increased, a reduction in σ will reduce the average number of units in the waiting line and improve the other operating characteristics of the system.

7.8   A MULTIPLE-CHANNEL MODEL WITH POISSON ARRIVALS, ARBITRARY SERVICE TIMES, AND NO WAITING LINE

An interesting variation of the waiting line models discussed so far involves a system in which no waiting is allowed. Arriving units or customers seek service from one of several service channels. If all channels are busy, arriving units are denied access to the system. In waiting line terminology, arrivals occurring when the system is full are **blocked** and are cleared from the system. Such customers may be lost or may attempt a return to the system later.

The specific model considered in this section is based on the following assumptions.

1. The system has k channels.
2. The arrivals follow a Poisson probability distribution, with mean arrival rate λ.
3. The service times for each channel may have any probability distribution.
4. The mean service rate μ is the same for each channel.
5. An arrival enters the system only if at least one channel is available. An arrival occurring when all channels are busy is blocked—that is, denied service and not allowed to enter the system.

With G denoting a general or unspecified probability distribution for service times, the appropriate model for this situation is referred to as an *M/G/k* model with "blocked customers cleared." The question addressed in this type of situation is, How many channels or servers should be used?

A primary application of this model involves the design of telephone and other communication systems where the arrivals are the calls and the channels are the number of telephone or communication lines available. In such a system, the calls are made to one telephone number, with each call automatically switched to an open channel if possible. When all channels are busy, additional calls receive a busy signal and are denied access to the system.

The Operating Characteristics for the *M/G/k* Model with Blocked Customers Cleared

We approach the problem of selecting the best number of channels by computing the steady-state probabilities that j of the k channels will be busy. These probabilities are

$$P_j = \frac{(\lambda/\mu)^j/j!}{\displaystyle\sum_{i=0}^{k} (\lambda/\mu)^i/i!} \tag{7.31}$$

where

$$\lambda = \text{the mean arrival rate}$$
$$\mu = \text{the mean service rate for each channel}$$
$$k = \text{the number of channels}$$
$$P_j = \text{the probability that } j \text{ of the } k \text{ channels are busy}$$
$$\text{for } j = 0, 1, 2, \ldots, k$$

With no waiting allowed, operating characteristics L_q and W_q considered in previous waiting line models are automatically zero regardless of the number of service channels. In this situation, the more important design consideration involves determining how the percentage of blocked customers is affected by the number of service channels.

The most important probability value is P_k, which is the probability that all k channels are busy. On a percentage basis, P_k indicates the percentage of arrivals that are blocked and denied access to the system.

Another operating characteristic of interest is the average number of units in the system; note that this number is equivalent to the average number of channels in use. Letting L denote the average number of units in the system, we have

$$L = \frac{\lambda}{\mu}(1 - P_k) \tag{7.32}$$

An Example. Microdata Software, Inc., uses a telephone ordering system for its computer software products. Callers place orders with Microdata by using the company's 800 telephone number. Assume that calls to this telephone number arrive at an average rate of $\lambda = 12$ calls per hour. The time required to process a telephone order varies considerably from order to order. However, each Microdata sales representative can be expected to handle an average of $\mu = 6$ calls per hour. Currently, the Microdata 800 telephone number has three internal lines or channels, each operated by a separate sales representative. Calls received on the 800 number are automatically transferred to an open line or channel if available.

Whenever all three lines are busy, callers receive a busy signal. In the past, Microdata's management has assumed that callers receiving a busy signal will call back later. However, recent research on telephone ordering has shown that a substantial number of callers who are denied access do not call back later. These lost calls represent lost revenues for the firm, so Microdata's management has requested an analysis of the telephone ordering system. Specifically, management wants to know the percentage of callers who are getting busy signals and are being blocked from the system. If management's goal is to provide sufficient capacity to handle 90% of the callers, how many telephone lines and sales representatives should Microdata use?

We can demonstrate the use of equation (7.31) by computing P_3, the probability that all three of the currently available telephone lines will be in use and additional callers will be blocked:

$$P_3 = \frac{(\frac{12}{6})^3/3!}{(\frac{12}{6})^0/0! + (\frac{12}{6})^1/1! + (\frac{12}{6})^2/2! + (\frac{12}{6})^3/3!} = \frac{1.3333}{6.3333} = 0.2105$$

With $P_3 = 0.2105$, approximately 21% of the calls, or slightly more than one in five calls, are being blocked. Only 79% of the calls are being handled immediately by the 3-line system.

Let us assume that Microdata expands to a 4-line system. Then, the probability that all four channels will be in use and that callers will be blocked is

$$P_4 = \frac{(\frac{12}{6})^4/4!}{(\frac{12}{6})^0/0! + (\frac{12}{6})^1/1! + (\frac{12}{6})^2/2! + (\frac{12}{6})^3/3! + (\frac{12}{6})^4/4!} = \frac{0.6667}{7} = 0.0952$$

Try Problem 30 to obtain practice in multiple-channel systems with no waiting line.

With only 9.52% of the callers blocked, 90.48% of the callers will reach the Microdata sales representatives. Thus, Microdata should expand its order-processing operation to 4 lines to meet management's goal of providing sufficient capacity to handle at least 90% of the callers. The average number of calls in the 4-line system and thus the average number of lines and sales representatives that will be busy is

$$L = \frac{\lambda}{\mu}(1 - P_4) = \frac{12}{6}(1 - 0.0952) = 1.8095$$

Although an average of less than 2 lines will be busy, the 4-line system is necessary to provide the capacity to handle at least 90% of the callers. We used equation (7.31) to calculate the probability that 0, 1, 2, 3, or 4 lines will be busy. These probabilities are summarized in Table 7.5.

As we discussed in Section 7.5, an economic analysis of waiting lines can be used to guide system design decisions. In the Microdata system, the cost of the additional line and additional sales representative should be relatively easy to establish. This cost can be balanced against the cost of the blocked calls. With 9.52% of the calls blocked and $\lambda = 12$ calls per hour, an 8-hour day will have an average of $8(12)(0.0952) = 9.1$ blocked calls. If Microdata can estimate the cost of possible lost sales, the cost of these blocked calls can be established. The economic analysis based on the service cost and the blocked-call cost can assist in determining the optimal number of lines for the system.

Table 7.5 PROBABILITIES OF BUSY LINES FOR THE MICRODATA 4-LINE SYSTEM

Number of Busy Lines	Probability
0	0.1429
1	0.2857
2	0.2857
3	0.1905
4	0.0952

NOTES and Comments

Many of the operating characteristics we have considered in previous sections are not relevant for the $M/G/k$ model with blocked customers cleared. In particular, the average time in the waiting line, W_q, and the average number of units in the waiting line, L_q, are no longer considered because waiting is not permitted in this type of system.

Spreadsheet Solution for the Microdata Software

Let us discuss the spreadsheet that can be used to compute the operating characteristics of a $M/G/k$ waiting line model with blocked customers cleared. Figure 7.9 shows the spreadsheet for the Microdata Software waiting line system. The assumptions of Poisson arrivals, arbitrary service times, and no waiting are shown in cells A4, A5, and A6. The three required input values and their cell locations are as follows: the number of channels, $k = 4$, shown in cell B8; the mean arrival rate, $\lambda = 12$ calls per hour, shown in cell B9; and the mean service rate, $\mu = 6$ calls per hour, shown in cell B10.

Equation 7.31, which shows the probability that j of the k channels are busy, is too complex to represent easily with a cell formula. As a result, we will develop a special Excel function to compute the value of P_j. The details of developing a function to compute P_j for the $M/G/k$ waiting line model with blocked customers cleared as shown in Appendix 7.1. Since the value of P_j is based on the number of channels k, the mean arrival rate λ, the mean service rate μ, and the number of channels busy j, the format of the function is $P_j(k, \lambda, \mu, j)$; we will refer to this function as the P_j function. Noting the cells that contain the values

| | | Figure 7.9 | SPREADSHEET SOLUTION FOR THE MICRODATA SOFTWARE PROBLEM |

**SPREADSHEET
MICRODATA
SOFTWARE**

	A	B	C
1	**Microdata Software**		
2			
3	**Assumptions**		
4	**Poisson Arrivals**		
5	**Arbitrary Service Times**		
6	**No Waiting**		
7			
8	Number of Channels	4	
9	Mean Arrival Rate	12	
10	Mean Service Rate Per Channel	6	
11			
12			
13	**Operating Characteristics**		
14		**Number of**	
15		**Channels Busy**	**Probability**
16		0	0.1429
17		1	0.2857
18		2	0.2857
19		3	0.1905
20		4	0.0952
21			
22	Probability that callers will be blocked		0.9048
23			
24	Average number of callers in the system, L		1.8095

of k, λ, and μ are B8, B9, and B10, we can enter the newly created P_j function for $j = 0$ channels busy in the spreadsheet as follows:

Cell C16   Probability that 0 channels are busy

$$=Pj(\$B\$8,\$B\$9,\$B\$10,B16)$$

As shown in Figure 7.9, this function provides the probability of no callers in the system with $P_0 = 0.1429$. After copying the contents of cell C16 to cells C17 through C20, these cells will provide the probability that 1, 2, 3, and 4 channels are busy, respectively. For example, the formula in cell C20, which provides the probability that all four channels are busy, is $=Pj(\$B\$8,\$B\$9,\$B\$10,B20)$; note that this value is 0.0952.

Since the probability that all four-channels will be in use and that callers will be blocked is equal to the value in cell C20, we can compute the probability an arriving caller is not blocked by entering the following formula into cell C22:

$$=1-C20$$

Thus, the probability that callers will be blocked is $1 - 0.0952 = 0.9048$.

Finally, to compute the average number of callers in the system, L, as given by equation 7.32, we entered the following formula into cell C24:

$$=(B9/B10)*C22$$

Note that the value obtained is 1.8095.

..../ /............

7.9   WAITING LINE MODELS WITH FINITE CALLING POPULATIONS

For the waiting line models introduced so far, the population of units or customers arriving for service has been considered to be unlimited. In technical terms, when no limit is placed on how many units may seek service, the model is said to have an **infinite calling population.** Under this assumption, the mean arrival rate λ remains constant regardless of how many units are in the waiting line system. This assumption of an infinite calling population is made in most waiting line models.

In other cases, the maximum number of units or customers that may seek service is assumed to be finite. In this situation, the mean arrival rate for the system changes, depending on the number of units in the waiting line, and the waiting line model is said to have a **finite calling population.** The formulas for the operating characteristics of the previous waiting line models must be modified to account for the effect of the finite calling population.

The finite calling population model discussed in this section is based on the following assumptions.

1. The arrivals for *each unit* follow a Poisson probability distribution, with mean arrival rate λ.
2. The service times follow an exponential probability distribution, with mean service rate μ.
3. The population of units that may seek service is finite.

The waiting line model that is appropriate in such cases is referred to as an $M/M/1$ model with a finite calling population.

The mean arrival rate for the $M/M/1$ model with a finite calling population is defined in terms of how often *each unit* arrives or seeks service. This situation differs from that for previous waiting line models in which λ denoted the mean arrival rate for the system. With a finite calling population, the mean arrival rate for the system varies, depending on the number of units in the system. Instead of adjusting for the changing system arrival rate, in the finite calling population model λ indicates the mean arrival rate for each unit.

> In previous waiting line models, the arrival rate λ was constant and independent of the number of units in the system. With a finite calling population, the arrival rate decreases as the number of units in the system increases because, with more units in the system, fewer units are in the population.

> The mean arrival rate λ is defined differently for the finite calling population model. Specifically, λ is defined in terms of the mean arrival rate for *each unit.*

The Operating Characteristics for the $M/M/1$ Model with a Finite Calling Population

The following formulas are used to determine the steady-state operating characteristics for an $M/M/1$ model with a finite calling population, where

$$\lambda = \text{the mean arrival rate for each unit}$$
$$\mu = \text{the mean service rate}$$
$$N = \text{the size of the population}$$

1. The probability that no units are in the system:

$$P_0 = \frac{1}{\displaystyle\sum_{n=0}^{N} \frac{N!}{(N-n)!} \left(\frac{\lambda}{\mu}\right)^n}$$

(7.33)

2. The average number of units in the waiting line:

$$L_q = N - \frac{\lambda + \mu}{\lambda}(1 - P_0)$$

(7.34)

3. The average number of units in the system:

$$L = L_q + (1 - P_0)$$

(7.35)

4. The average time a unit spends in the waiting line:

$$W_q = \frac{L_q}{(N - L)\lambda}$$

(7.36)

5. The average time a unit spends in the system:

$$W = W_q + \frac{1}{\mu}$$

(7.37)

6. The probability an arriving unit has to wait for service:

$$P_w = 1 - P_0$$

(7.38)

7. The probability of n units in the system:

$$P_n = \frac{N!}{(N-n)!}\left(\frac{\lambda}{\mu}\right)^n P_0 \quad \text{for } n = 0, 1, \ldots, N$$

(7.39)

One of the primary applications of the *M/M/*1 model with a finite calling population is referred to as the *machine repair problem.* In this problem, a group of machines is considered to be the finite population of "customers" that may request repair service. Whenever a machine breaks down, an arrival occurs in the sense that a new repair request is initiated. If another machine breaks down before the repair work has been completed on the first machine, the second machine begins to form a "waiting line" for repair service. Additional breakdowns by other machines will add to the length of the waiting line. The assumption of first-come, first-served indicates that machines are repaired in the order they break down. The *M/M/*1 model shows that one person or one channel is available to perform the repair service. To return the machine to operation, each machine with a breakdown must be repaired by the single-channel operation.

An Example.   The Kolkmeyer Manufacturing Company has a group of six identical machines; each machine operates an average of 20 hours between breakdowns. Thus, the mean arrival rate or request for repair service for each individual machine is $\lambda = \frac{1}{20} = 0.05$ per hour. With randomly occurring breakdowns, the Poisson probability distribution is used to describe the machine breakdown arrival process. One person from the maintenance department provides the single-channel repair service for the six machines. The exponentially distributed service times have a mean of 2 hours per machine or a mean service rate of $\mu = \frac{1}{2} = 0.50$ machines per hour.

With $\lambda = 0.05$ and $\mu = 0.50$, we use equations (7.33) through (7.38) to compute the operating characteristics for this system. Note that the use of equation (7.33) makes the computations involved somewhat cumbersome. Confirm for yourself that equation (7.30) provides the value $P_0 = 0.4845$. The computations for the other operating characteristics are

$$L_q = 6 - \left(\frac{0.05 + 0.50}{0.05}\right)(1 - 0.4845) = 0.3295 \text{ machine}$$

$$L = 0.3295 + (1 - 0.4845) = 0.8451 \text{ machine}$$

$$W_q = \frac{0.3295}{(6 - 0.845)0.05} = 1.279 \text{ hours}$$

$$W = 1.279 + \frac{1}{0.50} = 3.279 \text{ hours}$$

$$P_w = 1 - P_0 = 1 - 0.4845 = 0.5155$$

Finally, equation (7.39) can be used to compute the probabilities of any number of machines being in the repair system.

As with other waiting line models, the operating characteristics provide the manager with information about the waiting line operation. Whether these operating characteristics suggest that better repair service is needed depends on the cost of the idle machine waiting time compared to the cost of assigning an additional person to make the repair operation either a two-channel system or a faster one-channel system.

Spreadsheet Solution for Kolkmeyer Manufacturing Waiting Line Model

Figure 7.10 shows the spreadsheet for the Kolkmeyer Manufacturing machine repair problem. The assumptions of Poisson arrivals, exponential service times, and a finite calling population are shown in cells A4, A5, and A6. The three inputs and their cell locations are as follows: the mean arrival rate, $\lambda = 0.05$ machines per hour, shown in cell B8; the mean service rate, $\mu = 0.5$ machines per hour, shown in cell B9; and the finite population size, $N = 6$ machines, shown in cell B10. The operating characteristics that we compute for this model are dependent upon the values of λ, μ and N.

Equation 7.33, which shows the probability that no units are in the system, is too complex to represent easily with a cell function. As a result, we will develop a special Excel function to compute P_0. The details of developing the P_0 function for the $M/M/1$ waiting line model with a finite calling population are shown in Appendix 7.1. Because the value of P_0 is based on the mean arrival rate λ, the mean service rate μ, and population size N, the format of the function is P_0 Finite(λ, μ, N); we will refer to this function as the P_0 Finite function. Noting the cells that contain the values of λ, μ and N are B8, B9, and B10, we can enter the newly created P_0 Finite function into the spreadsheet as follows:

Cell C15   Probability that no units are in the system, P_0
    $=P0$Finite(B8,B9,B10)

Operating characteristics of an $M/M/1$ waiting line with a finite calling population are considered in Problem 34.

As shown in Figure 7.10, this function provides the probability of no units in the system with $P_0 = 0.5155$.

Figure 7.10	SPREADSHEET SOLUTION FOR THE KOLKMEYER SINGLE-CHANNEL PROBLEM

	A	B	C
1	**Kolkmeyer Single-Channel Waiting Line**		
2			
3	**Assumptions**		
4	**Poisson Arrivals**		
5	**Exponential Service Times**		
6	**Finite Calling Population**		
7			
8	Mean Arrival Rate	0.05	
9	Mean Service Rate	0.5	
10	Population Size	6	
11			
12			
13	**Operating Characteristics**		
14			
15	Probability that no machines are in the system, P_o		0.4845
16	Average number of machines in the waiting line, L_q		0.3297
17	Average number of machines in the system, L		0.8451
18	Average time a machine spends in the waiting line, W_q		1.2790
19	Average time a machine spends in the system, W		3.2790
20	Probability an arriving machine has to wait, P_w		0.5155

The operating characteristics provided by equations (7.34) through (7.38) can now be added to the spreadsheet by using the following cell equations:

Cell C16   Average number of machines in the waiting line, L_q
$$=B10-((B8+B9)/B8)*(1-C15)$$

Cell C17   Average number of machines in the system, L
$$=C16+(1-C15)$$

Cell C18   Average time a machine spends in the waiting line, W_q
$$=C16/((B10-C17)*B8)$$

Cell C19   Average time a machine spends in the system, W
$$=C18+1/B9$$

Cell C20   Probability an arriving machine has to wait for service, P_w
$$=1-C15$$

Extending this single-channel waiting line model to the multiple-channel finite calling population model requires additional and more complex operating characteristic equations. A computer solution based on four special Excel functions is required for this model. The interested reader can load the Excel file named Kolkmeyer Multiple Channel from the spreadsheet disk and review the equations and functions that are required. Figure 7.11 shows the Excel spreadsheet solution to the Kolkmeyer two-channel machine repair prob-

SPREADSHEET KOLKMEYER MULTIPLE CHANNEL

Figure 7.11	SPREADSHEET SOLUTION FOR THE KOLKMEYER TWO-CHANNEL PROBLEM

	A	B	C
1	**Kolkmeyer Multiple-Channel Waiting Line**		
2			
3	**Assumptions**		
4	**Poisson Arrivals**		
5	**Exponential Service Times**		
6	**Finite Calling Population**		
7			
8	Number of Channels	2	
9	Mean Arrival Rate	0.05	
10	Mean Service Rate	0.5	
11	Population Size	6	
12			
13			
14	**Operating Characteristics**		
15			
16	Probability that no machines are in the system, P_0		0.5602
17	Average number of machines in the waiting line, L_q		0.0227
18	Average number of machines in the system, L		0.5661
19	Average time a machine spends in the waiting line, W_q		0.0834
20	Average time a machine spends in the system, W		2.0834
21	Probability an arriving machine has to wait, P_w		0.1036

lem. By considering the cost of machine waiting or downtime and the cost of the repair personnel, management can determine whether the two-channel system is cost effective. As a final note, the spreadsheet shown in Figure 7.11 is the general *M/M/k* spreadsheet that can be used for any finite calling population problem; for example, if 1 is placed into cell B8, this spreadsheet provides the single-channel results shown previously in Figure 7.10.

SUMMARY

In this chapter we presented a variety of waiting line models that have been developed to help managers make better decisions concerning the operation of waiting lines. For each model, we presented formulas that could be used to develop operating characteristics or performance measures for the system being studied. Some of the operating characteristics presented were the

1. probability that no units are in the system,
2. average number of units in the waiting line,
3. average number of units in the system,
4. average time a unit spends in the waiting line,
5. average time a unit spends in the system, and
6. probability that arriving units will have to wait for service.

We also showed how an economic analysis of the waiting line could be conducted by developing a total-cost model that includes the cost associated with units waiting for service and the cost required to operate the service facility.

As many of the examples in this chapter show, the most obvious applications of waiting line models are situations in which customers arrive for service such as at a grocery checkout counter, bank, or restaurant. However, with a little creativity, waiting line models can be applied to many different situations such as telephone calls waiting for connections, mail orders waiting for processing, machines waiting for repairs, manufacturing jobs waiting to be processed, and money waiting to be spent or invested. The Management Science in Action article describes how a waiting line model provided the basis for improving productivity of a fire department in New Haven, Connecticut.

The complexity and diversity of waiting line systems found in practice often prevents an analyst from finding an existing waiting line model that fits the specific application being studied. Simulation, the topic discussed in Chapter 8, provides another approach to determining the operating characteristics of waiting line systems.

MANAGEMENT SCIENCE IN ACTION

IMPROVING FIRE DEPARTMENT PRODUCTIVITY*

The New Haven, Connecticut, Fire Department implemented a reorganization plan with cross-trained fire and medical personnel responding to both fire and medical emergencies. A waiting line model provided the basis for the reorganization by demonstrating that substantial improvements in emergency medical response time could be achieved with only a small reduction in fire protection. Annual savings were reported to be $1.4 million.

The model was based on Poisson arrivals and exponential service times for both fire and medical emergencies. It was used to estimate the average time that a person placing a call would have to wait for the appropriate emergency unit to arrive at the location. Waiting times were estimated by the model's prediction of the average travel time to reach each of the city's 28 census tracts.

The model was first applied to the original system of 16 fire units and 4 emergency medical units that operated independently. It was then applied to the proposed reorganization plan that involved cross-trained department personnel qualified to respond to both fire and medical emergencies. Results from the model demonstrated that average travel times could be reduced under the reorganization plan. Various facility location alternatives also were evaluated. When implemented, the reorganization plan reduced operating cost and improved public safety services.

*Based on A. J. Sweeney, L. Goldring, and E. D. Geyer, "Improving Fire Department Productivity: Merging Fire and Emergency Medical Units in New Haven," *Interfaces* 23, no. 1 (January–February 1993): 109–129.

GLOSSARY

Queue A waiting line.

Queuing theory The body of knowledge dealing with waiting lines.

Operating characteristics The performance measures for a waiting line including the probability that no units are in the system, the average number of units in the waiting line, the average waiting time and so on.

Single channel waiting line A waiting line with only one service facility.

Poisson probability distribution A probability distribution used to describe the arrival pattern for some waiting line models.

Exponential probability distribution A probability distribution used to describe the service time for some waiting line models.

First-come, first-served (FCFS) The queue discipline that serves waiting units on a first-come, first-served basis.

Transient period The start-up period for a waiting line, occurring before the waiting line reaches a normal or steady-state operation.

Steady-state operation The normal operation of the waiting line after it has gone through a start-up or transient period. The operating characteristics of waiting lines are computed for steady-state conditions.

Mean arrival rate The average number of customers or units arriving in a given period of time.

Mean service rate The average number of customers or units that can be served by one service facility in a given period of time.

Multiple-channel waiting line A waiting line with two or more parallel service facilities.

Blocked When arriving units cannot enter the waiting line because the system is full. Blocked units can occur when waiting lines are not allowed or when waiting lines have a finite capacity.

Infinite calling population The population of customers or units who may seek service has no specified upper limit.

Finite calling population The population of customers or units who may seek service has a fixed and finite value.

PROBLEMS

Note: The problems that follow can be solved by using the formulas for the operating characteristics of the various waiting line models presented in this chapter. If you would like to develop a spreadsheet solution for any of the problems, you can use the spreadsheet for the corresponding waiting line model exactly as it has been presented in this chapter. You will not need to modify or redesign new spreadsheets to develop the solutions for the following problems.

1. Willow Brook National Bank operates a drive-up teller window that allows customers to complete bank transactions without getting out of their cars. On weekday mornings, arrivals to the drive-up teller window occur at random, with a mean arrival rate of 24 customers per hour or 0.4 customer per minute.
   a. What is the mean or expected number of customers that will arrive in a 5-minute period?
   b. Assume that the Poisson probability distribution can be used to describe the arrival process. Use the mean arrival rate in part (a) and compute the probabilities that exactly 0, 1, 2, and 3 customers will arrive during a 5-minute period.
   c. Delays are expected if more than 3 customers arrive during any 5-minute period. What is the probability that delay will occur?

2. In the Willow Brook National Bank waiting line system (see Problem 1), assume that the service times for the drive-up teller follow an exponential probability distribution with a mean service rate of 36 customers per hour or 0.6 customer per minute. Use the exponential probability distribution to answer the following questions.
   a. What is the probability the service time is 1 minute or less?
   b. What is the probability the service time is 2 minutes or less?
   c. What is the probability the service time is more than 2 minutes?

3. Use the single-channel drive-up bank teller operation referred to in Problems 1 and 2 to determine the following operating characteristics for the system.
   a. The probability that no customers are in the system
   b. The average number of customers waiting
   c. The average number of customers in the system
   d. The average time a customer spends waiting
   e. The average time a customer spends in the system
   f. The probability that arriving customers will have to wait for service

4. Use the single-channel drive-up bank teller operation referred to in Problems 1–3 to determine the probabilities of 0, 1, 2, and 3 customers in the system. What is the probability that more than 3 customers will be in the drive-up teller system at the same time?

SELF TEST

5. The reference desk of a university library receives requests for assistance. Assume that a Poisson probability distribution with a mean rate of 10 requests per hour can be used to describe the arrival pattern and that service times follow an exponential probability distribution with a mean service rate of 12 requests per hour.
   a. What is the probability that no requests for assistance are in the system?
   b. What is the average number of requests that will be waiting for service?
   c. What is the average waiting time in minutes before service begins?
   d. What is the average time at the reference desk in minutes (waiting time plus service time)?
   e. What is the probability that a new arrival has to wait for service?

6. Trucks using a single-channel loading dock arrive according to a Poisson probability distribution. The time required to load/unload follows an exponential probability distribution. The mean arrival rate is 12 trucks per day, and the mean service rate is 18 trucks per day.
   a. What is the probability that no trucks are in the system?
   b. What is the average number of trucks waiting for service?
   c. What is the average time a truck waits for the loading/unloading service to begin?
   d. What is the probability that an arriving truck will have to wait for service?

7. A mail-order nursery specializes in European beech trees. New orders, which are processed by a single shipping clerk, have a mean arrival rate of 6 per day and a mean service rate of 8 per day. Assume that arrivals follow a Poisson probability distribution and that service times follow an exponential probability distribution.
   a. What is the average number of orders in the system?
   b. What is the average time that an order spends waiting before the clerk is available to begin service?
   c. What is the average time an order spends in the system?

8. For the Burger Dome single-channel waiting line in Section 7.2, assume that the arrival rate is increased to 1 customer per minute and that the mean service rate is increased to 1.25 customers per minute. Compute the following operating characteristics for the new system: P_0, L_q, L, W_q, W, and P_w. Does this system provide better or poorer service compared to the original system? Discuss any differences and the reason for these differences. Use the spreadsheet in Figure 7.2 to answer this question.

9. Marty's Barber Shop has one barber. Customers arrive at the rate of 2.2 customers per hour, and haircuts are given at the average rate of 5 per hour. Use the Poisson arrivals and exponential service times model to answer the following questions.
   a. What is the probability that no units are in the system?
   b. What is the probability that 1 customer is receiving a haircut and no one is waiting?
   c. What is the probability that 1 customer is receiving a haircut and 1 customer is waiting?
   d. What is the probability that 1 customer is receiving a haircut and 2 customers are waiting?
   e. What is the probability that more than 2 customers are waiting?
   f. What is the average time a customer waits for service?

10. Develop a spreadsheet based on Figure 7.2 to solve this problem. Trosper Tire Company has decided to hire a new mechanic to handle all tire changes for customers ordering a new set of

tires. Two mechanics have applied for the job. One mechanic has limited experience, can be hired for $14 per hour, and can service an average of 3 customers per hour. The other mechanic has several years of experience, can service an average of 4 customers per hour, but must be paid $20 per hour. Assume that customers arrive at the Trosper garage at the rate of 2 customers per hour.

a. What are the waiting line operating characteristics using each mechanic, assuming Poisson arrivals and exponential service times?

b. If the company assigns a customer waiting cost of $30 per hour, which mechanic provides the lower operating cost?

SELF TEST

11. Agan Interior Design provides home and office decorating assistance to its customers. In normal operation, an average of 2.5 customers arrive each hour. One design consultant is available to answer customer questions and make product recommendations. The consultant averages 10 minutes with each customer.

a. Compute the operating characteristics of the customer waiting line, assuming Poisson arrivals and exponential service times.

b. Service goals dictate that an arriving customer should not wait for service more than an average of 5 minutes. Is this goal being met? If not, what action do you recommend?

c. If the consultant can reduce the average time spent per customer to 8 minutes, what is the mean service rate? Will the service goal be met?

12. Pete's Market is a small local grocery store with only one checkout counter. Assume that shoppers arrive at the checkout lane according to a Poisson probability distribution, with a mean arrival rate of 15 customers per hour. The checkout service times follow an exponential probability distribution, with a mean service rate of 20 customers per hour.

a. Compute the operating characteristics for this waiting line.

b. If the manager's service goal is to limit the waiting time prior to beginning the checkout process to no more than 5 minutes, what recommendations would you provide regarding the current checkout system?

13. After reviewing the waiting line analysis of Problem 12, the manager of Pete's Market wants to consider one of the following alternatives for improving service. What alternative would you recommend? Justify your recommendation.

a. Hire a second person to bag the groceries while the cash register operator is entering the cost data and collecting money from the customer. With this improved single-channel operation, the mean service rate could be increased to 30 customers per hour.

b. Hire a second person to operate a second checkout counter. The two-channel operation would have a mean service rate of 20 customers per hour for each channel.

14. Keuka Park Savings and Loan currently has one drive-up teller window. The arrivals follow a Poisson probability distribution, with a mean arrival rate of 10 cars per hour. The service times follow an exponential probability distribution, with a mean service rate of 12 cars per hour.

a. What is the probability that no cars are in the system?

b. If you were to drive up to the facility, how many cars would you expect to see waiting and being served?

c. What is the average time a car spends in the waiting line?

d. What is the probability that an arriving car will have to wait for service?

e. As a potential customer of the system, would you be satisfied with the given waiting line characteristics? Why or why not?

15. To improve customer service, Keuka Park Savings and Loan (see Problem 14) managers want to investigate the effect of a second drive-up teller window. Assume a mean arrival rate of 10 cars per hour and a mean service rate of 12 cars per hour for each drive-up window. What effect would the addition of a new teller window have on the system? Does this system appear acceptable?

16. The new Fore and Aft Marina is to be located on the Ohio River near Madison, Indiana. Assume that Fore and Aft has decided to build a docking facility where one boat at a time can stop for gas and servicing. Assume that arrivals follow a Poisson probability distribution, with a mean of 5 boats per hour, and that service times follow an exponential probability distribution, with a mean of 10 boats per hour. Answer the following questions.
    a. What is the probability that no boats are in the system?
    b. What is the average number of boats that will be waiting for service?
    c. What is the average time a boat will spend waiting for service?
    d. What is the average time a boat will spend at the dock?
    e. If you were the manager of Fore and Aft Marina, would you be satisfied with the service level your system will be providing? Why or why not?

17. The manager of the Fore and Aft Marina in Problem 16 wants to investigate the possibility of enlarging the docking facility so that two boats can stop for gas and servicing simultaneously. Assume that the mean arrival rate is 5 boats per hour and that the mean service rate for each channel is 10 boats per hour.
    a. What is the probability that the boat dock will be idle?
    b. What is the average number of boats that will be waiting for service?
    c. What is the average time a boat will spend waiting for service?
    d. What is the average time a boat will spend at the dock?
    e. If you were the manager of Fore and Aft Marina, would you be satisfied with the service level your system will be providing? Why or why not?

18. The City Beverage Drive-Thru is considering a two-channel service system. Cars arrive according to the Poisson probability distribution, with a mean arrival rate of 6 cars per hour. The service times have an exponential probability distribution, with a mean service rate of 10 cars per hour for each channel.
    a. What is the probability that no cars are in the system?
    b. What is the average number of cars waiting for service?
    c. What is the average time waiting for service?
    d. What is the average time in the system?
    e. What is the probability that an arriving car will have to wait for service?

SELF TEST

19. Consider a two-channel waiting line with Poisson arrivals and exponential service times. The mean arrival rate is 14 units per hour, and the mean service rate is 10 units per hour for each channel.
    a. What is the probability that no units are in the system?
    b. What is the average number of units in the system?
    c. What is the average time a unit waits for service?
    d. What is the average time a unit is in the system?
    e. What is the probability of having to wait for service?

20. Refer to Problem 19. Assume that the system is expanded to a three-channel operation.
    a. Compute the operating characteristics for this waiting line system.
    b. If the service goal is to provide sufficient capacity so that no more than 25% of the customers have to wait for service, is the two- or three-channel system preferred?

SELF TEST

21. Refer to the Agan Interior Design situation in Problem 11. Agan's management would like to evaluate two alternatives:
    • Use one consultant with an average service time of 8 minutes per customer.
    • Expand to two consultants, each of whom has an average service time of 10 minutes per customer.
    If the consultants are paid $16 per hour and the customer waiting time is valued at $25 per hour for waiting time prior to service, should Agan expand to the two-consultant system? Explain.

22. Develop a spreadsheet to solve this problem. Use the format of the Burger Dome Multiple Channel spreadsheet in Figure 7.5. A fast-food franchise is considering operating a drive-up window food-service operation. Assume that customer arrivals follow a Poisson probability distribution,

with a mean arrival rate of 24 cars per hour, and that service times follow an exponential probability distribution. Arriving customers place orders at an intercom station at the back of the parking lot and then drive to the service window to pay for and receive their orders. The following three service alternatives are being considered.

- A single-channel operation in which one employee fills the order and takes the money from the customer. The average service time for this alternative is 2 minutes.
- A single-channel operation in which one employee fills the order while a second employee takes the money from the customer. The average service time for this alternative is 1.25 minutes.
- A two-channel operation with two service windows and two employees. The employee stationed at each window fills the order and takes the money for customers arriving at the window. The average service time for this alternative is 2 minutes for each channel.

Answer the following questions and recommend an alternative design for the fast-food franchise.

a. What is the probability that no cars are in the system?
b. What is the average number of cars waiting for service?
c. What is the average number of cars in the system?
d. What is the average time a car waits for service?
e. What is the average time in the system?
f. What is the probability that an arriving car will have to wait for service?

23. The following cost information is available for the fast-food franchise in Problem 22.
- Customer waiting time is valued at $25 per hour to reflect the fact that waiting time is costly to the fast-food business.
- The cost of each employee is $6.50 per hour.
- To account for equipment and space, an additional cost of $20 per hour is attributable to each channel.

What is the lowest-cost design for the fast-food business?

24. Patients arrive at a dentist's office at a mean rate of 2.8 patients per hour. The dentist can treat patients at the mean rate of 3 patients per hour. A study of patient waiting times shows that, on average, a patient waits 30 minutes before seeing the dentist.
a. What are the mean arrival and treatment rates in terms of patients per minute?
b. What is the average number of patients in the waiting room?
c. If a patient arrives at 10:10 A.M., at what time is the patient expected to leave the office?

SELF TEST

25. A study of the multichannel food-service operation at the Red Birds' baseball park shows that the average time between the arrival of a customer at the food-service counter and his or her departure with a filled order is 10 minutes. During the game, customers arrive at the average rate of 4 per minute. The food-service operation requires an average of 2 minutes per customer order.
a. What is the mean service rate per channel in terms of customers per minute?
b. What is the average waiting time in the line prior to placing an order?
c. On average, how many customers are in the food-service system?

26. Manning Autos operates an automotive service counter. While completing the repair work, Manning mechanics arrive at the company's parts department counter at the mean rate of 4 per hour. The parts coordinator spends an average of 6 minutes with each mechanic, discussing the parts the mechanic needs and retrieving the parts from inventory.
a. Currently, Manning has one parts coordinator. On average, each mechanic waits 4 minutes before the parts coordinator is available to answer questions and/or retrieve parts from inventory. Find L_q, W, and L for this single-channel parts operation.
b. A trial period with a second parts coordinator showed that, on average, each mechanic waited only 1 minute before a parts coordinator was available. Find L_q, W, and L for this two-channel parts operation.
c. If the cost of each mechanic is $20 per hour and the cost of each parts coordinator is $12 per hour, is the one-channel or the two-channel system more economical?

27. Gubser Welding, Inc., operates a welding service for construction and automotive repair jobs. Assume that the arrival of jobs at the company's office can be described by a Poisson probability distribution with a mean arrival rate of 2 jobs per 8-hour day. The time required to complete the jobs follows a normal probability distribution with a mean time of 3.2 hours and a standard deviation of 2 hours. Answer the following questions, assuming that Gubser uses one welder to complete all jobs.
    a. What is the mean arrival rate in jobs per hour?
    b. What is the mean service rate in jobs per hour?
    c. What is the average number of jobs waiting for service?
    d. What is the average time a job waits before the welder can begin working on it?
    e. What is the average number of hours between when a job is received and when it is completed?
    f. What percentage of the time is Gubser's welder busy?

28. Jobs arrive randomly at a particular assembly plant; assume that the mean arrival rate is 5 jobs per hour. Service times (in minutes per job) do not follow the exponential probability distribution. Two proposed designs for the plant's assembly operation are shown.

| | Service Time | |
Design	Mean	Standard Deviation
A	6.0	3.0
B	6.25	0.6

    a. What is the mean service rate in jobs per hour for each design?
    b. For the mean service rates in part (a), what design appears to provide the best or fastest service rate?
    c. What are the standard deviations of the service times in hours?
    d. Use the $M/G/1$ model in Section 7.7 to compute the operating characteristics for each design.
    e. Which design provides the best operating characteristics? Why?

29. Develop a spreadsheet based on Figure 7.8 to solve this problem. The Robotics Manufacturing Company operates an equipment repair business where emergency jobs arrive randomly at the rate of 3 jobs per 8-hour day. The company's repair facility is a single-channel system operated by a repair technician. The service time varies with a mean repair time of 2 hours and a standard deviation of 1.5 hours. The company's cost of the repair operation is $28 per hour. In the economic analysis of the waiting line system, Robotics uses $35 per hour cost for customers waiting during the repair process.
    a. What are the arrival rate and service rate in jobs per hour?
    b. Show the opearting characteristics including the total cost per hour.
    c. The company is considering purchasing a computer-based equipment repair system that would enable a constant repair time of 2 hours. For practical purposes, the standard deviation is 0. Because of the computer-based equipment, the company's cost of the new operation would be $32 per hour. The firm's director of operations has said no to the request for new equipment because the hourly cost is $4 higher and the mean repair time is the same. Do you agree? What effect will the new system have on the waiting line characteristics of the repair service?
    d. Does paying for the computer-based system to reduce the variation in service time make economic sense? How much will the new system save the company during a 40-hour work week?

30. A large insurance company has a central computing system that contains a variety of information about customer accounts. Insurance agents in a six-state area use telephone lines to access the customer information database. Currently, the company's central computer system allows 3 users to access the central computer simultaneously. Agents who attempt to use the system when it is full are denied access; no waiting is allowed. Management realizes that with its expanding business, more requests will be made to the central information system. Being denied

access to the system is inefficient as well as annoying for agents. Access requests follow a Poisson probability distribution, with a mean of 42 calls per hour. The mean service rate per line is 20 calls per hour.

a. What is the probability that 0, 1, 2, and 3 access lines will be in use?
b. What is the probability that an agent will be denied access to the system?
c. What is the average number of access lines in use?
d. In planning for the future, management wants to be able to handle $\lambda = 50$ calls per hour; in addition, the probability that an agent will be denied access to the system should be no greater than the value computed in part (b). How many access lines should this system have?

31. Develop a spreadsheet based on Figure 7.9 to solve this problem. Mid-West Publishing Company publishes college textbooks. The company operates an 800 telephone number whereby potential adopters can ask questions about forthcoming texts, request examination copies of texts, and place orders. Currently, two extension lines are used, with two representatives handling the telephone inquiries. Calls occurring when both extension lines are being used receive a busy signal; no waiting is allowed. Each representative can accommodate an average of 12 calls per hour. The mean arrival rate is 20 calls per hour.

a. How many extension lines should be used if the company wants to handle 90% of the calls immediately?
b. What is the average number of extension lines that will be busy if your recommendation in part (a) is used?
c. What percentage of calls receive a busy signal for the current telelphone system with two extension lines?

32. City Cab, Inc., uses two dispatchers to handle requests for service and to dispatch the cabs. The telephone calls that are made to City Cab use a common telephone number. When both dispatchers are busy, the caller hears a busy signal; no waiting is allowed. Callers who receive a busy signal can call back later or call another cab service. Assume that the arrival of calls follows a Poisson probability distribution, with a mean of 40 calls per hour, and that each dispatcher can handle a mean of 30 calls per hour.

a. What percentage of time are both dispatchers idle?
b. What percentage of time are both dispatchers busy?
c. What is the probability callers will receive a busy signal if 2, 3, or 4 dispatchers are used?
d. If management wants no more than 12% of the callers to receive a busy signal, how many dispatchers should be used?

33. Use the spreadsheet entitled Kolkmeyer Multiple-Channel to solve this problem. Kolkmeyer Manufacturing Company (see Section 7.9) is considering adding 2 machines to its manufacturing operation. This addition will bring the number of machines to 8. Mr. Andrews, president of Kolkmeyer, has asked for a study of the need to add a second employee to the repair operation. The mean arrival rate is 0.05 machine per hour for each machine, and the mean service rate for each individual assigned to the repair operation is 0.50 machine per hour.

a. Compute the operating characteristics if the company retains the single-employee repair operation.
b. Compute the operating characteristics if a second employee is added to the machine repair operation.
c. Each employee is paid $20 per hour. Machine downtime is valued at $80 per hour. From an economic point of view, should one or two employees handle the machine repair operation? Explain.

SELF TEST

34. Five administrative assistants use an office copier. The average time between arrivals for each assistant is 40 minutes, which is equivalent to a mean arrival rate of $1/40 = 0.025$ arrivals per minute. The mean time each assistant spends at the copier is 5 minutes, which is equivalent to a mean service rate of $^1/_5 = 0.20$ users per minute. Use the *M/M/*1 model with a finite calling population to determine the following:

a. The probability that the copier is idle
b. The average number of administrative assistants in the waiting line

    c.   The average number of administrative assistants at the copier

    d.   The average time an assistant spends waiting for the copier

    e.   The average time an assistant spends at the copier

    f.   During an 8-hour day, how many minutes does an assistant spend at the copier? How much of this time is waiting time?

    g.   Should management consider purchasing a second copier? Explain.

Case Problem   AIRLINE RESERVATIONS

Regional Airlines is establishing a new telephone system for handling flight reservations. During the 10:00 A.M. to 11:00 A.M. time period, calls to the reservation agent occur randomly at an average of one call every 3.75 minutes. Historical service time data show that a reservation agent spends an average of 3 minutes with each customer. The waiting line model assumptions of Poisson arrivals and exponential service times appear reasonable for the telephone reservation system.

Regional Airlines' management believes that offering an efficient telephone reservation system is an important part of establishing an image as a service-oriented airline. If the system is properly implemented, Regional Airlines will establish good customer relations, which in the long run will increase business. However, if the telephone reservation system is frequently overloaded and customers have difficulty contacting an agent, a negative customer reaction may lead to an eventual loss of business. The cost of a ticket reservation agent is $20 per hour. Thus, management wants to provide good service, but it does not want to incur the cost of overstaffing the telephone reservation operation by using more agents than necessary.

At a planning meeting, Regional's management team agreed that an acceptable customer service goal is to answer at least 85% of the incoming calls immediately. During the planning meeting, Regional's vice president of administration pointed out that the data show that the average service rate for an agent is faster than the average arrival rate of the telephone calls. The vice president's conclusion was that personnel costs could be minimized by using one agent and that the single agent should be able to handle the telephone reservations and still have some idle time. The vice president of marketing restated the importance of customer service and expressed support for at least two reservation agents.

The current telephone reservation system design does not allow callers to wait. Callers who attempt to reach a reservation agent when all agents are occupied receive a busy signal and are blocked from the system. A representative from the telephone company suggested that Regional Airlines consider an expanded system that accommodates waiting. In the expanded system, when a customer calls and all agents are busy, a recorded message tells the customer that the call is being held in the order received and that an agent will be available shortly. The customer can stay on the line and listen to background music while waiting for an agent. Regional's management will need more information before switching to the expanded system.

Managerial Report

Prepare a managerial report for Regional Airlines analyzing the telephone reservation system. Evaluate both the system that does not allow waiting and the expanded system that allows waiting. Include the following information in your report.

1. A detailed analysis of the operating characteristics of the reservation system with one agent as proposed by the vice president of administration. What is your recommendation concerning a single-agent system?

2. A detailed analysis of the operating characteristics of the reservation system based on your recommendation regarding the number of agents Regional should use.

3. What appear to be the advantages or disadvantages of the expanded system? Discuss the number of waiting callers the expanded system would need to accommodate.

4. The telephone arrival data presented are for the 10:00 A.M. to 11:00 A.M. time period; however, the arrival rate of incoming calls is expected to change from hour to hour. Describe how your waiting line analysis could be used to develop a ticket agent staffing plan that would enable the company to provide different levels of staffing for the ticket reservation system at different times during the day. Indicate the information that you would need to develop this staffing plan.

Appendix 7.1   CREATING SPECIAL FUNCTIONS WITH EXCEL

If an equation used for a spreadsheet calculation is relatively simple, the equation can be entered directly into a cell as a cell formula. However, if an equation is too complex to be expressed as a cell formula, the equation can be evaluated using a specially created spreadsheet function. As you will see, creating such a function requires the user to program the function in the Visual Basic programming language. Using this procedure, we are able to evaluate very complex functions and have the value of the function displayed in a spreadsheet cell.

In this appendix, we show how to create the P_0 function for the multiple-channel waiting line model in Section 7.3, the P_j function for the no waiting line model in Section 7.8, and the P_0 function for the finite calling population model in Section 7.9. We begin with the details of creating the P_0 function for the multiple-channel waiting line model in Section 7.3.

Function for the Multiple-Channel Waiting Line Model (Section 7.3)

The equation used to compute P_0 for the multiple-channel waiting line model in Section 7.3 is

$$P_0 = \frac{1}{\displaystyle\sum_{n=0}^{k-1} \frac{(\lambda/\mu)^n}{n!} + \frac{(\lambda/\mu)^k}{k!}\left(\frac{k\mu}{k\mu - \lambda}\right)}$$

Note that the number of channels k, the mean arrival rate λ (lambda), and the mean service rate μ (mu) must be known in order to compute P_0.

The steps required to create the P_0 function are as follows:

1. Select the **Tools** pull-down menu

2. Select the **Macro** option

3. Choose the **Visual Basic Editor**

4. When the Visual Basic Editor appears

   Select the **Insert** pull-down menu

   Choose the **Module** option

5. When the Module sheet appears enter

   Function Your_Function_Name(Arg1, Arg2, . . .)

   where Your_Function_Name is any name you wish to use for the function and where Arg1, Arg2, etc., are the arguments of the function or the inputs that you will need to evaluate the function. For the multiple-channel waiting line model, we named the function *P*0 and listed the three arguments or inputs as k, lamda, and mu. Thus, we entered the following:

   Function *P*0(k,lamda,mu)

6. Next write a Visual Basic program to evaluate the function. The exact statement sequence may vary and depends upon the programming skills of the user. The Visual Basic program we entered for P_0 is shown in Figure 7.12.

   End Function appears as the last line of the program

7. Select the **File** pull-down menu

   Choose the **Close and Return to Microsoft Excel** option

You will be returned to the spreadsheet application. You can now choose the cell where the P_0 function is to appear. Using the spreadsheet in Figure 7.5, the number of channels *k* appears in cell B7, the mean arrival rate lamda appears in cell B8 and the mean service rate mu appears in cell B9. Thus we entered the following function in order to place the value of P_0 into cell C14.

$$=\text{P0(B7,B8,B9)}$$

The value of the function will be determined based on the values of the arguments provided in cells B7, B8, and B9. The new function will be saved with the workbook when the workbook is saved.

Function for the No Waiting Line Model (Section 7.8)

The equation used to compute P_j for the no waiting line model in Section 7.8 is

$$P_j = \frac{(\lambda/\mu)^j/j!}{\sum_{i=0}^{k} (\lambda/\mu)^i/i!}$$

Note that the number of channels *k,* the mean arrival rate λ (lamda), the mean service rate μ (mu) and the number of channels busy *j* must be known in order to evaluate the function.

Figure 7.12   THE VISUAL BASIC PROGRAM FOR P_0 IN THE MULTIPLE-CHANNEL WAITING LINE MODEL IN SECTION 7.3

```
Function P0(k, lamda, mu)
Sum = 0
For n = 0 To k − 1
Sum = Sum + (lamda/mu) ^ n/Application.Fact(n)
Next
P0 = 1/(Sum + ((lamda/mu) ^ k/Application.Fact(k)) * (k * mu/(k * mu − lamda)))
End Function
```

Thus we created the function Pj(k,lamda,mu,ChannelsBusy) using the Excel procedure described previously.

Using the spreadsheet in Figure 7.9, we note that the number of channel k appears in cell B8, the mean arrival rate lamda appears in cell B9, and the mean service rate mu appears in cell B10. The number of channels busy appears in cell B16 to cell B20. Thus we entered the following function into cell C16.

$$=Pj(\$B\$8,\$B\$9,\$B\$10,B16)$$

Coping this cell formula for cells C17 to C20 provided the desired probabilities. The Visual Basic program for the P_j function is shown in Figure 7.13.

Function for the Finite Population Waiting Line Model (Section 7.9)

The equation used to compute P_0 for the finite population waiting line model in Section 7.9 is

$$P_0 = \frac{1}{\displaystyle\sum_{n=0}^{N} \frac{N!}{(N - n)!}\left(\frac{\lambda}{\mu}\right)^n}$$

Note that the mean arrival rate λ (lamda), the mean service rate μ (mu), and the population size N must be known in order to evaluate the function. Thus we created the function P0Finite(lamda,mu,N) using the Excel procedure described previously.

Figure 7.13   THE VISUAL BASIC PROGRAM FOR Pj IN THE NO WAITING LINE MODEL IN SECTION 7.8

```
Function Pj(k, lamda, mu, ChannelsBusy)
j = ChannelsBusy
Sum = 0
For i = 0 To k
Sum = Sum + (lamda/mu) ^ i/Application.Fact(i)
Next
Pj = ((lamda/mu) ^ j/Application.Fact(j))/Sum
End Function
```

Using the spreadsheet in Figure 7.10, we note that lamda, the mean arrival rate, appears in cell B8; mu, the mean service rate, appears in cell B9; and N, the population size, appears in cell B10. Thus we entered the following function into cell C15.

$$=P0Finite(B8,B9,B10)$$

The Visual Basic program for the $P0$Finite function is shown in Figure 7.14.

Figure 7.14   THE VISUAL BASIC PROGRAM FOR P_0 IN THE FINITE POPULATION WAITING LINE MODEL IN SECTION 7.9

```
Function P0Finite(lamda, mu, N)
Sum = 0
For i = 0 To N
Sum = Sum + (Application.Fact(N)/Application.Fact(N −i)) * (lamda/mu) ^ i
Next
P0Finite = 1/Sum
End Function
```

CITIBANK*

LONG ISLAND CITY, NEW YORK

Citibank, a major subsidiary of Citicorp, makes available a wide range of financial services, including checking and savings accounts, loans and mortgages, insurance, and investment services, within the framework of a unique strategy for delivering those services called Citibanking. Citibanking entails a consistent brand identity all over the world, consistent product offerings, and high-level customer service. Citibanking lets you manage your money anytime, anywhere, anyway you choose. Whether you need to save for the future or borrow for today, you can do it all at Citibank.

Citibanking's state-of-the-art automatic teller machines (ATMs) located in Citicard Banking Centers (CBCs), let customers do all their banking in one place with the touch of a finger, 24 hours a day, 7 days a week. More than 150 different banking functions from deposits to managing investments can be performed with ease. Citibanking ATMs are so much more than just cash machines that customers today use them for 80% of their transactions.

A Waiting Line Application

The New York franchise of U.S. Citibanking operates approximately 250 CBCs. Each CBC provides customers with one or more ATMs, called customer activated terminals (or CATs), which are capable of performing a variety of banking transactions. Approximately 70% of the CBCs are located in Manhattan, the Bronx, Brooklyn, Queens, and Staten Island. The remaining 30% are suburban CBCs located in Nassau, Suffolk, Orange, Rockland, and Westchester counties. Measuring performance

and service capacity at each CBC is an important part of Citibank's emphasis on providing superior access and convenience for its customers.

Each Citibank CBC operates as a waiting line system with randomly arriving customers seeking service at a CAT. Based on the use at each site, the number of CATs ranges from 1 to 20 with each site operating with a single queue. If 1 CAT is present, the system operates as a single-channel waiting line, with arriving customers waiting whenever the CAT is being used by another customer. At most CBC sites, multiple CATs provide a multiple-channel waiting line system.

A periodic CBC capacity study is used to determine the capacity needed at each center. The hardware supply at the center is measured in terms of the transactional volume the site is capable of supporting for a standard number of transactions per CAT per hour. Customer demand is measured in terms of the peak number of arrivals per hour at the site. Comparing supply and demand enables Citibank to classify each CBC as either

- Highly endangered—average peak hour waiting time exceeds 5 minutes.
- Borderline—average peak hour waiting time is 3–5 minutes.
- Sufficient—average peak hour waiting time is 3 minutes or less.

In a recent capacity study, demand data suggested approximately 6% of the CBCs should be classified as highly endangered and approximately 8% should be classified as borderline. In total, 34 sites were listed as candidates for possible capacity expansion with incremental CATs desired.

In order to make recommendations on the number of CATs to add at the selected sites, management needed

---

*The authors are indebted to Stacey Karter, Citibank, for providing this application.

additional information concerning the customer service levels at each site. Operating characteristics information provided by a waiting line model would be helpful in determining the number of CATs each center should have. Typical information provided by the model included:

- The average number of customers in the waiting line
- The average number of customers in the system
- The average time a customer spends in the waiting line
- The average time a customer spends in the system
- The probability that an arriving customer has to wait

In-house management information system (MIS) data on arrival rates and service times were collected to determine whether a multiple-channel waiting line model with Poisson arrivals and exponential service time could be used to model a CBC waiting line system. Customer arrivals were indeed random and adequately represented by a Poisson probability distribution. The mean arrival rate varied, depending on time of day and day of week. However, developing operating characteristic information for the peak or high demand periods was important. An average of the top 10 hourly demands was used to determine the mean arrival rate for each CBC site. Observed service times showed that the exponential probability distribution provided a reasonable approximation of the service time distribution.

For example, one midtown Manhattan branch site was classified as an endangered center operating with 5 CATs. Onsite observations were conducted to verify the MIS data and the peak arrival rate of 172 customers per hour. From the observed session times of 2 minutes per customer, the mean service rate per CAT was estimated to be 30 per hour. Five CATs were insufficient to meet this peak demand. A multiple-channel waiting line model with an expansion to 6 CATs showed that 88% of the customers would still have to wait and that the average waiting time would be 6 to 7 minutes. Expansion to 6 CATs still provided an unacceptable level of service. Expansion to 7 CATs provided acceptable service levels with an average of 2.4 customers in the waiting line. Hence, expansion to 8 CATs was not necessary at that time.

Even though peak demand periods were not always long enough to reach the steady-state conditions projected by the waiting line model, the operating characteristics indicated by the model provided general guidelines for capacity decisions. Use of the observed mean arrival and service rates unique to each site enabled the waiting line model to provide useful information for making the incremental CAT decisions at each CBC location.

Questions

1. How did Citibank's CBCs operate as a waiting line system?
2. How did Citibank ensure appropriate arrival and service time rates for the CBC waiting line operation?
3. What information did the waiting line model provide? How was this information helpful in making the incremental CAT decisions for each site?

8

SIMULATION

Simulation is one of the most widely used quantitative approaches to decision making. It is a method for learning about a real system by experimenting with a model that represents the system. The simulation model contains the mathematical expressions and logical relationships that describe how to compute the value of the output given the values of the inputs. Any simulation model has two inputs: controllable inputs and probabilistic inputs. Figure 8.1 shows a conceptual diagram of a simulation model.

In conducting a **simulation experiment,** values for the **controllable inputs** are selected by the decision maker. Then, values for the **probabilistic inputs** are randomly generated. Based upon the values for the controllable and probabilistic inputs, the model is used to compute the value, or values, of the output. Simulation has been successfully applied in a wide variety of applications. The following examples are typical.

1. **New Product Introduction**   The objective of this simulation is to determine the probability that a new product will be profitable. A model is developed relating profit (the output measure) to various probabilistic inputs such as demand, parts cost, and labor cost. The only controllable input is whether to introduce the product. A variety of possible values would be generated for the probabilistic inputs, and the resulting profit would be computed. We develop a simulation model for this type of application in Section 8.1.

2. **Airline Overbooking**   The objective of this simulation is to determine the number of reservations the airline should accept for a particular flight. A model is developed relating profit for the flight to a probabilistic input, the number of passengers that show up to use their reservations, and a

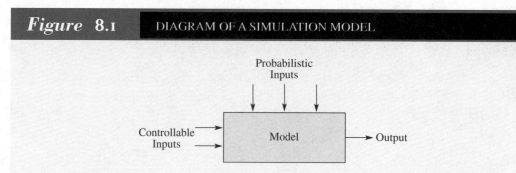

Figure 8.1   DIAGRAM OF A SIMULATION MODEL

controllable input, the number of reservations made. For each choice of a value for the controllable input, a variety of possible values would be generated for the number of passengers that show up, and the resulting profit would be computed. Similar models are applicable for hotel and car rental reservation systems.

3. **Inventory Policy**   The objective of this simulation is to choose an inventory policy that will provide good customer service at a reasonable cost. A model is developed relating cost and service level (2 output measures) to probabilistic inputs, such as product demand and delivery lead time from vendors, and controllable inputs, such as the order quantity and the reorder point. For each setting of the controllable inputs, a variety of possible values would be generated for the probabilistic inputs, and the resulting cost and service levels would be computed.

4. **Traffic Flow**   The objective of this simulation is to determine the effect of installing a left turn signal on the flow of traffic through a busy intersection. A model is developed relating waiting time for vehicles to get through the intersection to probabilistic inputs, such as the number of vehicle arrivals and the fraction that want to make a left turn, and controllable inputs, such as the length of time the left turn signal is on. For each setting of the controllable inputs, values would be generated for the probabilistic inputs, and the resulting vehicle waiting times would be computed.

5. **Waiting Lines**   The objective of this simulation is to determine the waiting times for customers at a bank's automatic teller machine (ATM). A model is developed relating customer waiting times to probabilistic inputs, such as customer arrivals and service times, and a controllable input, the number of ATM machines installed. For each value of the controllable input (a number of ATM machines), a variety of values would be generated for the probabilistic inputs and the customer waiting times would be computed. We develop a simulation model for this type of application in Section 8.3.

Simulation is not an optimization technique. It is a method that can be used to describe or predict how a system will operate given certain choices for the controllable inputs and randomly generated values for the probabilistic inputs. Management scientists often use simulation to determine values for the controllable inputs that are likely to lead to desirable system outputs. In this sense, simulation can be a very effective tool in designing a system to provide good performance.

In this chapter we begin by showing how simulation can be used for risk analysis; we use simulation to study the financial risks associated with a new product introduction. We continue with illustrations showing how simulation can be used to establish an effective inventory policy and how simulation can be used to design waiting line systems. Other issues such as verifying the simulation program, validating the model, and selecting a simulation software package are discussed in Section 8.4.

..../ /............

8.1   RISK ANALYSIS

Risk analysis is the process of predicting the outcome of a decision in the face of uncertainty. In this section, we describe a problem that involves considerable uncertainty: the introduction of a new product. We first show how risk analysis can be conducted without using simulation; then, we show how a much more comprehensive risk analysis can be conducted with the aid of simulation.

The PortaCom Printer

PortaCom manufactures personal computers and related equipment. PortaCom's product design group has developed a prototype for a high-quality portable printer with a 30-sheet paper feeder. The new printer has an innovative design and the potential to capture a significant share of the market. Preliminary marketing and financial analyses have led to establishing a selling price and budget for first-year administrative and advertising costs.

$$\text{Selling price} = \$249 \text{ per unit}$$
$$\text{Administrative cost} = \$400,000$$
$$\text{Advertising cost} = \$600,000$$

In the simulation model that we develop for the PortaCom problem, these values are treated as constants and referred to as **parameters** of the model.

The cost of direct labor, the cost of parts, and the first-year demand for the printer are not known with certainty and are considered probabilistic inputs. At this stage of the planning process, PortaCom's best estimates of these inputs are $45 per unit for the direct labor cost, $90 per unit for the parts cost, and 15,000 units for the first-year demand. PortaCom would like an analysis of the first-year profit potential for the printer. Because of a tight cash flow situation, company management is particularly concerned about the potential for a loss.

The What-If Approach

One approach to risk analysis is called **what-if analysis.** A what-if analysis here involves generating values for the three probabilistic inputs (direct labor cost, parts cost, and first-year demand) and computing the resulting value for profit. With a selling price of $249 per unit and administrative plus advertising costs equal to $400,000 + $600,000 = $1,000,000, the PortaCom profit model is

$$\text{Profit} = (\$249 - \text{Direct labor cost per unit} - \text{Parts cost per unit})(\text{Demand}) - \$1,000,000$$

Letting

$$c_1 = \text{direct labor cost per unit}$$
$$c_2 = \text{parts cost per unit}$$

and

$$x = \text{first-year demand}$$

the profit model for the first year can be written as follows:

$$\text{Profit} = (249 - c_1 - c_2)x - 1,000,000 \qquad (8.1)$$

Recall that PortaCom's best estimates of the direct labor cost per unit, the parts cost per unit, and first-year demand are $45, $90, and 15,000 units, respectively. These values constitute the **base-case scenario** for PortaCom. Substituting these values into equation (8.1) yields the following profit projection.

$$\text{Profit} = (249 - 45 - 90)(15{,}000) - 1{,}000{,}000 = 710{,}000$$

Thus, the base-case scenario leads to an anticipated profit of $710,000.

In risk analysis we are concerned with both the probability of a loss and the magnitude of a loss. Although the base-case scenario looks appealing, PortaCom might be interested in what happens if their estimates of the direct labor cost per unit, parts cost per unit, and first-year demand do not turn out to be as expected under the base-case scenario. For instance, suppose that PortaCom believes that direct labor costs could range from $43 to $47 per unit, parts cost could range from $80 to $100 per unit, and first-year demand could range from 1500 to 28,500 units. Using these ranges, what-if analysis can be used to evaluate a **worst-case scenario** and a **best-case scenario.**

The worst-case value for the direct labor cost is $47 (the highest value), the worst-case value for the parts cost is $100 (the highest value), and the worst-case value for demand is 1500 units (the lowest value). Thus, in the worst-case scenario, $c_1 = 47$, $c_2 = 100$, and $x = 1500$. Substituting these values into equation (8.1) leads to the following profit projection:

$$\text{Profit} = (249 - 47 - 100)(1500) - 1{,}000{,}000 = -847{,}000$$

So, the worst-case scenario leads to a projected loss of $847,000.

The best-case value for the direct labor cost is $c_1 = 43$ (the lowest value), the best-case value for the parts cost is 80 (the lowest value), and the best-case value for demand is 28,500 units (the highest value). Substituting these values into equation (8.1) leads to the following profit projection:

$$\text{Profit} = (249 - 43 - 80)(28{,}500) - 1{,}000{,}000 = 2{,}591{,}000$$

So, the best-case scenario leads to a projected profit of $2,591,000.

Problem 2 will give you practice with a what-if analysis application.

At this point the what-if analysis provides the conclusion that profits can range from a loss of $847,000 to a profit of $2,591,000 with a base-case scenario value of $710,000. The what-if analysis indicates that a substantial loss is possible, a substantial profit is possible, and the base-case profit of $710,000 is possible. Other scenarios that PortaCom might want to consider can also be evaluated. However, the difficulty with what-if analysis is that it does not tell us the likelihood of the various profit or loss values. In particular, we do not have any idea about the *probability* of a loss.

The Simulation Approach

The simulation approach to the PortaCom risk analysis problem is like playing out many what-if scenarios by randomly generating values for the probabilistic inputs. The advantage of the simulation approach is that it allows us to make an assessment of the probability of the possible profit and/or loss values. The PortaCom profit model can be depicted graphically as shown in Figure 8.2.

Using the what-if approach to risk analysis, we selected values for the probabilistic inputs [direct labor cost per unit (c_1), parts cost per unit (c_2), and first-year demand (x)], and

Figure 8.2   PORTACOM PROFIT MODEL

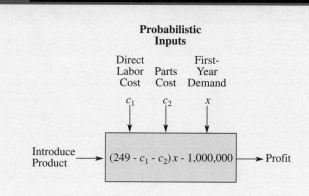

then computed the resulting profit. The three sets of values we used were the base-, worst-, and best-case scenarios. Applying simulation to the PortaCom problem requires generating values for the probabilistic inputs that are representative of what we might observe in practice. To generate such values, we must know the probability distribution for each probabilistic input. Further analysis by PortaCom has led to the following probability distributions for the direct labor cost per unit, the parts cost per unit, and first-year demand:

One advantage of simulation is the ability to use probability distributions that are unique to the system being studied.

Direct Labor Cost.   This cost ranges from $43 to $47 per unit and is described by the discrete probability distribution shown in Table 8.1. Thus, we see a 0.1 probability that the direct labor cost will be $43 per unit, a 0.2 probability that the direct labor cost will be $44 per unit, and so on. The highest probability of 0.4 is associated with a direct labor cost of $45 per unit.

Parts Cost.   This cost depends upon the general economy, the overall demand for parts, and the pricing policy of PortaCom's parts suppliers. Parts cost ranges from $80 to $100 per unit and is described by the uniform probability distribution shown in Figure 8.3. Values from $80 to $100 are equally likely.

First-Year Demand.   First-year demand is described by the normal probability distribution shown in Figure 8.4. The mean or expected value of first-year demand is 15,000 units. The standard deviation of 4500 units describes the variability in the first-year demand.

   To simulate the PortaCom problem, we must generate values for the three probabilistic inputs, and compute the resulting profit. Then generate another set of values for the

Table 8.1   PROBABILITY DISTRIBUTION FOR DIRECT LABOR COST PER UNIT FOR THE PORTACOM PRINTER

Direct Labor Cost per Unit	Probability
$43	0.1
$44	0.2
$45	0.4
$46	0.2
$47	0.1

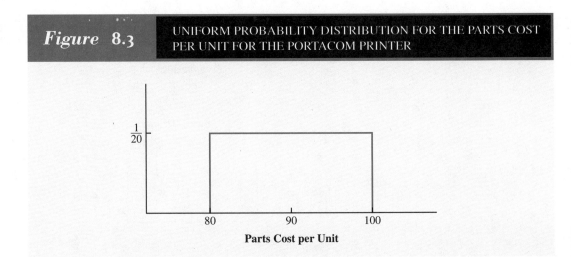

Figure 8.3 UNIFORM PROBABILITY DISTRIBUTION FOR THE PARTS COST PER UNIT FOR THE PORTACOM PRINTER

probabilistic inputs, compute a second value for profit, and so on. We continue this process until we are satisfied that enough trials have been conducted to provide a good picture of the distribution of profit values. This process of generating probabilistic inputs and computing the value of the output is called *simulation*. The sequence of logical and mathematical operations required to conduct a simulation is often depicted as a flowchart. A flowchart for the PortaCom simulation is depicted in Figure 8.5.

> A flowchart provides a graphical representation that helps describe the logic of the simulation model.

Following the logic described by the flowchart we see that the model parameters—selling price, administrative cost, and advertising cost—are set at their given values of $249, $400,000, and $600,000, respectively. These values will remain fixed throughout the simulation run.

The next three blocks depict the generation of values for the probabilistic inputs. First, a value for the direct labor cost (c_1) is generated. Then a value for the parts cost (c_2) is gen-

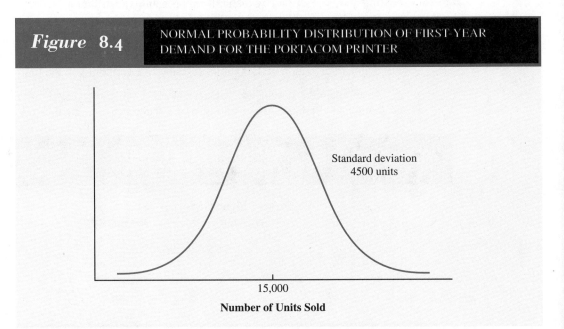

Figure 8.4 NORMAL PROBABILITY DISTRIBUTION OF FIRST-YEAR DEMAND FOR THE PORTACOM PRINTER

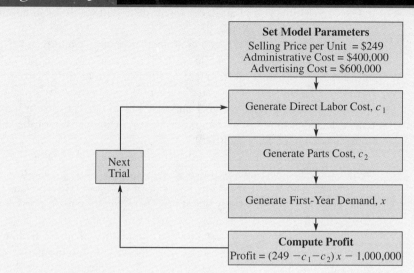

Figure 8.5   FLOWCHART FOR THE PORTACOM SIMULATION

Set Model Parameters
Selling Price per Unit = \$249
Administrative Cost = \$400,000
Advertising Cost = \$600,000

Generate Direct Labor Cost, c_1

Generate Parts Cost, c_2

Generate First-Year Demand, x

Compute Profit
Profit = $(249 - c_1 - c_2)x - 1{,}000{,}000$

Next Trial

erated, followed by a value for the first-year demand (x). These probabilistic input values are combined using the profit model given by equation (8.1).

$$\text{Profit} = (249 - c_1 - c_2)x - 1{,}000{,}000$$

The computation of profit completes one trial of the simulation run. We then return to the block where we generated the direct labor cost and begin another trial. This process is repeated until a satisfactory number of trials has been generated.

At the end of the simulation, output measures of interest can be developed. For example, we will be interested in computing the average profit and the probability of a loss. It should be clear that for the output measures to be meaningful, the values of the probabilistic inputs must have been representative of what is likely to happen when the PortaCom printer is introduced into the market. An essential part of the simulation procedure is the ability to generate representative values for the probabilistic inputs. We now discuss how to generate these values.

Random Numbers and Generating Probabilistic Input Values.   In running the PortaCom simulation, representative values must be generated for the direct labor cost per unit (c_1), the parts cost per unit (c_2), and the first-year demand (x). Random numbers and the probability distributions associated with each probabilistic input are used to generate representative values. To illustrate how to generate these values, we need to introduce the concept of *computer generated random numbers*.

Computer generated random numbers[1] are randomly selected over the interval from 0 up to, but not including, 1. Since each computer generated random number is equally likely, the computer generated random numbers are said to be uniformly distributed over the

---

1. Computer generated random numbers are called *pseudorandom numbers*. Since they are generated through the use of mathematical formulas, they are not technically random. The difference between random numbers and pseudorandom numbers is primarily philosophical, and we use the term *random numbers* regardless of whether they are generated by a computer.

interval from 0 to 1. Computer generated random numbers can be obtained using built-in functions available in computer simulation packages and spreadsheets. For instance, placing =RAND() in a cell of an Excel spreadsheet will result in a random number between 0 and 1 being placed into that cell.

Table 8.2 contains 500 random numbers generated using Excel. These numbers can be viewed as a random sample of 500 values from a uniform probability distribution that takes on values over the interval from 0 to 1. A uniform probability distribution over the interval from 0 to 1 has a mean or expected value of 0.5; moreover, 10% of the values are between 0.0 and 0.1, 10% are between 0.1 and 0.2, and so on. Thus, for a sample of 500 observations selected at random, we should expect to see about 10% of the values, or 50 observations, in each interval of width 0.1.

Table 8.3 shows the frequency distribution for the 500 computer generated random numbers in Table 8.2, and a histogram is shown in Figure 8.6. We should expect approximately 50 random numbers in each of the intervals of width 0.1. However, as you can see from the table, there is some variability about 50. Theoretically, the proportion in each interval will get closer and closer to 0.1 as more and more random numbers are generated. This same concept also applies in general to running any simulation. That is, the longer we run the simulation, the more likely the observed results will be representative of the system being simulated. We discuss these types of issues more thoroughly throughout the chapter.

Let us show how we use random numbers uniformly distributed over the interval from 0 to 1 to generate values for the PortaCom probability distributions. We begin by showing how to generate a value for the direct labor cost per unit. The approach described is applicable for generating values from any discrete probability distribution.

An interval of random numbers is assigned to each possible value of the direct labor cost in such a fashion that the probability of generating a random number in the interval is equal to the probability of the corresponding direct labor cost. Table 8.4 shows how this is done. The interval of random numbers 0.0 but less than 0.1 is associated with a direct labor cost of $43, the interval of random numbers 0.1 but less than 0.3 is associated with a direct labor cost of $44, and so on. With this assignment of random number intervals to the possible values of the direct labor cost, the probability of generating a random number in any interval is equal to the probability of obtaining the corresponding value for the direct labor cost. Thus, to generate a random value for the direct labor cost, we generate a random number between 0 and 1. If the random number is 0.0 but less than 0.1, we set the direct labor cost equal to $43. If the random number is 0.1 but less than 0.3, we set the direct labor cost equal to $44, and so on.

Each trial of the simulation requires a value for the direct labor cost. Suppose that on the first trial the random number generated is 0.9109. From Table 8.4, we see that the simulated value for the direct labor cost is $47 per unit. Suppose that on the second trial the random number is 0.2841. Since this random number is in the second interval of Table 8.4, the simulated value for the direct labor cost is $44 per unit. Table 8.5 shows the results obtained for the first 10 simulation trials.

Each trial in the simulation requires a value of direct labor cost, parts cost, and first-year demand. Let us now turn to the issue of generating values for parts cost. The probability distribution for parts cost is the uniform distribution shown in Figure 8.3. Since this random variable has a different probability distribution than direct labor cost, we use random numbers in a slightly different way to generate values for parts cost. With a uniform probability distribution, the following relationship between the random number and the associated value of the parts cost is used:

$$\text{Parts Cost} = a + r(b - a) \tag{8.2}$$

Because random numbers are equally likely, management scientists can assign ranges of random numbers to corresponding values of probabilistic inputs so that the probability of any input value to the simulation model is identical to the probability of its occurrence in the real system.

Problem 5 will give you the opportunity to establish intervals of random numbers and simulate demand from a discrete probability distribution.

Table	8.2		500 COMPUTER GENERATED RANDOM NUMBERS						
0.6953	0.5247	0.1368	0.9850	0.7467	0.3813	0.5827	0.7893	0.7169	0.8166
0.0082	0.9925	0.6874	0.2122	0.6885	0.2159	0.4299	0.3467	0.2186	0.1033
0.6799	0.1241	0.3056	0.5590	0.0423	0.6515	0.2750	0.8156	0.2871	0.4680
0.8898	0.1514	0.1826	0.0004	0.5259	0.2425	0.8421	0.9248	0.9155	0.9518
0.6515	0.5027	0.9290	0.5177	0.3134	0.9177	0.2605	0.6668	0.1167	0.7870
0.3976	0.7790	0.0035	0.0064	0.0441	0.3437	0.1248	0.5442	0.9800	0.1857
0.0642	0.4086	0.6078	0.2044	0.0484	0.4691	0.7058	0.8552	0.5029	0.3288
0.0377	0.5250	0.7774	0.2390	0.9121	0.5345	0.8178	0.8443	0.4154	0.2526
0.5739	0.5181	0.0234	0.7305	0.0376	0.5169	0.5679	0.5495	0.7872	0.5321
0.5827	0.0341	0.7482	0.6351	0.9146	0.4700	0.7869	0.1337	0.0702	0.4219
0.0508	0.7905	0.2932	0.4971	0.0225	0.4466	0.5118	0.1200	0.0200	0.5445
0.4757	0.1399	0.5668	0.9569	0.7255	0.4650	0.4084	0.3701	0.9446	0.8064
0.6805	0.9931	0.4166	0.1091	0.7730	0.0691	0.9411	0.3468	0.0014	0.7379
0.2603	0.7507	0.6414	0.9907	0.2699	0.4571	0.9254	0.2371	0.8664	0.9553
0.8143	0.7625	0.1708	0.1900	0.2781	0.2830	0.6877	0.0488	0.8635	0.3155
0.5681	0.7854	0.5016	0.9403	0.1078	0.5255	0.8727	0.3815	0.5541	0.9833
0.1501	0.9363	0.3858	0.3545	0.5448	0.0643	0.3167	0.6732	0.6283	0.2631
0.8806	0.7989	0.7484	0.8083	0.2701	0.5039	0.9439	0.1027	0.9677	0.4597
0.4582	0.7590	0.4393	0.4704	0.6903	0.3732	0.6587	0.8675	0.2905	0.3058
0.0785	0.1467	0.3880	0.5274	0.8723	0.7517	0.9905	0.8904	0.8177	0.6660
0.1158	0.6635	0.4992	0.9070	0.2975	0.5686	0.8495	0.1652	0.2039	0.2553
0.2762	0.7018	0.6782	0.4013	0.2224	0.4672	0.5753	0.6219	0.6871	0.9255
0.9382	0.6411	0.7984	0.0608	0.5945	0.3977	0.4570	0.9924	0.8398	0.8361
0.5102	0.7021	0.4353	0.3398	0.8038	0.2260	0.1250	0.1884	0.3432	0.1192
0.2354	0.7410	0.7089	0.2579	0.1358	0.8446	0.1648	0.3889	0.5620	0.6555
0.9082	0.7906	0.7589	0.8870	0.1189	0.7125	0.6324	0.1096	0.5155	0.3449
0.6936	0.0702	0.9716	0.0374	0.0683	0.2397	0.7753	0.2029	0.1464	0.8000
0.4042	0.8158	0.3623	0.6614	0.7954	0.7516	0.6518	0.3638	0.3107	0.2718
0.9410	0.2201	0.6348	0.0367	0.0311	0.0688	0.2346	0.3927	0.7327	0.9994
0.0917	0.2504	0.2878	0.1735	0.3872	0.6816	0.2731	0.3846	0.6621	0.8983
0.8532	0.4869	0.2685	0.6349	0.9364	0.3451	0.4998	0.2842	0.0643	0.6656
0.8980	0.0455	0.8314	0.8189	0.6783	0.8086	0.1386	0.4442	0.9941	0.6812
0.8412	0.8792	0.2025	0.9320	0.7656	0.3815	0.5302	0.8744	0.4584	0.3585
0.5688	0.8633	0.5818	0.0692	0.2543	0.5453	0.9955	0.1237	0.7535	0.5993
0.5006	0.1215	0.8102	0.1026	0.9251	0.6851	0.1559	0.1214	0.2628	0.9374
0.5748	0.4164	0.3427	0.2809	0.8064	0.5855	0.2229	0.2805	0.9139	0.9013
0.1100	0.0873	0.9407	0.8747	0.0496	0.4380	0.5847	0.4183	0.5929	0.4863
0.5802	0.7747	0.1285	0.0074	0.6252	0.7747	0.0112	0.3958	0.3285	0.5389
0.1019	0.6628	0.8998	0.1334	0.2798	0.7351	0.7330	0.6723	0.6924	0.3963
0.9909	0.8991	0.2298	0.2603	0.6921	0.5573	0.8191	0.0384	0.2954	0.0636
0.6292	0.4923	0.0276	0.6734	0.6562	0.4231	0.1980	0.6551	0.3716	0.0507
0.9430	0.2579	0.7933	0.0945	0.3192	0.3195	0.7772	0.4672	0.7070	0.5925
0.9938	0.7098	0.7964	0.7952	0.8947	0.1214	0.8454	0.8294	0.5394	0.9413
0.4690	0.1395	0.0930	0.3189	0.6972	0.7291	0.8513	0.9256	0.7478	0.8124
0.2028	0.3774	0.0485	0.7718	0.9656	0.2444	0.0304	0.1395	0.1577	0.8625
0.6141	0.4131	0.2006	0.2329	0.6182	0.5151	0.6300	0.9311	0.3837	0.7828
0.2757	0.8479	0.7880	0.8492	0.6859	0.8947	0.6246	0.1574	0.4936	0.8077
0.0561	0.0126	0.6531	0.0378	0.4975	0.1133	0.3572	0.0071	0.4555	0.7563
0.1419	0.4308	0.8073	0.4681	0.0481	0.2918	0.2975	0.0685	0.6384	0.0812
0.3125	0.0053	0.9209	0.9768	0.3584	0.0390	0.2161	0.6333	0.4391	0.6991

Table 8.3	FREQUENCY DISTRIBUTION FOR 500 COMPUTER GENERATED RANDOM NUMBERS

Interval	Frequency
0.0 but less than 0.1	53
0.1 but less than 0.2	47
0.2 but less than 0.3	56
0.3 but less than 0.4	44
0.4 but less than 0.5	43
0.5 but less than 0.6	49
0.6 but less than 0.7	54
0.7 but less than 0.8	52
0.8 but less than 0.9	53
0.9 but less than 1.0	49
Total	500

Figure 8.6	HISTOGRAM OF 500 RANDOM NUMBERS

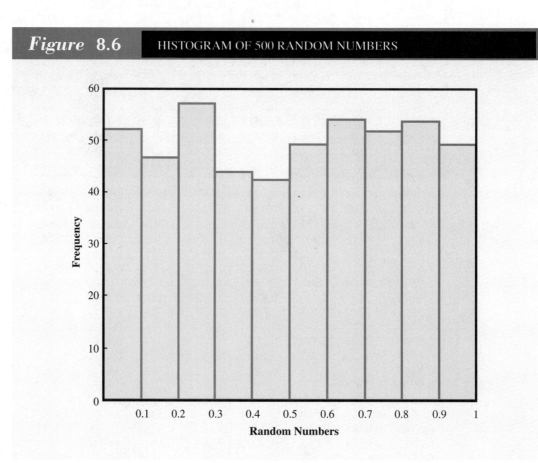

Table 8.4	RANDOM NUMBER INTERVALS FOR GENERATING VALUES OF DIRECT LABOR COST PER UNIT FOR THE PORTACOM PRINTER

Direct Labor Cost per Unit	Probability	Interval of Random Numbers
$43	0.1	0.0 but less than 0.1
$44	0.2	0.1 but less than 0.3
$45	0.4	0.3 but less than 0.7
$46	0.2	0.7 but less than 0.9
$47	0.1	0.9 but less than 1.0

Table 8.5	RANDOM GENERATION OF TEN VALUES FOR THE DIRECT LABOR COST PER UNIT

Trial	Random Number	Direct Labor Cost ($)
1	0.9109	47
2	0.2841	44
3	0.6531	45
4	0.0367	43
5	0.3451	45
6	0.2757	44
7	0.6859	45
8	0.6246	45
9	0.4936	45
10	0.8077	46

where

$$r = \text{random number between 0 and 1}$$

$$a = \text{smallest value for parts cost}$$

$$b = \text{largest value for parts cost}$$

For PortaCom, the smallest value for parts cost is $80, and the largest value is $100. Applying equation (8.2) with $a = 80$ and $b = 100$ leads to the following formula for generating parts cost given a random number, r.

$$\text{Parts Cost} = 80 + r(100 - 80) = 80 + r20 \qquad (8.3)$$

Let us use equation (8.3) to generate a value for parts cost. Suppose that a random number of 0.2680 is obtained. The value we would generate for the parts cost per unit is

$$\text{Parts Cost} = 80 + 0.2680(20) = 85.36 \text{ per unit}$$

Suppose that a random number of 0.5842 is generated on the next trial. The value we would generate for the parts cost is

$$\text{Parts Cost} = 80 + 0.5842(20) = 91.68 \text{ per unit}$$

With appropriate choices of a and b, equation (8.2) can be used to generate values for any uniform probability distribution. Table 8.6 shows the generation of ten values for parts cost.

Finally, we need a random number procedure for generating the first-year demand. Since first-year demand is normally distributed with a mean of 15,000 units and a standard deviation of 4500 units (see Figure 8.4), we need a procedure for generating random values from a normal probability distribution. Because of the mathematical complexity, a detailed discussion of the procedure for generating random values from a normal probability distribution is omitted. However, computer simulation packages and spreadsheets include a built-in function that provides randomly generated values from a normal probability distribution. In most cases the user only needs to provide the mean and standard deviation of the normal distribution. For example, using Excel the following formula can be placed into a cell to obtain a value for a probabilistic input that is normally distributed:

$$=\text{NORMINV(RAND(),Mean,Standard Deviation)}$$

Since the mean for the first-year demand in the PortaCom problem is 15,000 and the standard deviation is 4500, the Excel statement

$$=\text{NORMINV(RAND(),15000,4500)} \tag{8.4}$$

will provide a normally distributed value for first-year demand. For example, if RAND() generates the random number 0.7005, the Excel function shown in equation (8.4) will generate a first-year demand of 17,366 units. If RAND() generates the random number 0.3204, a first-year demand of 12,900 is generated. Table 8.7 shows the results for the first ten randomly generated values for demand. Note that random numbers less than 0.5 generate first-year demand values below the mean and that random numbers greater than 0.5 generate first-year demand values greater than the mean.

Running the Simulation Model.   Running the simulation model means implementing the sequence of logical and mathematical operations described in the flowchart in Figure 8.5. The model parameters are set at $249 per unit for the selling price, $400,000 for the administrative cost, and $600,000 for the advertising cost. Each trial in the simulation involves randomly generating values for the probabilistic inputs (direct labor cost, parts cost, and first-year demand) and computing profit. The simulation is complete when a satisfactory number of trials have been conducted.

> Spreadsheet packages such as Excel have built-in functions that make simulations based on probability distributions such as the normal probability distribution relatively easy.

Table 8.6	RANDOM GENERATION OF TEN VALUES FOR THE PARTS COST PER UNIT

Trial	Random Number	Parts Cost ($)
1	0.2680	85.36
2	0.5842	91.68
3	0.6675	93.35
4	0.9280	98.56
5	0.4180	88.36
6	0.7342	94.68
7	0.4325	88.65
8	0.1186	82.37
9	0.6944	93.89
10	0.7869	95.74

Table 8.7	RANDOM GENERATION OF TEN VALUES FOR FIRST-YEAR DEMAND

Trial	Random Number	Demand
1	0.7005	17,366
2	0.3204	12,900
3	0.8968	20,686
4	0.1804	10,888
5	0.4346	14,259
6	0.9605	22,904
7	0.5646	15,732
8	0.7334	17,804
9	0.0216	5,902
10	0.3218	12,918

Let us compute the profit for one trial assuming the following values have been generated for the probabilistic inputs:

Direct Labor Cost: $c_1 = 47$

Parts Cost: $c_2 = 85.36$

First-Year Demand: $x = 17,366$

Referring to the flowchart in Figure 8.5, we see that the profit obtained is

Profit $= (249 - c_1 - c_2)x - 1,000,000 = (249 - 47 - 85.36)17,366 - 1,000,000 = 1,025,570$

The first row of Table 8.8 shows the result of this first trial of the PortaCom simulation.

The simulated profit for the PortaCom printer if the direct labor cost is $47 per unit, the parts cost is $85.36 per unit, and first-year demand is 17,366 units is $1,025,570. This is the same profit value we would get from generating a what-if scenario with the given values

Table 8.8	PORTACOM SIMULATION RESULTS FOR TEN TRIALS

Trial	Direct Labor Cost per Unit ($)	Parts Cost per Unit ($)	Units Sold	Profit ($)
1	47	85.36	17,366	1,025,570
2	44	91.68	12,900	461,828
3	45	93.35	20,686	1,288,906
4	43	98.56	10,888	169,807
5	45	88.36	14,259	648,911
6	44	94.68	22,904	1,526,769
7	45	88.65	15,732	814,686
8	45	82.37	17,804	1,165,501
9	45	93.89	5,902	−350,131
10	46	95.74	12,918	385,585
Total	449	912.64	151,359	7,137,432
Average	$44.90	$91.26	$15,136	$713,743

for the probabilistic inputs. The difference is, with simulation, the values generated for the probabilistic inputs appear with the same likelihood that they would be expected to occur in practice. Of course, one simulation trial does not provide a complete understanding of the possible profit and loss levels. Since other values are possible for the probabilistic inputs, we can benefit from more simulation trials.

Suppose that on a second simulation trial, random numbers of 0.2841, 0.5842, and 0.3204 are generated for the direct labor cost, the parts cost, and first-year demand, respectively. These random numbers will generate values for the probabilistic inputs of $44 for the direct labor cost, $91.68 for the parts cost, and 12,900 for first-year demand. These values provide a simulated profit of $461,828 on the second simulation trial (see the second row of Table 8.8).

Repetition of the simulation process with different values for the probabilistic inputs is an essential part of any simulation. Through the repeated trials, management will begin to understand what might happen when the product is introduced into the real world. We have shown the results of ten simulation trials in Table 8.8. For these 10 cases, we find a profit as high as $1,526,769 for the 6th trial and a loss of $350,131 for the 9th trial. Thus, we see both the possibility of a profit and a loss. Some summary statistics for the ten trials are presented at the bottom of the table. We see that the total profit is $7,137,432 and the average profit is $713,743. The probability of a loss is 0.10, since one of the ten trials (the 9th) resulted in a loss. We note also that the average values for labor cost, parts cost, and first-year demand are fairly close to their means of $45, $90, and 15,000, respectively.

Simulation of the PortaCom Problem

Using an Excel spreadsheet, we simulated the PortaCom project 500 times. The spreadsheet used to carry out the simulation is shown in Figure 8.7. Note that simulation trials between 5 and 496 have been hidden so that the results can be shown in a reasonably sized figure. If desired, the rows for these trials can be shown and the simulation results displayed for all 500 trials. Let us describe the details of the Excel spreadsheet that provided the PortaCom simulation.

First, the PortaCom data are presented in the first 14 rows of the spreadsheet. The selling price per unit, administrative cost, and advertising cost parameters are entered directly into cells C3, C4, and C5. The discrete probability distribution for the direct labor cost per unit is shown in a tabular format. Note that the random number intervals are entered first followed by the corresponding cost per unit. For example, 0.0 in cell A10 and 0.1 in cell B10 show that a cost of $43 per unit will be assigned if the random number is in the interval 0.0 but less than 0.1. Thus, approximately 10% of the simulated direct labor costs will be $43 per unit. The uniform probability distribution with a smallest value of $80 in cell E8 and a largest value of $100 in cell E9 describes the parts cost per unit. Finally, a normal probability distribution with a mean of 15,000 units in cell E13 and a standard deviation of 4500 units in cell E14 describes the first-year demand distribution for the product. At this point we are ready to insert the Excel formulas that will carry out each simulation trial.

Simulation information for the first trial appears in row 21 of the spreadsheet. The cell formulas for row 21 are as follows:

        Cell A21   Enter 1 for the first simulation trial.

        Cell B21   Simulate the direct labor cost per unit[2]
                     =VLOOKUP(RAND(),$A$10:$C$14,3)

        Cell C21   Simulate the parts cost per unit (uniform distribution)
                     =$E$8+($E$9−$E$8)*RAND()

        Cell D21   Simulate the first-year demand (normal distribution)
                     =NORMINV(RAND(),$E$13,$E$14)

Figure 8.7   SPREADSHEET SIMULATION FOR THE PORTACOM PROBLEM

**SPREADSHEET
PORTACOM RISK
ANALYSIS**

	A	B	C	D	E	F
1	**PortaCom Risk Analysis**					
2						
3	Selling Price per Unit		$249			
4	Administrative Cost		$400,000			
5	Advertising Cost		$600,000			
6						
7	**Direct Labor Cost**			**Parts Cost (Uniform Distribution)**		
8	Lower	Upper		Smallest Value	$80	
9	Random No.	Random No.	Cost per Unit	Largest Value	$100	
10	0.0	0.1	$43			
11	0.1	0.3	$44			
12	0.3	0.7	$45	**Demand (Normal Distribution)**		
13	0.7	0.9	$46	Mean	15000	
14	0.9	1.0	$47	Standard Dev	4500	
15						
16						
17	**Simulation Trials**					
18						
19		Direct Labor	Parts	First-Year		
20	Trial	Cost Per Unit	Cost Per Unit	Demand	Profit	
21	1	47	$85.36	17,366	$1,025,570	
22	2	44	$91.68	12,900	$461,828	
23	3	45	$93.35	20,686	$1,288,906	
24	4	43	$98.56	10,888	$169,807	
25	5	45	$88.36	14,259	$648,911	
516	496	44	$98.67	8,730	($71,659)	
517	497	45	$94.38	19,257	$1,110,841	
518	498	44	$90.85	14,920	$703,102	
519	499	43	$90.37	13,471	$557,662	
520	500	46	$92.50	18,614	$1,056,927	
521						
522			**Summary Statistics**			
523			Mean Profit		$698,457	
524			Standard Deviation		$520,485	
525			Minimum Profit		($785,234)	
526			Maximum Profit		$2,367,058	
527			Number of Losses		51	
528			Probabilitiy of Loss		0.1020	

2. The VLOOKUP function generates a random number using the RAND() function. Then, using the table defined by the region from cells $A$10 to $C$14, the function identifies the row containing the RAND() random number and assigns the corresponding direct labor cost per unit shown in column 3.

Cell E21   The profit obtained for the first trial
$$=(\$C\$3-B21-C21)*D21-\$C\$4-\$C\$5$$

Cells A21:E21 can be copied to A520:E520 in order to provide the 500 simulation trials.

Ultimately, summary statistics will be collected in order to describe the results of the 500 simulated trials. Using the standard Excel functions, the following summary statistics are computed for the 500 simulated profits appearing in cells E21 to E520.

Cell E523   The mean profit per trial
$$=\text{AVERAGE(E21:E520)}$$

Cell E524   The standard deviation of profit
$$=\text{STDEV(E21:E520)}$$

Cell E525   The minimum profit
$$=\text{MIN(E21:E520)}$$

Cell E526   The maximum profit
$$=\text{MAX(E21:E520)}$$

Cell E527   The count of the number of trials where a loss occurred (i.e., profit $< \$0$)
$$=\text{COUNTIF(E21:E520,"<0")}$$

Cell E528   The percentage or probability of a loss based on the 500 trials
$$=\text{E527/500}$$

Simulation Results

The simulation results in Figure 8.7 provide information about the risk associated with PortaCom's new printer. The worst result obtained in a simulation of 500 trials is a loss of $785,234, and the best result is a profit of $2,367,058. The mean profit is $698,457. Fifty-one of the trials resulted in a loss; thus, the estimated probability of a loss is $51/500 = 0.1020$.

Simulation studies enable an objective estimate of the probability of a loss, which is an important aspect of risk analysis.

Excel's Data Analysis Histogram routine was used to generate the histogram of simulated profit values shown in Figure 8.8. We note that the distribution of profit values is fairly symmetric with a large number of values in the range of $250,000 to $1,250,000. The probability of a large loss or a large gain is small. Only 3 trials resulted in a loss more than $500,000, and only 3 trials resulted in a profit greater than $2,000,000. However, the probability of a loss is significant. Forty-eight of the 500 trials resulted in a loss in the $0 to $500,000 range—almost 10%. The modal category, the one with the largest number of values, is the range of profits between $750,000 and $1,000,000.

In comparing the simulation approach to risk analysis to the what-if approach, we see that much more information is obtained by using simulation. With the what-if anaylsis, we learned that the base-case scenario projected a profit of $710,000. The worst-case scenario projected a loss of $847,000, and the best-case scenario projected a profit of $2,591,000. From the 500 trials of the simulation run, we see that the worst- and best-case scenarios, although possible, are very unlikely. None of the 500 trials provided a loss as low as the worst-case or a profit as high as the best-case. Indeed, the advantage of simulation for risk analysis is the information it provides on the likely values of the output. We now know the probability of a loss, how the profit values are distributed over their range, and what profit values are most likely.

Figure 8.8   HISTOGRAM OF SIMULATED PROFIT FOR 500 TRIALS OF THE PORTACOM SIMULATION

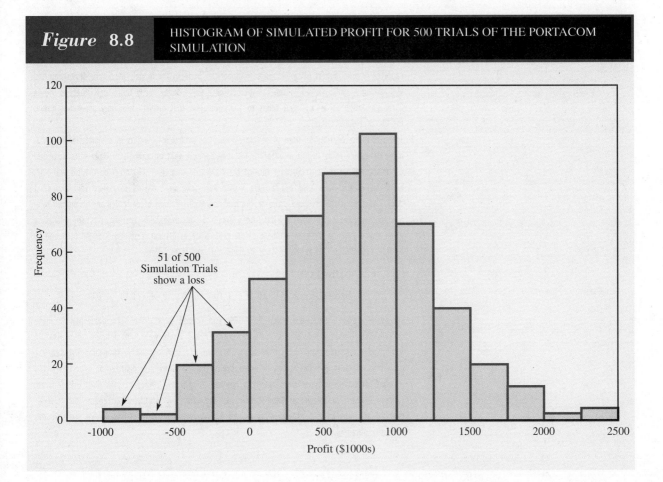

You should be able to work Problems 9 and 14 at this point.

The simulation results help PortaCom's management better understand the profit/loss potential of the PortaCom portable printer. The 0.1020 probability of a loss may be acceptable to management given a probability of almost 0.80 (see Figure 8.8) that profit will exceed $250,000. If not, PortaCom might want to conduct further market research before deciding whether to introduce the product. In any case, the simulation results should be a help in reaching an appropriate decision.

A Note about Simulation with Spreadsheets

In most cases calculation of spreadsheets is done automatically. Thus, if a simulation spreadsheet is reopened or if a cell entry is changed, the random numbers provided by RAND() will be updated and a completely new set of simulation results will be provided. In general, the results will be different but close to the results provided by the previous simulation. If the user wishes to turn the automatic calculation off, the Excel **Tools** and **Options** menus can be used to select **Manual** rather than **Automatic Calculation.** Regardless of whether **Manual** or **Automatic** is selected, the user can press the F9 key any time to obtain a completely new set of simulation results.

1. The PortaCom simulation model is based on independent trials in which what happens during one trial does not affect what happens in subsequent trials. Historically, simulation studies such as this were referred to as *Monte Carlo simulations*. The term *Monte Carlo simulation* was used because early practitioners of simulation saw similarities between the models they were developing and the gambling games played in the casinos of Monte Carlo. Today, many individuals interpret Monte Carlo simulation as a term that refers to any simulation that involves randomly generating values for the probabilistic inputs.

2. The probability distribution used to generate values for probabilistic inputs in a simulation model is often developed using historical data. For instance, suppose that an analysis of daily sales at a new car dealership for the past 50 days showed: On 2 days no cars were sold; on 5 days 1 car was sold; on 9 days 2 cars were sold; on 24 days 3 cars were sold; on 7 days 4 cars were sold; and on 3 days 5 cars were sold. We can estimate the probability distribution of daily demand using the relative frequencies for the observed data. An estimate of the probability that no cars are sold on a given day is $2/50 = 0.04$, an estimate of the probability that 1 car is sold is $5/50 = 0.10$ and so on. The probability distribution of daily demand obtained is as follows:

Daily Sales	0	1	2	3	4	5
Probability	0.04	0.10	0.18	0.48	0.14	0.06

3. Spreadsheet add-in packages such as @RISK® and Crystal Ball® have been developed to make spreadsheet simulation easier. For instance, using Crystal Ball® we could simulate the PortaCom new product introduction by first entering the formulas showing the relationships between the probabilistic inputs and the output measure, profit. Then, a probability distribution type is selected for each probabilistic input from among a number of available choices. Crystal Ball will generate random values for each probabilistic input, compute the profit, and repeat the simulation for as many trials as specified. Graphical displays and a variety of descriptive statistics can be easily obtained.

8.2   AN INVENTORY SIMULATION

In this section we describe how simulation can be used to establish an inventory policy for a product that has an uncertain demand. The product is a home ventilation fan distributed by the Butler Electrical Supply Company. Each fan costs Butler $75 and sells for $125. Thus Butler realizes a gross profit of $125 - $75 = $50 for each fan sold. Monthly demand for the fan is described by a normal probability distribution with a mean of 100 units and a standard deviation of 20 units.

Butler receives monthly deliveries from its supplier and replenishes its inventory to a level of Q at the beginning of each month. This beginning inventory level is referred to as the replenishment level. If monthly demand is less than the replenishment level, an inventory holding cost of $15 is charged for each unit that is not sold. However, if monthly demand is greater than the replenishment level, a stockout occurs and a shortage cost is incurred. Since Butler assigns a goodwill cost of $30 for each customer turned away, a shortage cost of $30 is charged for each unit of demand that cannot be satisfied. Management would like to use a simulation model to determine the average monthly net profit resulting from using a particular replenishment level. Management would also like information on the percentage of total demand that will be satisfied. This percentage is referred to as the *service level*.

The controllable input to the Butler simulation model is the replenishment level, Q. The probabilistic input is the monthly demand, D. There are two output measures: the average monthly net profit and the service level. Computation of the service level requires that we keep track of the number of fans sold each month and the total demand for fans for each month. The service level will be computed at the end of the simulation run as the ratio of total units sold to total demand. A diagram showing the relationship between the inputs and the outputs is shown in Figure 8.9.

When demand is less than or equal to the replenishment level ($D \leq Q$), D units are sold, and an inventory holding cost of $15 is incurred for each of the $Q - D$ units that remain in inventory. Net profit for this case is computed as follows:

Case 1: $D \leq Q$

$$\text{Gross Profit} = \$50D$$

$$\text{Holding Cost} = \$15(Q - D)$$

$$\text{Net Profit} = \text{Gross Profit} - \text{Holding Cost} = \$50D - \$15(Q - D) \qquad (8.5)$$

When demand is greater than the replenishment level ($D > Q$), Q fans are sold, and a shortage cost of $30 is imposed for each of the $D - Q$ units of demand not satisfied. Net profit for this case is computed as follows:

Case 2: $D > Q$

$$\text{Gross Profit} = \$50Q$$

$$\text{Shortage Cost} = \$30(D - Q)$$

$$\text{Net Profit} = \text{Gross Profit} - \text{Shortage Cost} = \$50Q - \$30(D - Q) \qquad (8.6)$$

Figure 8.10 shows a flowchart that defines the sequence of logical and mathematical operations required to simulate the Butler inventory system. Each trial in the simulation represents one month of operation. The simulation is run for 300 months using a given replenishment level, Q. Then, the average profit and service level output measures are computed. Let us describe the steps involved in the simulation by illustrating the results for the first two months of a simulation run using a replenishment level of $Q = 100$.

The first block of the flowchart in Figure 8.10 sets the values of the model parameters: gross profit = $50 per unit, holding cost = $15 per unit, and goodwill cost = $30 per unit. The next block shows that a replenishment level of Q is selected; in our illustration, $Q = 100$. Then, a value for monthly demand is generated. Since monthly demand is normally distributed with a mean of 100 units and a standard deviation of 20 units, we can use the Excel function = NORMINV(RAND(),100,20), as described in Section 8.1, to generate

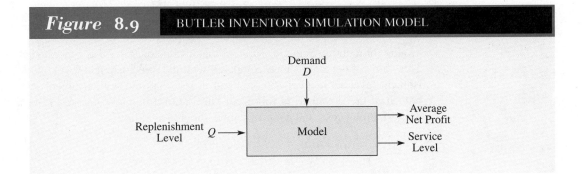

Figure 8.9   BUTLER INVENTORY SIMULATION MODEL

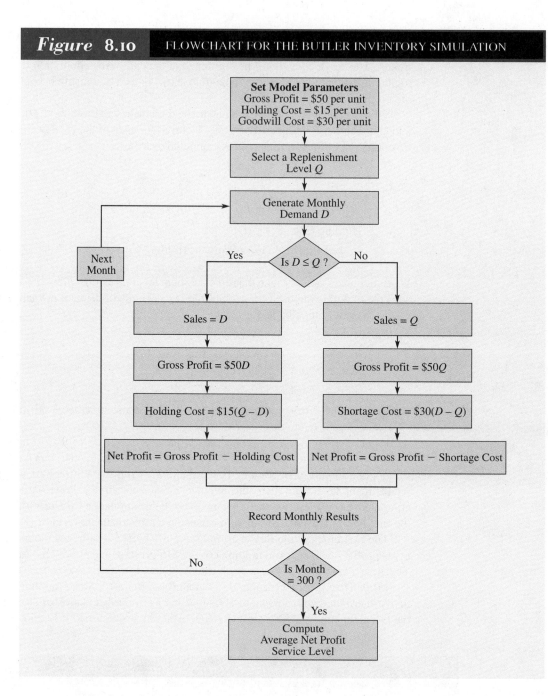

Figure 8.10 FLOWCHART FOR THE BUTLER INVENTORY SIMULATION

a value for monthly demand. Suppose that a value of $D = 79$ is generated on the first trial. This value of demand is then compared with the replenishment level, Q. With the replenishment level set at $Q = 100$, demand is less than the replenishment level, and the left branch of the flowchart is followed. Sales are set equal to demand (79), and then gross profit, holding cost, and net profit are computed as follows:

$$\text{Gross Profit} = 50D = 50(79) = 3950$$

$$\text{Holding Cost} = 15(Q - D) = 15(100 - 79) = 315$$

$$\text{Net Profit} = \text{Gross Profit} - \text{Holding Cost} = 3950 - 315 = 3635$$

The values of demand, sales, gross profit, holding cost, and net profit are recorded for the first month. The first row of Table 8.9 summarizes the information for this first trial.

For the second month, suppose that a value of 111 is generated for monthly demand. Since demand is greater than the replenishment level, the right branch of the flowchart is followed. Sales are set equal to the replenishment level (100), and then gross profit, shortage cost, and net profit are computed as follows:

$$\text{Gross Profit} = 50Q = 50(100) = 5000$$
$$\text{Shortage Cost} = 30(D - Q) = 30(111 - 100) = 330$$
$$\text{Net Profit} = \text{Gross Profit} - \text{Shortage Cost} = 5000 - 330 = 4670$$

The values of demand, sales, gross profit, holding cost, shortage cost, and net profit are recorded for the second month. The second row of Table 8.9 summarizes some of the information generated in the second trial.

Results for the first 5 months of the simulation are shown in Table 8.9. The totals show that we have an accumulated total profit of $22,310, which is an average monthly profit of $22,310/5 = $4,462. Total unit sales are 472, and total demand is 501. Thus, the service level is 472/501 = .942, or 94.2%.

Simulation of the Butler Inventory Problem

Using an Excel spreadsheet, we simulated the Butler inventory operation for 300 months. The spreadsheet used to carry out the simulation is shown in Figure 8.11. Note that simulation months between 5 and 296 have been hidden so that the results can be shown in a reasonably sized figure. If desired, the rows for these months can be shown and the simulation results displayed for all 300 months. Let us describe the details of the Excel spreadsheet that provided the Butler inventory simulation.

First, the Butler inventory data are presented in the first 11 rows of the spreadsheet. The gross profit per unit, holding cost per unit, and shortage cost per unit data are entered directly into cells C3, C4, and C5. The replenishment level is entered into cell C7, and the mean and standard deviation of the normal probability distribution for demand are entered into cells B10 and B11. At this point we are ready to insert Excel formulas that will carry out each simulation month or trial.

Table **8.9**	BUTLER INVENTORY SIMULATION RESULTS FOR FIVE TRIALS WITH $Q = 100$					
Month	**Demand**	**Sales**	**Gross Profit ($)**	**Holding Cost ($)**	**Shortage Cost ($)**	**Net Profit ($)**
1	79	79	3950	315	0	3635
2	111	100	5000	0	330	4670
3	93	93	4650	105	0	4545
4	100	100	5000	0	0	5000
5	118	100	5000	0	540	4460
Totals	501	472	23,600	420	870	22,310
Average	100	94	$4,720	$ 84	$174	$4,462

	SPREADSHEET SIMULATION FOR THE BUTLER INVENTORY
Figure 8.11	PROBLEM

	A	B	C	D	E	F	G
1	**Butler Inventory**						
2							
3	Gross Profit per Unit		$50				
4	Holding Cost per Unit		$15				
5	Shortage Cost per Unit		$30				
6							
7	**Replenishment Level**		100				
8							
9	**Demand (Normal Distribution)**						
10	Mean	100					
11	Standard Dev	20					
12							
13							
14	**Simulation**						
15							
16	Month	Demand	Sales	Gross Profit	Holding Cost	Shortage Cost	Net Profit
17	1	79	79	$3,950	$315	$0	$3,635
18	2	111	100	$5,000	$0	$330	$4,670
19	3	93	93	$4,650	$105	$0	$4,545
20	4	100	100	$5,000	$0	$0	$5,000
21	5	118	100	$5,000	$0	$540	$4,460
312	296	89	89	$4,450	$165	$0	$4,285
313	297	91	91	$4,550	$135	$0	$4,415
314	298	122	100	$5,000	$0	$660	$4,340
315	299	93	93	$4,650	$105	$0	$4,545
316	300	126	100	$5,000	$0	$780	$4,220
317							
318	**Totals**	30,181	27,917		**Summary Statistics**		
319					Mean Profit		$4,293
320					Standard Deviation		$658
321					Minimum Profit		($206)
322					Maximum Profit		$5,000
323					Service Level		92.5%

Simulation information for the first month or trial appears in row 17 of the spreadsheet. The cell formulas for row 17 are as follows:

Cell A17   Enter 1 for the first simulation month

Cell B17   Simulate demand (normal distribution)

=NORMINV(RAND(),$B$10,$B$11)

Next compute the sales, which is equal to demand (cell B17) if demand is less than or equal to the replenishment level, or is equal to the replenishment level (cell C7) if demand is greater than the replenishment level.

Cell C17   Compute sales

$$=IF(B17<=\$C\$7,B17,\$C\$7)$$

Cell D17   Calculate gross profit

$$=\$C\$3*C17$$

Cell E17   Calculate the holding cost if demand is less than or equal to the replenishment level

$$=IF(B17<=\$C\$7,\$C\$4*(\$C\$7-B17),0)$$

Cell F17   Calculate the shortage cost if demand is greater than the replenishment level

$$=IF(B17<=\$C\$7,0,\$C\$5*(B17-\$C\$7))$$

Cell G17   Calculate net profit

$$=D17-E17-F17$$

Cells A17:G17 can be copied to cells A316:G316 in order to provide the 300 simulation months.

Finally, summary statistics will be collected in order to describe the results of the 300 simulated trials. Using the standard Excel functions, the following totals and summary statistics are computed for the 300 months.

Cell B318   Total Demand

$$=SUM(B17:B316)$$

Cell C319   Total Sales

$$=SUM(C17:C316)$$

Cell G319   The mean profit per month

$$=AVERAGE(G17:G316)$$

Cell G320   The standard deviation of profit

$$=STDEV(G17:G316)$$

Cell G321   The minimum profit

$$=MIN(G17:G316)$$

Cell G322   The maximum profit

$$=MAX(G17:G316)$$

Cell G323   The service level

$$=C318/B318$$

Simulation Results

The simulation results in Figure 8.11 show what can be anticipated over 300 months if Butler operates its inventory using a replenishment level of 100. The average net profit is $4,293 per month. Since 27,917 units of the total demand of 30,181 units were satisfied, the service level is 27,917/30,181 = 92.5%. We are now ready to use the simulation model to consider other replenishment levels that may improve the net profit and the service level.

At this point, we conducted a series of simulation experiments by repeating the Butler inventory simulation with replenishment levels of 110, 120, 130, and 140 units. The average

Table 8.10	BUTLER INVENTORY SIMULATION RESULTS FOR 300 TRIALS

Replenishment Level	Average Net Profit ($)	Service Level (%)
100	4293	92.5
110	4524	96.5
120	4575	98.6
130	4519	99.6
140	4399	99.9

Simulation allows the user to consider different operating policies and changes to model parameters and then to observe the impact of the changes on output measures such as profit or service level.

monthly net profits and the service levels are shown in Table 8.10. The highest monthly net profit of $4,575 occurs with a replenishment level of $Q = 120$. The associated service level is 98.6%. On the basis of these results, Butler selected a replenishment level of $Q = 120$.

Experimental simulation studies, such as this one for Butler's inventory policy, can help identify good operating policies and decisions. Butler's management has used simulation to choose a replenishment level of 120 for its home ventilation fan. With the simulation model in place, management can also explore the sensitivity of this decision to some of the model parameters. For instance, we assigned a shortage cost of $30 for any customer demand not met. With this shortage cost, the replenishment level was $Q = 120$ and the service level was 98.6%. If management felt a more appropriate shortage cost was $10 per unit, running the simulation again using $10 as the shortage cost would be a simple matter. In this case, we would expect a smaller value of Q yielding the best results.

We mentioned earlier that simulation is not an optimization technique. Even though we have used simulation to choose a replenishment level, we have no guarantee that this choice is optimal. All possible replenishment levels were not tested. Perhaps a manager would like to consider additional simulation runs with replenishment levels of $Q = 115$ and $Q = 125$ to search for an even better inventory policy. Also, we have no guarantee that with another set of 300 demand values generated the replenishment level with the highest profit would not change. However, with a large number of simulation trials, we should find a very good and, at least, near optimal solution.

Problem 18 will give you a chance to develop a different simulation model and design a new spreadsheet.

8.3   A WAITING LINE SIMULATION

The simulation models discussed thus far have been based on independent trials in which the results for one trial do not affect what happens on subsequent trials. In this sense, the system being modeled does not change or evolve over time. These simulation models are referred to as **static simulation models.** In this section, we develop a simulation model of a waiting line system where the state of the system, including the number of customers in the waiting line and whether the service facility is busy or idle, changes or evolves over time. To incorporate time into the simulation model, we use a simulation clock to record the time that each customer arrives for service as well as the time that each customer completes service. Whenever a simulation clock is used to keep track of the time that events occur and whenever the model is used to record how the system changes or evolves over time, the simulation model is referred to as a **dynamic simulation model.** Since the arrivals and departures of customers are **events** that occur at *discrete* points in time, the simulation model is also referred to as a **discrete-event simulation model.**

In Chapter 7, we presented formulas that could be used to compute the steady-state operating characteristics of a waiting line, including the average waiting time, the average number of units in the waiting line, the probability of waiting, and so on. In most cases, the waiting line formulas were based on specific assumptions about the probability distribution for arrivals, the probability distribution for service times, the queue discipline, and so on. Simulation is an alternative for studying waiting lines that is more flexible. In applications where the assumptions required by the waiting line formulas are not reasonable, simulation may be the only feasible approach to the study of the waiting line system. In this section we discuss the simulation of the waiting line for the Hammondsport Savings Bank automated teller machine (ATM).

The Hammondsport Savings Bank ATM Waiting Line

Hammondsport Savings Bank will open several new branch banks during the coming year. Each new branch is designed to have one automated teller machine (ATM). A concern is that during busy periods several customers may have to wait to use the ATM. This concern has led the bank to undertake a study of the ATM waiting line system. The bank's vice president wants to determine whether one ATM will be sufficient. The bank has established service guidelines for its ATM system stating that the average customer waiting time for an ATM should be one minute or less. Let us show how a simulation model can be used to study the ATM waiting line at a particular branch.

Customer Arrival Times

One probabilistic input to the ATM simulation model is the arrival times of customers who want to use the ATM. In waiting line simulations, arrival times are determined by randomly generating the time between two successive arrivals, referred to as the *interarrival time.* For the branch bank being studied, the customer interarrival times are uniformly distributed between 0 and 5 minutes as shown in Figure 8.12. With r denoting a random number between 0 and 1, an interarrival time for two successive customers can be simulated using the formula presented in Section 8.1 for generating values from a uniform probability distribution.

$$\text{Interarrival Time} = a + r(b - a)$$

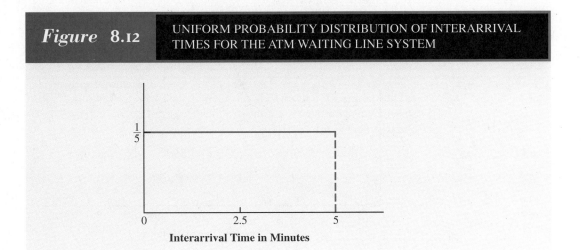

Figure 8.12   UNIFORM PROBABILITY DISTRIBUTION OF INTERARRIVAL TIMES FOR THE ATM WAITING LINE SYSTEM

where

$$r = \text{random number between 0 and 1}$$
$$a = \text{minimum interarrival time}$$
$$b = \text{maximum interarrival time}$$

A uniform probability distribution of interarrival times is used here to simplify the simulation computations. Actually, any interarrival time probability distribution can be assumed, and the logic of the waiting line simulation model will not change.

For the Hammondsport ATM system, the minimum interarrival time is $a = 0$ minutes, and the maximum interarrival time is $b = 5$ minutes; therefore, the formula for generating an interarrival time is

$$\text{Interarrival Time} = 0 + r(5 - 0) = 5r$$

Assume that the simulation run begins at time $= 0$. A random number of $r = 0.2804$ generates an interarrival time of $5(0.2804) = 1.4$ minutes for customer 1. Thus, customer 1 arrives 1.4 minutes after the simulation run begins. A second random number of $r = 0.2598$ generates an interarrival time of $5(0.2598) = 1.3$ minutes, indicating that customer 2 arrives 1.3 minutes after customer 1. Thus, customer 2 arrives $1.4 + 1.3 = 2.7$ minutes after the simulation begins. Continuing, a third random number of $r = 0.9802$ indicates that customer 3 arrives 4.9 minutes after customer 2, which is 7.6 minutes after the simulation begins.

Customer Service Times

Another probabilistic input in the ATM simulation model is the service time, which is the time a customer spends using the ATM machine. The service time does not include waiting time. Past data from similar ATMs indicates that a normal probability distribution with a mean of 2 minutes and a standard deviation of 0.5 minutes, as shown in Figure 8.13, can be used to describe service times. As discussed in the previous sections, values from a normal probability distribution with mean 2 and standard deviation 0.5 can be generated using the

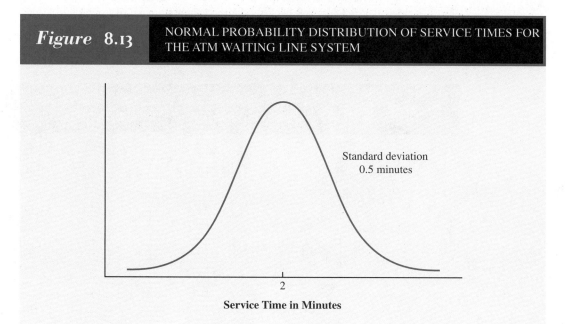

Figure 8.13   NORMAL PROBABILITY DISTRIBUTION OF SERVICE TIMES FOR THE ATM WAITING LINE SYSTEM

Standard deviation 0.5 minutes

2

Service Time in Minutes

Excel function =NORMINV(RAND(),2,0.5). For example, the random number of 0.7257 generates a customer service time of 2.3 minutes.

The Simulation Model

The probabilistic inputs to the Hammondsport Savings Bank ATM simulation model are the values of the interarrival time and the service time. The controllable input is the number of ATMs used. The output will consist of various operating characteristics such as the probability of waiting, the average waiting time, the maximum waiting time and so on. We show a diagram of the ATM simulation model in Figure 8.14.

Figure 8.15 shows a flowchart that defines the sequence of logical and mathematical operations required to simulate the Hammondsport ATM system. The flowchart uses the following notation:

$$IAT = \text{Interarrival Time generated}$$
$$\text{Arrival Time } (i) = \text{Time at which customer } i \text{ arrives}$$
$$\text{Start Time } (i) = \text{Time at which customer } i \text{ starts service}$$
$$\text{Wait Time } (i) = \text{Waiting time for customer } i$$
$$ST = \text{Service Time generated}$$
$$\text{Completion Time } (i) = \text{Time at which customer } i \text{ completes service}$$
$$\text{System Time } (i) = \text{System time for customer } i \text{ (waiting time + service time)}$$

Referring to Figure 8.15, we see that the simulation is initialized in the first block of the flowchart. Then a new customer is created. An interarrival time is generated to determine the time since the preceding customer arrived.[3] The arrival time for the new customer is then computed by adding the interarrival time to the arrival time of the preceding customer.

The arrival time for the new customer must be compared to the completion time of the preceding customer to determine whether the ATM is idle or busy. If the arrival time of the new customer is greater than the completion time of the preceding customer, the preceding customer will have finished service prior to the arrival of the new customer. In this case, the ATM will be idle, and the new customer can begin service immediately. The service starting time for the new customer is equal to the arrival time of the new customer. However, if the arrival time for the new customer is not greater than the completion time of the preceding

The decision rule for deciding whether the ATM is idle or busy is the most difficult aspect of the logic in a waiting line simulation model.

Figure 8.14   HAMMONDSPORT SAVINGS BANK ATM SIMULATION MODEL

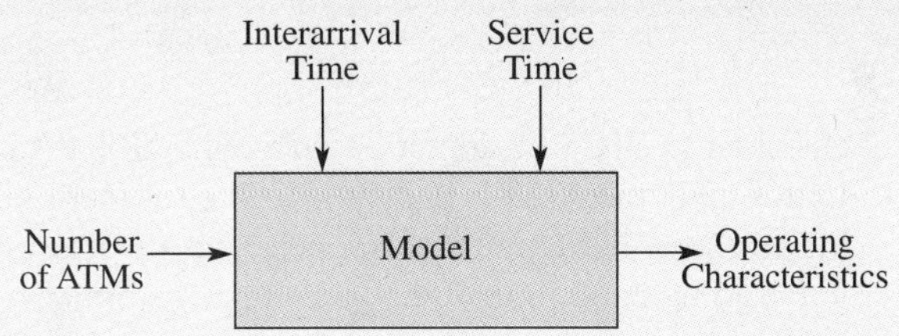

3. For the first customer, the interarrival time determines the time since the simulation started. Thus, the first interarrival time determines the time the first customer arrives.

Figure 8.15   FLOWCHART OF THE HAMMONDSPORT SAVINGS BANK ATM WAITING LINE SIMULATION

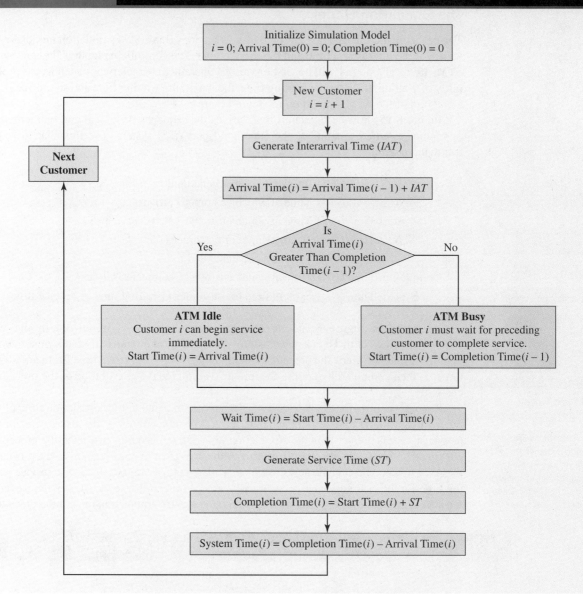

customer, the new customer has arrived before the preceding customer has finished service. In this case, the ATM is busy; the new customer must wait to use the ATM until the preceding customer has completed service. The service starting time for the new customer is equal to the completion time of the preceding customer.

Note that the time the new customer has to wait to use the ATM is the difference between the customer's service starting time and the customer's arrival time. At this point, the customer is ready to use the ATM, and the simulation run continues with the generation of the customer's service time. The time at which the customer begins service plus the service time generated determine the customer's completion time. Finally, the total time the customer spends in the system is the difference between the customer's service completion time and the customer's arrival time. At this point, the computations are complete for the current customer, and the simulation continues with the next customer. The simulation is continued until a specified number of customers have been served by the ATM.

Simulation results for the first ten customers are shown in Table 8.11. We discuss the computations for the first 3 customers to illustrate the logic of the simulation model and to show how the information in Table 8.11 was developed.

Customer 1

- An interarrival time of IAT = 1.4 minutes is generated.
- Since the simulation run begins at time 0, the arrival time for customer 1 is $0 + 1.4$ = 1.4 minutes.
- Customer 1 may begin service immediately with a start time of 1.4 minutes.
- The waiting time for customer 1 is the start time minus the arrival time: $1.4 - 1.4 = 0$ minutes.
- A service time of ST = 2.3 minutes is generated for customer 1.
- The completion time for customer 1 is the start time plus the service time: $1.4 + 2.3$ = 3.7 minutes.
- The time in the system for customer 1 is the completion time minus the arrival time: $3.7 - 1.4 = 2.3$ minutes.

Customer 2

- An interarrival time of IAT = 1.3 minutes is generated.
- Since the arrival time of customer 1 is 1.4, the arrival time for customer 2 is $1.4 + 1.3$ = 2.7 minutes.
- Since the completion time of customer 1 is 3.7 minutes, the arrival time of customer 2 is not greater than the completion time of customer 1; thus, the ATM is busy when customer 2 arrives.

Table 8.11 — SIMULATION RESULTS FOR TEN ATM CUSTOMERS

Customer	Interarrival Time	Arrival Time	Service Start Time	Waiting Time	Service Time	Completion Time	Time in System
1	1.4	1.4	1.4	0.0	2.3	3.7	2.3
2	1.3	2.7	3.7	1.0	1.5	5.2	2.5
3	4.9	7.6	7.6	0.0	2.2	9.8	2.2
4	3.5	11.1	11.1	0.0	2.5	13.6	2.5
5	0.7	11.8	13.6	1.8	1.8	15.4	3.6
6	2.8	14.6	15.4	0.8	2.4	17.8	3.2
7	2.1	16.7	17.8	1.1	2.1	19.9	3.2
8	0.6	17.3	19.9	2.6	1.8	21.7	4.4
9	2.5	19.8	21.7	1.9	2.0	23.7	3.9
10	1.9	21.7	23.7	2.0	2.3	26.0	4.3
Totals	21.7			11.2	20.9		32.1
Averages	2.17			1.12	2.09		3.21

- Customer 2 must wait for customer 1 to complete service before beginning service. Since customer 1 completes service at 3.7 minutes, the starting time for customer 2 is 3.7 minutes.
- The waiting time for customer 2 is the start time minus the arrival time: $3.7 - 2.7 = 1$ minute.
- A service time of $ST = 1.5$ minutes is generated for customer 2.
- The completion time for customer 2 is the start time plus the service time: $3.7 + 1.5 = 5.2$ minutes.
- The time in the system for customer 2 is the completion time minus the arrival time: $5.2 - 2.7 = 2.5$ minutes.

Customer 3

- An interarrival time of $IAT = 4.9$ minutes is generated.
- Since the arrival time of customer 2 was 2.7 minutes, the arrival time for customer 3 is $2.7 + 4.9 = 7.6$ minutes.
- The completion time of customer 2 is 5.2 minutes, so the arrival time for customer 3 is greater than the completion time of customer 2. Thus, the ATM is idle when customer 3 arrives.
- Customer 3 begins service immediately with a start time of 7.6 minutes.
- The waiting time for customer 3 is the start time minus the arrival time: $7.6 - 7.6 = 0$ minutes.
- A service time of $ST = 2.2$ minutes is generated for customer 3.
- The completion time for customer 3 is the start time plus the service time: $7.6 + 2.2 = 9.8$ minutes.
- The time in the system for customer 3 is the completion time minus the arrival time: $9.8 - 7.6 = 2.2$ minutes.

Using the totals in Table 8.11, we computed an average waiting time for the 10 customers of $11.2/10 = 1.12$ minutes, and an average time in the system of $32.1/10 = 3.21$ minutes. Seven of the ten customers had to wait. The total time for the ten-customer simulation is given by the completion time of the tenth customer: 26.0 minutes. However, at this point, we realize that a simulation for ten customers is much too short a period to draw any firm conclusions about the operation of the waiting line.

Simulation of the Hammondsport Savings Bank ATM Problem

Using an Excel spreadsheet, we simulated the operation of the Hammondsport ATM waiting line system for 1000 customers. The spreadsheet used to carry out the simulation is shown in Figure 8.16. Note that the simulation rows for customers between 5 and 996 have been hidden so that the results can be shown in a reasonably sized figure. If desired, the rows for these customers can be shown and the simulation results displayed for all 1000 customers. Let us describe the details of the Excel spreadsheet that provided the Hammondsport ATM simulation.

The data are presented in the first 9 rows of the spreadsheet. The interarrival times are described by a uniform distribution with a smallest time of 0 minutes (cell B4) and a largest time of 5 minutes (cell B5). A normal probability distribution with a mean of 2 minutes (cell B8) and a standard deviation of 0.5 minutes (cell B9) describes the service time distribution.

Figure 8.16 SPREADSHEET SIMULATION OF THE HAMMONDSPORT SAVINGS BANK WITH ONE ATM

SPREADSHEET
HAMMONDSPORT
1 ATM

	A	B	C	D	E	F	G	H
1	**Hammondsport Savings Bank with One ATM**							
2								
3	**Interarrival Times (Uniform Distribution)**							
4	Smallest Value	0						
5	Largest Value	5						
6								
7	**Service Times (Normal Distribution)**							
8	Mean	2						
9	Standard Dev	0.5						
10								
11								
12	**Simulation**							
13								
14		Interarrival	Arrival	Service	Waiting	Service	Completion	Time
15	Customer	Time	Time	Start Time	Time	Time	Time	in System
16	1	1.4	1.4	1.4	0.0	2.3	3.7	2.3
17	2	1.3	2.7	3.7	1.0	1.5	5.2	2.5
18	3	4.9	7.6	7.6	0.0	2.2	9.8	2.2
19	4	3.5	11.1	11.1	0.0	2.5	13.6	2.5
20	5	0.7	11.8	13.6	1.8	1.8	15.4	3.6
1011	996	0.5	2496.8	2498.1	1.3	0.6	2498.7	1.9
1012	997	0.2	2497.0	2498.7	1.7	2.0	2500.7	3.7
1013	998	2.7	2499.7	2500.7	1.0	1.9	2502.5	2.8
1014	999	3.7	2503.4	2503.4	0.0	2.5	2505.8	2.5
1015	1000	4.1	2507.4	2507.4	0.0	1.9	2509.3	1.9
1016								
1017		**Summary Statistics**						
1018		Number Waiting			549			
1019		Probability of Waiting			0.6100			
1020		Average Waiting Time			1.59			
1021		Maximum Waiting Time			13.5			
1022		Utilization of ATM			0.7860			
1023		Number Waiting > 1 Min			393			
1024		Probability of Waiting > 1 Min			0.4367			

Simulation information for the first customer appears in row 16 of the spreadsheet. The cell formulas for row 16 are as follows:

Cell A16   Enter 1 for the first customer

Cell B16   Simulate the interrarival time for customer 1 (uniform distribution)

=$B$4 + RAND()*($B$5−$B$4)

> Cell C16   Compute the arrival time for customer 1
> =B16
>
> Cell D16   Compute the starting time for customer 1
> =C16
>
> Cell E16   Compute the waiting time for customer 1
> =D16−C16
>
> Cell F16   Simulate the service time for customer 1 (normal distribution)
> =NORMINV(RAND(),$B$8,$B$9)
>
> Cell G16   Compute the completion time for customer 1
> =D16+F16
>
> Cell H16   Compute the time in the system for customer 1
> =G16−C16

Simulation information for the second customer appears in row 17 of the spreadsheet. The cell formulas for row 17 are as follows:

> Cell A17   Enter 2 for the second customer
> Cell B17   Simulate the interarrival time for customer 2 (uniform distribution)
> =$B$4+RAND()*($B$5−$B$4)
>
> Cell C17   Compute the arrival time for customer 2
> =C16+B17
>
> Cell D17   Compute the starting time for customer 2
> =IF(C17>G16, C17, G16)
>
> Cell E17   Compute the waiting time for customer 2
> =D17−C17
>
> Cell F17   Simulate the service time for customer 2 (normal distribution)
> =NORMINV(RAND(),$B$8,$B$9)
>
> Cell G17   Compute the completion time for customer 2
> =D17+F17
>
> Cell H17   Compute the time in the system for customer 2
> =G17−C17

Cells A17:H17 can be copied to cells A1015:H1015 in order to provide the 1000 customer simulation.

Ultimately, summary statistics will be collected in order to describe the results of 1000 customers. Before collecting the summary statistics, let us point out that most simulation studies of dynamic systems focus on the operation of the system during its long-run or steady-state operation. To ensure that the effect of start-up conditions are not included in the steady-state calculations, a dynamic simulation model is usually run for a specified period without collecting any data about the operation of the system. The length of the start-up period can vary depending on the application. For the Hammondsport Savings Bank ATM simulation, we treated the results for the first 100 customers as the start-up period. The simulation information for customer 100 appears in row 115 of the spreadsheet. Cell

G115 shows that the completion time for the 100th customer is 240.8. Thus the length of the start-up period is 240.8 minutes.

Summary statistics are collected for the next 900 customers corresponding to rows 116 to 1015 of the spreadsheet. Figure 8.16 shows the summary statistics collected. The following Excel formulas provided the summary statistics.

Cell E1018	Number of customers who had to wait (i.e., waiting time > 0)
	=COUNTIF(E116:E1015,">0")
Cell E1019	Probability of waiting
	=E1018/900
Cell E1020	The average waiting time
	=AVERAGE(E116:E1015)
Cell E1021	The maximum waiting time
	=MAX(E116:E1015)
Cell E1022	The utilization of the ATM[4]
	=SUM(F116:F1015)/(G1015−G115)
Cell E1023	The number of customers who had to wait more than 1 minute
	=COUNTIF(E116:E1015,">1")
Cell E1024	Probability of waiting more than 1 minute
	=E1023/900

Simulation Results

The simulation results in Figure 8.16 show that with 1 ATM 549 of the 900 Hammondsport customers had to wait. This result provides a 549/900 = 0.61 probability that a customer will have to wait for service. Or, in other words, approximately 61% of the customers will have to wait because the ATM is in use. The average waiting time is 1.59 minutes per customer with at least one customer waiting the maximum time of 13.5 minutes. The utilization rate of 0.7860 indicates that the ATM is in use 78.6% of the time. Finally, 393 of the 900 customers had to wait more than 1 minute (43.67% of all customers). Using Excel's Histogram data analysis tool for the waiting time data in cells E116 to E1015, we developed the histogram shown in Figure 8.17. This figure shows that 45 customers (5%) had a waiting time greater than six minutes.

The simulation supports the conclusion that the branch will have a busy ATM system. With an average customer waiting time of 1.59 minutes, the branch does not satisfy the bank's customer service guideline. This branch is a good candidate for installation of a second ATM.

Simulation with Two ATMs

We extended the simulation model to the case of two ATMs. For the second ATM we also assume that the service time is normally distributed with a mean of 2 minutes and a standard deviation of 0.5 minutes. Table 8.12 shows the simulation results for the first ten customers. In comparing the 2-ATM system results in Table 8.12 with the single ATM simulation results shown in Table 8.11, we see that 2 additional columns are needed. These

---

4. The proportion of time the ATM is in use is equal to the sum of the 900 customer service times in column F divided by the total elapsed time required for the 900 customers to complete service. This total elapsed time is the difference between the completion time of customer 1000 and the completion time of customer 100.

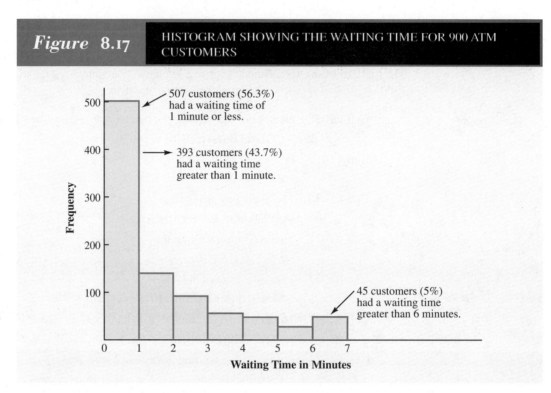

Figure 8.17 HISTOGRAM SHOWING THE WAITING TIME FOR 900 ATM CUSTOMERS

507 customers (56.3%) had a waiting time of 1 minute or less.

393 customers (43.7%) had a waiting time greater than 1 minute.

45 customers (5%) had a waiting time greater than 6 minutes.

Frequency

Waiting Time in Minutes

two columns show when each ATM becomes available for customer service. We assume that, when a new customer arrives, the customer will be served by the ATM that frees up first. When the simulation begins, the first customer is assigned to ATM 1.

Table 8.12 shows that customer 7 is the first customer that has to wait to use an ATM. We describe how customers 6, 7, and 8 are processed to show how the logic of the simulation run for two ATMs differs from that with a single ATM.

Table 8.12 SIMULATION RESULTS FOR TEN CUSTOMERS FOR A TWO-ATM SYSTEM

Customer	Interarrival Time	Arrival Time	Service Start Time	Waiting Time	Service Time	Completion Time	Time in System	Time Available ATM 1	ATM 2
1	1.7	1.7	1.7	0.0	2.1	3.8	2.1	3.8	0.0
2	0.7	2.4	2.4	0.0	2.0	4.4	2.0	3.8	4.4
3	2.0	4.4	4.4	0.0	1.4	5.8	1.4	5.8	4.4
4	0.1	4.5	4.5	0.0	0.9	5.4	0.9	5.8	5.4
5	4.6	9.1	9.1	0.0	2.2	11.3	2.2	5.8	11.3
6	1.3	10.4	10.4	0.0	1.6	12.0	1.6	12.0	11.3
7	0.6	11.0	11.3	0.3	1.7	13.0	2.0	12.0	13.0
8	0.3	11.3	12.0	0.7	2.2	14.2	2.9	14.2	13.0
9	3.4	14.7	14.7	0.0	2.9	17.6	2.9	14.2	17.6
10	0.1	14.8	14.8	0.0	2.8	17.6	2.8	17.6	17.6
Totals	14.8			1.0	19.8		20.8		
Averages	1.48			0.1	1.98		2.08		

Customer 6

- An interarrival time of 1.3 minutes is generated, and customer 6 arrives 9.1 + 1.3 = 10.4 minutes into the simulation.
- From the customer 5 row, we see that ATM 1 frees up at 5.8 minutes, and ATM 2 will free up at 11.3 minutes into the simulation. Since ATM 1 is free, customer 6 does not wait and begins service on ATM 1 at the arrival time of 10.4 minutes.
- A service time of 1.6 minutes is generated for customer 6. So customer 6 has a completion time of 10.4 + 1.6 = 12.0 minutes.
- The time ATM 1 will next become available is set at 12.0 minutes; the time available for ATM 2 remains 11.3 minutes.

Customer 7

- An interarrival time of 0.6 minutes is generated, and customer 7 arrives 10.4 + 0.6 = 11.0 minutes into the simulation.
- From the previous row, we see that ATM 1 will not be available until 12.0 minutes, and ATM 2 will not be available until 11.3 minutes. So customer 7 must wait to use an ATM. Since ATM 2 will free up first, customer 7 begins service on that machine at a start time of 11.3 minutes. With an arrival time of 11.0 and a service start time of 11.3, customer 7 experiences a waiting time of 11.3 − 11.0 = 0.3 minutes.
- A service time of 1.7 minutes is generated leading to a completion time of 11.3 + 1.7 = 13.0 minutes.
- The time available for ATM 2 is updated to 13.0 minutes, and the time available for ATM 1 remains at 12.0 minutes.

Customer 8

- An interarrival time of 0.3 minutes is generated, and customer 8 arrives 11.0 + 0.3 = 11.3 minutes into the simulation.
- From the previous row, we see that ATM 1 will be the first available. Thus, customer 8 starts service on ATM 1 at 12.0 minutes resulting in a waiting time of 12.0 − 11.3 = 0.7 minutes.
- A service time of 2.2 minutes is generated resulting in a completion time of 12.0 + 2.2 = 14.2 minutes and a system time of 0.7 + 2.2 = 2.9 minutes.
- The time available for ATM 1 is updated to 14.2 minutes, and the time available for ATM 2 remains at 13.0 minutes.

From the totals in Table 8.12, we see that the average waiting time for these ten customers is only 1.0/10 = 0.1 minutes. Of course, a much longer simulation will be necessary before any conclusions can be drawn.

Simulation Results with Two ATMs

The Excel spreadsheet that we used to conduct a simulation for 1000 customers is shown in Figure 8.18. Results for the first 100 customers were discarded to account for the start-up period. With 2 ATMs, the number of customers who had to wait was reduced from 549 to 78. This reduction provides a 78/900 = 0.0867 probability that a customer will have to wait for service when 2 ATMs are used. The 2-ATM system also reduced the average waiting time to 0.07 minutes (4.2 seconds) per customer. The maximum waiting time was reduced from 13.5 to 2.9 minutes, and each ATM was in use 40.84% of the time. Finally, only 23 of the 900 customers had to wait more than 1 minute for an ATM to become available. Thus, only 2.56% of customers had to wait more than one minute. The

Figure 8.18   SPREADSHEET SIMULATION OF THE HAMMONDSPORT SAVINGS BANK WITH 2 ATMs

	A	B	C	D	E	F	G	H	I	J
1	**Hammondsport Savings Bank with Two ATMs**									
2										
3	**Interarrival Times (Uniform Distribution)**									
4	Smallest Value	0								
5	Largest Value	5								
6										
7	**Service Times (Normal Distribution)**									
8	Mean	2								
9	Standard Dev	0.5								
10										
11										
12	**Simulation**									
13										
14		Interarrival	Arrival	Service	Waiting	Service	Completion	Time	Time Available	
15	Customer	Time	Time	Start Time	Time	Time	Time	in System	ATM 1	ATM 2
16	1	1.7	1.7	1.7	0.0	2.1	3.8	2.1	3.8	0.0
17	2	0.7	2.4	2.4	0.0	2.0	4.4	2.0	3.8	4.4
18	3	2.0	4.4	4.4	0.0	1.4	5.8	1.4	5.8	4.4
19	4	0.1	4.5	4.5	0.0	0.9	5.4	0.9	5.8	5.4
20	5	4.6	9.1	9.1	0.0	2.2	11.3	2.2	5.8	11.3
1011	996	3.3	2483.2	2483.2	0.0	2.2	2485.4	2.2	2485.4	2482.1
1012	997	4.5	2487.7	2487.7	0.0	1.9	2489.6	1.9	2485.4	2489.6
1013	998	3.7	2491.5	2491.5	0.0	3.2	2494.7	3.2	2494.7	2489.6
1014	999	0.0	2491.5	2491.5	0.0	2.4	2493.9	2.4	2494.7	2493.9
1015	1000	2.6	2494.1	2494.1	0.0	2.8	2496.9	2.8	2494.7	2496.9
1016										
1017		**Summary Statistics**								
1018		Number Waiting			78					
1019		Probability of Waiting			0.0867					
1020		Average Waiting Time			0.07					
1021		Maximum Waiting Time			2.9					
1022		Utilization of ATMs			0.4084					
1023		Number Waiting > 1 Min			23					
1024		Probability of Waiting > 1 Min			0.0256					

simulation results provide evidence that Hammondsport Savings Bank needs to expand to the 2-ATM system.

The spreadsheet simulation of the Hammondsport Savings Bank with 2 ATMs is available in the file Hammondsport—2 ATMs. Slight variations of this spreadsheet can be used to simulate a variety of two-channel waiting line systems. We will not go into the details of the cell formulas necessary for this waiting line simulation model. The interested reader can load the Excel file from the spreadsheet disk and review the cell formulas if desired.

Finally, the simulation models that we have developed can now be used to study the ATM operation at other branch banks. In each case, assumptions must be made about the appropriate interarrival time and service time probability distributions. However, once appropriate assumptions have been made, the same simulation models can be used to determine the operating characteristics of the ATM waiting line system. The Red Cross simulation model described in the Management Science in Action possesses many of the same characteristics as the ATM simulation models.

MANAGEMENT SCIENCE IN ACTION

RED CROSS USES SIMULATION TO IMPROVE BLOODMOBILE SERVICES*

The American Red Cross collects more than 6 million units of blood each year in the United States, making it the largest blood-product supplier in the country. Blood is collected daily at some 400 fixed and mobile sites.

The Red Cross relies heavily on repeat donations by the same group of individuals. A particular concern to the Red Cross was the length of the waiting times occurring at bloodmobile temporary sites sponsored by businesses, schools, and community groups. If bloodmobile waiting lines and times are excessive, blood donor dissatisfaction with the process could significantly decrease the number of future blood donations.

The Red Cross bloodmobile operation was simulated to study ways of reducing the waiting line and waiting times. Data were collected on the number of donor arrivals during 30-minute periods of time. The donors selected their own times to visit the bloodmobile, with these nonscheduled (random) visits described by a nonstationary Poisson probability distribution. Data on arrival rates and service times at the bloodmobile were based on the study of actual blood-mobile operations in Atlanta, Georgia; Charlotte, North Carolina; and Washington, D.C.

The GPSS® computer simulation language was used to model the waiting line at the bloodmobile. After testing and validating the simulation model, the project team varied setup procedures, staff allocation, and work rules to determine how each change would affect the waiting line operating characteristics at the bloodmobile. Through a series of experiments with the simulation model, the project team developed recommendations for improved processing. Implementation of the recommendations markedly reduced waiting times. Improved blood donor satisfaction was noted, with the majority of donors reporting both less waiting time and less processing (service) time compared to previous visits.

*Based on J. F. Brennan, B. L. Golden, and H. K. Rappoport, "Go with the Flow: Improving Red Cross Bloodmobiles Using Simulation Analysis," *Interfaces* 22, no. 5 (September–October 1992): 1–13.

NOTES and Comments

1. The ATM waiting line model was based on uniformly distributed interarrival times and normally distributed service times. One advantage of simulation is its flexibility in accommodating a variety of different probability distributions. For instance, if we believe an exponential distribution is more appropriate for interarrival times, the ATM simulation could be repeated by simply changing the way the interarrival times are generated.

2. At the beginning of this section, we defined *discrete-event simulation* as involving a dynamic system that evolves over time. The simulation computations focus on the sequence of events as they occur at discrete points in time. In the ATM waiting line example, customer arrivals and the customer service completions were the discrete events. Referring to the arrival times and completion times in Table 8.11, we see that the first 5 discrete events for the ATM waiting line simulation were as follows:

Event	Description	Time Event Occurred
1	Customer 1 arrives	1.4
2	Customer 2 arrives	2.7
3	Customer 1 completes service	3.7
4	Customer 2 completes service	5.2
5	Customer 3 arrives	7.6

---

3. We did not keep track of the number of customers in the ATM waiting line as we carried out the ATM simulation computations on a customer-by-customer basis. However, we can determine the average number of customers in the waiting line from other information in the simulation output. The following relationship is valid for any waiting line system:

(Average Number in Waiting Line)(Total Time of Simulation) = Total Waiting Time

For the system with 1 ATM, the total time of the simulation for 900 customers was $2509.3 - 247.8 = 2261.5$ minutes, and the average waiting time was 1.59 minutes. Since 900 customers were served during the simulation, the total waiting time is $900(1.59) = 1431$ minutes. Therefore, the average number of customers in the waiting line is

Average Number in Waiting Line $= 1431/2261.5 = 0.63$ customers

8.4   OTHER SIMULATION ISSUES

Because simulation is one of the most widely used management science techniques, a variety of software tools have been developed to help people implement a simulation model on a computer. In this section we comment on the software available and discuss some issues involved in verifying and validating a simulation model. We close the section with a discussion of some of the advantages and disadvantages of using simulation to study a real system.

Computer Implementation

The use of spreadsheets for simulation has grown rapidly in recent years, and third-party software vendors have developed spreadsheet add-ins that make building simulation models on a spreadsheet much easier. These add-in packages provide an easy facility for generating random values from a variety of probability distributions and provide a rich array of statistics describing the simulation output. Two popular spreadsheet add-ins are Crystal Ball® from Decisioneering and @RISK® from Palisade Corporation. Although spreadsheets can be a valuable tool for some simulation studies, they are generally limited to smaller, less complex systems.

> The computational and record-keeping aspects of simulation models are assisted by special simulation software packages. The packages ease the tasks of developing a computer simulation model.

With the growth of simulation applications, both users of simulation and software developers began to realize that computer simulations have many common features: model development, generating values from probability distributions, maintaining a record of what happens during the simulation, and recording and summarizing the simulation output. A variety of special-purpose simulation packages are available, including GPSS®, SIMSCRIPT®, SLAM®, and Arena®. These packages have built-in simulation clocks, simplified methods for generating probabilistic inputs, and procedures for collecting and summarizing the simulation output. Special-purpose simulation packages enable management scientists to simplify the process of developing and implementing the simulation model.

Simulation models can also be developed using general-purpose computer programming languages such as BASIC, FORTRAN, PASCAL, C, and C++. The disadvantage of using these languages is that special simulation procedures are not built in. One command in a special-purpose simulation package often performs the computations and record-keeping tasks that would require several BASIC, FORTRAN, PASCAL, C, or C++ statements to duplicate. The advantage of using a general-purpose programming language is that they offer greater flexibility in terms of being able to model more complex systems.

To decide which software to use, an analyst will have to consider the relative merits of a spreadsheet, a special-purpose simulation package, and a general-purpose computer programming language. The goal is to select the method that is easy to use while still providing an adequate representation of the system being studied.

Verification and Validation

An important aspect of any simulation study involves confirming that the simulation model accurately describes the real system. Inaccurate simulation models cannot be expected to provide worthwhile information. Thus, before using simulation results to draw conclusions about a real system, one must take steps to verify and validate the simulation model.

Verification is the process of determining that the computer procedure that performs the simulation calculations is logically correct. Verification is largely a debugging task to make sure that no errors are in the computer procedure that implements the simulation. In some cases, an analyst may compare computer results for a limited number of events with independent hand calculations. In other cases, tests may be performed to verify that the probabilistic inputs are being generated correctly and that the output from the simulation model seems reasonable. The verification step is not complete until the user has developed a high degree of confidence that the computer procedure is error free.

Validation is the process of ensuring that the simulation model provides an accurate representation of a real system. Validation requires an agreement among analysts and managers that the logic and the assumptions used in the design of the simulation model accurately reflect how the real system operates. The first phase of the validation process is done prior to, or in conjunction with, the development of the computer procedure for the simulation process. Validation continues after the computer program has been developed with the analyst reviewing the simulation output to see if the simulation results closely approximate the performance of the real system. If possible, the output of the simulation model is compared to the output of an existing real system to make sure that the simulation output closely approximates the performance of the real system. If this form of validation is not possible, an analyst can experiment with the simulation model and have one or more individuals experienced with the operation of the real system review the simulation output to determine whether it is a reasonable approximation to what would be obtained with the real system under similar conditions.

Verification and validation are not tasks to be taken lightly. They are key steps in any simulation study and are necessary to ensure that decisions and conclusions based on the simulation results are appropriate for the real system.

Advantages and Disadvantages of Using Simulation

The primary advantages of simulation are that it is easy to understand and that the methodology can be used to model and learn about the behavior of complex systems that would be difficult, if not impossible, to deal with analytically. Simulation models are flexible; they can be used to describe systems without requiring the simplifying assumptions, or approximations, that are often required by mathematical models. In general, the larger the number of probabilistic inputs a system has, the more likely that a simulation model will provide the best approach for studying the system. Another advantage of computer simulation is that a simulation model provides a convenient experimental laboratory for the real system. Changing assumptions or operating policies in the simulation model and rerunning it can provide results that help predict how such changes will affect the operation of the real system. Experimenting directly with a real system is often not feasible. The Management Science in Action describes how simulation was used to select manufacturing configurations and to design new plants at Mexico's Vilpac Truck Company.

Simulation is not without some disadvantages. For complex systems, the process of developing, verifying, and validating a simulation model can be time-consuming and expensive. In addition, each simulation run only provides a sample of how the real system will operate. As such, the summary of the simulation data only provides estimates or approximations about the real system. Consequently, computer simulation does not guarantee an optimal solution. Nonetheless, the danger of obtaining poor solutions is slight if the analyst exercises good judgment in developing the simulation model and if the simulation process is run long enough under a wide variety of conditions so that the analyst has sufficient data to predict how the real system will operate.

Using simulation, we can ask what-if questions and project how the real system will behave. Although simulation does not guarantee optimality, it will usually provide near-optimal solutions. In addition, simulation models often warn against poor decision strategies by projecting disastrous outcomes such as system failures, large financial losses, and so on.

MANAGEMENT SCIENCE IN ACTION

SIMULATION AT VILPAC TRUCK COMPANY*

In increasing numbers, U.S. firms are joining diverse geographical and cultural partners in Western Europe, Asia, and Mexico to capitalize on each other's advantages and remain competitive in world markets. Mexico, the United States' third largest trading partner, offers a unique opportunity for integrating manufacturing operations. For example, Mexican and U.S. firms have been working together to turn the Mexican truck company, Vilpac, into a world-class manufacturing firm.

The selection of manufacturing configurations and the design of new plants at Vilpac is being guided by a simulation model of the firm's manufacturing operations. A network simulation language, SIMNET II®, has been used to model the manufacturing system that comprises some 95 machines and 1900 parts. Various simulation runs were used to validate the model. When applied to a plant that was producing 20 trucks per day, the simulation model accurately predicted production at 19.8 trucks per day.

The three interrelated modules of the simulation model include operations, corrective maintenance, and preventive maintenance. Various components of the model include capabilities for handling changes in customer demand, manufacturing cost, capacity, and work-in-process and inventory levels. Experimentation with the model investigated capacity requirements, product-mix effects, new products, inventory policies, product flow, setup times, production planning and control strategies, plant expansion, and new plant design. Tangible benefits include an increase in production of 260%, a reduction in work-in-process of 70%, and an increase in market share.

*Based on J. P. Nuno, D. L. Shunk, J. M. Padillo, and B. Beltran, "Mexico's Vilpac Truck Company Uses a CIM Implementation to Become a World Class Manufacturer," *Interfaces* no. 1 (January–February 1993): 59–75.

SUMMARY

Simulation is a method for learning about a real system by experimenting with a model that represents the system. Some of the reasons simulation is frequently used are:

1. It can be used for a wide variety of practical problems.
2. The simulation approach is relatively easy to explain and understand. As a result, management confidence is increased, and acceptance of the results is more easily obtained.
3. Spreadsheet packages now provide another alternative for model implementation, and third-party vendors have developed add-ins that expand the capabilities of the spreadsheet.
4. Computer software developers have produced simulation packages that make it easier to develop and implement simulation models for more complex problems.

We first showed how simulation can be used for risk analysis by analyzing a situation involving the introduction of a new product: the PortaCom printer. We then showed how simulation can be used to select an inventory replenishment level that would provide both a good profit and a good customer service level. Finally, we developed a simulation model for the Hammondsport Savings Bank ATM waiting line system. This model is an example of a dynamic simulation model in which the state of the system changes or evolves over time.

Our approach was to develop a simulation model that contained both controllable inputs and probabilistic inputs. Procedures were developed for randomly generating values for the probabilistic inputs, and a flowchart was developed to show the sequence of logical and mathematical operations that describe the steps of the simulation process. Simulation results were obtained by running the simulation for a suitable number of trials or length of time. Results were obtained and conclusions were drawn about the operation of the real system.

··/ /············

GLOSSARY

Simulation A method for learning about a real system by experimenting with a model that represents the system.

Simulation experiment The generation of a sample of values for the probabilistic inputs of a simulation model and computing the resulting values of the model output. Conducting a simulation experiment is sometimes referred to as *running the simulation model.*

Controllable input Input to a simulation model that is selected by the decision maker.

Probabilistic input Input to a simulation model that is subject to uncertainty. A probabilistic input is described by a probability distribution.

Risk analysis The process of predicting the outcome of a decision in the face of uncertainty.

Parameters Numerical values that appear in the mathematical relationships of a model. Parameters are considered known and remain constant over all trials of a simulation.

What-if analysis A trial-and-error approach to learning about the range of possible outputs for a model. Trial values are chosen (these are the "what-ifs") for the model inputs and the value of the output(s) is computed.

Base-case scenario Determining the output given the most likely values for the probabilistic inputs of a model.

Best-case scenario Determining the output given the best values that can be expected for the probabilistic inputs of a model.

Worst-case scenario Determining the output given the worst values that can be expected for the probabilistic inputs of a model.

Static simulation model A simulation in which the state of the system at one point in time does not affect the state of the system at future points in time. Each trial in the simulation run is independent.

Dynamic simulation model A simulation in which the state of the system affects how the system changes or evolves over future points in time.

Event An instantaneous occurrence that changes the state of the system in a simulation model.

Discrete-event simulation model A simulation that describes how a system evolves over time by using events that occur at discrete points in time to update the state of the system.

Verification The process of determining that a computer program implements a simulation model as it is intended.

Validation The process of determining that a simulation model provides an accurate representation of a real system.

..../ /..............

PROBLEMS

Note: Problems 1–12 are designed to give you practice at setting up a simulation model and demonstrating how random numbers can be used to generate values for the probabilistic inputs. These problems, which ask you to provide a small number of simulation trials, can be done with hand calculations. This approach should give you a good understanding of the simulation process, but the simulation results will not be sufficient for you to draw final conclusions or make decisions about the situation. Problems 13–24 are more realistic in that they ask you to generate simulation outputs for a large number of trials enabling you to draw conclusions about the behavior of the system being studied. These problems require the use of a computer to carry out the simulation computations. The ability to use Excel or some other spreadsheet package will be necessary when you attempt Problems 13–24.

1. Consider the PortaCom project discussed in Section 8.1
    a. An engineer on the product development team believes that first-year sales for the new printer will be 20,000 units. Using estimates of $45 per unit for the direct labor cost and $90 per unit for the parts cost, what is the first-year profit using the engineer's sales estimate?
    b. The financial analyst on the product development team is more conservative, indicating that parts cost may well be $100 per unit. In addition, the analyst suggests that a sales volume of 10,000 units is more realistic. Using the most likely value of $45 per unit for the direct labor cost, what is the first-year profit using the financial analyst's estimates?
    c. Why is the simulation approach to risk analysis preferable to generating a variety of what-if scenarios such as those suggested by the engineer and the financial analyst?

SELF TEST

2. The management of Madeira Manufacturing Company is considering the introduction of a new product. The fixed cost to begin the production of the product is $30,000. The variable cost for the product is expected to be between $16 and $24 with a most likely value of $20 per unit. The product will sell for $50 per unit. Demand for the product is expected to range from 300 units to 2100 units, with 1200 units the most likely demand.
    a   Develop the profit model for this product.
    b. Provide the base-case, worst-case, and best-case analyses.
    c. Discuss why a simulation risk analysis would be desirable. Problem 14 asks you to develop a spreadsheet to conduct a risk analysis for the Madeira project.

3. Use the random numbers 0.3753, 0.9218, 0.0336, 0.5145, 0.7000 to generate 5 simulated values for the PortaCom direct labor cost per unit.

4. A retail store experiences the following probability distribution for sales of a product.

Sales (units)	0	1	2	3	4	5	6
Probability	0.08	0.12	0.28	0.24	0.14	0.10	0.04

    a. Set up intervals of random numbers that can be used to simulate sales.
    b. Random numbers generated for the first 10 days of a simulation are as follows: 0.4627, 0.8745, 0.4479, 0.6712, 0.4557, 0.8435, 0.2162, 0.1699, 0.1338, 0.2278. What is the sales value generated for each day?
    c. What are the total sales over the 10-day period?

SELF TEST

5. The price of a share of a particular stock listed on the New York Stock Exchange is currently $39. The following probability distribution shows how the price per share is expected to change over a three-month period.

Stock Price Change	Probability
−2	0.05
−1	0.10
0	0.25
+1	0.20
+2	0.20
+3	0.10
+4	0.10

    a. Set up intervals of random numbers that can be used to generate the change in stock price over a three-month period.

    b. With the current price of $39 per share and the random numbers 0.1091, 0.9407, 0.1941, and 0.8083, simulate the price per share for each on the next four 3-month periods. What is the ending simulated price per share?

6. The Statewide Auto Insurance Company has the following probability distribution for automobile collision claims paid during the past year.

Payment ($)	Probability
0	0.83
500	0.06
1,000	0.05
2,000	0.02
5,000	0.02
8,000	0.01
10,000	0.01

    a. Set up intervals of random numbers that can be used to generate automobile claim payments.

    b. Using the first 20 random numbers in column 4 of Table 8.2, simulate the claims for 20 policyholders. How many claims are paid and what is the total amount paid to the policyholders?

7. A variety of routine maintenance checks are made on commercial airplanes prior to each take-off. A particular maintenance check of an airplane's landing gear requires between 10 and 18 minutes of a maintenance engineer's time. In fact, the exact time required is uniformly distributed over this interval. As part of a larger simulation model designed to determine total on-ground maintenance time for an airplane, we will need to simulate the actual time required to perform this maintenance check on the airplane's landing gear. Using random numbers of 0.1567, 0.9823, 0.3419, 0.5572, and 0.7758, compute the time required for each of five simulated maintenance checks of the airplane's landing gear.

8. Baseball's World Series is a maximum of 7 games, with the winner being the first team to win 4 games. Assume that the Atlanta Braves are in the World Series and that the first 2 games are to be played in Atlanta; the next 3 games at the opponent's ball park; and the last 2 games, if necessary, back in Atlanta. Taking into account the projected starting pitchers for each game and the homefield advantage, the probabilities of Atlanta winning each game are as follows:

Game	1	2	3	4	5	6	7
Probability of Win	0.60	0.55	0.48	0.45	0.48	0.55	0.50

a. Set up random number intervals that can be used to determine the winner of each game. Let the smaller random numbers indicate that Atlanta wins the game. For example, the random number interval "0.00 but less than 0.60" corresponds to Atlanta winning game 1.

b. Use the random numbers in column 6 of Table 8.2 beginning with 0.3813 to simulate the playing of the World Series. Do the Atlanta Braves win the series? How many games are played?

c. Discuss how repeated simulation trials could be used to estimate the overall probability of Atlanta winning the series as well as the most likely number of games in the series.

SELF TEST

9. A project has four activities (A, B, C, and D) that must be performed sequentially. The probability distributions for the time required to complete each of the activities are as follows:

Activity	Activity Time (weeks)	Probability
A	5	0.25
	6	0.35
	7	0.25
	8	0.15
B	3	0.20
	5	0.55
	7	0.25
C	10	0.10
	12	0.25
	14	0.40
	16	0.20
	18	0.05
D	8	0.60
	10	0.40

a. Provide the base-case, the worst-case, and best-case calculations for the time to complete the project.

b. Use the random numbers 0.1778, 0.9617, 0.6849, and 0.4503 to simulate the completion time of the project in weeks.

c. Discuss how simulation could be used to estimate the probability the project can be completed in 35 weeks or less.

10. Larkin Corporation conducted a test designed to evaluate the effectiveness of a new television advertisement for one of its household products. The particular television advertisement was shown in a test market for a two-week period. In a follow-up study, randomly selected individuals were contacted by telephone and asked a series of questions to determine whether they could recall the message in the television advertisement and how likely they were to purchase the product. The test market study provided the following probabilities.

Individual could recall the message   0.40

Individual could not recall the message   0.60

Response to the question of how likely they were to purchase the product provided the following probabilities.

If	Purchase		
	Definitely No	**Uncertain**	**Definitely Yes**
Could recall message	0.30	0.30	0.40
Could not recall message	0.50	0.40	0.10

a. Set up intervals of random numbers that can be used to determine whether a sampled individual could recall the message and then how the individual responded to the likelihood of purchase question.

b. Use the following pairs of random numbers to simulate the results for three sampled individuals: individual 1 (0.5521, 0.6318), individual 2 (0.2189, 0.8432), individual 3 (0.3812, 0.1831). Which individual, if any, answered "definitely yes" to the likelihood to purchase question?

c. Discuss how a large number of simulation trials could be used to estimate the overall probability of an individual answering "definitely yes" to the likelihood of purchase question.

11. A bowler has the following probability distribution for the number of pins knocked over on the first ball thrown.

Number of Pins	Probability
7	0.12
8	0.15
9	0.18
10	0.55

The probability distributions for the number of pins on the second ball are as follows:

First-Ball Pins	Second-Ball Pins			
	0	**1**	**2**	**3**
7	0.02	0.10	0.45	0.43
8	0.04	0.20	0.76	
9	0.06	0.94		

a. Set up intervals of random numbers that can be used to generate the number of pins on each ball.

b. The first two random numbers in column 6 of Table 8.2 are 0.3813 and 0.2159. Use these to simulate what the bowler did on the first two balls rolled.

c. Assume that the results in part (b) are for the first bowling frame. If you know how bowling scores are computed, continue to use the random numbers in Table 8.2 to compute the bowler's score for a full 10-frame game. The bowler's opponent rolled a 206 game. Did the simulated bowler beat the opponent?

12. The management of Brinkley Corporation is interested in using a simulation model that will help estimate the profit per unit for a new product. Probability distributions for the purchase cost, the labor cost, and the transportation cost are as follows:

Purchase Cost ($)	Probability	Labor Cost ($)	Probability	Transportation Cost ($)	Probability
10	0.25	20	0.10	3	0.75
11	0.45	22	0.25	5	0.25
12	0.30	24	0.35		
		25	0.30		

Assume that these are the only costs and that the selling price for the product will be $45 per unit.

a. Provide the base-case, worst-case, and best-case calculations for the profit per unit.

b. Set up intervals of random numbers that can be used to randomly generate the three cost components.

c. Using the random numbers 0.3726, 0.5839 and 0.8275, calculate the profit per unit.

d. Using the random numbers 0.1862, 0.7466, and 0.6171, calculate the profit per unit.

e. Management believes the project may not be profitable if the profit per unit is less than $5. Explain how simulation can be used to estimate the probability the profit per unit will be less than $5.

13. Using the PortaCom Risk Analysis spreadsheet in Figure 8.7, develop your own spreadsheet for the PortaCom simulation model.

a. Compute the mean profit, the minimum profit, and the maximum profit.

b. What is your estimate of the probability of a loss?

SELF TEST

14. Develop a spreadsheet simulation for the following problem. The management of Madeira Manufacturing Company is considering the introduction of a new product. The fixed cost to begin the production of the product is $30,000. The variable cost for the product is uniformly distributed between $16 and $24 per unit. The product will sell for $50 per unit. Demand for the product is best described by a normal probability distribution with a mean of 1200 units and a standard deviation of 300 units. Use a spreadsheet simulation similar to Figure 8.7. Use 500 simulation trials to answer the following questions.

a. What is the mean profit for the simulation?

b. What is the probability the project will result in a loss?

c. What is your recommendation concerning the introduction of the product?

15. Use a spreadsheet to simulate the rolling of dice. Use the VLOOKUP function as described in Section 8.2 to select the outcome for each die. Place the number for the first die in column B and the number for the second die in column C. Show the sum in column D. Repeat the simulation for 1000 rolls of the dice. What is your simulation estimate of the probability of rolling a 7?

16. Based on experience, the time required to complete a college statistics exam is normally distributed with a mean of 42 minutes and a standard deviation of 8 minutes. A class has 70 students. Use a spreadsheet to simulate the exam completion times for 70 students. How many students are still working when the professor stops the exam at 50 minutes?

17. Grear Tire Company has produced a new tire with an estimated mean lifetime mileage of 36,500 miles. Management also believes that the standard deviation is 5000 miles and that tire mileage is normally distributed. Use a spreadsheet to simulate the miles obtained for a sample of 500 tires.

a. Use the Excel COUNTIF function to determine the number of tires that last longer than 40,000 miles. What is your estimate of the percentage of tires that will exceed 40,000 miles?

b. Use COUNTIF to find the number of tires that obtain mileage less than 32,000 miles, then find the number with less than 30,000 miles and the number with less than 28,000 miles.

c. If management would like to advertise a tire mileage guarantee such that approximately 10% of the tires would obtain mileage low enough to qualify for the guarantee, what tire mileage considered in part (b) would you recommend for the guarantee?

SELF TEST

18. A building contractor is preparing a bid on a new construction project. Two other contractors will be submitting bids for the same project. Based on past bidding practices, bids from the other contractors can be described by the following probability distributions:

Contractor	Probability Distribution of Bid
A	Uniform probability distribution between $600,000 and $800,000
B	Normal probability distribution with a mean bid of $700,000 and a standard deviation of $50,000

a. If the building contractor submits a bid of $750,000, what is the probability the building contractor will obtain the bid? Use a spreadsheet to simulate 1000 repeats of the contract bidding process.

b. The building contractor is also considering bids of $775,000 and $785,000. If the building contractor would like to bid such that the probability of winning the bid is about 0.80, what bid would you recommend? Repeat the simulation process with bids of $775,000 and $785,000 to justify your recommendation.

19. Develop your own spreadsheet for the Butler inventory simulation model shown in Figure 8.11. Suppose that management prefers not to charge for loss of goodwill. Run the Butler inventory simulation model with replenishment levels of 110, 115, 120, and 125. What is your recommendation?

20. In preparing for the upcoming holiday season, Mandrell Toy Company has designated a new doll called Freddy. The fixed cost to produce the doll is $100,000. The variable cost, which includes material, labor, and shipping costs, is $34 per doll. During the holiday selling season, Mandrell will sell the dolls for $42 each. If Mandrell overproduces the dolls, the excess dolls will be sold in January through a distributor who has agreed to pay Mandrell $10 per doll. Demand for new toys during the holiday selling season is extremely uncertain. Forecasts are for expected sales of 60,000 dolls with a standard deviation of 15,000. The normal probability distribution is assumed to be a good description of the demand.

a. Create a spreadsheet similar to the inventory spreadsheet in Figure 8.11. Include columns showing demand, sales, revenue from sales, amount of surplus, revenue from sales of surplus, total cost, and net profit. Use your spreadsheet to simulate the sales of the Freddy doll using a production quantity of 60,000 units. Using 500 simulation trials, what is the estimate of the mean profit associated with the production quantity of 60,000 dolls?

b. Before making a final decision on the production quantity, management has requested an analysis of a more aggressive 70,000 unit production quantity and a more conservative 50,000 unit production quantity. Run your simulation with these two production quantities. What is the mean profit associated with each? What is your recommendation on the production of the Freddy doll?

c. Assuming that Mandrell's management adopts your recommendation, what is the probability of a stockout and a shortage of the Freddy dolls during the holiday season?

21. South Central Airlines operates a commuter flight between Atlanta and Charlotte. The plane holds 30 passengers, and the airline makes a $100 profit on each passenger on the flight. When South Central takes 30 reservations for the flight, experience has shown an average of 2 passengers do not show up. As a result, with 30 reservations, South Central is averaging 28 passengers with a profit of 28(100) = $2800 per flight. The airline operations office has asked for an evaluation of an overbooking strategy where they would accept 32 reservations even though

the airplane holds only 30 passengers. The probability distribution for the number of passengers showing up when 32 reservations are accepted is shown below.

Passengers Showing Up	Probability
28	0.05
29	0.25
30	0.50
31	0.15
32	0.05

The airline will receive a profit of $100 for each passenger on the flight up to the capacity of 30 passengers. The airline will incur a cost for any passenger denied seating on the flight. This cost covers added expenses of rescheduling the passenger as well as loss of goodwill, estimated to be $150 per passenger. Develop a spreadsheet model that will simulate the performance of the overbooking system. Simulate the number of passengers showing up for each of 500 flights by using the VLOOKUP function. Use the results to compute the profit for each flight.

a. Does your simulation recommend the overbooking strategy? What is the mean profit per flight if overbooking is implemented?

b. Explain how your simulation model can be used to evaluate other overbooking levels such as 31, 33, 34 and ultimately recommending a best overbooking strategy.

22. Develop your own one-ATM and two-ATM waiting line simulation models for the Hammondsport Savings Bank problem (See Figures 8.16 and 8.18). Assume that a new branch is expected to open with interarrival times uniformly distributed between 0 and 4 minutes. The service times at this branch are anticipated to be normal with a mean of 2 minutes and a standard deviation of 0.5 minutes.

a. Simulate the operation of this system for 600 customers using one ATM. What is your assessment of the ability to operate this branch with one ATM? What happens to the average waiting time for customers near the end of the simulation period?

b. Simulate the operation of this system for 600 customers using two ATMs. What is the average waiting time for customers? What is your recommendation for the ATM operation?

23. The Burger Dome waiting line model in Section 7.1 studies the waiting time of customers at its fast-food restaurant. Burger Dome's single-channel waiting line system has a mean of 0.75 arrivals per minute and a service rate of 1 customer per minute.

a. Use a spreadsheet based on Figure 8.16 to simulate the operation of this waiting line. Assuming that customer arrivals follow a Poisson probability distribution, the interarrival times can be simulated with the cell formula $-(1/\lambda)*LN(RAND())$, where $\lambda = 0.75$. Assuming that the service time follows an exponential probability distribution, the service times can be simulated with the cell formula $-\mu*LN(RAND())$, where $\mu = 1$. Run the Burger Dome simulation for 500 customers. The analytical model in Chapter 7 indicates an average waiting time of 3 minutes per customer. What average waiting time does your simulation model show?

b. One advantage of using simulation is that a simulation model can be altered easily to reflect other assumptions about the probabilistic inputs. Assume that the service time is more accurately described by a normal probability distribution with a mean of 1 minute and a standard deviation of 0.2 minutes. This distribution has less service time variability than the exponential probability distribution used in part (a). What is the impact of this change on the average waiting time?

24. Telephone calls come into an airline reservations office randomly at the mean rate of 15 calls per hour. The time between calls follows an exponential distribution with a mean of 4 minutes. When the two reservations agents are busy, a telephone message tells the caller that the call is important and to please wait on the line until the next reservation agent becomes available. The

service time for each reservation agent is normally distributed with a mean of 4 minutes and a standard deviation of 1 minute. Use a two-channel waiting line simulation model to evaluate this waiting line system. Use the spreadsheet design shown in Figure 8.18. The cell formula $=-4*LN(RAND())$ can be used to generate the interarrival times. Simulate the operation of the telephone reservation system for 600 customers. Discard the first 100 customers and collect data over the next 500 customers.

a.   Compute the mean interval arrival time and the mean service time. If your simulation model is operating correctly, both of these should have means of approximately 4 minutes.

b.   What is the mean customer waiting time for this system?

c.   Use the =COUNTIF function to determine the number of customers who have to wait for a reservation agent. What percentage of the customers have to wait?

Case Problem   COUNTY BEVERAGE DRIVE-THRU

County Beverage Drive-Thru, Inc., operates a chain of beverage supply stores in Northern Illinois. Each store has a single service lane; cars enter at one end of the store and exit at the other end. Customers pick up soft drinks, beer, snacks, and party supplies without getting out of their cars. When a new customer arrives at the store, the customer waits until the preceding customer's order is complete and then drives into the store for service.

Typically, three employees operate each store during peak periods; two clerks take and fill orders; and a third clerk serves as cashier and store supervisor. County Beverage is considering a revised store design in which computerized order-taking and payment are integrated with specialized warehousing equipment. Management hopes that the new design will permit operating each store with one clerk. To determine whether the new design is beneficial, management has decided to build a new store using the revised design.

County Beverage's new store will be located near a major shopping center. Based on experience at other locations, management believes that during the peak late afternoon and evening hours, the time between arrivals follows an exponential probability distribution with a mean of 6 minutes. These peak hours are the most critical time period for the company; most of their profit is generated during these peak hours.

Most of County Beverage's business is generated from people stopping on the way home from work and picking up just a few items. However, occasionally a larger order is placed. An extensive study of times required to fill orders with a single clerk has led to the following probability distribution of service times.

Service Time (minutes)	Probability
2	0.24
3	0.20
4	0.15
5	0.14
6	0.12
7	0.08
8	0.05
9	0.02
Total	1.00

In case customer waiting times prove too long with just a single clerk, County Beverage's management is considering two alternatives: add a second clerk to help with bagging, taking orders, etc., or enlarge the drive-thru area so that two cars can be served at once (a two-channel system). With either of these options, two clerks will be needed. With the two-channel option, service times are expected to be the same for each channel. With the second clerk helping with a single channel, service times will be reduced. The following probability distribution describes service times given that option.

Service Time (minutes)	Probability
1	0.20
2	0.35
3	0.30
4	0.10
5	0.05
Total	1.00

County Beverage's management would like you to develop a spreadsheet simulation model of the new system and use it to compare the operation of the system using the following three designs:

Design
A One channel, one clerk
B One channel, two clerks
C Two channels, each with one clerk

Management is especially concerned with how long customers have to wait for service. Research has shown that 30% of the customers will wait no longer than 6 minutes and that 90% will wait no longer than 10 minutes. As a guideline, management requires the average waiting time to be less than 1.5 minutes.

Managerial Report

Prepare a report that discusses the general development of the spreadsheet simulation model, and make any recommendations that you have regarding the best store design and staffing plan for County Beverage. One additional consideration is that the design allowing for a two-channel system will cost an additional $10,000 to build.

1. List the information the spreadsheet simulation model should generate so that a decision can be made on the store design and the desired number of clerks.
2. Run the simulation for 1000 customers for each alternative considered. You may want to consider making more than one run with each alternative. [*Note:* Values from an exponential probability distribution with mean μ can be generated in Excel using the following function: $=-\mu*LN(RAND())$]
3. Be sure to note the number of customers County Beverage is likely to lose due to long customer waiting times with each design alternative.

THE UPJOHN COMPANY*

KALAMAZOO, MICHIGAN

The Upjohn Company is a worldwide supplier of high-quality, innovative pharmaceutical products. Although its largest business is in prescription pharmaceutical products, Upjohn also operates related businesses in animal health care products, agronomic and vegetable seeds, and specialty chemical products. Founded in 1886, the company has approximately 19,000 employees worldwide, with major manufacturing facilities in Kalamazoo, Puerto Rico, and Belgium, and research laboratories in Kalamazoo, England, and Japan. Committed to total quality improvement—in service to its customers, its products, and its performance in the workplace—Upjohn is also dedicated to conducting businesses in an environmentally and socially responsible manner.

Management Science at Upjohn

The management science function at Upjohn is part of the Management Information and Office Services organization and offers a high-quality, professional problem-solving service to any part of the corporation. The mission of the group is to provide decision-making support for the company's customers, strategies, and priorities by using quantitative techniques to solve business problems and exploit business opportunities in a cost-effective manner. The primary areas of application are problem definition and analysis, modeling and simulation, capacity planning, resource allocation, scheduling, and project management.

A Computer Simulation Application

Demand for one of Upjohn's long-standing products had remained stable for several years at a level easily

satisfied by the company's manufacturing facility. However, changes in market conditions caused an increase in demand to a level beyond the capacity of the current facility. In the discussion that follows, we describe a simulation study successfully undertaken to determine the most cost-effective means of increasing production to meet the new level of demand.

The production process is shown in Figure 8.19. It consists of three independent subprocesses: raw material processing, bulk processing, and spent material reprocessing. Raw material processing takes purchased material as input and transforms it into material that can be used in bulk processing. Bulk processing (shown within the dashed line in Figure 8.19), which involves initial processing, assay, and final processing, converts the raw materials into a finished product. The key step occurs when an assay of the initial bulk processing output or intermediate is performed to determine whether the lot is ready for final processing. If the assay is acceptable, the lot proceeds to final processing and completion. If the assay is not acceptable, the intermediate is returned to initial bulk processing and several steps are repeated. The new intermediate material, which is input during the repeat processing, is obtained by reprocessing one of the spent materials generated during a prior initial bulk processing.

Each time the initial bulk process is run, a quantity of spent material is generated for possible reprocessing. Although the primary use of the reprocessed material is as input for repeat bulk processing, it also can be used as a replacement for the original raw material at the start of the bulk processing. Since the cost of the reprocessed material is significantly less than the cost of new raw material, using as much reprocessed material as possible is beneficial.

*The authors are indebted to Dr. David B. Magerlein, Dr. James M. Magerlein, and Mr. Michael J. Goodrich of The Upjohn Company for providing this application.

Figure 8.19   A PRODUCTION PROCESS AT UPJOHN

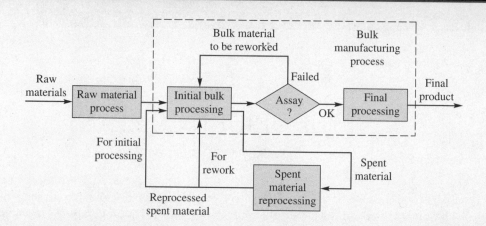

A simulation model of the production process was developed, and these questions were addressed:

1. What is the maximum throughput of the existing facility?
2. How can the production process be modified to increase the throughput of the existing facility?
3. How much equipment (tanks and centrifuges) must be added to the current facility to increase the capacity to meet the forecasted demand?
4. How should the reprocessed spent material be used to minimize the total production cost?
5. If a new facility is required, what is the optimal size and configuration?

The scope of the simulation model included the raw material, bulk- and spent-material processes already defined. The model was built in a modular flexible manner that allowed for the evaluation of resource levels within the facility, staffing levels and hours, changes in process times or equipment usage, changes in lot size, and/or yield changes. The logic of the process flow served as the core of the model and was developed in collaboration with the lead operators and supervisors of the production area. Since a good logical model is the key to good simulation results, a significant amount of time was spent defining the logic of the process flow. The model development process provided a secondary benefit in that production personnel got to review and evaluate the process as they explained it.

The computer simulation model has been used on several occasions over the past two years. Simulation results have assisted management in addressing capacity,

resource allocation, and operating policy issues. Each time a request to evaluate an issue is made, a detailed experimental design is developed that defines the alternatives to be evaluated. The appropriate simulation runs are made, the results are evaluated and presented to production management and personnel, and follow-up actions defined.

The computer simulation model was developed using the SLAMSYSTEM® Version 3.0 simulation language from the Pritsker Corporation. All simulation runs were made on a personal computer.

Benefits of the Simulation Model

The ongoing investigation of the production process using computer simulation has resulted in numerous benefits to the company, including the following:

1. Optimizing the use of reprocessed spent material to replace fresh raw material. Total material costs were reduced by approximately $3 million per year.
2. Demonstrating that the current facility, with some operating policy improvements, was large enough to satisfy the increased demand for the next several years. Expansion to a new facility was not necessary.
3. Determining the impact on facility throughput from alternative process changes. Numerous potential changes were investigated. The simulation model predicted how each change would affect total facility throughput. One change was identi-

fied that would increase throughput beyond what was needed for the 5-year forecasted demand.

4. Determining appropriate staffing levels within the facility. The model determined the number of operators that will be required as the production level increases in the future. This ensures that the proper number of operators will be trained by the time they are needed.

5. Determining the required size and configuration for a new facility. Although the current facility was found adequate to meet demand, the model still allowed management to determine the cost required to build a new facility.

The final actions taken based on the simulation results included alterations in policies for using re- processed spent material, priority implementation of the process change that most impacted increasing facility throughput, establishment of appropriate staffing levels, and cost minimization because the expense of building a new or expanded facility was avoided.

Questions

1. Briefly describe the Upjohn production operation.
2. What is the primary reason Upjohn conducted a study of this operation?
3. Describe some of the factors that had to be included in the simulation model.
4. What were the advantages of computer simulation to Upjohn?

9

DECISION ANALYSIS

Decision analysis can be used to determine an optimal strategy when a decision maker is faced with several decision alternatives and an uncertain or risk-filled pattern of future events. For example, the manager of a retail business with seasonal clothing products would like to order a large quantity of a particular product if demand for the product will be high. Conversely, the manager would like to order a much smaller quantity if demand for the product will be low. Unfortunately, seasonal clothing products require the manager to make an order quantity decision and place an order with the supplier before demand is known. If fact, the actual demand for the product will not be known until the product has been placed into the store and customers have had the opportunity to purchase it. The selection of the best order quantity when the manager is faced with an uncertain demand is a problem suited for decision analysis.

We begin the study of decision analysis by considering problems having reasonably few decision alternatives and reasonably few possible future events. We introduce the concept of a payoff table to provide a structure for a decision problem and to illustrate the fundamentals of decision analysis. We then introduce decision trees as a way to structure more complex decision problems. Ultimately, we show how an analysis of a decision tree will identify an optimal decision strategy for a problem.

..../ /.............

9.1   STRUCTURING THE DECISION PROBLEM

Pittsburgh Development Corporation (PDC) has purchased land for a luxury, riverfront condominium complex. The site provides a spectacular view of downtown Pittsburgh and the Golden Triangle where the Allegheny and Monongahela rivers meet to form the Ohio River. The individual condominium units will be priced from \$300,000 to \$1,200,000, depending on the floor the unit is located on, the square footage of the unit, and optional features such as fireplaces and large balconies.

The company has had preliminary architectural drawings developed for three different project sizes: 6 floors with 30 units, 12 floors with 60 units, and 18 floors with 90 units. The financial success of the project will depend heavily on the decision that PDC makes regarding the size of the condominium project. Let us consider how decision analysis can help PDC determine which size project to develop.

The first step in the decision analysis approach is to identify the decision alternatives that are being considered. PDC has three alternatives:

d_1 = a small condominium complex with 6 floors and 30 units

d_2 = a medium condominium complex with 12 floors and 60 units

d_3 = a large condominium complex with 18 floors and 90 units

A key factor in selecting one of these decision alternatives involves management's assessment of the demand for the condominiums.

When asked about possible market acceptance of the condominium project, management viewed the possible acceptance of the project as an all-or-nothing situation. That is, management believes that market acceptance will be one of two possibilities: high market acceptance of the project and hence a substantial demand for the condominiums, or low market acceptance of the project and hence a limited demand for the condominiums. Although management can exercise some influence over market acceptance with advertising, the high prices for the units mean that demand will likely depend on a variety of other factors over which PDC will have no control.

In decision analysis, events that may occur but which the decision maker cannot control are referred to as **states of nature.** The list of possible states of nature includes everything that can happen, and individual states of nature are defined so that only one will actually occur. For the PDC condominium project, the two states of nature are

s_1 = high market acceptance and hence a substantial demand for the units

s_2 = low market acceptance and hence a limited demand for the units

Payoff Tables

Given the three decision alternatives and the two states of nature, which condominium size should PDC select? To answer this question, PDC will need information on the profit associated with each combination of a decision alternative and a state of nature. For example, what profit would PDC realize if it constructs a large condominium complex (d_3) and market acceptance turns out to be high (s_1)? But what would happen to the profit if PDC constructs a large condominium complex (d_3) and market acceptance turns out to be low (s_2)? In decision analysis, we refer to the outcome that results from a specific decision alternative and the occurrence of a particular state of nature as a **payoff.** A table showing the payoffs for all combinations of the decision alternatives and states of nature is a **payoff table.**

Using the best information available, management has estimated the payoffs, or profits, for the PDC condominium project. These estimates, with profits expressed in millions of dollars, are presented in Table 9.1. In general, entries in a payoff table can be stated in terms of profit, cost, time, distance, or any other measure of output that may be appropriate for the situation being analyzed. We will refer to the payoff associated with decision alternative i and state of nature j as V_{ij}. For example, Table 9.1 shows that $V_{31} = 20$, indicating that a \$20 million profit is anticipated if the large complex is constructed (d_3) and a high market acceptance (s_1) occurs. However, $V_{32} = -9$ shows an anticipated loss of \$9 million if the large complex is constructed (d_3) and a low market acceptance (s_2) occurs.

Decision Trees

A **decision tree** provides a graphical representation of the decision-making process. Figure 9.1 presents a decision tree for the PDC problem. Note that the decision tree shows the natural or logical progression that will occur over time. First, PDC must make a decision regarding the size of the condominium complex (d_1, d_2, or d_3). Then, after the decision is implemented, either state of nature s_1 or s_2 will occur. The number at each end point of the tree indicates the payoff associated with a particular sequence. For example the topmost payoff of 8 indicates that an \$8 million profit is anticipated if PDC constructs a small condominium complex (d_1) and market acceptance turns out to be high (s_1). The next payoff of 7 indicates an anticipated profit of \$7 million if PDC constructs a small condominium complex (d_1) and market acceptance turns out to be low (s_2). Thus, the decision tree shows graphically the sequences of decision alternatives and states of nature that provide the six possible outcomes and payoffs for PDC.

If you have a payoff table, you should be able to develop a decision tree. Try Problem 1(a).

We refer to an intersection or junction point of the decision tree as a **node** and the arc or connector between nodes as a **branch.** Figure 9.1 shows the PDC decision tree with the nodes numbered 1–4. When the branches *leaving* a node are decision branches, we refer to the node as a *decision node* and represent it by a square. Similarly, when the branches leaving a node are state-of-nature branches, we refer to the node as a *state-of-nature node* and represent it by a circle. Hence, node 1 is a decision node, whereas nodes 2, 3, and 4 are state-of-nature nodes.

The identification of the decision alternatives, the states of nature, and the payoff associated with each decision alternative and state-of-nature combination are the first three steps in the decision-analysis process. We now turn to this question: How can the decision maker best utilize the information presented in the payoff table or the decision tree to arrive at a decision? Several approaches may be used.

Table 9.1	PAYOFF TABLE FOR THE PDC CONDOMINIUM PROJECT (PAYOFFS IN \$ MILLION)

Decision Alternative	State of Nature	
	High Acceptance s_1	Low Acceptance s_2
Small complex, d_1	8	7
Medium complex, d_2	14	5
Large complex, d_3	20	−9

Figure 9.1   DECISION TREE FOR THE PDC CONDOMINIUM PROJECT (PAYOFFS IN $ MILLION)

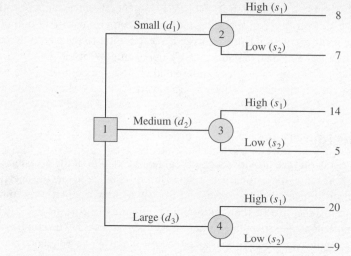

N O T E S
and Comments

1. Experts in problem solving agree that the first step in solving a complex problem is to decompose it into a series of smaller subproblems. Decision trees provide a useful way to show how the problem can be decomposed and the sequential nature of the decision process.

2. People often view the same problem from different perspectives. Thus, the discussion regarding the development of a decision tree may provide additional insight about the problem.

9.2   DECISION MAKING WITHOUT PROBABILITIES

In this section we consider approaches to decision making that do not require knowledge of the probabilities of the states of nature. These approaches are appropriate in situations in which the decision maker has little confidence in the ability to assess the probabilities of the various states of nature, or in which considering best- and worst-case analyses that are independent of state-of-nature probabilities is desirable. Because different approaches sometimes lead to different decision recommendations, the decision maker needs to understand the approaches available and then select the specific approach that, according to the decision maker's judgment, is the most appropriate.

Many people think of a good decision as one in which the outcome is good. However, in some instances, a good, well-thought-out decision may still lead to a bad or undesirable outcome.

Optimistic Approach

The **optimistic approach** evaluates each decision alternative in terms of the *best* payoff that can occur. The decision alternative that is recommended is the one that provides the best possible payoff. For a problem in which maximum profit is desired, as in the PDC problem, the optimistic approach would lead the decision maker to choose the alternative corresponding to the largest profit. For problems involving minimization, this approach leads to choosing the alternative with the smallest payoff.

For a maximization problem, the optimistic approach often is referred to as the *maximax approach;* for a minimization problem, the corresponding terminology is *minimim*.

To illustrate the optimistic approach, we use it to develop a recommendation for the PDC problem. First, we determine the maximum payoff for each decision alternative; then we select the decision alternative that provides the overall maximum payoff. These steps systematically identify the decision alternative that provides the largest possible profit. Table 9.2 illustrates these steps.

Since 20, corresponding to d_3, is the largest payoff, the decision to construct the large condominium complex is the recommended decision alternative using the optimistic approach.

Conservative Approach

The **conservative approach** evaluates each decision alternative in terms of the *worst* payoff that can occur. The decision alternative recommended is the one that provides the best of the worst possible payoffs. For a problem in which the output measure is profit, as in the PDC problem, the conservative approach would lead the decision maker to choose the alternative that maximizes the minimum possible profit that could be obtained. For problems involving minimization, this approach identifies the alternative that will minimize the maximum payoff.

For a maximization problem, the conservative approach is often referred to as the *maximin approach;* for a minimization problem, the corresponding terminology is *minimax*.

To illustrate the conservative approach, we use it to develop a recommendation for the PDC problem. First, we identify the minimum payoff for each of the decision alternatives; then we select the decision alternative that maximizes the minimum payoff. Table 9.3 illustrates these steps for the PDC problem.

Because 7, corresponding to d_1, yields the maximum of the minimum payoffs, the decision alternative of a small condominium complex is recommended. This decision approach is considered conservative because it identifies the worst possible payoffs and then recommends the decision alternative that avoids the possibility of extremely "bad" payoffs. In the conservative approach, PDC is guaranteed a profit of at least $7 million. Although PDC may make more, it *cannot* make less than $7 million.

Minimax Regret Approach

Minimax regret is an approach to decision making that is neither purely optimistic nor purely conservative. Let us illustrate the minimax regret approach by showing how it can be used to select a decision alternative for the PDC problem.

Table 9.2	MAXIMUM PAYOFF FOR EACH PDC DECISION ALTERNATIVE

Decision Alternative	Maximum Payoff	
Small complex, d_1	8	
Medium complex, d_2	14	
Large complex, d_3	20	← Maximum of the maximum payoff values

Table 9.3	MINIMUM PAYOFF FOR EACH PDC DECISION ALTERNATIVE

Decision Alternative	Minimum Payoff	
Small complex, d_1	7	← Maximum of the minimum payoff values
Medium complex, d_2	5	
Large complex, d_3	−9	

Suppose that the PDC constructs a small condominium complex (d_1) and market acceptance turns out to be high (s_1). Table 9.1 shows that the resulting profit for PDC would be $8 million. However, we now know that the high acceptance state of nature (s_1) has occurred, so we realize that the decision to construct a large condominium complex (d_3), yielding a profit of $20 million, would have been the best decision. The difference between the payoff for the best decision alternative ($20 million) and the payoff for the decision to construct a small condominium complex ($8 million) is the **opportunity loss,** or **regret,** associated with decision alternative d_1 when state of nature s_1 occurs; thus, for this case, the opportunity loss or regret is $20 million $-$ $8 million $=$ $12 million. Similarly, if PDC makes the decision to construct a medium condominium complex (d_2) and the high acceptance state of nature (s_1) occurs, the opportunity loss, or regret, associated with d_2 would be $20 million $-$ $14 million $=$ $6 million.

In general the following expression represents the opportunity loss, or regret.

$$R_{ij} = \left| V_j^* - V_{ij} \right| \tag{9.1}$$

where

R_{ij} = the regret associated with decision alternative d_i and state of nature s_j

V_j^* = the payoff value[1] corresponding to the best decision for the state of nature s_j

V_{ij} = the payoff corresponding to decision alternative d_i and state of nature s_j

Note the role of the absolute value in equation (9.1). That is, for minimization problems, the best payoff, V_j^*, is the smallest entry in column j. Because this value always is less than or equal to V_{ij}, the absolute value of the difference between V_j^* and V_{ij} ensures that the regret is always the magnitude of the difference.

Using equation (9.1) and the payoffs in Table 9.1, we can compute the regret associated with each combination of decision alternative d_i and state of nature s_j. Since the PDC problem is a maximization problem, V_j^* will be the largest entry in column j of the payoff table. Thus, to compute the regret, we simply subtract each entry in a column from the largest entry in the column. Table 9.4 shows the opportunity loss, or regret, table for the PDC problem.

The next step in applying the minimax regret approach is to list the maximum regret for each decision alternative; Table 9.5 shows the results for the PDC problem. Selecting the decision alternative with the *minimum* of the *maximum* regret values—hence, the name *minimax regret*—yields the minimax regret decision. For the PDC problem, the alternative to construct the medium condominium complex, with a corresponding maximum regret of $6 million, is the recommended minimax regret decision.

Note that the three approaches discussed in this section provide different recommendations, which in itself isn't bad. It simply reflects the difference in decision-making philosophies that underlie the various approaches. Ultimately, the decision maker will have to choose the most appropriate approach and then make the final decision accordingly. The main criticism of the approaches discussed in this section is that they do not consider any information about the probabilities of the various states of nature. In the next section we discuss an approach that utilizes probability information in selecting a decision alternative.

You should be able to develop a decision recommendation using the optimistic, conservative, and minimax regret approaches. Try Problem 1(b).

---

1. In maximization problems, V_j^* will be the largest entry in column j of the payoff table. In minimization problems, V_j^* will be the smallest entry in column j of the payoff table.

Table 9.4	OPPORTUNITY LOSS, OR REGRET, TABLE FOR THE PDC CONDOMINIUM PROJECT ($ MILLION)

| | State of Nature | |
Decision Alternative	High Acceptance s_1	Low Acceptance s_2
Small complex, d_1	12	0
Medium complex, d_2	6	2
Large complex, d_3	0	16

Table 9.5	MAXIMUM REGRET FOR EACH PDC DECISION ALTERNATIVE

Decision Alternative	Maximum Regret	
Small complex, d_1	12	
Medium complex, d_2	6	← Minimum of the maximum regret
Large complex, d_3	16	

Spreadsheet Solution for the PDC Problem

The spreadsheet solution using the optimistic approach is shown in Figure 9.2. The payoff table with appropriate headings is placed in cell A4 through cell C8. The Excel formulas that provide the calculations and optimal solution recommendation are as follows:

Cell D6	Compute the maximum payoff
	=MAX(B6:C6) (Copy D6 to D7:D8)
Cell D10	Compute the best payoff
	=MAX(D6:D8)
Cell E6	Determine which decision alternative is recommended
	=IF(D6=$D$10,A6,"") (Copy E6 to E7:E8)

If the maximum payoff in cell D6 is equal to the best payoff in cell D10, the words "Small complex" will be displayed in cell E6; otherwise, this cell will be left blank. As Figure 9.2 shows, the optimistic approach recommends the large complex decision alternative with a best payoff value of 20.

Figure 9.3 shows a similar spreadsheet design for the PDC problem using the conservative approach. The only difference between the spreadsheets in Figure 9.2 and 9.3 is that the conservative approach finds the minimum payoff in each decision alternative. Thus, cell D6 contains MIN(B6:C6), which is copied to cells D7 and D8. With this change, the spreadsheet in Figure 9.3 shows that the conservative approach recommends the small complex decision alternative with a best payoff value of 7.

Figure 9.4 shows the spreadsheet for the PDC problem using the minimax regret approach. The payoff table with appropriate headings is again presented in cell A4 through

| | Figure 9.2 | SPREADSHEET SOLUTION FOR THE PDC PROBLEM USING THE OPTIMISTIC APPROACH |

	A	B	C	D	E
1	**PDC Problem - Optimistic Approach**				
2					
3	**Payoff Table**				
4		**State of Nature**		**Maximum**	**Recommended**
5	**Decision Alternative**	High acceptance	Low acceptance	**Payoff**	**Decision**
6	Small complex	8	7	8	
7	Medium complex	14	5	14	
8	Large complex	20	-9	20	Large complex
9					
10	**Best Payoff**			20	

SPREADSHEET
PDC
OPTIMISTIC

cell C8. The minimax regret approach requires the computation of an opportunity loss or regret table. The Excel formulas for this table are as follows:

Cell B14   Compute the opportunity loss for the high acceptance state of nature
            =MAX($B$6:$B$8)−B6   (Copy B14 to B15:B16)

Cell C14   Compute the opportunity loss for the low acceptance state of nature
            =MAX($C$6:$C$8)−C6   (Copy C14 to C15:C16)

Cell D14   Compute the maximum regret
            =MAX(B14:C14)   (Copy D14 to D15:D16)

Cell D18   Compute the minimum of the maximum regret values
            =MIN(D14:D16)

| | Figure 9.3 | SPREADSHEET SOLUTION FOR THE PDC PROBLEM USING THE CONSERVATIVE APPROACH |

	A	B	C	D	E
1	**PDC Problem - Conservative Approach**				
2					
3	**Payoff Table**				
4		**State of Nature**		**Minimum**	**Recommended**
5	**Decision Alternative**	High acceptance	Low acceptance	**Payoff**	**Decision**
6	Small complex	8	7	7	Small complex
7	Medium complex	14	5	5	
8	Large complex	20	-9	-9	
9					
10	**Best Payoff**			7	

SPREADSHEET
PDC
CONSERVATIVE

Figure 9.4 — SPREADSHEET SOLUTION FOR THE PDC PROBLEM USING THE MINIMAX REGRET APPROACH

SPREADSHEET
PDC MINIMAX
REGRET

	A	B	C	D	E
1	**PDC Problem - Minimax Regret Approach**				
2					
3	**Payoff Table**				
4		**State of Nature**			
5	**Decision Alternative**	High acceptance	Low acceptance		
6	Small complex	8	7		
7	Medium complex	14	5		
8	Large complex	20	-9		
9					
10					
11	**Opportunity Loss Table**				
12		**State of Nature**		**Maximum**	**Recommended**
13	**Decision Alternative**	High acceptance	Low acceptance	**Regret**	**Decision**
14	Small complex	12	0	12	
15	Medium complex	6	2	6	Medium complex
16	Large complex	0	16	16	
17					
18	**Minimax Regret Value**			6	

Column E contains the IF formulas that were used in Figures 9.2 and 9.3 to determine which decision alternative provides the recommended decision.

> Cell E14   Determine which decision alternative is recommended
>   =IF(D14=$D$18,A14,"")   (Copy E14 to E15:E16)

Figure 9.4 shows that the minimax regret approach recommends the medium complex decision alternative.

Spreadsheets for larger payoff tables use the same logic and same general cell formulas. Inserting necessary rows for decision alternatives and/or necessary columns for states of nature and copying the corresponding cell formulas can easily expand Figure 9.2, 9.3, and 9.4 into spreadsheets for larger decision-analysis problems.

We do not present detailed cell formulas for payoff tables with a minimization objective. However, Figure 9.2 and 9.3 can be easily converted to minimization problems by changing MAX functions to MIN functions and by changing MIN functions to MAX functions. These changes only effect column D of the spreadsheet. For a minimax regret *minimization* problem, the formula in cell B14 of Figure 9.4 would be changed to

$$=B6-MIN(\$B\$6:\$B\$8)$$

Similar cell formulas will be needed in the opportunity loss table in cell B14 to cell C16. No changes would be required in column D to obtain the optimal minimax regret decision.

9.3   DECISION MAKING WITH PROBABILITIES

In many decision-making situations, we can obtain probability estimates for the states of nature. When such probabilities are available, we can use the **expected value approach** to identify the best decision alternative. Let us first define the expected value of a decision alternative and then apply it to the PDC problem.

Let

$$N = \text{the number of states of nature}$$
$$P(s_j) = \text{the probability of state of nature } s_j$$

Since one and only one of the N states of nature can occur, the probabilities must satisfy two conditions:

$$P(s_j) \geq 0 \qquad \text{for all states of nature} \tag{9.2}$$

$$\sum_{j=1}^{N} P(s_j) = P(s_1) + P(s_2) + \cdots + P(s_N) = 1 \tag{9.3}$$

The **expected value (EV)** of decision alternative d_i is defined as follows.

$$EV(d_i) = \sum_{j=1}^{N} P(s_j)V_{ij} \tag{9.4}$$

In words, the expected value of a decision alternative is the sum of weighted payoffs for the decision alternative. The weight for a payoff is the probability of the associated state of nature and therefore the probability that the payoff will occur. Let us return to the PDC problem to see how the expected value approach can be applied.

PDC is optimistic about the potential for the luxury high-rise condominium complex. Suppose that this optimism provides an initial subjective probability assessment of 0.8 that market acceptance will be high (s_1) and a corresponding probability of 0.2 that market acceptance will be low (s_2). Thus, $P(s_1) = 0.8$ and $P(s_2) = 0.2$. Using the payoff values in Table 9.1 and equation (9.4), we compute the expected value for each of the three decision alternatives as follows:

$$EV(d_1) = 0.8(8) + 0.2(7) = 7.8$$
$$EV(d_2) = 0.8(14) + 0.2(5) = 12.2$$
$$EV(d_3) = 0.8(20) + 0.2(-9) = 14.2$$

Thus, using the expected value approach, we find that the large condominium complex, with an expected value of $14.2 million, is the recommended decision.

You should now be able to use the expected value approach to develop a decision recommendation. Try Problem 5.

The calculations required to identify the decision alternative with the best expected value can be conveniently carried out on a decision tree. Figure 9.5 shows the decision tree for the PDC problem with state-of-nature branch probabilities. Working backward through the decision tree, we first compute the expected value at each state-of-nature node. That is, at each state-of-nature node, we weight each possible payoff by its chance of occurrence. By doing so, we obtain the expected values for nodes 2, 3, and 4, as shown in Figure 9.6.

Since the decision maker controls the branch leaving decision node 1 and since we are trying to maximize the expected profit, the best decision branch at node 1 is d_3. Thus, the

Figure 9.5   PDC DECISION TREE WITH STATE-OF-NATURE BRANCH PROBABILITIES

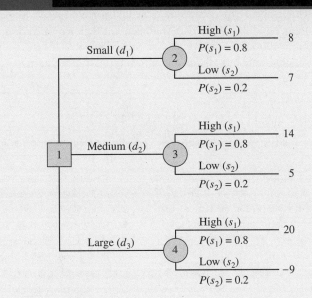

decision tree analysis leads to a recommendation of d_3 with an expected value of $14.2 million. Note that this is the same recommendation obtained with the expected value approach in conjunction with the payoff table.

Other decision problems may be substantially more complex than the PDC problem, but if a reasonable number of decision alternatives and states of nature are present, you can use the decision tree approach outlined here. First, draw a decision tree consisting of decision and state-of-nature nodes and branches that describe the sequential nature of the

Figure 9.6   APPLYING THE EXPECTED VALUE APPROACH USING DECISION TREES

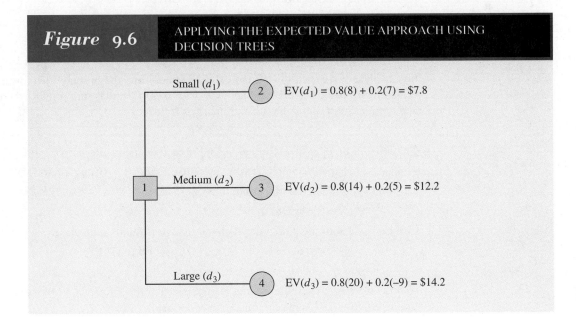

problem. If you use the expected value approach, the next step is to determine the probabilities for each of the state-of-nature branches and compute the expected value at each state-of-nature node. Then select the decision branch leading to the state-of-nature node with the best expected value. The decision alternative associated with this branch is the recommended decision. The Management Science in Action article on decision analysis and the selection of home mortgages describes how the decision analysis approach can be used to help home buyers select the best type of mortgage.

MANAGEMENT SCIENCE IN ACTION

DECISION ANALYSIS AND THE SELECTION OF HOME MORTGAGES*

Purchasing a new home can be a stressful experience, especially when it may commit the new owners to a mortgage contract for the next 20 to 30 years. The decision is further complicated by the fact that mortgages have varying interest rates that range from traditional fixed-rate mortgages (FRM) to adjustable-rate mortgages (ARM) with a wide variety of special features.

A decision analysis approach to selecting the best type of mortgage involves the development of a decision tree that includes one branch for each mortgage alternative available. For example, if the buyer is considering three different mortgage contracts—fixed rate, variable rate with a 3-year adjustment, and variable rate with a 5-year adjustment—the decision tree begins with three decision alternative branches.

The future events that indicate what can happen to interest rates over time are the states of nature branches for the decision tree. For instance, variable-rate mortgage branches have state-of-nature branches that indicate possible interest rate increases and decreases. The complete decision tree shows the outcomes for each mortgage alternative and its associated cost.

Using decision analysis criteria reflecting a conservative or an optimistic perspective, a prospective home buyer can select a recommended mortgage alternative. If probability estimates are available for the future mortgage rates, the expected value approach will use the probability information to recommend the best mortgage alternative.

*Robert E. Luna, and Richard A. Reid, "Mortgage Selection Using a Decision Tree Approach," *Interfaces* 16, no. 3 (May–June 1986): 73–81.

Spreadsheet Solution for the PDC Problem Using the Expected Value Approach

This spreadsheet solution is shown in Figure 9.7. The payoff table with appropriate headings is placed into cell A4 through cell C8. In addition, the probabilities for the two states of nature are placed in cells B9 and C9. The Excel formulas that provide the calculations and optimal solution recommendation are as follows:

Cell D6   Compute the expected value for each decision alternative.
             =SUMPRODUCT($B$9:$C$9,B6:C6)   (Copy D6 to D7:D8)

Cell D11   Compute the maximum expected value.
             =MAX(D6:D8)

Cell E6   Determine which decision alternative is the recommended.
             =IF(D6=$D$11,A6,"")   (Copy E6 to E7:E8)

As Figure 9.7 shows, the expected value approach recommends the larger complex decision alternative with a maximum expected value of 14.2.

Problem 8 uses a spreadsheet to learn how the optimal decision changes as the state-of-nature probabilities change. This process is called *sensitivity analysis*.

The only change required to the convert the spreadsheet in Figure 9.7 into a minimization analysis is to change the formula in cell D11 to =MIN(D6:D8). With this change, the decision alternative with the minimum expected value will be shown in column E.

Expected Value of Perfect Information

Suppose that PDC has the opportunity to conduct a market research study that would help evaluate buyer interest in the condominium project and provide information that management could use to improve the probability assessments for the states of nature. To determine the potential value of this information, we begin by assuming that the study could provide *perfect information* regarding the states of nature; that is, we assume for the moment that PDC could determine with certainty which state of nature is going to occur. To make use of this perfect information, we will develop a decision strategy that PDC should follow once it knows which state of nature will occur. As we show, a decision strategy is simply a decision rule that specifies the decision alternative to be selected after the new information becomes available.

To help determine the decision strategy for PDC, we have reproduced PDC's payoff table as Table 9.6. Note that, if PDC knew for sure that state of nature s_1 would occur, the best decision alternative would be d_3, with a payoff of \$20 million. Similarly, if PDC knew for sure that state of nature s_2 would occur, the best decision alternative would be d_1, with a payoff of \$7 million. Thus, we can state PDC's optimal decision strategy based on perfect information as follows:

$$\text{If } s_1, \text{ select } d_3.$$
$$\text{If } s_2, \text{ select } d_1.$$

What is the expected value for this decision strategy? To compute the expected value with perfect information, we return to the original probability estimates for the states of nature: $P(s_1) = 0.8$, and $P(s_2) = 0.2$. Based on these probabilities, there is a 0.8 probability that the perfect information will indicate state of nature s_1. In this case, the resulting decision alternative d_3 will provide a \$20 million profit. Similarly, with a 0.2 probability for state

SPREADSHEET
PDC EXPECTED
VALUE

Figure 9.7	SPREADSHEET SOLUTION FOR THE PDC PROBLEM USING THE EXPECTED VALUE APPROACH

	A	B	C	D	E
1	**PDC Problem - Expected Value Approach**				
2					
3	**Payoff Table**				
4		**State of Nature**		**Expected**	**Recommended**
5	**Decision Alternative**	High acceptance	Low acceptance	**Value**	**Decision**
6	Small complex	8	7	7.8	
7	Medium complex	14	5	12.2	
8	Large complex	20	-9	14.2	Large complex
9	**Probability**	0.8	0.2		
10					
11	**Maximum Expected Value**			14.2	

Table 9.6	PAYOFF TABLE FOR THE PDC CONDOMINIUM PROJECT ($ MILLION)

Decision Alternative	State of Nature	
	High Acceptance s_1	Low Acceptance s_2
Small complex, d_1	8	7
Medium complex, d_2	14	5
Large complex, d_3	20	−9

of nature s_2, the resulting decision alternative d_1 will provide a $7 million profit. Thus, from equation (4.4), the expected value of the decision strategy that uses perfect information is

$$0.8(20) + 0.2(7) = 17.4$$

We refer to the expected value of $17.4 million as the *expected value with perfect information* (EVwPI).

Earlier in this section we showed that the recommended decision using the expected value approach is decision alternative d_3, with an expected value of $14.2 million. Because this decision recommendation and expected value computation were made without the benefit of perfect information, $14.2 million is referred to as the *expected value without perfect information* (EVwoPI).

The expected value with perfect information is $17.4 million, and the expected value without perfect information is $14.2; therefore, the expected value of the perfect information (EVPI) is $17.4 − $14.2 = $3.2 million. In other words, $3.2 million represents the additional expected value that can be obtained if perfect information were available about the states of nature.

Figure 9.8 shows the spreadsheet for the PDC problem expanded to include the expected value of perfect information. The following cell formulas are added in row 14.

Cell B14	=MAX(B6:B8)
Cell C14	=MAX(C6:C8)
Cell D14	=SUMPRODUCT($B$9:$C$9,B14:C14)−D11

You should be able to determine the expected value of perfect information. Try Problem 12.

Generally speaking, a market research study will not provide "perfect" information; however, if the market research study is a good one, the information gathered might be worth a sizable portion of the $3.2 million. Given the EVPI of $3.2 million, PDC should seriously consider the market survey as a way to obtain more information about the states of nature.

In general, the expected value of perfect information is computed as follows:

$$EVPI = |EVwPI - EVwoPI| \tag{9.8}$$

where

EVPI = expected value of perfect information

EVwPI = expected value *with* perfect information about the states of nature

EVwoPI = expected value *without* perfect information about the states of nature

Figure 9.8	SPREADSHEET SOLUTION FOR THE PDC PROBLEM SHOWING THE EXPECTED VALUE OF PERFECT INFORMATION

SPREADSHEET
PDC EXPECTED
VALUE

	A	B	C	D	E
1	**PDC Problem - Expected Value Approach**				
2					
3	**Payoff Table**				
4		**State of Nature**		**Expected**	**Recommended**
5	**Decision Alternative**	High acceptance	Low acceptance	**Value**	**Decision**
6	Small complex	8	7	7.8	
7	Medium complex	14	5	12.2	
8	Large complex	20	-9	14.2	Large complex
9	**Probability**	0.8	0.2		
10					
11	**Maximum Expected Value**			14.2	
12					
13	**Expected Value of**	**Maximum Payoff**			
14	**Perfect Information**	20	7	3.2	

Note the role of the absolute value in equation (9.8). That is, for minimization problems the expected value with perfect information is always less than or equal to the expected value without perfect information. In this case, EVPI is the magnitude of the difference between EVwPI and EVwoPI, or the absolute value of the difference as shown in equation (9.8).

N O T E S
and Comments

We restate the *opportunity loss*, or *regret*, table for the PDC problem (see Table 9.4) as follows.

Decision Alternative	State of Nature	
	High Acceptance	Low Acceptance
	s_1	s_2
Small complex, d_1	12	0
Medium complex, d_2	6	2
Large complex, d_3	0	16

Using $P(s_1)$, $P(s_2)$, and the opportunity loss values, we can compute the *expected opportunity loss* (EOL) for each decision alternative. With $P(s_1) = 0.8$ and $P(s_2) = 0.2$, the expected opportunity loss for each of the three decision alternatives is

$$EOL(d_1) = 0.8(12) + 0.2(0) = 9.6$$
$$EOL(d_2) = 0.8(6) + 0.2(2) = 5.2$$
$$EOL(d_3) = 0.8(0) + 0.2(16) = 3.2$$

Regardless of whether the decision analysis involves maximization or minimization, the *minimum* expected opportunity loss always provides the best decision alternative. Thus, with $EOL(d_3) = 3.2$, d_3 is the recommended decision. In addition, the minimum expected opportunity loss always is *equal to the expected value of perfect information.* That is, EOL(best decision) = EVPI; for the PDC problem, this value is $3.2 million.

..../ /..............

9.4   DECISION ANALYSIS WITH SAMPLE INFORMATION

In applying the expected value approach, we have shown how probability information about the states of nature affects the expected value calculations and thus the decision recommendation. Frequently, decision makers have preliminary or **prior probability** estimates for the states of nature that are the best probability values available. However, to make the best possible decision, the decision maker may want to seek additional information about the states of nature. This new information can be used to revise or update the prior probabilities so that the final decision is based on more accurate probability estimates for the states of nature. Most often, additional information is obtained through experiments designed to provide s**ample information** about the states of nature. Raw material sampling, product testing, and market research studies are examples of experiments that may enable management to revise or update the state-of-nature probabilities. These *revised* probabilities are called **posterior probabilities.**

Let us return to the PDC problem and assume that management is considering a six-month market research study designed to evaluate market acceptance of the PDC condominium project. Management anticipates that the market research study will provide one of the following two results:

1. Favorable report: A significant number of the individuals contacted express interest in purchasing a PDC condominium.
2. Unfavorable report: Very few of the individuals contacted express interest in purchasing a PDC condominium.

By introducing the possibility of conducting a market research study, the PDC problem has become more complex. First, PDC's management must decide whether the market research should be conducted. If it is conducted, PDC's management must be prepared to make a decision about the size of the condominium project if the market research report is favorable and possibly a different decision about the size of the condominium project if the market research report is unfavorable. The decision tree in Figure 9.9 shows this PDC decision problem. The squares are *decision nodes* and the circles are *probability nodes*. At each decision node, the branch of the tree that is taken is based on the decision made. At each probability node, the branch of the tree that is taken is based on probability or chance. For example, decision node 1 shows that PDC must first make the decision of whether to conduct the market research study. If the market research study is undertaken, probability node 2 indicates that both the favorable report branch and the unfavorable report branch are not under PDC's control and will be determined by chance. Node 3 is a decision node, indicating that PDC must make the decision to construct the small, medium, or large complex if the market research report is favorable. Node 4 is a decision node showing that PDC must make the decision to construct the small, medium, or large complex if the market research report is unfavorable. Node 5 is a decision node indicating that PDC must make the decision to construct the small, medium, or large complex if the market research is not undertaken. Nodes 6 to 14 are probability nodes indicating that the high acceptance or low acceptance state-of-nature branches will be determined by chance.

At this point, the analysis of the decision tree requires that we know the branch probabilities corresponding to all probability nodes. PDC's estimates of the branch probabilities are as follows.

Figure 9.9   THE PDC DECISION TREE INCLUDING THE MARKET RESEARCH STUDY

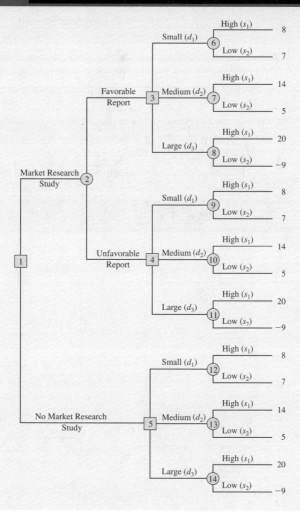

If the market research study is undertaken

$$P(\text{Favorable report}) = 0.77$$
$$P(\text{Unfavorable report}) = 0.23$$

If the market research report is Favorable

$$P(\text{High acceptance given a Favorable report}) = 0.94$$
$$P(\text{Low acceptance given a Favorable report}) = 0.06$$

If the market research report is Unfavorable

$$P(\text{High acceptance given an Unfavorable report}) = 0.35$$
$$P(\text{Low acceptance given an Unfavorable report}) = 0.65$$

If the market research report is not undertaken

$$P(\text{High acceptance}) = 0.80$$
$$P(\text{Low acceptance}) = 0.20$$

The branch probabilities are shown on the decision tree in Figure 9.10.

The approach used to determine the optimal decision strategy is based on a backward pass through the decision tree using the following steps:

1. At a probability node, compute the expected value at the node by multiplying the payoff at the end of each branch by the corresponding branch probabilities.
2. At a decision node, select the decision branch that leads to the best expected value. This expected value becomes the expected value at the decision node.

Figure 9.10   THE PDC DECISION TREE WITH BRANCH PROBABILITIES

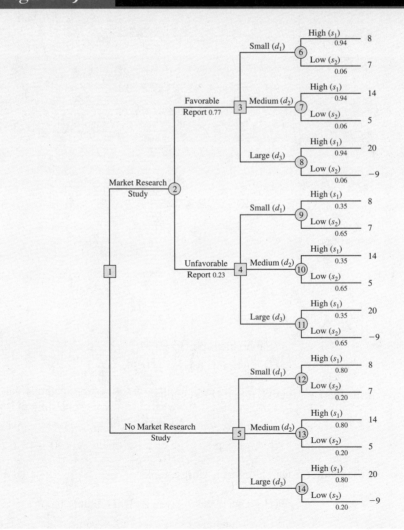

Starting the backward pass calculations by computing the expected values at probability nodes 6 to 16 provides the following results.

$$
\begin{aligned}
\text{EV(Node 6)} &= 0.94(8) &+ 0.06(7) &= 7.94 \\
\text{EV(Node 7)} &= 0.94(14) &+ 0.06(5) &= 13.46 \\
\text{EV(Node 8)} &= 0.94(20) &+ 0.06(-9) &= 18.26 \\
\text{EV(Node 9)} &= 0.35(8) &+ 0.65(7) &= 7.35 \\
\text{EV(Node 10)} &= 0.35(14) &+ 0.65(5) &= 8.15 \\
\text{EV(Node 11)} &= 0.35(20) &+ 0.65(-9) &= 1.15 \\
\text{EV(Node 12)} &= 0.80(8) &+ 0.20(7) &= 7.80 \\
\text{EV(Node 13)} &= 0.80(14) &+ 0.20(5) &= 12.20 \\
\text{EV(Node 14)} &= 0.80(20) &+ 0.20(-9) &= 14.20
\end{aligned}
$$

Next move to decision nodes 3, 4, and 5. For each of these nodes, we select the decision alternative branch that leads to the best expected value. For example, at node 3 we have the choice of the small complex branch with EV(Node 6) = 7.94, the medium complex branch with EV(Node 7) = 13.46, and the large complex branch with EV(Node 8) = 18.26. Thus, we select the large complex decision alternative branch and the expected value at node 3 becomes EV(Node 3) = 18.26.

For node 4, we select the best expected value from nodes 9, 10, and 11. The best decision alternative is the medium complex branch which provides EV(Node 4) = 8.15. For node 5, we select the best expected value from nodes 12, 13, and 14. The best decision alternative is the large complex branch which provides EV(Node 5) = 14.20.

The expected value at probability node 2 can now be computed as follows:

$$
\begin{aligned}
\text{EV(Node 2)} &= 0.77\text{EV(Node 3)} + 0.23\text{EV(Node 4)} \\
&= 0.77(18.26) + 0.23(8.15) = 15.93
\end{aligned}
$$

Finally, the decision can be made at decision node 1 by selecting the best expected values from nodes 2 and 5. This action leads to the decision alternative to conduct the market research study which provides an overall expected value of 15.93.

The optimal decision for PDC is to conduct the market research study and then carry out the following decision strategy:

Decision Strategy
If the market research is favorable, construct the large condominium complex.
If the market research is unfavorable, construct the medium condominium complex.

Problem 4 will test your ability to develop an optimal decision strategy.

The analysis of the PDC decision tree describes the methods that can be used to analyze any decision problem. First, draw a decision tree consisting of decision and probability nodes and branches that describe the sequential nature of the problem. Determine the probabilities for all probability branches. Then, by working backward through the tree, compute expected values at all probability nodes and select the best decision branch at all decision nodes. The sequence of optimal decision branches determines the optimal decision strategy for the problem. The Management Science in Action article on drug testing for student athletes describes how Santa Clara University used decision analysis to make a decision regarding whether to implement a drug testing program for student athletes.

MANAGEMENT SCIENCE IN ACTION

DECISION ANALYSIS AND DRUG TESTING FOR STUDENT ATHLETES*

The athletic governing board of Santa Clara University considered whether to implement a drug-testing program for the university's intercollegiate athletes. The decision analysis framework contains two decision alternatives: implement a drug-testing program and do not implement a drug-testing program. Each student athlete is either a drug user or not a drug user, so these two possibilities are considered to be the states of nature for the problem.

If the drug-testing program is implemented, student athletes will be required to take a drug-screening test. Results of the test will be either positive (test indicates a potential drug user) or negative (test does not indicate a potential drug user). The test outcomes are considered to be the sample information in the decision problem. If the test result is negative, no follow-up action will be taken. However, if the test result is positive, follow-up action will be taken to determine whether the student athlete actually is a drug user. The payoffs include the cost of not identifying a drug user and the cost of falsely identifying a nonuser.

Decision analysis showed that if the test result is positive, a reasonably high probability still exists that the student athlete is not a drug user. The cost and other problems associated with this type of misleading test result were considered significant. Consequently, the athletic governing board decided not to implement the drug-testing program.

*Charles D. Feinstein, "Deciding Whether to Test Student Athletes for Drug Use," *Interfaces* 20, no. 3 (May–June 1990): 80–87.

Expected Value of Sample Information

In the PDC problem, the market research study is the sample information that provides the optimal decision strategy. The expected value associated with the market research study is $15.93. In Section 9.3 we showed that the best expected value if the market research study is *not* undertaken is $14.20. Thus, we can conclude that the difference, $15.93 − $14.20 = $1.73, is the **expected value of sample information.** In other words, conducting the market research study adds $1.73 million to the PDC expected value. In general, the expected value of sample information is as follows:

$$\text{EVSI} = |\text{EVwSI} - \text{EVwoSI}| \tag{9.9}$$

where

$$\text{EVSI} = \text{expected value of sample information}$$
$$\text{EVwSI} = \text{expected value } \textit{with} \text{ sample information about the states of nature}$$
$$\text{EVwoSI} = \text{expected value } \textit{without} \text{ sample information about the states of nature}$$

Note the role of the absolute value in equation (9.9). That is, for minimization problems the expected value with sample information always is less than or equal to the expected value without sample information. In this case, EVSI is the magnitude of the difference between EVwSI and EVwoSI; thus, by taking the absolute value of the difference as shown in equation (9.9), we can handle both the maximization and minimization cases with one equation.

Efficiency of Sample Information

In Section 9.3 we showed that the expected value of perfect information (EVPI) for the PDC problem is $3.2 million. We never anticipated that the market research report would obtain perfect information, but we can use an **efficiency** measure to express the value of the market research information. With perfect information having an efficiency rating of 100%, the efficiency rating E for sample information is computed as follows.

$$E = \frac{EVSI}{EVPI} \times 100 \tag{9.10}$$

For the PDC problem,

$$E = \frac{1.73}{3.2} \times 100 = 54.1\%$$

In other words, the information from the market research study is 54.1% as efficient as perfect information.

Low efficiency ratings for sample information might lead the decision maker to look for other types of information. However, high efficiency ratings indicate that the sample information is almost as good as perfect information and that additional sources of information would not yield significantly better results.

Spreadsheet Solution for the PDC Decision Tree

The PDC decision tree with branch probabilities is shown in Figure 9.10. In Figure 9.11 we present the spreadsheet that can be used to perform the decision tree computations and identify the optimal decision strategy. The payoff table and probability information are shown in the first 19 rows of the spreadsheet.

Beginning in cell A25 we list and identify the 14 nodes of the decision tree. The rows corresponding to the four decision nodes (1, 3, 4, and 5) are shaded. We input a title or description of each node so that we can easily recall the node in the decision tree. For example, the node 3 title "Market Research Favorable: Decision S, M, or L" indicates that node 3 is a decision node that is reached if PDC finds that the market research report is favorable. At this node, a decision to construct the small (S), medium (M), or large (L) condominium complex must be made. The node 6 title "Market Research/Favorable/Small Complex" indicates that node 6 is a probability node that is reached if the market research study has a favorable outcome and the decision is made to construct the small complex. Other node titles or descriptions have similar interpretations.

Column B contains the cell formulas that compute the expected value at each node of the decision tree. Let us begin with node 6.

Cell B30	Compute the expected value of node 6	
	=SUMPRODUCT($B$18:$C$18,B6:C6)	(Copy B30 to B31:B32)
Cell B33	Compute the expected value of node 9	
	=SUMPRODUCT($B$19:$C$19,B6:C6)	(Copy B33 to B34:B35)
Cell B36	Compute the expected value of node 12	
	=SUMPRODUCT($B$9:$C$9,B6:C6)	(Copy B36 to B37:B38)
Cell B27	Compute the expected value of node 3	
	=MAX(B30:32)	
Cell B28	Compute the expected value of node 4	
	=MAX(B33:35)	

Figure 9.11   SPREADSHEET SOLUTION FOR THE PDC DECISION TREE

SPREADSHEET PDC DECISION TREE

	A	B	C
1	**PDC Problem - Decision Tree Analysis**		
2			
3	**Payoff Table**		
4		**State of Nature**	
5	**Decision Alternative**	High acceptance	Low acceptance
6	Small complex	8	7
7	Medium complex	14	5
8	Large complex	20	-9
9	**Probability**	0.8	0.2
10			
11	**Probability Information**		
12			
13	**Market Research Outcomes**	Favorable	Unfavorable
14		0.77	0.23
15			
16		**State of Nature**	
17	**If Market Research is**	High acceptance	Low acceptance
18	Favorable	0.94	0.06
19	Unfavorable	0.35	0.65
20			
21			
22	**Decision Tree Analysis**		
23		**Expected**	**Recommended**
24	**Node**	**Value**	**Decision**
25	1. Decision Market Research or No Market Research	15.93	Market Research
26	2. Market Research	15.93	
27	3. Market Research Favorable: Decision S, M or L	18.26	Large Complex
28	4. Market Research Unfavorable: Decision S, M or L	8.15	Medium Complex
29	5. No Market Research: Decision S, M or L	14.20	Large Complex
30	6. Market Research/Favorable/Small Complex	7.94	
31	7. Market Research/Favorable/Medium Complex	13.46	
32	8. Market Research/Favorable/Large Complex	18.26	
33	9. Market Research/Unfavorable/Small Complex	7.35	
34	10. Market Research/Unfavorable/Medium Complex	8.15	
35	11. Market Research/Unfavorable/Large Complex	1.15	
36	12. No Market Research/Small Complex	7.80	
37	13. No Market Research/Medium Complex	12.20	
38	14. No Market Research/Large Complex	14.20	

Cell B29   Compute the expected value of node 3
        =MAX(B36:38)

Cell B26   Compute the expected value of node 2
        =B14*B27+C14*B28

Cell B25   Compute the overall best expected value
        =MAX(B26,B29)

Column C identifies the decision made at each decision node. We begin with decision node 1.

Cell C25   Determine if the decision is to conduct the market research study

=IF(B25=B26, "Market Research", "No Market Research")

If B25 = B26, we know the overall best expected value is from cell B26 which corresponds to the market research decision. If B25 ≠ B26, we know the overall best expected value is not from cell B26 and therefore must be from cell B29, which corresponds to the no market research decision. Next, consider decision node 3.

Cell C27   Determine the decision alternative if the market research is favorable

=IF(B27=B30,"Small Complex",
  IF(B27=B31,"Medium Complex","Large Complex"))

This cell formula determines if the expected value for decision node 3 is based on cell B30 for the small complex, cell B31 for the medium complex, or cell B32 for the large complex. Similar formulas for decision nodes 4 and 5 are as follows:

Cell C28   Determine the decision alternative if the market research is unfavorable

=IF(B28=B33,"Small Complex",
  IF(B28=B34,"Medium Complex","Large Complex"))

Cell C29   Determine the decision alternative if the market research is not used

=IF(B29=B36,"Small Complex",
  IF(B29=B37,"Medium Complex","Large Complex"))

The results in Figure 9.11 can be used to identify the optimal decision strategy. For decision node 1, the recommended decision is to conduct the market research study. If the market research is favorable, node 3 shows that the recommended decision is to construct the large complex. If the market research is unfavorable, node 4 shows that the recommended decision is to construct the medium complex. Cell B25 shows that the expected value of this recommendation is $15.93 million. Note that the expected value of 14.20 in cell B30 indicates that $14.20 million is the expected value if the market research is not undertaken. Thus, we can conclude that the expected value of the market research study is $15.93 − $14.20 = $1.73 million.

Although Figure 9.11 contains the spreadsheet for the PDC decision tree, its logic can be modified to perform the expected value calculation for any decision tree problem. The cell formulas in column B compute the expected value of each probability node and select the best decision branch for each decision node. The PDC maximization problem can be easily converted to a minimization problem by using the MIN function for the decision nodes rather than the MAX function.

9.5   COMPUTING BRANCH PROBABILITIES

In Section 9.4 the branch probabilities for the PDC decision tree probability nodes were specified in the problem description. No computations were required to determine these probabilities. In this section we show how **Bayes Theorem,** a topic that is covered in most introductory courses on probability, can be used to compute the branch probabilities for decision trees.

The PDC decision tree is shown again in Figure 9.12. Let

$$F = \text{Favorable market research report}$$
$$U = \text{Unfavorable market research report}$$
$$s_1 = \text{High acceptance (state of nature 1)}$$
$$s_2 = \text{Low acceptance (state of nature 2)}$$

At probability node 2, we need to know the branch probabilities $P(F)$ and $P(U)$. At probability nodes 6, 7, and 8, we need to know the branch probabilities $P(s_1 \mid F)$, the probability of state of nature 1 given a favorable market research report, and $P(s_2 \mid F)$, the probability

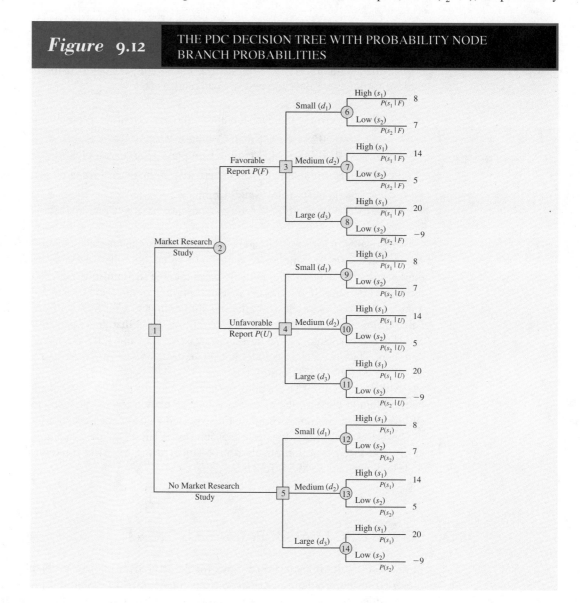

Figure 9.12 THE PDC DECISION TREE WITH PROBABILITY NODE BRANCH PROBABILITIES

of state of nature 2 given a favorable market research report. $P(s_1 \mid F)$ and $P(s_2 \mid F)$ are referred to as **conditional probabilities.** At probability nodes 9, 10, and 11, we need to know the branch probabilities $P(s_1 \mid U)$ and $P(s_2 \mid U)$; note that these are also conditional probabilities, denoting the probabilities of the two states of nature *given* that the market research report is unfavorable. Finally at probability nodes 12, 13, and 14, we need the probabilities for the states of nature, $P(s_1)$ and $P(s_2)$, if the market research study is not undertaken.

In making the probability computations, we need to know PDC's best estimates of the probabilities for the two states of nature, $P(s_1)$ and $P(s_2)$; these probabilities will be referred to as the **prior probabilities.** In addition, we must know the conditional probability of the market research outcomes (the sample information) *given* each state of nature. For example, we need to know the conditional probability of a favorable market research report given that the state of nature is high acceptance of the PDC project; note that this is the conditional probability of F given state of nature s_1, written $P(F \mid s_1)$. To carry out the probability calculations, we will need conditional probabilities for all sample outcomes given all states of nature, that is, $P(F \mid s_1)$, $P(F \mid s_2)$, $P(U \mid s_1)$ and $P(U \mid s_2)$. In the PDC problem, we assume that the following estimates are available for these conditional probabilities.

State of Nature	Market Research	
	Favorable, F	Unfavorable, U
High acceptance, s_1	$P(F \mid s_1) = 0.90$	$P(U \mid s_1) = 0.10$
Low acceptance, s_2	$P(F \mid s_2) = 0.25$	$P(U \mid s_2) = 0.75$

Note that the above probability estimates provide a reasonable degree of confidence in the market research study. If the true state of nature is s_1, the probability of a favorable market research report is 0.90, and the probability of an unfavorable market research report is 0.10. If the true state of nature is s_2, the probability of a favorable market research report is 0.25, and the probability of an unfavorable market research report is 0.75. The reason for a 0.25 probability of a potentially misleading favorable market research report for state of nature s_2 is that when some potential buyers first hear about the new condominium project, their enthusiasm may lead them to overstate their real interest in it. A potential buyer's initial favorable response can change quickly to a "no thank you" when later faced with the reality of signing a purchase contract and making a down payment.

In the following discussion, we present a tabular approach as a convenient method for carrying out the probability computations. The computations for the PDC problem based on a favorable market research report (F) are summarized in Table 9.7. The steps used to develop this table are as follows.

Step 1 In column 1 enter the states of nature. In column 2 enter the **prior probabilities** for the states of nature. In column 3 enter the **conditional probabilities** of a favorable market research report (F) given each state of nature.

Step 2 In column 4 compute the **joint probabilities** by multiplying the prior probability values in column 2 by the corresponding conditional probability values in column 3.

Step 3 Sum the joint probabilities in column 4 to obtain the probability of a favorable market research report, $P(F)$.

Step 4 Divide each joint probability in column 4 by $P(F) = 0.77$ to obtain the revised or **posterior probabilities,** $P(s_1 \mid F)$ and $P(s_2 \mid F)$.

Table 9.7	BRANCH PROBABILITIES FOR THE PDC CONDOMINIUM PROJECT BASED ON A FAVORABLE MARKET RESEARCH REPORT			

States of Nature s_j	Prior Probabilities $P(s_j)$	Conditional Probabilities $P(F \mid s_j)$	Joint Probabilities $P(F \cap s_j)$	Posterior Probabilities $P(s_j \mid F)$
s_1	0.8	0.90	0.72	0.94
s_2	0.2	0.25	0.05	0.06
			$P(F) = 0.77$	

Table 9.7 shows that the probability of obtaining a favorable market research report is $P(F) = 0.77$. In addition, $P(s_1 \mid F) = 0.94$ and $P(s_2 \mid F) = 0.06$. In particular, note that if the market report is favorable, there is a revised or posterior probability of 0.94 that the market acceptance of the condominium will be high, s_1.

The tabular probability computation procedure must be repeated for each possible sample information outcome. Thus, Table 9.8 shows the computations of the branch probabilities of the PDC problem based on an unfavorable market research report. Note that the probability of obtaining an unfavorable market research report is $P(U) = 0.23$. If an unfavorable report is obtained, the posterior probability of a high market acceptance, s_1, is 0.35 and of a low market acceptance, s_2, is 0.65. The branch probabilities from Table 9.7 and 9.8 were shown on the PDC decision tree in Figure 9.10. These probabilities were also used in the spreadsheet computation shown in Figure 9.11.

Problem 22 asks you to compute posterior probabilities.

The previous discussion shows an underlying relationship between the probabilities of the various probability branches in a decision tree. To assume different prior probabilities, $P(s_1)$ and $P(s_2)$, without determining how these changes would alter $P(F)$ and $P(U)$, as well as the posterior probabilities $P(s_1 \mid F)$, $P(s_2 \mid F)$, $P(s_1 \mid U)$ and $P(s_2 \mid U)$ would be inappropriate. Fortunately, a spreadsheet can be very helpful in making the computations required to update these probabilities.

Spreadsheet Computation of Branch Probabilities

In Figure 9.13 we show the spreadsheet that can be used to compute the branch probabilities for the PDC problem. The prior probabilities are entered into cells B5 and B6. The four conditional probabilities are entered into cells B11, B12, C11, and C12. The following cell

Table 9.8	BRANCH PROBABILITIES FOR THE PDC CONDOMINIUM PROJECT BASED ON AN UNFAVORABLE MARKET RESEARCH REPORT			

States of Nature s_j	Prior Probabilities $P(s_j)$	Conditional Probabilities $P(U \mid s_j)$	Joint Probabilities $P(U \cap s_j)$	Posterior Probabilities $P(s_j \mid U)$
s_1	0.8	0.10	0.08	0.35
s_2	0.2	0.75	0.15	0.65
			$P(U) = 0.23$	

| **Figure 9.13** | SPREADSHEET SOLUTION FOR THE PDC PROBLEM PROBABILITY CALCULATIONS |

SPREADSHEET PDC BAYES

	A	B	C	D	E
1	**PDC Problem - Bayes' Probability Calculations**				
2					
3		Prior			
4	**States of Nature**	Probabilities			
5	High Acceptance	0.8			
6	Low Acceptance	0.2			
7					
8	**Conditional Probabilities**				
9			Market Research		
10	If State of Nature is	Favorable	Unfavorable		
11	High Acceptance	0.90	0.10		
12	Low Acceptance	0.25	0.75		
13					
14					
15	**Market Research Favorable (F)**				
16		Prior	Conditional	Joint	Posterior
17	State of Nature	Probabilities	Probabilities	Probabilities	Probabilities
18	High Acceptance	0.8	0.90	0.72	0.94
19	Low Acceptance	0.2	0.25	0.05	0.06
20				P(F) =	0.77
21					
22					
23	**Market Research Unfavorable (U)**				
24		Prior	Conditional	Joint	Posterior
25	State of Nature	Probabilities	Probabilities	Probabilities	Probabilities
26	High Acceptance	0.8	0.10	0.08	0.35
27	Low Acceptance	0.2	0.75	0.15	0.65
28				P(U) =	0.23

formulas perform the probability calculations for the PDC problem based on a favorable market research report, shown previously in Table 9.7.

Cells B18 and B19   Enter the prior probabilities

=B5

=B6

Cells C18 and C19   Enter the conditional probabilities for a favorable market research report

=B11

=B12

Cells D18 and D19   Compute the joint probabilities

=B18*C18

=B19*C19

Cell D20   Compute the probability of a favorable market research report
=SUM(D18:D19)

Cells E18 and E19   Compute the posterior probabilities for each state of nature
=D18/D20
=D19/D20

The same logic was used to perform the probability calculations based on an unfavorable market research report shown in cells B23:E28.

The probabilities $P(F) = 0.77$, $P(U) = 0.23$, and the four posterior probabilities 0.94, 0.06, 0.35, and 0.65 shown in the spreadsheet become the probability information input for the PDC decision tree spreadsheet in Figure 9.11. Since the PDC decision tree spreadsheet shown in Figure 9.11 and the PDC probability calculation spreadsheet shown in Figure 9.13 are related, an experienced user could place the two spreadsheets in the same Excel workbook. The two spreadsheets could then be set up to exchange data automatically. For example, the user of the decision tree spreadsheet might want to determine what would happen to the optimal decision strategy if the states of nature probabilities were actually $P(s_1) = 0.60$ and $P(s_2) = 0.40$. The user could enter these values into cells B9 and C9 of the decision tree spreadsheet. The workbook could be set up to automatically send this change to the probability calculation spreadsheet, with the new state-of-nature probabilities appearing in cells B5 and B6. The probability calculation spreadsheet would automatically update $P(F)$, $P(U)$, and the four posterior probabilities. These changes could then be sent automatically to the decision tree spreadsheet where they would appear in cells B14, C14, B18, B19, C18, and C19. Based on this change, the decision analysis section of the spreadsheet would be updated and a new optimal decision strategy would be developed. With this set-up, the probability calculation spreadsheet would provide the necessary probability revisions automatically, and the revised decision strategy would be displayed immediately on the decision tree spreadsheet.

SUMMARY

In this chapter we showed how decision analysis can be used to solve problems with reasonably few decision alternatives and reasonably few states of nature. The goal of decision analysis is to identify the best decision alternative in the face of uncertain or risk-filled future events known as *states of nature.*

We presented three approaches—optimistic, conservative, and minimax regret—for decision making without probabilities. When probability information about the states of nature was available, we used the expected value approach to determine the best decision alternative. In Section 9.4, we introduced the use of sample information to develop an optimal decision strategy. This approach results in a more complex decision problem which can be solved by using a decision tree. A decision tree approach is general and can be used to solve a wide variety of decision analysis problems. Spreadsheets were shown to be effective in performing the decision analysis computations.

In the last section, we pointed out that probabilities of probability node branches can be interrelated such that changes in some of the branch probabilities may alter other branch probabilities. We presented a tabular computational procedure that could be used to compute the branch probabilities. A spreadsheet was also presented as a way of performing these probability revision computations.

··/ /············

GLOSSARY

States of nature Uncontrollable future events that affect the payoff associated with a decision alternative.

Payoff An outcome measure such as profit, cost, or time. Each combination of a decision alternative and a state of nature has an associated payoff.

Payoff table A tabular representation of the payoffs for a decision problem.

Decision tree A graphical representation of the decision problem that shows the sequential nature of the decision-making situation.

Node An intersection or junction point of a decision tree.

Branch A line or arc connecting nodes of a decision tree.

Optimistic approach An approach to choosing a decision alternative without using probabilities. For a maximization problem, it leads to choosing the decision alternative corresponding to the largest payoff; for a minimization problem, it leads to choosing the decision alternative corresponding to the smallest payoff.

Conservative approach An approach to choosing a decision alternative without using probabilities. For a maximization problem, it leads to choosing the decision alternative that maximizes the minimum payoff; for a minimization problem, it leads to choosing the decision alternative that minimizes the maximum payoff.

Minimax regret approach An approach to choosing a decision alternative without using probabilities. For each alternative, the maximum regret is computed. This approach leads to choosing the decision alternative that minimizes the maximum regret.

Opportunity loss, or regret The amount of loss (lower profit or higher cost) from not making the best decision for each state of nature.

Expected value approach An approach to choosing a decision alternative that is based on the expected value of each decision alternative. The recommended decision alternative is the one that provides the best expected value.

Expected value (EV) For a decision alternative, it is the weighted average of the payoffs. The weights are the state-of-nature probabilities.

Expected value of perfect information (EVPI) The expected value of information that would tell the decision maker exactly which state of nature is going to occur (i.e., perfect information).

Expected value of sample information (EVSI) The difference between the expected value of an optimal strategy based on sample information and the "best" expected value without any sample information.

Efficiency The ratio of EVSI to EVPI; perfect information is 100% efficient.

Prior probabilities The probabilities of the states of nature prior to obtaining sample information.

Conditional probabilities The probabilities of the sample information, given an assumed state of nature.

Joint probabilities The probabilities of both sample information and a particular state of nature occurring simultaneously.

Posterior (revised) probabilities The probabilities of the states of nature after revising the prior probabilities based on given indicator information.

Sample information New information obtained through research or experimentation that enables an updating or revision of the state of nature probabilities.

Bayes theorem A probability expression that enables the use of sample information to revise prior probabilities.

PROBLEMS

Note: The problems that follow can be solved using the calculation procedures presented in this chapter. All problems can be modeled and solved with spreadsheets. In general, the spreadsheets will be very similar to spreadsheets presented in this chapter. However, some modification or redesign may be necessary due to the size and complexity of the problem.

SELF TEST

1. The following payoff table shows profit for a decision analysis problem with two decisions and three states of nature.
   a. Construct a decision tree for this problem.
   b. If the decision maker knows nothing about the probabilities of the three states of nature, what is the recommended decision using the optimistic, conservative, and minimax regret approaches?

Decision Alternative	State of Nature		
	s_1	s_2	s_3
d_1	250	100	25
d_2	100	100	75

2. Suppose that a decision maker faced with four decision alternatives and four states of nature develops the following profit payoff table.

Decision Alternative	State of Nature			
	s_1	s_2	s_3	s_4
d_1	14	9	10	5
d_2	11	10	8	7
d_3	9	10	10	11
d_4	8	10	11	13

   a. If the decision maker knows nothing about the probabilities of the four states of nature, what is the recommended decision using the optimistic, conservative, and minimax regret approaches?
   b. Which approach do you prefer? Explain. Is establishing the most appropriate approach before analyzing the problem important for the decision maker? Explain.
   c. Assume that the payoff table provides *cost* rather than profit payoffs. What is the recommended decision using the optimistic, conservative, and minimax regret approaches?

3. Southland Corporation's decision to produce a new line of recreational products has resulted in the need to construct either a small plant or a large plant. The selection of plant size depends on how the marketplace reacts to the new product line. To conduct an analysis, marketing man-

agement has decided to view the possible long-run demand as either low, medium, or high. The following payoff table shows the projected profit in millions of dollars:

Decision Alternative	Long-Run Demand		
	Low	Medium	High
Small plant	150	200	200
Large plant	50	200	500

a. Construct a decision tree for this problem.
b. Recommend a decision based on the use of the optimistic, conservative, and minimax regret approaches.

4. Develop spreadsheets that can be used to solve the following problem. Investment Advisors, Inc., has three investment strategies under consideration. Profits from the strategies will depend on what happens to the prime interest rate over the next three months. Payoffs (in thousand of dollars) are shown.

Decision Alternative	State of Nature		
	Rate Decrease, s_1	No Change, s_2	Rate Increase, s_3
Strategy, d_1	50	70	40
Strategy, d_2	55	35	80
Strategy, d_3	15	60	70

What investment strategy would you recommend based on the use of the optimistic, pessimistic, and minimax regret approaches?

5. The profit payoff table presented in Problem 1 is shown below. Suppose that the decision maker has obtained the probability estimates: $P(s_1) = 0.65$, $P(s_2) = 0.15$, and $P(s_3) = 0.20$. Use the expected value approach to determine the optimal decision.

Decision Alternative	State of Nature		
	s_1	s_2	s_3
d_1	250	100	25
d_2	100	100	75

6. The profit payoff table presented in Problem 2 is repeated here.

Decision Alternative	State of Nature			
	s_1	s_2	s_3	s_4
d_1	14	9	10	5
d_2	11	10	8	7
d_3	9	10	10	11
d_4	8	10	11	13

Suppose that the decision maker obtains information that enables the following probability estimates to be made: $P(s_1) = 0.5$, $P(s_2) = 0.2$, $P(s_3) = 0.2$, and $P(s_4) = 0.1$.

a. Use the expected value approach to determine the optimal decision.

b. Now assume that the entries in the payoff table are costs; use the expected value approach to determine the optimal decision.

7. Develop a spreadsheet that can be used to solve the following problem. Hudson Corporation is considering three options for managing its data processing operation: continuing with its own staff, hiring an outside vendor to do the managing (referred to as *outsourcing*), or using a combination of its own staff and an outside vendor. The cost of the operation depends on future demand. The annual cost of each decision alternative and state of nature (in thousands of dollars) is as follows.

Decision Alternative	State of Nature		
	High Demand s_1	Medium Demand s_2	Low Demand s_3
Own staff, d_1	650	650	600
Vendor, d_2	900	600	300
Combination, d_3	800	650	500

If the demand probabilities are 0.2, 0.5, and 0.3, which decision alternative will minimize the expected cost of the data processing operation? What is the expected annual cost associated with that recommendation?

8. The following payoff table shows the profit for a decision problem with two states of nature and two decision alternatives.

SELF TEST

Decision Alternative	State of Nature	
	s_1	s_2
d_1	10	1
d_2	4	3

Develop a spreadsheet for this problem by deleting row 7 of the PDC Expected Value spreadsheet in Figure 9.7. After row 7 is deleted, the probabilities of the states of nature will appear in row 8 of the spreadsheet. Place the cell formula $=1-B8$ into cell C8. This formula will guarantee that the sum of the probabilities for the states of nature equal 1.

Use the spreadsheet to try a variety of values for the probability of state of nature s_1. This process will enable you to learn how sensitive the optimal decision is to the state-of-nature probabilities. What range of probabilities for $P(s_1)$ make d_1 the optimal decision and what range of probabilities for $P(s_1)$ make d_2 the optimal decision?

9. The following payoff table shows the profit for a decision problem with two states of nature and three decision alternatives.

Decision Alternative	State of Nature	
	s_1	s_2
d_1	80	50
d_2	65	85
d_3	30	100

Develop a spreadsheet for this problem by modifying the PDC Expected Value spreadsheet in Figure 9.7. Place the cell formula $=1-B9$ into cell C9. This formula will guarantee that the sum of the probabilities for the states of nature equal 1.

Use the spreadsheet to try a variety of values for the probability of state of nature s_1. This process will enable you to learn how sensitive the optimal decision is to the state-of-nature probabilities. What range of probabilities for $P(s_1)$ make d_1 the optimal decision, what range of probabilities for $P(s_1)$ make d_2 the optimal decision, and what range of probabilities for $P(s_1)$ make d_3 the optimal decision?

10. Political Systems, Inc., is a new firm specializing in information services such as surveys and data analysis for individuals running for political office. The firm is opening its headquarters in Chicago and is considering three office locations that differ in cost due to square footage and office equipment requirements. The profit projections shown (in thousands of dollars) for each location were based on both high demand and low demand states of nature.

Decision Alternative	State of Nature	
	High Demand s_1	Low Demand s_2
Location A	200	−20
Location B	120	10
Location C	100	60

Develop a spreadsheet for this problem by modifying the PDC Expected Value spreadsheet in Figure 9.7. Place the cell formula $=1-B9$ into cell C9. This formula will guarantee that the sum of the probabilities for the states of nature equal 1.

a. Use the spreadsheet to try a variety of values for the probability of state of nature s_1. This process will enable you to learn how sensitive the optimal decision is to the state-of-nature probabilities. What range of probabilities for $P(s_1)$ make d_1 the optimal decision, what range of probabilities for $P(s_1)$ make d_2 the optimal decision, and what range of probability for $P(s_1)$ make d_3 the optimal decision?

b. After further review, the best estimate of the probability of a high demand was established at 0.65. However, with some uncertainty in this probability, a manager felt that 0.55 to 0.75 was a better way to state the probability of a high demand. Based on your results in part (a), which location should be selected? Why? What is the expected value of the decision based on the best estimate of 0.65?

11. Six months ago, Reynold's Properties purchased an option to buy a tract of land that has the potential of becoming very desirable commercial property. Currently, another real estate investment firm has offered to purchase Reynolds' option. If Reynold's sells its option, it will experience a $250,000 profit. On the other hand, if Reynold's keeps the option, the success of the project depends upon what happens to the real estate market over the next year. In the worst case, Reynold's could lose $1.5 million, while in the best case Reynold's could have a $4 million profit. The decision alternatives, states of nature, and payoffs in $ millions are as follows:

Decision Alternative	State of Nature		
	Market Down	Market Steady	Sell option
Sell option	0.25	0.25	0.25
Keep option	−1.50	1.00	4.00

a. If Reynold's managers believe that the probabilities of the real estate market being down, steady, and up are 0.6, 0.3, and 0.1, respectively, what decision alternative is recommended? What is the expected value of this recommendation?

b. Suppose that the three probabilities are revised to 0.5, 0.3, and 0.2. What should Reynold's do? Repeat this question if the three probabilities are revised to 0.4, 0.4, and 0.2. What do the results suggest about Reynold's decision?

c. Suppose that after further consideration, Reynold's managers conclude that 0.1 is a realistic probability of the market being up. What would the probability of the market being down have to be for the sell option to be the recommended decision alternative? Would this information be helpful in making a final decision regarding whether to sell or keep the option? Explain.

SELF TEST

12. The profit payoff table presented in Problems 1 and 5 is repeated below.

Decision Alternative	State of Nature		
	s_1	s_2	s_3
d_1	250	100	25
d_2	100	100	75

The probabilities for the states of nature are: $P(s_1) = 0.65$, $P(s_2) = 0.15$, and $P(s_3) = 0.20$.

a. What is the optimal decision strategy if perfect information were available?

b. What is the expected value for the decision strategy developed in part (a)?

c. Using the expected value approach, what is the recommended decision? What is its expected value?

d. What is the expected value of perfect information?

13. The profit payoff table presented in Problems 2 and 6 is repeated below. The probabilities are $P(s_1) = 0.5$, $P(s_2) = 0.2$, $P(s_3) = 0.2$, and $P(s_4) = 0.1$.

a. What is the optimal decision strategy if perfect information were available?

b. What is the expected value for the decision strategy developed in part (a)?

c. Using the expected value approach, what is the recommended decision? What is its expected value? What is the value of perfect information?

Decision Alternative	State of Nature			
	s_1	s_2	s_3	s_4
d_1	14	9	10	5
d_2	11	10	8	7
d_3	9	10	10	11
d_4	8	10	11	13

14. Consider a variation of the PCD decision tree shown in Figure 9.12. The company must first decide whether to undertake the market research study. If the market research study is conducted, the outcome will either be favorable (F) or unfavorable (U). Assume that there are only two decision alternatives d_1 and d_2 and two states of nature s_1 and s_2. The payoff table showing profit is as follows:

Decision Alternative	State of Nature	
	State s_1	State s_2
Decision d_1	100	300
Decision d_2	400	200

a. Show the decision tree.
b. Using the following probabilities, what is the optimal decision strategy?

$P(F) = 0.56$ $P(s_1 \mid F) = 0.57$ $P(s_1 \mid U) = 0.18$ $P(s_1) = 0.40$

$P(U) = 0.44$ $P(s_2 \mid F) = 0.43$ $P(s_2 \mid U) = 0.82$ $P(s_2) = 0.60$

15. A real estate investor has the opportunity to purchase land that is currently zoned residential. If the county board approves a request to rezone the property as commercial within the next year, the investor will be able to lease the land to a large discount firm that wants to open a new store on the property. However, if the zoning change is not approved, the investor will have to sell the property at a loss. Profits (in thousands of dollars) are shown in the following payoff table.

Decision Alternative	State of Nature	
	Rezoning Approved s_1	Rezoning Not Approved s_2
Purchase, d_1	600	−200
Do not purchase, d_2	0	0

a. If the probability that the rezoning will be approved is 0.5, what decision is recommended? What is the expected profit?
b. The investor can purchase an option to buy the land. Under the option, the investor maintains the rights to purchase the land anytime during the next 3 months while learning more about possible resistance to the rezoning proposal from area residents. Historical probabilities are as follows.

Decision Alternative	State of Nature	
	Rezoning Approved s_1	Rezoning Not Approved s_2
High resistance to rezoning H	0.18	0.82
Low resistance to rezoning L	0.89	0.11

Suppose $P(H) = 0.55$ and $P(L) = 0.45$. What is the optimal decision strategy if the investor uses the option period to learn more about the resistance from area residents before making the purchase decision?
c. If the option will cost the investor an additional $10,000, should the investor purchase the option? Why or why not? What is the maximum that the investor should be willing to pay for the option?

16. McHuffter Condominiums, Inc., of Pensacola, Florida, recently purchased land near the Gulf of Mexico and is attempting to determine the size of the condominium development it should build. It is considering three sizes of developments: small, d_1; medium, d_2; and large, d_3. At the same time, an uncertain economy makes ascertaining the demand for the new condominiums difficult. McHuffter's management realizes that a large development followed by low demand could be very costly to the company. However, if McHuffter makes a conservative small-development decision and then finds a high demand, the firm's profits will be lower than they might have been. With the three levels of demand—low, medium, and high—McHuffter's management has prepared the following profit (in thousands of dollars) payoff table.

Decision Alternatives	State of Nature		
	Low, s_1	Medium, s_2	High, s_3
Small Condo, d_1	400	400	400
Medium Condo, d_2	100	600	600
Large Condo, d_3	−300	300	900

The probabilities for the states of nature are $P(s_1) = 0.20$, $P(s_2) = 0.35$, and $P(s_3) = 0.45$. Suppose that before making a final decision, McHuffter is considering conducting a survey to help evaluate the demand for the new condominium development. The survey report is anticipated to indicate one of three levels of demand: weak (W), average (A), or strong (S). The relevant probabilities are as follows:

$P(W) = 0.30$	$P(s_1 \mid W) = 0.39$	$P(s_1 \mid A) = 0.16$	$P(s_1 \mid S) = 0.06$
$P(A) = 0.38$	$P(s_2 \mid W) = 0.46$	$P(s_2 \mid A) = 0.37$	$P(s_2 \mid S) = 0.22$
$P(S) = 0.32$	$P(s_3 \mid W) = 0.15$	$P(s_3 \mid A) = 0.47$	$P(s_3 \mid S) = 0.72$

a. Construct a decision tree for this problem.
b. Develop a spreadsheet that can be used to solve this problem.
c. What is the recommended decision if the survey is not undertaken? What is the expected value?
d. What is the expected value of perfect information?
e. What is McHuffter's optimal decision strategy?
f. What is the expected value of the survey information?
g. What is the efficiency of the survey information?

17. Hale's TV Productions is considering producing a pilot for a comedy series at a major television network. The network may decide to reject the series, but it may also decide to purchase the rights to the series for either one or two years. At this point in time, Hale may either produce the pilot and wait for the network's decision or transfer the rights for the pilot and series to a competitor for $100,000. Hale's decision alternatives and profits (in thousands of dollars) are as follows:

Decision Alternative	State of Nature		
	Reject, s_1	1 Year, s_2	2 Years, s_3
Produce Pilot, d_1	−100	50	150
Sell to Competitor, d_2	100	100	100

The probabilities for the states of nature are $P(s_1) = 0.20$, $P(s_2) = 0.30$, and $P(s_3) = 0.50$. For a consulting fee of $5,000, an agency will review the plans for the comedy series and indicate the overall chances of a favorable network reaction to the series. Assume that the agency review will result in a favorable (F) or an unfavorable (U) review and that the following probabilities are relevant.

$P(F) = 0.69$	$P(s_1 \mid F) = 0.09$	$P(s_1 \mid U) = 0.45$
$P(U) = 0.31$	$P(s_2 \mid F) = 0.26$	$P(s_2 \mid U) = 0.39$
	$P(s_3 \mid F) = 0.65$	$P(s_3 \mid U) = 0.16$

  a. Construct a decision tree for this problem.
  b. What is the recommended decision if the agency opinion is not used? What is the expected value?
  c. What is the expected value of perfect information?
  d. What is Hale's optimal decision strategy assuming the agency's information is used?
  e. What is the expected value of the agency's information?
  f. Is the agency's information worth the $5,000 fee? What is the maximum that Hale should be willing to pay for the information?
  g. What is the recommended decision?

18. Martin's Service Station is considering entering the snowplowing business for the coming winter season. Martin can purchase either a snowplow blade attachment for the station's pick-up truck or a new heavy-duty snowplow truck. Martin has analyzed the situation and believes that either alternative would be a profitable investment if the snowfall is heavy. Smaller profits would results if the snowfall is moderate, and losses would result if the snowfall is light. The following profits have been determined.

Decision Alternatives	State of Nature		
	Heavy, s_1	Moderate, s_2	Light, s_3
Blade Attachment, d_1	3500	1000	−1500
New Snowplow, d_2	7000	2000	−9000

The probabilities for the states of nature are $P(s_1) = 0.4$, $P(s_2) = 0.3$, and $P(s_3) = 0.3$. Suppose that Martin decides to wait until September before making a final decision. Estimates of the probabilities associate with a normal (N) or unseasonably cold (U) September are as follows:

$$P(N) = 0.80 \qquad P(s_1 \mid N) = 0.35 \qquad P(s_1 \mid U) = 0.62$$
$$P(U) = 0.20 \qquad P(s_2 \mid N) = 0.30 \qquad P(s_2 \mid U) = 0.31$$
$$P(s_3 \mid N) = 0.35 \qquad P(s_3 \mid U) = 0.07$$

  a. Construct a decision tree for this problem.
  b. What is the recommended decision if Martin does not wait until September? What is the expected value?
  c. What is the expected value of perfect information?
  d. What is Martin's optimal decision strategy if the decision is not made until the September weather is determined? What is the expected value of this decision strategy?

19. Joseph Software, Inc. (JSI), has been investigating the possibility of developing a grammar-and-style checker for use on microcomputers. Based on its experience with other software projects, JSI estimates that the total cost to develop a prototype is $200,000. If the performance of the prototype is somewhat better than existing software, referred to as a *moderate success*, JSI believes that it could sell the rights to the software to a larger software developer for $600,000. If the performance of the prototype is significantly better than existing software, referred to as a *major success*, JSI believes that it can sell the software for $1.2 million. However, if the performance of the prototype does not exceed the performance of existing software, referred to as a *failure*, JSI will not be able to sell the software and hence will lose all its development costs.
  a. If the best estimates of the states of nature are $P(\text{failure}) = 0.70$, $P(\text{moderate success}) = 0.20$, and $P(\text{major success}) = 0.10$, what should JSI do if it uses the expected value approach?

Suppose that JSI can hire an independent consultant to review its ideas for the new software. For a fee of $20,000, the consultant will make a recommendation as to whether JSI should develop a prototype.

$$\text{Let } D = \text{recommendation to develop the prototype}$$
$$N = \text{recommendation to not develop the prototype}$$
$$s_1 = \text{failure}$$
$$s_2 = \text{moderate success}$$
$$s_3 = \text{major success}$$

Based on experience with this consultant, JSI has assigned the following probabilities:

$P(D) = 0.35$	$P(s_1 \mid D) = 0.40$	$P(s_1 \mid N) = 0.86$
$P(N) = 0.65$	$P(s_2 \mid D) = 0.34$	$P(s_2 \mid N) = 0.12$
	$P(s_3 \mid D) = 0.26$	$P(s_3 \mid N) = 0.02$

  b. Should JSI hire the consultant? Explain.
  c. What is the optimal strategy?

20. Milford Trucking Company of Chicago has requests to haul two shipments, one to St. Louis and one to Detroit. Because of a scheduling problem, Milford will be able to accept only one of these assignments. The St. Louis customer has guaranteed a return shipment, but the Detroit customer has not. Thus, if Milford accepts the Detroit shipment and cannot find a Detroit–Chicago return shipment, the truck will return to Chicago empty. The payoff table showing profit is as follows.

Shipment	Return Shipment from Detroit s_1	No Return Shipment from Detroit s_2
St. Louis, d_1	2000	2000
Detroit, d_2	2500	1000

  a. If the probability of a Detroit return shipment is 0.4, what should Milford do?
  b. What is the expected value of perfect information that would tell Milford Trucking whether Detroit has a return shipment?

Milford can telephone a Detroit truck dispatch center and determine whether the general Detroit shipping activity is busy (B) or slow (S). If shipping activity is busy, the chances of obtaining a return shipment will increase. Suppose that the conditional probabilities are

$P(B) = 0.42$	$P(s_1 \mid B) = 0.57$	$P(s_1 \mid S) = 0.28$
$P(S) = 0.58$	$P(s_2 \mid B) = 0.43$	$P(s_2 \mid S) = 0.72$

  c. What should Milford do?

21. Lawson's Department Store faces a buying decision for a seasonal product for which demand can be high, medium, and low. The purchaser for Lawson's can order 1, 2, or 3 lots of the product before the season begins but cannot reorder later. Profit projections (in thousands of dollars) are shown.

Decision Alternative	State of Nature		
	High Demand s_1	Medium Demand s_2	Low Demand s_3
Order 1 lot, d_1	60	60	50
Order 2 lots, d_2	80	80	30
Order 3 lots, d_3	100	70	10

a. If the prior probabilities for the three states of nature are 0.3, 0.3, and 0.4, respectively, what is the recommended order quantity?

b. At each preseason sales meeting, the vice president of sales provides his personal opinion regarding potential demand for this product. Because of his enthusiasm and optimistic nature, his predictions of market conditions have always been either "excellent" (E) or "very good" (V). Probabilities are as follows. What is the optimal decision strategy?

$$P(E) = 0.70 \qquad P(s_1 \mid E) = 0.34 \qquad P(s_1 \mid V) = 0.20$$
$$P(V) = 0.30 \qquad P(s_2 \mid E) = 0.32 \qquad P(s_2 \mid V) = 0.26$$
$$P(s_3 \mid E) = 0.34 \qquad P(s_3 \mid V) = 0.54$$

c. Use the efficiency of sample information and discuss whether the firm should consider a consulting expert who could provide independent forecasts of market conditions for the product.

22. Suppose that you are given a decision situation with three possible states of nature: s_1, s_2, and s_3. The prior probabilities are $P(s_1) = 0.2$, $P(s_2) = 0.5$, and $P(s_2) = 0.3$. With sample information I, $P(I \mid s_1) = 0.1$, $P(I \mid s_2) = 0.05$, and $P(I \mid s_3) = 0.2$. Compute the revised or posterior probabilities: $P(s_1 \mid I)$, $P(s_2 \mid I)$, and $P(s_3 \mid I)$.

23. In the following profit payoff table for a decision problem with two states of nature and three decision alternatives, the prior probabilities for s_1 and s_2 are $P(s_1) = 0.8$ and $P(s_2) = 0.2$.

Decision Alternative	State of Nature	
	s_1	s_2
d_1	15	10
d_2	10	12
d_3	8	20

a. What is the optimal decision?
b. Find the EVPI.
c. Suppose that sample information I is obtained, with $P(I \mid s_1) = 0.2$, $P(I \mid s_2) = 0.75$. Find the posterior probabilities $P(s_1 \mid I)$ and $P(s_2 \mid I)$. Recommend a decision alternative based on these probabilities.

24. To save on expenses, Rona and Jerry agreed to form a carpool for traveling to and from work. Rona preferred to use the somewhat longer but more consistent Queen City Avenue. Although Jerry preferred the quicker expressway, he agreed with Rona that they should take Queen City Avenue if the expressway had a traffic jam. The following payoff table provides the one-way times estimate in minutes for traveling to or from work.

Decision Alternative	State of Nature	
	Expressway Open s_1	Expressway Jammed s_2
Queen City Avenue, d_1	30	30
Expressway, d_2	25	45

Based on their experience with traffic problems, Rona and Jerry agreed on a 0.15 probability that the expressway would be jammed.

In addition, they agreed that weather seemed to affect the traffic conditions on the expressway. Let

$$C = \text{clear}$$
$$O = \text{overcast}$$
$$R = \text{rain}$$

The following conditional probabilities apply.

$P(C \mid s_1) = 0.8$	$P(O \mid s_1) = 0.2$	$P(R \mid s_1) = 0.0$
$P(C \mid s_2) = 0.1$	$P(O \mid s_2) = 0.3$	$P(R \mid s_2) = 0.6$

a. Use the Bayes' probability revision procedure to compute the probability of each weather condition and the conditional probability of the expressway open s_1 or jammed s_2 given each weather condition.
b. Show the decision tree for this problem.
c. What is the optimal decision strategy and what is the expected travel time?

25. The Gorman Manufacturing Company must decide whether to manufacture a component part at its Milan, Michigan, plant or purchase the component part from a supplier. The resulting profit is dependent upon the demand for the product. The following payoff table shows the projected profit in thousands of dollars

Decision Alternatives	State of Nature		
	Low Demand s_1	Medium Demand s_2	High Demand s_3
Manufacture, d_1	−20	40	100
Purchase, d_2	10	45	70

The state-of-nature probabilities are $P(s_1) = 0.35$, $P(s_2) = 0.35$, and $P(s_3) = 0.30$.

Gorman is considering using a market research study to forecast the demand for the product. The study will predict either a favorable or an unfavorable condition. The following conditional probabilities apply.

$P(F \mid s_1) = 0.1$	$P(U \mid s_1) = 0.9$
$P(F \mid s_2) = 0.4$	$P(U \mid s_2) = 0.6$
$P(F \mid s_3) = 0.6$	$P(U \mid s_3) = 0.4$

a. Use the Bayes' probability revision procedure to compute the probability of a favorable report, unfavorable report, and the conditional probability of the demand given each report. What is the probability that the market research report will be favorable?
b. Show the decision tree for this problem.
c. What is Gorman's optimal strategy?
d. What is the expected value of the market research information?
e. What is the efficiency of the information?

Case Problem   PROPERTY PURCHASE STRATEGY

Glenn Foreman, president of Oceanview Development Corporation, is considering submitting a bid to purchase property that will be sold by sealed bid at a county tax foreclosure. Glenn's initial judgment is to submit a bid of $5 million. Based on his experience, Glenn estimates that a bid of $5 million will have a 0.2 probability of being the highest bid and securing the property for Oceanview. The current date is June 1. Sealed bids for the property must be submitted by August 15. The winning bid will be announced on September 1.

If Oceanview submits the highest bid and obtains the property, the firm plans to build and sell a complex of luxury condominiums. However, a complicating factor is that the property is currently zoned for single-family residences only. Glenn believes that a referendum could be placed on the voting ballot in time for the November election. Passage of the referendum would change the zoning of the property and permit construction of the condominiums.

The sealed-bid procedure requires the bid to be submitted with a certified check for 10% of the amount bid. If the bid is rejected, the deposit is refunded. If the bid is accepted, the deposit is the down payment for the property. However, if the bid is accepted and the bidder does not follow through with the purchase and meet the remainder of the financial obligation within six months, the deposit will be forfeited. In this case, the county will offer the property to the next highest bidder.

To determine whether Oceanview should submit the $5 million bid, Glenn has done some preliminary analysis. This preliminary work provided an estimate of 0.3 for the probability that the referendum for a zoning change will be approved and resulted in the following estimates of the costs and revenues that will be incurred if the condominiums are built.

Cost and Revenue Estimates	
Revenue from condominium sales	$15,000,000
Cost	
Property	$5,000,000
Construction expenses	$8,000,000

If Oceanview obtains the property and the zoning change is rejected in November, Glenn believes that the best option would be for the firm not to complete the purchase of the property. In this case, Oceanview would forfeit the 10% deposit that accompanied the bid.

Because the likelihood that the zoning referendum will be approved is such an important factor in the decision process, Glenn has suggested that the firm hire a market research service to conduct a survey of voters. The survey would provide a better estimate of the likelihood that the referendum for a zoning change would be approved. The market research firm that Oceanview Development has worked with in the past has agreed to do the study for $15,000. The results of the study will be available August 1, so that Oceanview will have this information before the August 15 bid deadline. The results of the survey will be either a prediction that the zoning change will be approved or a prediction that the zoning change will be rejected. After considering the record of the market research service in previous studies conducted for Oceanview, Glenn has developed the following probability estimates concerning the accuracy of the market research information.

$$P(A \mid s_1) = 0.9 \qquad P(N \mid s_1) = 0.1$$
$$P(A \mid s_2) = 0.2 \qquad P(N \mid s_2) = 0.8$$

where

A = prediction of zoning change approval

N = prediction that zoning change will not be approved

s_1 = the zoning change is approved by the voters

s_2 = the zoning change is rejected by the voters

Managerial Report

Perform an analysis of the problem facing the Oceanview Development Corporation, and prepare a report that summarizes your findings and recommendations. Include the following items in your report:

1. A decision tree that shows the logical sequence of the decision problem
2. A recommendation regarding what Oceanview should do if the market research information is not available
3. A decision strategy that Oceanview should follow if the market research is conducted
4. A recommendation as to whether Oceanview should employ the market research firm, along with the value of the information provided by the market research firm. Include the details of your analysis as an appendix to your report.

OHIO EDISON COMPANY*

AKRON, OHIO

Ohio Edison Company is an investor-owned electric utility headquartered in northeastern Ohio. Ohio Edison and a Pennsylvania subsidiary provide electrical service to more than two million people. Most of this electricity is generated by coal-fired power plants. To meet evolving air-quality standards, Ohio Edison replaced existing particulate control equipment at most of its generating plants with more efficient equipment. The combination of this program to upgrade air-quality control equipment with the continuing need to construct new generating plants to meet future power requirements resulted in a large capital investment program.

Management Science activities at Ohio Edison are distributed throughout the company rather than centralized in a specific department, and are more or less evenly divided among the following areas: fossil and nuclear fuel planning, environmental studies, capacity planning, large equipment evaluation, and corporate planning. Applications include decision analysis, optimal ordering strategies, computer modeling, and simulation.

A Decision Analysis Application

The flue gas emitted by coal-fired power plants contains small ash particles and sulfur dioxide (SO_2). Federal and state regulatory agencies have established emission limits for both particulates and sulfur dioxide. In the late 1970s, Ohio Edison developed a plan to comply with new air-quality standards at one of its largest power plants. This plant, which consists of seven coal-fired units (most of which were constructed in the 1960s), constitutes about one-third of the generating capacity of Ohio Edison and

its subsidiary company. Although all units were initially constructed with particulate emission control equipment, that equipment was no longer capable of meeting new particulate emission requirements.

A decision had already been made to burn low-sulfur coal in four of the smaller units (units 1–4) at the plant in order to meet SO_2 emission standards. Fabric filters were to be installed on these units to control particulate emissions. Fabric filters, also known as baghouses, use thousands of fabric bags to filter out the particulates; they function in much the same way as a household vacuum cleaner.

It was considered likely, although not certain, that the three larger units (units 5–7) at this plant would burn medium- to high-sulfur coal. A method of controlling particulate emissions at these units had not yet been selected. Preliminary studies narrowed the particulate control equipment choice to a decision between fabric filters and electrostatic precipitators (which remove particulates suspended in the flue gas by passing the flue gas through a strong electric field). This decision was affected by a number of uncertainties, including the following:

- Uncertainty in the way some air-quality laws and regulations might be interpreted
- Potential requirements that either low-sulfur coal or high-sulfur Ohio coal (or neither) be burned in units 5–7
- Potential future changes to air quality laws and regulations
- An overall plant reliability improvement program already under way at this plant
- The outcome of this program itself, which would affect the operating costs of whichever pollution control technology was installed in these units

*The authors are indebted to Thomas J. Madden and M. S. Hyrnick of Ohio Edison Company, Akron, Ohio, for providing this application.

- Uncertain construction costs of the equipment, particularly since limited space at the plant site made it necessary to install the equipment on a massive bridge deck over a four-lane highway immediately adjacent to the power plant
- Uncertain costs associated with replacing the electrical power required to operate the particulate control equipment
- Various other factors, including potential accidents and chronic operating problems that could increase the costs of operating the generating units (the degree to which each of these factors could affect operating costs varied with the choice of technology and with the sulfur content of the coal).

Particulate Control Decision

The air-quality program involved a choice between two types of particulate control equipment (fabric filters and electrostatic precipitators) for units 5–7. Because of the complexity of the problem, the high degree of uncertainty associated with factors affecting the decision, and the importance (because of potential reliability and cost impact on Ohio Edison) of the choice, decision analysis was used in the selection process.

The decision measure used to evaluate the outcomes of the particulate technology decision analysis was the annual revenue requirements for the three large units over their remaining lifetime. Revenue requirements are the monies that would have to be collected from the utility customers to recover costs resulting from the decision. They include not only direct costs but also the cost of capital and return on investment.

A decision tree was constructed to represent the particulate control decision and its uncertainties and costs. A simplified version of this decision tree is shown in Figure 9.14. The decision and state-of-nature nodes are indicated. Note that to conserve space, a type of shorthand notation is used. The coal sulfur content state-of-nature node should actually be located at the end of each branch of the capital cost state-of-nature node, as the dashed lines indicate. Each state-of-nature node actually represents several probabilistic cost models or submodels. The total revenue requirements are the sum of the revenue requirements for capital and operating costs. Costs associated with these models were obtained from engineering calculations or estimates. Probabilities were obtained from exist-

ing data or the subjective assessments of knowledgeable persons.

Results

A decision tree similar to that shown in Figure 9.14 was used to generate cumulative probability distributions for the annual revenue requirements outcomes calculated for each of the two particulate control alternatives. Careful study of these results led to the following conclusions:

- The expected value of annual revenue requirements for the electrostatic precipitator technology was approximately $1 million lower than that for the fabric filters.
- The fabric filter alternative had a higher upside risk—that is, a higher probability of high revenue requirements—than did the precipitator alternative.
- The precipitator technology had nearly an 80% probability of lower annual revenue requirements than the fabric filters.
- Although the capital cost of the fabric filter equipment (the cost of installing the equipment) was lower than for the precipitator, this cost was more than offset by the higher operating costs associated with the fabric filter.

These results led Ohio Edison to select the electrostatic precipitator technology for the generating units in question. Had the decision analysis not been performed, the particulate control decision might have been based chiefly on capital cost, a decision measure that would have favored the fabric filter equipment. Decision analysis offers a means for effectively analyzing the uncertainties involved in a decision. Because of this analysis, the use of decision analysis methodology in this application resulted in a decision that yielded both lower expected revenue requirements and lower risk.

Questions

1. Why was decision analysis used in the selection of particulate control equipment for units 5, 6, and 7?
2. List the decision alternatives for the decision analysis problem developed by Ohio Edison.
3. What were the benefits of using decision analysis in this application?

Figure 9.14   SIMPLIFIED PARTICULATE CONTROL EQUIPMENT
DECISION TREE

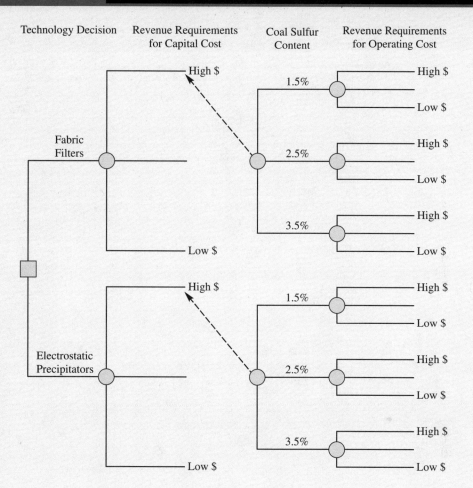

10

MULTICRITERIA DECISION MAKING

The majority of the management science problems considered thus far have involved a single decision criterion such as the maximization of profit, the minimization of cost, or the minimization of time. The objective was to find a solution that provided the best value for the single criterion. In this chapter we consider decision problems involving two or more criteria that are often in conflict as the decision maker attempts to identify the best decision alternative. In this case, a trade-off among the multiple criteria is often necessary because no one solution is best for every criterion. We show how management science techniques can be used to quantify the importance of each criterion and then evaluate how each decision alternative contributes to each criterion. The goal is a prioritizing, or ranking, of the decision alternatives so that the decision alternative that comes closest to meeting the multiple criteria can be identified.

We first consider a scoring model as a quick and relatively easy way to identify a decision alternative for a multicriteria problem. Then we introduce a method known as the **analytical hierarchy process (AHP),** which allows the user to make pairwise comparisons among the criteria and a series of pairwise comparisons among the decision alternatives in order to arrive at a prioritizing or ranking of the decision alternatives. We show Excel spreadsheets that can be used to implement both the scoring model and AHP procedures.

···/ /············

10.1 A SCORING MODEL FOR JOB SELECTION

Assume that a graduating college student with a double major in finance and accounting has received job offers for the following three positions:

- A financial analyst for an investment firm located in Chicago
- An accountant for a manufacturing firm located in Denver
- An auditor for a CPA firm located in Houston

When asked about which job is preferred, the student made the following comments: "The financial analyst position in Chicago provides the best opportunity for my long-run career advancement. However, I would prefer living in Denver rather than in Chicago or Houston. On the other hand, I liked the management style and philosophy at the Houston CPA firm the best." The student's statement points out that this example is clearly a multi-criteria decision problem. Considering only the *long-run career advancement* criterion, the financial analyst position in Chicago is the preferred decision alternative. Considering only the *location* criterion, the best decision alternative is the accountant position in Denver. Finally, considering only the *management style* criterion, the best alternative is the auditor position with the CPA firm in Houston. For most individuals, a multicriteria decision problem that requires a trade-off among the several criteria is difficult to solve. In this section, we describe how a **scoring model** can assist in analyzing a multicriteria decision problem and help identify the preferred decision alternative.

The steps required to develop a scoring model are as follows:

1. List the criteria for the decision-making process. The criteria are the factors that the decision maker considers relevant for evaluating each decision alternative.
2. Assign a weight to each criterion that describes the criterion's relative importance in the decision-making process. Let

$$w_i = \text{the weight for criterion } i$$

> A *scoring model* enables a decision maker to identify the criteria and indicate the weight or importance of each criterion.

3. Assign a rating for each criterion that shows how well each decision alternative satisfies the criterion. Let

$$r_{ij} = \text{the rating for criterion } i \text{ and decision alternative } j$$

4. Compute the score for each decision alternative. Let

$$S_j = \text{score for decision alternative } j$$

The equation used to compute S_j is as follows:

$$S_j = \sum_i w_i \, r_{ij} \qquad (10.1)$$

5. Order the decision alternatives from highest score to lowest score to provide the scoring model's ranking of the decision alternatives. The decision alternative with the highest score is the recommended decision alternative.

Let us return to the multicriteria job-selection problem the graduating student was facing and illustrate the use of a scoring model to assist in the decision-making process. In carrying out Step 1 of the scoring model procedure, the student listed seven criteria as important factors in the decision making process. These criteria are as follows:

- Career advancement
- Location
- Management style
- Salary
- Prestige
- Job security
- Enjoy the work

In Step 2, a weight is assigned to each criterion to indicate its relative importance in the decision-making process. For example, using the five-point scale shown below, the following question would be posed for the career advancement criterion.

Relative to the other criteria you are considering, how important is career advancement?

Importance	Weight
Very important	5
Somewhat important	4
Average importance	3
Somewhat unimportant	2
Very unimportant	1

By repeating this question for each of the seven criteria, the student provided the criterion weights shown in Table 10.1. Using this table, we see that career advancement and enjoy the work are the two most important criteria, each receiving a weight of 5. The management style and job security criteria are both considered somewhat important, and thus each received a weight of 4. Location and salary are considered average in importance, each receiving a weight of 3. Finally, since prestige is considered to be somewhat unimportant, it received a weight of 2.

The weights shown in Table 10.1 are subjective values provided by the student. A different student would most likely choose to weight the criteria differently. One of the key advantages of a scoring model is that it uses the subjective weights that most closely reflect the preferences of the individual decision maker.

In Step 3, each decision alternative is rated in terms of how well it satisfies each criterion. For example, using a nine-point scale, the specific question for the "financial analyst in Chicago" alternative and the career advancement criterion would be as follows:

Table 10.1   WEIGHTS FOR THE SEVEN JOB SELECTION CRITERIA

Criterion	Importance	Weight (w_i)
Career advancement	Very important	5
Location	Average importance	3
Management style	Somewhat important	4
Salary	Average importance	3
Prestige	Somewhat unimportant	2
Job security	Somewhat important	4
Enjoy the work	Very important	5

To what extent does the financial analyst position in Chicago satisfy your career advancement criterion?

Level of Satisfaction	Rating
Extremely high	9
Very high	8
High	7
Slightly high	6
Average	5
Slightly low	4
Low	3
Very low	2
Extremely low	1

A score of 8 on this question would indicate that the student believes the financial analyst position would be rated "very high" in terms of satisfying the career advancement criterion.

This scoring process must be completed for each combination of decision alternative and decision criterion. Since there are seven decision criteria and three decision alternatives, $7 \times 3 = 21$ ratings must be provided. Table 10.2 summaries the student's responses. Scanning this table provides some insights about how the student rates each decision criterion and decision alternative combination. For example, a rating of 9, corresponding to an extremely high level of satisfaction, only appears for the management style criterion and the auditor position in Houston. Thus, considering all combinations, the student rates the auditor position in Houston as the very best in terms of satisfying the management criterion. The lowest rating in the table is a 3 that appears for the location criterion and the financial analyst position in Chicago. This rating indicates that Chicago is rated "low" in terms of satisfying the student's location criterion. Other insights and interpretations are possible, but the question at this point is how does a scoring model use the data in Tables 10.1 and 10.2 to identify the best overall decision alternative.

Step 4 of the procedure shows that equation (10.1) is used to compute the score for each decision alternative. The data in Table 10.1 provide the weight for each criterion (w_i) and

Table 10.2	RATINGS FOR EACH DECISION CRITERIA AND EACH DECISION ALTERNATIVE COMBINATION

Criterion	Decision Alternative		
	Financial Analyst Chicago	Accountant Denver	Auditor Houston
Career Advancement	8	6	4
Location	3	8	7
Management style	5	6	9
Salary	6	7	5
Prestige	7	5	4
Job security	4	7	6
Enjoy the work	8	6	5

the data in Table 10.2 provides the ratings of each decision alternative for each criterion (r_{ij}). Thus for decision alternative 1, the score for the financial analyst position in Chicago is

$$S_1 = \sum_i w_i \, r_{i1} = 5(8) + 3(3) + 4(5) + 3(6) + 2(7) + 4(4) + 5(8) = 157$$

By comparing the scores for each criterion, a decision maker can learn why a particular decision alternative has the highest score.

The scores for the other decision alternatives are computed in the same manner. The computations are summarized in Table 10.3.

From Table 10.3, we see that the highest score of 167 corresponds to the accountant position in Denver. Thus, the accountant position in Denver is the recommended decision alternative. The financial analyst position in Chicago, with a score of 157, is ranked second, and the auditor position in Houston, with a score of 149, is ranked third.

Spreadsheet Solution for the Job Selection Scoring Model

Problem 1 will test your understanding of the scoring model calculations.

A spreadsheet for the job selection scoring model is shown in Figure 10.1 The criteria weights are placed into cells B6 to B12. The ratings for each criterion and decision alternative are entered into cells C6 to E12.

The calculations used to compute the score for each decision alternative are shown in the bottom portion of the spreadsheet. The calculation for cell C18 is provided by the cell formula

$$=\$B6*C6$$

This cell formula can be copied from cell C18 to cells C18:E24 to provide the results shown in rows 18 to 24. The score for the financial analyst position in Chicago is found by placing the following formula in cell C26:

$$=SUM(C18:C24)$$

Copying cell C26 to cells D26:E26 provides the scores for the accountant in Denver and the auditor in Houston positions.

Table 10.3	COMPUTATION OF SCORES FOR THE THREE DECISION ALTERNATIVES						
Criterion		**Decision Alternative**					
		Financial Analyst Chicago		Accountant Denver		Auditor Houston	
	Weight w_i	Rating r_{i1}	Score $w_i r_{i1}$	Rating r_{i2}	Score $w_i r_{i2}$	Rating r_{i3}	Score $w_i r_{i3}$
Career advancement	5	8	40	6	30	4	20
Location	3	3	9	8	24	7	21
Management style	4	5	20	6	24	9	36
Salary	3	6	18	7	21	5	15
Prestige	2	7	14	5	10	4	8
Job security	4	4	16	7	28	6	24
Enjoy the work	5	8	40	6	30	5	25
Score			157		167		149

| | *Figure* 10.1 | | SPREADSHEET SOLUTION FOR THE JOB SELECTION SCORING MODEL | | |

	A	B	C	D	E
1	**Job Selection Scoring Model**				
2					
3				**Ratings**	
4			**Analyst**	**Accountant**	**Auditor**
5	**Criteria**	**Weight**	**Chicago**	**Denver**	**Houston**
6	Career Advancement	5	8	6	4
7	Location	3	3	8	7
8	Management Style	4	5	6	9
9	Salary	3	6	7	5
10	Prestige	2	7	5	4
11	Job Security	4	4	7	6
12	Enjoy the Work	5	8	6	5
13					
14					
15	**Scoring Calculations**				
16			**Analyst**	**Accountant**	**Auditor**
17	**Criteria**		**Chicago**	**Denver**	**Houston**
18	Career Advancement		40	30	20
19	Location		9	24	21
20	Management Style		20	24	36
21	Salary		18	21	15
22	Prestige		14	10	8
23	Job Security		16	28	24
24	Enjoy the Work		40	30	25
25					
26	**Score**		157	167	149

Figure 10.1 shows that the accountant position in Denver, with a score of 167, is the recommended decision alternative. The spreadsheet provides the advantage of allowing the decision maker to review the criteria weights and all decision alternative criteria ratings to make sure they are consistent with the decision maker's beliefs and preferences. If changes are desired in the entries in the top portion of the spreadsheet, the decision maker can enter the revised data and immediately determine how the changes affect the score for each decision alternative.

10.2 THE ANALYTIC HIERARCHY PROCESS

The analytic hierarchy process (AHP), developed by Thomas L. Saaty,[1] is designed to solve complex multicriteria decision problems. AHP requires the decision maker to provide judg-

---

1. T.L. Saaty, *The Analytic Hierarchy Process* (New York: McGraw-Hill, 1988).

ments about the relative importance of each criterion and then specify a preference for each decision alternative using each criterion. The output of AHP is a prioritized ranking of the decision alternatives based on the overall preferences expressed by the decision maker.

To introduce AHP, we consider a car purchasing decision problem faced by Diane Payne. After a preliminary analysis of the makes and models of several used cars, Diane has narrowed her list of decision alternatives to three cars: a Honda Accord, a Saturn, and a Chevrolet Cavalier. Table 10.4 summarizes the information Diane has collected about these cars.

Diane decided that the following criteria were relevant for her car-selection decision process:

- Price
- Miles per gallon (MPG)
- Comfort
- Style

Data regarding the Price and MPG are provided in Table 10.4. However, measures of the Comfort and Style cannot be specified so directly. Diane will need to consider factors such as the car's interior, type of audio system, ease of entry, seat adjustments, and driver visibility in order to determine the comfort level of each car. The style criterion will have to be based on Diane's subjective evaluation of the color and the general appearance of each car.

Even when a criterion such as price can be as easily measured, subjectivity becomes an issue whenever a decision maker indicates his or her personal preference for the decision alternatives based on price. For instance, the price of the Accord ($13,100) is $3600 more than the price of the Cavalier ($9500). The $3600 difference might represent a great deal of money to one person, but not very much of a difference to another person. Thus, whether the Accord is considered "extremely more expensive" than the Cavalier or perhaps only "moderately more expensive" than the Cavalier depends upon the financial status and the subjective opinion of the person making the comparison. An advantage of AHP is that it can handle situations such as this in which the unique subjective judgments of the individual decision maker constitute an important part of the decision-making process.

> AHP allows a decision maker to express personal preferences and subjective judgments about the various aspects of a multicriteria problem.

Developing the Hierarchy

The first step in AHP is to develop a graphical representation of the problem in terms of the overall goal, the criteria to be used, and the decision alternatives. Such a graph depicts the **hierarchy** for the problem. Figure 10.2 shows the hierarchy for the car selection problem. Note that the first level of the hierarchy shows that the overall goal is to select the best car.

Table 10.4   INFORMATION FOR THE CAR SELECTION PROBLEM

Characteristics	Decision Alternatives		
	Accord	Saturn	Cavalier
Price	$13,100	$11,200	$9500
Color	Black	Red	Blue
Miles per Gallon	19	23	28
Interior	Deluxe	Above Average	Standard
Body Type	4-door midsize	2-door sport	2-door compact
Sound System	AM/FM, tape, CD	AM/FM	AM/FM

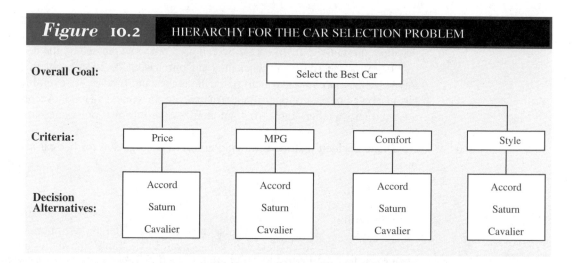

Figure 10.2   HIERARCHY FOR THE CAR SELECTION PROBLEM

At the second level, the four criteria (Price, MPG, Comfort, and Style) each contribute to the achievement of the overall goal. Finally, at the third level, each decision alternative—Accord, Saturn, and Cavalier—contributes to each criterion in a unique way.

Using AHP, the decision maker specifies judgments about the relative importance of each of the four criteria in terms of its contribution to the achievement of the overall goal. At the next level, the decision maker indicates a preference for each decision alternative based on each criterion. A mathematical process is used to synthesize the information on the relative importance of the criteria and the preferences for the decision alternatives to provide an overall priority ranking of the decision alternatives. In the car selection problem, AHP will use Diane's personal preferences to provide a priority ranking of the three cars in terms of how well each car meets the overall goal of being the *best* car.

10.3   ESTABLISHING PRIORITIES USING AHP

In this section we show how AHP uses pairwise comparisons expressed by the decision maker to establish priorities for the criteria and priorities for the decision alternatives based on each criterion. Using the car selection example, we show how AHP determines priorities for each of the following:

1. How the four criteria contribute to the overall goal of selecting the best car
2. How the three cars compare using the Price criterion
3. How the three cars compare using the MPG criterion
4. How the three cars compare using the Comfort criterion
5. How the three cars compare using the Style criterion

In the following discussion, we demonstrate how to establish priorities for the four criteria in terms of how each contributes to the overall goal of selecting the best car. The priorities of the three cars using each criterion can be determined similarly.

Pairwise Comparisons

Pairwise comparisons form the fundamental building blocks of AHP. In establishing the priorities for the four criteria, AHP will require Diane to state how important each criterion is relative to each other criterion when the criteria are compared two at a time (pairwise).

That is, with the four criteria (Price, MPG, Comfort, and Style) Diane must make the following pairwise comparisons:

> Price compared to MPG
>
> Price compared to Comfort
>
> Price compared to Style
>
> MPG compared to Comfort
>
> MPG compared to Style
>
> Comfort compared to Style

In each comparison, Diane must select the more important criterion and then express a judgment of how much more important the selected criterion is.

For example, in the Price-MPG pairwise comparison, assume that Diane indicates that Price is more important than MPG. To measure how much more important Price is compared to MPG, AHP uses scale with values from 1 to 9. Table 10.5 shows how the decision maker's verbal description of the relative importance between the two criteria are converted into a numerical rating. In the car selection example, suppose that Diane states that Price is "moderately more important" than MPG. In this case, a numerical rating of 3 is assigned to the Price-MPG pairwise comparison. Using Table 10.5, we see "strongly more important" receives a numerical rating of 5 while "very strongly more important" receives a numerical rating of 7. Intermediate judgments such as "strongly to very strongly more important" are possible and would receive a numerical rating of 6.

Table 10.6 provides a summary of the six pairwise comparisons Diane provided for the car selection problem. Using the information in this table, Diane has specified that

> Price is moderately more important than MPG
>
> Price is equally to moderately more important than Comfort
>
> Price is equally to moderately more important than Style
>
> Comfort is moderately to strongly more important than MPG
>
> Style is moderately to strongly more important than MPG
>
> Style is equally to moderately more important than Comfort

AHP uses the numerical ratings from the pairwise comparisons to establish a priority or importance measure for each criterion.

This is a good time to comment on the flexibility of AHP to accommodate to the unique preferences of each individual decision maker. First, the choice of the criteria that are considered can vary depending upon the decision maker. Not everyone would agree that Price,

Table 10.5 COMPARISON SCALE FOR THE IMPORTANCE OF CRITERIA USING AHP

Verbal Judgment	Numerical Rating
Extremely more important	9
	8
Very strongly more important	7
	6
Strongly more important	5
	4
Moderately more important	3
	2
Equally important	1

| Table 10.6 | SUMMARY OF DIANE PAYNE'S PAIRWISE COMPARISONS OF THE FOUR CRITERIA FOR THE CAR SELECTION PROBLEM | | |

Pairwise Comparison	More Important Criterion	How Much More Important	Numerical Rating
Price-MPG	Price	Moderately	3
Price-Comfort	Price	Equally to moderately	2
Price-Style	Price	Equally to moderately	2
MPG-Comfort	Comfort	Moderately to strongly	4
MPG-Style	Style	Moderately to strongly	4
Comfort-Style	Style	Equally to moderately	2

MPG, Comfort, and Style are the only criteria to be considered in a car selection problem. Perhaps you would want to add safety, resale value, and/or other criteria if you were making the car selection decision. AHP can accommodate any set of criteria specified by the decision maker. Of course, if additional criteria are added, more pairwise comparisons will be necessary. In addition, if you agree with Diane that Price, MPG, Comfort, and Style are the four criteria to use, you would probably disagree with her as to the relative importance of the criteria. Using the format of Table 10.6, you could provide your own assessment of the importance to each pairwise comparison, and AHP would adjust the numerical ratings to reflect your personal preferences.

The Pairwise Comparison Matrix

To determine the priorities for the four criteria, we need to construct a matrix of the pairwise comparison ratings provided in Table 10.6. Using the four criteria, the **pairwise comparison matrix** will consist of four rows and four columns as shown below:

	Price	MPG	Comfort	Style
Price				
MPG				
Comfort				
Style				

Each of the numerical ratings in Table 10.6 must be entered into the pairwise comparison matrix. To illustrate how this is done, consider the numerical rating of 3 for the Price-MPG pairwise comparison. Table 10.6 shows that for this pairwise comparison that Price is the most important criterion. Thus, we must enter a 3 into the row label Price and the column labeled MPG into the pairwise comparison matrix. In general, the entries in the column labeled Most Important Criterion in Table 10.6 indicate which row of the pairwise comparison matrix the numerical rating must be placed in. As another illustration, consider the MPG-Comfort pairwise comparison. Table 10.6 shows that Comfort is the most important criterion for this pairwise comparison and that the numerical rating is 4. Thus, we enter a 4 into the row labeled Comfort and into the column labeled MPG. Following this procedure for the other pairwise comparisons shown in Table 10.6, we obtain the following pairwise comparison matrix.

	Price	MPG	Comfort	Style
Price		3	2	2
MPG				
Comfort		4		
Style		4	2	

Since the diagonal elements are comparing each criterion to itself, the diagonal elements of the pairwise comparison matrix are always equal to 1. For example, if Price is compared to Price, the verbal judgment would be "equally important" with a rating of 1; thus, a 1 would be placed into the row labeled Price and into the column labeled Price in the pairwise comparison matrix. At this point, the pairwise comparison matrix appears as follows:

	Price	MPG	Comfort	Style
Price	1	3	2	2
MPG		1		
Comfort		4	1	
Style		4	2	1

All that remains is to complete the entries for the remaining cells of the matrix. This is easy to do when we realize that the Price row compared to the MPG column has a rating of 3. This rating implies that the MPG row compared to Price column should have a rating of ⅓. That is, since Diane has already indicated Price is moderately more important that MPG (a rating of 3), we can infer that a pairwise comparison of MPG relative to Price should be ⅓. Similarly, since the Comfort row comparison to the MPG column has a rating of 4, the MPG row comparison to the Comfort column would be ¼. Thus the complete pairwise comparison matrix for the car selection criteria is as follows:

	Price	MPG	Comfort	Style
Price	1	3	2	2
MPG	⅓	1	¼	¼
Comfort	½	4	1	½
Style	½	4	2	1

Synthesization

Using the pairwise comparison matrix, we can now calculate the priority of each criterion in terms of its contribution to the overall goal of selecting the best car. This aspect of AHP is referred to as **synthesization.** The exact mathematical procedure required to perform synthesization is beyond the scope of this text. However, the following three-step procedure provides a good approximation of the synthesization results.

1. Sum the values in each column of the pairwise comparison matrix.
2. Divide each element in the pairwise comparison matrix by its column total; the resulting matrix is referred to as the **normalized pairwise comparison matrix.**
3. Compute the average of the elements in each row of the normalized pairwise comparison matrix; these averages provide the estimates of the priorities for the criteria.

To show how the synthesization process works, we carry out this three-step procedure for the criteria pairwise comparison matrix.

Step 1: Sum the values in each column.

	Price	MPG	Comfort	Style
Price	1	3	2	2
MPG	⅓	1	¼	¼
Comfort	½	4	1	½
Style	½	4	2	1
Sum	2.333	12.000	5.250	3.750

Step 2: Divide each element of the matrix by its column total.

	Price	MPG	Comfort	Style
Price	0.429	0.250	0.381	0.533
MPG	0.143	0.083	0.048	0.067
Comfort	0.214	0.333	0.190	0.133
Style	0.214	0.333	0.381	0.267

Step 3: Average the elements in each row to determine the priority of each criterion.

	Price	MPG	Comfort	Style	Priority
Price	0.429	0.250	0.381	0.533	0.398
MPG	0.143	0.083	0.048	0.067	0.085
Comfort	0.214	0.333	0.190	0.133	0.218
Style	0.214	0.333	0.381	0.267	0.299

The AHP synthesization procedure has provided the priority of each criterion in terms of its contribution to the overall goal of selecting the best car. Thus, using Diane's pairwise comparisons provided in Table 10.6, AHP has determined that Price with a priority of 0.398 is the most important criterion in the car selection process. Style with a priority of 0.299 ranks second in importance and is closely followed by Comfort with a priority of 0.218. MPG is the least important criterion with a priority of 0.085.

Consistency

A key step in AHP is the making of several pairwise comparisons as previously described. An important consideration in this process is the **consistency** of the pairwise judgments provided by the decision maker. For example, if criterion A compared to criterion B has a numerical rating of 3 and if criterion B compared to criterion C has a numerical rating of 2, perfect consistency of criterion A compared to criterion C would have a numerical rating of $3 \times 2 = 6$. If the A to C numerical rating assigned by the decision maker was 4 or 5, some inconsistency would exist among the pairwise comparisons.

With numerous pairwise comparisons, perfect consistency is very difficult to achieve. In fact, some degree of inconsistency can be expected to exist in almost any set of pairwise comparisons. To handle the consistency issue, AHP provides a method for measuring the degree of consistency among the pairwise comparisons provided by the decision maker. If the degree of consistency is unacceptable, the decision maker should review and revise the pairwise comparisons before proceeding with the AHP analysis.

AHP provides a measure of the consistency for the pairwise comparisons by computing a **consistency ratio.** This ratio is designed in such a way that a value **greater than** 0.10 indicates an inconsistency in the pairwise judgments. Thus, if the consistency ratio is 0.10 or less, the consistency of the pairwise comparisons is considered reasonable, and the AHP process can continue with the synthesization computations.

Although the exact mathematical computation of the consistency ratio is beyond the scope of this text, an approximation of the ratio can be obtained with little difficulty. The step-by-step procedure for estimating the consistency ratio for the criteria of the car selection problem follows.

A consistency ratio greater than 0.10 indicates inconsistency in the pairwise comparisons. In such cases, the decision maker should review the pairwise comparisons information before proceeding.

Step 1: Multiply each value in the first column of the pairwise comparison matrix by the priority of the first item; multiply each value in the second column of the pairwise comparison matrix by the priority of the second item; continue this process for all columns of the pairwise comparison matrix. Sum the values across the rows to obtain a vector of values labeled "weighted sum." This computation for the car selection problem is as follows:

$$
0.398 \begin{bmatrix} 1 \\ \frac{1}{3} \\ \frac{1}{2} \\ \frac{1}{2} \end{bmatrix} + 0.085 \begin{bmatrix} 3 \\ 1 \\ 4 \\ 4 \end{bmatrix} + 0.218 \begin{bmatrix} 2 \\ \frac{1}{4} \\ 1 \\ 2 \end{bmatrix} + 0.299 \begin{bmatrix} 2 \\ \frac{1}{4} \\ \frac{1}{2} \\ 1 \end{bmatrix} =
$$

$$
\begin{bmatrix} 0.398 \\ 0.133 \\ 0.199 \\ 0.199 \end{bmatrix} + \begin{bmatrix} 0.255 \\ 0.085 \\ 0.340 \\ 0.340 \end{bmatrix} + \begin{bmatrix} 0.436 \\ 0.054 \\ 0.218 \\ 0.436 \end{bmatrix} + \begin{bmatrix} 0.598 \\ 0.075 \\ 0.149 \\ 0.299 \end{bmatrix} = \begin{bmatrix} 1.687 \\ 0.347 \\ 0.907 \\ 1.274 \end{bmatrix}
$$

Step 2: Divide the elements of the weighted sum vector obtained in Step 1 by the corresponding priority for each criterion.

$$\text{Price} \qquad \frac{1.687}{0.398} = 4.236$$

$$\text{MPG} \qquad \frac{0.347}{0.085} = 4.077$$

$$\text{Comfort} \qquad \frac{0.907}{0.218} = 4.163$$

$$\text{Style} \qquad \frac{1.274}{0.299} = 4.264$$

Step 3: Compute the average of the values found in step 2; this average is denoted λ_{max}.

$$\lambda_{max} = \frac{(4.236 + 4.077 + 4.163 + 4.264)}{4} = 4.185$$

Step 4: Compute the consistency index (CI) as follows:

$$CI = \frac{\lambda_{max} - n}{n - 1}$$

where n is the number of items being compared. Thus, we have

$$CI = \frac{4.185 - 4}{4 - 1} = 0.0616$$

Step 5: Compute the consistency ratio, which is defined as

$$CR = \frac{CI}{RI}$$

where RI is the consistency index of a *randomly* generated pairwise comparison matrix. The value of RI depends on the number of items being compared and is given as follows:

n	3	4	5	6	7	8
RI	0.58	0.90	1.12	1.24	1.32	1.41

Thus, for the car selection problem with $n = 4$ criteria, we have RI = 0.90 and a consistency ratio

Problem 8 will give you practice with the synthesization calculations and determining the consistency ratio.

$$CR = \frac{0.0616}{0.90} = 0.068$$

As mentioned previously, a consistency ratio of 0.10 or less is considered acceptable. Since the pairwise comparisons for the car selection criteria show CR = 0.068, we can conclude that the degree of consistency in the pairwise comparisons is acceptable.

Other Pairwise Comparisons for the Car Selection Problem

Continuing with the AHP analysis of the car selection problem, we need to use the pairwise comparison procedure to determine the priorities for the three cars using each of the criteria: Price, MPG, Comfort, and Style. Determining these priorities requires Diane to express pairwise comparison preferences for the cars using each criterion one at a time. For example, using the price criterion, Diane must make the following pairwise comparisons:

> the Accord compared to the Saturn
>
> the Accord compared to the Cavalier
>
> the Saturn compared to the Cavalier

In each comparison, Diane must select the more preferred car and then express a judgment of how much more preferred the selected car is.

For example, using the Price as the basis for comparison, assume that Diane considers the Accord-Saturn pairwise comparison and indicates that the less expensive Saturn is more preferred. Table 10.7 shows how AHP uses Diane's verbal description of the preference between the Accord and Saturn to determine a numerical rating of the preference. For example, suppose that Diane states that based on Price, the Saturn is "moderately more preferred" to the Accord. Thus, using the Price criterion, a numerical rating of 3 is assigned to the Saturn row and Accord column of the pairwise comparison matrix.

Table 10.8 shows the summary of the car pairwise comparisons that Diane provided for each criterion of the car selection problem. Using this table and referring to selected pairwise comparison entries, we see that Diane has stated the following preferences:

In terms of Price, the Cavalier is moderately to strongly preferred to the Accord.

In terms of the MPG, the Cavalier is moderately preferred to the Saturn.

In terms of Comfort, the Accord is very strongly to extremely preferred to the Cavalier.

In terms of Style, the Saturn is moderately preferred to the Accord.

Using the pairwise comparison matrixes in Table 10.8, many other insights may be gained about the preferences Diana has expressed for the cars. However, at this point, AHP continues by synthesizing each of the four pairwise comparison matrixes in Table 10.8 in order to determine the priority of each car using each criterion. A synthesization is conducted for each pairwise comparison matrix using the three-step procedure described previously

Table 10.7	PAIRWISE COMPARISON SCALE FOR THE PREFERENCE OF DECISION ALTERNATIVES USING AHP

Verbal Judgment	Numerical Rating
Extremely preferred	9
	8
Very strongly preferred	7
	6
Strongly preferred	5
	4
Moderately preferred	3
	2
Equally preferred	1

Table 10.8	PAIRWISE COMPARISON MATRIXES SHOWING PREFERENCES FOR THE CARS USING EACH CRITERION

Price

	Accord	Saturn	Cavalier
Accord	1	1/3	1/4
Saturn	3	1	1/2
Cavalier	4	2	1

MPG

	Accord	Saturn	Cavalier
Accord	1	1/4	1/6
Saturn	4	1	1/3
Cavalier	6	3	1

Comfort

	Accord	Saturn	Cavalier
Accord	1	2	8
Saturn	1/2	1	6
Cavalier	1/8	1/6	1

Style

	Accord	Saturn	Cavalier
Accord	1	1/3	4
Saturn	3	1	7
Cavalier	1/4	1/7	1

Table 10.9	PRIORITIES FOR EACH CAR USING EACH CRITERION

	Criterion			
	Price	MPG	Comfort	Style
Accord	0.123	0.087	0.593	0.265
Saturn	0.320	0.274	0.341	0.656
Cavalier	0.557	0.639	0.065	0.080

for the criteria pairwise comparison matrix. Four synthesization computations provide the four sets of priorities shown in Table 10.9. Using this table, we see that the Cavalier is the preferred alternative based on Price (0.557), the Cavalier is the preferred alternative based on MPG (0.639), the Accord is the preferred alternative based on Comfort (0.593), and the Saturn is the preferred alternative based on Style (0.656). At this point, no car is the clear, overall best. The next section shows how to combine the priorities for the criteria and the priorities in Table 10.9 to develop an overall priority ranking for the three cars.

You should be able to set up a pairwise comparison matrix and determine whether judgments are consistent. Try problem 12.

10.4 USING AHP TO DEVELOP AN OVERALL PRIORITY RANKING

In Section 10.3, we used Diane's pairwise comparisons of the four criteria to develop the priorities of 0.398 for Price, 0.085 for MPG, 0.281 for Comfort, and 0.299 for Style. We now want to use these priorities and the priorities shown in Table 10.9 to develop an overall priority ranking for the three cars.

The procedure used to compute the overall priority is to weight each car's priority shown in Table 10.9 by the corresponding criterion priority. For example, the Price criterion has a priority of 0.398, and the Accord has a priority of 0.123 in terms of the Price criterion. Thus, $0.398 \times 0.123 = 0.049$ is the priority value of the Accord based on the Price criterion. To obtain the overall priority of the Accord, we need to make similar computations for the MPG, Comfort, and Style criteria and then add the values to obtain the overall priority. This calculation is as follows:

Overall Priority of the Accord:

$$0.398(0.123) + 0.085(0.087) + 0.218(0.593) + 0.299(0.265) = 0.265$$

Repeating this calculation for the Saturn and the Cavalier, we obtain the following results:

Overall Priority of the Saturn:

$$0.398(0.32) + 0.085(0.274) + 0.218(0.341) + 0.299(0.655) = 0.421$$

Overall Priority of the Cavalier:

$$0.398(0.557) + 0.085(0.639) + 0.218(0.066) + 0.299(0.080) = 0.314$$

Ranking these priorities, we have the AHP ranking of the decision alternatives:

Car	Priority
1. Saturn	0.421
2. Cavalier	0.314
3. Accord	0.265

These results provide a basis for Diane to make a decision regarding the purchase of a car. As long as Diane believes that her judgments regarding the importance of the criteria and her preferences for the cars using each criterion are valid, the AHP priorities show that the Saturn is preferred. In addition to the recommendation of the Saturn as the best car, the AHP analysis has helped Diane gain a better understanding of the trade-offs in the decision-making process and a clearer understanding of why the Saturn is the AHP recommended alternative.

Work problem 16 and determine the AHP priorities for the two decision alternatives.

NOTES *and Comments*

The scoring model in Section 10.1 used the following equation to compute the overall score of a decision alternative.

$$S_j = \sum_i w_i\, r_{ij}$$

where

w_i = the weight for criterion i

r_{ij} = the rating for criterion i and decision alternative j

In Section 10.2 AHP used the same calculation to determine the overall priority of each decision alternative. The difference between the two approaches is that the scoring model required the decision maker to estimate the values of w_i and r_{ij} directly. AHP used synthesization to compute the criterion priorities w_i and the decision alternative priorities r_{ij} based on the pairwise comparison information provided by the decision maker.

..../ /...............

10.5   SPREADSHEET SOLUTION FOR THE CAR SELECTION PROBLEM

Figure 10.3 shows the spreadsheet solution using AHP solve the car selection problem. The format of the spreadsheet is unique to the car selection problem. However, this spreadsheet can be used for any multicriteria problem where four criteria are used to evaluate three decision alternatives. Understanding this spreadsheet will help you modify it and use AHP to solve other multicriteria problems.

The criteria pairwise comparison matrix appears in cells B7:E10. The cell formulas used to perform the AHP calculations for the criteria are as follows:

Cell B11   Compute the sum of the pairwise comparison data for the price criterion

      =SUM(B7:B10)

This formula is copied to cells C11:E11 to compute the sum of the pairwise comparison data for the other criteria.

Cell H7   Compute the normalized matrix value for the price criterion

      =B7/B$11

This formula is copied to complete the normalized matrix in cells H7:K10.

Cell L7   Compute the priority for the Price criterion

      =AVERAGE(H7:K7)

This formula is copied to cells L8:L10 to provide the priorities for the other criteria.

Cell N7   Compute the weighted sum of Price for the consistency ratio calculation

      =B7*$L$7+C7*$L$8+D7*$L$9+E7*$L$10

This formula is copied to cells N8:N10 to compute the weighted sums for the other criteria.

Cell O7   Compute the consistency measure for the Price criterion

      =N7/L7

This formula is copied to cells O8:O10 to compute the consistency measures for the other criteria.

Cell O11   Compute the consistency ratio for the four criteria (with $n = 4$, the random index RI = 0.9)

      =((AVERAGE(O7:O10)−4)/3)/0.9

This completes the criteria section of the spreadsheet.

Figure 10.3 — SPREADSHEET SOLUTION FOR THE AHP CAR SELECTION PROBLEM

SPREADSHEET
CAR SELECTION
AHP

	A	B	C	D	E	F	G	H	I	J	K	L	M	N	O
1	**Car Selection Using AHP**														
2															
3	**Pairwise Comparison Matrices**						**Normalized Matrices**							**Consistency Ratios**	
4															
5	**Criteria**	**Criteria**												Weighted	Consistency
6		Price	MPG	Comfort	Style			Price	MPG	Comfort	Style	Priorty		Sum	Measure
7	Price	1.000	3.000	2.000	2.000		Price	0.429	0.250	0.381	0.533	0.398		1.687	4.236
8	MPG	0.333	1.000	0.250	0.250		MPG	0.143	0.083	0.048	0.067	0.085		0.347	4.077
9	Comfort	0.500	4.000	1.000	0.500		Comfort	0.214	0.333	0.190	0.133	0.218		0.907	4.163
10	Style	0.500	4.000	2.000	1.000		Style	0.214	0.333	0.381	0.267	0.299		1.274	4.264
11	Sum	2.333	12.000	5.250	3.750									**CR**	0.068
12															
13															
14	**Price**						**Price**							Weighted	Consistency
15		Accord	Saturn	Cavalier				Accord	Saturn	Cavalier		Priorty		Sum	Measure
16	Accord	1.000	0.333	0.250			Accord	0.125	0.100	0.143		0.123		0.369	3.006
17	Saturn	3.000	1.000	0.500			Saturn	0.375	0.300	0.286		0.320		0.967	3.019
18	Cavalier	4.000	2.000	1.000			Cavalier	0.500	0.600	0.571		0.557		1.688	3.030
19	Sum	8.000	3.333	1.750										**CR**	0.016
20															
21															
22	**MPG**						**MPG**							Weighted	Consistency
23		Accord	Saturn	Cavalier				Accord	Saturn	Cavalier		Priorty		Sum	Measure
24	Accord	1.000	0.250	0.167			Accord	0.091	0.059	0.111		0.087		0.262	3.013
25	Saturn	4.000	1.000	0.333			Saturn	0.364	0.235	0.222		0.274		0.835	3.049
26	Cavalier	6.000	3.000	1.000			Cavalier	0.545	0.706	0.667		0.639		1.982	3.100
27	Sum	11.000	4.250	1.500										**CR**	0.047
28															
29															
30	**Comfort**						**Comfort**							Weighted	Consistency
31		Accord	Saturn	Cavalier				Accord	Saturn	Cavalier		Priorty		Sum	Measure
32	Accord	1.000	2.000	8.000			Accord	0.615	0.632	0.533		0.593		1.799	3.032
33	Saturn	0.500	1.000	6.000			Saturn	0.308	0.316	0.400		0.341		1.030	3.020
34	Cavalier	0.125	0.167	1.000			Cavalier	0.077	0.053	0.067		0.065		0.196	3.003
35	Sum	1.625	3.167	15.000										**CR**	0.016
36															
37															
38	**Style**						**Style**							Weighted	Consistency
39		Accord	Saturn	Cavalier				Accord	Saturn	Cavalier		Priority		Sum	Measure
40	Accord	1.000	0.333	4.000			Accord	0.235	0.226	0.333		0.265		0.802	3.028
41	Saturn	3.000	1.000	7.000			Saturn	0.706	0.677	0.583		0.656		2.007	3.062
42	Cavalier	0.250	0.143	1.000			Cavalier	0.059	0.097	0.083		0.080		0.239	3.007
43	Sum	4.250	1.476	12.000										**CR**	0.028
44															
45															
46	**Priority Summary**														
47		Price	MPG	Comfort	Style		**Overall Priorities**								
48	Priority	0.398	0.085	0.218	0.299										
49	Accord	0.123	0.087	0.593	0.265		Accord	0.265							
50	Saturn	0.320	0.274	0.341	0.656		Saturn	0.421							
51	Cavalier	0.557	0.639	0.065	0.080		Cavalier	0.314							

Cell formulas can now be entered to determine the priorities for the three cars using each of the criteria and the corresponding consistency ratios.

Cell locations differ but the logic is the same. We do not present the detailed cell formulas here. Instead, let us continue with the Priority Summary section of the spreadsheet shown in rows 46 to 51. Row 48 contains the criteria priorities previously shown in cells L7 to L10. Thus the following cell formulas are used in row 48:

$$\text{Cell B48} \quad =\text{L7}$$
$$\text{Cell C48} \quad =\text{L8}$$
$$\text{Cell D48} \quad =\text{L9}$$
$$\text{Cell E48} \quad =\text{L10}$$

The matrix located in cell B49 to cell E51 contains the priorities computed earlier in the spreadsheet. For example,

$$\text{Cell B49} \quad =\text{L16}$$
$$\text{Cell C49} \quad =\text{L24}$$
$$\text{Cell D49} \quad =\text{L32}$$
$$\text{Cell E49} \quad =\text{L40}$$

Cell B49 to cell E49 can be copied to rows 50 and 51 to complete the matrix.

The overall priorities can now be computed.

Cell I49   Compute the overall priority for the Accord

=SUMPRODUCT($B$48:$E$48,B49:E49)

This formula can be copied to cells I50 and I51 to compute the overall priorities for the other two cars.

The overall priorities shown in Figure 10.3 agree with the AHP priorities computed in Section 10.4. The Saturn is the preferred car with an overall priority of 0.421. The Cavalier is the second choice, followed by the Accord. Note that the consistency ratios in all cases are less than 0.10 and considered to be reasonable values.

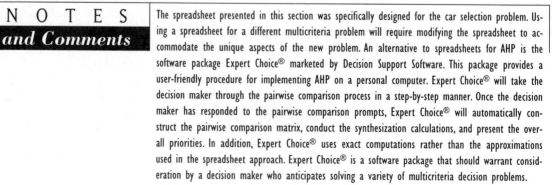

N O T E S *and Comments*

The spreadsheet presented in this section was specifically designed for the car selection problem. Using a spreadsheet for a different multicriteria problem will require modifying the spreadsheet to accommodate the unique aspects of the new problem. An alternative to spreadsheets for AHP is the software package Expert Choice® marketed by Decision Support Software. This package provides a user-friendly procedure for implementing AHP on a personal computer. Expert Choice® will take the decision maker through the pairwise comparison process in a step-by-step manner. Once the decision maker has responded to the pairwise comparison prompts, Expert Choice® will automatically construct the pairwise comparison matrix, conduct the synthesization calculations, and present the overall priorities. In addition, Expert Choice® uses exact computations rather than the approximations used in the spreadsheet approach. Expert Choice® is a software package that should warrant consideration by a decision maker who anticipates solving a variety of multicriteria decision problems.

SUMMARY

This chapter is concerned with decision making when two or more criteria are important in the decision-making process. A scoring model was presented as a quick and relatively easy way to identify the most desired decision alternative in a multicriteria problem. The decision maker provides a subjective weight indicating the importance of each criterion. Then the decision maker rates each decision alternative in terms of how well it satisfies each criterion. The end result is a score for each decision alternative that indicates the preference for the decision alternative considering all criteria.

We also presented an approach to multicriteria decision making called the *analytic hierarchy process (AHP)*. We showed that a key part of AHP is the development of judgments concerning the relative importance of, or preference for, the elements being compared. A consistency ratio is computed to determine the degree of consistency exhibited by the decision maker in making the pairwise comparisons. Values of the consistency ratio less than or equal to 0.10 are considered acceptable.

Once the set of all pairwise comparisons has been developed, a process referred to as synthesization is used to determine the priorities for the elements being compared. The final step of the analytic hierarchy process involves multiplying the priority levels established for the decision alternatives relative to each criterion by the priority levels reflecting the importance of the criteria themselves; the sum of these products over all the criteria provides the overall priority level for each decision alternative. We concluded the chapter with a description of how a spreadsheet can be used to perform the computational steps of AHP.

GLOSSARY

Scoring model An approach to multicriteria decision making that requires the user to assign weights to each criterion that describes the criterion's relative importance and to assign a rating that shows how well each decision alternative satisfies each criterion. The output is a score for each decision alternative.

Analytic hierarchy process (AHP) An approach to multicriteria decision making based on pairwise comparisons for elements in a hierarchy.

Hierarchy A diagram that shows the levels of a problem in terms of the overall goal, the criteria, and the decision alternatives.

Pairwise comparison matrix A matrix that consists of the preference, or relative importance, ratings provided during a series of pairwise comparisons.

Synthesization A mathematical process that uses the preference or relative importance values in the pairwise comparison matrix to develop priorities.

Normalized pairwise comparison matrix The matrix obtained by dividing each element of the pairwise comparison matrix by its column total. This matrix is computed as an intermediate step in the synthesization of priorities.

Consistency A concept developed to assess the quality of the judgments made during a series of pairwise comparisons. It is a measure of the internal consistency of these comparisons.

Consistency ratio A numerical measure of the degree of consistency in a series of pairwise comparisons. Values less than or equal to 0.10 are considered reasonable.

PROBLEMS

Note: The problems that follow can be solved using either hand calculations or spreadsheets. In general, the spreadsheets will be very similar to the spreadsheets presented in this chapter. However, some modification may be necessary due to the size and complexity of the problem.

SELF TEST

1. One advantage of using the multicriteria decision-making methods presented in this chapter is that the criteria weights and the decision alternative ratings may be modified to reflect the unique interests and preferences of each individual decision maker. For example, assume that another graduating college student had the same three job offers described in Section 10.1. This student provided the following scoring model information. Rank the overall preference for the three positions. Which position is recommended?

Criteria	Weight	Analyst Chicago	Accountant Denver	Auditor Houston
		Ratings		
Career advancement	5	7	4	4
Location	2	5	6	4
Management style	5	6	5	7
Salary	4	7	8	4
Prestige	4	8	5	6
Job security	2	4	5	8
Enjoy the work	4	7	5	5

2. The Kenyon Manufacturing Company is interested in selecting the best location for a new plant. After a detailed study of ten sites, the three location finalists are Georgetown, Kentucky; Marysville, Ohio; and Clarksville, Tennessee. The Kenyon management team provided the following data on location criteria, criteria importance, and location ratings. Use a scoring model to determine the best location for the new plant.

Criteria	Weight	Georgetown Kentucky	Marysville Ohio	Clarksville Tennessee
		Ratings		
Land cost	4	7	4	5
Labor cost	3	6	5	8
Labor availability	5	7	8	6
Construction cost	4	6	7	5
Transportation	3	5	7	4
Access to customers	5	6	8	5
Long-range goals	4	7	6	5

3. The Davis Family of Atlanta, Georgia, is planning its annual summer vacation. Three vacation locations along with criteria weights and location ratings follow. What is the recommended vacation location?

Criteria	Weight	Ratings		
		Myrtle Beach South Carolina	Smokey Mountains	Branson Missouri
Travel distance	2	5	7	3
Vacation cost	5	5	6	4
Entertainment available	3	7	4	8
Outdoor activities	2	9	6	5
Unique experience	4	6	7	8
Family fun	5	8	7	7

4. A high school senior is considering attending one of four colleges or universities listed below. Eight criteria, criteria weights, and school ratings are also shown below. What is the recommended choice?

Criteria	Weight	Ratings			
		Midwestern University	State College at Newport	Handover College	Tecumseh State
School prestige	3	8	6	7	5
Number of students	4	3	5	8	7
Average class size	5	4	5	8	7
Cost	5	5	8	3	6
Distance from home	2	7	8	7	6
Sports program	4	9	5	4	6
Housing desirability	4	6	5	7	6
Beauty of campus	3	5	3	8	5

5. Mr. and Mrs. Brinkley are interested in purchasing condominium property in Naples, Florida. The three most preferred condominiums are listed below along with criteria weights and rating information. Which condominium is preferred?

Criteria	Weight	Ratings		
		Park Shore	The Terrace	Gulf View
Cost	5	5	6	5
Location	4	7	4	9
Appearance	5	7	4	7
Parking	2	5	8	5
Floor plan	4	8	7	5
Swimming pool	1	7	2	3
View	3	5	4	9
Kitchen	4	8	7	6
Closet space	3	6	8	4

6. Clark and Julie Anderson are interested in purchasing a new boat and have limited their choice to one of three boats manufactured by Sea Ray, Inc.: the 220 Bowrider, the 230 Overnighter, and the 240 Sundancer. The Bowrider weights 3100 pounds, has no overnight capability, and has a price of $28,500. The 230 Overnighter weights 4300 pounds, has a reasonable overnight capability, and has a price of $37,500. The 240 Sundancer weights 4500 pounds, has a excellent overnight capability (kitchen, bath, and bed), and has a price of $48,200. The Andersons provided the scoring model information separately as shown below.

Clark Anderson

		Ratings		
Criteria	Weight	220 Bowrider	230 Overnighter	240 Sundancer
Cost	5	8	5	3
Overnight capability	3	2	6	9
Kitchen/bath facilities	2	1	4	7
Appearance	5	7	7	6
Engine/speed	5	6	8	4
Towing/handling	4	8	5	2
Maintenance	4	7	5	3
Resale value	3	7	5	6

Julie Anderson

		Ratings		
Criteria	Weight	220 Bowrider	230 Overnighter	240 Sundancer
Cost	3	7	6	5
Overnight capability	5	1	6	8
Kitchen/bath facilities	5	1	3	7
Appearance	4	5	7	7
Engine/speed	2	4	5	3
Towing/handling	2	8	6	2
Maintenance	1	6	5	4
Resale value	2	5	6	6

a. Which boat does Clark Anderson prefer?
b. Which boat does Julie Anderson prefer?

7. Use the pairwise comparison matrix for the price criterion shown in Table 10.8 to verify that the priorities after synthesization are 0.123, 0.320, and 0.557. Compute the consistency ratio and comment on its acceptability.

8. Use the pairwise comparison matrix for the style criterion as shown in Table 10.8 to verify that the priorities after synthesization are 0.265, 0.656, and 0.080. Compute the consistency ratio and comment on its acceptability.

SELF TEST

9. Dan Joseph was considering entering one of two graduate schools of business to pursue studies for an MBA degree. When asked how he compared the two schools with respect to reputation, he responded that he preferred school A strongly to very strongly to school B.

    a.   Set up the pairwise comparison matrix for this problem.

    b.   Determine the priorities for the two schools relative to this criterion.

10.   An organization was investigating relocating its corporate headquarters to one of three possible cities. The following pairwise comparison matrix shows the president's judgments regarding the desirability for the three cities.

	City 1	City 2	City 3
City 1	1	5	7
City 2	1/5	1	3
City 3	1/7	1/3	1

    a.   Develop a spreadsheet to determine the priorities for the three cities.

    b.   Is the president consistent in terms of the judgments provided? Explain.

11.   The following pairwise comparison matrix contains the judgments of an individual regarding the fairness of two proposed tax programs, A and B.

	A	B
A	1	3
B	1/3	1

    a.   Determine the priorities for the two programs.

    b.   Are the individual's judgments consistent? Explain.

SELF TEST

12.   Asked to compare three soft drinks with respect to flavor, an individual stated that

        A is moderately more preferable than B,

        A is equally to moderately more preferable than C, and

        B is strongly more preferable than C.

    a.   Set up the pairwise comparison matrix for this problem.

    b.   Determine the priorities for the soft drinks with respect to the flavor criterion.

    c.   Compute the consistency ratio. Are the individual's judgments consistent? Explain.

13.   Refer to Problem 12. Suppose that the individual had stated the following judgments instead of those given in Problem 12.

        A is strongly more preferable than C.

        B is equally to moderately more preferable than A.

        B is strongly more preferable than C.

Answer parts (a), (b), and (c) as stated in Problem 12.

14.   The national sales director for Jones Office Supplies needs to determine the best location for the next national sales meeting. Three locations have been proposed: Dallas, San Francisco, and New York. One criterion considered important in the decision is the desirability of the location in terms of restaurants, entertainment, and so on. The national sales manager made the following judgments with regard to this criterion.

        New York is very strongly more preferred than Dallas.

        New York is moderately more preferred than San Francisco.

        San Francisco is moderately to strongly more preferred than Dallas.

a. Set up the pairwise comparison matrix for this problem.
b. Determine the priorities for the desirability criterion.
c. Compute the consistency ratio. Are the sales manager's judgments consistent? Explain.

15. A study comparing four personal computers resulted in the following pairwise comparison matrix for the performance criterion.

	1	2	3	4
1	1	3	7	1/3
2	1/3	1	4	1/4
3	1/7	1/4	1	1/6
4	3	4	6	1

a. Develop a spreadsheet to determine the priorities for the four computers relative to the performance criterion.
b. Compute the consistency ratio. Are the judgments regarding performance consistent? Explain.

SELF TEST

16. An individual was interested in determining which of two stocks to invest in, Central Computing Company (CCC) or Software Research, Inc. (SRI). The criteria thought to be most relevant in making the decision are the potential yield of the stock and the risk associated with the investment. The pairwise comparison matrices for this problem are

Criterion	Yield	Risk
Yield	1	2
Risk	1/2	1

Yield	CCC	SRI
CCC	1	3
SRI	1/3	1

Risk	CCC	SRI
CCC	1	1/2
SRI	2	1

a. Develop a spreadsheet to compute the priorities for each pairwise comparison matrix.
b. Determine the overall priority for the two investments, CCC and SRI. Which investment is preferred based on yield and risk?

17. The vice president of Harling Equipment needs to select a new director of marketing. The two possible candidates are Bill Jacobs and Sue Martin, and the criteria thought to be most relevant in the selection are leadership ability (L), personal skills (P), and administrative skills (A). The following pairwise comparison matrices were obtained.

Criterion	L	P	A
L	1	1/3	1/4
P	3	1	2
A	4	1/2	1

Leadership	Jacobs	Martin
Jacobs	1	4
Martin	1/4	1

Personal	Jacobs	Martin
Jacobs	1	1/3
Martin	3	1

Administrative	Jacobs	Martin
Jacobs	1	2
Martin	1/2	1

a. Compute the priorities for each pairwise comparison matrix.
b. Determine an overall priority for each candidate. Which candidate is preferred?

18. A woman considering the purchase of a custom sound stereo system for her car looked at three different systems (A, B, and C) that varied in terms of price, sound quality, and FM reception. The following pairwise comparison matrices were developed.

Criterion	Price	Sound	Reception
Price	1	3	4
Sound	⅓	1	3
Reception	¼	⅓	1

Price	A	B	C
A	1	4	2
B	¼	1	⅓
C	½	3	1

Sound	A	B	C
A	1	½	¼
B	2	1	⅓
C	4	3	1

Reception	A	B	C
A	1	4	2
B	¼	1	1
C	½	1	1

a. Compute the priorities for each pairwise comparison matrix.
b. Determine an overall priority for each system. Which stereo system is preferred?

Chapter 1   Introduction

Churchman, C. W., R. L. Ackoff, and E. L. Arnoff. *Introduction to Operations Research.* New York: John Wiley & Sons, 1957.

Leon, Linda, Z. Przasnyski, and K. C. Seal. "Spreadsheets and OR/MS Models: An End-User Perspective," *Interfaces* (Mar.–Apr., 1996).

Powell, S. G. "Innovative Approaches to Management Science." *OR/MS Today* (October 1996).

Savage, S. "Weighing the Pros and Cons of Decision Technology and Spreadsheets." *OR/MS Today* (February 1997).

Winston, W. L., "The Teachers' Forum: Management Science with Spreadsheets for MBAs at Indiana University." *Interfaces* (Mar.–Apr., 1996).

Chapters 2 to 6   Linear Programming, Transportation, Assignment, Transshipment and Integer Programming Problems

Bazarra, M. S., J. J. Jarvis, and H. D. Sherali. *Linear Programming and Network Flows.* 2nd ed. New York: John Wiley & Sons, 1990.

Carino, H. F., and C. H. Le Noir, Jr. "Optimizing Wood Procurement in Cabinet Manufacturing." *Interfaces* (March–April 1988): 10–19.

Dantzig, G. B. *Linear Programming and Extensions.* Princeton, N.J.: Princeton University Press, 1963.

Geoffrion, A., and G. Graves. "Better Distribution Planning with Computer Models." *Harvard Business Review* (July–August 1976).

Greenberg, H. J. "How to Analyze the Results of Linear Programs—Part 1: Preliminaries." *Interfaces* 23, no. 4 (Jul–Aug 1993): 56–67.

Greenberg, H. J. "How to Analyze the Results of Linear Programs—Part 2: Price Interpretation." *Interfaces* 23, no. 5 (Sept–Oct 1993): 97–114.

Greenberg, H. J. "How to Analyze the Results of Linear Programs—Part 3: Infeasibility Diagnosis." *Interfaces* 23, no. 6 (Nov–Dec 1993): 120–139.

Nemhauser, G. L., and L. A. Wolsey. *Integer and Combinatorial Optimization.* New York: John Wiley & Sons, 1988.

Sherman, H. D. "Hospital Efficiency Measurement and Evaluation." *Medical Care* 22, no. 10 (October 1984): 922–938.

Winston, W. L. *Operations Research: Applications and Algorithms.* 3rd ed. Belmont, Calif.: Duxbury Press, 1994.

Chapter 7   Waiting Lines

Cox, D. R., and W. L. Smith. *Queues.* New York: John Wiley & Sons, 1965.

Hall, R. *Queuing Methods for Service and Manufacturing.* Englewood Cliffs, N.J.: Prentice-Hall, 1991.

Kao, E. P. C. *An Introduction to Stochastic Processes,* Belmont; Duxbury Press, 1997.

Hillier, F., and G. J. Lieberman. *Introduction to Operations Research.* Book and Disk, 6th ed., McGraw Hill, 1995.

Chapter 8   Simulation

Cochran, J. K., G. T. Mackulak, and Paul A. Savory. "Simulation Project Characteristics in Industrial Settings." *Interfaces* 25, no. 4 (July–August 1995).

Kelton, W. D., R. P. Sandowski, and D. A. Sandowski. *Simulation with ARENA.* Boston: McGraw-Hill, 1998.

Law, A. M., and W. D. Kelton. *Simulation Modeling and Analysis.* 2d ed. New York: McGraw-Hill, 1991.

Naylor, T. H., J. L. Balintfy, D. S. Burdick, and K. Chu. *Computer Simulation Techniques.* New York: John Wiley & Sons, 1968.

Thesen, A., and L. Travis. *Simulation for Decision Making.* St. Paul: West Publishing, 1992.

Winston, W. L., and S. C. Albright. *Practical Management Science.* Belmont, Calif.: Duxbury Press, 1997.

Chapters 9 and 10   Decision Analysis and Multicriteria

Baird, B. F., *Managerial Decisions Under Uncertainty.* New York: John Wiley & Sons, 1989.

Berger, J. O. *Statistical Decision Theory and Bayesian Analysis.* 2d ed. New York: Springer-Verlag, 1985.

Bunn, D. *Applied Decision Analysis.* New York: McGraw-Hill, 1984.

Dyer, J. S. "A Clarification of Remarks on the Analytic Hierarchy Process." *Management Science* 36, no. 3 (March 1990): 274–275.

Dyer, J. S. "Remarks on the Analytic Hierarchy Process." *Management Science* 36, no. 3 (March 1990): 249–258.

French, S. *Decision Theory.* New York: John Wiley & Sons, 1986.

Harker, P. T., and L. G. Vargas. "The Theory of Ratio Scale Estimation: Saaty's Analytic Hierarchy Process." *Management Science* 33, no. 11 (November 1987): 1383–1403.

Harker, P. T., and L. G. Vargas. "Reply to Remarks on the Analytic Hierarchy Process by J. S. Dyer." *Management Science* 36, no. 3 (March 1990): 269–273.

Raiffa, H. *Decision Analysis: Introductory Lectures on Choices Under Uncertainty.* Reading, Mass.: Addison-Wesley, 1968.

Saaty, T. *The Analytic Hierarchy Process.* Pittsburgh, Pa., 1988.

Saaty, T. L. "An Exposition of the AHP in Reply to the Paper Remarks on the Analytic Hierarchy Process." *Management Science* 36, no. 3 (March 1990): 259–268.

Saaty, T. L. "How to Make a Decision: The Analytic Hierarchy Process." *Interfaces* 24, no. 6 (Nov–Dec 1994): 19–43.

Schlaifer, R. *Analysis of Decisions under Uncertainty.* New York: McGraw-Hill, 1969.

Weiss, E. N., and V. R. Rao. "AHP Design Issues for Large-Scale Systems." *Decision Sciences* 18 (1987): 43–61.

Winkler, R. L. "Decision Modeling and Rational Choice: AHP and Utility Theory." *Management Science* 36, no. 3 (March 1990): 247–248.

Zahedi, F. "Analytic Hierarchy Process—A Survey of the Method and its Applications." *Interfaces* 16, no. 4 (August 1986): 96–108.

Chapter 1

2. Methodological developments based on research and advances in computer technology

4. The problem is large, complex, important, new, and repetitive

6. Iconic—scale model of a new building
   Analog—barometer
   Mathematical—inventory cost equation

8. **a.** Max $10x + 5y$
   s.t.
   $$5x + 2y \leq 40$$
   $$x \geq 0, y \geq 0$$
   b. Controllable inputs: x and y
   Uncontrollable inputs: profit, labor hours per unit, and total labor hours available
   d. $x = 0, y = 20$, profit $= \$100$

10. If $a = 3$, $x = 13\frac{1}{3}$ and profit $= \$133$
    If $a = 4$, $x = 10$ and profit $= \$100$
    If $a = 5$, $x = 8$ and profit $= \$80$
    If $a = 6$, $x = 6\frac{2}{3}$ and profit $= \$67$
    Since a is unknown, the actual values of x and profit are not known with certainty.

12. A deterministic model with d = distance, m = miles per gallon, and c = cost per gallon, where total cost = $(2d/m)c$

14. Quicker to formulate, easier to solve, and/or more easily understood

16. **b.** 100

18. **b.** 4706

20. **b.** 30

22. **a.** $s_j = s_{j-1} + x_j - d_j$
    or $s_j - s_{j-1} - x_j + d_j = 0$
    b. $x_j \leq c_j$
    c. $s_j \geq I_j$

Chapter 2

8. $x_1 = 12/7, x_2 = 15/7$, value $= 69/7$

10. **a.** $x_1 = 3, x_2 = 1.5$, value $= 13.5$
    b. $x_1 = 0, x_2 = 3$, value $= 18$
    c. Four extreme points: (0, 0), (4, 0), (3, 1.5), and (0, 3)

12. **a.** $x_1 = 3, x_2 = 1$, value $= 5$
    b. 14, 0, 10.5, 0
    c. $x_1 = 6, x_2 = 2$, value $= 34$

14. **a.** $S = 300, D = 400$, profit $= \$10,560$
    b. $S = 708, D = 0$, profit $= \$14,160$
    c. Sewing constraint is redundant; optimal solution does not change

16. **a.** Max $5R + 8C$
    s.t.
    $$1R + \tfrac{3}{2}C \leq 900$$
    $$\tfrac{1}{2}R + \tfrac{1}{3}C \leq 300$$
    $$\tfrac{1}{8}R + \tfrac{1}{4}C \leq 100$$
    $$R, C \geq 0$$
    b. $R = 500, C = 150$
    c. $\$3700$
    d. 725, 300, 100
    e. 175, 0, 0

18. **a.** Min $A + 2.5B$
    s.t.
    $$2A + 1.5B \geq 1.7$$
    $$2A + 3B \leq 2.8$$
    $$4A + 3B \leq 3.6$$
    $$A + B = 1$$
    $$A, B \geq 0$$
    b. $A = 0.6, B = 0.4$, value $= \$0.022$
    c. 0.1, 0.4, 0, 0
    d. $\$0.176$

20. **a.** $S = 0, M = 15,000$, total risk $= 45,000$
    b. $S = 9,000, M = 7,500$, total risk $= 94,500$
    c. $S = 4,000, M = 10,000$, total risk $= 70,000$
    d. $S = 3,636, M = 10,417$, total risk $= 60,341$

22. **a.** $= B8*B15+C8*C15$
    b. Cutting and sewing: $=B5*B15+C5*C15$
    Finishing: $=B6*B15+C6*C15$
    Package and shipping: $=B7*B15+C7*C15$
    c. $=D5; =D6; =D7$
    d. After rounding: Regular = 500, Catcher's = 150, Profit = $3700

24. **a.** Max $0.06B + 0.10S$
    s.t.
    $$B \geq 3$$
    $$0.06B + 0.10S \geq 0.075$$
    $$B + S = 1$$
    $$B, S \geq 0$$
    b. $B = 0.3, S = 0.7$, value $= 0.088$ or 8.8%

26. a. Max $1W + 1.25M$
   s.t.
$$5W + 7M \leq 4480$$
$$3W + 1M \leq 2080$$
$$2W + 2M \leq 1600$$
$$W, M \geq 0$$
b. $W = 560$, $M = 240$, value $= 860$

28. a. Max $40X + 50Y$
   s.t.
$$3X + 5Y \leq 600$$
$$X \geq 25$$
$$Y \geq 25$$
$$X, Y \geq 0$$
b. $X = 158.33$, $Y = 25$, profit $= \$7,583$
c. $X = 75$, $Y = 75$, profit $= \$6,750$

30. a. Min $2P_1 + 3P_2$
   s.t.
$$P_1 \geq 125$$
$$P_1 + P_2 \geq 350$$
$$2P_1 + P_2 \leq 600$$
$$P_1, P_2 \geq 0$$
b. $P_1 = 250$, $P_2 = 100$, total cost $= \$800$
c. Surplus of 125 gallons of product 1

32. a. Max $1R + 1.5D$
   s.t.
$$1R + 1D \leq 150$$
$$1/4R + 1/2D \leq 50$$
$$R \geq 50$$
$$D \geq 25$$
$$R, D \geq 0$$
b. $R = 100$, $D = 50$, profit $= \$175$

34. Unbounded

36. b. Unbounded
c. $x_1 = 3$, $x_2 = 0$, value $= 3$
d. No

38. current $= 225,000$, new $= 50,000$, sales $= \$8,750$

40. a. Max $1.2R + 1N$
   s.t.
$$R + N \leq 80$$
$$25R + 8N \geq 800$$
$$N \geq 0.60R$$
b. $R = 50$, $N = 30$, customers contacted $= 90$

Chapter 3

2. Shadow price $= 4.375$

4. 1.5, 0

6. 0.333, 0.333, 0

8. a. $x_1 = 9$, $x_2 = 4$
b. 0, 0.0769

10. a. $x_1 = 0$, $x_2 = 10$, value $= 100$
b. No change

12. a. 4 to 12 and 3.33 to 10
c. 725 to No Upper Limit; 133.33 to 400; 75 to 135
d. \$560

14. a. More than \$7.00
b. More than \$3.50
c. None

16. a. $P_1 = 30$, $P_2 = 25$; \$55
b. 0.5 to No Upper Limit
   0.0 to 2
c. 0.50; 0.50; 0.0
d. No change
e.

Min RHS	Max RHS
70	No Upper Limit
0	40
No Lower Limit	25

18. a. $x_1 = 0$, $x_2 = 25$, $x_3 = 125$, $x_4 = 0$, value $= 525$
b. 1 and 3
c. 2; 425 hours
d. Yes

20. a. $x_1 = 7.30$, $x_2 = 0$, $x_3 = 1.89$, value $= 139.73$
b. Two and three
c. 0, 3.41, and 4.43
d. Decrease the right-hand side of constraint 3 from 20 to 19

22. a. All Pro: 1000; College: 200; High School: 0
b. Sewing and minimum All Pro production require-ment
c. 4000 minutes of unused cutting and dyeing time; all the sewing time is being used; 5200 minutes of unused inspection and packaging time; only the minimum number of All Pro models is being produced.
d. No Lower Limit to 5
   5 to No Upper Limit
   No Lower Limit to 4

24. a. $P_1 = 25$, $P_2 = 0$, $P_3 = 25$, profit $= \$1,250$
b. Machine 1: 31.25, machine 2: 37.50
c. \$12.50
d. $P_1 = 24$, $P_2 = 8$, $P_3 = 16$, profit $= \$1,440$

26. a. 333.3, 0, 833.3, 2500; risk $= 14,666.7$, return $= 18,000$ (9%)
b. 1000, 0, 0, 2500; risk $= 18,000$, return $= 22,000$ (11%)
c. \$4,000

28. b.

	San Diego	Tampa
Regular	20,000	18,000
Stiff	75,000	0

  c. Yes
  d. No effect

30. a. Relevant
  b. $W = 10,000$, $R = 6,000$, $F = 4,000$, profit = $29,000
  c. $2.90 is the maximum premium (over the normal price of $1.00) that LaJolla Beverage Products should be willing to pay to obtain one additional gallon of wine.
  d. No
  e. Requiring 50% plus one gallon of white wine would reduce profit by $2.40.
  f. The problem would have to be resolved if management allows the amount of fruit juice to exceed 20% by one gallon.

32. a. $B = 4,181$, $J = 41,806$, $L = 30,000$
  c. Total cost will decrease by $0.2210

Chapter 4

2. a. $P_1 = 77.89$, $P_2 = 63.16$, $3284.21
  b. Department A $15.79; department B $47.37
  c. $P_1 = 87.21$, $P_2 = 65.12$, $3341.34
    Department A 10 hours; department B 3.2 hours

4. a. $B_1 = 500$, $B_2 = 300$, $B_3 = 200$, $550
  b. $0.55
  c. Aroma 75; taste 84.4
  d. $0.60

6. 50 units of product 1; 0 units of product 2; 300 hours department A; 600 hours department B

8. Schedule 19 officers as follows:
    3 begin at 8:00 A.M.; 3 begin at noon; 7 begin at 4:00 P.M.; 4 begin at midnight, 2 begin at 4:00 A.M.

10.

Product	New Line	Old Line
1	500	0
2	300	400

  Cost = $3850

12. a. Purchase 5000 bases
  b. Same solution with objective function increased by $80
  c. Yes; total cost = $24,293.33; $FCP = 1333$ and $FCM = 1667$

14. b.

Quarter	Production	Ending Inventory
1	4000	2100
2	3000	1100
3	2000	100
4	1900	500

16. x_i = number of 10-inch rolls processed by cutting alternative i
  a. $x_1 = 0$, $x_2 = 125$, $x_3 = 500$, $x_4 = 1500$, $x_5 = 0$, $x_6 = 0$, $x_7 = 0$; 2125 rolls with waste of 750 inches
  b. 2500 rolls with no waste; however, 1½-inch size is overproduced by 3000 units

18. a. 5 Super, 2 Regular, and 3 Econo-Tankers
  b. Optimal solution: 7⅓ Super Tankers, Round up to 8

20. Produce 10,250 units in March, 10,250 units in April, and 12,000 units in May

22. $TW100 = 48$, $TW200 = 96$, $456
    Assembler times: 480, 480, and 456

24. Investment strategy: 45.8% of A and 100% of B
    Objective function = $4340.40
    Savings/Loan Schedule

	Period			
	1	2	3	4
Savings	242.11	—	—	341.04
Funds from loan	—	200.00	127.58	—

26. a. Solution does not indicate that General Hospital is relatively inefficient.
  b. General Hospital

28. c. No; E = 1 indicates that the amount of resources used by Hospital E are required to produce the outputs of Hospital E.
  d. Hospital E is the only hospital in the composite.

Chapter 5

2. a. Min $14x_{11} + 9x_{12} + 7x_{13} + 8x_{21} + 10x_{22} + 5x_{23}$
    s.t.

$$
\begin{aligned}
x_{11} + x_{12} + x_{13} & & & \leq 30 \\
& x_{21} + x_{22} + x_{23} & & \leq 20 \\
x_{11} & + x_{21} & & = 25 \\
x_{12} & + x_{22} & & = 15 \\
x_{13} & + x_{23} & & = 10
\end{aligned}
$$

$x_{11}, x_{12}, x_{13}, x_{21}, x_{22}, x_{23} \geq 0$
  b. $x_{11} = 5$, $x_{12} = 15$, $x_{13} = 10$, $x_{21} = 20$

4. b. $x_{12} = 300$, $x_{21} = 200$, $x_{22} = 100$, $x_{23} = 200$, $x_{33} = 100$
Cost = $10,400

6. b.
Seattle–Denver	4000;	Seattle–Los Angeles	5000;
Columbus–Mobile	4000;	New York–Pittsburgh	3000;
New York–Mobile	1000;	New York–Los Angeles	1000;
New York–Washington	3000		

Cost = $150,000

c.
Seattle–Denver	4000;	Seattle–Los Angeles	5000;
Columbus–Mobile	5000;	New York–Pittsburgh	4000;
New York–Los Angeles	1000;	New York–Washington	3000

Cost actually decreases by $9,000

8. Clifton Springs–D_2 4000;   Clifton Springs–D_4 1000;
Danville–D_1 2000;   Danville–D_4 1000;
Customer 2 has a shortfall of 1000; customer 3's demand is not satisfied

10. 1–A 300; 1–C 1200; 2–A 1200; 3–A 500; 3–B 500

12. b. Jackson–2, Ellis–1, Smith–3 Total completion time = 64

14. b. Bostock–Southwest, Miller–Northwest

16.
Toys	Location 2
Auto Parts	Location 4
Housewares	Location 3
Videos	Location 1
Profit	61
Shoes	Unassigned

18. 1-B, 2-C, 3-A, 4-D; 74 hours required

20. A to MS, B to Ph.D., C to MBA, D to undergrad
Maximum total rating = 13.3

22. a.

	Division				
Supplier	1	2	3	4	5
1	614	603	865	532	720
2	660	639	830	553	648
3	534	702	775	511	684
4	680	693	850	581	693
5	590	693	900	595	657
6	630	630	930	553	747

b. Optimal Solution:

Supplier 1–Division 2	$ 603
Supplier 2–Division 5	648
Supplier 3–Division 3	775
Supplier 5–Division 1	590
Supplier 6–Division 4	553
Total	$3169

24. c. $x_{14} = 320$, $x_{25} = 600$, $x_{47} = 300$, $x_{49} = 20$, $x_{56} = 300$, $x_{58} = 300$, $x_{39} = 380$
Cost = $11,220

26. c. Note: Augusta: 1, Tupper Lake: 2, Albany: 3, Portsmouth: 4, Boston: 5, New York: 6, Philadelphia: 7

Variable	Value	Variable	Value
x_{13}	50	x_{36}	0
x_{14}	250	x_{37}	150
x_{23}	100	x_{45}	150
x_{24}	0	x_{46}	100
x_{35}	0	x_{47}	0

Objective function = 4300

28.

Optimal Solution	Units Shipped	Cost
Muncie–Cincinnati	1	6
Cincinnati–Concord	3	84
Brazil–Louisville	6	18
Louisville–Macon	2	88
Louisville–Greenwood	4	136
Xenia–Cincinnati	5	15
Cincinnati–Chatham	3	72
	Total	419

Two rail cars must be held at Muncie until a buyer is found

32. b. Regular-month 1: 275; overtime—month 1: 25; inventory—end of month 1: 150
Regular-month 2: 200; overtime—month 2: 50; inventory—end of month 2: 150
Regular-month 3: 100; overtime—month 3: 50; inventory—end of month 3: 0
Cost: $46,750
c. There are 75 units of unused overtime capacity in month 1

Chapter 6

2. b. $x_1 = 1.43$, $x_2 = 4.29$; value = 41.47
Rounded: $x_1 = 1$, $x_2 = 4$; value = 37
c. $x_1 = 0$, $x_2 = 5$, value = 40
Not the same

4. a. $x_1 = 3.67$, $x_2 = 0$, value = 36.7
Rounded: $x_1 = 3$, $x_2 = 0$; value = 30
Lower bound = 30; upper bound = 36.7

b. $x_1 = 3, x_2 = 2$; value = 36

c. Alternative optimal solutions: $x_1 = 0, x_2 = 5$
$$x_1 = 2, x_2 = 4$$

6. b. $x_1 = 1.96, x_2 = 5.48$; value = 7.44
Rounded: $x_1 = 1.96, x_2 = 5$; value = 6.96
Lower bound = 6.96; upper bound = 7.44

c. $x_1 = 1.29, x_2 = 6$; value = 7.29

8. a. $x_3 = 1, x_4 = 1, x_6 = 1$; value = 17,500

b. Add $x_1 + x_2 \leq 1$

c. Add $x_3 - x_4 = 0$

10. b. Choose locations B and E

12. a. $P \leq 15 + 15y_1$
$D \leq 15 + 15y_2$
$J \leq 15 + 15y_3$
$Y_P + Y_D + Y_J \leq 1$

b. $P = 15, D = 15, J = 30$
$Y_P = 0, Y_D = 0, Y_J = 1$; value = 50

14. b. Modernize plants 1 and 3 or plants 4 and 5

d. Modernize plants 1 and 3

16. b. Use all part-time employees
Bring on as follows: 9:00 A.M.–6, 11:00 A.M.–8, 1:00 P.M.–1, 3:00 P.M.–6
Cost = $672

c. Same as in part (b)

d. New solution is to bring on 1 full-time employee at 9:00 A.M., 4 more at 11:00 A.M., and part-time employees as follows:
9:00 A.M.–5, 1:00 P.M.–5, and 3:00 P.M.–2

18. a. New objective function: Min $25x_1 + 40x_2 + 40x_3 + 40x_4 + 25x_5$

b. $x_4 = x_5 = 1$; modernize the Ohio and California plants

c. Add the constraint $x_2 + x_3 = 1$

d. $x_1 = x_3 = 1$

20. $x_1 + x_2 + x_3 = 3y_1 + 5y_2 + 7y_3$
$y_1 + y_2 + y_3 = 1$

Chapter 7

2. a. 0.4512

b. 0.6988

c. 0.3012

4. 0.3333, 0.2222, 0.1481, 0.0988, 0.1976

6. a. 0.3333

b. 1.3333

c. 0.1111 days (53.3 minutes)

d. 0.6667

8. 0.20, 3.2, 4, 3.2, 4, 0.80
Slightly poorer service

10. a. New: 0.3333, 1.3333, 2, 0.6667, 1, 0.6667
Experienced: 0.50, 0.50, 1, 0.25, 0.50, 0.50

b. New $74; experienced $50; hire experienced

12. a. 0.25, 2.25, 3, 0.15 hours, 0.20 hours, 0.75

b. The service needs improvement

14. a. 0.1667

b. 5

c. 0.4167 hours (25 minutes)

d. 0.8333

e. No; the service was poor since W_q = 25 minutes

16. a. 0.50

b. 0.50

c. 0.10 hours (6 minutes)

d. 0.20 hours (12 minutes)

e. Yes, W_q = 6 minutes is most likely acceptable for a marina.

18. a. 0.5385

b. 0.0593

c. 0.0099 hours (0.59 minutes)

d. 0.1099 hours (6.59 minutes)

e. 0.1385

20. a. 0.2360, 0.1771, 1.5771, 0.0126 hours, 0.1126 hours

b. P(wait) = 0.2024 for a 3-channel system

22.

Characteristic		A	B	C
a.	P_0	0.2000	0.5000	0.4286
b.	L_q	3.2000	0.5000	0.1524
c.	L	4.0000	1.0000	0.9524
d.	W_q	0.1333	0.0208	0.0063
e.	W	0.1667	0.0417	0.0397
f.	P_w	0.8000	0.5000	0.2286

The two-channel System C provides the best service.

24. a. 0.0466, 0.05

b. 1.4

c. 11:00 A.M.

26. a. 0.2668, 10 minutes, 0.6667

b. 0.0667, 7 minutes, 0.4669

c. $25.33; $33.34; one-channel

28. a. 10, 9.6

b. Design A with $\mu = 10$

c. 0.05, 0.01

d. A: 0.5, 0.3125, 0.8125, 0.0625, 0.1625, 0.5
B: 0.4792, 0.2857, 0.8065, 0.0571, 0.1613, 0.5208

e. Design B has slightly less waiting time

30. a. 0.1460, 0.3066, 0.3220, 0.2254

b. 0.2254

c. 1.6267

d. 4; 0.1499

32. a. 31.03%
  b. 27.59%
  c. 0.2759, 0.1092, 0.0351
  d. 3, 10.92%

34. a. 0.4790
  b. 0.3110
  c. 0.8321
  d. 2.9854 minutes
  e. 7.9854 minutes
  f. 95.8 minutes; 35.8 minutes
  g. Yes, assistants spend too much time waiting at the copier

Chapter 8

2. a. Profit $= (50 - c)x - 30,000$
  b. 6000, $-22,200$, 41,400
  c. Helps estimate probability of loss

4. a. 0.00–0.08, 0.08–0.20, 0.20–0.48, 0.48–0.72, 0.72–0.86, 0.86–0.96, 0.96–1.00
  b. 2, 5, 2, 3, 3, 2, 4, 2, 1, 1, 2
  c. 24 units

6. a. 0.00–0.83, 0.83–0.89, 0.89–0.94, 0.94–0.96, 0.96–0.98, 0.98–0.99, 0.99–1.00
  b. 4 claims paid, total $= \$22,000$

8. a. Atlanta wins each game if random number is in interval 0.00–0.60, 0.00–0.55, 0.00–0.48, 0.00–0.45, 0.00–0.48, 0.00–0.55, 0.00–0.50.
  b. Atlanta wins games 1, 2, 4, and 6
  Atlanta wins series 4 to 2
  c. Repeat many times; record % of Atlanta wins

10. a. 0.00–0.40 for Yes; 0.40–1.00 for No
  If Yes, 0.00–0.30, 0.30–0.60, 0.60–1.00
  If No, 0.00–0.50, 0.50–0.90, 0.90–1.00
  b. Uncertain, definitely yes, definitely no
  c. Repeat many times; record % of definitely yes

12. a. \$7, \$3, \$12
  b. Purchase: 0.00–0.25, 0.25–0.70, 0.70–1.00
  Labor: 0.00–0.10, 0.10–0.35, 0.35–0.70, 0.70–1.00
  Transportation: 0.00–0.75, 0.75–1.00
  c. \$5
  d. \$7
  e. Provide probability profit less than \$5/unit

14. a. Most simulations between \$5,500 and \$6,500
  b. Most simulations between 0.24 and 0.30
  c. Project is too risky

16. Most simulations between 6 and 16 still working; 11 is the expected number.

18. a. Most simulations between 0.60 and 0.65
  b. \$775,000 roughly 0.82; \$785,000 roughly 0.88
  Select \$775,000

20. a. Results vary with each simulation run;
  Approximate results: 50,000 provided \$230,000
      60,000 provided \$190,000
      70,000 less than \$100,000
  b. Recommend 50,000 units
  c. Roughly 0.75

22. a. Very poor operation; some customers wait 30 minutes or more.
  b. Average wait is from 0.10 to 0.13 minutes; 2 ATMs do a good job

24. a. Both should be approximately four minutes.
  b. Approximately 0.8 minutes; other simulations may vary slightly
  c. Most simulations between 150 and 170; roughly 30% to 35% wait

Chapter 9

2. a. Optimistic: d_1
  Conservative: d_3
  Minimax regret: d_3
  c. Optimistic: d_1
  Conservative: d_2 or d_3
  Minimax regret: d_2

4. Optimistic: d_2
  Conservative: d_1
  Minimax regret: d_2

6. a. d_1 **b.** d_4

8. If $P(s_1) < .25$, d_2
  If $P(s_1) = .25$, d_1 or d_2
  If $P(s_1) > .25$ d_1

10. a. If $p > 0.44$, location A; if $p < 0.44$, location C
  b. Location A because $0.65 > 0.44$

12. a. If s_1, then d_1; if s_2, then d_1 or d_2; if s_3, then d_2
  b. 192.5
  c. d_1; 182.5
  d. 10

14. b. If favorable, d_2
  If unfavorable, d_1
  EV $= 292$

16. c. d_2, 500
  d. 195
  e. If weak, then d_2; if average, then d_2; if strong, then d_3
  f. 41.8
  g. 21%

18. b. d_1, 1250
  c. 1700
  d. If N, d_1
  If U, d_2; 1666

20. a. d_1, 2000
  b. 200
  c. d_1, 2000;
   don't call

22. 0.1915, 0.2381, 0.5714

24. a. 0.695, 0.215, 0.090
   0.98, 0.02
   0.79, 0.21
   0.00, 1.00
  c. If C, Expressway
   If O, Expressway
   If R, Queen City
   26.6 minutes

Chapter 10

2. 178, 184, 151,
  Marysville

4. 170, 168, 190, 183
  Handover College

6. a. 220 Bowrider (194)
  b. 240 Sundancer (144)

8. CR = 0.028, acceptable

10. a. 0.724, 0.193, 0.083
  b. CR = 0.057, yes

12. a.

	A	B	C
A	1	3	2
B	1/3	1	5
C	1/2	1/5	1

  b. 0.503, 0.348, 0.148
  c. CR = 0.415, no

14. a.

	D	S	N
D	1	1/4	1/7
S	4	1	1/3
N	7	3	1

  b. 0.080, 0.265, 0.656
  c. Since CR = 0.028, yes

16. a. Criterion: 0.667, 0.033
   Yield: 0.750, 0.250
   Risk: 0.333, 0.667
  b. CCC, 0.611; SRI, 0.389
   CCC is preferred

18. a. Criterion: 0.608, 0.272, 0.120
   Price: 0.557, 0.123, 0.320
   Sound: 0.137, 0.239, 0.623
   Reception: 0.579, 0.187, 0.046
  b. 0.446, 0.162, 0.392
   System A is preferred

Chapter 1

4. A quantitative approach may be considered for the following reasons: the problem is large and complex; the problem is very important; the problem is new and no experience exists; the problem is repetitive

8. a. Max $10x + 5y$
      s.t. $5x + 2y \leq 40$
                $x \geq 0, y \geq 0$
   b. Controllable inputs: x and y
      Uncontrollable inputs: profit (10, 5), labor hours (5, 2), and labor hour availability (40)
   d. $x = 0, y = 20$; profit $= \$100$
      (Solution by trial-and-error)

15. a. $TC = 1000 + 30x$
    b. $P = 40x - (1000 + 30x) = 10x - 1000$
    c. Break even when $P = 0$
       Thus $10x - 1000 = 0$
       $$10x = 1000$$
       $$x = 100$$

Chapter 2

1. Parts (a), (b), and (e) are acceptable linear programming relationships.
   Part (c) is not acceptable because of $-2x_2^2$.
   Part (d) is not acceptable because of $3\sqrt{x_1}$.
   Part (f) is not acceptable because of $1x_1x_2$.
   Parts (c), (d), and (f) could not be found in a linear programming model because they have the above nonlinear terms.

2. a.

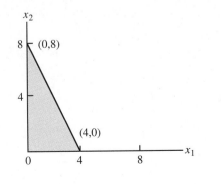

b.

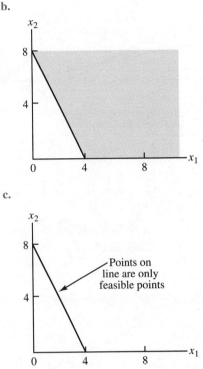

c.

Points on line are only feasible points

5. Slope of objective function: $-c_1/c_2$
   For $7x_1 + 10x_2$, slope $= -7/10$
   For $6x_1 + 4x_2$,   slope $= -6/4 = -3/2$
   For $-4x_1 + 7x_2$, slope $= 4/7$

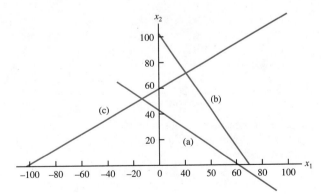

6.

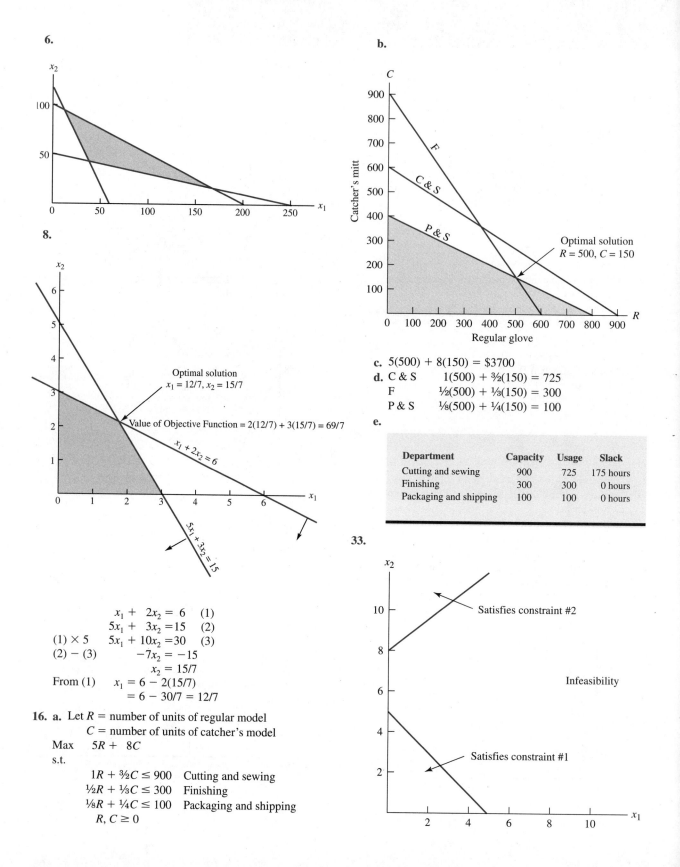

8.

$$x_1 + 2x_2 = 6 \quad (1)$$
$$5x_1 + 3x_2 = 15 \quad (2)$$
$$(1) \times 5 \quad 5x_1 + 10x_2 = 30 \quad (3)$$
$$(2) - (3) \quad -7x_2 = -15$$
$$x_2 = 15/7$$
From (1) $x_1 = 6 - 2(15/7)$
$$= 6 - 30/7 = 12/7$$

16. a. Let R = number of units of regular model
    C = number of units of catcher's model

Max $5R + 8C$
s.t.

$1R + \frac{3}{2}C \le 900$ Cutting and sewing
$\frac{1}{2}R + \frac{1}{3}C \le 300$ Finishing
$\frac{1}{8}R + \frac{1}{4}C \le 100$ Packaging and shipping
    $R, C \ge 0$

b.

c. $5(500) + 8(150) = \$3700$

d. C & S $1(500) + \frac{3}{2}(150) = 725$
    F $\frac{1}{2}(500) + \frac{1}{3}(150) = 300$
    P & S $\frac{1}{8}(500) + \frac{1}{4}(150) = 100$

e.

Department	Capacity	Usage	Slack
Cutting and sewing	900	725	175 hours
Finishing	300	300	0 hours
Packaging and shipping	100	100	0 hours

33.

34.

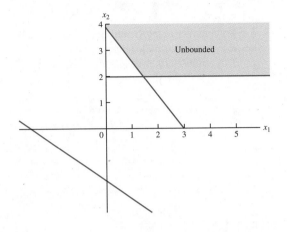

Chapter 3

3. a.

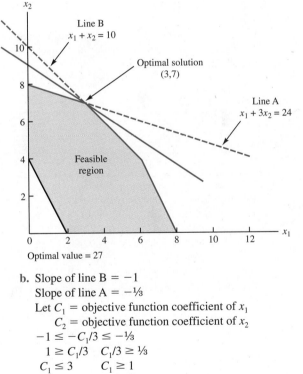

Optimal value = 27

b. Slope of line B = −1
Slope of line A = −⅓
Let C_1 = objective function coefficient of x_1
   C_2 = objective function coefficient of x_2
$-1 \leq -C_1/3 \leq -\frac{1}{3}$
$1 \geq C_1/3 \quad C_1/3 \geq \frac{1}{3}$
$C_1 \leq 3 \quad\quad C_1 \geq 1$
Range: $1 \leq C_1 \leq 3$

c. $-1 \leq -2/C_2 \leq -\frac{1}{3}$
$1 \geq 2/C_2 \quad 2/C_2 \geq \frac{1}{3}$
$C_2 \geq 2 \quad\quad C_2 \leq 6$
Range: $2 \leq C_2 \leq 6$

d. Since this change leaves C_1 in its range of optimality, the same solution ($x_1 = 3$, $x_2 = 7$) is optimal

e. This change moves C_2 outside its range of optimality; the new optimal solution is shown below:

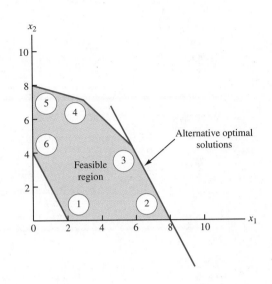

Alternative optimal solutions exist; extreme points 2 and 3 and all points on the line segment between them are optimal

4. By making a small increase in the right-hand side of constraint 1 and resolving, we find a shadow price of 1.5 for the constraint; thus, the objective function will improve at the rate of 1.5 per unit increase in the right-hand side. Since constraint 2 is not binding, its shadow price is zero. To determine the range over which these shadow prices are applicable, you must obtain the range of feasibility.

11. a. Regular glove = 500; Catcher's mitt = 150;
value = 3700

b. The finishing, packaging, and shipping constraints are binding; there is no slack

c. Cutting and sewing = 0
Finishing = 3
Packaging and shipping = 28
Additional finishing time is worth $3 per unit, and additional packaging and shipping time is worth $28 per unit

d. In the packaging and shipping department, each additional hour is worth $28

12. a. 4 to 12
3.33 to 10

b. As long as the profit contribution for the regular glove is between $4.00 and $12.00, the current solution is optimal. As long as the profit contribution for the catcher's mitt stays between $3.33 and $10.00, the current solution is optimal. The optimal solution is not sensitive to small changes in the profit contributions for the gloves.

c. The shadow prices for the resources are applicable over the following ranges.

Constraint	Range of Feasibility
Cutting and sewing	725 to No Upper Limit
Finishing	133.33 to 400
Packaging and shipping	75 to 135

d. Amount of increase = (28)(20) = $560

16. a. $P_1 = 30$, $P_2 = 25$, minimum production cost = $55
    b.

Variable	Range of Optimality
P_1	0.5 to No Upper Limit
P_2	0.0 to 2

c. 0.50; 0.50; 0.0
d.

Constraint	Range of Feasibility
Raw material	70 to No Upper Limit
Product 1 minimum	0.0 to 40.0
Product 2 minimum	No Lower Limit to 25.0

18. a. $x_1 = 0$; $x_2 = 25$; $x_3 = 125$; $x_4 = 0$
    Value of solution = 525.0
    b. The constraints on machine 1 and machine 3 hours are binding
    c. Machine 2 has 425 hours of excess capacity
    d. Yes, the allowable increase is only 0.05

19. a.

Variable	Range of Optimality
x_1	No Lower Limit to 4.05
x_2	5.923 to 9
x_3	2 to 12
x_4	No Lower Limit to 4.5

b.

Constraint	Range of Feasibility
Machine A hours	133.33 to 800
Machine B hours	275 to No Upper limit
Machine C hours	137.5 to 825

c. An increase of 300 exceeds the allowable increase of 250; the problem will have to be resolved.

Chapter 4

1. Media Selection
   a. Let T = number of television spot advertisements
      R = number of radio advertisements
      N = number of newspaper advertisements

Max $100{,}000T + 18{,}000R + 40{,}000N$
s.t.

$$2{,}000T + 300R + 600N \le 18{,}200 \quad \text{Budget}$$
$$R \le .5(T + R + N) \quad \text{Max 50\% radio}$$
$$T \ge .1(T + R + N) \quad \text{Min 10\% TV}$$
$$T \le 10 \quad \text{Max TV}$$
$$R \le 20 \quad \text{Max radio}$$
$$N \le 10 \quad \text{Max news}$$
$$T, R, N \ge 0$$

	Budget $
Solution: $T = 4$	$8,000
$R = 14$	4,200
$N = 10$	6,000
	$18,200 Audience = 1,052,000.

The spreadsheet formulation and solution are shown in Figure S4.1.

9. Portfolio Selection
   a. Let each decision variable, A, P, M, H and G, represent the fraction or proportion of the total investment placed in each investment alternative.

Max $.073A + .103P + .064M + .075H + 0.45G$
s.t.

$$A + P + M + H + G = 1$$
$$A + P \le .5 \ (A + P + M + H)$$
$$M + H \le .5 \ (A + P + M + H)$$
$$P \le .6 \ (A + P)$$
$$G \ge .25 \ (M + H)$$
$$A, P, M, H, G \ge 0$$

Solution: Objective function = 0.079
Atlantic Oil   = 0.178
Pacific Oil   = 0.267
Midwest Steel   = 0.000
Huber Steel   = 0.444
Government Bonds = 0.111

The spreadsheet formulation and solution are shown in Figure S4.9.

b. For a total investment of $100,000 we show
Atlantic Oil   = $17,800
Pacific Oil   = 26,700
Midwest Steel   =   0.000
Huber Steel   = 44,400
Government Bonds = 11,100
Total $100,000

c. Total earnings = $100,000 (.079) = $7,900
d. Marginal rate of return is .079

	SPREADSHEET FORMULATION AND SOLUTION FOR THE WESTCHESTER PROBLEM
Figure S4.1	

	A	B	C	D	E	F	G	H	I
1	Westchester Chamber of Commerce								
2									
3			Media						
4		Television	Radio	Newspaper					
5	Audience per Ad	100000	18000	40000		Budget	18200		
6	Cost per Ad	2000	300	600		Max Radio Ads	50%		
7	Availability	10	20	10		Min TV Ads.	10%		
8									
9									
10	Model								
11									
12		Television	Radio	Newspaper					
13	Ads Placed	4	14	10					
14									
15	Max Audience	1052000							
16									
17	Constraints	LHS		RHS					
18	Budget	18200	<=	18200					
19	Max 50% Radio	14	<=	14					
20	Min 10% TV	4	>=	2.8					
21									

SPREADSHEET WESTCHESTER

	SPREADSHEET FORMULATION AND SOLUTION FOR THE WELTE MUTUAL FUNDS PROBLEM
Figure S4.9	

	A	B	C	D	E	F	G
1	**Welte Mutual Funds**						
2							
3							
4	Investment	Projected Rate of Return					
5	Atlantic Oil	0.073		Available Funds		1	
6	Pacific Oil	0.103		Oil Max		50%	
7	Midwest Steel	0.064		Steel Max		50%	
8	Huber Steel	0.075		Pacific Oil Max		0.6	
9	Gov't Bonds	0.045		Gov't Bonds Min		0.25	
10							
11	**Model**						
12							
13	Investment	Amount Invested		Constraints	LHS		RHS
14	Atlantic Oil	0.178		Avl. Funds	1	=	1
15	Pacific Oil	0.267		Oil Max	0.44444	<=	0.44444
16	Midwest Steel	0.000		Steel Max	0.44444	<=	0.44444
17	Huber Steel	0.444		Pacific Oil	0.26667	<=	0.26667
18	Gov't Bonds	0.111		Gov't Bonds	0.11111	>=	0.11111
19							
20	Max Total Return	0.079					

SPREADSHEET WELTE

12. Make or Buy

a. The only change is in the objective function with the price per unit for the number of bases purchased (BP) lowered from 0.60 to 0.55. The solution for the new model provides an objective function value of $24,276.67, which is an overall savings of $166.66 compared to the previous solution. Janders will now purchase all 5000 bases from the supplier. In addition, Janders will increase the manufacturing of financial cartridges from 667 to 2333 units to take advantage of the manufacturing capacity freed by the fact that the company no longer needs to manufacture bases.

The spreadsheet formulation and solution are shown in Figure S4.12.

b. By referring to the sensitivity report in Figure 4.15, we can answer the question without modifying and re-solving the original problem. The range of optimality for the objective function coefficient for TTP is $0.685 to No Upper Limit. Since the price increase to $0.82 is within the range, there will be no change in the manufacturing and purchasing plan. However, Janders purchases 2000 Technician tops. Thus, the price increase from $0.78 to $0.82 per unit will add $0.04(2000) = $80 to the total cost

c. The only change in the original problem is to reduce the objective function coefficient for overtime (OT) premium from $9 to $2 per hour. This change enables Janders to use all 50 hours of overtime for manufac-

**SPREADSHEET
JANDERS**

Figure S4.12 SPREADSHEET FORMULATION AND SOLUTION FOR THE JANDERS COMPANY PROBLEM

	A	B	C	D	E	F	G
1	**Janders Make-or-Buy**						
2							
3			**Cost per Unit**	**Mfg. Time**			
4	**Component**	Make	Buy	**in Minutes**		**Calculator**	**Demand**
5	Base	$0.50	$0.55	1.0		Financial	3000
6	Fin. Cart.	$3.75	$4.00	3.0		Technician	2000
7	Tech. Cart.	$3.30	$3.90	2.5			
8	Fin. Top	$0.60	$0.65	1.0		**Time Available (Hours)**	
9	Tech.Top	$0.75	$0.78	1.5		Regular	Overtime
10						200	50
11							
12						**Overtime Cost per Hour:**	9
13							
14	**Model**						
15							
16							
17		**Min Cost**	24276.66667				
18							
19				**Number**		**Number**	
20	**Component**	Make	Buy	**Available**		**Required**	
21	Base	0	5000	5000	=	5000	
22	Fin. Cart.	2333.3333	666.6666667	3000	=	3000	
23	Tech. Cart.	2000	0	2000	=	2000	
24	Fin. Top	0	3000	3000	=	3000	
25	Tech.Top	0	2000	2000	=	2000	
26							
27	**Overtime Used**	0					
28							
29				**Time Used**		**Time Avl.**	
30			Overtime	0	<=	50	
31			Mfg. Time	12000	<=	12000	

turing. The total cost is further reduced to $24,293.33. The company still needs purchases of 1333 financial cartridges (FCP), 3000 financial tops (FTP), and 2000 technician tops (TTP). The overtime is used to increase the manufacturing of financial cartridges (FCM) from 667 to 1667 units.

15. Blending Problem

Let x_{11} = gallons of crude 1 used to produce regular
x_{12} = gallons of crude 1 used to produce high octane
x_{21} = gallons of crude 2 used to produce regular
x_{22} = gallons of crude 2 used to produce high octane

$$\text{Min} \quad 0.10x_{11} + 0.10x_{12} + 0.15x_{21} + 0.15x_{22}$$
s.t.

Each gallon of regular must have at least 40% A.

$x_{11} + x_{21}$ = amount of regular produced
$0.4(x_{11} + x_{21})$ = amount of A required for regular
$0.2x_{11} + 0.50x_{21}$ = amount of A in $(x_{11} + x_{21})$ gallons of regular gas
$0.2x_{11} + 0.50x_{21} \geq 0.4x_{11} + 0.40x_{21}$ [1]

Each gallon of high octane can have at most 50% B

$x_{12} + x_{22}$ = amount high octane
$0.5(x_{12} + x_{22})$ = amount of B required for high octane
$0.60x_{12} + 0.30x_{22}$ = amount of B in $(x_{12} + x_{22})$ gallons of high octane

$$0.60x_{12} + 0.30x_{22} \leq 0.5x_{12} + 0.5x_{22} \quad [2]$$
$$x_{11} + x_{21} = 800{,}000 \quad [3]$$
$$x_{12} + x_{22} = 500{,}000 \quad [4]$$
$$x_{11}, x_{12}, x_{21}, x_{22} \geq 0$$

Optimal solution: x_{11} = 266,667; x_{12} = 333,333; x_{21} = 533,333; x_{22} = 166,667

Cost = $165,000
The spreadsheet formulation and solution are shown in Figure S4.15.

19. a. Multiple-Period Planning

Let x_{11} = amount of men's model in month 1
x_{21} = amount of women's model in month 1
x_{12} = amount of men's model in month 2
x_{22} = amount of women's model in month 2
s_{11} = inventory of men's model at end of month 1
s_{21} = inventory of women's model at end of month 1
s_{12} = inventory of men's model at end of month 2
s_{22} = inventory of women's model at end of month

The model formulation for part (a) is given.

$$\text{Min} \quad 120x_{11} + 90x_{21} + 120x_{12} + 90x_{22} + 2.4s_{11} + 1.8s_{21} + 2.4s_{12} + 1.8s_{22}$$
s.t.

$20 + x_{11} - s_{11} = 150$		[1]
$30 + x_{21} - s_{21} = 125$		[2]
$s_{11} + x_{12} - s_{12} = 200$		[3]
$s_{21} + x_{22} - s_{22} = 150$		[4]
$s_{12} \geq 25$	Ending Inventory	[5]
$s_{22} \geq 25$	Requirement	[6]

Labor hours: Men's 2.0 + 1.5 = 3.5
    Women's 1.6 + 1.0 = 2.6

$3.5x_{11} + 2.6x_{21} - 1000 \leq 100$	Labor Smoothing	[7]
$1000 - 3.5x_{11} - 2.6x_{21} \leq 100$	Month 1	[8]
$3.5x_{11} + 2.6x_{21} - 3.5x_{12} - 2.6x_{22} \leq 100$	Labor Smoothing	[9]
$-3.5x_{11} - 2.6x_{21} + 3.5x_{12} + 2.6x_{22} \leq 100$	Month 2	[10]

$$x_{11}, x_{12}, x_{21}, x_{22}, s_{11}, s_{12}, s_{21}, s_{22} \geq 0$$

SPREADSHEET
SEASTRAND OIL

Figure S4.15   SPREADSHEET FORMULATION AND SOLUTION FOR THE SEASTRAND OIL PROBLEM

	A	B	C	D	E	F	G	H	I
1	Seastrand Oil								
2									
3									
4	Crude Oil	Cost	Ingredient A	Ingredient B			Regular	High Octane	
5	1	$0.10	20%	60%		Min A	40%		
6	2	$0.15	50%	30%		Max B		50%	
7						Demand	800000	500000	
8									
9									
10	Model								
11									
12			Blending Plan			Blending			
13	Crude Oil	Regular	High Octane	Total		Requirements	Amount In		Requireme
14	1	266666.67	333333.33	600000		Min A-Reg	320000	>=	320000
15	2	533333.33	166666.67	700000		Max B-High	250000	<=	250000
16	Total	800000	500000						
17		=	=						
18	Demand	800000	500000		Min Cost	165000			

Figure **S4.19**	SPREADSHEET FORMULATION AND SOLUTION FOR THE SILVER STAR BICYCLE PROBLEM	

	A	B	C	D	E	F	G	H	I
1	Silver Star Bicycle								
2									
3		Production Cost		Inventory Cost			Labor Reqmts. (hrs.)		
4		Month 1	Month 2	Month 1	Month 2		Manufacturing	Assembly	
5	Men's	$120	$120	$2.40	$2.40		2.00	1.5	
6	Women's	$90	$90	$1.80	$1.80		1.6	1	
7									
8		Demand		Beginning	Min Ending		Labor Usage Month 0 (hrs.):		1000
9		Month 1	Month 2	Inventory	Inventory		Max Labor Hours Change:		100
10	Men's	150	200	20	25				
11	Women's	125	150	30	25				
12									
13									
14	Model								
15									
16		Production		Ending Inventory					
17		Month 1	Month 2	Month 1	Month 2			Labor Utilization	
18	Men's	192.92857	162.07143	62.928571	25			Month 1	Month 2
19	Women's	95	175	0	25		Usage	922.25	1022.25
20							Increase	-77.75	100.00
21	Min Cost	67156.029						<=	<=
22							Max Increase	100	100
23		Beg. Inv. + Prod. - End. Inv.		Demand					
24	Men/Mo.1	150	=	150			Decrease	77.75	-100.00
25	Men/Mo.2	200	=	200				<=	<=
26	Women/Mo.1	125	=	125			Max Decrease	100	100
27	Women/Mo.2	150	=	150					
28									
29				End. Inv.					
30		End. Inv.		Rqmt.					
31	Men's	25	>=	25					
32	Women's	25	>=	25					

The spreadsheet formulation and solution are given in Figure S4.19. It calls for production of 193 of the men's model in month 1 and 162 in month 2. The optimal production schedule calls for 95 units of the women's model in month 1 and 175 in month 2.

Inventory Schedule

Month 1	63 Men's	0 Women's
Month 2	25 Men's	25 Women's

Labor Levels

Previous month	1000.00 hours
Month 1	922.25 hours
Month 2	1022.25 hours

b. To accommodate this new policy, the right-hand sides of constraints [7] to [10] must be changed to 50, 50, 50, and 50, respectively. The revised optimal solution is given.

$$x_{11} = 201$$
$$x_{21} = \ 95$$
$$x_{12} = 154$$
$$x_{22} = 175 \quad \text{Total Cost} = \$67,175$$

We produce more men's models in the first month and carry a larger men's model inventory; the added cost however is only $19. This seems to be a small expense to have less drastic labor force fluctuations. The new labor levels are 1000, 950, and 994.5 hours each month. Since the added cost is only $19, management might want to experiment with the labor force smoothing restrictions to enforce even less fluctuations. You may want to experiment yourself to see what happens.

Chapter 5

1. The network model is shown.

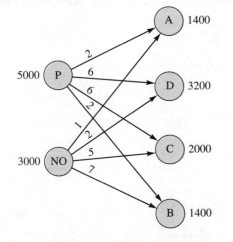

2. a. Let x_{11} = Amount shipped from Jefferson City to Des Moines

x_{12} = Amount shipped from Jefferson City to Kansas City

.
.
.

x_{23} = Amount shipped from Omaha to St. Louis

Min $14x_{11} + 9x_{12} + 7x_{13} + 8x_{21} + 10x_{22} + 5x_{23}$
s.t.

$$
\begin{aligned}
x_{11} + x_{12} + x_{13} &\leq 30 \\
x_{21} + x_{22} + x_{23} &\leq 20 \\
x_{11} \qquad\qquad + x_{21} &= 25 \\
x_{12} \qquad\qquad + x_{22} &= 15 \\
x_{13} \qquad\qquad + x_{23} &= 10 \\
x_{11}, x_{12}, x_{13}, x_{21}, x_{22}, x_{23} &\geq 0
\end{aligned}
$$

b. The spreadsheet formulation and solution are shown in Figure S5.2 on page 514.

8. The linear programming formulation, the network model, and the spreadsheet solution are shown. Note that the third constraint corresponds to the dummy origin. The variables $x_{31}, x_{32}, x_{33},$ and x_{34} are the amounts shipped out of the dummy origin; they do not appear in the objective function since they are given a coefficient of zero.

Max $32x_{11} + 34x_{12} + 32x_{13} + 40x_{14} + 34x_{21} + 30x_{22} + 28x_{23} + 38x_{24}$
s.t.

$$
\begin{aligned}
x_{11} + x_{12} + x_{13} + x_{14} &\leq 5000 \\
x_{21} + x_{22} + x_{23} + x_{24} &\leq 3000 \\
x_{31} + x_{32} + x_{33} + x_{34} &\leq 4000 \quad \text{Dummy} \\
x_{11} \qquad + x_{21} \qquad + x_{31} &= 2000 \\
x_{12} \qquad + x_{22} \qquad + x_{32} &= 5000 \\
x_{13} \qquad + x_{23} \qquad + x_{33} &= 3000 \\
x_{14} \qquad + x_{24} \qquad + x_{34} &= 2000 \\
x_{ij} &\geq 0 \quad \text{for all } i, j
\end{aligned}
$$

The spreadsheet formulation and solution are shown in Figure S5.8 on page 514.

Customer 2 demand has a shortfall of 1000

Customer 3 demand of 3000 is not satisfied

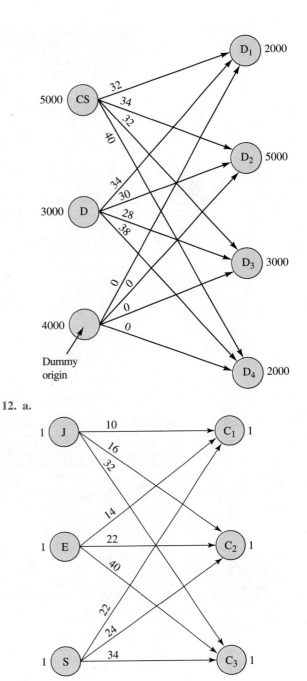

Dummy origin

12. a.

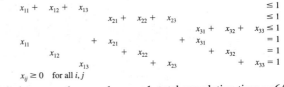

b.

Min $10x_{11} + 16x_{12} + 32x_{13} + 14x_{21} + 22x_{22} + 40x_{23} + 22x_{31} + 24x_{32} + 34x_{33}$
s.t.

$$
\begin{aligned}
x_{11} + x_{12} + x_{13} &\leq 1 \\
x_{21} + x_{22} + x_{23} &\leq 1 \\
x_{31} + x_{32} + x_{33} &\leq 1 \\
x_{11} \qquad + x_{21} \qquad + x_{31} &= 1 \\
x_{12} \qquad + x_{22} \qquad + x_{32} &= 1 \\
x_{13} \qquad + x_{23} \qquad + x_{33} &= 1 \\
x_{ij} \geq 0 \quad \text{for all } i, j
\end{aligned}
$$

Solution $x_{12} = 1, x_{21} = 1, x_{33} = 1$; total completion time = 64

Figure S5.2	SPREADSHEET FORMULATION AND SOLUTION FOR THE TRANSPORTATION PROBLEM

	A	B	C	D	E	F	G
1	**Transportation**						
2							
3			**Destination**				
4	**Origin**	Des Moines	Kansas City	St. Louis	**Supply**		
5	Jefferson City	14	9	7	30		
6	Omaha	8	10	5	20		
7	**Demand**	25	15	10			
8							
9							
10	**Model**						
11							
12		**Min Cost**	435				
13							
14			**Destination**				
15	**Origin**	Des Moines	Kansas City	St. Louis	**Total**		**Supply**
16	Jefferson City	5	15	10	30	<=	30
17	Omaha	20	0	0	20	<=	20
18	**Total**	25	15	10			
19		=	=	=			
20	**Demand**	25	15	10			

SPREADSHEET
TRANSPORTATION

Figure S5.8	SPREADSHEET FORMULATION AND SOLUTION FOR THE KLEIN CHEMICALS PROBLEM

	A	B	C	D	E	F	G	H
1	**Klein Chemicals**							
2								
3			**Customer**					
4	**Plant**	D1	D2	D3	D4	**Capacity**		
5	Clifton Springs	32	34	32	40	5000		
6	Danville	34	30	28	38	3000		
7	Dummy	0	0	0	0	4000		
8	**Demand**	2000	5000	3000	2000			
9								
10								
11	**Model**							
12								
13		**Max Profit**	282000					
14								
15			**Customer**					
16	**Plant**	D1	D2	D3	D4	**Total**		**Supply**
17	Clifton Springs	0	4000	0	1000	5000	<=	5000
18	Danville	2000	0	0	1000	3000	<=	3000
19	Dummy	0	1000	3000	0	4000	<=	4000
20	**Total**	2000	5000	3000	2000			
21		=	=	=	=			
22	**Demand**	2000	5000	3000	2000			

SPREADSHEET
KLEIN
CHEMICALS

The spreadsheet formulation and solution are shown in Figure S5.12 on page 516.

23. a.

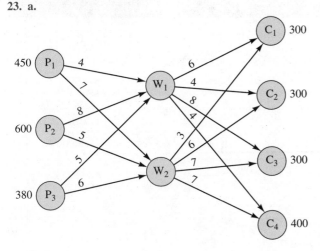

b.

$$\text{Min } 4x_{14}+7x_{15}+8x_{24}+5x_{25}+5x_{34}+6x_{35}+6x_{46}+4x_{47}+8x_{48}+4x_{49}+3x_{56}+6x_{57}+7x_{58}+7x_{59}$$

s.t.

$$
\begin{array}{lr}
x_{14}+\ x_{15} & \leq 450 \\
x_{24}+\ x_{25} & \leq 600 \\
x_{34}+\ x_{35} & \leq 380 \\
-x_{14}\ -\ x_{24}\ -\ x_{34}\ +\ x_{46}+\ x_{47}+\ x_{48}+\ x_{49} & =\ 0 \\
-\ x_{15}\ -\ x_{25}\ -\ x_{35}\ +\ x_{56}+\ x_{57}+\ x_{58}+\ x_{59} & =\ 0 \\
-\ x_{46}\ -\ x_{56} & =-300 \\
-\ x_{47}\ -\ x_{57} & =-300 \\
-\ x_{48}\ -\ x_{58} & =-300 \\
-\ x_{49}\ -\ x_{59} & =-400
\end{array}
$$

c. The spreadsheet formulation and solution are shown in Figure S5.23 on page 516.

Chapter 6

2. a.

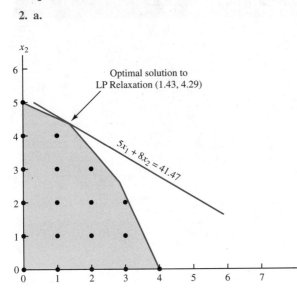

b. The optimal solution to the LP Relaxation is given by $x_1 = 1.43$, $x_2 = 4.29$ with an objective function value of 41.47. Rounding down gives the feasible integer solution $x_1 = 1$, $x_2 = 4$; its value is 37

c.

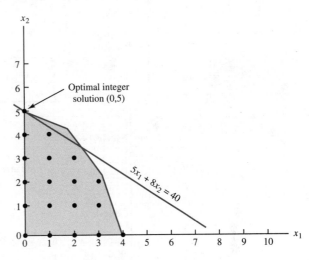

The optimal solution is given by $x_1 = 0$, $x_2 = 5$; its value is 40. This is not the same solution as that found by rounding down; it provides a 3-unit increase in the value of the objective function

5. a. The feasible mixed-integer solutions are indicated by the boldface vertical lines in the graph

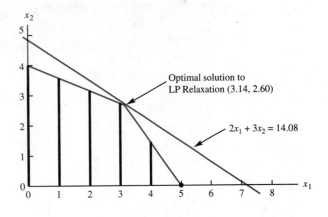

b. The optimal solution to the LP Relaxation is given by $x_1 = 3.14$, $x_2 = 2.60$; its value is 14.08

Rounding down the value of x_1 to find a feasible mixed-integer solution yields $x_1 = 3$, $x_2 = 2.60$ with a value of 13.8; this solution is clearly not optimal; with $x_1 = 3$, x_2 can be made larger without violating the constraints

Figure S5.12 SPREADSHEET FORMULATION AND SOLUTION FOR THE SCOTT AND ASSOCIATES PROBLEM

	A	B	C	D	E	F	G	H
1	**Scott and Associates**							
2								
3			**Client**					
4	**Project Leader**	1	2	3				
5	Jackson	10	16	32				
6	Ellis	14	22	40				
7	Smith	22	24	34				
8								
9								
10	**Model**							
11								
12		**Min Time**	64					
13								
14			**Client**					
15	**Project Leader**	1	2	3	**Total**			
16	Jackson	0	1	0	1	<=	1	
17	Ellis	1	0	0	1	<=	1	
18	Smith	0	0	1	1	<=	1	
19	**Total**	1	1	1				
20		=	=	=				
21		1	1	1				

SPREADSHEET SCOTT AND ASSOCIATES

Figure S5.23 SPREADSHEET FORMULATION AND SOLUTION FOR THE HERMAN COMPANY PROBLEM

	A	B	C	D	E	F	G	H	I	J	K
1	**Herman Company**										
2											
3		**Route**		**Units**							
4	Start Node	End Node	Cost	Shipped							
5	Plant1	Warehouse 1	4	450			**Units Shipped**		**Net**		**Net**
6	Plant 1	Warehouse 2	7	0		**Node**	In	Out	**Shipments**		**Supply**
7	Plant 2	Warehouse 1	8	0		Plant 1		450	450	<=	450
8	Plant 2	Warehouse 2	5	600		Plant 2		600	600	<=	600
9	Plant 3	Warehouse 1	5	250		Plant 3		250	250	<=	380
10	Plant 3	Warehouse 2	6	0		Warehouse 1	700	700	0	=	0
11	Warehouse 1	Customer 1	6	0		Warehouse 2	600	600	0	=	0
12	Warehouse 1	Customer 2	4	300		Customer 1	300		-300	=	-300
13	Warehouse 1	Customer 3	8	0		Customer 2	300		-300	=	-300
14	Warehouse 1	Customer 4	4	400		Customer 3	300		-300	=	-300
15	Warehouse 2	Customer 1	3	300		Customer 4	400		-400	=	-400
16	Warehouse 2	Customer 2	6	0							
17	Warehouse 2	Customer 3	7	300							
18	Warehouse 2	Customer 4	7	0							
19											
20											
21								**Total Cost**	11850		

SPREADSHEET HERMAN COMPANY

c. The optimal solution to the MILP is given by $x_1 = 3$, $x_2 = 2.67$; its value is 14. See the graph below.

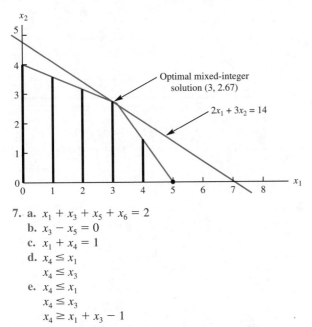

7. a. $x_1 + x_3 + x_5 + x_6 = 2$
   b. $x_3 - x_5 = 0$
   c. $x_1 + x_4 = 1$
   d. $x_4 \leq x_1$
      $x_4 \leq x_3$
   e. $x_4 \leq x_1$
      $x_4 \leq x_3$
      $x_4 \geq x_1 + x_3 - 1$

13. a. Add the following multiple-choice constraint to the problem
    $y_1 + y_2 = 1$
    New optimal Solution: $y_1 = 1, y_3 = 1, x_{12} = 10$,
    $x_{31} = 30, x_{52} = 10, x_{53} = 20$
    Value = 940
    b. Since one plant is already located in St. Louis, it is only necessary to add the following constraint to the model
    $y_3 + y_4 \leq 1$
    New Optimal Solution: $y_4 = 1, x_{42} = 20, x_{43} = 20$,
    $x_{51} = 30$
    Value = 860

Chapter 7

5. a. $P_0 = 1 - \dfrac{\lambda}{\mu} = 1 - \dfrac{10}{12} = 0.1667$

   b. $L_q = \dfrac{\lambda^2}{\mu(\mu - \lambda)} = \dfrac{10^2}{12(12 - 10)} = 4.1667$

   c. $W_q = \dfrac{L_q}{\lambda} = 0.4167$ hour (25 minutes)

   d. $W = W_q + \dfrac{1}{\mu} = 0.5$ hour (30 minutes)

   e. $P_w = \dfrac{\lambda}{\mu} = \dfrac{10}{12} = 0.8333$

Spreadsheet: Burger Dome Single Channel Figure 7.2.

11. a. $\lambda = 2.5$; $\mu = \dfrac{60}{10} = 6$ customers per hour

    $P_0 = 1 - \dfrac{\lambda}{\mu} = 1 - \dfrac{2.5}{6} = 0.5833$

    $L_q = \dfrac{\lambda^2}{\mu(\mu - \lambda)} = \dfrac{(2.5)^2}{6(6 - 2.5)} = 0.2976$

    $L = L_q + \dfrac{\lambda}{\mu} = 0.7143$

    $W_q = \dfrac{L_q}{\lambda} = 0.1190$ hours (7.14 minutes)

    $W = W_q + \dfrac{1}{\mu} = 0.2857$ hours

    $P_w = \dfrac{\lambda}{\mu} = \dfrac{2.5}{6} = 0.4167$

    b. No; $W_q = 7.14$ minutes; firm should increase the mean service rate (μ) for the consultant or hire a second consultant

    c. $\mu = \dfrac{60}{8} = 7.5$ customers per hour

    $L_q = \dfrac{\lambda^2}{\mu(\mu - \lambda)} = \dfrac{(2.5)^2}{7.5(7.5 - 2.5)} = 0.1667$

    $W_q = \dfrac{L_q}{\lambda} = 0.0667$ hour (4 minutes)

    The service goal is being met
    Spreadsheet: Burger Dome Single Channel Figure 7.2.

19. a. $k = 2$; $\lambda/\mu = 14/10 = 1.4$
    From table, $P_0 = 0.1765$

    b. $L_q = \dfrac{(\lambda/\mu)^2 \lambda \mu}{1!(2\mu - \lambda)^2} P_0 = \dfrac{(1.4)^2(14)(10)}{(20 - 14)^2}(0.1765)$
    $= 1.3451$

    $L = L_q + \dfrac{\lambda}{\mu} = 1.3451 + \dfrac{14}{10} = 2.7451$

    c. $W_q = \dfrac{L_q}{\lambda} = \dfrac{1.3453}{14} = 0.961$ hours (5.77 minutes)

    d. $W = W_q + \dfrac{1}{\mu} = 0.0961 + \dfrac{1}{10}$
    $= 0.1961$ hours (11.77 minutes)

    e. $P_0 = 0.1765$

    $P_1 = \dfrac{(\lambda/\mu)^1}{1!} P_0 = \dfrac{14}{10}(0.1765) = 0.2470$

    $P(\text{wait}) = P(n \geq 2) = 1 - P(n \leq 1)$
    $= 1 - 0.4235 = 0.5765$

Spreadsheet: Burger Dome Multiple Channel Figure 7.5.

21. From Problem 11, a service time of 8 minutes has
$\mu = 60/8 = 7.5$

$$L_q = \frac{\lambda^2}{\mu(\mu - \lambda)} = \frac{(2.5)^2}{7.5(7.5 - 2.5)} = 0.1667$$

$$L = L_q + \frac{\lambda}{\mu} = 0.50$$

Total cost = $25L + $16
      $= 25(0.50) + 16 = 28.50
Two channels: $\lambda = 2.5$; $\mu = 60/10 = 6$
Using $P_0 = 0.6552$

$$L_q = \frac{(\lambda/\mu)^2 \lambda \mu}{1!(2\mu - \lambda)^2} P_0 = 0.0189$$

$$L = L_q + \frac{\lambda}{\mu} = 0.4356$$

Total cost = $25(0.4356) + 2(16) = 42.89
Use one consultant with an 8-minute service time
Spreadsheet: Burger Dome Multiple Channel Figure 7.5.

25. $\lambda = 4$, $W = 10$ minutes
  a. $\mu = \frac{1}{2} = 0.5$
  b. $W_q = W - 1/\mu = 10 - 1/0.5 = 8$ minutes
  c. $L = \lambda W = 4(10) = 40$

27. a. $\lambda = \frac{2}{8}$ hours $= 0.25$ per hour
  b. $\mu = \frac{1}{3.2}$ hours $= 0.3125$ per hour

  c. $L_q = \dfrac{\lambda^2 \sigma^2 + (\lambda/\mu)^2}{2(1 - \lambda/\mu)}$

  $$= \frac{(0.25)^2(2)^2 + (0.25/0.3125)^2}{2(1 - 0.25/0.3125)} = 2.225$$

  d. $W_q = \dfrac{L_q}{\lambda} = \dfrac{2.225}{0.25} = 8.9$ hours

  e. $W = W_q + \dfrac{1}{\mu} = 8.9 + \dfrac{1}{0.3125} = 12.1$ hours

  f. Same as $P_w = \dfrac{\lambda}{\mu} = \dfrac{0.25}{0.3125} = 0.80$

    80% of the time the welder is busy
  Spreadsheet: See Hartlage Seafood in Figure 7.8.

30. a. $\lambda = 42$; $\mu = 20$

i	$(\lambda/\mu)^i/i!$
0	1.0000
1	2.1000
2	2.2050
3	1.5435
Total	6.8485

j	P_j	
0	1/6.8485	= 0.1460
1	2.1/6.8485	= 0.3066
2	2.2050/6.8485	= 0.3220
3	1.5435/6.8485	= 0.2254
		1.0000

  b. $P_3 = 0.2254$
  c. $L = \lambda/\mu(1 - P_3) = 42/20(1 - 0.2254) = 1.6267$
  d. Four lines will be necessary; the probability of denied access is 0.1499
Spreadsheet: See Microdata Software in Figure 7.9

34. $N = 5$; $\lambda = 0.025$; $\mu = 0.20$; $\lambda/\mu = 0.125$
  a.

n	$\dfrac{N}{(N-n)!}\left(\dfrac{\lambda}{\mu}\right)^n$
0	1.0000
1	0.6250
2	0.3125
3	0.1172
4	0.0293
5	0.0037
Total	2.0877

$P_0 = 1/2.0877 = 0.4790$

  b. $L_q = N - \left(\dfrac{\lambda + \mu}{\lambda}\right)(1 - P_0)$

  $$= 5 - \left(\frac{0.225}{0.025}\right)(1 - 0.4790) = 0.3110$$

  c. $L = L_q + (1 - P_0) = 0.3110 + (1 - 0.4790)$
    $= 0.8321$

  d. $W_q = \dfrac{L_q}{(N - L)\lambda} = \dfrac{0.3110}{(5 - 0.8320)(0.025)}$
    $= 2.9854$ minutes

  e. $W = W_q + \dfrac{1}{\mu} = 2.9854 + \dfrac{1}{0.20} = 7.9854$ minutes

  f. Trips/day = (8 hours)(60 minutes/hour)(λ)
        $= (8)(60)(0.025) = 12$ trips
    Time at copier: $12 \times 7.9854 = 95.8$ minutes/day
    Wait time at copier: $12 \times 2.9854 = 35.8$ minutes/day

g. Yes, five assistants $\times$ 35.8 = 179 minutes (3 hours/day), so 3 hours per day are lost to waiting
(35.8/480)(100) = 7.5% of each assistant's day is spent waiting for the copier

Spreadsheet: Kolkmeyer Single-Channel Figure 7.10.

Chapter 8

2. a. c = variable cost per unit
x = demand
Profit = $(50 - c)x - 30,000$

b. Base: Profit = $(50 - 20)1200 - 30,000 = 6,000$
Worst: Profit = $(50 - 24)300 - 30,000 = -22,200$
Best: Profit = $(50 - 16)2100 - 30,000 = 41,400$

c. Simulation will be helpful in estimating the probability of a loss

5. a.

Stock Price Change	Interval
-2	0.00 but less than 0.05
-1	0.05 but less than 0.15
0	0.15 but less than 0.40
$+1$	0.40 but less than 0.60
$+2$	0.60 but less than 0.80
$+3$	0.80 but less than 0.90
$+4$	0.90 but less than 1.00

b. Beginning price $39
0.1091 indicates -1 change; $38
0.9407 indicates $+4$ change; $42
0.1941 indicates 0 change; $42
0.8083 indicates $+3$ change; $45 (ending price)

9. a. Base-case based on most likely;
Time = 6 + 5 + 14 + 8 = 33 weeks
Worst: Time = 8 + 7 + 18 + 10 = 43 weeks
Best: Time = 5 + 3 + 10 + 8 = 26 weeks

b. 0.1778 for A — 5 weeks
0.9617 for B — 7 weeks
0.6849 for C — 14 weeks
0.4503 for D — 8 weeks; Total = 24 weeks

c. Simulation will provide an estimate of the probability of 35 weeks or less

14.

Selected cell formulas for the spreadsheet shown in Figure 8.14 are as follows:

Cell	Formula
B13	=$C$7+RAND()*($C$8−$C$7)
C13	=NORMINV(RAND(),$G$7,$G$8)
D13	=($C$3−B13)*C13−$C$4

a. The mean profit should be approximately $6,000. Simulation results will vary with most simulations having a mean profit between $5,500 and $6,500.

b. 120 to 150 of the 500 simulation trials should show a loss. Thus, the probability of a loss should be between 0.24 and 0.30.

c. This project appears too risky.

***Figure* S8.14** SPREADSHEET FOR THE MADEIRA MANUFACTURING COMPANY

	A	B	C	D	E	F	G
1	**Madeira Manufacturing Company**						
2							
3	Selling Price per Unit		$50				
4	Fixed Cost		$30,000				
5							
6	**Variable Cost (Uniform Distribution)**				**Demand (Normal distribution)**		
7	Smallest Value		$16		Mean		1200
8	Largest Value		$24		Standard Deviation		300
9							
10	**Simulation Trials**						
11		Variable					
12	Trial	Cost per Unit	Demand	Profit			
13	1	$17.81	788	($4,631)			
14	2	$18.86	1078	$3,580			

SPREADSHEET
MADEIRA
MANUFACTURING
COMPANY

18.

	A	B	C	D	E	F	G	H
	Figure S8.18					SPREADSHEET FOR THE CONTRACTOR BIDDING		
1	**Contractor Bidding**							
2								
3	**Contractor A (Uniform Distribution)**					**Contractor B (Normal Distribution)**		
4	Smallest Value		$600			Mean		$700
5	Largest Value		$800			Standard Deviation		$50
6								
7								
8	**Simulation**					**Results**		
9		Contractor	Contractor	Highest		Contractor's	Number	Probability
10	Trial	A's Bid	B's Bid	Bid		Bid	of Wins	of Winning
11	1	$673.4	$719.8	$719.8		750	629	0.629
12	2	$756.9	$654.8	$756.9		775	824	0.824
13	3	$705.5	$791.1	$791.1		785	887	0.887
14	4	$638.0	$677.1	$677.1				

Caption: Figure S8.18 SPREADSHEET FOR THE CONTRACTOR BIDDING

Selected cell formulas for the spreadsheet shown in Figures 8.18 are as follows:

Cell	Formula
B11	=$C$4+RAND()*($C$5−$C$4)
C11	=NORMINV(RAND(),$H$4,$H$5)
D11	=MAX(B11:C11)
G11	=COUNTIF(D11:D1010,"<750")
H11	=G11/COUNT(D11:D1010)

a. $750,000 should win roughly 600 to 650 of the 1000 times. The probability of winning the bid should be between 0.60 and 0.65.

b. The probability of $775,000 winning should be roughly 0.82, and the probability of $785,000 winning should be roughly 0.88. A contractor's bid of $775,000 is recommended.

Chapter 9

1. a.

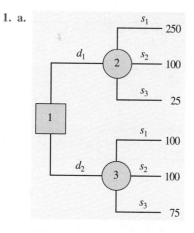

b. Spreadsheet: See PDC Spreadsheets in Figures 9.2, 9.3, and 9.4

Decision	Maximum Profit	Minimum Profit
d_1	250	25
d_2	100	75

Optimistic approach: Select d_1
Conservative approach: Select d_2
Regret or opportunity loss table:

Decision	s_1	s_2	s_3
d_1	0	0	50
d_2	150	0	0

Maximum regret: 50 for d_1 and 150 for d_2; select d_1

5. a. Spreadsheet: See PDC Expected Value in Figure 9.7.
   $EV(d_1) = 0.65(250) + 0.15(100) + 0.20(25) = 182.5$
   $EV(d_2) = 0.65(100) + 0.15(100) + 0.20(75) = 95$
   The optimal decision is d_1

8. Modify spreadsheet PDC Expected Value in Figure 9.7.
   Use trial-and-error values for $P(s_1)$
   $EV(d_1) = 10P(s_1) + 1(1 − P(s_1))$
   $EV(d_2) = 4 P(s_1) + 3(1 − P(s_1))$
   At $P(s_1) = 0.25$, $EV(d_1) = EV(d_2) = 3.25$
   If $P(s_1) < 0.25$, $EV(d_2)$ is greater.
   If $P(s_1) > 0.25$, $EV(d_1)$ is greater.

12. Spreadsheet: See PDC Expected Value in Figure 9.8.
   a. If s_1, then d_1; if s_2, then d_1 or d_2; if s_3, then d_2
   b. $EVwPI = 0.65(250) + 0.15(100) + 0.20(75) = 192.5$

c. From the solution to Problem 5, we know that $EV(d_1) = 182.5$ and $EV(d_2) = 95$; thus, recommended decision is d_1; hence, $EVwoPI = 182.5$

d. $EVPI = EVwPI - EVwoPI = 192.5 - 182.5 = 10$

14. a.

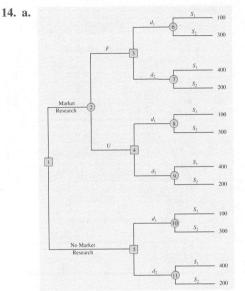

b. Use spreadsheet S9.14 Decision Tree on page 522.

$EV(\text{node } 6) = 0.57(100) + 0.43(300) = 186$
$EV(\text{node } 7) = 0.57(400) + 0.43(200) = 314$
$EV(\text{node } 8) = 0.18(100) + 0.82(300) = 264$
$EV(\text{node } 9) = 0.18(400) + 0.82(200) = 236$
$EV(\text{node } 10) = 0.40(100) + 0.60(300) = 220$
$EV(\text{node } 11) = 0.40(400) + 0.60(200) = 280$
$EV(\text{node } 3) = \max(186, 314) = 314 \quad d_2$
$EV(\text{node } 4) = \max(264, 236) = 264 \quad d_1$
$EV(\text{node } 5) = \max(220, 280) = 280 \quad d_2$
$EV(\text{node } 2) = 0.56(314) + 0.44(264) = 292$
$EV(\text{node } 1) = \max(292, 280) = 292$ Market Research
Conduct Market Research,
    If F, d_2; If U, d_1

22. Use spreadsheet S9.22 Bayes on page 523.

Chapter 10

1. Spreadsheet: See Job Selection in Figure 10.1

Scoring Calculations

Criteria	Analyst Chicago	Accountant Denver	Auditor Houston
Career advancement	35	20	20
Location	10	12	8
Management	30	25	35
Salary	28	32	16
Prestige	32	20	24
Job security	8	10	16
Enjoy the work	28	20	20
Totals	171	139	139

The analyst position in Chicago is recommended.

8. Spreadsheet: Car Selection AHP Figure 10.3.
Step 1: Column totals are $17/4$, $31/21$, and 12
Step 2:

Style	Accord	Saturn	Cavalier
Accord	$4/17$	$7/31$	$4/12$
Saturn	$12/17$	$21/31$	$7/12$
Cavalier	$1/17$	$3/31$	$1/12$

Step 3:

Style	Accord	Saturn	Cavalier	Row Average
Accord	0.235	0.226	0.333	0.265
Saturn	0.706	0.677	0.583	0.656
Cavalier	0.059	0.097	0.083	0.080

Consistency Ratio
Step 1:

$$0.265 \begin{bmatrix} 1 \\ 3 \\ 1/4 \end{bmatrix} + 0.656 \begin{bmatrix} 1/3 \\ 1 \\ 1/7 \end{bmatrix} + 0.080 \begin{bmatrix} 4 \\ 7 \\ 1 \end{bmatrix}$$

$$\begin{bmatrix} 0.265 \\ 0.795 \\ 0.066 \end{bmatrix} + \begin{bmatrix} 0.219 \\ 0.656 \\ 0.094 \end{bmatrix} + \begin{bmatrix} 0.320 \\ 0.560 \\ 0.080 \end{bmatrix} = \begin{bmatrix} 0.802 \\ 2.007 \\ 0.239 \end{bmatrix}$$

Step 2: $0.802/0.265 = 3.028$
    $2.007/0.656 = 3.062$
    $0.239/0.080 = 3.007$
Step 3: $\lambda_{max} = (3.028 + 3.062 + 3.002)/3 = 3.032$
Step 4: $CI = (3.032 - 3)/2 = 0.016$
Step 5: $CR = 0.016/0.58 = 0.028$
Since $CR = 0.028$ is less than 0.10, the degree of consistency exhibited in the pairwise comparison matrix for style is acceptable

12. a.

Flavor	Flavor		
	A	B	C
A	1	3	2
B	$1/3$	1	5
C	$1/2$	$1/5$	1

Figure S9.14 — DECISION TREE ANALYSIS

	A	B	C
1	**Decision Tree Analysis**		
2			
3	**Payoff Table**		
4		**State of Nature**	
5	**Decision Alternative**	State s1	State s2
6	Decision d1	100	300
7	Decision d2	400	200
8	**Probability**	0.4	0.6
9			
10	**Probability Information**		
11			
12	**Market Research Outcomes**	Favorable	Unfavorable
13		0.56	0.44
14			
15		**State of Nature**	
16	**If Market Research is**	State s1	State s2
17	Favorable	0.57	0.43
18	Unfavorable	0.18	0.82
19			
20			
21	**Decision Tree Analysis**		
22		**Expected**	**Recommended**
23	**Node**	**Value**	**Decision**
24	1. Decision Market Research or No Market Research	292	Market Research
25	2. Market Research	292	
26	3. Market Research Favorable: Decision d1 or d2	314	Decision d2
27	4. Market Research Unfavorable: Decision d1 or d2	264	Decision d1
28	5. No Market Research: Decision d1 or d2	280	Decision d2
29	6. Market Research/Favorable/Decision d1	186	
30	7. Market Research/Favorable/Decision d2	314	
31	8. Market Research/Unfavorable/Decision d1	264	
32	9. Market Research/Unfavorable/Decision d2	236	
33	10. No Market Research/Decision d1	220	
34	11. No Market Research/Decision d2	280	

b. Step 1: Column totals are $11/6$, $21/5$, and 8

Step 2:

Flavor

Flavor	A	B	C
A	$6/11$	$15/21$	$2/8$
B	$2/11$	$5/21$	$5/8$
C	$3/11$	$1/21$	$1/8$

Step 3:

Flavor

Flavor	A	B	C	Row Average
A	0.545	0.714	0.250	0.503
B	0.182	0.238	0.625	0.348
C	0.273	0.048	0.125	0.148

Figure S9.22   BAYES PROBABILITY

	A	B	C	D	E
1	**Bayes' Probability Calculations**				
2					
3		Prior			
4	**States of Nature**	Probabilities			
5	State s1	0.2			
6	State s2	0.5			
7	State s3	0.3			
8					
9	**Conditional Probabilities**				
10		Indicator			
11	If State of Nature is	I			
12	State s1	0.10			
13	State s2	0.05			
14	State s3	0.20			
15					
16					
17	**Indicator I**				
18		Prior	Conditional	Joint	Posterior
19	State of Nature	Probabilities	Probabilities	Probabilities	Probabilities
20	State s1	0.2	0.10	0.020	0.19
21	State s2	0.5	0.05	0.025	0.24
22	State s3	0.3	0.20	0.060	0.57
23				**P(I) =**	0.105

SPREADSHEET
BAYES
PROBABILITY

c. Step 1:

$$0.503 \begin{bmatrix} 1 \\ \frac{1}{3} \\ \frac{1}{2} \end{bmatrix} + 0.348 \begin{bmatrix} 3 \\ 1 \\ \frac{1}{5} \end{bmatrix} + 0.148 \begin{bmatrix} 2 \\ 5 \\ 1 \end{bmatrix}$$

$$\begin{bmatrix} 0.503 \\ 0.168 \\ 0.252 \end{bmatrix} + \begin{bmatrix} 1.044 \\ 0.348 \\ 0.070 \end{bmatrix} + \begin{bmatrix} 0.296 \\ 0.740 \\ 0.148 \end{bmatrix} = \begin{bmatrix} 1.845 \\ 1.258 \\ 0.470 \end{bmatrix}$$

Step 2: 1.845/0.503 = 3.668
        1.258/0.348 = 3.615
        0.470/0.148 = 3.123
Step 3: λ_{max} = (3.668 + 3.615 + 3.123)/3 = 3.469
Step 4: CI = (3.469 − 3)/2 = 0.235
Step 5: CR = 0.235/0.58 = 0.415
Step 6: Since CR = 0.415 is greater than 0.10, the individual's judgments are not consistent.

16. Use spreadsheet in Figure S10.16 Stock Selection located on page 524.

Criteria: Yield and Risk
Step 1: Column totals are 1.5 and 3
Step 2:

	Yield	Risk	Priority
Yield	0.667	0.667	0.667
Risk	0.333	0.333	0.333

With only 2 criteria, CR = 0; no need to compute CR

Above calculations for Yield and Risk provide

Stocks	Yield Priority	Risk Priority
CCC	0.750	0.333
SRI	0.250	0.667

Overall Priorities:
  CCC 0.667 (0.750) + 0.333 (0.333) = 0.611
   SRI 0.667 (0.250) + 0.333 (0.667) = 0.387
CCC is preferred

SPREADSHEET
Stock Selection

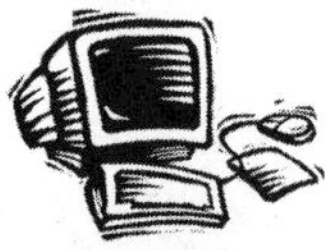

Figure S10.16 STOCK SELECTION

	A	B	C	D	E	F	G	H	I
1	**Stock Selection Using AHP**								
2									
3	**Pairwise Comparison Matrices**					**Normalized Matrices**			
4									
5	**Criteria**	**Criteria**							
6		Yield	Risk				Yield	Risk	Priority
7	Yield	1.000	2.000			Yield	0.667	0.667	0.667
8	Risk	0.500	1.000			Risk	0.333	0.333	0.333
9	Sum	1.500	3.000						
10									
11									
12	**Yield**					**Yield**			
13		CCC	SRI				CCC	SRI	Priority
14	CCC	1.000	3.000			CCC	0.750	0.750	0.750
15	SRI	0.333	1.000			SRI	0.250	0.250	0.250
16	Sum	1.333	4.000						
17									
18									
19	**Risk**					**Risk**			
20		CCC	SRI				CCC	SRI	Priority
21	CCC	1.000	0.500			CCC	0.333	0.333	0.333
22	SRI	2.000	1.000			SRI	0.667	0.667	0.667
23	Sum	3.000	1.500						
24									
25									
26	**Priority Summary**								
27		Yield	Risk			**Overall Priorities**			
28	Priority	0.667	0.333						
29	CCC	0.750	0.333			CCC	0.611		
30	SRI	0.250	0.667			SRI	0.389		

INDEX